Equity & Trusts Law

DIRECTIONS

6th Edition

GARY WATT MA (Oxon)

Professor of Law University of Warwick
National Teaching Fellow

OXFORD
UNIVERSITY PRESS

OXFORD
UNIVERSITY PRESS

Great Clarendon Street, Oxford, OX2 6DP,
United Kingdom

Oxford University Press is a department of the University of Oxford.
It furthers the University's objective of excellence in research, scholarship,
and education by publishing worldwide. Oxford is a registered trade mark of
Oxford University Press in the UK and in certain other countries

Third edition 2012
Fourth edition 2014
Fifth edition 2016

Impression: 1

Published in the United States of America by Oxford University Press
198 Madison Avenue, New York, NY 10016, United States of America

British Library Cataloguing in Publication Data
Data available

Library of Congress Control Number: 2019930160

ISBN 978–0–19–880470–3

Printed in Great Britain by
Bell & Bain Ltd., Glasgow

To my students

Guide to using the book

Equity & Trusts Law Directions is enriched with a range of special features designed to support and reinforce your learning. This brief guide to those features will help you use the book to the full and get the most out of your study.

Learning objectives

Each chapter begins with a list of learning objectives to enable you to draw out the main themes of the chapter. They should also be helpful when you are revising as a quick check that you have a grasp of the key knowledge requirements.

> **☐ LEARNING OBJECTIVES**
>
> **By the end of this chapter you should be able to:**
> - outline the major stages in the historical development of equity
> - appreciate that the theoretical distinction between equity and th law is largely concerned with their different functions;

Definition boxes

Key terms are highlighted in colour and clearly explained when they first appear. These terms are then collated into a glossary which appears at the end of the book for your ease of reference.

> *in personam* A remedy, such as an injunction, is said to operate *in person* against a defendant personally. An *in personam* action is normally contraste which is a claim against property held by the defendant regardless of the de to comply with the injunction is a direct contempt of court punishable by f more on injunctions, see Chapter 20.

Outside the box

This innovative feature shows that philosophy, literature, theatre and film can illuminate issues in equity and trusts law. Hopefully it will stimulate your imagination and inspire you to learn more. It will at least offer some light relief!

> **☐ OUTSIDE THE BOX**
>
> Charles Dickens, *Bleak House*, 1852–3
>
> *Chapter 1 – In Chancery*
>
> Never can there come fog too thick, never can there come mud and mire

Case close-up

Summaries of landmark cases are highlighted for enhanced impact and ease of reference.

> **🔍 CASE CLOSE-UP**
>
> **P. Birks, *Civil Wrongs: A New World*, The Butterworth Lectures 1990-**
>
> It is dangerous, not to say absurd, almost 120 years after the Judicature sist in habits of thought calculated to submerge and conceal one or othe law . . . Meagher, Gummow and Lehane . . . did not attempt to say th

Statutes

Boxed extracts or summaries of key pieces of legislation are provided throughout for ease of reference and recall.

> **➡ STATUTE**
>
> **The Hague Convention on the Law Applicable to Trusts and on their Recognition, Article 2**
>
> For the purposes of this Convention the term 'trust' refers to the legal relationshi ated—*inter vivos* or on death—by a person, the settlor, when assets have been under the control of a trustee for the benefit of a beneficiary or for a specified purp

Cross references

Crucial connections between topics are carefully cross-referenced to provide a fully integrated understanding of the subject. Links are highlighted to aid quick and accurate navigation through the book.

> **❱ CROSS REFERENCE**
>
> For detailed consideration
> of the remedy of
> specific performance,
> see Chapter 20.

Thinking point

This feature gives you the opportunity to pause and reflect upon how well you have digested the law. A thinking point usually takes the form of a question, but the author won't leave you dangling for long—the answer can be found in the adjacent text.

 THINKING POINT

How would you define the trust concept in your own words? For what it is worth, and incomplete though it must be, this author would offer the following definition of a private trust:

A private trust is the legal relationship between the formal owner(s) of assets ('the trustee' or 'trustees') and the beneficial owner(s) of those assets ('the beneficiary' or 'ben-

Tables and figures

Tables and figures are presented across the book to help with your learning and revision, graphically presenting some of the key cases, concepts, and principles of the law.

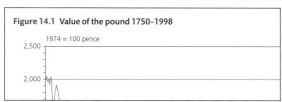

Table 6.1 Statutory lives in being

To Mandy's first daughter to qualify as a doctor	Mandy
	All of Mandy's daughters alive at the date of the testator's
	The father (or fathers) of every one of Mandy's daughters a the date of the testator's death

Figure 14.1 Value of the pound 1750–1998

1974 = 100 pence

2,500

2,000

Summaries

The brief summaries at the end of each chapter help to reinforce your understanding of each topic.

 Summary

The historical development of equity and trusts

- Where the King's common law caused injustice in individual cases, with consequent embarrassment to the King's conscience, the task of providing a just remedy fell to the Chancellor. The Chancellor came to dispense justice on his own authority from Westminster, and so the Court of Chancery, the Chancellor's court, developed.
- Competition between Chancery and the common law courts came to a head in the early

Summative assessment exercises

Here you are given the opportunity to put some of the theory into practice and therefore to assess how you are progressing. You can check your answers against those the author has suggested in the online resources.

 Summative assessment exercise

Herbert Chance, wishing to make future provision for his adult son, entered into the following covenant in a deed to which his friends Allan Smith and Clifford Overy were the only other parties: 'I promise to settle the sum of £100,000 in cash, or assets of equivalent value, for the benefit of my son for his life, to his issue in remainder. This bounty to be held on trust by Allan Smith and Clifford Overy in accordance with the terms of the settlement annexed hereto.'

Some years later Herbert fell grievously ill. As he lay on his death bed, his friend, Mr Overy,

The bigger picture

This feature shows you how you can deepen and contextualise your new legal understanding.

 The bigger picture

Does it seem strange that the law struggles to understand something as socially straightforward as an unincorporated association? Does it surprise us that the law's default solution, when it comes to explaining the ways in which people gather socially into groups for non-profit purposes, is to look for the 'contract' that binds them together? Perhaps it shouldn't surprise us when we consider that since The Enlightenment (and the work of the French political philosopher Jean-Jacques Rousseau, see *Du contrat social ou Principes du droit politique*) the 'Social Contract' has been a preferred mode of understanding political

Further reading

Selected further reading is included at the end of each chapter to provide a springboard for further study. The author has annotated the list to explain why a certain book or article might be useful to you in your studies.

Further reading

Barton, J.L. 'Trusts and Covenants' (1975) 91 LQR 236
an in-depth analysis of the relationship between covenants and the constituti

Borkowski, A. *Deathbed Gifts: The Law of Donatio Mortis Causa* (19 Blackstone Press
an engaging and detailed examination of the doctrine of *donatio mortis caus*

Guide to the Online Resources

The online resources that accompany this book provides students and lecturers with ready-to-use teaching and learning resources. They are free of charge and are designed to maximise the learning and teaching experience.

www.oup.com/uk/watt_directions6e/

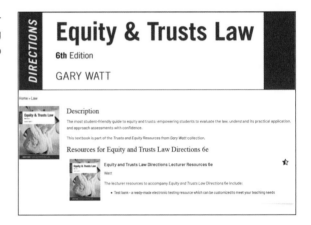

For students

Accessible to all, with no registration or password required, enabling students to get the most from this textbook.

Updates

An indispensable resource providing access to recent cases and developments in the law that have occurred since publication of the book.

> Updates covering recent developments in the law since book publication will be added to this page. Sign up to be alerted when a new update is added by clicking on the link below.
> ✉ Keep me updated

Pointers to answering self-assessment questions and exercises

All the questions and exercises that appear at the end of each chapter in the book have some suggestions on how you might answer them.

> Chapter 1 Multiple choice questions
>
> What is the meaning of the word 'equity'?
> ◌ The ability to make exceptions to the legal rule
> ◌ A body of law developed by the Court of Chancery
> ◌ Fairness
> ◌ A share in a company
>
> How did the Lord Chancellor become a judge?
> ◌ He dealt with petitions to the king

Introducing the author

Meet Gary Watt—active researcher, experienced writer and passionate teacher. In a short video clip he introduces himself, equity and trusts law and this textbook, setting the scene for your studies.

Guidance on answering essay questions and problem scenarios

The author offers his thoughts on how best to approach exam questions to achieve the best possible grade.

General guidance on answering problem scenarios

The points made about structure and clarity in relation to essay answers apply equally to answers to problem scenarios. The first point of reference in any problem-type question is to be clear what it is you are being asked to do. If you are asked to advise a particular party or parties make sure that your answer very definitely approaches the facts from their point of view. This is not to suggest that your use of the law should be unbalanced or biased. You must discuss all relevant and realistic legal issues arising from the facts whether in favour of your client or against them. If you are not sure whether the facts of the problem raise an issue because the facts are incomplete or ambiguous it is advisable expressly to state your belief that there is uncertainty and then to outline all alternative (and of course relevant and realistic) interpretations and approaches.

Once you are clear who it is you are required to advise the key to a good answer is a methodical approach, lucid expression and clear structure. You should identify the issues, state the issues, cite the relevant law, briefly discuss any debate as to the relevant law (making reference to the legal authorities and to any relevant academic commentary) and then - most crucial of all - you should apply the relevant law to the facts and reach a conclusion. It will do no harm expressly to state 'applying case Y to fact X...it would appear that / I would conclude that.' You should follow this process, or something like it, with every issue raised by the problem. It is crucial, however, that you tackle the issues in a logical order. Sometimes the form of question will insist upon a certain order (issues may be listed a, b.

Flashcard glossary

The online flashcards help you familiarise yourself with the definitions of the key terms used throughout the book. Click through the randomised definitions and see if you can identify which key term they describe. And then try it the other way round!

Flashcard glossary

13 of 69 Card(s)

Flip Card
Next Card
Previous Card
Toggle Mode
Shuffle Deck

certum est quod certum reddi potest

Web links

The author has selected links to useful websites so you can go directly to reliable sources of online information and direct your online study in order to work efficiently and effectively.

10 Trusteeship - introductory web links

Futter & Anor v Revenue and Customs [2013] UKSC 26 (9 May 2013)
http://www.bailii.org/uk/cases/UKSC/2013/26.html
Important case on the review of trustee decisions

The following is a link to Law Commission Consultation Paper 171 Trustee Exemption Clauses 2nd December 2002.
http://lawcommission.justice.gov.uk/areas/trustee-exemption-clauses.htm

Charity Commission leaflet CC3 - Responsibilities of Charity Trustees
http://www.charitycommission.gov.uk/publications/cc3.aspx

Multiple choice questions

Comprising of nearly 200 multiple-choice questions with answers and feedback, this is a great way to test your understanding.

Which of the following statements is false?
- The relationship between law and equity broadly corresponds to the relationship between certainty and justice.
- The relationship between law and equity broadly corresponds to the relationship between form and substance.
- The relationship between law and equity broadly corresponds to the relationship between general and particular.
- The relationship between law and equity broadly corresponds to the relationship between rules and morality.

Which of the following statements was made by the seventeenth century jurist, John Selden?
- "Equity in Law, is the same that the Spirit is in Religion, what every one pleases to make it".
- "Equity is the slipper of the Law, absent which the Law is but a poor foot on hard ground".
- "Equity is like a fixed rule by which is measured the rightness of this Changeling Law".
- "Equity is the Pole-star or the compass which guides the footsteps of the judge".

New to this edition

A wide range of new case law, including:

- *Akers* v *Samba Financial Group* [2017], Supreme Court on The Hague Convention on the Law Applicable to Trusts and on Their Recognition
- *Patel* v *Mirza* [2016], Supreme Court on the right to recover wealth transferred between parties to an illegal scheme
- *Bailey* v *Angove's PTY Ltd* [2016], Supreme Court on the distinction between contractual debt and constructive trust
- *Burnden Holdings (UK) Ltd* v *Fielding* [2018] UKSC 14; [2018] 2 WLR 885, Supreme Court on limitation of actions
- *First Subsea Ltd* v *Balltec Ltd* [2017], Court of Appeal on trust, fiduciary duty and limitation of actions
- *Barnett* v *Creggy* [2016], Court of Appeal on breach of trust and limitation of actions
- *Singha* v *Heer* [2016], Court of Appeal on facts giving rise to declaration of trust
- *Davies* v *Davies* [2016], Court of Appeal on the nature and basis of proprietary estoppel
- *Clydesdale Bank plc* v *John Workman* [2016], Court of Appeal on dishonest assistance in a breach of trust
- *Bathurst* v *Bathurst* [2016], on variation of trusts
- *Newman* v *Clarke* [2016], on fiduciary conflict of interest
- *Daniel* v *Tee* [2016], on relieving trustees of liability for imprudent investment
- *Akita Holdings Ltd* v *Attorney General of the Turks and Caicos Islands* [2017], Privy Council on knowing receipt of assets fraudulently transferred at an undervalue
- *RBC Trustees (CI) Ltd* v *Stubbs* [2017], on rectification of a trust deed on the ground of mistake
- *Bainbridge* v *Bainbridge* [2016], on rescission of a contract on the ground of mistake
- *Erlam* v *Rahman* [2016] EWHC 111, on 'sham' trusts
- *JSC Mezhdunarodniy Promyshlenniy Bank* v *Pugachev* [2017] EWHC 2426 (Ch), on 'sham' trusts

Coverage of recent legislation, including:

- The 2017 Money Laundering, Terrorist Financing and Transfer of Funds Regulations (SI 2017/692)
- The EU Fourth Money Laundering Directive ((EU) 2015/849), as amended by the EU Fifth Money Laundering Directive ((EU) 2018/843)

Plus references to recent scholarship and the work of relevant commissions, including:

- The Law Commission's ongoing consultation on electronic execution of documents
- The Law Commission's 2017 initial consultation on reform of the law governing the making of wills
- The Law Commission's proposed project 'Modernising Trust Law for a Global Britain'
- The Charity Commission for England and Wales, 'Trust in Charities' (2018)

Preface

Despite its medieval origins, the trust concept boasts a multiplicity of contemporary uses and these will form the main focus of this book: trusts in commerce, insolvency, pensions and cohabitation figure prominently. Indeed, one of my greatest satisfactions as a teacher of equity and trusts has been to demonstrate that a subject that students sometimes expect to be archaic, insignificant and impenetrable is in fact highly relevant to contemporary commercial and family life, and, what is more, is interesting and can be clearly understood. You might even conclude, as I have, that the flexibility and utility of the trust goes beyond that of any other judge-made creature. One piece of evidence for this claim is the fact that within this volume you will discover whether a trust to promote the works of the classical composer Delius is charitable and, at the other extreme, whether the manager of a young and vulnerable pop star owes their protégé a trust-like ('fiduciary') duty.

Just as the substance of this book emphasises that which is current and relevant to the modern world, so also the form of the book takes advantage of the latest advances in teaching and learning. The use of 'thinking points', diagrams, end-of-chapter summaries, the 'bigger picture' feature and so forth is designed to reinforce learning at every stage.

An especially unusual and novel feature of this book is the inclusion of non-legal materials, including extracts from film and literature, under the label 'outside the box'. Why are they included? One reason is simply to introduce a little light refreshment. Another is to stimulate the reader's imagination. Thinking 'outside the box' is always a good thing, and the inclusion of non-legal literature is bound to exercise the imagination. If issues of trusts law and equity have been interesting enough to stimulate creative writers throughout history, the reader is challenged to imagine how the subject might be stimulating and significant today. A third reason is to remind us that the law does not (or should not) exist in a vacuum. The 'outside the box' materials put you in touch with a wider world beyond the sometimes narrow confines of legal studies. A fourth reason, related to the last, is the sense of responsibility this writer feels to ensure that legal education resists the general trend towards conformity. Considerations of time and cost tend to channel 'formal' education into predictable, uniform lines. This tendency towards the rigid is sometimes overwhelming, but the 'outside the box' materials represent a small opportunity for resistance. Malvina Reynolds once wrote a song entitled 'Little Boxes on the Hillside', which is a satire on suburbia (a somewhat sanctimonious satire, it has been said). The second verse recites:

> the people in the houses all go to university, and they all get put in boxes, little boxes, all the same. And there's doctors and there's lawyers and business executives, and they're all made out of ticky-tacky and they all look just the same.

Law is a discipline that depends upon order, and lawyers, law teachers and law students have a responsibility to organise concepts into little boxes, but, as the eminent American judge Felix Frankfurter said, '[n]o less important for a lawyer is the cultivation of the imaginative faculties by reading poetry, seeing great paintings and listening to great music'. In other words, there is no need for the lawyer to live in the box. One of the greatest American jurists, Oliver Wendell Holmes, captured the essence of this when, speaking on 'The Use of Law Schools' in 1886, he described the 'noblest' graduates of law as those who acknowledge their dependence upon 'abstract thought, of science, of beauty, of poetry and art, of every flower of civilisation'.

Some other features in the book require a little explanation.

The 'definitions' feature provides definitions for unfamiliar phrases as and when they appear in the text. If the phrase is not an English one, I have included a suggested pronunciation. The pronunciation is the sort that I would expect an English judge to use in court, and is therefore probably not the sort of which a linguist or Classics scholar would approve. The guide to pronunciation uses standard English words where appropriate—a method borrowed from Glanville Williams, who employed it in his celebrated text *Learning the Law*. The best example is provided by the French law term *cestuis que trust* (meaning 'beneficiary of a trust'), which Professor Williams rendered 'settee-key-trust'.

Online resources accompany this book. Where the online resources symbol appears in the text, the student has the opportunity to consult the website for further materials including web links to full statutes, Law Commission reports and House of Lords decisions. Included in the online resources is a bank of multiple-choice questions and it will include regular updates to the text, so the book will remain as up to date as possible. The online resources also contain a few short podcasts to help reinforce your reception and understanding of certain subtle aspects of the subject.

There is enough in this book and the accompanying online resources to satisfy the demands of a typical undergraduate degree course in equity and trusts, but if the student is hungry for more, he or she may wish to consult books that address current debates in even greater depth. My own textbook *Trusts and Equity*, also published by Oxford University Press, is one. For even greater depth, the student may consult specialist monographs on particular areas of the subject (Lionel Smith on *The Law of Tracing*, Robert Chambers on *Resulting Trusts* and Peter Birks and Arianna Pretto (eds) on *Breach of Trust* are all excellent examples, and others are mentioned in the 'further reading' section appearing at the end of each chapter). The leading journals on the subject (for example, *The Law Quarterly Review* and *The Conveyancer and Property Lawyer*) should also be consulted.

Finally, the reader will notice that the front cover of the book features a baker kneading a ball of dough. The image provides a clue to my philosophy of education—which is to encourage students to strengthen their thinking by stretching themselves. Trusts and equity can be a puzzling subject to begin with, but stretching the mind strengthens the mind just as stretching dough strengthens the proteins in the mixture and makes for better bread. Teasing and releasing—puzzling and resolving—is pleasing in itself. The form of this book, with its thinking points, case studies and encouragements to think outside the box, all contributes to an active working with the subject—getting a grasp of it—rather than simply receiving it passively. The dough also serves as a good metaphor for the relationship between common law and equity. The pulling and pushing apart of a ball of dough at its opposite ends produces a certain polarity or contrast, but it is a productive one. So it is with the relationship between common law and equity. They are defined in opposition to each other, but it is a productive opposition. An effective and just legal system needs both. The curved shape of the ball of dough is also significant—no straight lines here! More than two thousand years ago Aristotle contrasted the rigid, straight-line rule of law with the flexible rule of equity. Equity, he said, is like a rule made of lead. It bends to meet practical needs. The beauty of equity is that it works in practice precisely because it isn't perfectly straight. The very fact that the cover image is seemingly unrelated to the topic is designed to set up a puzzle that will be pleasing to work out. For the same reason, you will find a photograph at the start of every chapter, but with no obvious clue as to why it has been included. You will have to read the chapter to find out why it's there.

I wish you every success in your studies.
Gary Watt, University of Warwick, January 2019

Outline contents

Detailed contents

Acknowledgements

Grateful acknowledgement is made to all the authors and publishers of copyright material which appears in this book, and in particular to the following for permission to reprint material from the sources indicated:

The *New Statesman* for the extract from the article 'Giving it all away', which first appeared in the *New Statesman*.

Trust Law & Practice for the extract from the article 'Some reflections on choosing trustees'.

Every effort has been made to trace and contact copyright holders prior to publication. If notified, the publisher will undertake to rectify any errors or omissions at the earliest opportunity.

Table of cases

Table of primary legislation

Table of secondary legislation

UK Statutory Instruments

Table of european legislation

Table of international treaties and conventions

1 Introduction to equity and trusts

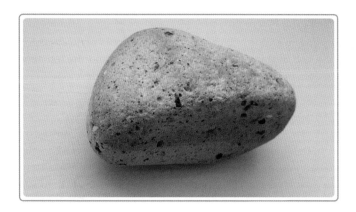

☐ LEARNING OBJECTIVES

By the end of this chapter you should be able to:

- outline the major stages in the historical development of equity and trusts;
- appreciate that the theoretical distinction between equity and the common law is largely concerned with their different functions;
- explain the correct way to use the maxims and doctrines of equity;
- distinguish between equity as an inventive, flexible, remedial branch of law, and equitable institutions which are now settled and established, such as the mortgage and the trust;
- identify the place of equity in the modern world and anticipate its possible future development.

Introduction

Suppose your parents are about to take a once-in-a-lifetime boat trip down the Amazon river. Before they depart they hand a large sum of money to a trusted friend, saying 'hold onto this and if we don't return within three months invest it wisely and use the income to look after our children'. Suppose now that your parents do not return within the three months and you approach the trusted friend for financial assistance. As a matter of law he is within his rights to say 'I became the legal owner of your parents' money the moment it came into my possession—so go away!' Thankfully, though, his legal rights aren't the end of the story. He agreed to hold the money for your benefit, so his legal right to the fund is subject to your rights in it. We say that he holds his legal rights to (and powers over) the fund 'on trust' for you. He is the trustee and you are the beneficiary (sometimes called the *cestui que trust*). This is a simple example of 'a trust', which is the main focus of this book.

> ### *cestui que trust*
> The one who trusts, i.e. the beneficiary of a trust (pronounced 'settee key trust').

In the next chapter we will see that trusts are everywhere in modern life: they encompass charities, pensions, home ownership and commercial deals. Wherever somebody is the legal owner of property in which someone else has some beneficial ownership, there one finds a trust.

⟩ CROSS REFERENCE

Equity imposes a number of positive duties on trustees, including duties of loyalty, care and good faith (see Chapters 11 and 12).

The trust is only one invention, albeit a very important one, of the branch of law known as equity. By the end of this chapter you should understand the function of equity in our law and be able to say where it originated and how it developed.

Equity is a wide-ranging concept—it appears in one form or another in the Bible, ancient philosophy and great works of literature. In this book we are concerned with equity as a particular branch of English law. In that sense it is contrasted with, albeit compatible with, the general body of English law—known as the common law. 'Common law' can be a confusing term because it carries at least three distinct meanings (see Figure 1.1). The first meaning distinguishes common law jurisdictions such as the UK, US and Australia, in which the law is developed on a case-by-case basis and consolidated and amended by statute, from civil law jurisdictions such as Germany, France and Italy, where the law is primarily codified or statutory. The second meaning of 'common law' applies within common law jurisdictions and contrasts common law in the sense of 'law found in cases' with law found in statutes; this meaning is not very helpful, but it is still sometimes used. The third meaning is the one which we will employ throughout the remainder of this book. It contrasts common law in the sense of 'general law' (whether based in statute or case law) with equity in the sense of 'law which modifies the general common law rules where the general rules cause practical hardship in the particular case'. Wherever any right or power exists at common law, the role of equity is to restrain the *unconscionable* exercise of the right and to keep the power in check.

⟩ CROSS REFERENCE

To see what the outcome of this case would be, look up 'proprietary estoppel' at 17.6.

Figure 1.1 What does 'common law' mean?

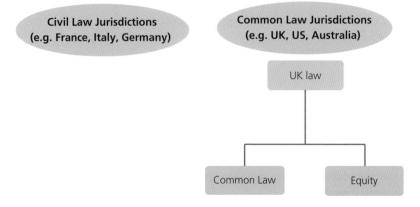

> **unconscionable** This is a hard word to define, but in the opinion of this author it describes the conduct of asserting a legal right or power in a way which in the particular context is oppressive or otherwise unjust to the party against whom the right or power is asserted.

Consider this example of equity in action: imagine that the absolute owner of a legal estate in a certain plot of land invites you to build a house on that land and promises that your reward will be the right to live in that house for the rest of your life. Suppose you build the house in the expectation that the promise will be fulfilled, but instead the owner of the land goes back on the promise. The building having been completed, the landowner shows you the formal deed of title to the land, saying 'this proves that I am the **fee simple** owner of this land. You have got no deed of title to this land, so I say that you are a trespasser and must leave immediately.' As a matter of strict law, there is no doubt that you are a trespasser and must leave the land. The law will compensate you for your time and expenditure, to make sure that the landowner is not unjustly enriched at your expense, but it will not give you that hoped-for lifelong entitlement to reside in the land. Some would describe the landowner's behaviour as clever and cunning; most, one suspects, would consider it an immoral breach of a promise. Neither opinion is relevant in a court of law, since a court of law is not a court of morality. However, what is relevant in a court of law is that the person who made the promise is using the strictness of the law to abuse you (the builder). The landowner is relying on the fact that you have not complied with the statute that requires a transfer of land to be by formal deed. If it were not for that rule of law, he would not be able to abuse you, and that is why equity gets involved. It is not because the landowner's behaviour is immoral, but because it brings the law into disrepute. The whole point of equity in a court of law is to prevent the law itself from being turned into an instrument of abuse. Hence the **maxim**: 'Equity will not permit a statute to be used as an instrument of fraud.'

> **fee simple**
> The largest and best form of land ownership in English law.

> ❯ CROSS REFERENCE
> Maxims are considered in depth later in this chapter. Equitable doctrines and remedies are considered in depth in the final chapter of the book.

> **equitable maxim** This is a traditional judicial principle developed in the old Court of Chancery which serves as a guide to the exercise of discretion in the application of equitable doctrines and the award of equitable remedies.

1.1 The historical development of equity and trusts

An appreciation of the historical development of equity and trusts is crucial to a true understanding of the law as it currently is. What is more, the rational future development of the law depends upon an understanding of its origins. We will see through the course of this chapter that the future development of equity and trusts is very much a live issue.

1.1.1 The historical development of equity

The history of equity is characterised by its continual ebb and flow between compatibility and competition with the common law. (See Table 1.1.)

Table 1.1 Historical overview of equity and trusts

12th century—Chancellor advises the King in Privy Council.

13th century—As keeper of the King's 'Great Seal', the Chancellor frames common law writs. The 'use' (precursor of the 'trust') of land is established.

14th century—As keeper of the King's conscience, the Chancellor remedies the strictness of the common laws in particular cases.

15th century—Growth of the Chancellor's court (Court of Chancery) at Westminster.

16th century—At the start of the century, Chancellors were clerics; by the end they were lawyers and the Chancellor's equitable jurisdiction was established as a branch of law rather than a branch of ecclesiastic morality. Henry VIII attempts to abolish uses of land.

17th century—Equity is established as supreme in cases of conflict between equity and the common law. Methods for indirectly enforcing uses of land become accepted and the modern trust is established.

18th century—Equity develops in a manner supplemental to the common law; modern trust doctrine and mortgage doctrine is developed and established.

19th century—Chancery and common law courts are subsumed within a new Supreme Court of Judicature. Procedures are united, but both branches of law remain functionally distinct.

20th century—Statutory consolidation and reform of the general law governing the creation and operation of trusts.

21st century—Increasing and on-going international popularity of the trust as a commercial device, even in jurisdictions without the English tradition of equity.

(NB: some events were of an on-going nature and were not limited to the indicative dates.)

1.1.1.1 Twelfth to thirteenth centuries

In the twelfth century the royal court was largely itinerant (i.e. it rarely stayed in one place for very long). The itinerary of Henry I, for instance, took him as far afield as Carlisle, Norwich, Southampton and Normandy, all within the years 1119–23, whilst still allowing time to campaign for war in Wales. Effective government required that the King and his courtiers travelled the length and breadth of the realm collecting taxes, dispensing justice and generally asserting royal authority. One of the chief courtiers was the King's 'Chancellor', a learned cleric (usually a bishop) who would advise the King and his Council. One celebrated Chancellor was St Thomas à Becket, the Archbishop of Canterbury, who was infamously assassinated by supporters of King Henry II in 1170. The Chancellor was keeper of the King's Great Seal, and beneath him were the Chancery scribes who were responsible for the King's paperwork (or parchment work as it was then).

1.1.1.2 Fourteenth to fifteenth centuries

By the early fourteenth century the King's common law was fairly well established and where it caused injustice in individual cases, with consequent embarrassment to the King's conscience, the task of providing a just remedy fell to the Chancellor. By the end of that century the Chancellor was dispensing justice on his own authority from his base in Westminster, his concern being still to remedy the rigid common law position on grounds of conscience. The petitions to the Chancellor grew in number throughout the fifteenth century and the Court of Chancery, the Chancellor's court, grew.

THINKING POINT

Is the relationship between law and equity at heart an attempt to reconcile certainty and justice?

The certainty–justice debate: The complaint against the uncertainty caused by equity's (or, more accurately, the Lord Chancellor's) interference in the common law was most memorably expressed by John Selden in the seventeenth century, when he said:

> Equity is a roguish thing. For Law we have a measure, know what to trust to; Equity is according to the conscience of him that is Chancellor, and as that is larger or narrower, so is Equity. 'T is all one as if they should make the standard for the measure we call a 'foot' a Chancellor's foot; what an uncertain measure would this be! One Chancellor has a long foot, another a short foot, a third an indifferent foot. 'T is the same thing in the Chancellor's conscience.

It is often said that the development of law is characterised by the on-going search for a balance between justice and certainty, or, to be more precise, a balance between justice in the individual case and that justice for the civilian population at large which flows from certainty in the law. The gradual move away from such ad hoc justice towards certainty led Bagnall J to suggest in *Cowcher* v *Cowcher* [1972] 1 WLR 425 at 431 that in modern times '[in] the field of equity the Chancellor's foot has been measured or is capable of measurement'. He was careful to add, however, that '[t]his does not mean that equity is past childbearing; simply that its progeny must be legitimate—by precedent out of principle'. Some few years later Browne-Wilkinson J expressed a similar view: 'Doing justice to the litigant who actually appears in court by the invention of new principles of law ought not to involve injustice to the other persons who are not litigants . . . but whose rights are fundamentally affected by the new principles' (*Re Sharpe (a bankrupt)* [1980] 1 WLR 219 at 227).

1.1.1.3 Sixteenth century

Common law suits were at this time subject to technical and inflexible forms of action, with the result that a just cause might fail due to the lack of some formality. Throughout the sixteenth century increasing numbers of petitions were brought to remedy the harshness of the common law. Chancery's ad hoc dispensation of justice prompted the accusation that equity was undermining the certainty of the law. This led William Lambarde, a sixteenth-century chancery lawyer, to ponder:

> Whether it be meet that the Chancellor should appoint unto himselfe, and publish to others any certaine Rules & Limits of Equity, or no; about the which men both godly and learned doe varie in opinion: For on the one part it is thought as hard a thing to prescribe to Equitie any certaine bounds, as it is to make one generall Law to be a meet measure of Justice in all particular cases. (quoted in S.F.C. Milsom, *Historical Foundations of the Common Law*, 2nd edn, London: Oxford University Press, 1981, p. 94)

1.1.1.4 Seventeenth century

The competition between Chancery and the common law courts came to a head in the early seventeenth century with the *Earl of Oxford's Case* (1615) 1 Rep Ch 1. Chief Justice Coke had indicted a defendant in a common law action who had deigned to apply to Lord Chancellor Ellesmere for an injunction against a common law judgment on the grounds of fraud. Lord

Ellesmere's response was to reason that such an injunction did not offend the common law courts at all—that it was effective merely *in personam* against the person who had been successful in the common law court: 'The office of the chancellor is to correct men's consciences for frauds, breaches of trust, wrongs and oppressions of what nature soever they be, and to soften and mollify the extremity of the law.'

> ***in personam*** A remedy, such as an injunction, is said to operate *in personam* because it is enforced against a defendant personally. An *in personam* action is normally contrasted with an action *in rem*, which is a claim against property held by the defendant regardless of the defendant's identity. Failure to comply with the injunction is a direct contempt of court punishable by fine or imprisonment. For more on injunctions, see Chapter 20.

In the end, the dispute between the Chief Justice and the Lord Chancellor was referred, in 1616, to King James I. The King resolved the dispute in favour of Lord Ellesmere, on the advice of his Attorney-General, Sir Francis Bacon. (Bacon went on, in fact, to succeed Lord Ellesmere as Chancellor.) It was thereby established that where equity and common law conflict, equity shall prevail.

1.1.1.5 Eighteenth century

In the eighteenth century equity matured through the careful Chancellorship of, amongst others, Heneage Finch, Lord Nottingham, who has been called the 'father' of modern equity (W. Holdsworth, *History of English Law*, vi, London: Methuen, p. 547). During the eighteenth century equity developed in a manner harmonious with the common law, rather than in competition with it. Chancery appears to have been a beneficiary of the so-called 'Enlightenment' philosophy which emerged in that century.

1.1.1.6 Nineteenth century

Somewhat a victim of its own success, by the early nineteenth century the Court of Chancery had become hopelessly busy, despite the appointment in 1729 of the chief Chancery Master, the Master of the Rolls, to sit as a second judge. In 1813 a Vice-Chancellor was appointed. There were now three judges presiding in Chancery, where once there had been the Chancellor alone. Yet the first Vice-Chancellor, upon being asked whether the three judges could cope, is said to have replied: 'No; not three angels.'

 OUTSIDE THE BOX

Charles Dickens, *Bleak House*, 1852–3

Chapter 1—In Chancery

Never can there come fog too thick, never can there come mud and mire too deep, to assort with the groping and floundering condition which this High Court of Chancery, most pestilent of hoary sinners, holds this day in the sight of heaven and earth . . . Well may the court be dim, with wasting candles here and there; well may the fog hang heavy in it, as if it would never get out; well may the stained-glass windows lose their colour and admit no light of day into the place; well may the uninitiated from the streets, who peep in through the glass panes in the door, be deterred from entrance by its owlish aspect and by the drawl, languidly echoing to the roof from the padded dais where the Lord High Chancellor looks into the lantern that has no light in it and where the attendant wigs are all stuck in a fog-bank! This is the Court of Chancery, which has its decaying houses and its blighted lands in every shire, which has its worn-out lunatic in every madhouse and its dead in every churchyard, which has its ruined suitor with his slipshod heels and threadbare dress borrowing and begging through the round of every man's acquaintance, which gives to monied might the means abundantly of wearying out the right, which so exhausts finances, patience, courage, hope, so overthrows the brain and breaks the heart, that there is not an honourable man among its practitioners who would not give—who does not often give—the warning, 'Suffer any wrong that can be done you rather than come here!'

The Court of Chancery Act 1850 and the Court of Chancery Procedure Act 1852 were early attempts to wrestle with the procedural problems in the Court of Chancery. But the great step towards expediting the procedure of Chancery came when Lord Chancellor Selborne introduced the Judicature Act 1873 into Parliament. Ironically, it was due to administrative delays that the statute did not in fact come into force until 1875, when it was re-enacted with amendments. We now refer collectively to the Judicature Acts 1873–5. By these enactments the Supreme Court of Judicature was established with concurrent jurisdiction to administer the rules of equity and law.

1.1.1.7 **Twentieth century**

It is of vital importance to realise that the Judicature Acts did not do away with the distinction between law and equity; equity and law still have their distinct functions. True, this book is primarily concerned with equitable doctrines, remedies and institutions having their origin in the old Court of Chancery, but nowadays we should expect to find the equity function flourishing in every court and every corner of the law. The leading legal historian Professor J.H. Baker has observed that, as the business of the Chancery Division of the High Court increasingly concerns commerce and property, where certainty is mostly highly prized, nowadays 'Chancery judges are the least likely to administer equity in the broad sense'. There is some truth in that, but on the other hand we have learned that equity is needed *most* where the law is *most* certain.

1.1.2 **The historical development of the trust**

The ancestor of the *trust* was the *use*. The *use* of land has existed since at least the early thirteenth century, and became an important device during the Crusades. When Guille de Pends left for battle he might well have left title to his landed estate in the name of a trusted friend, to be held for the use and benefit of Guille's family during his absence. The use might have read: 'I convey all my lands to Richard de Livers for the use of Lady de Pends and her children.' Nevertheless, the use of land, though recognised by Chancery, differed from the trust of land in one important respect, as Professor Simpson (*op. cit.* at p. 170) has said:

> The use had originated as a personal confidence or trust placed by one person in the other, and even when a use became a species of property it continued to bear marks of this origin. Thus it never came to bind the land itself; rather, it was conceived to bind the conscience of persons into whose hands the land came.

In 1535 Henry VIII pushed through the Statute of Uses with a view to abolishing uses of land, because landowners were employing uses effectively to separate the benefit of the land from legal title so as to keep the benefits for themselves whilst avoiding the payment of fees which the Crown levied against legal title. The effect of the statute was to transfer legal title to the beneficiary of the use, thereby bringing the use to an end or 'executing' it. By means of this statute Henry VIII executed a great many uses, but, as with his wives, he didn't execute them all. The only uses that were executed were those concerning land where there was a single named beneficiary, usually the original absolute owner, and which therefore represented a sham device for avoiding the payment of fees to the Crown. Eventually, of course, inventive legal draftsmen found creative ways of avoiding the statute entirely. One such was a 'use upon a use' in the form: 'to A to the use of B to the use of C.' The Statute of Uses only executed the first use (by vesting legal title in B) but B would still then hold it to the use of the intended beneficiary, C. Thus the statute was bypassed and Chancery came to recognise the 'use upon a use', which in time became known as the trust. The trust was not, however, a mere replication of the old use under a new name. Crucially, the trust did not have to be established *in personam* against every person into whose hands it came; rather, the trust bound the land itself. In the Court of Chancery the ***bona fide*** purchaser for valuable consideration of legal title to the land would take free of the trust if he had purchased without notice of the trust (*per* James LJ in *Pilcher v Rawlins* (1872) 7 Ch App 259 at 268–9). This person was known, accordingly, as 'equity's darling', and is sometimes still referred to as such today (see, for example, *Griggs Group Ltd v Evans* [2005] FSR 31, [2005] EWCA Civ 11, Court of Appeal, *per* Jacob LJ at para. 7).

> **bona fide**
> Good faith (bona fide is pronounced 'bone-a fyde' or 'bonna fye-dee').

THINKING POINT

Jeffrey Hackney (in *Understanding Equity and Trusts*, London: Fontana, 1987) argues that the Court of Chancery afforded special status to the *bona fide* purchaser because it had no jurisdiction to question the legal title of such a person. In other words, he suggests that equity's darling is in truth the darling of the common law. Do you agree?

The situation had been reached whereby the Court of Chancery acknowledged the existence of a separate equitable title under a trust which the equitable (beneficial) owner could enforce against the legal owner (the trustee) and against third parties who acquired the legal title with notice of the equitable interest binding upon it. Where Chancery recognised two or more parties as having competing equitable claims of equal merit, the Chancery judge would give priority to whichever claim came first in time.

> **CROSS REFERENCE**
> See the maxim *qui prior est tempore potior est jure* at 1.3.10.

The court's approach to disputes between legal owners and equitable owners and disputes between equitable owners *inter se* was neatly summarised in *Liverpool Marine Credit Co v Wilson* (1872) 7 Ch App 507 at 511: 'The legal owner's right is paramount to every equitable charge not affecting his own conscience; the equitable owner, in the absence of special circumstances, takes subject to all equities prior in date to his own estate or charge.' The point is that equitable 'title' is by no means the equal and opposite of legal title, but is rather in the nature of a restriction on the legal owner that has limited proprietary status as regards third parties.

Through this scheme of priority to claims in land, Chancery created a law of property where previously there had existed only the common law concept of formal title. In the eighteenth and nineteenth centuries the trust was used extensively in relation to land to effect settlements according to which land could be kept within families for generation after generation. Changes in social attitudes, not to mention fiscal considerations and the onset of endemic inflation, have seen a dramatic decline in the use of trusts for this purpose. However, it is because of equity's willingness to acknowledge property behind legal title that trusts, despite their origins as medieval land obligations, are nowadays asserted with regularity in modern commercial contexts, and in particular in the context of insolvency.

1.2 Equity and trusts today

'It can no longer be doubted that equity has moved out of the family home and the settled estate and into the market place'—Sir Peter Millett, 'Equity—The Road Ahead' (1995) 9 TLI 35 at 36.

1.2.1 **The commercial context**

In 1995, in *Royal Brunei Airlines* v *Tan* [1995] 3 WLR 64 (see 19.5), Lord Nicholls of Birkenhead observed that '[t]he proper role of equity in commercial transactions is a topical question'. It is, of course, but it is also a rather old one. In 1927, Atkin LJ criticised the introduction of equitable principles into commercial sale of goods transactions as a migration 'into territory where they are trespassers' (*Re Wait* [1927] 1 Ch 606 at 635). Against this Sir Peter Millett has suggested (in the article quoted at the top of this section) that '[t]he intervention of equity in commercial transactions, long resisted by common lawyers, can no longer be withstood'.

On both sides of the modern debate there is an implicit assumption that the intervention of equity in the field of commerce is something of a new development. In fact, equity has always felt free to wander through that particular field. Professor Baker observed in *An Introduction to English Legal History* (3rd edn, London: Butterworths, 1990, pp. 119–21) that, throughout the fifteenth century, tort and commercial cases featured as prominently in Chancery as property disputes. He records that 'the typical petition complained of weakness or poverty or the abuse of position by an opponent'. It is interesting that some of the leading modern cases in which equitable principles have been developed still involve precisely the same kinds of plea. See, for instance, *O'Sullivan* v *MAM* [1985] QB 428 (see 12.1.2), where a pop star was granted equitable rescission of an unfavourable contract he had signed as a young and inexperienced artist when subject to the undue influence of his manager.

> **CROSS REFERENCE**
>
> Despite reluctance to extend equity in commerce, commercial agents such as banks, solicitors, directors etc. may in some circumstances be treated 'as if' they were trustees (see in Chapter 19).

As for the introduction of *trusts* into commerce, Bramwell LJ had this to say:

> Now I do not desire to find fault with the various intricacies and doctrines concerned with trusts, but I should be very sorry to see them introduced into commercial transactions, and an agent in a commercial case turned into a trustee with all the troubles that attend that relation. (*New Zealand & Australian Land Co* v *Watson* (1881) 7 QBD 374 at 382)

1.2.2 **The dualism/fusion debate**

Professor Ashburner set out the dualist position in his *Principles of Equity* (2nd edn, London: Butterworth, 1933), where he famously described the common law and equity as two streams of jurisdiction which 'though they run in the same channel run side by side and do not mingle their waters'. Regardless of the substantial merits of his analysis, Professor Ashburner's metaphor is not a particularly helpful one. The picture of two streams running in the same channel without mingling is a hard one to imagine. Half a century later, Lord Diplock took the metaphor to its logical conclusion when he stated, *obiter*, that 'it may be possible for a short distance to discern the source from which each part of the combined stream came, but . . . the waters of the confluent streams of law and equity have surely mingled now' (*United Scientific Holdings Ltd* v *Burnley Borough Council* [1978] AC 904 at 924–5). I prefer the metaphor of the horse and rider (see *Equity Stirring* in Further reading). The common law is the horse and equity is the rider. The common law is the main muscle of the justice system and does most of the work. The common law walks straight on, following the rigid rule, and the rider is content to sit back in the

dualism
In its most extreme form, the belief that, despite the Judicature Acts, equity remains utterly distinct from the common law.

fusion
In its most extreme form, the belief that, after the Judicature Acts, equity and the law are indistinguishable.

saddle where the law maintains a just course. 'Equity follows the law', as a maxim puts it. Only where the straight course of the law is going to cause harm in a particular case, as if a person were about to be unconscionably trampled by the weight of the law, does equity intervene. Equity, the rider, steers the law in such a case. As another maxim puts it: 'where Law and Equity conflict, equity prevails.'

The dualists took up arms again when Meagher, Gummow and Lehane, authors of the leading Australian textbook *Equity: Doctrines and Remedies*, described their Lordships' decision in *United Scientific* as 'the low water mark of modern English jurisprudence' (2nd edn, London: LexisNexis Butterworths, 1984, p. xi), to which Professor Peter Birks gave the following characteristically quotable response:

P. Birks, *Civil Wrongs: A New World*, The Butterworth Lectures 1990–1, p. 55

It is dangerous, not to say absurd, almost 120 years after the Judicature Acts, to persist in habits of thought calculated to submerge and conceal one or other half of our law . . . Meagher, Gummow and Lehane . . . did not attempt to say why the properties and dispositions of equity, which they rightly admire, should be confined to something less than the whole law. They did not attempt it because it cannot be done, any more than the courts might justify themselves in doing alpha justice on Mondays and Tuesdays and something less for the rest of the week.

In *Elders Pastoral Ltd* v *Bank of New Zealand* [1989] 2 NZLR 180 at 193, Somer J provided a more conciliatory summary of the current relationship between law and equity, when he observed that '[n]either law nor equity is now stifled by its origin and the fact that both are administered by one Court has inevitably meant that each has borrowed from the other in furthering the harmonious development of the law as a whole'.

Sir Anthony Mason has argued (in 'The Place of Equity and Equitable Remedies in the Contemporary Common Law World' (1994) 110 LQR 238) that the Judicature Acts are an opportunity for equity to progress ahead of the common law. He argues that 'Equity has yielded to the common law some ground that conceivably it might have claimed for itself', including the territory appropriated by the 'boundless expansion of the tort of negligence, based on the existence of a duty of care to one's neighbour'. Consider the 'thinking point', next.

 THINKING POINT

Is Sir Anthony's expansive version of equity a correct one, bearing in mind the way that equity operated historically in relation to the common law?

It is submitted that it is not correct. Equity and law are concerned to remedy similar ideas of negligence, but in quite different contexts. Unlike the law of tort, equity does not prescribe minimum standards of civilian behaviour, let alone suggest a paradigm 'neighbourhood principle'. In equity there is no gold standard of conscientious conduct equivalent to the objective opinion of the reasonable man in tort, the so-called man on the Clapham omnibus. Equity does not concern itself with civil conduct generally, but only with conduct in relation to pre-existing legal rights, powers and duties. In short, there never is equity without law. As the maxim tells us, 'equity follows the law' (see 1.3.2).

One problem with an expansive ambition for the equitable jurisdiction is that equity can too easily become confused with the quite distinct concept of morality. This is a distinction that the next section seeks to clarify.

1.2.3 Equity, common law and morality

It should be clear from the preceding discussion that equity is most certainly a branch of law and not a branch of morality (see Figure 1.2). However, largely due to its ecclesiastical origins and use of the language of 'unconscionability', it is a branch of law that has a moral flavour not so evident in the common law—although Sir Peter Millett opined in *Trustee of the Property of F.C. Jones and Sons (a firm)* v *Jones* [1997] Ch 159 that it would 'be a mistake to suppose that the common law courts disregarded considerations of conscience'. Just one example of equity's concern with matters of conscience is the requirement that, in relation to investment, trustees should 'take such care as an ordinary prudent person would take who was minded to invest for the benefit of another for whom he felt *morally* obliged to provide' (emphasis added) (*per* Lindley LJ in *Re Whiteley*, see 11.3.1).

Equitable 'morality' is limited to the restraint of unconscionability in legal contexts. Equity will not enforce a bare moral promise (*Taylor* v *Dickens* [1998] 1 FLR 806; see also 17.4). In fact, equity will sometimes encourage a trustee to break a non-legal promise ('gentlemen's agreement') if to do so would be in the best financial interest of beneficiaries (*Buttle* v *Saunders* [1950] 2 All ER 193). How can this be reconciled with the fact that equity, being unable to countenance the breaking of certain types of a promise made in a legal contract, will enforce the contract according to the maxim that *equity sees as done that which ought to be done* (see 1.3.8)? The answer is that equity is not concerned with immoral conduct generally, but only with the unconscionable abuse of *legal* power or position. A great deal of immoral conduct is prohibited neither in law nor in equity. In fact, despite the ecclesiastical origins of equity, only three of the Ten Commandments (see Exodus, chapter 20) have any real force today in English law, and even then in limited form. Equity cannot even claim the three survivors. 'Do not steal', 'do not kill' and 'do not accuse falsely' are to be found in the *common law*: as theft, homicide and perjury!

Figure 1.2 Equity is not morality

 THINKING POINT

Do you think it would it be right for equity to assume to regulate wrongs such as infringement of privacy?

Equity is not the appropriate solution to such a wrong—it is down to the common law, or Parliament, to provide a general remedy for a general civil wrong, if it is thought that one is required. Equity should be restricted to restraining the unconscionable abuse of an established legal right or power. The creation of a modern law of 'breach of confidence' should not have been undertaken (as it has been undertaken—see, for instance, the case of *Douglas v Hello! Ltd* [2001] QB 967, CA) in the name of 'equity'. Indeed, the House of Lords has acknowledged that the equitable label 'breach of confidence' is inappropriate in this context. Lord Nicholls suggests that '[t]he essence of the tort is better encapsulated now as misuse of private information' (*Campbell v MGN Ltd* [2004] 2 AC 457, HL, at paras 13–14), although that message appears to have been overlooked in an appeal in the *Douglas v Hello!* litigation (*Douglas v Hello! Ltd* [2005] EWCA Civ 595, CA).

Equity is morally ambiguous because it is selective in its recognition of unconscionable behaviour as between different legal contexts. Sometimes commercial sharp practice goes unchecked by equity, even if oppressive, and even if advantage has been taken of a legal entitlement. So, for example, in *Liverpool Marine Credit Co v Hunter* (1867–8) 3 Ch App 479 the defendants, the owners of a ship subject to a mortgage, deliberately sent the ship to be sold in Louisiana, knowing that Louisiana did not recognise mortgages of ships. The claimant argued that the defendant had committed a positive fraud. The judge held (at 487) that the defendant owed no duty of care to the claimant: 'I do not . . . see how Equity could properly interfere to restrain the actions which, however oppressive . . . arose out of remedies employed by the plaintiff for the recovery of his debt, of which the law entitled him to avail himself.'

The fact must be faced that equity's scrutiny of conscience varies dramatically according to the context in which legal powers are exercised and duties discharged. In *Barnes v Addy* (1874) 9 Ch App 244, a case of alleged accessory liability against an agent who had acted for a trustee who had breached his trust, Lord Selborne said that 'strangers are not to be made constructive trustees merely because they act as the agents of trustees in *transactions within their legal powers*, transactions, perhaps of which a Court of Equity may disapprove' (emphasis added).

1.2.4 Concurrent rights in equity and common law

So long as law and equity remain to any extent distinct, they must function alongside each other. It is also true that rights recognised in law and equity must co-exist alongside each other.

 CASE CLOSE-UP

Walsh v Lonsdale (1882) 21 ChD 9

The facts were that a landlord and tenant had entered into a contract for a seven-year lease, the tenant had gone into possession, but the parties had forgotten to execute the formal deed needed for a valid legal lease. Despite the absence of the deed, the landlord claimed rent in advance in accordance with the contract and attempted to enforce his claim by exercising the *legal* right to distress for rent (which is the right to take and sell the tenants' goods in lieu of rent). The tenant claimed that in the absence of a *legal* deed there could be no *legal* right to claim rent in advance, and that rent should be payable in arrears, so he sought an injunction against the distress.

Sir George Jessel MR, one of the leading equity judges of all time, stated (at pp. 14–15): 'There are not two estates as there were formerly . . . There is only one Court, and the equity rules prevail in it. The tenant holds under an agreement for a lease. He holds, therefore, under the same terms in equity as if a lease had been granted.' Ironically, the *tenant* had sought the aid of equity (in the form of an injunction), but the *landlord* actually received it (in the form of an equitable lease). Paradoxically, the landlord was permitted to exercise the traditionally *legal* right to levy distress for rent against the tenant of an *equitable* lease. Sir George based his judgment on the maxim that *equity sees as done that which ought to be done* (see 1.3.8).

Of special interest to us is the fact that Sir George acknowledged that alongside the tenant's fixed-term equitable lease, the tenant *also* had a periodic legal tenancy which arose at law from the fact that the tenant was in possession and paying rent. Thus equitable and legal leases can co-exist. (The legal tenancy could be brought to an end by giving notice, so the equitable lease was more valuable—hence the litigation!)

For a further example of the co-existence of legal and equitable rights, see the next Case Close-Up.

 CASE CLOSE-UP

Barclays Bank v Quistclose Investments Ltd [1970] AC 567

The facts were, briefly, that Quistclose made a loan to a company (RR Ltd) on the brink of insolvency for the express purpose of paying a dividend that the company had declared in favour of its shareholders. Had the loan been repaid in the normal course of events, the case would have been just like any other in which common law contractual obligations had been discharged. However, the borrowing company became insolvent before the dividend had been paid. At that point one might assume, as did Barclays Bank, that Quistclose's contractual claim would have to join the queue of personal claims against the estate of the insolvent company. In fact, a majority of their Lordships favoured quite the opposite result.

Lord Wilberforce, delivering the leading speech, held that the arrangement gave rise to a primary trust in favour of the shareholders in whose favour the dividend had been declared, and a secondary trust in favour of Quistclose arising in the event of the company's insolvency. What type of trust this secondary trust might be is considered at 2.3.4.2. What is significant for present purposes is that a trust of *any* sort was held to exist *alongside* the common law contractual debt. Lord Wilberforce held (at 582) that '[t]here is surely no difficulty in recognising the co-existence in one transaction of legal and equitable rights and remedies'. No doubt it has never been a difficulty to recognise the existence of concurrent legal and equitable rights, but whether as a matter of policy it *should* be recognised is quite a different matter.

 THINKING POINT

Can you think of any policy reasons for and against the decision in *Quistclose*?

The consequence of Lord Wilberforce's analysis was, of course, to take Quistclose out of the queue of general creditors and to promote its claim to the status of proprietary right. *Against* this it could be argued that the borrowing company had unfairly preferred Quistclose to its other creditors (including, notably, its long-term banker Barclays). In *favour* it could be argued that to save a company from insolvency is for the good of all its creditors, and is to the benefit of society generally, and that special protection should therefore be advanced to those creditors who lend money to companies on the brink of insolvency.

1.2.5 Co-operative remedies in equity and common law

Equitable remedies are considered in depth in the final chapter of this book. Here it is worth pointing out that law and equity take a co-operative approach to remedies. At law, contracts do not have to be performed—each party has the option to breach their contract and pay common law damages to the other party. Equity follows the law, but the court will exceptionally decree (order) **specific performance**, which requires the contract to be performed according to its terms or according to the terms of the court order.

▶ CROSS REFERENCE

For detailed consideration of the remedy of specific performance, see Chapter 20.

> **specific performance** An equitable remedy taking the form of an order of the court requiring performance of a contract; it is awarded where the court will not permit the defendant to breach his contract and pay common law damages by way of remedy.

The diagram in Figure 1.3 summarises the position:

Where common law damages would provide an *adequate* remedy, specific performance will not be awarded. The court will only decree specific performance where 'it can by that means do more and complete justice' than the common law (*Wilson v N & BJ Rly Co* (1874) 9 Ch App 279 at 284). For this reason a number of specific performance cases relate to land, for all land is unique and damages are therefore presumed to be inadequate compensation for breach of a contract to convey land.

Figure 1.3 Specific performance

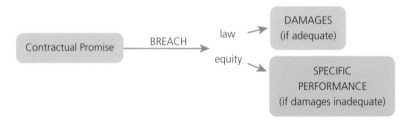

▶ CROSS REFERENCE

The Contracts (Rights of Third Parties) Act 1999 now permits persons in Mrs Beswick's position (i.e. an identified third-party beneficiary of a contract) to enforce the contract in some cases.

Q | CASE CLOSE-UP

Beswick v Beswick [1968] AC 58

The facts were that Mr B gave his coal merchant business to his nephew, in consideration of which the nephew agreed to look after Mr B's widow after Mr B's death, to the order of £5 per week. In due course Mr B died and his widow sought to enforce the nephew's promise. The House of Lords granted the equitable remedy of specific performance of the contract in favour of the widow, because the defendant had received the whole benefit of the contract and as a matter of conscience the court would ensure that he carried out his promise so as to achieve 'mutuality' between the contracting parties. However, the widow could not enforce the contract in her own person, but only in her capacity as Mr B's personal representative. The doctrine of privity of contract would not permit her to sue in her own right. The fact that the widow was suing in her husband's place meant that common law damages would have been merely nominal (the husband, being dead, had suffered no real loss); damages being inadequate, specific performance was ordered.

Incidentally, Lord Reid acknowledged that had the case involved a trust for the benefit of Mrs B, as opposed to a contract for her benefit, she would have been entitled to sue in her own person. However, counsel for Mrs B did not argue that there was a trust, and so their Lordships restricted their deliberations to the contract issue.

Equity's co-operation with the common law in this context receives extra assistance from statute. According to the Chancery Amendment Act 1858 (known as Lord Cairns' Act), courts can award common law-type damages in lieu of an injunction or decree of specific performance (see, now, s 50 of the Senior Courts Act 1981).

1.2.6 **Equity and crime**

The court of equity is not a court of punishment (see *Vyse* v *Foster* (1872–3) 8 LR Ch App 309 at 333). However, equity's traditional concern for matters of conscience has led to some interesting points of overlap with the criminal law. For one thing, it is well established that a killer will not be permitted to take their victim's property by will or **intestacy** (*Re Sigsworth* [1935] Ch 89). Furthermore, if the killer's innocent children were next in line to inherit under the victim's intestacy, they will receive nothing if the killer is still alive, with the result that the estate may pass to some more remote relative of the victim in ways the victim would never have intended. This seems unfair, so the Law Commission recommended that where a potential heir is disqualified under this so-called forfeiture rule the estate should be distributed on the fictional assumption that the killer is dead ('The Forfeiture Rule and the Law of Succession Report' (Law Com Report No 295), 27 July 2005). This reform has now been enacted by the Estates of Deceased Persons (Forfeiture Rule and Law of Succession) Act 2011, which came into force in February 2012.

> **intestacy**
> The legal scheme for distributing the estates of people who die without leaving a valid will.

If equity takes note of criminal behaviour, then it is equally true that the criminal courts take notice of equity, if only in as much as dishonest breach of trust or **fiduciary** duty is an aggravating factor in cases of theft. (See, for example, *R* v *Clark* [1998] Crim LR 227.)

> **fiduciary** (As an adjective) descriptive of a duty of exclusive loyalty owed in law by one person to another and descriptive also of certain offices (the paradigm being trusteeship) under which a fiduciary duty is always one of the duties owed. (As a noun) descriptive of persons owing a fiduciary duty: although a trustee is the paradigm fiduciary, the term 'fiduciary' is often used as shorthand to indicate 'a fiduciary other than a trustee'.

1.2.7 **Equity and restitution**

Restitution is a remedy that operates by reversing unjust enrichment. In the leading case *Banque Financière de la Cité* v *Parc (Battersea) Ltd* [1999] 1 AC 221, Lord Steyn set out the following list of questions that a court will ask when considering a restitutionary claim: (a) Has the defendant benefited, in the sense of being enriched? (b) Was the enrichment at the claimant's expense? (c) Was the enrichment unjust? (d) Are there any defences? In simple terms, a claim for restitution will be successful if the answers to (a), (b) and (c) are all 'yes', and if the answer to (d) is 'no'. (*Banque Financière* was approved by the Supreme Court in *Investment Trust Companies* v *Revenue and Customs Commissioners* [2017] UKSC 29, which held that consumers have no right to make a claim in restitution directly against HMRC for overpaid VAT, but should claim against the supplier unless it would be 'impossible or excessively difficult'.) An interesting example of a case in which **restitution** was awarded to reverse an unjust enrichment is *Cressman* v *Coys of Kensington* [2004] All ER (D) 69, Court of Appeal, in which the purchaser of a car that had been mistakenly transferred with a valuable personalised number plate was liable to account for the value of the number plate because he knew of the mistake at the time of the purchase.

---

restitution There is no simple definition of restitution, and if there is, it is disputed on account of its simplicity. For present purposes we will adopt Professor Andrew Burrows' simple (and disputed) proposition that '[r]estitution is the law concerned with reversing a defendant's unjust enrichment at the plaintiff's expense' (*The Law of Restitution*, London: Butterworths, 1993, p. 1).

Supporters of the development of restitution as a coherent body of English law in its own right play down the distinction between the legal and equitable nature of restitutionary remedies and the routes to asserting them. The emphasis is upon remedial justice for the claimant, be it achieved by requiring the defendant to disgorge his unjustified receipts under, for example, a common law 'action for money had and received', or as a constructive or resulting trustee in equity. This aspect of restitution was met with some scepticism in *Westdeutsche Landesbank Girozentrale* v *Islington London Borough Council* [1996] 2 WLR 802, where Lord Browne-Wilkinson commented that 'the search for a perceived need to strengthen the remedies of a plaintiff claiming in restitution involves, to my mind, a distortion of trust principles'.

Nevertheless, the House of Lords in *Lipkin Gorman (a firm)* v *Karpnale Ltd* [1991] 3 WLR 10 did appear to acknowledge a general remedy of restitution based on the concept of unjust enrichment.

🔍 CASE CLOSE-UP

Lipkin Gorman (a firm) v *Karpnale Ltd* [1991] 3 WLR 10, House of Lords

A partner in a firm of solicitors (the claimants) had used monies from the firm's client account in order to gamble at the 'Playboy' casino (run by the first defendant, Karpnale Ltd). The House of Lords decided that the casino had to pay back the monies it had received to the extent that it had been unjustly enriched by them. However, it did not have to pay back monies to the extent that it had changed its position in good faith as a result of receiving them (the so-called change of position defence). It was permitted to deduct a sum equivalent to the winnings it had paid out to the fraudulent solicitor before making restitution to his firm.

> Lord Goff of Chieveley: 'In these circumstances it is right that we should ask ourselves: why do we feel that it would be unjust to allow restitution in cases such as these? The answer must be that, where an innocent defendant's position is so changed that he will suffer an injustice if called upon to repay or to repay in full, the injustice of requiring him so to repay outweighs the injustice of denying the plaintiff restitution. If the plaintiff pays money to the defendant under a mistake of fact, and the defendant then, acting in good faith, pays the money or part of it to charity, it is unjust to require the defendant to make restitution to the extent that he has so changed his position. Likewise, on facts such as those in the present case, if a thief steals my money and pays it to a third party who gives it away to charity, that third party should have a good defence to an action for money had and received. In other words, *bona fide* change of position should of itself be a good defence in such cases as these. The principle is widely recognised throughout the common law world . . . The time for its recognition in this country is, in my opinion, long overdue.'

According to one of the leading academic advocates of a substantive law of restitution, Professor Peter Birks, '[t]heir Lordships [in *Lipkin*] looked forward to the day in which there might be a synthesis of common law and equity relating to restitution of misapplied funds' (*Civil Wrongs: A New World*, The Butterworth Lectures 1990–1, pp. 55, 56). Certainly this was the view of Lord Goff (the co-author, with Professor Gareth Jones, of *Goff and Jones on Restitution*). His Lordship, having accepted that the solicitors' claim was founded upon the unjust enrichment of the club, and that the club was entitled to defend that claim to the extent that it had changed its position in good faith, said:

> The recognition of change of position as a defence should be doubly beneficial. It will enable a more generous approach to be taken to the recognition of the right to restitution, in the knowledge that the defence is, in appropriate cases, available; and, while recognising the different functions of property at law and in equity, there may also in due course develop a more consistent approach to tracing claims, in which common defences are recognised as available to such claims, whether advanced at law or in equity.

❯ CROSS REFERENCE
For detailed consideration of the tracing procedure, see Chapter 18.

 THINKING POINT

What does 'unjust' mean in 'unjust enrichment'? If a fundamental principle of civil justice is that nobody should be deprived of their legal or equitable property rights except by voluntary transfer or agreement, can we really imagine a future English law in which 'unjust enrichment' can be established without first respecting the very distinction between equity and law that some proponents of the restitutionary remedy would seek to abolish?

1.3 The maxims of equity

The remedial jurisdiction of equity was predicated not upon the recognition of formal entitlement, but upon the exercise of the court's discretion; and in the exercise of discretion, maxims are more useful than rules.

1.3.1 **Equity will not suffer a wrong without a remedy**

The Latin version of this maxim suggests equity to be the healer of all ills: *nullus recedat e curia cancellariae sine remedio* (nobody leaves the Court of Chancery without remedy). The reality, of course, is that equity does not concern itself with every type of wrong (see 1.2.1). However, where an activity is one with which the law is concerned, and in relation to which the law provides no sufficient remedy, equity will endeavour to supplement the shortcomings of the common law.

1.3.2 **Equity follows the law**

The judge in *Leech* v *Schweder* (1873) 9 LR Ch App 463 gave the following useful exposition of this maxim (at 475): 'I always supposed that where a right existed at law and a person only came into equity because the Court of Equity had a more convenient remedy than a court of law . . . there equity followed the law, and the person entitled to the right had no greater right in equity than at law.'

1.3.3 **Equity looks to substance not form**

In *Walsh* v *Lonsdale* (1882) 21 ChD 9 we have already considered one of the most dramatic illustrations of this principle (see 1.2.4). Another nice illustration is provided by *Locking* v *Parker* (1873) 8 LR Ch App 30, where the question arose whether a real security in the form of a trust for sale of land was or was not a mortgage. The judge held that 'it is not for a Court of Equity to be making distinctions between forms instead of attending to the real substance and essence of the transaction. Whatever form the matter took, I am of the opinion that this was solely a mortgage transaction.'

It should not be assumed, however, that the common law is blind to substance. In *Street* v *Mountford* [1985] 1 AC 809 Lord Templeman famously refused to recognise an occupier's right in land to be a personal 'licence', even though it had been labelled a 'licence' and was intended by the parties to be such. Instead he held that it was a lease, because an examination of the substantial relationship between the parties revealed that the tenant had in fact got exclusive possession of the landlord's premises. The name the parties used could not alter the substantial nature of the transaction. As Shakespeare put it in *Romeo and Juliet* (Act II, scene ii): 'What's in a name? That which we call a rose by any other name would smell as sweet.' Lord Templeman preferred another gardening metaphor: 'The manufacture of a five-pronged implement for manual digging results in a fork even if the manufacturer, unfamiliar with the English language, insists that he intended to make and has made a spade.'

Nevertheless, if we take the example of a ten-year lease of land contained in a document labelled 'licence', the fact remains that the common law will only recognise the document as creating a valid legal lease if the document itself is in the *form* of a deed. It is in relation to statutory formality requirements such as these that equity is able to take a less constrained approach to fulfilling the substantial intentions of the parties. See the next section.

1.3.4 **Equity will not permit a statute to be used as an instrument of fraud**

This maxim usually applies to restrain a defendant from relying in bad faith upon the absence of some statutory formality in order to defeat the claimant's just claim. The leading authority is

Rochefoucauld v *Boustead* [1897] 1 Ch 196, which was applied in *Bannister* v *Bannister* [1948] 2 All ER 133 and *Lyus* v *Prowsa Developments* [1982] 1 WLR 1044. See, generally, Chapter 3 at 3.2.1–3.2.3.

A more radical, and relatively unknown, possibility is that equity might, by virtue of its *in personam* jurisdiction, have power not simply to prevent existing statutes from being used as instruments of fraud, but to restrain an improper application to Parliament for the enactment of a new private Act of Parliament. The possibility was admitted in *Re London, Chatham and Dover Railway Arrangement Act* (1869–70) 5 LR Ch App 671, although the court thought it difficult to conceive of a case in which it would be right for the court to exercise the power.

1.3.5 Equity acts *in personam*

One of the most useful modern applications of equity's *in personam* jurisdiction has been in relation to international freezing injunctions (formerly known as *Mareva* injunctions: *Mareva Compania Naviera SA* v *International Bulkcarriers SA* [1975] 2 Lloyd's Rep 509; [1980] 1 All ER 2). The injunction is effective *in personam* against any person made a defendant to proceedings in an English court, and is not defeated by the mere fact that the assets subject to the injunction are based outside the jurisdiction of the English court (although *freezing* injunctions are usually used to prevent assets from being taken outside the English jurisdiction). See Chapter 20 at 20.2.3.7.

1.3.6 Those who come to equity must come with clean hands

In *Lee* v *Haley* (1869) 5 LR Ch App 155 the claimants failed when they sought an injunction to protect their trade as coal merchants. The court held that they had 'unclean hands', not because of the coal, but because they had been dishonestly selling their customers short. As the judge said (at 158): 'if the Plaintiffs had been systematically and knowingly carrying on a fraudulent trade, and delivering short weight [of coal], it is beyond all question that this court would not interfere to protect them in carrying on such trade.'

The maxim applies in the case of injunctions and on applications for specific performance because the award of such remedies lies in the discretion of the court. The maxim will not be applied to prevent a claimant from bringing an action under an established equitable right (*Rowan* v *Dann* 64 P & CR 202).

It is crucial to realise that equity only insists on the good behaviour of those who *come to equity* seeking a remedy. It does not insist that the successful equitable claimant must continue to use his equitable interest with probity after the award. This is perhaps nowhere better illustrated than in the case of *Williams* v *Staite*.

1.3.7 Those who come to equity must do equity

The 1877 edition of Story's *Commentaries on Equity Jurisprudence* states, in the context of rescission and specific performance, that:

> the interference of a court of equity is a matter of mere discretion . . . And in all cases of this sort . . . the court will, in granting relief, impose such terms upon the party as it deems the real justice of the case to require . . . The maxim here is emphatically applied—he who seeks equity must do equity.

> ### 🔍 CASE CLOSE-UP
>
> **Williams v Staite [1979] Ch 291**
>
> The facts of that case were that the holders of an equitable right to occupy a cottage for life persistently interfered with their neighbour's enjoyment of an adjoining cottage. The neighbour had purchased the legal titles to *both* cottages from the person against whom the bad neighbours had established their equitable interest. On account of the harassment that he had suffered, the legal owner sought to evict his bad neighbours. The judge at first instance held that the equitable rights of the bad neighbours should be revoked by reason of their conduct, and he awarded possession to the claimant. The defendants successfully appealed.
>
> Goff LJ held that, after the appropriate award has been made in satisfaction of the equity (based on estoppel; see 17.6), subsequent 'excessive user or bad behaviour towards [the legal owner] cannot bring the equity to an end or forfeit it'. Denning LJ thought that the equitable award might be revoked in 'some circumstances' (he did not specify what they might be) but held that the remedies available to the legal owner in this case would be to bring an action at common law for nuisance, trespass and so forth.

The Court of Appeal in *O'Sullivan* v *Management Agency Ltd* [1985] QB 428 (see 12.1.2), in exercising its jurisdiction to set aside (rescind) a contract (see 20.2.4), required the successful claimant to allow the other party to retain some benefits made under the contract. Their Lordships stated that, by means of the maxim *he who comes to equity must do equity*, 'the court can achieve practical justice between the parties' (*per* Dunn LJ) and 'the court will do what is practically just in the individual case' (*per* Fox LJ). For further illustrations of the maxim see *Sledmore* v *Dalby* (1996) 72 P & CR 196, *Cheese* v *Thomas* [1994] 1 WLR 129 at 136 and *Vadasz* v *Pioneer Concrete (SA) Pty Ltd* (1995) 69 ALR 678.

1.3.8 Equity sees as done that which ought to be done

CROSS REFERENCE

For examples of this maxim in operation, see the case of *Re Hallett's Estate* (1880) 13 ChD 696, CA (18.3.3.3) and, in Chapter 20, the equitable remedies of 'performance' and 'satisfaction'.

Equity sees as done that which *ought* to be done, not as a matter of morality, but as a matter of law. (See *Walsh* v *Lonsdale* (1882) 21 ChD 9, CA, at 1.2.4.) Although normally applied to private transactions, this maxim has occasionally been applied to treat a court order to transfer property as taking immediate effect in equity, so as to impose a constructive trust on the person subject to the order (*Mountney* v *Treharne* [2003] Ch 135, CA; *Re Flint (a bankrupt)* [1993] Ch 319).

1.3.9 Equity imputes an intention to fulfil an obligation

Equity imputes an intention to fulfil a *legal*, but not a *moral*, obligation.

1.3.10 Where the equities are equal the first in time prevails (*Qui prior est tempore potior est jure*)

This maxim is sometimes paraphrased as *the first in time is the first in right*. Its use can be illustrated by taking the straightforward case of equitable mortgagees competing against each other for priority. Suppose that A grants an equitable mortgage of property to B and later grants a mortgage of the same property to C. In the usual course of events, B's mortgage will have priority over C's, in accordance with the maxim. In theory the maxim only applies if the competing equities are equal, but Kay J, in *Taylor* v *Russell* [1890] 1 Ch 8 at 17, stated that nothing less than 'gross negligence' must be proved by a later equitable mortgagee against a prior mortgagee to give priority to a later one. What is being referred to here is, for example, the sort of gross neglect that might have fooled C into thinking that B had no prior mortgage. Earlier authorities which appear to suggest that B might cede priority to C, if C's equity is merely *technically* superior to B's, must be doubtful. See, for example, *Pease* v *Jackson* (1867–83) Ch App 576.

1.3.11 Where the equities are equal the law prevails

This maxim, like the previous one, operates more like a rule than a principle, and works in the context of determining priority between competing equitable claims. If we take our previous hypothetical case, where A granted an equitable mortgage to B and then another to C, the present maxim allows C to gain priority over B by the simple expedient of purchasing the legal title from A (see *Bailey* v *Barnes* [1894] 1 Ch 25 and *Taylor* v *Russell* [1893] AC 244).

One exception to this maxim is the rule in *Dearle* v *Hall* (1828) 3 Russ 1. According to this rule, priority between competing assignees of a *debt* is awarded to the first one to give notice to the debtor. It matters not that one of the competitors has a legal interest and the other merely an equitable one.

1.3.12 Where equity and law conflict, equity shall prevail

Established as a result of a 1616 decision of King James I (see 1.1.1.4), this maxim is now enshrined in s 49 of the Senior Courts Act 1981, which provides that:

> [e]very Court exercising jurisdiction in England and Wales in any civil cause or matter shall continue to administer law and equity on the basis that, wherever there is any conflict or variance between the rules of equity and the rules of common law with reference to the same matter, the rules of equity shall prevail.

THINKING POINT

Note how, more than a century after the Judicature Acts, Parliament thought it quite appropriate for this section to draw a distinction between the rules of law and the rules of equity.

1.3.13 Equality is equity

For illustrations of the maxim 'Equality is equity', see the CA decisions in *IRC* v *Broadway Cottages Trust* (4.4.1.1) and the decision of the HL in *Stack* v *Dowden* (17.5.3.1).

1.3.14 Delay defeats equities

The processes of law are notorious for delay. Shakespeare's Hamlet lists 'the law's delay' among the chief woes of life in his famous 'to be, or not to be' soliloquy. More than two centuries later administrative delay effectively crippled Chancery procedure. This may in part explain the requirement, enshrined in the maxim 'delay defeats equities', that a person seeking an equitable remedy should not be lax in bringing their claim. In practice, however, the doctrine of **laches** is more often resorted to (to defeat stale claims) than is this maxim (see J. Brunyate, *The Limitation of Actions in Equity*, London, 1932).

CROSS REFERENCE

For detailed consideration of laches, limitation and the effect of delay on equitable claims, see 15.2.

> **laches** Delay or 'laxness' in bringing a claim. A claim against a defendant will be barred by reason of the claimant's laches if there was such a delay in bringing the claim as is likely to prejudice the defendant's fair trial or otherwise offend the public interest in finality of litigation.

1.3.15 Equity will not assist a volunteer

Considered in detail in Chapter 5.

1.3.16 There is no equity to perfect an imperfect gift

Considered in detail in Chapter 5.

1.3.17 Equity abhors a vacuum in ownership

Considered in detail in Chapter 5.

 ## Summary

The historical development of equity and trusts

- Where the King's common law caused injustice in individual cases, with consequent embarrassment to the King's conscience, the task of providing a just remedy fell to the Chancellor. The Chancellor came to dispense justice on his own authority from Westminster, and so the Court of Chancery, the Chancellor's court, developed.

- Competition between Chancery and the common law courts came to a head in the early seventeenth century with the *Earl of Oxford's Case*, reported at (1615) 1 Rep Ch 1. The dispute between the Chief Justice and the Lord Chancellor was referred, in 1616, to King James I. The King resolved the dispute in favour of Lord Ellesmere, thereby establishing that where equity and common law conflict, equity shall prevail.

- In the eighteenth century equity developed in a manner supplemental to the common law and modern trust doctrine and mortgage doctrine was established. The success of Chancery rendered it too busy to cope, and so, by the Judicature Acts 1873–5, Chancery and the common law courts were subsumed within a new Supreme Court of Judicature. Procedures were unified, but equity and common law remain functionally distinct.

Equity and the common law

- 'Neither law nor equity is now stifled by its origin and the fact that both are administered by one court has inevitably meant that each has borrowed from the other in furthering the harmonious development of the law as a whole' (*Elders Pastoral Ltd* v *Bank of New Zealand* [1989] 2 NZLR 180 at 193, *per* Somer J).

- Equity is a branch of law and not a branch of morality. Equitable 'morality' is limited to the restraint of unconscionability in legal contexts. Equity will not enforce a bare moral promise. In fact, equity will sometimes encourage a trustee to break a non-legal promise ('gentlemen's agreement'), if to do so would be in the best financial interest of the trust beneficiaries (*Buttle* v *Saunders* [1950] 2 All ER 193).

? Summative assessment exercise

The maxims of equity

We scrutinised the maxims of equity at the end of the chapter, but can you remember them all? As a final exercise, the following list of maxims contains DELIBERATE MISTAKES. Put a cross next to any of the maxims in the following list which is not accurately expressed—and underline the mistake in each case:

- equity will not suffer a moral wrong without a remedy;
- equity leads the law;
- equity looks to substance and never to form;
- equity will not enforce the Statute of Frauds;
- equity acts *in personam*;
- those who come to equity must come with clean hands;
- those who come to equity must do good;
- equity sees as done that which ought morally to be done;
- equity imputes an intention to fulfil an obligation;
- where the equities are equal it is a draw;
- where equity and law conflict, equity follows the law;
- equality is equity;
- delay defeats equities;
- equity will mend a bad bargain;
- equity will not assist a volunteer;
- equity will perfect an imperfect gift.

 Full specimen answers can be found at www.oxfordtextbooks.co.uk/orc/watt_directions5e/.

▢ The bigger picture

In this chapter we have seen how the relative flexibility and creativity of equity jurisprudence calls for the use of metaphors to understand the relationship of law to equity. Note that Lord Toulson began his speech in the Supreme Court in *AIB Group (UK) plc v Mark Redler and Co Solicitors* [2014] UKSC 58; [2014] 3 WLR 1367 with the observation that '140 years after the Judicature Act 1873, the stitching together of equity and the common law continues to cause problems at the seams'.

Rather than fear metaphor in law as if it were less than ideal, maybe we should accept that metaphor is the best language we have to appreciate the nature of equity (see Gary Watt, *Equity Stirring: The Story of Justice beyond Law* (Oxford: Hart Publishing, 2009)). In this chapter we have seen that metaphors from 'streams of water' to 'horse and rider' to 'fusion' have been used to describe law's relationship to equity. You might find it a useful learning exercise to attempt to identify your own metaphor for equity and its relationship to law.

Further reading

Baker, J.H. 'The Court of Chancery and Equity' (Chapter 6) in *An Introduction to English Legal History* 3rd edn (2002) London: Butterworths
a wonderful overview from the leading modern text on legal history

Edelman, J. 'Two Fundamental Questions for the Law of Trusts' (2013) 129 LQR 66
cautions that 'equitable title' is a misleading term, because equitable ownership is in the nature of a restriction on the title of the legal owner

Halliwell, M. *Equity and Good Conscience* 2nd edn (2004) London: Old Bailey Press
an engagingly written and hopeful vision for greater moral conscience in law

Harding, M. 'Manifesting Trust' (2009) 29(2) *Oxford Journal of Legal Studies* 245
explores the distinction between trust and entrusting, comparing law with life in general

Holdsworth, W.S. 'Relation of the Equity Administered by the Common Law Judges to the Equity Administered by the Chancellor' (1916) 26 Yale LJ 1
a classic piece by one of the academic fathers of modern legal history. It examines the surprising fact that the common law judges have always exercised their own brand of equity

Martin, J. 'Fusion, Fallacy and Confusion: A Comparative Study' [1994] Conv 13
a clear and helpful contribution to the debate regarding the fusion of law and equity

McGhee, J. (ed), *Snell's Equity* 33rd edn (2017) London: Sweet & Maxwell/Thomson Reuters
classic text on equity which was 150 years old in 2018

Watt, G. *Equity Stirring: The Story of Justice Beyond Law* (2009) Oxford: Hart Publishing
an interdisciplinary study of the nature and history of equity drawing on a range of legal and non-legal sources, including Aristotle, Dickens and Shakespeare

 For links to selected cases, statutes, academic papers and official reports mentioned in this chapter please visit the online resources at www.oup.com/uk/watt_directions6e/.

2 Understanding trusts

☐ LEARNING OBJECTIVES

By the end of this chapter you should understand:

- the usefulness of the trust;
- the difference between the trust and other legal concepts;
- the variety of trust types, e.g. pension trusts, protective trusts;
- the role of trusts in asset protection;
- the social significance of trusts.

Introduction

If we were asked what is the greatest and most distinctive achievement performed by Englishmen in the field of jurisprudence I cannot think that we should have any better answer to give than this, namely the development from century to century of the trust idea.

Maitland, 'The Unincorporate Body' in *Collected Papers*, vol. III, p. 272

THINKING POINT

If you have already studied land law you may think that you already know all there is to know about trusts. To see if you're right, place a tick next to whichever of the following propositions you believe is always true:

- the trustee holds legal title to the trust asset;
- the trustee must discharge the purposes for which trust property is held;
- the trustee is not a beneficiary of his own trust.

You get full marks if you didn't tick any of them! The first two propositions are almost always true, and the third proposition is very often true, but it is possible for a person to be a trustee of an equitable interest, to hold property for purposes which they are not obliged to fulfil (see 7.2) and to have a beneficial interest under their own trust (Trustee Act 1925, s 68(17)). You should have remembered the last point from your knowledge of land law, for where two or more persons purchase land in their joint names each of them is presumed to have an equitable ('beneficial') interest in the land and to hold their legal title subject to the equitable interests of every other co-owner. They hold the legal title as trustees for themselves.

Trusts come in all shapes and sizes. Indeed, it is very much at issue whether we have now a coherent law of the trust, or several laws of trusts. There are certainly very significant differences between private family trusts of the orthodox type and special trusts such as pension trusts and charitable trusts and the so-called NHS trust. The diversity within the law of trusts stems from the diversity of functions performed by trusts.

 THINKING POINT

To give yourself some idea of the breadth of functions performed by the law of trusts, why not take a sheet of paper and attempt to list some of the uses to which trusts might be put, and the contexts in which they occur. It might assist you to consider whether or not you have personally had any contact or dealings with trusts.

Did your list contain any (or all) of the following?

- to provide for property to be held for the benefit of persons subject to legal disability. For example, minors are not permitted to hold the legal estate in land, but are permitted to be beneficiaries under a trust of land (see 'capacity' in Chapter 3 at 3.1);
- to provide for property to be held for persons in succession, e.g. 'to A for life, to A's children in remainder';
- to provide for property to be held by a number of owners concurrently, e.g. co-ownership of land: see Chapter 17;
- to protect family property from the bankruptcy or extravagance of particular beneficiaries (i.e. protective or 'spendthrift' trusts: see 2.3.2);
- to take into account possible changes in the future circumstances of beneficiaries when making a gift, instead of making an outright gift (see Chapters 9 and 13);

- to apply property for purposes, rather than for persons (e.g. charitable purposes: see Chapters 7 and 8);

- to make collective investment (e.g. pension funds, see 2.3.3, and trade union funds);

- to enable clubs (unincorporated, non-profit associations) to receive and hold property (see 7.5);

- to minimise tax liability by restructuring property ownership (see Chapter 9);

- to protect assets from creditors in the event of insolvency (see 2.3.4);

- to concentrate managerial power (in relation to, for example, pension funds, trade unions and clubs);

- to achieve privacy in dealings with property (hiding true beneficial ownership behind legal ownership) (see, for example, secret trusts at 3.2.3);

- to function as trading trusts and voting trusts (these topics are outside the scope of this book, but see, for example, The Hon. Mr Justice B.H. McPherson, 'The Insolvent Trading Trust' in P.D. Finn, *Essays in Equity* (Sydney: Law Book Co Ltd, 1985)).

It is some evidence of the ongoing importance of trusts that 'Modernising Trust Law for a Global Britain' is one of the projects in the Law Commission's 13th Programme of Law Reform launched in December 2017. It is designed to make the English trust more commercially competitive post-Brexit.

2.1 Trusts: to define or describe?

Given the very wide range of functions performed by trusts, and the great variety of contexts in which they are to be found, do you think it is possible to define the trust concept?

The definition of 'trust' is fraught with difficulty. To define must always mean to describe the essence of the thing, and so any definition must necessarily be incomplete and/or circular. (As to the problem of paraphrase in legal reasoning, see H.L.A. Hart, 'Definition and Theory in Jurisprudence' (1954) 70 LQR 37.)

 THINKING POINT

How would you define the trust concept in your own words? For what it is worth, and incomplete though it must be, this author would offer the following definition of a private trust:

A private trust is the legal relationship between the formal owner(s) of assets ('the trustee' or 'trustees') and the beneficial owner(s) of those assets ('the beneficiary' or 'beneficiaries'). The hallmark of the trust is that every trustee is obliged in equity to employ every incident of their formal (typically 'legal') ownership for the exclusive benefit of the beneficiaries. A trustee might himself be one of the beneficiaries, but cannot be the sole beneficiary of the trust.

We can say, in short, that trustees have all the powers that come with being the owner of property 'at law' (including, to name a few, the power to sell, the power to lease and the power to bring a common law action to protect the trust property), but that these powers must be exercised for the exclusive benefit of the beneficiaries, who are said to own 'in equity'. Lord Mance points out that 'where a trust exists, the legal and beneficial interests are distinct, and what affects the former does not necessarily affect the latter' (*Akers* v *Samba Financial Group* [2017] UKSC 6, at para. [51]). The trust's quality of having two different natures at the same time is rather strange; hence Lord Neuberger has said that 'it is fair to say that the concept of equitable proprietary rights is in some respects paradoxical' (*FHR European Ventures LLP* v *Cedar Capital Partners LLC* [2014] UKSC 45; [2015] AC 250, Supreme Court, at para. [32]). It always seems paradoxical to think of a thing (e.g. a trust) that is two things at once (i.e. title at law and property in equity), but a picture can help us to appreciate the paradox. Picture the trust as a banana in which the trustee owns the outer or 'formal' banana skin of legal title, whereas the beneficiary owns the inner beneficial part. Absolute owners are entitled to exercise their legal powers for their own benefit, but trustees' powers must be exercised for the benefit of the beneficiaries. So in the case of a trustee, as in the case of Peter Parker (a.k.a. Spider-man), 'with great power comes great responsibility'. To put it another way, the formal 'banana skin' of legal title is something which brings the trustee no personal benefit (although professional trustees are presumed to be entitled to payment: see Chapter 12), but which might cause them to slip up and become personally liable (see, generally, Chapter 15 on 'breach of trust'). The beneficiaries are entitled 'in equity' but not 'at law' (unless they happen also to be trustees), so they have no direct right to bring common law claims. However, if the trustees are for some technical reason unwilling or unable to use their legal powers to assist the beneficiaries, the beneficiaries can compel them to, say, bring a legal action on behalf of the beneficiaries. In special circumstances the beneficiaries can even step into the trustees' shoes to exercise indirectly the trustees' legal powers to, say, recover common law damages for loss caused to the trust (*Colour Quest Ltd* v *Total Downstream UK Plc* [2010] EWCA Civ 180; [2010] 3 All ER 793, Court of Appeal; *Roberts* v *Gill & Co* [2010] UKSC 22; [2010] 2 WLR 1227, Supreme Court). Beneficiaries can even agree to remove the trustees or (as we saw in Chapter 1) agree to bring the trust to an end if the beneficiaries are all competent adults who between them are absolutely entitled to the benefit of the trust property.

 STATUTE

The Hague Convention on the Law Applicable to Trusts and on their Recognition, Article 2

For the purposes of this Convention the term 'trust' refers to the legal relationship created—*inter vivos* or on death—by a person, the settlor, when assets have been placed under the control of a trustee for the benefit of a beneficiary or for a specified purpose. A trust has the following characteristics—(a) the assets constitute a separate fund and are not part of the trustee's estate; (b) title to the trust assets stands in the name of the trustee or in the name of another person on behalf of the trustee; (c) the trustee has the power and the duty, in respect of which he is accountable, to manage, employ or dispose of the assets in accordance with the terms of the trust and the special duties imposed upon him by law. Neither the reservation by the settlor of certain rights and powers nor the fact that the trustee may himself have rights as a beneficiary are necessarily inconsistent with the existence of a trust.

The Hague Convention (which is incorporated into English law by the Recognition of Trusts Act 1987) identifies a number of important features of expressly created trusts, but it does not attempt to define or describe the many significant trusts, such as constructive and resulting trusts, which arise in the absence of an express intention to create them. The Convention enables non-common law states to recognise common law trusts. The states that are currently signed up as parties to the Convention number a bare dozen. Lord Collins has observed that 'it says much about the likely principal uses of the Convention' [i.e. tax avoidance] 'that they include Liechtenstein, Luxembourg, Monaco, San Marino and Switzerland' (*Akers* v *Samba Financial Group* [2017] UKSC 6; [2017] AC 424, Supreme Court, at para. [100]).

2.2 Trusts compared to other concepts

Probably the best way to understand the nature of the trust is to contrast and compare it with other legal concepts. This is the task of the following sections.

2.2.1 Trusts compared with contracts

A contract is a private relationship between the parties under which their rights and obligations are generally enforceable only against each other (*Beswick* v *Beswick* [1968] AC 58), whereas it is of the essence of a trust that a settlor can give property to a trustee on trust for a *third party*, and thereby grant the *third party* (the beneficiary) rights against the trustee to see that the trust is properly discharged. It is true that by virtue of the Contracts (Rights of Third Parties) Act 1999 third parties can in certain circumstances enforce their rights under a contract to which they were not a party, but they cannot enforce those rights against a person who is not a party to the contract. The beneficiary of a trust, on the other hand, can enforce their property right in the trust assets against all comers except a person who innocently purchases trust property without notice of the trust (*Pilcher* v *Rawlins* (1872) 7 Ch App 259).

2.2.1.1 Are trusts merely a special type of contract?

Having noted the orthodox conceptual distinction between the contract and the trust, we should nevertheless be aware that many commentators have been impressed by the close relationship between the two concepts. Maitland thought it 'utterly impossible for us to frame any definition of a contract which shall not include the acts by which ninety-nine out of every hundred trusts are created' (F.W. Maitland, *Equity: A Course of Lectures*, revised by J. Brunyate, 2nd edn, Cambridge, 1936, p. 111).

Professor Kevin Gray suggested that 'every gift, lease, trust and security has its origins in some arrangement of consent or assent' ('Property in Thin Air' (1991) 50(2) CLJ 252 at 302) and a leading American academic went so far as to suggest that 'the deal between settlor and trustee is functionally indistinguishable from the modern third-party beneficiary contract. Trusts are contracts' (J.H. Langbein, 'Contractarian Basis of the Law of Trusts' (1995) 105 *Yale Law Journal* 625 at 627). The enactment of the Contracts (Rights of Third Parties) Act 1999 gives some support for Langbein's view, because it allows certain third party beneficiaries of contracts made by other people to enforce their rights directly, but there are still good reasons for distinguishing trusts from contracts.

It may well be true that every *express* trust has 'its origins in' a transaction entered into by the settlor consensually, either voluntarily or for contractual consideration. The creation of any express trust is predicated upon a finding that the settlor (the original legal owner) intended its creation (see 4.2), and therefore the consent of the settlor is always a feature of such trusts. However, many non-express trusts do not originate with the consent of the original legal owner, and some (constructive trusts being the prime example) are even created against the legal owner's true intentions (see Chapter 16).

If, for the sake of argument, we were to accept that all trusts *originate* in contract-like agreement, this would only go a little way towards illuminating the essential nature of trusts. For even where trusts are *created* consensually, even contractually, they *operate* quite differently from contracts, not least because the trust creates *property* rights whereas the rights arising under a contract are merely personal. (See 2.2.2 for consideration of the different status of contractual (personal) and trust (proprietary) claims against the estates of insolvent persons.) His Lordship clearly objects to the idea that the trust is a contract! His Lordship also added, as a further objection, the fact that that the contract theory gives 'little weight to the fact that a trustee, whether paid or unpaid, is under no obligation, contractual or otherwise, to provide future services to the trust' (see 'retirement' at 10.3).

🔍 CASE CLOSE-UP

Re Duke of Norfolk's ST [1982] Ch 61

In *Re Duke of Norfolk's ST* [1982] Ch 61 Fox LJ considered the contractual analysis of express trusts to be 'artificial': 'it may have some appearance of reality in relation to a trustee who, at the request of the settlor, agrees to act before the settlement is executed and approves the terms of the settlement. But very frequently executors and trustees of wills know nothing of the terms of the will until the testator is dead; sometimes in the case of corporate trustees such as banks, they have not even been asked by the testator whether they will act. It is difficult to see with whom, in such cases, the trustees are to be taken to be contracting. The appointment of a trustee by the court also gives rise to problems as to the identity of the contracting party.'

2.2.2 Trust compared with debt

A creditor's right to recover a **debt** is always a mere personal right against the debtor. Enforcement of a personal (or *in personam*) right, because it is enforced against a defendant in his personal capacity, may be defeated if the defendant is personally insolvent. The beneficiary's rights under a trust include proprietary rights (sometimes called rights **in rem**) in the assets themselves. The distinction between debt and trust is the distinction between 'owing' and 'owning'. A debt exists where A *owes* money to B. A trust exists where A holds formal title to assets beneficially *owned* by B.

---

debt 'A monetary obligation owed by one person to another which is an item of value because it can be transferred to a third party by way of sale or security for a loan' (Michael Bridge, *Personal Property Law*, 2nd edn, Oxford: Blackstone Press, 1996, p. 4).

> **in rem** A right is an *in rem* right (also known as a 'proprietary right') where it is enforced against assets in the defendant's hands in which or over which the claimant has a proprietary interest, thus it is not defeated by the defendant's personal insolvency.

The possibility of assigning a debt to a third party merits further consideration. The fact that a debt may be assigned means that a debtor may be obliged to make payment to a person with whom he has had no dealings whatsoever. At common law the assignee (new creditor) of a debt can bring proceedings against the debtor in the name of the assignor (original creditor), and if the assignor tries to resist this, he can, *in equity*, be compelled to comply (*Three Rivers District Council* v *Bank of England* [1996] QB 292). In this respect there is a passing similarity with the trust (under which the trustee must account to a beneficiary with whom he may have had no personal dealings), but the differences between trust and debt are still vast.

Despite these differences, and in a sense by virtue of them, a number of important cases have acknowledged that trust and debt can co-exist in the same transaction in certain commercial contexts. The leading case is *Barclays Bank Ltd* v *Quistclose Investments Ltd* [1970] AC 567: see 2.3.4.2. You should recall that the House of Lords held that: (1) the monies were held by RR Ltd on trust for its shareholders, and that when that trust failed the monies were held by RR Ltd on resulting trust for QI Ltd. BB Ltd had notice of that trust and therefore held the monies on trust for QI Ltd, and (2) *the fact that the transaction, had it succeeded, would have given rise to a standard common law debt owed by RR Ltd to QI Ltd did not preclude the co-existence of a trust remedy in equity*. The finding of a trust in that case had been absolutely crucial to the lender's recovery of the sums loaned. This is because the finding of a trust gave the lender a proprietary claim. Had the lender QI had to rely upon its personal debt claim against the borrower (RR Ltd), it would have been forced to join the long queue of RR Ltd's personal creditors.

Commenting on this case, Meagher J has said that 'whilst previously it might have been thought that debt and trust were distinct and disparate norms, it was thereafter clear that in a given case the transaction under analysis might bear a dual character' (*Re Australian Elizabethan Theatre Trust* (1991) 102 ALR 681 at 693).

2.2.3 **Trusts compared with powers**

A trustee is bound to discharge his trust. If the trustee fails to do so the court will intervene to ensure that the trust is fulfilled. In contrast, the court will not compel the exercise of a mere power to distribute the fund (sometimes called a 'power of appointment'). In *Re Hay's Settlement Trusts* [1982] 1 WLR 202, Sir Robert Megarry V-C observed that powers of appointment can be *general* (exercisable in favour of anybody at all) or *special* (exercisable in favour of a specific class of persons, no matter how numerically large that class might be) or *hybrid/intermediate* (exercisable generally, or in favour of a specific class, but not exercisable in favour of specific named individuals or an excluded sub-class of persons).

 THINKING POINT

The defining characteristic of a power is that the holder has the option to exercise it or not—but do you think that changes where the power of appointment is given to a trustee?

> ### 🔍 CASE CLOSE-UP
>
> #### *Re Manisty's Settlement* [1974] 1 Ch 17, Chancery Division
>
> The settlement under consideration in this case gave trustees a discretionary power to apply the trust fund for the benefit of a small class of the settlor's near relations, save that any member of a smaller 'excepted class' was to be excluded from the class of beneficiaries.
>
> The trustees were also given power at their absolute discretion to declare that any person, corporation or charity (except a member of the excepted class or a trustee) should be included in the class of beneficiaries. A summons was brought to determine whether the intermediate power in this case was void for uncertainty. The power to extend the class of beneficiaries was held to be valid.
>
> Templeman J: 'The court cannot insist upon any particular consideration being given by the trustees to the exercise of the power. If a settlor creates a power exercisable in favour of his issue, his relations and the employees of his company, the trustees may in practice for many years hold regular meetings, study the terms of the power and the other provisions of the settlement, examine the accounts and either decide not to exercise the power or to exercise it only in favour, for example, of the children of the settlor … In my judgment it cannot be said that the trustees in those circumstances have committed a breach of trust and that they ought to have advertised the power or looked beyond the people who are most likely to be the objects of the bounty of the settlor …
>
> If a person within the ambit of the power is aware of its existence he can require the trustees to consider exercising the power and in particular to consider a request on his part for the power to be exercised in his favour. The trustees must consider this request, and if they decline to do so or can be proved to have omitted to do so, then the aggrieved person may apply to the court which may remove the trustees and appoint others in their place …
>
> The court may also be persuaded to intervene if the trustees act 'capriciously', that is to say, act for reasons which I apprehend could be said to be irrational, perverse or irrelevant to any sensible expectation of the settlor; for example, if they chose a beneficiary by height or complexion or by the irrelevant fact that he was a resident of Greater London.'

This was considered in *Re Hay's Settlement Trusts* [1982] 1 WLR 202. It was held that a trustee does not have to exercise a power, and will not be compelled to do so by the court, but that a trustee who holds a power must periodically consider whether or not to exercise the power. If the power is actually exercised the trustee must ensure that he or she acts in accordance with the terms of the power, and must consider both the range of potential beneficiaries and whether each individual appointment is appropriate. In that case the terms of the trust provided that if the trustees were to choose not to exercise their power of appointment the fund would pass to the settlor's nieces and nephews. The presence of this kind of 'gift over' or 'trust over' to other persons in default of the exercise of the power is in practice often the easiest way to distinguish between a trust and a power. In the case of a trust, where the fund *must* be distributed, there will generally be no provision for what should happen in default of distribution.

The court is not so reluctant to insist upon the exercise of a power where it is held by a trustee in the pension context. In *Mettoy Pension Trustees v Evans* [1990] 1 WLR 1587 a mere power in the hands of trustees was described as being a 'fiduciary power' and it was held that the court might in some circumstances intervene to ensure that the power is exercised. In that case, Warner J stepped in to give directions to the trustees of a pension fund as to the appropriate distribution of the pension fund surplus (see 2.3.3).

2.2.4 Trusts compared to agency

An agent owes fiduciary duties and duties of good faith to their principal, and will often have some degree of managerial control over the principal's property. Crucially, however, a trustee's holding or control of the trust property is more fundamental than that of a mere agent, and is in the nature of entitlement to the property, albeit merely legal entitlement. One of the clearest indicators of a trust (or agency in the nature of a trust), as distinct from simple non-trust agency, is an obligation on the agent to keep the beneficiary's funds separate from the agent's private funds. For instance, in *HMRC* v *Annabel's (Berkeley Square) Ltd* (2008) ICR 1076, a 'troncmaster' who used a *dedicated* bank account to hold tips paid to staff at an exclusive London nightclub was held to be a trustee of the tips. *Bailey* v *Angove's PTY Ltd* [2016] UKSC 47, UK Supreme Court, is a contrasting case in which debts collected by an agent for its principal were held to be owned absolutely, subject to contractual obligations to account, and not held on trust.

2.2.5 Trust and corporation

The corporation bears a close resemblance to the trust in so far as they both may involve the management of assets and wealth by a few for the benefit of many. However, for all their functional similarities, there are fundamental differences between the corporation and the trust. First, a corporation has a separate legal personality, which means that it is treated as a distinct person for purposes of law: it is sued and sues in its own name. A private trust, in contrast, has no legal personality apart from that of the trustees. Second, a trustee is the legal owner and manager of trust property, which is held on trust for the beneficiaries as beneficial owners of the trust property in equity. A corporation, on the other hand, is the absolute owner of its business assets and the shareholders are absolute owners of quite different assets: shares in the corporation. Third, a director of a company is not a trustee of the company's assets. However, a director is in a fiduciary position to the company, and if a director takes personal advantage of a business opportunity 'belonging' to the company, the director is accountable just as if he or she were a trustee of someone else's property (*Foster Bryant Surveying Ltd* v *Bryant* [2007] EWCA Civ 200; approving *CMS Dolphin Limited* v *Simonet* [2001] 2 BCLC 704). Fourth, a company must be entered on a public register, whereas no register of private trusts is accessible to the general public (see 2.3.4.4).

2.3 Special categories of trusts and trustees

Hopefully the preceding sections have helped elucidate the distinction between trusts and other legal concepts with which you may already have been familiar. If only trusts were all of one sort, the study of trusts would hereinafter be a relatively straightforward matter. In fact some basic conceptual and functional distinctions exist between different kinds of trust. The following sections examine categories of trusts which are not considered in depth elsewhere in this text. It should be borne in mind, however, that many other categories of trusts—constructive trusts, secret trusts, resulting trusts and express trusts, to name but a few—receive special attention in future chapters.

2.3.1 **Bare trusts**

A bare trust exists where a trustee holds the trust property on trust for a single beneficiary who is *sui juris* (adult and not subject to any legal disability) and absolutely entitled to the trust fund. The beneficiary under such a trust has the right to terminate the trust on giving notice to the trustee, provided the beneficiary has mental capacity to exercise that right (see *Saunders* v *Vautier*, at 9.1.1). Accordingly, the trustee of a bare trust is under no obligation to invest it or otherwise manage it for the medium to long term, but merely to hold it until called for. Bare trusts most frequently occur when settlement trusts come to an end. So, for example, upon the death of B in a trust 'To A to hold on trust for B for life and C in remainder', the trustee will hold the trust fund for the benefit of C under a bare trust. Bare trusts also arise in commercial contexts. So, for example, a solicitor holds a client's monies under a bare trust for the client.

2.3.2 **Protective trusts**

> [M]ost men, like spendthrift heirs, are apt to judge a little in hand better than a great deal to come; and so, for small matters in possession, part with greater ones in reversion.
>
> John Locke, *An Essay Concerning Human Understanding*, 1690

Typically, the beneficiary of a **protective trust** has a life interest in the income of a trust fund which will determine if ever the income of the fund becomes payable to another person, e.g. the beneficiaries' creditors. It follows that the most common 'determining event' will be the personal bankruptcy of the beneficiary, including some bad bargain which will lead to personal insolvency. When the life interest determines, a discretionary trust 'springs up' under which the original beneficiary (together with certain members of his or her family) has a hope of being reappointed as a beneficiary by the trustees of the discretionary trust.

> **protective trust** A trust established by the settlor to protect the beneficiary (who cannot be the settlor) from the beneficiary's creditors. Sometimes called a 'spendthrift' trust, because it was traditionally employed to protect spendthrift children of the settlor. Protective trusts are used to protect beneficiaries from financial calamity and their own folly. It has been said that 'a protective trust shows the furthest extent to which English law will permit property to be denied to creditors': *Maudsley & Burn's Trusts and Trustees* (5th edn, Oxford: Oxford University Press, 1996).

Where a settlor calls his trust a 'protective trust' or uses very similar words, the terms of the trust will be presumed to be those set out in s 33 of the Trustee Act 1925. That section provides that income held on trust for the principal beneficiary of a protective trust will pass to a discretionary trust in the event of the principal beneficiary committing some act (e.g. an act of bankruptcy) by which his interest is forfeit. The principal beneficiary will be a potential beneficiary under the discretionary trust, together with members of his close family (or, if he has none, those persons who would have been entitled to the original trust in the event of the death of the principal beneficiary).

Where the settlor describes the trust in his own terms, those terms will be given their natural construction even if they differ from those provided by s 33 of the Trustee Act. In *Re Balfour's Settlement* [1938] Ch 928, B had a life interest in the income of the settled fund until he should 'do or suffer something whereby the same or some part thereof would through his act or default or by operation or process of law or otherwise … become vested in or payable to some other person'. It was provided, further, that in the event of determination a discretionary trust would spring up.

In that case the trustees paid capital of the fund to B in breach of their trust, and later impounded income due to B to remedy that breach (see 15.3.5 on impounding). The question arose whether the impounding of B's income had been a determining event under the protective trust. Farwell J held that it had been. The impounding of the income had effected a forfeiture of B's life interest under the terms of the protective trust.

THINKING POINT

Consider the facts of *Re Baring's ST* [1940] Ch 737. Mrs Baring had a protected life interest under a family settlement. When she absconded abroad with the children of the family and ignored a court order to return them to England, Mr Baring obtained a court order against her property. Eventually Mrs Baring returned. Do you think that Mrs Baring had forfeited her life interest?

Morton J held that the settlor had intended that his property should be continuously available to his family, and that when the court order deprived Mrs Baring, albeit temporarily, of her interest in the income of the settlement, the settlor's intentions could only be met by forfeiting her life interest at that point. She was left with a mere hope of an interest under the discretionary trust which arose on the determination of her life interest.

Similarly, in *Gibbon v Mitchell* [1990] 1 WLR 1304, Mr Gibbon had a life interest under a protective trust. On the advice of his accountants and solicitors, he executed a deed purporting to surrender his life interest in favour of his children. The surrender was held to have forfeited his interest, and so his children could not take under the deed.

Further, the law does not recognise protective trusts which are *conditional* upon the solvency of the life beneficiary. The protective trust is only valid if it grants a *determinable* life interest. A life interest which is limited to take effect *until* bankruptcy will be valid, whereas a *condition* in a trust which purports to forfeit the life interest in the event of the bankruptcy of the life tenant will be void (*Re Leach* [1912] 2 Ch 422).

THINKING POINT

Do you think that protective trusts should be prohibited on the ground that they defraud creditors?

In recognising the validity of protective trusts Parliament has sought to balance the settlor's right to make provision for his or her family against the rights of the family's creditors. Whether the balance achieved is a fair one might be doubted. However, the law does stop short of recognising the validity of a trust under which the settlor purports to appoint *himself* as principal beneficiary under a protective trust.

2.3.3 **Pension fund trusts**

An employee pension fund can exist without a trust, but in most cases a trust is a practical necessity.

 CASE CLOSE-UP

Air Jamaica Ltd **v** *Charlton* **[1999] 1 WLR 1399, Privy Council**

'A pension scheme can, in theory at least, be established by contract between the employer and each employee and without using the machinery of a trust. Such a scheme would have to be very simple. It would look very like a self-employed pension policy. There would be no trust fund and no trustees. The employer would simply contract with each of his employees that, if the employee made weekly payments to the employer, the employer would pay the employee a pension on retirement or a lump sum on death. The employer would not make any contributions itself, since there would be no one to receive them.'

2.3.3.1 **The advantages and disadvantages of holding pension funds under a trust**

 THINKING POINT

The quotation in the preceding section suggests that a trust is useful because it allows employee and employer to make contributions to the same fund. The use of trusts for holding pension funds yields a number of other advantages. Can you imagine any?

Trusts are a useful vehicle for pension provision because they allow the managerial control of large funds to be concentrated in the hands of a few trustees. But the great advantage in the use of a trust over most other instrumentalities (such as a corporation) is the fact that the beneficiaries under a trust have a proprietary interest in the fund. This gives them security in the event of the insolvency of the employer corporation, and allows them to leave their entitlement to another in the event of their own death.

The use of a trust also brings with it the added advantage of subjecting the pension fund manager to strict equitable obligations (see D. Pollard, 'Review and Disclosure of Decisions by Pension Trustees' (1997) 11(2) TLI 42 and see *Express Newspapers Pensions Trustees Ltd* v *Express Newspapers plc* [1999] PLR 9).

 CASE CLOSE-UP

Edge **v** *Pensions Ombudsman* **[2000] Ch 602 at 622–3, Court of Appeal**

Chadwick LJ: 'the task of the trustees is to maintain a balance between assets and liabilities valued on [an] actuarial basis; so that, so far as the future can be foreseen, they will be in a position to provide pensions and other benefits in accordance with the rules throughout the life of the scheme. That task is to be performed by setting appropriate levels for employers' and members' contributions. If that task could be performed with perfect foresight there would be no surpluses and no deficits. But, because the task has to be performed in the real world, surpluses and deficits are bound to arise from time to time and prudent trustees will aim to ensure that the likelihood of surplus outweighs the risk of deficit. Nevertheless, it is no part of the trustees' function, in a fund of this nature, to set levels for contributions which will generate surpluses beyond those properly required as a reserve against contingencies.'

THINKING POINT

Can you think of any disadvantages in holding pension funds by means of a trust?

The main problems in relation to occupational pension schemes stem from the potential for fraudulent use of the (often vast) funds involved. The potential for abuse stems in turn from the fact that in the usual case half the scheme trustees will be representatives of the employer company, and the employer very often has the power to appoint new trustees. If the employee's representatives are not astute to spot a fraud on the fund (and fraud, by its very nature, is often hard to detect), the trust fund can be wrongfully employed for the employer's personal purposes (see, for example, *HRT Ltd* v *J Alsford Pension Trustees* Ltd (1997) 11(2) TLI 48). This sort of fraudulent activity lay at the root of the Maxwell scandal in the late 1980s, and prompted the Report of the Pension Law Review Committee chaired by Professor Roy Goode (and known as 'The Goode Report'), published in September 1993, which in turn led to the enactment of the Pensions Act 1995 which provided greater protection for employees and pensioners.

2.3.3.2 Are pension trusts different from other trusts?

This is the assumption that Sir Robert Megarry made when he said in *Cowan* v *Scargill* [1985] Ch 270 at 290:

> I can see no reason for holding that different principles apply to pension fund trusts from those which apply to other trusts. Of course, there are many provisions in pension schemes which are not to be found in private trusts, and to these the general law of trusts will be subordinated. But subject to that, I think that the trusts of pension funds are subject to the same rules as other trusts.

Subsequent cases took a different view. See, for example, *Imperial Group Pension Trust Ltd* v *Imperial Tobacco Ltd* [1991] 1 WLR 589, where Browne-Wilkinson V-C held that:

> [p]ension schemes are of a quite different nature to traditional trusts. The traditional trust is one under which the settlor, by way of bounty, transfers property to trustees to be administered for the beneficiaries as objects of his bounty … a pension scheme is quite different. Pension benefits are part of the consideration which an employee receives in return for the rendering of his services … contractual and trust rights can exist in parallel.

See, further, Graham Moffat, 'Pension Funds: A Fragmentation of Trust Law' (1993) 56(4) MLR 471 and I. Pittaway, 'Pension Funds—Is a Separate Branch of Trust Law Evolving?' (1990) 4 *Trust*

Law & Practice 156. In the *Air Jamaica* case (see 2.3.3) it was stressed that the use of trusts in the pension context:

> is not to say that the trust is like a traditional family trust under which a settlor voluntarily settles property for the benefit of the object of his bounty. The employee members of an occupational pension scheme are not voluntary settlors. As has been repeatedly observed, their rights are derived from their contracts of employment as well as from the trust instrument. Their pensions are earned by their services under their contracts of employment as well as by their contributions. They are often not inappropriately described as deferred pay. This does not mean, however, that they have contractual rights to their pensions. It means only that, in construing the trust instrument, regard must be had to the nature of an occupational pension and the employment relationship that forms its genesis.

2.3.4 Asset protection trusts

> He who lends money to a trading company neither wishes nor expects it to become insolvent. Its prosperous trading is the best assurance of the return of his money with interest. But against an evil day he wants the best security the company can give him consistently with its ability to trade meanwhile.
>
> Nourse LJ in *Re New Bullas Trading Ltd* [1994] BCC 36

The 'evil day' referred to in the quote usually means the day that the borrowing company is wound up insolvent. We will consider asset protection for this purpose first, but insolvency is not the only evil from which assets might be protected.

2.3.4.1 Protecting assets from creditors

Where party A incurs a debt to party B, A will be subject to a *personal* obligation to repay the debt to B. But if A becomes insolvent before repaying the debt to B, B will have to 'join the queue' of all the creditors with personal claims against A's assets. If, however, A is a trustee (and not merely a debtor) of assets held by A for the benefit of B, the situation is very different. In such a case B, as beneficiary of the trust, will have *proprietary* rights in those assets. B will no longer have to join the queue of A's general creditors, because the assets will be treated as having never belonged to A.

2.3.4.2 *Barclays Bank v Quistclose*

We have already considered the case of *Barclays Bank v Quistclose Investments Ltd* [1970] AC 567. Look back to 1.2.4 to remind yourself of the facts. They are summarised diagrammatically in Figure 2.1:

Figure 2.1 The facts and decision of *Quistclose*

CASE CLOSE-UP

Barclays Bank v Quistclose Investments Ltd [1970] AC 567, House of Lords

Lord Wilberforce: 'The transaction, it was said, between the respondents and Rolls Razor Ltd, was one of loan, giving rise to a legal action of debt. This necessarily excluded the implication of any trusts enforceable in equity, in the respondents' favour: a transaction may attract one action or the other, it could not admit of both … I should be surprised if an argument of this kind—so conceptualist in character—had ever been accepted. In truth it has plainly been rejected by the eminent judges who from 1819 onwards have permitted arrangements of this type to be enforced, and have approved them as being for the benefit of creditors and all concerned. There is surely no difficulty in recognising the co-existence in one transaction of legal and equitable rights and remedies: when the money is advanced, the lender acquires an equitable right to see that it is applied for the primary designated purpose (see *Re Rogers*, 8 Morr 243 where both Lindley LJ and Kay LJ recognised this): when the purpose has been carried out (i.e. the debt paid) the lender has his remedy against the borrower in debt: if the primary purpose cannot be carried out, the question arises if a secondary purpose (i.e. repayment to the lender) has been agreed, expressly or by implication: if it has, the remedies of equity may be invoked to give effect to it, if it has not (and the money is intended to fall within the general fund of the debtor's assets) then there is the appropriate remedy for recovery of a loan. I can appreciate no reason why the flexible interplay of law and equity cannot let in these practical arrangements, and other variations if desired: it would be to the discredit of both systems if they could not. In the present case the intention to create a secondary trust for the benefit of the lender, to arise if the primary trust, to pay the dividend, could not be carried out, is clear and I can find no reason why the law should not give effect to it.'

THINKING POINT

Barclays Bank v *Quistclose* is a case where an equitable interest was held to co-exist with a common law contractual debt. What was the nature of the equitable interest?

Lord Wilberforce held that there was a 'primary trust' in favour of the shareholders. The trouble with that analysis is that it is unclear why the corporate insolvency should have rendered that purpose incapable of being fulfilled. If the trust was in favour of the shareholders personally, they should have been able to claim their beneficial entitlement under the trust even after the company's insolvency.

Writing extrajudicially (i.e. outside his official functions as a judge) Sir Peter Millett, as he then was, suggested another analysis. Namely, this was that, apart from where the lender (A) has a private interest of its own, separate and distinct from any interest of the borrowing company (B), in seeing that the loaned sums are applied for the stated purpose, 'the purpose of the arrangements [such as those in *Quistclose*] would be fulfilled if they were treated as leaving the beneficial interest in the fund in A throughout, but subject to a power in B, revocable by A at any time, to apply the fund for the stated purpose'. In other words, the beneficial interest only leaves the lender if the borrowing company actually applies the loaned monies in favour of the beneficiaries (Sir Peter Millett, 'The Quistclose Trust: Who Can Enforce It?' (1985) 101 LQR 269 at 275–6). This 'revocable power' analysis goes some way towards providing a solution to the problem expressed by Peter Gibson J in *Carreras Rothmans Ltd* v *Freeman Mathews Ltd* [1985] 1 Ch 207 at 223 when commenting on Lord Wilberforce's analysis: 'I do not comprehend how a trust, which on no footing could the plaintiff revoke unilaterally, and which was expressed as a trust to pay third parties and was still capable of performance, could nevertheless leave the beneficial interest in the plaintiff which had parted with the monies.'

THINKING POINT

Does Lord Millett's revocable licence analysis appear in any way unorthodox?

Lord Millett's analysis is probably the best attempt to date to provide a rationale for the *Quistclose* trust (and his Lordship has approved it judicially at the highest level—*Twinsectra Ltd* v *Yardley* [2002] 2 AC 164, House of Lords). However, Lord Millett's 'revocable power' analysis is hardly compatible with Lord Wilberforce's 'primary trust' label. Trusts and powers are in theory quite different legal ideas, with very different practical consequences. (There are, having said that, other contexts in which the distinction between them has been downplayed for practical reasons: see 4.4.2.1.) Nevertheless, the usual reason for insisting upon a clear distinction between powers and trusts is that a clear distinction ensures that trustees and holders of powers know what is expected of them. This consideration does not arise in cases like *Quistclose*, where the contractual terms of the loan arrangement leave the trustee in no doubt as to what it *ought* to do. The *Quistclose* trust only becomes significant when the trustee has already failed to do that which it ought to have done. In *Twinsectra Ltd* v *Yardley* [2002] 2 AC 164 Lord Millett held that the borrower is generally not obliged to *apply* the loan for the particular specified purpose (hence there is no primary trust), but rather he is obliged to *refrain from applying* the loan for any purpose other than the particular specified purpose (188, para. [87]).

The search for an orthodox legal conceptual rationale for the *Quistclose* case will probably never reach an entirely satisfactory conclusion (see, further, Rickett, 'Different Views on the Scope of the Quistclose Analysis' (1991) 107 LQR 608; W. Swadling (ed.), *The Quistclose Trust: Critical Essays* (Oxford: Hart, 2004)). The *Quistclose* trust is a very unorthodox equitable incursion into the world of commercial contracting, especially when one considers the general principle that equity should not be relied upon to enlarge or mend a contract (see, for example, *Hageman* v *Holmes* [2009] EWHC 50 (Ch)). The brevity and content of Lord Wilberforce's speech in *Quistclose*, and the striking brevity with which his learned brothers concurred, suggests a decision driven by policy and pragmatism rather than one based on legal doctrine.

THINKING POINT

What might have been the policy concern driving the decision in *Quistclose*?

The likely policy concern is the desire to protect lenders who make emergency loans to corporations on the brink of insolvency, for '*Quistclose* trusts are frequently beneficial in the sense of providing an injection of capital which may rescue a company in financial difficulties' (Janet Ulph, 'Equitable Proprietary Rights in Insolvency: The Ebbing Tide?' [1996] JBL 482 at 495). A rescued company is a rescued trader and a rescued employer. A failed company very often results in unemployment and consequent social ills. The only persons with personal claims against the estate of the insolvent company who are likely to be fully satisfied are the insolvency practitioners themselves.

In *Quistclose*, the broad social and commercial benefits of corporate rescue may have been seen to outweigh the disadvantages of granting 'emergency lenders' priority rights in the event of insolvency. Yet despite the supposed political desirability of the *Quistclose* trusts, the irony is that if the *Quistclose* loan had actually been applied to pay the dividend to the shareholders, the lender would at that point have lost its priority over other creditors even though the loan had not at that time been repaid. The *Quistclose* trust provides, at best, only a short-term form of security. It is perhaps this feature that more than any other explains judicial willingness to recognise *Quistclose* trusts despite the conceptual difficulties they raise for orthodox trust law.

2.3.4.3 Cases after *Quistclose*

Quistclose was followed in *Re EVTR Ltd, Gilbert v Barber* [1987] BCLC 646, decided after the Insolvency Act 1986. There the Court of Appeal considered another claim to a proprietary interest in insolvency. EVTR Ltd was in trouble financially and B (who had just won a small fortune on his premium bonds) agreed to assist it. He deposited £60,000 with EVTR's solicitors and authorised them to release the monies 'for the sole purpose of buying new equipment'. This they did. However, EVTR went into receivership before the equipment was delivered. The receivers recovered a large part of the monies which had been paid to the equipment suppliers. The trial judge held that the sums so recovered should be held as part of the general assets of the company. B successfully appealed. The Court of Appeal held that B had paid the monies to EVTR for the specific purpose of purchasing equipment. When this purpose failed, EVTR held the monies on trust for B. Through merely contracting to purchase the equipment EVTR had not fulfilled the purpose for which the monies had been provided; the true purpose had been the acquisition of equipment, and that had failed. As Dillon LJ put it, 'I do not see why the final whistle should be blown at half time.'

 THINKING POINT

What would have been the outcome if EVTR had acquired the equipment?

This would have left the lender with a mere *personal* claim under the loan agreement. However, surely his intended purpose in making the loan to a company in financial difficulties was not that the company would acquire equipment, but that he, the lender, would be repaid. In other words, it could be argued that the Court of Appeal in this case still blew the whistle at half time as far as the lender was concerned. However, it would surely be going too far to recognise the priority of the lender's claim right up until the date of repayment of the loaned monies, that is, even after all special conditions attaching to the loan had been met.

So far we have been considering asset protection trusts in cases where the monies had been advanced to assist failing companies. We have already suggested that granting priority to the lender can be justified on grounds of policy and principle because of the perceived social and commercial benefits of successful corporate rescue. In fact, asset protection trusts have also been recognised in other circumstances.

An example is *Carreras Rothmans Ltd v Freeman Mathews Treasure Ltd* [1985] 1 Ch 207. In that case, CR, a cigarette manufacturer, had for many years employed FMT to advertise its products, for which service FMT received an annual fee. The annual fee was paid on a monthly basis. FMT eventually fell into financial difficulties and was unable to meet its own monthly debts to third party agents. Fearing that it would lose the custom of CR, FMT set up a special account into which CR would henceforth make its monthly payments and out of which FMT would finance advertising on CR's behalf. Ultimately, however, FMT went into creditors' voluntary liquidation and the special account was frozen. CR was obliged thereafter to pay FMT's agents directly to maintain the advertising campaign. CR brought an action against FMT and its liquidators claiming a declaration that the balance of monies in the special account had been held by FMT on trust to pay for CR's advertising and, that trust having failed, the monies were now held by FMT on resulting trust for CR. It was held that the monies in the special account had never been held by FMT for its own benefit, but rather had been held for a specific purpose. Accordingly, the monies were not available to FMT's general creditors, but were held by the liquidator on trust for CR. Sir Peter Millett QC, as he then was, appeared for the successful claimant.

THINKING POINT

In the absence of the policy benefit of corporate rescue, can you think of any principled justification for allowing CR to recover its funds ahead of FMT's general creditors?

Peter Gibson J was of the opinion that 'the principle in all these cases is that equity fastens on the conscience of the person who receives from another property transferred for a specific purpose only and not for the recipient's own purposes, so that such person will not be permitted to treat the property as his own or to use it for other than the stated purpose' (p. 222).

CASE CLOSE-UP

Twinsectra Ltd v Yardley [2002] 2 AC 164, House of Lords

Facts: Twinsectra Ltd made a loan to Mr Yardley through the agency of solicitors. The solicitors to whom the loan monies were paid gave an undertaking that the loan monies would be retained by them until such time as they were applied in the acquisition of property on behalf of their client. They also undertook that '[t]he loan monies will be utilised solely for the acquisition of property on behalf of our client and for no other purposes'. In the event, the loan monies were not applied exclusively towards the acquisition of property and the question arose whether the solicitor had breached a trust and whether another solicitor involved in the transaction at a later stage might be liable for having dishonestly assisted in a breach of that trust (on this aspect see Chapter 19).

Held: the undertaking by the recipient solicitors gave rise to a trust of the *Quistclose* variety, the terms of the undertaking corresponding to the terms of the trust. The Court of Appeal in *Challinor* v *Juliet Bellis & Co* [2015] EWCA Civ 59, following Lord Millett's analysis in *Twinsectra*, has summarised the *Quistclose* trust in the following terms (*per* Briggs LJ, at para. [63]):

> Where property is transferred on terms that do not leave it at the free disposal of the transferee then the *Quistclose*-type trust thereby established is one under which the beneficial interest in the property remains in the transferor unless and until the purposes for which it has been transferred have been fulfilled: see *Twinsectra* at paragraph 100. That beneficial interest ceases to exist if and to the extent that the property is used for the stated purposes, but not otherwise. The application of the property for the stated purpose is a power vested in the transferee, not (usually at least) a primary purpose trust.

The outcome in *Twinsectra* should be contrasted with that in *Gabriel v Little & Ors* [2013] EWCA Civ 1513, where money was loaned to a company in the belief that it would be used to develop property, but without any express restriction to a 'sole' or 'exclusive' purpose. The claim of a *Quistclose* trust failed.

THINKING POINT

The courts sometimes seem over-generous in recognising a *Quistclose* trust in cases where the policy concerns are not as clear as they were in the original *Quistclose* case. For example, in *Cooper v PRG Powerhouse* [2008] EWHC 498, the departing managing director of a company paid money to the company on the understanding that it would be paid onwards to complete the private purchase by the director of his company car. The company went insolvent before the money was paid. What should have been the outcome, do you think?

A *Quistclose* trust was held in the director's favour. If the justification for the radically unorthodox *Quistclose* trust is that it serves the public interest in saving failing companies, one has to question whether the former director of an insolvent company should be able to use such a trust to get a good deal on a company car in priority to the company's general creditors. Another case where a *Quistclose* trust was upheld almost as if it were a resulting trust of first resort is *Wise v Jimenez* [2013] All ER (D) 123. The successful claimant, the former professional footballer Dennis Wise, recovered money given to his business partner on the (unfulfilled) understanding that it would be used to develop a golf course to their mutual profit.

2.3.4.4 Asset protection for reasons other than priority in insolvency

In the previous section we saw that a commercial lender might wish to use a trust as an asset protection facility to protect the loaned monies from the borrower's general creditors.

THINKING POINT

Write down a brief list of any other reasons why an international commercial enterprise might wish to protect its assets.

For an international commercial enterprise another reason for using an asset protection trust is to protect its assets from political risks in particular jurisdictions (Harry Wiggin, 'Asset Protection for Multinational Corporations' in E. McKendrick (ed.), *Commercial Aspects of Trusts and Fiduciary Obligations*, Oxford: Clarendon Press, 1992).

THINKING POINT

Can you think of any advantages that a trust might have over a corporation in this context?

By means of a trust, it is possible to create an asset protection structure under which the trustees, the trust fund, the settlor and the governing law are based in different jurisdictions. The governing law of a trust is a matter of the settlor's choice, whereas that of a corporation is determined by its domicile. Multi-jurisdictional asset protection works because those claiming the protected assets lose the will to litigate in the face of complexity. (For an illustrative hypothetical example, see D. McNair, 'Risk Assessment in Multi-Jurisdictional Asset Protection Structures', in *Trusts and Trustees and International Asset Management* (1996) 2(1), 15.) Of course, one major problem with international asset protection structures is that the more complex they are, the more able they are to assist in the laundering of money:

OUTSIDE THE BOX

Lethal Weapon II (Warner Bros) 1989, starring Mel Gibson

(screenplay by Jeffrey Boam; story by Shane Black and Warren Murphy)

LEO:	I also launder money.
RIGGS:	How'd you do it?
LEO:	Okay. They bring the cash into the bank and deposit it into the account of a dummy Finance Company licensed out of the Bahamas. Sometimes this takes all day, because we can't do it all in one deposit.
MURTAUGH:	Why not?
LEO:	The Bank Secrecy Act. All cash deposits or withdrawals of ten thousand dollars or more will generate a CTR ... 'Currency Transaction Record' ... which goes to the IRS.
MURTAUGH:	That's good.
LEO:	No, that's bad. Made my job a lot harder.
RIGGS:	That's what's good about it, Leo.
LEO:	Anyway ... after all the deposits have been made, I turn around and issue them a cashier's cheque for the amount of the total deposits minus a commission. Cashiers' cheques are wonderful instruments. As good as cash, but they don't generate a report to the IRS.
MURTAUGH:	So now the money is washed, right?
LEO:	Yeah. But there's more ... The cashier's cheque is treated as a *loan*. The 'lender' is the dummy Finance Company. There's loan documents to support it. They can even take a tax deduction on the interest payments they're not making.
MURTAUGH:	Leo ... you're a crook.

The EU Fourth Money Laundering Directive ((EU) 2015/849)) seeks to strengthen EU defences against money laundering and terrorist financing. In compliance with this Directive, HMRC introduced new regulations requiring the registration of trusts by the end of January 2018 (The 2017 Money Laundering, Terrorist Financing and Transfer of Funds Regulations (SI 2017/692)). Under the regulations, all trusts with a UK tax liability must be registered on the new Trusts Registration Service (TRS) online portal held by HMRC. The information will be available to UK law enforcement authorities, but, crucially, the register of trusts is not accessible to the public. Hence trusts remain essentially private.

Whether this will remain the case following the EU Fifth Money Laundering Directive (EU) 2018/843) ('5MLD') is debatable. It might depend upon the legal effects of 'Brexit'. The Directive came into force on 9 July 2018 and EU Member States had 18 months to implement it into national law (with a deadline of 10 January 2020). 5MLD requires Member States, including the UK, to extend registration of beneficial ownership of trusts to all UK resident express trusts and non-EU resident express trusts that own UK real estate or that have a business relationship with an entity obliged to carry out customer (anti-money laundering) due diligence, such as a bank, estate agent or accountant. It requires Member States to share data from the register under certain defined circumstances, in particular as part of customer due diligence requirements.

Summary

- We have seen that the trust is a flexible and useful legal instrument and that it is conceptually and functionally distinct from other legal concepts such as contract, agency and debt.

- The distinctiveness of the trust is seen most clearly where it is employed as a means of prioritising the beneficiaries' claims against their trustee in the event of the trustee's insolvency. Personal claims against the trustee's personal wealth brought by the trustee's personal creditors are relegated behind the claims of trust beneficiaries to recover their *own* property from the trustee's hands.

- This proprietary dimension of trust law (the fact that the beneficiaries' interest under the trust is their property to keep or transfer and takes priority in the event of the trustee's insolvency), combined with the high standard of care demanded of trustees, has seen the trust employed for such diverse ends as the provision of occupational pension funds and the recovery of loans in commerce (e.g. *Quistclose*).

? Summative assessment exercise

'Of all the exploits of Equity the largest and the most important is the invention and development of the Trust. It is an 'institute' of great elasticity and generality; as elastic, as general as contract. This perhaps forms the most distinctive achievement of English lawyers.'

F.W. Maitland, *'Uses and Trusts' in Equity: A Course of Lectures* (rev. J. Brunyate, Cambridge, 1936)

Critically discuss this statement.

 Full specimen answers can be found at www.oxfordtextbooks.co.uk/orc/watt_directions5e/.

The bigger picture

As Rudyard Kipling wrote in the 1891 poem *The English Flag*, what do 'they know of England who only England know'? You might find it useful to your understanding of the English law of trusts to examine the nature of the trust in other jurisdictions. Overseas scholars frequently bring a very insightful 'comparative law' perspective to the subject which throws the unique points of the English trust into sharp relief. See, for example, Professor Lionel Smith's book *Reimagining the Trust: Trusts in Civil Law* (Cambridge: Cambridge University Press, 2012). The New Zealand Law Commission's *Review of the Law of Trusts: A Trusts Act for New Zealand* (R130) August 2013 recommends the introduction of a new Trusts Act to replace the New Zealand Trustee Act 1956. The new Act will be a comprehensive statute that modernises the law of trusts in a number of areas and addresses key matters that are currently only governed by case law. The New Zealand proposals are very clearly set out and include a comprehensive overview of trusts law (much of which also applies to the law of England and Wales). You might find it useful to consult the proposals for a lucid outsider commentary and critique of trusts law.

 The New Zealand proposals can be accessed at www.lawcom.govt.nz/our-projects/law-trusts and via the Online Resource Centre accompanying this book.

Further reading

Harris, J. 'The Hague Trusts Convention after *Akers v Samba*' (2018) 24(4) *Trusts & Trustees* 346–63

Hayton, D. 'Pension Trusts and Traditional Trusts: Drastically Different Species of Trusts' (2005) 18 Conv 229
more analysis of the distinction between pension trusts and traditional trusts

Jaffey, P. 'Explaining the Trust' (2015) 131 LQR 377–401
an argument that 'the beneficiary's equitable interest consists of distinct personal and property rights' and that the relevant personal rights should be regarded as essentially contractual

Langbein, J.H. 'The Contractarian Basis of the Law of Trusts' (1995) 105 *Yale Law Journal* 625
controversial argument that the trust is functionally indistinguishable from the modern third party beneficiary contract

Nolan, R.C. 'Property in a Fund' (2004) 120 LQR 108
a stimulating re-examination of the fundamentals of the trust

Sealy, L.S. 'The Director as Trustee' (1967) 25 CLJ 83
an older article, but still a very useful and insightful analysis of the points of overlap and distinction between corporation and trust

Stevens, R. 'The Contracts (Rights of Third Parties) Act 1999' (2004) 120 LQR 292
a scholarly examination of the implications of the statute

Swadling, W. (ed.) *The Quistclose Trust: Critical Essays* (2004) Oxford: Hart
a variety of sometimes complementary and sometimes conflicting analyses of the *Quistclose* trust by several leading international scholars

 For links to selected cases, statutes, academic papers and official reports mentioned in this chapter please visit the online resources at www.oup.com/uk/watt_directions6e/.

3 Capacity and formality requirements

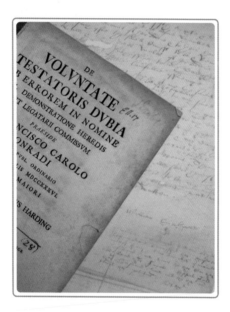

□ **LEARNING OBJECTIVES**

By the end of this chapter you should be able to:

● advise whether a would-be settlor is legally capable of setting up a trust;

● create a trust of any type of property in compliance with the proper formalities;

● deal with the equitable interest under a trust in compliance with the proper formalities;

● recognise the numerous trusts for which there are no formality requirements;

● identify valid 'mutual wills' and 'secret trusts'.

Introduction

Perhaps you have recently split up with a boyfriend or girlfriend and you are keen to recover that signed limited edition CD which was your gift to them last Valentine's day. You are a law student, so how hard can it be? Surely all you have to do is knock on their door wearing a sharp suit with your briefcase at your side and announce that the CD has to be returned because you accidentally failed to complete official gift form Val2014a. By all means try, but legally speaking you haven't got a leg to stand on. The generous act of giving is rightly a private one, and where a gift is made by a living person (as opposed to by the will of a dead person) the law does not insist upon any formality. The mechanics of transfer might require a form to be filled out in certain cases—usually in order to authorise a change in the name of the registered owner (for example, if transferring a car or company shares: see Chapter 5)—but that is quite a different thing from saying that the *intention to give* must somehow be set out in writing. So it is with trusts. Expressly created trusts are really just a special form of gift; it would therefore be an unwarranted intrusion into our private affairs for the law to require us to fill out a form to declare to the world that we have created a trust. Even an express trust of *land* can be declared without any formality, although if you want to *enforce* an express trust of land in court, the settlor or his agent must have confirmed the declaration of trust in signed writing. In short, formality is not very important with regard to the *creation* of express trusts. And why should it be? After all, equity is said to look to substance, not form. But beware! Formality is extremely important with regard to the *subsequent transfer* of beneficial interests once a trust has been created. Formality is also very important with regard to trusts made by will (so-called testamentary trusts), although that is true of all dispositions, including absolute gifts, made on death. Where formality is required (to evidence the lifetime or *inter vivos* creation of trusts of land, or to effect testamentary dispositions or to make lifetime dispositions of interests under existing trusts), it is because our freedom to transact informally must occasionally give way to the need to produce certainty and to prevent fraud.

---

inter vivos Also known as a 'lifetime' trust. A trust is said to be *inter vivos* if it is effective within the lifetime of the settlor. The person setting up an *inter vivos* trust is called a 'settlor'.

testamentary Any trust which comes into effect upon the death of the person setting up the trust is said to be 'testamentary'. The person setting up such a trust is called a 'testator' (if male) and a 'testatrix' (if female).

3.1 Capacity

Before we turn to consider formalities, which is the main topic of this chapter, we must briefly note that not everybody has the capacity to create a binding trust.

capacity
'Legal competency or qualification' (Oxford English Dictionary).

The two most common reasons for lack of capacity are poor mental health and minority (infancy). These are considered next. However, even so-called 'artificial' persons, such as corporations, might also lack capacity if the legal documentation according to which they are constituted restricts or excludes their powers. So, for example, the 'objects clause' in the memorandum of a limited liability company might expressly or impliedly exclude the company's power to act as a trustee.

3.1.1 **Mental incapacity**

Medical evidence as to the mental state of property owners may raise a presumption that they lack the mental capacity necessary to make valid dispositions of their property. Unless this presumption is rebutted by other evidence, any purported dispositions will be ineffective to transfer the beneficial interests in the property (see *Simpson* v *Simpson* [1992] 1 FLR 601; *Kostic* v *Conservative Party Association* [2007] EWHC 2298 Ch). The Mental Capacity Act 2005 authorises the Court of Protection to deal with the property of a person judged to be incapacitated in this way. For the purposes of the 2005 Act, 'a person lacks capacity in relation to a matter if at the material time he is unable to make a decision for himself in relation to the matter because of an impairment of, or a disturbance in the functioning of, the mind or brain' (s 2(1)). The Act does not apply to people under the age of 16.

3.1.2 **Minority**

Since 1 January 1970 a minor is any person who has not yet attained 18 years of age, known as the age of majority (Family Law Reform Act 1969, s 1). Before 1970, legal minority did not come to an end until the age of 21. Minors lack the capacity to hold the legal estate to land, and cannot create a trust of land (Law of Property Act 1925, s 1(6)). Further, a formal trust made by a minor since 1 January 1970, though not void from the outset, is voidable if the minor repudiates (renounces) the trust within a reasonable time of attaining majority.

3.2 Formalities

One of the maxims of equity is that *equity looks to substance not form* (see 1.3.3) and we have already noted that an express trust can be created during the lifetime of the settlor without any formality (subject to what was said about express trusts of *land*). I could, for example, declare orally: 'See this gold pen of mine, I henceforth hold it on trust for the benefit of my baby son.' Assuming the context showed that I had intended to create legal relations, these words would be sufficient to move the beneficial (equitable) ownership of the pen from me to my son. I would be a trustee of the pen for him. On account of a few words I would no longer be entitled to the use and enjoyment of the pen, even though I will probably keep the pen in my physical possession. However, we also noted that there are certain documentary formalities governing the creation of testamentary trusts and the lifetime transfer of interests under existing trusts. These formalities are contained in the Wills Act 1837 and the Law of Property Act 1925, respectively. One reason is to prevent fraud (it is assumed that informality and secrecy tend to foster fraud). A related reason is to be able to identify with certainty the people who are entitled to the benefit of property. Another reason, related to the last, is that the Inland Revenue is keen to ascertain who is entitled to claim the benefit of property, so that the benefit may be taxed! (You will notice as you progress through this section the remarkable proportion of cases in which the Inland Revenue appeared as claimant.)

There are, however—to the probable chagrin of the Inland Revenue—exceptional cases in which the statutory formalities do not apply. Thus the formality requirements laid down in the

Law of Property Act 1925, which we shall shortly be considering in depth, do not apply to the creation or operation of resulting, implied or constructive trusts (informal trusts are considered further in Chapters 16 and 17), and the formality requirements laid down in the Wills Act 1837, s 9 (as amended by the Administration of Justice Act 1982, s 17) do not apply to the creation or operation of so-called 'secret trusts' (considered later in this chapter).

3.2.1 *Inter vivos* transactions

 STATUTE

Law of Property Act 1925, s 53

(1) Subject to the provisions hereinafter contained [notably those concerning short leases contained in s 54] with respect to the creation of interests in land by parol—

   (a) no interest in land can be created or disposed of except by writing signed by the person creating or conveying the same, or by his agent thereunto lawfully authorised in writing, or by will, or by operation of law;

   (b) a declaration of trust respecting any land or any interest therein must be manifested and proved by some writing signed by some person who is able to declare such trust or by his will;

   (c) a disposition of an equitable interest or trust subsisting at the time of the disposition, must be in writing signed by the person disposing of the same, or by his agent thereunto lawfully authorised in writing or by will.

(2) This section does not affect the creation or operation of resulting, implied or constructive trusts.

 THINKING POINT

Consider s 53 of the Law of Property Act 1925, set out immediately above. You will see that the section describes a number of transactions and prescribes formalities which must be met for each of those transactions. In Table 3.1 you will see two columns headed TRANSACTION and FORMALITY, respectively. Simply take your pen and draw lines to join the transactions to their corresponding formality requirement(s). Then compare your choices with the solution which follows.

Hopefully you correctly observed that a *declaration* of trust respecting any land or any interest therein must be manifested and proved by some writing signed by some person who is able to declare such trust or by his will (s 53(1)(b)). A and C should have been linked with 2.

Further, a *disposition* of an equitable interest or trust already subsisting at the time of the disposition must be in writing signed by the person disposing of the same, or by his agent lawfully authorised in writing or by will (s 53(1)(c)). B should have been linked with 3.

Table 3.1 Law of Property Act s 53

Transaction	Formality
A declaration of trust of a legal interest in land	1 no formality
B disposition of an interest under an existing trust	2 must be proved by a document signed by the settlor (or proved by the testator's will)
C declaration of trust of a subsisting equitable interest in land	3 must be made in a document signed by the settlor or the settlor's agent (or made in the testator's will)
D transaction giving rise to a constructive trust	

You should also have noted that the formality requirements in s 53(1) do not affect the creation or operation of resulting, implied or constructive trusts. D should have been linked with 1.

The words 'declaration' and 'disposition' have been emphasised because they are easily confused. Declaration of a trust creates the trust, and hence creates the equitable interests under

THINKING POINT

Between 1949 and 1950 H set up six settlement trusts in favour of his grandchildren. On 1 February 1955 H transferred 18,000 £1 shares to the trustees. On 18 February H orally and irrevocably directed that the shares should be held on the trusts of the six settlements, 3,000 shares to each settlement. On 25 March the trustees made written declarations of trust in accordance with H's directions. Which transaction transferred H's equitable interest in the shares?

the trust, whereas disposition refers to the disposition of an equitable interest under a trust which already exists. Before a trust has been declared of property, it does not make sense to describe the equitable interest under that trust as already 'subsisting'.

These are the facts of *Grey v Inland Revenue Commissioners* [1960] AC 1, a case which was heard in the House of Lords. Grey was one of the trustees of the six settlements. The instruments of 25 March, by which the trustees declared the six trusts of 3,000 shares each, were formal documents which would be taxed if they had passed any 'value'. The crucial question was whether the 25 March instruments had actually transferred value, or whether they had been mere formal confirmation of a substantial transfer that had already taken place on 18 February. The Inland Revenue had assessed the 25 March instruments to *ad valorem* stamp duty. Grey had appealed. Their Lordships held that H's oral direction of 18 February had been an attempted 'disposition' of his equitable interest in the shares, but that it had been ineffective for failing to satisfy the requirement of writing established by s 53(1)(c) of the Law of Property Act 1925. Accordingly, only the later *formal* declarations by the trustees on 25 March were effective to transfer H's equitable interest in the shares. Those formal declarations constituted 'instruments' for the purposes of the Stamp Act 1891 and had been rightly assessed to **ad valorem stamp duty**.

> **ad valorem stamp duty**
> A tax charged as a percentage of the value transferred by a document.

CASE CLOSE-UP

Oughtred v Inland Revenue Commissioners [1960] AC 206

Facts: 200,000 shares in a private company were held upon trust for Mrs Oughtred for life, thereafter for her son absolutely. Mrs Oughtred also owned 72,700 shares absolutely. To avoid estate duty payable on the shares in the event of Mrs Oughtred's death, the parties determined by an oral agreement to exchange their interests. Mrs Oughtred promised to transfer the 72,700 shares to her son, and he in turn promised to transfer his remainder interest in the 200,000 shares to Mrs Oughtred. Two documents of transfer were executed at a later date. The first document recorded the transfer of legal title in the 200,000 shares from the trustees to Mrs Oughtred in consideration of the sum of ten shillings. The second document recorded the transfer of Mrs Oughtred's 72,700 shares to her son's nominees.

The Inland Revenue claimed *ad valorem* stamp duty on the document recording the transfer of the legal title in the 200,000 shares. Mrs Oughtred argued that no value had passed by virtue of that document, the equitable interest having been transferred by the earlier oral agreement, and accordingly that there was no basis on which to charge *ad valorem* stamp duty against the document.

 CASE CLOSE-UP

Oughtred v Inland Revenue Commissioners [1960] AC 206

Decision: The House of Lords could not agree on the result. Two of the five law lords dissented. One of the speeches in dissent was delivered by Lord Radcliffe, who had delivered the leading speech in *Grey v IRC*. The majority held that Mrs Oughtred did not have a beneficial interest in the 200,000 shares until the execution of the later documents. It followed, therefore, that the document relating to the transfer of the 200,000 shares was an instrument transferring value, and should be subjected to *ad valorem* stamp duty.

Mrs Oughtred had argued that inasmuch as the oral agreement was an agreement of sale and purchase it gave rise in equity to a constructive trust of the remainder interest in her favour, subject only to Mrs Oughtred performing her side of the agreement to transfer the 72,700 shares to her son.

The gist of Mrs Oughtred's argument ran something like this: because the shares in the case were shares in a *private* company they were unique (inasmuch as it could not be guaranteed that replacement shares could be obtained on the open market). It followed from the uniqueness of the shares that common law damages would not be an adequate remedy for failure to fulfil the oral agreement. Equity would therefore grant specific performance of the contract. Having granted specific performance, equity pretends that the performance has already occurred (in accordance with the maxim *equity sees as done that which ought to be done* (see 1.3.8)), with the result that the oral agreement was immediately effective in equity. Consequently, Mrs Oughtred was, according to equity, from the date of the oral agreement no longer the beneficial owner of the shares in her possession. The necessary conclusion was that Mrs Oughtred held those shares not for her own benefit, but upon trust for her son, with whom the oral agreement had been made. This was not an expressly created trust, but a constructive trust. Even if the oral agreement had, strictly speaking, amounted to a 'disposition' within s 53(1)(c), nevertheless it would be valid without writing because s 53(2) disapplies s 53(1)(c) where the disposition operates by virtue of a constructive trust.

Her argument can be represented diagrammatically as in Figure 3.1.

Figure 3.1 Mrs Oughtred's argument

Contract for private company shares	Unique	Common law damages inadequate	Equitable remedy of specific performance	Equity sees as done that which ought to be done	Contract deemed to be already performed	Equitable ownership passes	Vendor holds shares under constructive trust

A bare majority of their Lordships rejected her argument. By analogy with the 'simple case of a contract for sale of land' they pointed out that the deed which comes after the contract and completes the sale has never been regarded as 'not stampable *ad valorem*'. It followed, on this reasoning, that the later instrument of transfer to Mrs Oughtred had transferred real value and was stampable *ad valorem* as the Inland Revenue had contended.

Lord Radcliffe, who (together with Lord Cohen) had dissented from the majority view, observed that Mrs Oughtred need never have called for the subsequent written instrument of transfer, and that she could have simply called upon the trustees of the settlement of the 200,000 shares to transfer the bare legal title to her. For Lord Radcliffe the subsequent written transfer by the son was nothing more than a transfer of the bare legal title to Mrs Oughtred; it did not transfer any equitable interest at all and should not have been assessed to *ad valorem* stamp duty.

Q | CASE CLOSE-UP

***Oughtred v Inland Revenue Commissioners* [1960] AC 206, House of Lords**

Lord Jenkins: 'The parties to a transaction of sale and purchase may, no doubt, choose to let the matter rest in contract. But if the subject-matter of a sale is such that the full title to it can only be transferred by an instrument, then any instrument they execute by way of transfer of the property sold ranks for stamp duty purposes as a conveyance on sale, not-withstanding the constructive trust in favour of the purchaser which arose on the conclusion of the contract.'

THINKING POINT

Do you think that *Oughtred v IRC* would have been decided differently if Mrs Oughtred had not executed the subsequent written instrument of transfer?

The Court of Appeal has since had an opportunity to consider this possibility, or something very similar to it, in *Neville v Wilson* [1996] 3 WLR 460. Neville carried on business through N Ltd. Shortly before Neville's death N Ltd acquired all the issued share capital in U Ltd, 120 shares in U Ltd being held by nominees of N Ltd, the remaining shares in U Ltd being held by N Ltd as registered owner. In 1969 N Ltd was informally liquidated by shareholder agreement, its liabilities discharged and its assets divided between the shareholders. N Ltd was later struck off the register and formally dissolved. Some years later, after profitable business and after U Ltd's assets had been reduced to cash, Neville's children (who had been shareholders in N Ltd) commenced proceedings against ex-shareholders in N Ltd to determine, inter alia, the beneficial ownership of the 120 shares in U Ltd held by nominees.

It was held that the informal 1969 agreement had made the shareholders in N Ltd implied or constructive trustees for each other of the assets of N Ltd, the equitable interest of each shareholder under the constructive trust being of a size proportional to his shareholding in N Ltd. Accordingly, s 53(2) of the Law of Property Act 1925 saved the 1969 agreement from being rendered ineffectual by the formality requirements contained in s 53(1). Consequently, the money representing the shares did not pass to the Crown as *bona vacantia*, but was divided between the shareholders as they had agreed.

> *bona vacantia* (pronounced 'bone-a vak-ansh-ee-a' or 'bonna vak-ant-ee-a') Vacant goods, i.e. ownerless property. In England and Wales ownerless property will usually pass to the Crown or the Duchy of Lancaster.

The decision of the Court of Appeal in *Neville* v *Wilson* lends indirect support to Mrs Oughtred's sophisticated line of argument, for the oral agreement in *Neville* v *Wilson* was held to give rise to a constructive trust, thus taking the agreement out of the remit of s 53(1)(c). On this view Mrs Oughtred's mistake was to execute a deed of transfer subsequent to her oral agreement. Although intended by her merely to confirm that the disposition of her equitable interest had already been effected orally, it gave an apparently irresistible opportunity to the House of Lords to decide, albeit by a bare majority, that *ad valorem* stamp duty should be paid on the deed. Whether as a matter of principle Mrs Oughtred's argument should ever be permitted to succeed is another matter.

3.2.1.1 Section 53(1)(b)

You should remember that s 53(1)(b) of the Law of Property Act 1925 provides as follows:

> a declaration of trust respecting any land or any interest therein must be manifested and proved by some writing signed by some person who is able to declare such trust or by his will; . . .

It is important to appreciate that the actual declaration of trust need not be *made* in writing. The requirement is merely that the declaration be manifested and *proved* by some authorised signed writing. Indeed, the written proof of the declaration could quite possibly come a long time after the declaration; it might even be contained within the will of the person who declared the trust. Without written proof of the declaration of a trust of land, the trust is not *enforceable* in court against the trustee; it is however (for what it is worth) in all other respects valid.

Note that an electronic signature has the same legal status as a wet ink signature (Golden Ocean Group Ltd v Salgaocar Mining [2012] EWCA Civ 265, Court of Appeal) so that typing a name into an email satisfies a statutory requirement for a document to be signed (J Pereira Fernandes SA v Mehta [2006] EWHC 813 (Ch); Green (Liquidator of Stealth Construction Ltd) v Ireland [2011] EWHC 1305 (Ch)). In August 2018, the Law Commission reached the provisional conclusion, as part of its consultation on the electronic execution of documents, that electronic signatures are valid at common law without the need for legislation.

3.2.1.2 **Section 53(1)(c)**

One crucial question unites the cases of *Grey* v *IRC*, *Oughtred* v *IRC* and *Neville* v *Wilson* considered earlier. The question is this: 'What amounts to a "disposition" for the purposes of s 53(1)(c)?' It is a question of central importance because, as we have seen, 'dispositions' are ineffective unless made by writing. See Figure 3.2.

Compare your answers with the following:

I. The transfer by a beneficiary of their interest under a trust to some other person

II. A direction by a beneficiary to their trustee henceforth to hold the equitable interest on trust for some other person

Figure 3.2 Dispositions under s 53(1)(c)

Place a tick next to whichever of the following you consider will amount to a 'disposition' under s. 53(1)(c).

I. the transfer by a beneficiary of their interest under a trust to some other person

T

B1 ⟶ B2

II. a direction by a beneficiary to their trustee henceforth to hold the equitable interest on trust for some other person

T

B1   B2

III. a statement by a beneficiary that they hold the equitable interest to which they are entitled on trust for some other person

T1

↓

B1/T2

↓

B2

IV. in the case of a bare trust, a direction by a beneficiary to their trustee to transfer the legal estate to some other person, the intention being that the equitable interest should pass simultaneously

T ⟶ A

B

V. the disclaimer by a beneficiary of their equitable interest under a trust

T

B

Both of these transactions qualify as 'dispositions' of subsisting equitable interests within s 53(1)(c) of the Law of Property Act 1925. In both cases the original beneficiary, having made the transfer or given the direction, drops out of the picture, their equitable interest having been disposed of.

III. A statement by a beneficiary that they hold the equitable interest to which they are entitled on trust for some other person

The crucial question is whether this type of transaction is a declaration of trust (a sub-trust, in fact), which involves the creation of an entirely novel equitable interest, or whether it is the disposition of a subsisting equitable interest.

As we have seen, s 53(1) treats 'declarations' and 'dispositions' quite differently. Generally, where a trust is declared *inter vivos* there are no formality requirements at all; only if a trust is declared of land must there be some written evidence of the declaration. In contrast, dispositions of equitable interests, whether the equitable interest is in land or some other property, must be made in writing in order to be valid. Figure 3.3 seeks to illustrate this.

Figure 3.3 Declaration or disposition?

Whether or not a statement by a beneficiary that they hold the equitable interest to which they are entitled on trust for some other person is a 'declaration' or a 'disposition' depends upon the facts of each case. If the beneficiary, having made the declaration, has no on-going duties in relation to the equitable property, it would be nonsensical to describe the beneficiary as being a trustee of it. In such a case the equitable interest, though expressly stated to be held on trust, has in fact been disposed of outright (*Grainge* v *Wilberforce* (1889) 5 TLR 436). Further, for a statement of this sort to be recognised as a true declaration of trust the beneficiary must retain not only nominal duties, but duties which involve the real exercise of choice.

IV. In the case of a bare trust, a direction by a beneficiary to their trustee to transfer the legal estate to some other person, the intention being that the equitable interest should pass simultaneously

This transaction was one of the many matters considered by the House of Lords in *Vandervell* v *Inland Revenue Commissioners* [1967] 2 AC 291. In 1958 Mr Vandervell, the immensely wealthy controlling director and shareholder of VP Ltd, decided to give 100,000 of his shares in the company to the Royal College of Surgeons (RCS) to found a chair in pharmacology. The shares were currently held by his bank under a bare trust for him. Accordingly, V directed the bank to transfer 100,000 shares to the RCS. It was intended that the RCS should keep the shares for a limited period only, and should relinquish them after receiving £150,000 income on the shares by way of dividends.

As to whether the direction to the bank had been void for lack of written formality, the House of Lords held that s 53(1)(c) only applied to cases where the equitable interest in property had been disposed of independently of the legal interest in that property. The object of s 53(1)(c) was to prevent hidden oral transactions in equitable interests which might defraud other parties (such as the Inland Revenue). In cases, such as the present, where the equitable owner had directed his bare trustee to deal with the legal and equitable estates simultaneously, s 53(1)(c) had no application. (Contrast *Prest v Petrodel* [2013] UKSC 34 where A, having held legal title for the benefit of B, transferred it to C. It was held that B retained the benefit, because he had not intended to confer a benefit on C (per Lord Sumption at para. [49]).)

V. Where a person entitled to a beneficial interest disclaims that interest

It was held by the Court of Appeal in *Re Paradise Motor Co Ltd* [1968] 2 All ER 625 that a disclaimer of this sort operates by way of avoidance, not by way of disposition. Consequently, the disclaimer does not need to comply with s 53(1)(c).

3.2.1.3 Lack of formality cannot be pleaded to disguise a fraud

It follows from the maxim *equity will not permit a statute to be used as an instrument of fraud* (see 1.3.4) that a party will not be permitted to perpetrate a fraud against another person by relying on that other person's failure to comply with the formality requirements laid down in s 53(1) of the Law of Property Act 1925. The classic example of this principle is the case of *Rochefoucauld v Boustead* [1897] 1 Ch 196, a case in which s 7 of the Statute of Frauds (29 Car.2, c.3), the precursor to s 53(1) of the 1925 Act, was considered in the Court of Appeal.

In *Rochefoucauld v Boustead* [1897] 1 Ch 197, Lindley LJ held that 'the Statute of Frauds does not prevent proof of a fraud; and it is a fraud on the part of a person to whom land is conveyed as a trustee, and who knows it was so conveyed, to deny the trust and claim the land himself. Consequently, notwithstanding the statute, it is competent for a person claiming land conveyed to another to prove by parol [oral] evidence that it was so conveyed upon trust for the claimant.'

However, after the enactment of s 53(2) of the 1925 Act, *Rochefoucauld v Boustead* sits uneasily with the *letter* of the law. You will recall that s 53(2) disapplies s 53(1) in cases of 'resulting implied and constructive trusts'. It is arguable that, by the rule of statutory interpretation *expressio unius est exclusio alterius* (which in the present context might be translated as follows: *express admission of one exception precludes implied admission of another*), the wording of s 53(2) removes any possibility of an *express* trust like the one in *Rochefoucauld v Boustead* being excepted from the s 53(1) formality requirements.

 OUTSIDE THE BOX

E.M. Forster, *Howards End*, 1910

In silence they drew up to the breakfast-table. The events of yesterday—indeed, of this morning—suddenly receded into a past so remote that they seemed scarcely to have lived in it. Heavy breathings were heard. They were calming themselves. Charles, to steady them further, read the enclosure out loud: 'A note in my mother's handwriting, in an envelope addressed to my father, sealed. Inside: "I should like Miss Schlegel (Margaret) to have

Howards End." No date, no signature. Forwarded through the matron of that nursing home. Now, the question is –.' Dolly interrupted him. 'But I say that note isn't legal. Houses ought to be done by a lawyer, Charles, surely.'

Her husband worked his jaw severely. Little lumps appeared in front of either ear—a symptom that she had not yet learnt to respect, and she asked whether she might see the note. Charles looked at his father for permission, who said abstractedly, 'Give it her.' She seized it, and at once exclaimed: 'Why, it's only in pencil! I said so. Pencil never counts.'

3.2.2 Testamentary trusts

The testamentary disposition in *Howards End* failed, not because it was in pencil, but because it failed to comply with the formality requirements laid down in the Wills Act 1837. That said, in 2017, the Law Commission opened consultation on possible reforms to enable the court to dispense with formalities where the deceased's intentions are clear from available evidence.

 STATUTE

Wills Act 1837, s 9 (as substituted by the Administration of Justice Act 1982, s 17)

No will shall be valid, unless—

(a) it is in writing, and signed by the testator, or by some other person in his presence and by his direction; and

(b) it appears that the testator intended by his signature to give effect to the will; and

(c) the signature is made or acknowledged by the testator in the presence of two or more witnesses present at the same time; and

(d) each witness either—

    (i) attests and signs the will; or

    (ii) acknowledges his signature, in the presence of the testator (but not necessarily in the presence of any other witness), but no form of attestation shall be necessary.

3.2.2.1 Mutual wills

The *usual* case of mutual wills occurs where a husband and wife enter into a binding agreement, intended to be irrevocable by either party acting unilaterally, that they will both draft their wills in a particular way so as to ensure that on the death of the first to die the surviving spouse will receive the property of the deceased. Frequently the wills also provide that, on the death of the last surviving spouse, certain other named persons (often their children) will receive the property. The surviving spouse may receive a life interest in the property (see *Re Green* [1951] Ch 148) or an absolute interest (see *Dufour* v *Pereira* (1769) Dick 419) depending upon whether the particular facts of the case show that there was to be a gift over to other persons on the death of the last surviving spouse. Of course, the device is not restricted to spouses, nor even to couples. Several people could in theory create mutual wills with one another.

THINKING POINT

How can equity's recognition of the mutual wills agreement be justified where the agreement itself does not comply with the formalities of the Wills Act?

The traditional justification for equity's recognition of the agreement on which mutual wills are based is the prevention of fraud (see *Dufour v Pereira* (1769) Dick 419 at 421). It would be a fraud for the surviving party to rely on the lack of statutory formality as an excuse for reneging on the agreement, the deceased party having already performed their part of it. This rationale flows from the maxim *equity will not permit a statute to be used as an instrument of fraud* (see 1.3.4). So from the date of the death of the first party to die, the survivor is obliged to carry out his or her part of the agreement. The obligation is expressed in the form of a constructive trust binding on the survivor. This use of constructive trusts to avoid the Wills Act is similar to that underlying fully secret trusts (see 3.2.3.1).

CASE CLOSE-UP

Re Dale [1994] Ch 31

A husband and wife agreed that they would both draw up wills leaving their estates to their son and daughter equally. On his death the husband left his estate in accordance with the agreement. The wife, however, later drew up a new will, leaving the vast majority of the estate to her son, whom she also named as her executor. It was held that the husband and wife had entered into a binding agreement to create mutual wills, and that the son must hold his mother's estate on trust for himself and his sister equally. The most novel aspect of this decision was the acceptance that mutual wills could be created by persons who were not themselves named as beneficiaries under those wills.

Morritt J: 'There is no doubt that for the doctrine to apply there must be a contract at law. It is apparent from all the cases . . . that it is necessary to establish an agreement to make and not revoke mutual wills, some understanding or arrangement being insufficient . . . it is necessary to find consideration sufficient to support a contract at law . . . It is to be assumed that the first testator and the second testator had agreed to make and not to revoke the mutual wills in question. The performance of that promise by the execution of the will by the first testator is in my judgment sufficient consideration by itself.'

Contrast the strict contractual approach taken in *Re Dale* with the *inter vivos* creation of constructive trusts of land, where the trust may be based upon mere proof of an 'understanding or arrangement'! (See 17.4.1.)

It is clear from the *dictum* of Morritt J in *Re Dale* that for the doctrine of mutual wills to apply there must be evidence of an actual contractual agreement to that effect. Thus even the action of executing identical wills will not, without an agreement, suffice (*Re Oldham* [1925] Ch 75). However, the person who seeks to enforce a mutual will is not a party to the contract that created the mutuality of the wills. They claim under a trust; they are not seeking specific performance of a contract (*The Thomas and Agnes Carvel Foundation v Carvel* [2007] EWHC 1314 (Ch); *Olins v Walters* [2008] EWCA Civ 782; [2009] 2 WLR 1, Court of Appeal).

3.2.3 Secret trusts

Secret trusts are a means by which a testator is able to bypass the formality requirements laid down in the Wills Act 1837. As Danckwerts J put it in *Re Young* [1951] Ch 344, 'the whole theory of the formation of a secret trust is that the Wills Act has nothing to do with the matter'. Thus in *Re Young* a party who had witnessed the will was nevertheless permitted to take a benefit under the secret trust, contrary to the usual rule (Wills Act 1837, s 15). It is often said that secret trusts operate *dehors* (French: 'outside') the will. Typically, the reason for wanting secrecy arose where the testator wished to make a testamentary gift to a mistress or illegitimate child. (Note that the concept of 'illegitimacy' does not now exist: see the Family Law Reform Act 1987, s 1.)

---

secret trust This is a trust binding on property passed under a will, but which does not comply with the formalities required by the Wills Act. It is effective because it binds the conscience of the person to whom the property passes under the will, that person having accepted the trust when the testator was still alive.

fully secret trust This is where X formally leaves property to Y by his will in circumstances where Y is informally made aware by X during X's lifetime (and Y expressly or impliedly accepts) that Y is to hold the property as trustee for the benefit of Z.

half-secret trust This is where X formally leaves property by his will to Y expressly 'on trust' for another, but where Y is only informally made aware of the identity of that other. It will be clear on the face of the will that Y is not the beneficial owner of the property.

3.2.3.1 Fully secret trusts

On the face of the will, Y will appear to be the beneficial owner of the property. The equitable jurisdiction to enforce a secret trust is aimed at preventing fraud on the part of the alleged trustee, as the following case illustrates.

 CASE CLOSE-UP

McCormick v Grogan **(1869) LR 4 HL 82**

McCormick (M) left all his estate to Grogan (G) by a will in the briefest of terms. On his deathbed M instructed G that his will and a letter were to be found in his desk. The letter named various intended beneficiaries and the intended gifts to them, and concluded with the words: 'I do not wish you to act strictly on the foregoing instructions, but leave it entirely to your own good judgment to do as you think I would, if living, and as the parties are deserving.' G accepted the terms of the letter. Later, one of the intended beneficiaries named in the letter (another McCormick), whom G had thought it right to exclude, sued G. The House of Lords did not doubt that in an appropriate case the terms of a secret trust could be enforced against the alleged trustee. However, it had not been shown on the facts of the present case that G should be held to any trust. The jurisdiction to enforce a secret trust is aimed at preventing equitable fraud on the part of the alleged trustee. It was held that there had been no *malus animus* (bad conscience) on G's part so the secret trust would not be enforced against him.

As has already been said, although fully secret trusts have certain testamentary characteristics they are valid, despite lack of testamentary formalities, because the trustee accepts the trust during the settlor's lifetime. They are essentially *inter vivos* and therefore operate independently of the Wills Act 1837. *It is absolutely crucial, however, that the precise objects of the trust have been communicated, and the trust accepted, during the testator's lifetime.* In fact, the communication of the secret trust must satisfy all three certainties required for the creation of an express trust. There must be certain *intention* to create a trust, the *subject matter* (property) of the trust must be certain, and the *objects* (beneficiaries) of the trust must be certain.

In *Re Boyes* (1884) 26 ChD 531 there was no secret trust due to the absence of certainty of object. B had made an absolute gift to his executor by his will. The executor accepted that he was to hold the gift on trust for other persons, but the names of those persons were not communicated to the executor during B's lifetime. Only after B's death were informal letters found which detailed the intended objects of the gift. As Kay J observed, 'no case has ever yet decided that a testator can by imposing a trust upon his devisee or legatee, the objects of which he does not communicate to him, enable himself to evade the Statute of Wills by declaring those objects in an unattested paper found after his death.' Consider the 'thinking point' next.

 THINKING POINT

Do you think that *Re Boyes* would have been decided differently if B had placed a sealed envelope containing detailed instructions into his executor's hand before his death?

Placing a sealed envelope containing detailed instructions in the executor's hand would have constituted constructive notice of the trusts to the executor, and the executor would be deemed to have accepted the trusts as detailed in the letter. As Lord Wright observed in *Re Keen* [1937] Ch 236 at 242: 'a ship which sails under sealed orders, is sailing under orders though the exact terms are not ascertained by the captain until later.'

In *Ottaway v Norman* [1972] Ch 698 the testator, by his will, left his bungalow to his housekeeper together with a legacy of £1,500 and half the residue of his estate. On her death the housekeeper left her property to strangers. Ottaway sued the housekeeper's executor, Norman, alleging that the housekeeper had orally agreed with the testator that she would leave various assets to Ottaway in her will. It was held that there had been an arrangement between the testator and the housekeeper under which the latter had agreed to pass on the bungalow, furnishings and fixtures to Ottaway. However, the date of the alleged agreement between the housekeeper and the testator was uncertain, and may have come after the will was drawn up.

 THINKING POINT

Do you think that there was a valid secret trust in this case?

Brightman J held that the testator had created a valid secret trust and that Norman now held the bungalow under a *constructive* trust for the benefit of Ottaway. The essential elements which had to be proved were:

- the intention of the testator to subject the housekeeper to an obligation in favour of Ottaway in relation to certain property;

- communication of that intention to the housekeeper; and
- the acceptance of that obligation by her either expressly or by acquiescence.

It was immaterial whether the informal agreement had come before or after the execution of the will. Nor was it necessary to show that the housekeeper had committed a deliberate and conscious wrong. However, his Lordship did hold that clear evidence would be needed before the court would assume that the testator had not meant what he had said in his will. The standard of proof was analogous to that required before a court would rectify a written instrument. (Contrast *Re Snowden* [1979] Ch 528, where Sir Robert Megarry V-C expressed some doubt about how far rectification was a fair analogy to secret trusts when determining the appropriate standard of proof. Apart from cases where fraud had been alleged against the trustee, he preferred to apply the ordinary civil standard of proof, i.e. proof 'on the balance of probabilities'.)

 CASE CLOSE-UP

Re Snowden [1979] Ch 528

Sir Robert Megarry V-C: 'The whole basis of secret trusts, as I understand it, is that they operate outside the will, changing nothing that is written in it, and allowing it to operate according to its tenor, but then fastening a trust on to the property in the hands of the recipient. It is at least possible that very different standards of proof may be appropriate for cases where the words of a formal document have to be altered and for cases where there is no such alteration but merely a question whether, when the document has been given effect to, there will be some trust of the property with which it dealt . . . The proposition of Lord Westbury in *McCormick v Grogan* (1869) LR 4 HL 82, 97 with which Brightman J was pressed in *Ottaway v Norman* [1972] Ch 698 was that the jurisdiction in cases of secret trust was founded altogether on personal fraud. It is a jurisdiction by which a Court of Equity, proceeding on the ground of fraud, converts the party who has committed it into a trustee for the party who is injured by that fraud. Now, being a jurisdiction founded on personal fraud, it is incumbent on the court to see that a fraud, a *malus animus*, is proved by the clearest and most indisputable evidence.

. . . the law on the subject has not stood still since 1869 . . . it is now clear that secret trusts may be established in cases where there is no possibility of fraud. *McCormick v Grogan* (1869) LR 4 HL 82 has to be read in the light both of earlier cases that were not cited, and also of subsequent cases, in particular *Blackwell v Blackwell* [1929] AC 318. It seems to me that fraud comes into the matter in two ways. First, it provides an historical explanation of the doctrine of secret trusts: the doctrine was evolved as a means of preventing fraud. That, however, does not mean that fraud is an essential ingredient for the application of the doctrine: the reason for the rule is not part of the rule itself. Second, there are some cases within the doctrine where fraud is indeed involved. There are cases where for the legatee to assert that he is a beneficial owner, free from any trust, would be a fraud on his part.'

 THINKING POINT

Do you think that the secret trust in *Ottaway v Norman* was an express trust of land which, in accordance with s 53(1)(b) of the Law of Property Act 1925, should have been unenforceable for lack of written proof?

At first sight the housekeeper had accepted an *express* trust of the testator's property, including the land, thus rendering the trust of land unenforceable for lack of writing. However, the s 53(1)(b) requirement for written proof of the trust is rather inconvenient where one is attempting to achieve secrecy! Section 53(1)(b) was not actually considered in the case. The fact that the defendant, Norman, was held to be subject to a *constructive* trust (on the ground of preventing fraud) took the trust of land into s 53(2), and thereby removed the need to comply with s 53(1)(b).

3.2.3.2 Half-secret trusts

Remind yourself of the definition of this type of trust set out in the earlier definition box. Viscount Sumner in the House of Lords in *Blackwell* v *Blackwell* [1929] AC 318 saw no relevant distinction between fully secret and half-secret trusts. 'In both cases', he observed, 'the testator's wishes are incompletely expressed in his will. Why should equity, over a mere matter of words, give effect to them in one case and frustrate them in the other?' For his Lordship the 'fraud' to be prevented was the same in both cases. However that may be, we will see that there are in fact substantive differences between fully secret and half-secret trusts.

Blackwell v *Blackwell* is itself a classic case of a valid half-secret trust. The testator left a legacy of £12,000 to five persons by a codicil to his will, and directed them to apply the income 'for the purposes indicated by me to them', with power to apply two-thirds of the capital 'to such person or persons indicated by me to them'. The beneficiaries of the trusts (a mistress and her illegitimate son) were communicated orally by the testator to the intended trustees, with detailed instructions being given to one of the intended trustees. The intended trustees accepted the trusts before the execution of the codicil. The testator's widow challenged the validity of the half-secret trust and claimed the £12,000 for herself. The House of Lords held that the evidence of the oral arrangement was admissible and proved a valid half-secret trust in favour of the mistress and illegitimate son.

Q CASE CLOSE-UP

Re Keen [1937] Ch 236, Court of Appeal

In advance of the execution of his will, Keen (K) handed a sealed envelope to E. The envelope contained the name of a lady to whom K had not been married. E was aware of the contents of the envelope but did not actually open it until after K's death.

By a clause of his will K left £10,000 to certain friends, 'to be held upon trust and disposed of by them among such person, persons or charities as may be notified by me to them . . . during my lifetime'. This clause purported to reserve to K the power to make *future* testamentary dispositions by simply notifying the trustees during his lifetime of his intentions. Accordingly, the Court of Appeal held that the clause could not take effect because it purported to exclude the requirement of the Wills Act 1837 that a duly executed codicil be used to amend a will.

Despite the fact that the clause was ineffective, the Court of Appeal held that the half-secret trust had to fail because the communication via the envelope had *preceded* the execution of the will and was therefore inconsistent with the reference in the clause to the *future* declaration of trusts by the testator during his lifetime.

THINKING POINT

Re Keen is one of the few reported cases in which a court has consciously refused to give effect to the proved intention of the testator, and Lord Wright, the Master of the Rolls, did so with reluctance. In truth, the testator fell foul of his own choice of words. Had he expressly referred in his will to trusts which had been notified to his trusted friends in the past the sealed letter would probably have been admissible to prove the half-secret trust.

Re Bateman's WT [1970] 1 WLR 1463 was a similar case to *Re Keen*. There the testator directed his trustees to set aside £24,000 from his estate and to pay the income thereof 'to such persons and in such proportions as shall be stated by me in a sealed letter in my own handwriting addressed to my trustees'. The trustees received a sealed letter after the execution of the will, but before the testator's death. There was no evidence to show that the letter had been written before the execution of the will. Pennycuik V-C held that the direction to the trustees was invalid: 'once one must construe the direction as admitting of a future letter then the direction is invalid, as an attempt to dispose of the estate by a non-testamentary instrument'.

THINKING POINT

Are the modern cases on half-secret trusts consistent with the statement, with which we started this topic, that 'the whole theory of the formation of a secret trust is that the Wills Act has nothing to do with the matter'?

Half-secret trusts are effective only when they can be treated as having been incorporated in the will. It follows that they must precede the execution of the will and that inconsistency with the will renders the half-secret trust invalid. It follows that in relation to half-secret trusts, the Wills Act 1837 still has something 'to do with the matter'.

Certain transactions (e.g. the nomination of a beneficiary under a life insurance policy) are still analysed by analogy to secret trusts, as occurred in *Gold* v *Hill* [1999] 1 FLR 54, but cases of secret trust are nowadays quite rare. One such case is *Rawstron* v *Freud*, considered next.

CASE CLOSE-UP

Rawstron v Freud [2014] EWHC 2577 (Ch)

Facts: The case involved the multi-million-pound estate of the celebrated artist Lucian Freud. The testator's will trust left the residue of his estate to his daughter and solicitor (hereafter 'Y') in the simple form 'to Y'. One of the artist's illegitimate sons argued that, even if there is a fully secret trust where Y informally takes assets on trust under a will that formally purports to give the assets 'to Y absolutely', where the will (as here) simply says 'to Y' this might imply 'to Y on trust' and might be considered to create a half-secret trust. A finding that a half-secret trust had been intended would favour the son because the terms of a half-secret trust need to be accepted before the execution of the will, and in this case acceptance came later.

Held: The court decided against the claimant and confirmed that the will was valid and that Y had taken absolutely under it. In such circumstances there might be a fully secret trust, but there could be no half-secret trust and therefore no failure on account of the timing of the trustee's acceptance of the secret trust.

Summary

- Equity is more concerned with substance than form; hence trusts are *created* without any formality whatsoever.
- Where formality is required it is not because they are required for the creation of the trust per se, but because of other policy concerns such as the need for certainty in dealings with land and the need for certainty in testamentary dispositions.
- *Inter vivos* transactions—a summary of the formality requirements:
  - the creation of a trust requires no formality;
  - an expressly created trust of land is unenforceable without formal evidence of its creation;
  - the transfer of an equitable interest, such as an interest under a trust, must be made formally;
  - resulting, constructive and implied trusts are exempt from formality.
- Testamentary transactions: the Wills Act sets out strict statutory formality requirements with regard to testamentary dispositions. However, the courts have recognised a number of methods by which the testamentary formalities may be 'bypassed', including:
  - fully secret trusts;
  - mutual wills;
  - *donationes mortis causa* (examined in detail in the next chapter).

Summative assessment exercise

Explain, with reasons, the formalities (if any) that must be complied with in order to make the following actions valid and enforceable in a court of law:

- Bill, the freehold owner of Whitehouse, declares that he henceforth holds the legal title to Whitehouse on trust for his son, Charlton;
- Tony, the sole life beneficiary under a trust set up by his father, gives notice to the trustees that he disclaims his interest in favour of his son, to whom the trustees should henceforth pay all the income from the trust;
- Rob, who died recently, left property to Patrick by his will, having previously informed Patrick that he should secretly hold the property as trustee for the benefit of Rob's mistress;
- Bertie is the sole beneficial owner of a number of shares held in trust for him by a trust company wholly owned and controlled by him for the past 20 years. He now decides to instruct the company to transfer the shares to his wife.

Full specimen answers can be found at www.oxfordtextbooks.co.uk/orc/watt_directions.

The bigger picture

A major technical area under consideration in this chapter has been the secret trust. We have noted that traditionally a typical reason for wanting secrecy was the testator's desire to make a testamentary gift to a mistress or a child born out of wedlock. That basis for creating and recognising a secret trust is not so significant today. Since the Inheritance (Provision for Family and Dependants) Act 1975 (as enlarged by the Inheritance and Trustees' Powers Act 2014, s 6 and Sch. 2), dependents can expect to be awarded reasonable provision out of the deceased's estate without having to rely on the deceased's support expressed in the will or otherwise. Indeed, in *Ilott* v *Mitson* [2015] EWCA Civ 797, the court made provision for an independent adult child contrary to the mother's wishes expressed in a side letter to her will.

 For a blog on this case, see <http://blog.oup.com/2015/09/family-drama-and-the-law/>, which can be accessed via the Online Resource Centre accompanying this book.

 Further reading

Chung, B. 'Fraud Prevention? Dehors? Or What? Why Secret Trusts are Enforced?' (2018) 24(2) Trusts & Trustees 162–7
rejects the 'fraud prevention' and 'dehors the will' theories in favour of a basis in established equitable notions of conscience and estoppel (compare Pawlowski and Brown)

Critchley, P. 'Instruments of Fraud, Testamentary Dispositions, and the Doctrine of Secret Trusts' (1999) 115 LQR 631
argues that it makes more sense to understand secret trusts as operating outside the 'Wills Act' rather than outside the 'will'. Taking 'will' in the sense of 'intent', it is clear that secret trusts are very much within the testator's will

Green, B. 'Grey, Oughtred and Vandervell—A Contextual Reappraisal' (1984) 47 MLR 385
an engaging and thought-provoking contextual analysis of the key cases

Jaconelli, J. 'Problems in the Rule in Strong v Bird' (2006) 70 Conv 432
offers an explanation of the evolution and operation of the rule in *Strong v Bird*

Liew, Y.K. 'The Ambit of the Mutual Wills Doctrine' (2016) 132 LQR 664–77
analyses the operation of the mutual wills doctrine, whereby a constructive trust binds the survivor to the terms of the testator's agreement, including such aspects as the minimum requirements of the agreement and the parties' latitude to define its terms

Pawlowski, M. and Brown, J. 'Constituting Secret Trusts by Estoppel' [2004] Conv 388
examines the extent to which a secret trust may be constituted by estoppel

Rickett, C. 'Mutual Wills and the Law of Restitution' (1989) 105 LQR 534
provides an analysis of the mutual wills doctrine based on the law of restitution rather than trust

 For links to selected cases, statutes, academic papers and official reports mentioned in this chapter please visit the online resources at www.oup.com/uk/watt_directions6e/.

4 Certainty requirements

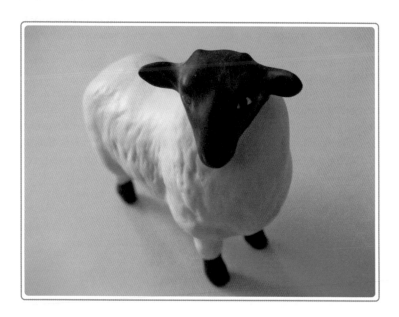

LEARNING OBJECTIVES

By the end of this chapter you should be able to:

- understand the three certainties that are prerequisite to the creation of an express trust, i.e. certainty of intention, subject and object;

- recognise the difference between conceptual and evidential uncertainty and the importance of that distinction;

- appreciate the consequences where a trust fails for lack of certainty;

- advise a settlor in drawing up a trust with sufficient certainty.

Introduction

You are not a gambler, but when out on a shopping trip you noticed that a horse called 'Equus Equity' was running in the Grand National and you couldn't resist placing £50 on it to win. In the event the horse came in at 100–1 and you returned home to your family with £5,000 and a broad smile. When your spouse demanded, 'did you buy Jimmy's birthday present, then?' you replied 'I've done better than that; I've earned £5,000 for him. I'll look after it until he's old enough.' The question is whether you have just declared an express trust of the £5,000. If you have created a trust, you should now keep the money separate from your own, and you certainly shouldn't use it (or interest earned on it) for your own benefit. There was, in fact, a case quite like this one, and the court held that there was no trust. We will see why later, but in essence it was because there will be no express trust unless an express trust was certainly intended.

Even if you actually transfer property to somebody with an obvious intention to part with the benefit, the court will presume the transfer to be an outright gift rather than presume that you intended the transferee to take on trust. Suppose, for example, that your grandmother hands you £30 at Christmas and accompanies the transfer with the words 'get yourself a nice jumper'. Do you think that she has created a trust of the £30? No, of course she hasn't. Your grandmother may have expressed her motive for making the gift, but there can be no doubt that the gift is an absolute gift. It follows that you are not a trustee of the £30 and do not have to purchase a jumper. The money is yours to do with as you wish. You may have a moral obligation to buy a jumper, but this is not enforceable against you in court (*Re Diggles* (1888) 39 ChD 253). According to Lord Langdale MR in *Knight* v *Knight* (1840) 3 Beav 171, courts will not acknowledge that an express trust has been created unless **the three certainties** are shown.

> **the three certainties**
> - certainty of intention = a certain intention to create a trust (i.e. words and conduct which create an imperative obligation);
> - certainty of subject = certainty with regard to the assets (property) subject to the trust and the shares in which they are to be held by the beneficiaries;
> - certainty of object = certainty with regard to beneficiaries or purposes of the trust.

The three certainties must be satisfied for the protection of the trustees. Imagine that you had been given a fund believing that it was an outright gift to you for your use and benefit. You would be in a lot of trouble if, having exhausted the fund, you were informed by a court that in fact you had been a trustee of that fund for the benefit of other persons. The requirement that the donor's intention be made certain is designed to prevent this sort of situation. The requirements of certain subject and certain object are similarly designed to protect the trustee, for if the trustee does not know the terms of the trust there is every chance that he or she will breach the trust and be personally liable for any loss (see Chapter 15).

The three certainties must also be satisfied for the benefit of the court. All trusts must be subject to control by the court: as Sir William Grant MR put it, '[t]here can be no trust over the exercise of which this court will not assume a control, for an uncontrollable power of disposition would be ownership and not trust' (*Morice* v *Bishop of Durham*

(1804) 9 Ves 399). For a trust to be controlled by the court, its object and subject must be certain.

In *Knight* v *Knight*, Lord Langdale MR suggested that there will be no difficulty in the application of his three certainties rule 'in simple cases'. He did acknowledge, however, that 'in the infinite variety of expressions which are employed … there is often the greatest difficulty in determining, whether the act desired or recommended is an act which the testator intended to be executed as a trust, or which the court ought to deem fit to be, or capable of being enforced as such'. He also stated that '[i]n the construction and execution of wills, it is undoubtedly the duty of this court to give effect to the intention of the testator whenever it can be ascertained'. It is to this that we now turn.

4.1 A question of construction

> If a man will begin with certainties, he shall end in doubts; but if he will be content to begin with doubts, he shall end in certainties.
>
> Sir Francis Bacon, *The Advancement of Learning*, 1605

When reading a document to discover whether the certainty requirements for a trust have been met, the document must be construed naturally—without straining the meaning of the words used.

4.1.1 Drafting background as evidence of proper construction

In *Rabin* v *Gerson* [1986] 1 WLR 526, the claimants took out a summons for the court's directions as to the proper construction of a charitable trust deed. During the proceedings the claimants sought to refer to the written opinions of the barristers who had originally drafted the trust deed. As the opinions had been written before the drafting of the deed, the claimants hoped that they might be used as evidence of the settlor's intentions in setting up the trust. The Court of Appeal held that, as it had not been disputed that the words used in the trust deed had been the words the testator had intended to use, the deed fell to be construed according to the natural meaning of those words. Counsel's written opinions could not be admitted as evidence that the settlor had intended to achieve a specific legal effect when such an effect did not otherwise flow from a natural reading of the deed.

> **CROSS REFERENCE**
> On the subject of rectification, see 20.2.5.

Incidentally, if a court does conclude that a deed does not reflect the settlor's intentions, the court might order the deed to be rectified.

4.1.2 The effect of precedent on construction

In *Re Hamilton* [1895] 2 Ch 370, Lindley LJ determined that in each case the wording of the disposition should be construed to find its proper meaning 'and if you come to the conclusion that no trust is intended, you say so, although previous judges have said the contrary on some wills more or less similar to the one which you have to construe'. In other words, the general rule is that previous cases should not determine the outcome in the present case, when it comes to determining what the writer of the document meant.

However, if a disposition is made in terms which reproduce exactly the peculiar wording of a disposition in a previous reported case, the court may infer that the person making the disposition intended to achieve the same result as that achieved in the previous reported case. In *Re Steele's Will Trusts* [1948] Ch 603, the testatrix left an heirloom to her son, to be held by him for his eldest son and so on 'as far as the rules of law and equity will permit', and with the request that the son should 'do all in his power by his will or otherwise to give effect to this my wish'. The phrasing of the gift exactly reproduced the wording of a disposition in a previous reported case where those words had been held to create a trust. It was held that, in choosing to adopt the precise wording used in a previous reported case, the testatrix had made clear her intention to achieve the result which was achieved in that previous case, namely a trust binding on her son. Accordingly, the wording of the present gift would take effect as a valid trust of the heirloom.

4.1.3 **A pragmatic approach to construction**

In *theory* the character of a disposition, whether it be an absolute gift or a trust, is determined from the outset on the basis of the words used by the settlor. In *practice* the question of construction does not come before the court at the moment that the disposition is drafted. It is generally not until quite some time later that the court is asked to declare the proper construction of the words used. This means that the court does not determine the nature of the gift in a logical vacuum, but rather with the full benefit of hindsight. The court knows at that point in time (far better than the settlor ever did) what the precise consequences will be of declaring the disposition to be either a trust or an absolute gift.

 THINKING POINT

The next two cases were decided at first instance and only five years apart, but the results in the cases were quite opposite. How do you account for the different decisions?

 CASE CLOSE-UP

***Re Trusts of the Abbott Fund* [1900] 2 Ch 326**

A doctor in Cambridge had collected £500 from various subscribers for 'the maintenance and support' of two elderly, deaf sisters. No arrangement was made as to the disposal of any sums surplus to their needs. In the event they died leaving a surplus of £367 in the fund. The question was whether the gift had been to the old ladies 'absolutely', or subject to a trust requiring that the monies be used for no other purpose than their 'maintenance and support'. If the gift was absolute, the surplus would form part of the sisters' estates. If the gift had been made on trust, the surplus would be held under a resulting trust for the contributors (for resulting trusts, see 16.1).

The decision was that the surplus in the account was held on a resulting trust for the subscribers to the fund in proportion to their contributions. The money had never been the property, absolutely, of the ladies 'so that they should be in a position to demand a transfer of it to themselves, or so that if they became bankrupt the trustee in bankruptcy should be able to claim it' (*per* Stirling J at 330).

CASE CLOSE-UP

Re Andrew's Trust [1905] 2 Ch 48

The Bishop of Jerusalem had died and a fund was set up to finance the education of his children. When all the children had grown up and their education had been completed, there remained a surplus of monies in the fund. Again, the question was whether the gift had been to the children 'absolutely', or subject to a trust requiring that the monies be used for no other purpose than their education. If the gift was absolute, the surplus would be available to the children for whatever purpose they wished. If the gift had been made on trust, the surplus would be held under a resulting trust for the contributors. In contrast to *Re Abbott*, it was held that the surplus in *Re Andrew's* should be divided equally between the Bishop's children. The donations were treated as an absolute gift to the children, albeit intended to be primarily for their education.

It is hard to see any justification for the different decisions in these two cases apart from the pragmatic one, namely that the donees (the persons receiving the gift) in *Re Abbott* had died by the time the court came to consider the nature of the donation, whereas the donees in *Re Andrew's* were alive. Indeed, Kekewich J, in *Re Andrew's*, distinguished the *Abbott* case on that very basis: 'Here I am dealing with different facts, including the fact that the children are still alive.'

THINKING POINT

What do you think a court would have decided in 1910 if faced with a settlement like that in *Re Andrew's* where the children had died before completing their education? Would the court still have concluded that the surplus should belong to the children absolutely and pass as part of their estates?

In the Court of Appeal in *Re Osoba* [1979] 1 WLR 247, Goff LJ eschewed any attempt to reconcile the *Abbott* case with *Re Andrew's*, accepting that '[b]oth cases may well have been right on their particular facts'. In *Osoba* the testator made a bequest to his wife of the residue of his estate and of the rents from certain leasehold properties for his wife's 'maintenance' and for his daughter's 'training … up to University grade'. His wife died and shortly thereafter his daughter completed her university education. The testator's son claimed a share of the residue which had not been used for the daughter's education.

It was held that the gift of residue was an absolute gift to the wife and daughter equally, the expression of the purposes for which the gift was to be used being merely an indication of the testator's motive for making the gift. Further, as there had been no words of severance of the gift as between the wife and her daughter, they were deemed to hold the residue as joint tenants. Accordingly, ever since her mother's death, the daughter had held the whole of the fund absolutely for her own benefit.

THINKING POINT

Read the following brief extract from the judgment of Buckley LJ in *Re Osoba*. To which factors did his Lordship attach special importance in coming to the conclusion he did?

 CASE CLOSE-UP

Re Osoba [1979] 1 WLR 247, Court of Appeal

Buckley LJ: 'If a testator has given the whole fund, whether of capital or income, to a beneficiary, whether directly or through the medium of a trustee, he is regarded, in the absence of any contra-indication, as having manifested an intention to benefit that person to the full extent of the subject matter, notwithstanding that he may have expressly stated that the gift is made for a particular purpose, which may prove to be impossible of performance or which may not exhaust the subject matter. This is because the testator has given the whole fund; he has not given so much of the fund as will suffice or be required to achieve the purpose, nor so much of the fund as a trustee or anyone else should determine, but the whole fund. This must be reconciled with the testator's having specified the purpose for which the gift is made. This reconciliation is achieved by treating the reference to the purpose as merely a statement of the testator's motive in making the gift. Any other interpretation of the gift would frustrate the testator's expressed intention that the whole subject matter shall be applied for the benefit of the beneficiary. These considerations have, I think, added force where the subject matter is the testator's residue, so that any failure of the gift would result in intestacy. The specified purpose is regarded as of less significance than the dispositive act of the testator, which sets the measure of the extent to which the testator intends to benefit the beneficiary.'

Did you identify the following?

- the testator had given the whole of the fund to the wife and daughter. This indicated that the monies were not limited to such amount as might be necessary to achieve the expressed purpose of the gift. The expressed 'purpose' was not, therefore, an imperative, overriding object of the gift, but 'merely a statement of the testator's motive in making the gift';

- the gift was a gift of the residue of the testator's estate. If it failed, the result would be an intestacy, which would be most undesirable;

- in summary, the act of outright disposition was of greater significance than the expression of the specific purpose.

It should also be borne in mind that the words 'up to university grade' might have been nothing more than an attempt by the testator to give helpful guidance to the trustees as to the timing of the final disposition of capital in favour of the wife and daughter, although a letter of wishes outside the will would have been a less formal and therefore more appropriate means of communicating such guidance.

4.2 Certainty of intention

It may already be clear to you from the preceding section that the courts will only enforce trust obligations against B if A had clearly intended such an outcome, and A will only be held to have intended to create a trust if his words impress an imperative obligation on B.

There are no hard and fast rules for determining whether words of disposition have created an absolute gift or a trust. It would help if donors always used the words 'absolute' or 'trust' to express their intentions, but even that is not foolproof, for there have even been confusing cases where property has been given to persons 'absolutely in trust'.

CROSS REFERENCE
For a case with similar facts, see *Comiskey* v *Bowring-Hanbury* [1905] AC 84, at 4.2.1.

A disposition from A to B 'on trust for C' would be a perfectly certain trust. There is no doubt, however, that a trust can be created without using the word 'trust': as Lord O'Hagan stated in the House of Lords in *Kinloch* v *Secretary of State for India* (1882) 7 App Cas 619, 'there is no magic in the word "trust"'. In *Re Kayford Ltd* [1975] 1 WLR 279, Megarry J held (at 282) that 'it is well settled that a trust can be created without using the words "trust" or "confidence" or the like: the question is whether in substance a sufficient intention to create a trust has been manifested'. (See, further, *Ong v Ping* [2017] EWCA Civ 2069.) If, on the other hand, a person disposing of property does use the word 'trust', it is still possible that he does not intend to create a trust. In *Singha* v *Heer* [2016] EWCA Civ 424; [2017] 1 FLR 1192, Court of Appeal, Mr Singha, a property developer, assured his business partner, Mr Heer, that he would hold property in their portfolio 'on trust' for him to reflect the latter's financial contribution. Singha had some legal training, but was not a qualified lawyer. Heer claimed that Singha's declaration of trust had made him a trustee of 100 per cent of the beneficial interest in the land in favour of Heer. The Court of Appeal rejected this. The letters between the partners might suggest that Singha held the asset subject to a charge in favour of Heer, but, despite express use of the term 'on trust', an intention to be bound by a juridical trust had not been established against Singha.

It is sometimes said that precatory words will not give rise to a trust. Precatory words are words of prayer or petition (the Latin verb at the root of the word 'precatory' means 'to beg').

THINKING POINT

Underline the precatory words in the following dispositions:
- I give my property to B hoping that B will look after my niece;
- I give my property to B desiring that B should distribute it amongst my cousins;
- I leave £100,000 to B feeling confident that B will look after my uncle;
- I leave my estate to my wife requesting that she should provide for the grandchildren.

You should have underlined the words 'hoping', 'desiring', 'feeling confident' and 'requesting'.

In the first half of the last century the courts were more willing to recognise trusts based on such precatory words. However, the attitude of the courts in the latter part of the last century hardened against trusts based on precatory words, and this remains the attitude of the courts today. Nevertheless, the test remains one of substance, to be applied on the facts of each case. Modern courts are still at liberty to recognise a trust based on precatory words if satisfied that the donor intended such a result. The courts will not determine the issue of construction on the basis of the precatory words alone, but will give the disposition its natural construction, taking the wording of the disposition as a whole.

In *Staden v Jones*, Arden LJ noted that 'a trust is a matter which is difficult to define, but which essentially imposes an obligation to deal with property in a particular way on behalf of another person'. Her Ladyship reiterated that it does not require the express use of the word 'trust' ([2008] EWCA Civ 936 para. [25]).

4.2.1 **Formal dispositions**

Formal dispositions are usually (though not exclusively) contained within wills. What has to be done in each case is, quite literally, to construe the *will* of the testator. As Goff LJ stated in *Re Osoba* [1979] 1 WLR 247, the court should 'endeavour to ascertain his intention from the words he has used … in the light of such knowledge of relevant facts as we know he must have had'.

 THINKING POINT

Outlined next are the brief facts of three cases involving dispositions made by will. In which, if any, of the cases do you think that the court held a trust to have been created?

- *Lambe* v *Eames* (1871) 6 Ch App 597, CA. The testator left his entire estate to his widow 'to be at her disposal in any way she may think best, for the benefit of herself and her family'. On her death she left part of the testator's estate to an illegitimate child of one of the testator's sons. Trust or no trust?

- *Re Adams and the Kensington Vestry* (1884) 27 ChD 394, CA. The testator provided by his will that all his property real and personal should pass to his wife, her heirs, personal representatives and assigns, 'in full confidence that she would do what was right as to the disposal thereof between his children, either in her lifetime or by will after her decease'. Trust or no trust?

- *Comiskey* v *Bowring-Hanbury* [1905] AC 84, HL. The testator left to his wife 'the whole of my real and personal estate and property absolutely in full confidence that she will make such use of it as I should have made myself and that at her death she will devise it to such one or more of my nieces as she may think fit and in default of any disposition by her thereof by her will or testament I hereby direct that all my estate and property acquired by her under this my will shall at her death be equally divided amongst the surviving said nieces'. Trust or no trust?

Here are the answers:

- in *Lambe* v *Eames* it was held that there was an absolute gift to the widow, not a trust. It was accepted that similar words had in previous cases been held to create a trust, but the will fell to be construed not according to precedent, but according to the testator's actual intention on a true construction of the will. To have found a trust in favour of the widow's family would have deprived the testator's 'illegitimate' grandchild of the gift made by the widow on her death. Compare *Re B (Child: Property Transfer)* [1999] 2 FLR 418, where a consent order transferring property from a husband to wife 'for the benefit of the child' of their marriage was held not to create a trust in favour of the child in the absence of clear words to that effect;

- in *Re Adams and the Kensington Vestry* the question was, yet again, whether the disposition in the will was an absolute gift in favour of the wife or a trust in favour of her children. It was held that the words created an absolute gift in favour of the widow, unfettered by any trust. The reference to the children had been made merely to call to his widow's attention the moral obligations which had weighed upon the testator in making an absolute gift to her. His intention was merely to make express his motivation for making the gift. It was acknowledged that a testator's 'confidence' in his donee might suggest a trust in some contexts, but in the present case, on a proper construction of the whole will, no trust had been intended;

- in *Comiskey* v *Bowring-Hanbury* it was held that, upon a true construction of the words of the will, the disposition took effect as a trust, under which the wife had a life interest. The initial part of the disposition (the gift 'absolutely in full confidence') may well have created an absolute gift if taken on its own. (The word 'confidence' is particularly ambiguous, for it can mean putting faith in another (confidence in the sense of trust) or it can mean the exact opposite, i.e. putting faith in oneself.) However, the additional direction that the nieces should acquire an interest in any event, showed that the wife was not intended to acquire an absolute interest in the estate.

It is important to appreciate that the settlor's intention is construed *objectively*. Thus in *Byrnes* v *Kendle* [2011] HCA 26 (High Court of Australia), the defendant failed in his attempt to deny that he had intended to create a trust. He was bound by an Acknowledgment of Trust that he had signed, even though he later claimed that he had not fully understood what he was creating.

4.2.2 Informal dealings

Whether or not a disposition was intended to take effect as a trust depends primarily upon the words used, but where the words do not appear in a formal document, special importance is attached to the context in which the words were used. *Jones* v *Lock* is a case in point.

 CASE CLOSE-UP

Jones v Lock (1865) 1 Ch App 25

Facts: Jones, an ironmonger, returned home from conducting some business in Birmingham. When criticised by his family for failing to bring a present for his nine-month-old son, he produced a cheque in the sum of £900 made payable to himself, said, 'I give this to baby for himself' and placed the cheque in the baby's hand. He then took the cheque and said, 'I am going to put it away for him'. Six days afterwards Jones died. The cheque was found amongst his possessions. At issue was whether the baby was entitled to the £900.

Held: The Court of Appeal held that there had been no valid gift or declaration of trust. Accordingly, the baby was not entitled to the money. Lord Cranworth, the Lord Chancellor, accepted that an oral 'declaration of trust of personalty may be perfectly valid even where voluntary' but refused to find an intention to declare a trust in 'loose conversations of this sort'. He observed that, had the father not died, he would have been very surprised to discover that he was not able to use the £900 for his own benefit, but rather that he was bound to hold it in trust for his baby son.

Contrast the approach of Lord Cranworth with the approach of Scarman LJ in the Court of Appeal in *Paul* v *Constance* [1977] 1 WLR 527. Several features of the reasoning of the Court of Appeal were rather odd—indeed, almost as odd as the fact that the case concerned a woman called Paul and a man called Constance!

 CASE CLOSE-UP

Paul v *Constance* **[1977] 1 WLR 527**

Facts: Mrs Paul and Mr Constance lived together as man and wife. When Constance received £950 in settlement of an action for personal injuries they decided to deposit the £950 in a bank account. The account was opened in the sole name of Constance, so as to avoid any embarrassment in view of the fact that Constance and Paul were unmarried (in fact, Constance had not actually been legally divorced from his estranged wife). *Constance frequently said to Paul that the money in the account 'is as much yours as mine'* and that she could make withdrawals with his written authority. In fact only one withdrawal was ever made from the account, the sum withdrawn being then divided equally between them both. On the other hand, further monies were paid into the account, notably their joint winnings from playing bingo. Constance eventually died intestate and his executors closed the bank account, the balance being then roughly equivalent to the original deposit of £950. Paul claimed that the money in the account had been held by Constance in trust for them both.

Held: The Court of Appeal held that the words used by Constance to assure Paul of her joint entitlement to the monies in the account were sufficient to constitute a declaration of trust. The absence of the word 'trust' was not fatal to the finding of an express declaration of trust, taking into account the 'unsophisticated character of the deceased and his relationship with the plaintiff'. In coming to the conclusion that there was a trust, the Court of Appeal acknowledged that this was a 'borderline' case. In the result it was held that Mrs Paul was entitled to claim half of the money in the account. The other half went to Mr Constance's estranged wife.

 THINKING POINT

Do you see any problems with this decision? Table 4.1 sets out some of the unusual features of the decision. Place a tick next to the ones you spotted, and count up your score.

For all the reasons set out in Table 4.1 the judgment of the Court of Appeal in *Paul* v *Constance* has rightly been criticised. The conclusion is inescapable that it was a highly pragmatic decision designed to achieve a rough form of justice between Mrs Paul and Mr Constance. In the absence of a trust in favour of Mrs Paul, Mr Constance would have been entitled to the balance standing in Mr Constance's account.

right of survivorship
This is where an asset, such as land or the balance of a bank account, is owned 'jointly' (i.e. not in shares) so that each owner can be said to own the whole of the asset; on the death of one joint tenant, the surviving joint tenant (or joint tenants) remains owner of the whole by 'right of survivorship'. It is important to realise that survivorship is not a process of inheritance. The joint tenant who survives does not inherit anything. He or she was already owner of the whole.

Table 4.1 Problems with *Paul* v *Constance*

According to *Jones* v *Lock*, the declaration of an express trust should not be recognised on the basis of 'loose conversations'. The conversations in *Paul* v *Constance* were of a very casual character. A case which illustrates that courts still find trusts in 'loose conversations' is *Gold v Hill* [1999] 1 FLR 54.	5 points
If there was a declaration of trust, it is far from clear when it occurred.	5 points
If there was a trust in this case it was at most an implied or constructive trust (Scarman LJ acknowledged that he was constrained by the pleadings to treat the claimant's claim, if there was to be a trust at all, as one based on an express trust).	10 points
What were the terms of the so-called express trust of the money in the bank? If the terms were that the money was 'as much his as it was hers' why was she awarded only *half* of the balance? Generally the holders of a joint bank account can withdraw as much or as little of the monies in the account as they like; there is no sense in which the account is divided into half-shares. The law generally treats the holders of a domestic joint bank account as joint tenants of the balance. One important aspect of this is that when one of them dies the other owns the whole balance, not *half*, by 'right of survivorship'.	20 points

4.2.3 Establishing express trusts in commercial contexts

Commerce brings with it the risk of insolvency and the risk that creditors of the insolvent party will not be able to recover their money or other property from the insolvent party. If the creditor can establish a trust of the money or property that it claims, the creditor can claim as a beneficiary to be entitled ahead of the claims of the general creditors of the insolvent party to the extent of the property subject to the trust.

🔍 CASE CLOSE-UP

Re Kayford Ltd (in liquidation) [1975] 1 WLR 279

Facts: K Ltd ran a mail order business, the customers of which paid either a deposit or the full price in advance. Fearing insolvency, the company sought independent advice and was advised to set up a 'Customers' Trust Deposit Account' to hold customers' monies until their goods were delivered to them. In fact, K Ltd paid customers' monies into one of its existing, dormant accounts. Only later was the name of the account changed to 'Customers' Trust Deposit Account'. Soon afterwards K Ltd went into voluntary liquidation. The liquidator raised the question whether the monies in the account belonged to the customers or to K Ltd's other creditors.

It was held that the customers were entitled to the balance of monies in the account. In the circumstances the intention to create a trust was held to have been manifestly clear, despite the failure to use a separate nominated 'trust' account from the outset. Megarry J stated (at 282A) that:

> [t]here is no doubt about the so-called 'three certainties' of a trust. The subject-matter to be held on trust is clear, and so are the beneficial interests therein, as well as the beneficiaries. As for the requisite certainty of words, it is well settled that a trust can be created without using the words 'trust' or 'confidence' or the like: the question is whether in substance a sufficient intention to create a trust has been manifested.

His Lordship's decision was firmly based on the fact that the trust had been set up for the benefit of members of the public who had paid money in advance of receipt of goods. It was accepted that different principles might apply to trade creditors.

THINKING POINT

Do you think his Lordship was right to suggest (as in effect he does) that there might be a greater element of trust involved in a case involving members of the public?

It appears that the *Re Kayford* approach need not be limited to members of the general public. In a similar case, but one where the 'subscribers' were shareholders (as opposed to customers) of the company in question, it was held that the company's promise to keep the subscribers' monies 'in a separate account' created a trust in their favour which took priority over the claims of the company's other creditors (*Re Nanwa Gold Mines Ltd* [1955] 1 WLR 1080).

THINKING POINT

As a purchaser of goods and services, what implications does *Re Kayford* have for you? The answer is that it would make good sense, whenever you make a payment in advance of delivery for the rendering of services, to make payments expressly 'on trust' for the provision of those goods or services. However, in the case of *OT Computers Ltd (in administration)* v *First National Tricity Finance Ltd* [2003] EWHC 1010 (Ch) the judge doubted whether even 'equity lawyers' do this! Thankfully, in the context of purchasing a holiday, where large sums of money are paid in advance, ABTA and ATOL travel and flight agents automatically hold consumers' monies on trust to purchase their particular holiday. The customers of Farepak, a mail order vendor of Christmas hampers, were not so lucky.

CASE CLOSE-UP

***Re Farepak Foods and Gifts Ltd (in administration)* [2006] EWHC 3272 (Ch)**
Farepak became insolvent just before Christmas 2006, creating anxiety for thousands of customers. In the three days leading up to the administration the directors sought to set up a trust of monies received by the customers' account in that period, but the deed mistakenly failed to identify the correct customer account. The judge held that the mistake could be remedied by rectification, but that monies received earlier in the year could not be subject to a trust in favour of customers because there was no obligation on Farepak to keep those monies in a separate customers' account.

》 CROSS REFERENCE

In *Farepak* the trust which was unsuccessfully asserted over monies received earlier in the year was a *Quistclose* trust: see 1.2.4 and 2.3.4.2.

4.2.4 **Consequence of failure of certainty of intention**

In the absence of a certain intention to create a trust, the donee takes the property beneficially (*Lassence* v *Tierney* (1849) 1 Mac & G 551), unless intended to take subject to a contractual or other legal obligation.

4.3 Certainty of subject matter

The lack of certainty of subject matter can take two forms. The property itself may be uncertain, in which case there will be no trust at all; or the beneficial entitlement of particular beneficiaries may be uncertain, in which case the trustees will hold the fund on resulting trust for the settlor (on resulting trusts, generally, see Chapter 16).

4.3.1 Uncertain property

We will treat traditional and commercial trusts separately.

4.3.1.1 Traditional trusts

The leading case is *Palmer* v *Simmonds* (1854) 2 Drew 221. In that case a testatrix left her residuary estate to Thomas Harrison 'for his own use and benefit', and expressing her 'confidence' (or trust) in him that he would leave the bulk of her residuary estate to certain named persons if he should die without issue. Kindersley V-C asked himself: 'What is the meaning then of bulk?' His conclusion was that 'what is meant is not the whole but the greater part ... When, therefore, the testatrix uses that term, can I say that she has used a term expressing a definite, clear, certain part of her estate, or the whole of her estate? I am bound to say that she has not designated the subject as to which she expresses her confidence; and I am therefore of the opinion that there is no trust.'

4.3.1.2 Commercial trusts

Difficulties arise where trusts are claimed out of homogeneous bulk, i.e. out of a mass of property comprising substantially identical parts (e.g. oxen from a herd, a sheep from a flock or an apple from a barrel of apples). If, for example, I declare that two sheep from my flock are held by me on trust for you, the trust will be uncertain because I have not identified *which* two sheep were intended to be held on trust. A fund of money does not raise the same difficulty, because money is not specific property. Thus a trust declared of £1,000 from my account does not fail for uncertainty, even though I have not identified which bank notes are to be held on trust.

OUTSIDE THE BOX

Charles de Secondat, Baron de Montesquieu, *The Spirit of Laws*, 1748, Book 22(ii)

Money is a sign which represents the value of all merchandises ... The Athenians, not having the use of metals, made use of oxen, and the Romans of sheep: but one ox is not the same as another ox, in the manner that one piece of metal may be the same as another.

In *Re Goldcorp Exchange (in receivership)* [1995] 1 AC 74, the claimants were ordinary members of the public who had been misled into investing in non-existent gold bullion. In return for their 'investments' they were presented with certificates which allowed them to claim their bullion on giving the requisite notice to the company. On the company's insolvency, the claimants claimed, inter alia, to have beneficial interests under a trust in any bullion matching the contractual description. The Privy Council held that because the contracts were for 'non-allocated' bullion there was no property which could be described with sufficient certainty as being impressed with a trust. (Another important issue was whether the company had owed any fiduciary duty such as would justify impressing a trust upon the company's stocks of gold.)

A somewhat similar case is *Re London Wine Co (Shippers) Ltd (1975)* [1986] PCC 121 where customers claimed, inter alia, to have beneficial interests under a trust of a number of cases of wine held in a warehouse. LW Ltd was a wine merchant which ran its business on the basis that wine ordered by customers was held on trust by the company from the date of each customer's order and until delivery to the customers. However, the cases representing each order were not physically separated from the company's stocks until delivery. So, for example, if a customer had ordered 20 cases of Chateau Lafite 1970 out of the company's bulk holding, the question to be determined was whether the subject matter was sufficiently certain for the company to be treated as trustee of that customer's order. This question was answered in the negative.

It was held that an express trust had certainly been *intended* by the company (the company's circulars referred to the customer as 'the beneficial owner' and to the company as merely having a lien, i.e. the right to keep the wine until paid). It can only make sense to talk of having a lien over property in one's possession if somebody else is entitled to the property, *but* the subject matter had not been removed from the company's general stock and there was insufficient certainty of subject matter.

According to Oliver J, for there to be a valid trust of property comprised within an homogeneous whole, it must be a trust *of the whole*. Thus, if the homogeneous whole comprised 80 cases, the company could have achieved a valid trust of 20 cases by declaring a trust of 'one-quarter of the cases'. According to the judge, the company would thereby become trustee of the whole homogeneous bulk, the terms of the trust being an equitable tenancy in common between the company and the beneficiary in shares of three-quarters to one-quarter respectively. His reasoning appears to be that the subject matter of the trust is certain because 'one-quarter' is a non-specific description so can be satisfied from *any* quarter of the property. In contrast, where the subject matter of the trust is '20 cases of wine', such a specific description produces uncertainty as to *which* 20 cases were intended to form the subject matter of the trust.

🔍 CASE CLOSE-UP

Re London Wine Co (Shippers) Ltd (1975) [1986] PCC 121

Oliver J: 'As it seems to me, to create a trust it must be possible to ascertain with certainty not only what the interest of the beneficiary is to be but to what property it is to attach. I cannot see how, for instance, a farmer who declares himself to be a trustee of two sheep (without identifying them) can be said to have created a perfect and complete trust whatever rights he may confer by such declaration as a matter of contract. And it would seem to me to be immaterial at the time he has a flock of sheep out of which he could satisfy the interest. Of course, he could by appropriate words, declare himself to be a trustee of a specified proportion of his whole flock and thus create an equitable tenancy in common between himself and the named beneficiary, so that a proprietary interest would arise in the beneficiary in an undivided share of all the flock and its produce. But the mere declaration that a given number of animals would be held upon trust could not, I should have thought, without very clear words pointing to such an intention, result in the creation of an interest in common in the proportion which that number bears to the number of the whole at the time of the declaration. And where the mass from which the numerical interest is to take effect is not itself ascertainable at the date of the declaration such a conclusion becomes impossible.'

THINKING POINT

If a shareholder declared an express trust of '50 shares' in a company, do you think that such a trust would fail for uncertainty of subject matter?

The answer appears to be that the trust would not fail, provided that the shares in the company were all identical (shares can be different if, for instance, certain shares attract better voting rights than others). Consider the decision of the Court of Appeal in *Hunter v Moss*.

 CASE CLOSE-UP

***Hunter v Moss* [1994] 1 WLR 452, Court of Appeal**

Facts: The defendant was the registered owner of 95 per cent of the issued share capital of a limited company. The trial judge held that the defendant had orally declared a valid trust of 50 of his shares (being 5 per cent of the total issued share capital of the company). The defendant applied by motion to have the judgment set aside, on the ground, inter alia, that there could not have been a valid declaration of trust because the subject matter of the trust was uncertain. The deputy judge dismissed the motion, whereupon the defendant appealed.

Held: The appeal was dismissed. The reason for the decision was that all the shares in the company were identical to each other, so it was quite valid to declare a trust of 50 shares without specifying which 50 shares were intended to form the subject matter of the trust. *Re London Wine Co (Shippers) Ltd* (1986) was distinguished.

 THINKING POINT

How can the different results in *Hunter v Moss* and *Re London Wine Co (Shipping) Ltd* be reconciled? In other words, why should cases of wine be regarded as distinct from each other while shares in a company are treated as being identical to each other? You might want to look again at the quote from de Montesquieu which appeared earlier in this section.

One obvious way to reconcile the different results in *Hunter v Moss* and *Re London Wine Co*, and the one which appealed to the judge in the *London Wine* case, was that, in the example of cases of wine, 'ostensibly similar or identical assets may in fact have characteristics which distinguish them from other assets in the class' ([1993] 1 WLR 934). So, for instance, certain cases may have been damaged or certain bottles been ruined. This distinction between tangible property (e.g. bottles) and intangible property (e.g. shares) was followed (apparently with some reluctance) in *Re Harvard Securities Ltd (in liquidation)* [1998] CC 567. There the court decided that while there could not be an equitable assignment of unappropriated chattels, it was none-theless possible to have a valid equitable assignment of unspecified shares, provided the shares are identical in type.

▶ CROSS REFERENCE

For more on *Hunter v Moss*, see 'The bigger picture' at the end of this chapter.

4.3.1.3 **Where a trust fails for uncertainty of property**

> **ab initio**
> From the beginning
> (pronounced 'ab
> in-ish-ee-oh').

In such a case the trust is said to fail **ab initio**. However, the fact that the trust attached to the gift has failed does not mean that the gift itself must fail. Thus, in *Palmer* v *Simmonds* (see 4.3.1.1), the court held that upon the failure of the trust of the testatrix's residuary estate, the fund was held by her husband *absolutely* and passed under his will to those claiming under him.

4.3.2 **Uncertain beneficial interests**

Sometimes, even where there is no difficulty in identifying the trust assets, the subject matter of the trust may be rendered uncertain because the beneficiaries' rights in those assets are unclear.

 THINKING POINT

In *Boyce* v *Boyce* (1849) 16 Sim 476 the testator left two houses to trustees to convey one each to Maria and Charlotte. Maria was to pick 'whichever she may think proper to choose or select', with the remaining house to go to Charlotte. Maria died before the testator without having made her choice. Do you think that the gift to Charlotte succeeded?

The gift to Charlotte did not succeed. It failed for uncertainty because, in the absence of Maria's choice, it could not be said with certainty which of the houses would have been the one remaining after Maria's election had been made.

In *Re Thomson's Estate* (1879) 13 ChD 144 the testator left realty and personality to his wife by his will 'for the term of her natural life to be disposed of as she may think proper for her own use and benefit', providing further that, 'in the event of her decease should there be anything remaining of the said property or any part thereof', the said remainder should pass to certain named persons.

It was held that the widow took a life interest with a power to dispose of the property during her lifetime, but that the provision as to the testamentary gift of the remainder would be void for uncertainty of subject matter. The widow's *power* was incompatible with a *trust duty* in relation to the property.

 THINKING POINT

Compare and contrast the facts of the following two cases. Can you explain the different results?

Sprange v *Bernard* (1789) 2 Bro CC 585

A testatrix left a legacy to her husband 'for his sole use' but went on to provide that 'at his death the remaining part of what is left that he does not want for his own wants and use' was to go to X. The Master of the Rolls held that no trust had been created. The husband was absolutely entitled to the legacy.

Re Last [1958] 1 All ER 316

A testatrix, L, left all her property to her brother, directing that upon his death 'anything that is left' should pass to her late husband's grandchildren. When L's brother died intestate, and without issue or relations, the grandchildren applied to court claiming the residue of L's estate. The Treasury Solicitor argued in response that on a true construction of her will L had made an absolute gift of her property to her brother, and that the Crown was therefore entitled now to the residue as *bona vacantia*. It was held that on a proper construction of the will L's brother had been entitled only to a life interest in the property and accordingly the applicants would be entitled to equal shares of the residue of L's estate. The judge was impressed by the absence of any words indicating the absolute nature of the gift to L's brother.

The decision in *Re Last* is at first sight hard to reconcile with that in *Sprange* v *Bernard*. However, the decision can probably be justified on the basis that the last thing the testatrix would have intended was that the property should have passed to the Crown.

Pragmatically the decision in *Re Last* may have been right. Conceptually, however, it is dubious. Karminski J can be criticised for apparently finding a trust because the words of the will did not suggest sufficient certainty of intention to make an absolute gift of the estate. The orthodox approach, as we have seen, is just the opposite—namely, to presume an absolute gift in the absence of certainty of intention to create a trust!

 THINKING POINT

From everything you have already learned in this section, do you think that the gift of income in *Re Golay* [1965] 1 WLR 969 failed for uncertainty of subject matter?

In *Re Golay* (1965) the testator directed his executor to let a certain woman enjoy one of his flats during her lifetime 'and to receive a reasonable income from my other properties'. The issue was obviously whether the direction to allow a 'reasonable' income was void for uncertainty. Ungoed-Thomas J held that the words 'reasonable income' invited an objective determination by either the trustees or the court. It was an objective determination which both were quite capable of carrying out. As the judge said, 'the court is constantly involved in making such objective assessments of what is reasonable'.

4.3.2.1 Where a trust fails because the beneficiary's interest is uncertain

One of the features of the cases which we have been considering is that, even where there is a certain intention to declare a trust, and even where the property is identified, the trust might still fail. See, for example, *Boyce* v *Boyce* (4.3.2). In such a case the property 'results' (literally 'jumps back': see 16.1.2.1) to the settlor or his estate under a resulting trust.

This is because the donee receives the property in such a case knowing that it was received in trust.

4.3.3 **Uncertain subject matter may indicate uncertain intention**

> **🔍 CASE CLOSE-UP**
>
> ***Mussoorie Bank Ltd v Raynor* (1882) 7 App Cas 321, Privy Council**
>
> Facts: a testator left the whole of his estate to his widow by his will stating that he felt 'confident' that she would 'act justly to our children in dividing the same when no longer required by her'. The question was whether his widow was obliged to hold the estate on trust for their children.
>
> Held: the precatory words 'feeling confident' raised a doubt as to whether a trust had certainly been intended, and the uncertainty of the subject matter cast further doubt on this intention. The widow took the estate absolutely, free from any trust.
>
> Sir Arthur Hobhouse: 'There is not only difficulty in the execution of the trust because the Court does not know upon what property to lay its hands, but the uncertainty in the subject of the gift has a reflex action upon the previous words, and throws doubt upon the intention of the testator, and seems to shew that he could not possibly have intended his words of confidence, hope, or whatever they may be—his appeal to the conscience of the first taker—to be imperative words.'

4.4 Certainty of object

The object of a trust might be to:

- benefit a legal person or legal persons (including corporate entities), i.e. to benefit 'beneficiaries'; or
- advance public purposes (for public, i.e. 'charitable' purposes, see Chapter 8); or
- advance private purposes (for 'private' purposes, see Chapter 7).

In any case, for the trust to be valid the object must be ascertainable. This means that the object must be certain from the outset, or capable of being made certain in accordance with the maxim ***certum est quod certum reddi potest***.

> ***certum est quod certum reddi potest***
> 'That is certain which can be made certain'
> (pronounced 'sir-tumm esst quad sir-tumm red-dee poh-test').

In the following sections we are mostly concerned with traditional non-commercial trusts, but it should be borne in mind that the same issues can arise in commercial contexts; thus in one case a company intended to set up a trust for its 'urgent suppliers', but the trust failed because that description failed to identify the objects with sufficient certainty (*OT Computers Ltd (in administration) v First National Tricity Finance Ltd* [2003] EWHC 1010 (Ch)).

4.4.1 **Fixed trusts**

These are trusts in which the trustees have no discretion as to the objects of the trust and no discretion as to how the trust fund is to be divided amongst the objects of the trust.

THINKING POINT

Which of the following do you think are fixed trusts? (tick your answer):

- to my trustees on trust for Betty and Bill in two-third and one-third shares respectively;
- to my trustees on trust for my employees in equal shares;
- to my trustees on trust for such of my nephews as my trustees may think fit.

Did you work out that the first two are fixed trusts? The third trust is a discretionary trust (for discretionary trusts, see 4.4.2).

4.4.1.1 The class ascertainability test

For trustees to divide a trust fund amongst a fixed class of beneficiaries in equal (or other fixed) shares, it is necessary to know how many beneficiaries there are. If the size of the class could not be ascertained with certainty, the trustees would not know how much of the fund to give to any particular employee. Because an overpayment would be a breach of trust, the trust would become effectively unworkable.

The test for certainty of objects in a fixed trust is thus the 'class ascertainability' or 'fixed-list' test. In other words, the trust will only be valid if it is possible to draw up a list containing every one of the beneficiaries. Of course, the trust does not fail for uncertainty merely because the beneficiaries on the list cannot be found. In an appropriate case the court might order that the share of the fund attributable to 'missing' beneficiaries should be distributed under a 'Benjamin Order' to those beneficiaries who have been located (see *Re Benjamin* [1902] 1 Ch 723). As an alternative to the cost and inconvenience of Benjamin Orders, courts have recommended the taking out of missing beneficiary insurance, especially where the estate is small (see *Re Evans* [1999] 2 All ER 777).

Note, however, that at one time the fixed-list or class ascertainability test was also applied to discretionary trusts. The reason given for applying the fixed-list test to discretionary trusts (where the whole point is that the testator or settlor did *not* intend that the fund should be divided equally or in other fixed shares) was that there are circumstances when a trust might fall to be carried out by the courts, and the courts, according to the orthodox view, cannot choose between potential beneficiaries but must effect an equal division of the fund, in keeping with the maxim *equality is equity*. Equal division obviously necessitates a complete fixed list of the members of the class of potential beneficiaries.

In *IRC* v *Broadway Cottages Trust* [1955] Ch 20, £80,000 was settled on trust to apply the income for the benefit of the members of a class of beneficiaries in such shares as the trustees in their absolute discretion saw fit. It was not possible to list all the members of the class at any one time but it was possible to say with certainty whether any particular claimant was or was not a member of the class. Two charities who had received monies from the trustees under the terms of the trust claimed to be exempt from income tax thereon. The Court of Appeal held that the trusts of the income were void for uncertainty of object and accordingly that the monies which the charities had received could not qualify as income for which they could claim exemption from income tax.

4.4.2 Discretionary trusts

Discretionary trusts are not always employed for the benefit of a large class of beneficiaries. A discretionary trust is also useful where it is not desirable (for tax and other financial planning reasons) for an individual beneficiary to have immediate beneficial enjoyment of an entire fund (for example, where damages for serious personal injury are designed to last a lifetime. See, e.g., *Lindsay* v *Wood* [2006] EWHC 2895, QB).

> **discretionary trust** This arises where there is an obligation upon the donee of certain property to distribute it amongst a certain class of beneficiaries, but with discretion as to the manner of distribution. The obligation to distribute makes it a trust; the discretion as to the manner of distribution makes it a discretionary trust. The trustee under such a trust 'is under a duty to select from among a class of beneficiaries those who are to receive, and the proportions in which they are to receive, income or capital of the trust property' (*per* Warner J in *Mettoy v Evans* [1990] 1 WLR 1587).

4.4.2.1 Adoption of the individual ascertainability test

As we have seen, the fixed list (class ascertainability) used to apply not only to fixed trusts but also to discretionary trusts. This caused a number of trusts to fail because a definitive list of beneficiaries could not be drawn up. However, with a discretionary trust the settlor does not want every potential beneficiary to receive a benefit, the whole point of such trusts being that the trustees should *choose* which of the potential beneficiaries should receive a benefit, and (generally) in what proportions. Thus the application of the fixed-list test to discretionary trusts all too often defeated the settlor's dispositive intentions.

A more flexible test for certainty of object was required, one that did not require the whole of the class to be ascertained. The courts could not find the appropriate test in the law relating to trusts but did find such a test in the law relating to powers of appointment, for a power of appointment will not fail simply because it is impossible to list all the potential objects of the power. Thereafter an artificial practice grew up under which courts would 'pretend' that a disposition was a power (when in fact it was a trust) in order to attract the more generous test of certainty of object applicable to powers.

The test of certainty for powers of appointment is to be found in the case of *Re Gestetner's Settlement* [1953] Ch 672. There the trustees had a power to distribute capital within a wide and diverse class of persons. Harman J stated that '[i]f ... there be no duty to distribute, but only a duty to consider ... there is no difficulty ... in ascertaining whether any given postulant is a member of the specified class'. In other words, the test of certainty in relation to powers is not a class ascertainability test, but an 'individual ascertainability test'.

Re Gestetner was followed by the House of Lords in *Re Gulbenkian's Settlement* [1970] AC 508, where the settlement contained a power to appoint in favour of, inter alia, the settlor's son. Lord Upjohn held (at 523) that 'with respect to mere powers, while the court cannot compel the trustees to exercise their powers, yet those entitled to the fund in default must clearly be entitled to restrain the trustees from exercising it save among those within the power. So the trustees or the court must be able to say with certainty who is within and who is without the power.'

> **Calouste Gulbenkian (1869–1955)**
>
> One of the richest men of his generation, having amassed a fortune through oil, he left millions of pounds to his descendants and the remainder of his wealth and a vast art collection were left to the Calouste Gulbenkian Foundation (<http://www.gulbenkian.org.uk/>).

An Armenian born in Istanbul, he also left money to restore the Echmiadzin Cathedral in Armenia. Lawyers and students of the law are also beneficiaries of his will, for it has been said that 'he left behind three enduring legacies: a vast fortune, a splendid art collection and, most fittingly of all, endless litigation over his will and the terms of his estate' (Daniel Yergin, *The Prize*, Simon & Schuster Ltd, 1991 at p. 419).

In a landmark decision of the House of Lords, Lord Wilberforce brought to an end the artificial practice of construing trusts to be powers. He 'cut the Gordian knot' by simply changing the test for certainty of object in discretionary trusts through adoption of the test which had previously been restricted to powers of appointment. The landmark decision came in the House of Lords in *McPhail* v *Doulton*. It was, however, 'a close-run thing', their Lordships eventually recognising the validity of the discretionary trust by a bare majority of three to two.

 CASE CLOSE-UP

McPhail v *Doulton (Re Baden's Deed Trusts No 1)* [1971] AC 424, House of Lords

Facts: Mr Baden had settled a trust for the benefit of certain persons connected with a company controlled by him. The deed granted the trustees an absolute discretion to apply the net income 'to or for the benefit of any officers and employees or ex-officers or ex-employees of the company or to any relatives or dependants of any such persons in such amounts at such times and on such conditions (if any) as they think fit'. The first question was whether the deed had (1) granted the trustees a power of appointment amongst the class, or (2) subjected them to a discretionary trust. The second question, which flowed from the first, was: 'is the gift void for uncertainty?' If the gift was in the form of a power, the trustees would have been able to appoint (distribute part of the fund to) any applicant of whom it could be said with certainty that they were or were not within the class of 'staff, relatives or dependants'. If, on the other hand, the gift was in the nature of a trust, the trustees would only have been able to appoint beneficiaries if every member of the class had been identified, in accordance with the 'fixed-list' test.

Held: the deed created a trust, not a power. However, the trust would not fail for uncertainty of object, even though it would not be possible to draw up a complete fixed list of every potential beneficiary within the class.

Lord Wilberforce: 'It is striking how narrow and in a sense artificial is the distinction, in cases such as the present, between trusts or as the particular type of trust is called, trust powers, and powers ... It does not seem satisfactory that the entire validity of a disposition should depend on such delicate shading ... As to powers, I agree with my noble and learned friend Lord Upjohn in *Re Gulbenkian's Settlement* that although the trustees may, and normally will, be under a fiduciary duty to consider whether or in what way they should exercise their power, the court will not normally compel its exercise. It will intervene if the trustees exceed their powers, and possibly if they are proved to have exercised it capriciously. But in the case of a trust power, if the trustees do not exercise it, the court will; I respectfully adopt as to this the statement in Lord Upjohn's opinion. I would venture to amplify this by saying that the court, if called on to execute the trust power, will do so in the manner best calculated to give effect to the settlor's or testator's intentions. It may do so by appointing new trustees, or by authorising or directing representative persons of the classes of beneficiaries to prepare a scheme of distribution, or even, should the proper basis for distribution appear, by itself directing the trustees so to distribute … Then, as to the trustees' duty of enquiry or ascertainment, in each case the trustees ought to make such a survey of the range of objects or possible beneficiaries as will enable them to carry out their further fiduciary duty … A wider and more comprehensive range of enquiry is called for in the case of trust powers than in the case of powers.

Two final points: first, as to the question of certainty, I desire to emphasise the distinction clearly made and explained by Lord Upjohn between linguistic or semantic uncertainty [to be discussed later in this section of the chapter] … and the difficulty of ascertaining the existence or whereabouts of members of the class, a matter with which the court can appropriately deal on an application for directions. There may be a third case where the meaning of the words used is clear but the definition of beneficiaries is so hopelessly wide as not to form "anything like a class" so that the trust is administratively unworkable.'

THINKING POINT

Isn't it fascinating to observe a brilliant judge at work? Notice how he artfully reduces the conceptual distance between the quite distinct concepts of trust and power by suggesting that there is nothing but 'delicate' shades of difference between them. At one point in his speech, his Lordship even describes discretionary trust by the label 'trust power' to suggest further that the concepts of trust and power are in this context virtually the same. He even observes, with no sense of irony, that the distinction between trusts and power is 'in a sense artificial'; this rhetorical technique is cleverly calculated to reassure his Lordship's audience that, far from perpetrating an artifice, he is actually opposing one.

Is the distinction between a trust and power really a 'narrow' and 'delicate' one? One way to find out is to play spot the difference. Which of the following dispositions is a mere power and which is a trust? (tick your answer):

- 10K to my wife to be distributed amongst my cousins as she may think fit;
- 10K to my wife to be distributed amongst my cousins if she may think fit.

Did you work out that the first disposition is a trust, because there must be a distribution, whereas the second disposition is a power, because distribution is not imperative? In the case of a discretionary trust ('trust power'), if the trustees do not exercise it, the court will *require* that it is exercised 'in the manner best calculated to give effect to the settlor's or testator's intentions'. In the case of a mere power, 'although the trustees may, and normally will, be under a duty to consider whether or in what way they should exercise their power, the court will not normally compel its exercise'. In the case of a mere power, the court will only intervene 'if the power is exceeded or exercised capriciously', although the courts have proven more willing to intervene in the pension context.

Now, it must be admitted that the gap between a discretionary trust and a power of appointment can be a narrower one than the preceding exercise in spot the difference suggests. Is the following disposition a power or a trust?

- £10K to my wife to be distributed amongst my cousins as she may think fit and any money not applied this year to be retained for future distribution.

This is a 'non-exhaustive' discretionary trust, and it is starting to look very like a power of appointment after all, is it not?

Having expertly reduced the (rather great) conceptual gap between trust and power to a mere hair's breadth, Lord Wilberforce nevertheless acknowledged a practical difference between them: 'such distinction as there is would seem to lie in the extent of the survey which the trustee is required to carry out … a wider and more comprehensive range of inquiry is called for in the case of trust powers than in the case of powers.' The trustee of a discretionary trust need not have a fixed list of all the beneficiaries, but must 'survey the field' to form a reasonable view as to the number of potential beneficiaries.

It is partly because of this duty to 'survey the field' that a discretionary trust will fail if the 'class' is so large as to be 'administratively unworkable' (see later in this section). In contrast, a mere power will not fail simply because the 'class' of potential beneficiaries is vast.

THINKING POINT

Why did Lord Wilberforce go to such lengths to force together the concepts of trust and power?

Obviously it was to validate more discretionary trusts and the best way to achieve this was to reject the rigid 'fixed-list' test of certainty which had traditionally applied to trusts, in favour of the relaxed 'individual ascertainability test' traditionally applied to powers of appointment. But how did his Lordship justify the rejection of the 'fixed-list' test? He did so by questioning the orthodox argument in favour of the fixed-list test, which was that a fixed list was required in order that the court might make a distribution in the event that the trust might fall to be carried out by the courts: 'Equal division is surely the last thing the settlor ever intended: equal division among all may, probably would, produce a result beneficial to none. Why suppose that the court would lend itself to a whimsical execution?' Rather, 'the court if called upon to execute the trust power, will do so in the manner best calculated to give effect to the settlor's or testator's intentions'.

In a move away from the orthodox approach, his Lordship held that the test of certainty of object which had hitherto been applied to powers (confirmed by the House of Lords in *Re Gulbenkian's Settlement* [1970] AC 508) should henceforth apply to discretionary trusts. He summarised that test, known as the 'individual ascertainability test', in the following terms: 'the trust will be valid if it can be said with certainty that any given individual is or is not a member of the class.'

THINKING POINT

But when can it 'be said with certainty' that any given individual is or is not a member of the class?

His Lordship agreed with the opinion of Lord Upjohn, who had identified two types of 'uncertainty' bearing upon the objects of discretionary trusts:

- first, 'linguistic or semantic uncertainty' (also called *conceptual uncertainty*), where the class of beneficiary is not susceptible of legal definition. An example of a conceptually certain class of beneficiaries would be 'my nephews'. An example of a conceptually un-certain class of beneficiaries would be 'my friends', for the latter is a term for which no usable definition can be agreed upon. This type of uncertainty *will* render the gift void;

- secondly, *evidential uncertainty*, which is the practical difficulty of ascertaining the exist-ence or whereabouts of beneficiaries. This type of uncertainty *will not* render the gift void;

- Lord Wilberforce also referred to a third case, not strictly speaking a case of uncertainty, where the meaning of the words is clear but the definition of beneficiaries is so hopelessly wide as not to form 'anything like a class' so that the trust is 'administratively unworkable'. One example of a trust that is administratively unworkable is a trust to benefit 'all the residents of Greater London'. A further example of administrative unworkability is illus-trated by the facts of *R* v *District Auditor, ex parte West Yorkshire Metropolitan County Council* [1986] RVR 24, where the council, before its abolition, purported to set up a trust 'for the benefit of any or all or some of the inhabitants of the county of West Yorkshire'.

THINKING POINT

Consider *McPhail* v *Doulton* again. On a separate sheet of paper, list any objections you can think of to Lord Wilberforce's reasoning in *McPhail* v *Doulton*, and against each try to identify a possible response (perhaps taken from his Lordship's speech). Compare your list to Table 4.2.

4.4.2.2 **Application of the individual ascertainability test**

Having considered Mr Baden's deed trusts in *McPhail* v *Doulton*, the House of Lords remitted the case to the High Court to apply the individual ascertainability test to determine, inter alia, whether the trust for the class of 'relatives' must fail for uncertainty. The judgment of the High Court was appealed against. The decision of the Court of Appeal appeared as *Re Baden's Deed Trusts (No 2)* [1973] Ch 9.

Table 4.2 *McPhail* v *Doulton:* **The reasoning of Lord Wilberforce**

Objection	Response
If all the trustees die, the court must administer the trust	It is nearly always possible to find new trustees
The court cannot exercise a private discretion	There are old authorities which suggest that it can
If the court exercises discretion it must do so on the basis of equal division	Equal division is the last thing that the testator wanted
The merits of the claim of every potential beneficiary must be considered	It is sufficient to make a survey of the field

Applying Lord Wilberforce's formulation of the 'individual ascertainability test', the Court of Appeal held that the term 'relatives' was conceptually certain and that the trust was valid.

However, their Lordships appeared to have different conceptions of the term. Stamp LJ preferred a narrow construction, namely 'legal next-of-kin' of the employees. However, Sachs LJ took the view that even if 'relatives' was given 'a very wide meaning', i.e. any persons who could 'trace legal descent from a common ancestor', there would not be conceptual uncertainty and the trust would be valid. For Sachs LJ, the problem of administrative unworkability in a class so large was automatically solved by the practical limitations on proof of relationship (i.e. family trees only ever go back so far, therefore the class would not in fact be administratively unworkable).

In *McPhail* v *Doulton*, Lord Wilberforce rejected any need for a fixed list of potential beneficiaries, but did he intend that a discretionary trust would be valid if a survey of the potential beneficiaries revealed that only *one* person may qualify for a benefit under the trust? Megaw LJ was alone amongst their Lordships in the Court of Appeal in picking up on this point, stating that '[t]o my mind, the test is satisfied if, as regards at least a *substantial number* of objects, it can be said with certainty that they fall within the trust' (emphasis added).

THINKING POINT

Can you see any possible grounds for criticising their Lordships' reasoning in *Re Baden (No 2)*?

You might make the following points:

- they held that the description 'relatives' was conceptually certain, even though they could not agree upon the meaning of the concept;

- if 'relatives' is taken to mean descendants from a common ancestor, the class must be administratively unworkable as being 'nothing like a class' since it could include everyone on earth;

- there is nothing in Lord Wilberforce's formulation of the individual ascertainability test to suggest, as Megaw LJ suggested, that a discretionary trust will only be valid where there is evidence that a 'substantial number' of beneficiaries will fall within the class;

- Stamp LJ took 'relatives' of X to mean X's statutory next of kin even though the membership of that class cannot be certain until the death of X. Seeking to address this objection, he suggested that if X is still alive his 'next-of-kin' are 'his nearest blood relations'. These two alternative meanings of 'next of kin' might be said to introduce conceptual uncertainty sufficient to render a trust for 'relatives' void.

THINKING POINT

Suppose someone were to give money to trustees on trust to divide as they might think fit amongst the 'friends' of 'Joe Bloggs'. Do you think that such a trust would be valid?

One of the greatest lawyers and humane thinkers ever to have lived, Marcus Tullius Cicero, had this to say on the subject of friendship:

OUTSIDE THE BOX

Cicero, *De Amicitia*—'On Friendship'

'Everyone has an idea how many goats and sheep he owns, but nobody can say how many friends he possesses' (… *amicos quot haberet, non posse dicere*).

Cicero was right. A trust for 'friends of Joe Bloggs' would fail for conceptual uncertainty. No court can presume to understand what a donor meant by the term 'friend' and therefore no court will enforce trust obligations against a donee in favour of an object of that description.

CASE CLOSE-UP

***Re Barlow's Will Trusts* [1979] 1 WLR 278 (see further 4.4.3.1)**

Browne-Wilkinson J: '[the word "friend"] has a great range of meanings; indeed, its exact meaning probably varies slightly from person to person. Some would include only those with whom they had been on intimate terms over a long period; others would include acquaintances whom they liked. Some would include people with whom their relationship was primarily one of business; others would not. Indeed, many people, if asked to draw up a complete list of their friends, would probably have some difficulty in deciding whether certain of the people they knew were really "friends".'

Even if one person could be found who on *any* definition would be regarded as a 'friend of Joe Bloggs' the trust would fail, because, being unsure of the size of the entire class, the trustees would be unsure how much it would be appropriate to give to the one identified friend.

THINKING POINT

Do you think that a trust 'for such persons as my wife considers to be my friends, in such shares as she thinks fit' would be valid?

This question is asking whether an otherwise conceptually uncertain term may be rendered certain by leaving the definition to one named person. The answer in the case of 'friends' must almost certainly be in the negative. The settlor's wife has more personal knowledge of the settlor and may be more expert at guessing the rough size of the class, but a rather more precise survey of the field is required in the case of a discretionary trust than the wife would be able to achieve by guesswork. She is no more able than a court to say with certainty whether *any* given individual is or is not within the class.

THINKING POINT

What if the discretionary trust had been expressed to be for the benefit of 'Jewish children resident in Greater Manchester, any dispute as to the Jewish status of the child to be determined by the Chief Rabbi'. Would such a trust be valid?

The point has not arisen for decision in relation to a discretionary trust, but a similar provision in a case of a conditional gift (the beneficiary of the gift had to be of the Jewish faith, married and living with an 'approved wife', the Chief Rabbi having jurisdiction to determine whether or not the beneficiary's wife was 'approved') was held to render the condition certain and the gift valid (*Re Tuck's Settlement Trusts* [1978] Ch 49). In favour of the application of the reasoning in *Re Tuck's* to discretionary trusts it could be said that 'Jewish', unlike 'friend', has a precise meaning which the Chief Rabbi is more expert to define than is the court. Against the application of *Re Tuck's* to discretionary trusts it could be argued that the Rabbi's expert opinion can only assist with evidential uncertainty and that the term 'Jewish' can be no more conceptually certain for the Chief Rabbi than for the court.

4.4.3 Gifts subject to conditions

Having considered the different tests which apply to fixed trusts (the 'fixed-list' or 'class ascertainability' test), discretionary trusts (the individual ascertainability test) and mere powers (the individual ascertainability test), it is appropriate to consider this final category of disposition. In fact, it is a category which must be further sub-divided into **gifts subject to conditions precedent** and **gifts subject to conditions subsequent**.

> **gift subject to conditions precedent** The intended donee of such a gift will not be entitled to the gift unless he or she first satisfies a particular condition, e.g. he or she might have to qualify as a barrister before the gift vests.
>
> **gift subject to conditions subsequent** Such a gift vests unconditionally in the donee, but will be forfeited if the donee subsequently breaches a condition to which the gift was subject, e.g. the gift of land to a person might come to an end in the event of their moving to live abroad.

4.4.3.1 Gifts subject to conditions precedent

 CASE CLOSE-UP

***Re Barlow's Will Trusts* [1979] 1 WLR 278**

Facts: A testatrix died leaving a collection of paintings in her will. Having made some specific bequests she gave the remainder of the paintings to her executor on trust for sale but subject to a direction that 'any members of my family and any friends of mine who may wish to do so' should be allowed to purchase any of the paintings at far below their market values. The executor took out a summons for a declaration as to whether the gift (i.e. the difference between the purchase price and the market price of the paintings) was void for uncertainty because the term 'friends' was itself uncertain. He also sought a direction as to the proper meaning of 'family' in the context of this gift.

Held: the condition did not fail for uncertainty. If it could be said with certainty that any particular claimant qualified as a 'friend', a sale of paintings to that claimant would be valid under the terms of the will. This was because uncertainty as to whether other persons may or may not be 'friends' would have no effect upon the quantum of the gift to those persons who clearly qualified as 'friends'.

The 'friends' in *Re Barlow's* were taking the *whole* of the individual gift. Beneficiaries under a discretionary trust or mere power, on the other hand, do not receive the whole subject matter of the gift, but merely a *share* of the fund, hence the necessity in such a case to be able to say with certainty of *any* person at all whether or not they fall within the class of potential beneficiaries. (Where a trustee has discretion as to how to divide a fund between potential beneficiaries, the trustee must be able to ascertain roughly how many beneficiaries there are!)

4.4.3.2 **Conditions subsequent**

Such a gift can raise issues of certainty of object where the condition, as is often the case, relates to a personal attribute of the donee. So, for example, in *Re Tepper's Will Trusts* [1987] 1 All ER 970 a gift was made on condition that the donee 'shall remain within the Jewish faith and shall not marry outside the Jewish faith'. The gift was valid because the term 'Jewish faith' could be understood in certain terms from the outset (following *Clayton v Ramsden* [1943] AC 320). There was no reference to an expert arbiter of the term 'Jewish' (compare *Re Tuck's* (see 4.4.2.2)), but Scott J admitted evidence of the testator's own practice as a Jew in order to render certain what the testator had meant by the term 'Jewish'.

4.4.4 **Uncertain object may indicate uncertain intention**

Where the objects of the trust are uncertain, this may indicate that there was no real intention to create a trust. Consider the disposition in *Lambe v Eames* (1871) 6 Ch App 597, which, as you will recall, was a gift by a testator to his widow of his entire estate 'to be at her disposal in any way she may think best, for the benefit of herself and her family'. If the testator intended this disposition to take effect as a trust it raises two questions: who are the intended beneficiaries of this trust (i.e. who are 'family'?) and what interests are those beneficiaries intended to have? We have seen that the courts *can* recognise such a disposition to be a valid discretionary trust for next of kin, but the fact that the settlor was so unclear as to the terms (in relation to the objects of the trust) might indicate, in a case where it is unclear whether a trust or an absolute gift was intended, that he did not intend to create a trust at all.

 Summary

- We have seen that there are three certainties that are prerequisite to the creation of an express trust:
  - certainty of intention—an outright gift is presumed unless a trust was clearly intended;
  - certainty of subject—which includes certainty of the assets and certainty as to the extent of the beneficiary's interest in those assets;
  - certainty of object—which may be to benefit a legal person or legal persons (including corporate entities), i.e. to benefit 'beneficiaries'; or to advance public purposes (i.e. charitable purposes, see Chapter 8); or, in special cases, to advance private purposes (see Chapter 7).
- When reading a document to discover whether the certainty requirements have been met, the document must be given its natural construction. We have seen that

the courts are willing to take a fairly generous approach to construction, and will construe that to be certain which can be rendered certain on a natural construction of the words used, but that the courts cannot overcome fundamental uncertainty in the concepts used, particularly in relation to the definition of the class of objects in a discretionary trust.

- In theory the character of a disposition, whether it be an absolute gift or a trust, is determined from the outset on the basis of the words used by the settlor. In practice, however, the question of construction does not come before the court until quite some time after the disposition was drafted. This means that the court does not determine the nature of the disposition in a logical vacuum, but rather with the full benefit of hindsight. Hence it is not unknown for a disposition to be construed pragmatically, i.e. 'to make it work'.

- We have seen that the consequences of uncertainty vary according to the type of uncertainty:

  - where the intention to create a trust is uncertain, the disposition will generally be effective as an absolute gift;

  - in the case where a trust fails for uncertainty of property the disposition is said to fail *ab initio*. Where a trust fails because the beneficiary's interest is uncertain the property will result to the settlor or his estate.

- Where the object of the trust is uncertain there will also be a resulting trust for the settlor or his estate.

? Summative assessment exercise

Vincent, a renowned artist, died in 2013. His will contains the following provisions:

- 'to my favourite artist, Theodore van Damme, I devise my country studio and gardens on the Isle of Mull absolutely in full confidence that he will make such use of them as I should have made myself and that at his death he will leave them to the Royal Academy and in default of any disposition by him thereof by his will or testament I hereby direct that all my estate and property acquired by him under this my will shall at his death be given to the Royal Academy absolutely';

- 'to my executors, my personal estate (excluding my art collection) to hold upon trust for such artists as they shall select having regard to their knowledge of my personal taste in art';

- 'to my executors, the greater part of my art collection to be held by them on trust for my favourite model, Lucille Gachet, subject to any pictures which my friends may choose'.

Consider the validity of each provision, and the consequences, where relevant, of invalidity.

Full specimen answers can be found at www.oxfordtextbooks.co.uk/orc/watt_directions5e/.

The bigger picture

One of the hard questions in this chapter has been the issue of certainty of subject matter in cases of 'homogenous bulk' (e.g. '50 of my 1,000 shares'). *Hunter* v *Moss* has been followed (e.g. *Re Lewis's of Leicester Ltd* [1995] 1 BCLC 428; *Re Lehman Brothers International (Europe) (In Administration)* [2011] EWCA Civ 1544), but it has also been subject to academic criticism such as that of David Hayton (see 'Further reading' at the end of this chapter), who argues that a trust of an unspecified 50 shares in a bulk is too uncertain, because the so-called trustee could sell 50 shares and the purchaser would not know if the shares were those subject to the trust or other shares owned by the vendor absolutely. *Hunter* v *Moss* has also been regarded as inconsistent with the Privy Council decision in *Re Goldcorp Exchange Ltd* [1995] 1 AC 74, where an argument was unsuccessfully advanced that a seller of gold bullion (who had gone into liquidation having taken money from the purchasers) had become a trustee of an undivided share in his stocks. Peter Birks ('Establishing a Proprietary Base' [1995] RLR 83) even went so far as to argue that, from the reasoning of the Privy Council in *Re Goldcorp Exchange Ltd*, '[o]ne inference is that the Court of Appeal's decision in *Hunter* v *Moss* [1994] 1 WLR 452 must be wrong'. Sarah Worthington (see 'Further reading') disagrees. She argues that the courts have traditionally found ways of making trusts sufficiently certain for practical purposes and that they did so successfully in *Hunter* v *Moss*. All that is required in theory and for practical workability is that the size of the total bulk be identified, as well as the size of the part to be held in trust (whether the part is identified by number of units or by a percentage proportion of the whole). Trustees can then be held to their fiduciary duty to keep the trust part separate from the rest.

 Further reading

Hardcastle, I.M. 'Administrative Unworkability—A Reassessment of an Abiding Problem' [1990] Conv 24
argues that administrative unworkability is a logical extension of evidential certainty

Hayton, D. 'Uncertainty of Subject-Matter of Trusts' (1994) 110 LQR 335
argues against *Hunter* v *Moss* that a trust of an unspecified 50 shares in a bulk is too uncertain

Matthews, P. 'All About Bare Trusts: Part 2' (2005) 6 *Private Client Business* 336
addresses the vexed question of formalities for sub-trusts and separate sub-funds

Worthington, S. 'Sorting Out Ownership Interests in a Bulk: Gifts, Sales and Trusts' [1999] *Journal of Business Law* 1
disagrees with Hayton's argument (see 'The bigger picture'), arguing that all that is required in a case like *Hunter* v *Moss* is to be able to identify the size of the total bulk and the size of the part to be held in trust

Yuen, P.W.C. 'Proprietary Interests in Fungible Shares: The Hong Kong Experience' (2002) 17(1) *Journal of International Banking Law* 24
discusses the certainty issues facing trust beneficiaries when the company shares they own are traded electronically

 For links to selected cases, statutes, academic papers and official reports mentioned in this chapter please visit the online resources at www.oup.com/uk/watt_directions6e/.

5 The constitution of trusts

Introduction

Suppose I were to telephone you on your birthday to say, 'I will give you a present when I see you tomorrow'. I am actually under no obligation to give you the promised present. You did not promise me anything in return, so I am under no contractual obligation to make the transfer. My promise was not contractual, but voluntary. This makes you a mere 'volunteer'. You have no right *at law* to compel me to fulfil my promise, and you will find no assistance in equity. Indeed, it is a maxim that *equity will not assist a volunteer*. (If equity did assist volunteers it would undermine the common law rule which says that a valid contract must be made for legal 'consideration'.) For my gift to be binding on me, it must be 'perfect'. This means that I must actually complete the transfer of the subject matter in favour of the intended donee or execute a formal 'deed of gift'. Another maxim states that *equity will not perfect an imperfect gift*. Similar rules apply to giving benefits by means of a trust. If I promise to create a trust of £10,000 in favour of a volunteer, the trust will not be enforceable (it will not be 'completely constituted') until I make an effective transfer of the £10,000 to the intended trustees or declare myself to be trustee of the £10,000. Because equity will not assist a volunteer, it will not enforce an incompletely constituted trust. Of course, if I actually transfer the £10,000 to the trustees or actually declare myself to be the trustee, the trust will then be completely constituted and the volunteer will become a beneficiary of the trust. The moment a volunteer becomes a beneficiary of a completely constituted trust, the volunteer no longer requires the assistance of equity; the beneficiary is from that moment *entitled* to enforce their beneficial interest against the trustee. Only when a trust is fully constituted is the trustee bound by it, the beneficiary entitled under it and the settlor deprived of the subject matter of it.

> **volunteer** Where a promise is made voluntarily in favour of a person, the person claiming the benefit of the promise is said to be a volunteer. A volunteer does not give contractual consideration for the performance of the promise.

5.1 The distinction between requirements of formality and constitution in the creation of trusts

The distinction between requirements of formality and constitution *in relation to the creation of trusts* is essentially one of function.

The formality requirements laid down in s 53(1) of the Law of Property Act 1925 and s 9 of the Wills Act 1837 are designed to defeat secret fraudulent dealings and to achieve certainty through the recording of transactions. In relation to the creation of trusts they come, as it were, 'extra to' the transaction itself. By way of contrast, if the requirements of valid constitution are not complied with, there is no trust at all. These requirements are a hurdle seemingly designed to prevent the casual creation of trusts. This is a sensible precaution when one considers the dramatic consequences of the *typical* express trust of property.

THINKING POINT

On a separate sheet of paper try to list the parties who may be affected by a validly created trust, and in your own words explain how they might be affected.

Did your list include the following?

- a person who creates a trust of his own property thereby terminates his right to benefit from that property (see *Re Bowden* [1936] Ch 71), except to the extent that he is identified as a beneficiary under the trust;
- the trust confers valuable rights upon persons who have not paid for them, i.e. the beneficiaries;
- the trust imposes onerous obligations on persons who may not have been paid to bear them, i.e. the trustees;
- in the rare case where no trustee can be found to administer the trust, the court may have to assume that function;
- trust property does not form part of the trustee's personal estate in the event of the trustee's death or insolvency, and will therefore not be available to satisfy the trustee's personal debts to third parties.

Imagine that you declare a trust of your land. You go on to produce a written memorandum of your declaration, thus complying with the formality requirement in s 53(1)(b).

If you declared yourself to be the sole trustee of the land there is nothing more that needs to be done, provided that the beneficiaries of the trust are certain. The trust is fully constituted because the legal title to the land is already in your name, therefore you already have everything you need to carry out the terms of the trust.

If, on the other hand, you declared that *other* named persons are to act as trustees, it will not be enough to have merely complied with the s 53(1)(b) formality requirement in relation to the setting up of the trust. You must, in addition, transfer the legal title in the land to the trustees so that they have everything they need in order to carry out the terms of the trust. (The legal title is needed to sell, exchange, mortgage or grant options against the legal estate.) This transfer of the legal title is said to be required for the *constitution* of an express trust. Failure to transfer the legal title to the trustees will render the trust incompletely constituted and for that reason void *ab initio*.

It is important not to confuse the requirement of valid constitution with the requirement of proper formality! It is true that where a trust of land is constituted by transfer of legal title to trustees the actual transfer must take the form of a deed (s 52 of the Law of Property Act 1925), but it would be a mistake to see this as a formality of trust creation. The fact is that whenever legal title to land is transferred *for whatever reason* (be it by way of sale, trust or absolute gift), the transfer must (apart from in the exceptional circumstances listed in ss 52(2) and 54 of the Law of Property Act 1925) be made by deed. The formality is a feature of transferring the particular type of property involved (i.e. land), not a feature of the instrumentality employed (i.e. trust).

5.2 Modes of constitution of trusts

It is crucially important to note that *a valid will automatically constitutes any will trust incorporated within it*, and that the trust thereby constituted is effective upon the death of the testator. *Inter vivos* trusts, on the other hand, must comply with one of the two modes of constitution. The first is where the settlor declares himself, or herself, to be a trustee for the benefit of the beneficiaries (a declaration of self as trustee). The second is where the settlor transfers the trust property to a trustee (or trustees) for the benefit of the beneficiaries (a declaration of trust by transfer to trustees).

5.2.1 Declaration of self as trustee

In Chapter 4, where we considered the certainty requirements prerequisite to the creation of a valid trust, we analysed a number of cases where the settlor declared himself to be a trustee. See, for instance, *Jones* v *Lock* (1865) 1 Ch App 25 (see 4.2.2) (where Lord Cranworth accepted that an oral 'declaration of trust of personalty may be perfectly valid even where voluntary') and *Paul* v *Constance* [1977] 1 WLR 527 (see 4.2.2). The fact that the requirements for valid constitution in such cases are so undemanding (because there is no need to transfer the trust property) means that the *certainty* requirements become paramount in determining the validity of trusts in such cases. The courts have to be very sure, before holding that legal owners of property are no longer entitled to the beneficial use and enjoyment of their property, that they certainly intended to declare themselves trustees.

In this chapter we will be far more concerned with the constitution of trusts where the trust property needs to be transferred to trustees. Usually this entails the transfer of legal title to the property, but it can involve the transfer of equitable property.

5.3 Constitution by transfer of legal title to trustees

In Chapter 3 we discovered that the creation of *inter vivos* trusts of land, and the creation of testamentary trusts generally, must usually be accompanied by formal documentation. Nevertheless, in Chapter 4 we noted that the creation of a trust does not depend upon any particular *form* of words. Whether or not an express trust was intended depends upon the *substance* of the words used, construed according to their context. In addition, there must be certainty of subject matter and certainty of object before a trust will be recognised. However, compliance with the formality and certainty requirements is not always sufficient to create an enforceable trust. Where the subject matter of the disposition is intended to pass to another person to hold as trustee, it is essential that it is passed to that person in accordance with the formal requirements for transfer of property of that type. The transfer formalities for trusts created by transfer of property to trustees vary according to the nature of the property transferred.

5.3.1 **Where the trust property consists of shares**

Many of the leading cases on incompletely constituted trusts and imperfect gifts have concerned trusts and gifts of shares. It is important to be aware that the general principles laid
down in those cases have been applied more widely to cover trusts and gifts of other forms of
property.

> **Q** | **CASE CLOSE-UP**
>
> *Milroy v Lord* (1862) 4 De G F & J 264
>
> Facts: a settlor owned shares in a bank which he purported to transfer to Lord by
> deed, to be held by him on trust for Milroy. The settlor later passed the share certifi-
> cates to Lord. Lord was the settlor's attorney and was therefore authorised to
> transfer the shares to Milroy, but ultimately the transfer could only be completed by
> registration, at the bank, of Milroy as owner of the shares. This registration never
> occurred. The issue was whether Milroy could claim the shares under a trust created
> by the settlor.
>
> Held: no valid trust had been created. Milroy had not provided consideration for the
> shares, the settlement was therefore made by the settlor 'voluntarily', and Milroy was
> therefore a mere 'volunteer' under the settlement. Applying the maxim that *equity
> does not assist a volunteer*, it followed that the settlement would not be binding on
> the settlor (even if he had wished it to be so) unless the settlor had 'done everything
> which, according to the nature of the property comprised in the settlement, was
> necessary to be done to transfer the property'. The settlor had tried to transfer the
> property to Lord upon trust for Milroy, but the transfer had failed because, according
> to the bank's own rules, there could be no valid transfer of the shares without
> registration.
>
> What is more, because the settlement was intended to take place *by transfer* the court
> would not give effect to it *by finding a valid declaration of trust*. It was held that if the
> settlor's chosen mode of disposition fails, the court will not perfect the settlement by al-
> lowing it to take effect by another of the modes.
>
> Turner LJ: 'Under the circumstances of this case, it would be difficult not to feel a strong
> disposition to give effect to this settlement to the fullest extent, and certainly I spared no
> pains to find the means of doing so, consistently with what I apprehend to be the law of
> the court; but, after full and anxious consideration, I find myself unable to do so. I take
> the law of this court to be well settled, that, in order to render a voluntary settlement valid
> and effectual, the settlor must have done everything which, according to the nature of
> the property comprised in the settlement, was necessary to be done in order to transfer
> the property and render the settlement binding upon him. He may of course do this by
> actually transferring the property to the persons for whom he intends to provide, and the
> provision will then be effectual, and it will be equally effectual if he transfers the property
> to a trustee for the purposes of the settlement, or declares that he himself holds it in trust
> for those purposes; and if the property be personal, the trust may, as I apprehend, be
> declared either in writing or by parol; but, in order to render the settlement binding, one
> or other of these modes must, as I understand the law of this court, be resorted to, for
> there is no equity in this court to perfect an imperfect gift. The cases I think go further to

this extent, that if the settlement is intended to be effectuated by one of the modes to which I have referred, the court will not give effect to it by applying another of those modes. If it is intended to take effect by transfer, the court will not hold the intended transfer to operate as a declaration of trust, for then every imperfect instrument would be made effectual by being converted into a perfect trust. These are the principles by which, as I conceive, this case must be tried.'

Shares in *public* companies must be transferred via the Stock Exchange. For most *private* companies the rule is that a transfer of shares in the company is only valid if the appropriate 'stock transfer form' is executed and delivered to the transferee (the trustee in our case) together with the share certificate, followed by the transfer of both documents by the trustee to the company. The company must then accept the transfer and register it in its books (see s 1 of the Stock Transfer Act 1963 and Part 21, especially s 771, of the Companies Act 2006). However, since the introduction of the CREST system on the London Stock Exchange in 1996 (see Chapter 14, Introduction) a great deal of share dealing takes place electronically. Part 21 of the Companies Act 2006 further facilitates this.

 THINKING POINT

Milroy v *Lord* is the foundational case in this area. What significant points are made about the constitution of trusts? Write down on a separate piece of paper anything that strikes you as being of particular importance. This is an exercise which will yield rich reward for the whole of this chapter.

It is clear from the leading judgment of Turner LJ that two equitable maxims underpinned these points, namely:

- equity will not assist a volunteer: 'in order to render a *voluntary* settlement valid and effectual, the settlor must have done everything which, according to the nature of the property comprised in the settlement, was necessary to be done in order to transfer the property and render the settlement binding upon him' (emphasis added);

- there is no equity to perfect an imperfect gift: 'the intention was that the trust should be vested in the defendant Samuel Lord, and I think therefore that we should not be justified in holding that by the settlement, or by any parol [oral] declaration made by the settlor, he himself became a trustee of these shares . . . by doing so we should be converting the settlement or the parol declaration to a purpose wholly different from that which was intended to be effected by it, and, as I have said, creating a perfect trust out of an imperfect transaction.'

 THINKING POINT

Consider the following two case studies and decide, in each case, whether you think that the settlor had 'done everything which, according to the nature of the property comprised in the settlement, was necessary to be done in order to transfer the property and render the settlement binding upon him'.

Case One

F, a resident of the United States, owned shares in an English company which he transferred by way of gift in favour of his son. By reason of wartime restrictions imposed upon the transfer of securities the English company was prohibited from registering (and refused to register) the transfer without Treasury consent. The forms necessary to obtain consent were sent to the donor to sign, which he duly did, and he returned them to the company. F died, however, before consent was obtained from the Treasury.

Case Two

In March 1943 R transferred 10,000 shares in an unlimited company to his wife and on the same day transferred a further 10,000 shares in the same company to trustees to hold upon the terms of a settlement. The transfers were in an authorised form. In the event, the transfers were not registered by the company until June 1943. R died in 1947, after which, in accordance with certain tax regulations, the Inland Revenue claimed estate duty on the shares because the gift had not been completed before April 1943.

The facts of Case One are taken from *Re Fry* [1946] Ch 312. In that case it was held that the transfer was ineffective and, consequently, that the intended gift was incomplete. The shares passed into F's residuary estate.

The facts of Case Two are from *Re Rose* [1952] Ch 499. The Court of Appeal held that R had done everything in his power to transfer his legal and equitable interest in the shares on the date of the transfer in March 1943. The factors which delayed the registration of the legal title until after April 1943 were beyond R's control. Counsel for the Inland Revenue had argued that the purported transfer must have been entirely ineffective according to *Milroy* v *Lord*, but the court held that *Milroy* v *Lord* would not invalidate a transfer in a case such as the present where the donor, after the purported transfer, would not have been permitted to assert any beneficial ownership in the shares at all. R had divested himself entirely of his equitable interest in the shares and accordingly his estate would not be liable to pay tax thereon.

 CASE CLOSE-UP

Re Rose **[1952] Ch 499, Court of Appeal**

Jenkins LJ: 'what was the position between the delivery of the transfers and the actual registration of the transferees as the holders of the shares? [Counsel for the Crown] has referred us to the well-known case of *Milroy* v *Lord*, which has been his sheet-anchor. He says that on this authority we must be forced to the conclusion that, pending registration, the transfers had no effect at all, and he arrives at that conclusion in this way: He says that these transfers, while purporting to be transfers of the property in the shares and not declarations of trust, did not transfer the property in the shares, because registration was necessary in order to get in the legal title. He says, further, that being transfers purporting to be transfers of the property in the shares and failing of their effect as such for want of registration, they could, pending registration, have no operation at all because in the case of *Milroy* v *Lord* it was held that a defective voluntary disposition purporting to operate as a transfer or assignment of the property in question would not be given effect to in equity as a declaration of trust. I agree with my Lord [Sir Raymond Evershed MR] that *Milroy* v *Lord*

> by no means covers the question with which we have to deal in the present case. If the deceased had in truth transferred the whole of his interest in these shares so far as he could transfer the same, including such right as he could pass to his transferee to be placed on the register in respect of the shares, the question arises, what beneficial interest had he then left? The answer can only be, in my view, that he had no beneficial interest left whatever: his only remaining interest consisted in the fact that his name still stood on the register as holder of the shares; but, having parted in fact with the whole of his beneficial interest, he could not, in my view, assert any beneficial title by virtue of his position as registered holder. In other words, in my view the effect of these transactions . . . must be that, pending registration, the deceased was in the position of a trustee of the legal title in the shares for the transferees.'

After *Re Rose* the *Milroy v Lord* requirement became: 'the settlor must have done everything *within his power* which, according to the nature of the property comprised in the settlement, was necessary to be done in order to transfer the property and render the settlement binding upon him' (emphasis added). In coming to his judgment, Sir Raymond Evershed MR purported to distinguish the facts of *Milroy v Lord* from those of *Re Rose*. His Lordship did not expressly desire to relax the application of the principles in *Milroy v Lord*, but that has undoubtedly been the effect of his reasoning.

In *Re Rose* the Court of Appeal held that the settlor had successfully divested himself of his property (he had done everything in his power 'to transfer the property and render the settlement binding upon him') but, also, that the trust property had not been transferred to the intended trustees. The result is that the equitable interest in the property appears to be hanging in mid-air between the date of the declaration of trust and the date when the legal title was finally registered with the company. This would all be well and good were it not for the fact that, as a matter of principle, the equitable interest in property must belong to somebody at all times. This principle is traditionally expressed in the maxim *equity abhors a vacuum in beneficial ownership*.

 THINKING POINT

Who do you think held the equitable interest in *Re Rose* between the declaration of trust and the date when the legal title was finally registered with the company?

It was stated in *Re Rose* that the settlor, Mr Rose, held the equitable interest between the declaration of trust and the date when the legal title was finally registered with the company. As Sir Raymond Evershed MR stated: 'If, as I have said, the phrase 'transfer the shares' is taken to be and to mean a transfer of all rights and interests in them, then I can see nothing contrary to the law in a man saying that so long as, pending registration, the legal estate remains in the donor, he was, by the necessary effect of his own deed, a trustee of the legal estate.' What type of trust this is, where the trustee has no trust obligations, it is hard to say. It isn't even a bare trust properly so-called because even if the beneficiary requested that the trust property be transferred to him, the settlor/'trustee' would be powerless to comply with the request. The best description of it might be that it is a 'nominal' trust, i.e. a trust in name only.

CASE CLOSE-UP

T Choithram International SA v Pagarani [2001] 1 WLR 1, Privy Council

Facts: Thakurdas Choithram Pagarani (TCP) was a successful businessman who had been diagnosed as having terminal cancer. He executed a trust deed at his bedside to establish a foundation as an umbrella organisation for a number of charities he had established during his life. Immediately after signing the deed he stated that all his wealth would now belong to the foundation (or words to that effect). TCP was a trustee of the foundation and the other trustees signed the deed the same day or shortly thereafter. Later, the directors of four companies controlled by TCP passed resolutions confirming that the companies' shares and assets would henceforth be held by the trustees of the foundation. TCP didn't actually transfer any shares during his lifetime. After TCP's death the companies registered the trustees of the foundation as shareholders.

Held: TCP had made an immediate, unconditional gift to the foundation.

Before proceeding to consider the transfer of other forms of property, it is important to note that the principles in *Milroy* v *Lord*, as interpreted in *Re Rose*, were stated in general terms and should be taken to apply to the constitution of all trusts, whatever the type of property involved, and not only to the constitution of trusts of company shares!

These general principles were applied again in *T Choithram International SA* v *Pagarani*.

 THINKING POINT

Do you see any problem with the decision in *T Choithram International SA* v *Pagarani*?

At first sight there had not been a valid transfer to all the trustees because TCP had not transferred the shares into their names. As he had not done everything he could have done, the transfer failed, and where a transfer fails equity will not constitute the transferor a trustee. However, their Lordships held that although equity will not aid a volunteer, neither would it strive officiously to defeat a gift. The words 'I give to the foundation' could have meant only one thing in the context of the case, namely 'I give to the trustees of the foundation' (for the foundation had no identity apart from its trustees). Although the words appeared to be words of outright gift, they really constituted a gift on trust. The fact that there had been no valid transfer to all the trustees was no obstacle to finding a trust on these facts because TCP was one of the trustees and therefore all the trust property had already vested in one of the trustees. As trustee TCP's conscience was bound to give effect to the trust, and the beneficiaries of the trust could enforce it. They were not mere volunteers.

The *Choithram* decision was approved by the Court of Appeal in *Pennington* v *Waine*.

 CASE CLOSE-UP

Pennington v Waine [2002] 1 WLR 2075

Facts: Mrs Ada Crampton told Mr Pennington that she wished to transfer 400 shares in a private company to her nephew, Harold. She signed a share transfer form and gave it to

Mr Pennington, who was a partner in the company's firm of auditors. He placed the form in a file and took no further action prior to Ada's death, apart from to write to Harold. In the letter he informed Harold that his firm had been instructed to arrange for the transfer of the 400 shares and that Harold need take no further action. Ada's will made no specific mention of the gift of 400 shares to Harold. It was held at first instance, in the absence of any evidence that the gift was intended to take effect in the future or subject to any condition precedent, that the gift of the 400 shares had taken effect *immediately* the share transfer forms had been executed, even though the form was never delivered to the intended donee or the company.

The Court of Appeal upheld that judgment, and in doing so it demonstrated generosity even greater than that which the courts had shown in *Re Rose* and *Choithram*. *Pennington* is more generous than *Re Rose* because in *Re Rose* there had actually been a transfer to the donee and all that remained to be done was to register the donee at the company, a step over which the donor had no control, and *Pennington* is more generous than *Choithram* because in *Choithram* there had at least been a notional 'transfer' from Mr Choithram in his capacity as donor to Mr Choithram in his capacity as trustee of the donee foundation. (Or, to explain the *Choithram* decision another way, it might be said—albeit none too convincingly in this author's opinion—that Mr Choithram was under a conscientious obligation because of his status as a trustee of the donee foundation not to assert his own claim to the subject matter of the donation at the foundation's expense.) In *Pennington* the donor had merely passed the share transfer form to her own agent. It is therefore hard to see how she could be said to have disposed outright of her beneficial interest in the shares when it remained open to her to revoke her instructions to Mr Pennington. (Whilst it is true that her death made it impossible for her to revoke her instructions, it also removed any binding obligation on Mr Pennington to carry them out.)

Arden LJ: 'The principle that, where a gift is imperfectly constituted, the court will not hold it to operate as a declaration of trust, does not prevent the court from construing it to be a trust if that interpretation is permissible as a matter of construction, which may be a benevolent construction. The same must apply to words of gift. An equity to perfect a gift would not be invoked by giving a benevolent construction to words of gift or, it follows, words which the donor used to communicate or give effect to his gift.

The cases to which Counsel have referred us do not reveal any, or any consistent single policy consideration behind the rule that the court will not perfect an imperfect gift. The objectives of the rule obviously include ensuring that donors do not by acting voluntarily act unwisely in a way that they may subsequently regret. This objective is furthered by permitting donors to change their minds at any time before it becomes completely constituted. This is a paternalistic objective, which can outweigh the respect to be given to the donor's original intention as gifts are often held by the courts to be incompletely constituted despite the clearest intention of the donor to make the gift. Another valid objective would be to safeguard the position of the donor: suppose, for instance, that (contrary to the fact) it had been discovered after Ada's death that her estate was insolvent, the court would be concerned to ensure that the gift did not defeat the rights of creditors . . . There must also be, in the interests of legal certainty, a clearly ascertainable point in time at which it can be said that the gift was completed, and this point in time must be arrived at on a principled basis.

There are countervailing policy considerations which would militate in favour of holding a gift to be completely constituted. These would include effectuating, rather than frustrating, the clear and continuing intention of the donor, and preventing the donor from acting in a manner which is unconscionable. As Mr McGhee points out, both these policy considerations are evident in *Choithram* . . .

"There can be no comprehensive list of factors which makes it unconscionable for the donor to change his or her mind: it must depend on the court's evaluation of all the relevant considerations."'

 THINKING POINT

On what basis was the Court of Appeal able to conclude that Ada had divested herself entirely of her interest in the 400 shares?

The main basis relied upon by the Court of Appeal was 'unconscionability' pure and simple. According to Arden LJ, unconscionability is a 'policy consideration' which militates in favour of holding a gift to be constituted. On the facts of the case her Ladyship held that by the time of Ada's death it would have been unconscionable of her to change her mind about making the disposition, because by that date she had 'not only told Harold about the gift and signed a form of transfer which she delivered to Mr Pennington for him to secure registration', but also her agent had 'told Harold that he need take no action. In addition Harold agreed to become a director of the company without limit of time, which he could not do without shares being transferred to him.'

Whilst it may be broadly accurate to say that equity's notion of unconscionability promotes fundamental policy concerns, such as the prevention of the abuse of legal rights and powers, it must not be forgotten that unconscionability does not *operate* at the level of policy. On the contrary, it operates *in personam*, on a case-by-case or context-by-context basis. In fact, despite her Ladyship's equation of policy and unconscionability, she clearly had in mind the *in personam* nature of unconscionability when, in the very next part of her judgment, she sought to identify the specific factors which in her judgment would have made it unconscionable for the particular donor in this case to have denied the donee's beneficial interest in the 400 shares. Those factors were as follows:

- Ada made the donation of her own free will;
- she signed the share transfer form and delivered it to Mr Pennington to secure registration;
- she told Harold about the gift;
- Mr Pennington told Harold that he need take no further action to perfect the gift;
- Harold signed a form of consent to become a director without limit of time (knowing he could not become a director without shares in the company).

If the first three factors, taken together or alone, were sufficient to bind Ada's conscience it would surely never be safe for a competent person voluntarily to promise to make a gift, let alone to instruct his agent to take steps preliminary to making a gift. They are not sufficient to bind Ada's conscience because it cannot be unconscionable to resile from a promise in circumstances where the promisee has suffered no detriment in reliance on it. This brings us to factors four and five. Factor four was no doubt a representation, but was it a representation on which Harold had relied to his detriment so that Ada's conscience would be affected? That must be doubtful. There was in fact nothing Harold could have done to perfect the gift in his favour, so his omission to do that which he could not have done can hardly be regarded as detrimental reliance. What, then, of the fifth factor? Here at last is a candidate. By accepting the director-ship it is certainly arguable that Harold acted to his detriment in reliance on an expectation that he would acquire some shares in the company. However, assuming that there had been a rep-resentation plus detrimental reliance thereon, this would normally be said to raise an estoppel binding on the conscience of the representor, but their Lordships made no reference to estop-pel, preferring instead to base their decision on the more general notion of unconscionability. That, with the greatest respect, will not suffice where a concept as vague as unconscionability is being applied in relation to something as dependent upon certainty as the transfer of benefi-cial ownership. However, if the 'unconscionability' approach survives it will no doubt come to represent a significant exception to the maxims *equity does not assist a volunteer* and *equity will not perfect an imperfect gift.*

Arden LJ was similarly generous and broad in her interpretation of the maxim *equity does not assist a volunteer* in *Staden v Jones* [2008] All ER (D) 176. A daughter found herself in a Cinder-ella-like predicament. When her mother and father divorced, the family house was put in the father's name on the understanding that it would be held for the daughter's benefit. The father remarried and when he died intestate, the house devolved on the stepmother, who (like the fairy-tale villain) purported to refuse the daughter any share in the house. The judge at first instance held that the daughter was a mere volunteer whom equity would not assist. The Court of Appeal found in favour of the daughter. Arden LJ acknowledged that a trust is hard to define, but held that it involves the assumption of an obligation to hold property for the benefit of another and decided, accordingly, that the father had held the house on trust for the daughter, so she could claim her share of the house.

The decision of the Court of Appeal in *Kaye v Zeital* [2010] EWCA Civ 159; [2010] 2 BCLC 1 was more orthodox, holding that an intended transfer of the beneficial interest in company shares failed because the transferor had done none of the actions necessary to effect such a transfer. He had not declared himself a trustee of the beneficial interest; neither had he assigned it in writing by way of gift or trust. *Kaye v Zeital* was followed in *Curtis v Pulbrook* (see next).

Q | CASE CLOSE-UP

Curtis v Pulbrook [2011] EWHC 167 (Ch); [2011] 1 BCLC 638

Briggs J (acknowledging that *Pennington v Waine* had identified three ways to perfect apparently imperfect donations): 'The first is where the donor has done everything neces-sary to enable the donee to enforce a beneficial claim without further assistance from the donor . . . The second is where some detrimental reliance by the donee upon an apparent although ineffective gift may so bind the conscience of the donor to justify the imposition of a constructive trust . . . The third is where by a benevolent construction an effective gift or implied declaration of trust may be teased out of the words used' (at para. [43]).

5.3.2 **Where trust property comprises land**

The basic rule has always been that 'all conveyances of land or of any interest therein are void for the purpose of conveying or creating a legal estate unless made by deed'. This rule is now contained in the Law of Property Act 1925, s 52(1).

CASE CLOSE-UP

Richards v Delbridge (1874) LR 18 Eq 11

Delbridge was the tenant of certain premises and the owner of a business which he carried on at those premises. He purported to make a gift of his lease and business to his grandson, Richards, who was an infant at the time. To give effect to the gift Delbridge endorsed and signed the following memorandum on the lease: 'This deed and all thereto belonging I give to Edward Bennetto Richards from this time forth, with all the stock-in-trade.' He then delivered the deed to Richards' mother to hold for her son. Delbridge later died, making no reference to the gift in his will. At issue was whether the lease and the business should pass to Richards, by gift or trust, or whether the property should pass to other persons under the will.

 THINKING POINT

In view of the Law of Property Act 1925, s 52(1), and bearing in mind the principles in *Milroy v Lord*, do you think that the transaction detailed in *Richards v Delbridge* was effective?

It was held that the property passed under the will, there being no valid gift or declaration of trust in favour of Richards. Richards had not given any consideration for the property and was therefore a mere 'volunteer', whom equity would not assist. Accordingly, Richards would only have been entitled to take the property if there had been evidence of a valid gift or a trust of the property. On the facts there had not been a perfect gift because there had been no formal conveyance of the legal title to Richards. There could not be a validly constituted trust imposed upon Richards' mother because there had been no conveyance of the legal title to her. Further, there could not be a validly constituted *inter vivos* trust binding on Delbridge (and binding now on his executors) because Delbridge had not expressed with sufficient certainty his intention to constitute himself a trustee by declaration of trust. Sir George Jessel MR followed *Milroy v Lord* and refused to spell out a trust from a failed gift. The following passage from his judgment, though quite long, is worth reciting here in full. It is a very clear summary of the applicable law:

> A man may transfer his property, without valuable consideration, in one of two ways: he may do such acts as amount in law to a conveyance or assignment of the property, and thus completely divest himself of the legal ownership, in which case the person who by those acts acquires the property takes it beneficially, or on trust, as the case may be; or the legal owner of the property may, by one or other of the modes recognised as amounting to a valid declaration of trust, constitute himself a trustee and, without an actual transfer of the legal title, may so deal with the property as to deprive himself of its beneficial ownership, and declare that he will hold it from that time forward on trust for the other person. It is true he need not use the words, 'I declare myself a trustee' but he must do something which is equivalent to it, and use expressions which have that meaning; for, however anxious the court may be to carry out a man's intention, it is not at liberty to construe words otherwise than according to their proper meaning.

In relation to land with registered title, in addition to the use of a deed, it is prerequisite to a valid transfer of the legal estate that the transfer of the estate be completed by the registrar entering the transferee on the register as the new proprietor (Land Registration Act 2002, s 7(1): 'If the requirement of registration is not complied with, the transfer, grant or creation becomes void as regards the transfer, grant or creation of a legal estate' (a similar provision appeared in the Land Registration Act 1925, now repealed)). Despite this, the Court of Appeal in *Mascall v*

Mascall (1985) 49 P & CR 119, applying the *Re Rose* interpretation of *Milroy* v *Lord*, held that a transfer of a registered estate had been effected (as far as the transferor was concerned at any rate) by the mere execution of the deed of transfer and the physical handing over of the land certificate to the transferee. Lawton LJ observed that '[the transferor] had done everything in his power in the ordinary way of the transfer of registered property and, in the ordinary way, it was for the [transferee] to get the Land Registry to register him as the proprietor of the property'.

5.3.3 Where the trust property is an ordinary chattel

Traditionally we celebrate the anniversary of a friend's birthday by making a gift to him or her. Usually such a gift takes the form of a 'chattel', by which we mean a movable object of personal property. Examples would include books, furniture and even animals (such as 'cattle', from which the word is derived, although nowadays they do not make ideal presents).

THINKING POINT

At what point do you think that the transfer of legal title in such a gift becomes effective?

To transfer legal title in a chattel there must be:

- physical delivery coupled with the requisite intention (i.e. the intention to make an outright gift); or
- a formally executed deed of gift. Words alone are insufficient to effect a valid transfer.

Do you recall the scenario with which we started this chapter? If I *telephone* you on your birthday and say 'happy birthday, I've just bought a present for you. I am holding it right now and I'll bring it over later', are those words legally binding on me? No, they are not. Despite my clear *intention* to make a gift to you, the gift will not be effective until I actually transfer the chattel to you. Alternatively, the gift could be effected by means of a formally executed deed of gift (although, apart from where law students are giving presents to each other, this would be rare).

CASE CLOSE-UP

Re Cole [1964] 1 Ch 175, Court of Appeal

In this case a husband bought a house in London whilst his wife and family were living elsewhere. Some time later his wife came to London and he took her to the house and showed her round. The wife was particularly impressed by certain chattels, namely a silk carpet and a card table. After the tour of the house the husband announced to her: 'It's all yours.' Some 16 years later the husband was declared bankrupt. In the year after the bankruptcy the wife sold the movable contents of the house. This action was brought by the trustee in bankruptcy to recover from the wife the proceeds of sale of the chattels.

It was held that, words of gift being in themselves insufficient to perfect a gift of chattels, the wife would have to prove some act of delivery or change of possession as would unequivocally show the husband's intention to transfer title to the wife. In the absence of evidence of such an act, legal title to the chattels must be said to have remained with the husband and to have vested in his trustee in bankruptcy. Some of their Lordships' reasoning would not, however, be well received today, as where Harman LJ held that '[i]n the ordinary case where a wife lives with her husband in a house owned and furnished by him, she has the use of the furniture by virtue of her position as wife, but that gives her no more possession of it than a servant who uses the furniture'. The rule of law remains, however, that the possession of chattels used by both husband and wife is deemed to be with the spouse who has legal title to that chattel. Provided possession is actually delivered, the transfer will be valid if delivery is made prior to, contemporaneous with or subsequent to the words of gift. In fact, pre-existing possession by the donee, followed by words of gift, may amount to a valid gift by transfer, even though possession of the chattel actually changed hands a long time ago.

The Court of Appeal rejected the novel submission of R. E. Megarry QC that it is enough for the donee to be brought to the chattels, rather than the chattels to the donee, although Harman LJ did accept that if the chattels be numerous or bulky there may be 'symbolical delivery'. He gave the example of a case involving a church organ, 'where the donor put his hand upon it in the presence of the donee and accompanied his gesture with words of gift'.

In some circumstances, where the court takes a very pragmatic view, it may not even be necessary to transfer physical possession of the chattel at all. In *Jaffa v Taylor Galleries Ltd* (1990) Times, 21 March, it was held that a trust of a painting had been validly constituted where the trust had been declared formally in a document (not a deed), of which the trustees each had a copy, even though the painting had not been physically transferred to the trustees. The judge commented that he 'could not conceive that a physical transfer had to take place and indeed it would be absurd so to find when one trustee was in Northern Ireland, another in England and when the third owner was the adult third plaintiff'. This very relaxed approach to the requirement of physical delivery will no doubt be restricted to cases where there is a formal document detailing the transfer and where it would be very inconvenient to require an actual change of physical possession of the chattel. Such cases will be very rare, most such gifts or trusts being effected by means of a properly executed deed of transfer as an alternative to physical delivery.

5.3.4 Where the trust property is a chose in action

A chose in action is a personal right of one person against another which can be sold, given away, subjected to a trust etc. as if it were property. Hence the name 'chose' (the French word for 'a thing'). Common examples include patent, copyright and debt. For a less typical example see *Don King Productions Inc v Warren* [2000] Ch 291. The chose in action in that case was the benefit of being a party to a contract to promote boxing. The Court of Appeal held that the benefit could be held on trust, even though the contract itself could not be assigned to the partnership (due to the contract having been entered into with a third party and having by its terms been expressly rendered non-assignable).

 STATUTE

Law of Property Act 1925, s 136(1)

Any absolute assignment by writing under hand of the assignor . . . of any debt or other legal thing in action, of which express notice has been given to the debtor . . . or other person from whom the assignor would have been entitled to claim such debt or thing in action, is effectual in law . . . to pass and transfer from the date of such notice . . . the legal right to such debt or thing in action.

❯ CROSS REFERENCE

Before starting 5.3.5, revise the formality requirement for the disposition of a subsisting equitable interest (s 53(1)(c), Law of Property Act 1925) at 3.2.1.2.

A special rule applies to those choses in action known as bills of exchange. A bill of exchange is an unconditional order in writing requiring one person to pay money to another. To be transferred they must be *endorsed* in favour of the transferee (Bills of Exchange Act 1882, s 31).

5.3.5 Constitution by transfer where the subject of the gift or trust is an equitable interest

Where the equitable interest is an interest under a trust, the transfer of the equitable interest is not complete until the trustees of the trust have been given notice of the transfer.

Q   **CASE CLOSE-UP**

Re McArdle [1951] 1 Ch 669

Facts: the testator, McArdle, left his residuary estate upon trust for his widow for life, remainder to his five children in equal shares. During the lifetime of the widow, one of the children, Monty, carried out improvements to a farm forming part of the testator's residuary estate. The testator's other children signed a document in these terms: 'To Monty . . . In consideration of your carrying out certain alterations and improvements to the . . . Farm . . . at present occupied by you, we the beneficiaries under the will of William Edward McArdle hereby agree that the executors . . . shall repay to you from the said estate when so distributed the sum of £488 in settlement of the amount spent on such improvements.' Accordingly, when the widow died, Monty claimed the £488. However, the other children of McArdle objected to the claim.

The questions which arose for consideration were, first, whether the signed document could take effect as a binding contract, and secondly, in the alternative, if it failed as a contract, could the document constitute an effective assignment of an equitable interest to Monty?

Held: the document did not constitute an enforceable contract because the works of improvement had been completed *before* the execution of the document and therefore the consideration for the agreement was wholly *past*. Nor could the document constitute a perfect gift of the equitable interest. The document had been expressed in the form of a contract for valuable consideration so it would be artificial to construe it as a valid equitable assignment (*there is no equity to perfect an imperfect gift*). Regrettably, Monty had no entitlement in law or equity to receive the £488. To remedy this the beneficiaries should have authorised the executors to pay the £488. As they did not do so, they had not done everything within their power to dispose of their interest in the £488.

Lord Evershed MR: 'I am for myself sorry that the other parties have been able, as I think they have, to evade the obligation which they imposed on themselves in 1945. But that is a matter for their conscience and not for this court.'

5.4 Assistance from the common law

There have been a number of cases in which people have promised to settle trusts in the future for the benefit of certain persons. If the latter have not given legal consideration for the promise, they will have no legal right to enforce the promise under the common law of contract. They will also be mere volunteers in the eyes of equity, claiming under a promise voluntarily made in their favour, and equity will not assist them. However, the following persons are not mere volunteers, and can sue at common law for performance of the promise to set up the trust (provided that they sue within the limitation period laid down by the Limitation Act 1980):

- persons who have provided money or money's worth in consideration of the promise;
- persons who are parties to a deed in which a **covenant** was made.

> **covenant** A promise contained within a deed is called a 'covenant'. A covenantee (i.e. a person to whom a promise is made by deed) is not a mere volunteer because the deed itself (or, traditionally, the seal on the deed) is deemed to satisfy the common law requirement of consideration. Any party to the deed can enforce the covenant against the person who made the promise (the covenantor). A person is a party to a deed when they are named in the deed and signed it.

Although the common law grants the right to sue in these cases, common law damages will be inadequate where the trust relates to specific property. Ironically, then, the appropriate remedy in such a case will be the *equitable* remedy of specific performance of the promise. A further irony is the fact that once the trust has been constituted by one of the common law methods referred to, even *volunteer* beneficiaries under the trusts will be entitled to claim their interests under the trusts, and the settlor will not be able to stop them (*Paul* v *Paul* (1882) 20 ChD 742).

Where a settlor promises an intended trustee that he will settle property on the trustee for the benefit of an intended beneficiary, it is arguable that there is a contract conferring a benefit on a third party. Since the Contracts (Rights of Third Parties) Act 1999 came into force, the volunteer beneficiary might be tempted to try to enforce this contract under the Act. However, any such claim is likely to fail on the ground that the contract does not confer a benefit as such, but creates a trust. It is the trust, not the contract, that confers the benefit. The volunteer's anticipated benefit under the contract would therefore be too indirect to claim under the Act.

5.4.1 Claims of persons within the marriage consideration

Persons within the **marriage consideration** include the husband and wife and the **issue of the marriage**.

> **issue of the marriage and marriage consideration** Issue will include children and even grandchildren, but not children of a previous marriage (unless their interests are 'interwoven' with those of the children of the marriage (AG v Jacob Smith [1895] 2 QB 341)), nor, it seems, 'illegitimate' children (despite the Family Law Reform Act 1987). The notion that children of a marriage have provided consideration is, according to Buckley J in Re Cook's ST [1965] Ch 902, a deliberate 'fiction'. In fact, the treatment of marriage as consideration is itself a fiction, not least because it functions as if it were common law consideration, even though strictly speaking it was a creation of the Court of Chancery.

Like all consideration, marriage consideration will be legally ineffective if given in the past in exchange for a present promise.

 OUTSIDE THE BOX

Jane Austen, *Pride and Prejudice*

Elizabeth read on: 'I have seen them both. They are not married, nor can I find there was any intention of being so; but if you are willing to perform the engagements which I have ventured to make on your side, I hope it will not be long before they are. All that is required of you is, to assure to your daughter, by settlement, her equal share of the five thousand pounds secured among your children after the decease of yourself and my sister; and, moreover, to enter into an engagement of allowing her, during your life, one hundred pounds per annum . . . If, as I conclude will be the case, you send me full powers to act in your name throughout the whole of this business, I will immediately give directions to Haggerston for preparing a proper settlement.'

marriage settlement
'A legal arrangement by which property is given or secured when a couple get married' (The Oxford Dictionary of English, 2nd edn, Oxford University Press).

For a **marriage settlement** to be truly made in consideration of marriage it must be made before the marriage takes place. One exception may be where the marriage settlement is made after the marriage but in accordance with a pre-marital (ante-nuptial) agreement to create the settlement.

Consider the following case studies. The core facts of the cases are basically the same: X executes a marriage settlement to which the trustees are parties, in which X covenants to settle any after-acquired property on trust for X, X's spouse and the issue of the marriage.

🔍 **CASE CLOSE-UP**

***Re Plumtre* [1910] 1 Ch 609**

Plumtre and his wife executed a marriage settlement to which the trustees were also parties. In the deed the wife covenanted to settle her after-acquired property on trust for herself, her husband, their prospective children and ultimately her next of kin. Some years later the husband made a gift to his wife of certain valuable stock. The wife sold this and reinvested the proceeds in other stock which remained registered in her sole name right up until her death. She died not having had children. After her death, letters of administration were granted to her husband and the stock was placed in his name. An action was brought by her next of kin, claiming to be entitled to the stock under the terms of the marriage settlement. It was held that the next of kin did not fall within the marriage consideration and therefore were mere volunteers. As such they were not entitled to enforce the covenant to settle. It was held that a voluntary contract (covenant) to create a trust under which the next of kin might get an interest must be distinguished from a declaration of trust in favour of the next of kin. The next of kin were not beneficiaries under the settlement and in the result the husband could keep the stock.

The next of kin in *Re Plumtre* would probably have had more success if there had been children of the marriage. Such children would have fallen within the marriage consideration and accordingly would not have been mere volunteers. They would have been entitled to enforce the covenant to settle, with resulting benefit not only for themselves, but also for other prospective beneficiaries such as the next of kin. In *Re D'Angibau* (1880) 15 ChD 228 the Court of Appeal acknowledged the possibility that prospective beneficiaries might benefit indirectly in this way even if they are mere volunteers.

CASE CLOSE-UP

Pullan v Koe [1913] 1 Ch 9

Facts: by a marriage settlement of 1859 a husband and wife covenanted to settle the wife's after-acquired property upon trusts for the benefit of the husband, the wife and their future children. In 1879 the wife's mother made a gift to her of £285 which the wife paid into her husband's bank account. A portion of this money was later invested in two bearer bonds which remained at the bank (gathering interest) until the husband's death in 1909. The trustees of the marriage settlement brought the present action against the husband's estate claiming that the bonds should be held for the benefit of the beneficiaries of the marriage settlement.

Held: that under the Statute of Limitations, the trustees were far too late to sue at common law for damages on the covenant. However, the husband had received the bonds with notice of the trusts of the marriage settlement and took them subject to the trusts of the marriage settlement. Accordingly, even though the trustees' legal action had been time barred, they were able to claim the bonds in equity on behalf of the beneficiaries. Whilst it is true that the court will not assist a volunteer, here the claimants (the trustees) were parties to the deed, and were acting on behalf of persons within the marriage consideration.

This case is further authority for the proposition that a person can covenant (or contract for valuable consideration) to settle property which is to come into existence in the future, and when it comes into existence, *equity sees as done that which ought to be done* and will insist upon the specific performance of the covenant.

THINKING POINT

Could the principle in *Pullan v Koe* have been used by the trustees in *Re Plumtre* so as to permit the trustees to take proceedings to enforce the covenant for the benefit of the next of kin?

In *Re Pryce* [1917] 1 Ch 234 the trustees sought the directions of the court to determine whether the principle in *Pullan v Koe* could be used so as to permit the trustees to take proceedings to enforce the covenant for the benefit of the next of kin. The facts of *Re Pryce* are very similar to those of *Re Plumtre* (earlier). The court directed the trustees *not* to take steps to enforce the covenant for the benefit of the next of kin. The next of kin were not within the marriage consideration. Being mere volunteers, they had no direct means of enforcing the covenant. As they could not enforce the covenant by direct means the court refused to allow them to acquire the benefit of it by indirect means.

In *Re Kay's Settlement* [1939] Ch 329, the judge, applying *Re Pryce*, also directed the trustees not to take steps to enforce a covenant on behalf of volunteers. For clarity he also added a further direction that the trustees should not sue for damages for breach of the covenant.

5.4.2 **Claims of persons who are parties to the covenant to settle**

Where a person covenants to create a settlement in the future, the proposed trustees of that settlement are often joined as parties to the deed in which the covenant is contained. We have seen that this gives the trustees a legal right to enforce the covenant against the covenantor. This legal right may be time barred under the Limitation Act, but even where it has not been time barred the trustees should not seek to enforce the right for the benefit of mere volunteers who would be beneficiaries under the settlement. It is quite a different matter if the beneficiaries are themselves parties to the deed in which the covenant is made, as the case of *Cannon v Hartley* illustrates.

> ### 🔍 CASE CLOSE-UP
>
> **Cannon v Hartley [1949] 1 Ch 213**
>
> Facts: Hartley and his wife executed a deed of separation on the breakdown of their marriage. Their daughter, Cannon, was also a party to the settlement. The deed contained the following covenant to settle after-acquired property: 'If and whenever during the lifetime of the wife or the daughter the husband [Hartley] shall become entitled . . . under the will . . . of either of his parents to any money exceeding in net amount or value £1,000 he will forthwith . . . settle one half of such money or property upon trust for himself for life and for the wife for life after his death and subject thereto in trust for the daughter absolutely.' In due course Hartley became entitled to a valuable share of his mother's estate. Shortly thereafter his wife died, whereupon Hartley refused to execute a settlement in accordance with his covenant. His daughter brought this action claiming damages for breach of the covenant.
>
> Held: because the daughter had been a party to the deed and a direct covenantee of the covenant to settle, she was entitled to a significant award of compensatory damages at common law. Although equity will not assist a mere volunteer, in the present case *the daughter did not require the assistance of equity*; she was entitled, as a party to the covenant, to enforce directly her common law right to the benefits of the covenant. The problems associated with the daughter being a mere volunteer in equity simply did not arise.

5.4.3 **The rule in *Strong v Bird***

> ### 🔍 CASE CLOSE-UP
>
> **Strong v Bird (1874) LR 18 Eq 315**
>
> Facts: Bird borrowed the sum of £1,100 from his stepmother. She lived in his house and paid rent quarterly and so it was agreed that Bird would repay the loan by deducting £100 from each quarter's rental payment. The deduction was made on two consecutive quarter days but on the third quarter day the stepmother insisted upon paying her full rent without deduction. She continued to make full payments of rent on every quarter day until her death, four years later. Bird was appointed as his stepmother's sole executor. This action was brought by Strong, the stepmother's next of kin, alleging that Bird should be charged with a debt of £900, representing the unpaid portion of the loan. It was held by Sir George Jessel MR that Bird owed no debt to the stepmother's estate. His Lordship reasoned that the appointment of Bird as executor had released the debt at law, whilst the stepmother's

continuing intention (up until her death) to make a gift of the £900 to Bird had released the debt in equity. Her continuing intention to make such a gift was amply evidenced by her making nine quarterly payments of the full rent without deduction.

Held: [The Master of the Rolls made it clear that Bird had not required the assistance of equity]: 'when a testator makes his debtor executor, and thereby releases the debt at law, he is no longer liable at law. It is said that he would be liable in this Court [i.e. Chancery]: and so he would, unless he could shew some reason for not being made liable. Then what does he shew here? Why he proves to the satisfaction of the Court a continuing intention to give, and it appears to me that there being the continuing intention to give, and there being a legal act which transferred the ownership or released the obligation—for it is the same thing—the transaction is perfected, and he does not want the aid of a Court of Equity to carry it out, or to make it complete, because it is complete already, and there is no equity against him to take the property away from him.'

THINKING POINT

Try to identify the two main criteria for the rule in *Strong* v *Bird* in the preceding extract. Compare your answer to the following:

- there must be evidence of the donor's intention to make an immediate *inter vivos* gift (if the gift is testamentary in nature it will fail for lack of formality: see Chapter 3);

- the intention to make the gift must have continued right up until the donor's death. The donor must not have treated the property as his own during the relevant period.

Re Stewart [1908] 2 Ch 251 confirms that the rule in *Strong* v *Bird* is not restricted to the release of a debt, but can apply to a regular gift, and that it is irrelevant that the intended donee is not a sole executor, but one of many. Neville J explained the 'double character' of the reasoning in *Strong* v *Bird* (at 254, 255):

> first, that the vesting of the property in the executor at the testator's death completes the imperfect gift made in the lifetime, and, secondly, that the intention of the testator to give the beneficial interest to the executor is sufficient to countervail the equity of beneficiaries under the will, the testator having vested the legal estate in the executor.

Farwell J in *Re James* [1935] 1 Ch 449 at 451 confirmed that the donee in such a case does not call for the assistance of equity: 'equity will not aid the donee, but on the other hand if the donee gets the legal title to the property vested in him he no longer wants the assistance of equity and is entitled to rely on his legal title as against the donor or persons claiming through him.' In *Re James* the rule in *Strong* v *Bird* was extended to perfect a gift to an administratix.

Arguably, the application of the rule to benefit an administrator or administratix goes too far. An administrator is appointed by the court, whereas an executor is appointed by the donor personally. In *Re Gonin* [1979] Ch 16 Walton J observed that *Strong* v *Bird* had proceeded on the basis that at law the appointment of a person as executor effected a release of the executor's debt to the appointor, a doctrine which had never been applied to administrators: 'The appointment of an administrator . . . is not an act of the deceased but of the law. It is often a matter of pure chance which of many persons equally entitled to a grant of letters of administration finally takes them out.'

> **THINKING POINT**
>
> Later in the same judgment his Lordship refers to the rule in *Strong* v *Bird* as a 'simple rule of equity'. Is he right?

No. The donee who relies upon the rule in *Strong* v *Bird* is not relying upon the assistance of equity: he claims his entitlement at common law. It is true that equity recognises this entitlement, as indeed it recognises all legal entitlement which is unencumbered by a superior claim in equity, but only in this limited sense can the rule be seen to be a 'simple rule of equity'. Incidentally, in *Re Gonin* itself the rule in *Strong* v *Bird* failed to assist because the donor gave away part of the subject matter of the gift to someone other than the claimant, thus rebutting any presumption that the donor had intended to make the donation in favour of the claimant right up until the time of his death.

> **CASE CLOSE-UP**
>
> ***Day* v *Royal College of Music* [2013] EWCA Civ 191; [2014] Ch 211, Court of Appeal**
>
> Facts: The case concerned a dispute between the adult children of the composer Sir Malcolm Arnold and his former carer, Mr Day. The dispute related to manuscript musical scores which had been deposited with the Royal College since the 1980s. Mr Day claimed that he had become owner of the manuscripts through a 1998 document executed by Sir Malcolm which recorded a gift in Mr Day's favour. However, Mr Day conceded that he never had physical possession of the manuscripts and that the 1998 document had not been executed as a deed.
>
> Held: The Court of Appeal upheld the judge's decision that the rule in *Strong* v *Bird* operated to perfect the formal imperfections of the gift when, upon Sir Malcolm's death, Mr Day became an executor under Sir Malcolm's will.

Whether the rule in *Strong* v *Bird* should apply to trusts as well as to absolute gifts has not been conclusively decided, but it appears that it should. Cast your mind back to the 'double character' of the reasoning in *Strong* v *Bird*, as delineated in *Re Stewart*. On the first line of reasoning, that the vesting of the property in the executor at the testator's death completes the imperfect gift made in the lifetime, there would appear to be no reason in principle why the rule should not be effective to transfer the legal title to trustees in the appropriate case. On the second line of reasoning, that the intention of the testator to give the beneficial interest to the executor is sufficient to defeat the equity of beneficiaries under the will, there would likewise be no difficulty in applying the rule to effect an *inter vivos* declaration of trust. The equities of the beneficiaries under that trust would take priority over the equitable claims of the beneficiaries under the will, for *the first equity in time will prevail where the equities are equal*.

As to authority, it has been suggested that in the case of *Re Ralli's Will Trusts* [1964] Ch 288 the rule in *Strong* v *Bird* was indeed applied to constitute a trust. See Figure 5.1.

Re Ralli's Will Trusts [1964] Ch 288

Facts: the testator, Ralli, left his residuary estate to trustees on trust for his wife for life, remainder to his daughters H and I. H, by a marriage settlement, covenanted to settle her share on trustees for the benefit of her own children and ultimately for the children of I. A clause of the marriage settlement declared that all property within the terms of the covenant should be subject to the terms of the trusts pending assignment to the trustees. H died childless. Later, a trustee who had been a party to H's marriage settlement was additionally appointed trustee under the will of Ralli. That trustee, who also happened to be I's husband, brought the present action, seeking directions as to whether H's share of her father's residuary estate should be held by him on the trusts of the marriage settlement, or under the terms of H's will. He claimed that the property should be held on the trusts of the marriage settlement. H's personal representatives claimed that H's estate should be entitled, in accordance with H's will.

Figure 5.1 *Re Ralli's WT*

If H has no children, if Ralli's wife is dead, and if H is dead, do you think that I's husband holds H's remainder interest for H's estate (in accordance with the will trust) or for I's children (in accordance with the marriage settlement)?

As we noted earlier, it is sometimes said that *Re Ralli's WT* is a case where the rule in *Strong* v *Bird,* which normally applies to gifts, was applied to a trust. Do you agree with that assertion?

CASE CLOSE-UP

***Re Ralli's Will Trusts* [1964] Ch 288**

Decision: it was held that the claimant (I's husband) held H's share of Ralli's estate on the trusts of the marriage settlement. Those trusts had become fully constituted when the legal title to the property had vested in the claimant in his capacity as trustee of Ralli's will trusts. The fact that the constitution had been purely fortuitous did not matter. If it had been necessary to enforce performance of the covenant, equity would not have done so at the request of the beneficiaries under the settlement, as they were mere volunteers. In the present case, however, there had been no need to invoke the assistance of equity to enforce performance of the covenant. On the contrary, it had been for the defendants to invoke equity to show that it would be 'unconscientious' for the claimant to perform the covenant. It was held not to be unconscientious for the claimant to exercise his legal authority to perform the covenant and to carry out the settlement trusts.

This line of reasoning should strictly speaking be regarded as, if not *obiter dicta*, then an alternative *ratio decidendi*. For Buckley J was in fact prepared to dispose of the case on the more straightforward assumption that H's remainder interest under Ralli's will was vested, not after-acquired, property at the date of execution of the marriage settlement. Accordingly, H had held that property as trustee when she was alive because the execution of the marriage settlement had constituted a declaration of trust binding *upon her* pending transfer of her interest to the trustees of the settlement. That trust would now be binding upon her successors in title, i.e. her personal representatives.

In *Re James* the housekeeper was able, somewhat fortuitously, to claim a gift under the rule in *Strong v Bird*. *Re James* was cited with no dissent by Buckley J in *Re Ralli's WT*. However, according to Walton J in *Re Gonin* [1979] Ch 16, *Re James* was 'only used as an illustration' in *Re Ralli's*. It remains a moot point whether *Re Ralli's* is an application of the rule in *Strong v Bird*.

Re Ralli's should be contrasted with *Re Brooks' Settlement Trusts* [1939] Ch 993, in which a person with a contingent interest under a trust purported to divest himself of that interest by voluntary settlement. The settlement was held to be not binding on him because his share was not yet his to give at the time of the purported voluntary settlement.

5.4.4 Assistance from the common law: summative exercise

Consider the following thinking point by way of summary to this section. You should be able to draw upon many of the points you have learned so far.

 THINKING POINT

Imagine that you are a court faced with the following facts, taken from *Re Cook's Settlement Trusts* [1965] Ch 902. The trustees have taken out a summons for directions as to what action they should take if the Rembrandt is sold during FC's lifetime and the proceeds are then not paid to the trustees. How will you direct the trustees?

HC and his son FC executed a settlement under which it was agreed that FC's reversionary interest under a will should be exchanged for other property of equal value and that some of the new (replacement) property should be settled by FC on trust for certain named beneficiaries. That part of the new property which was not required to be so settled (primarily comprising valuable paintings) was to be held by FC for his own benefit, but FC covenanted for valuable consideration that the proceeds of the sale of any of the paintings, if sold during FC's lifetime, should be paid to the trustees of the settlement to be held by them on the trusts of the settlement. FC later made a gift of one of the paintings (a Rembrandt) to his wife and she has since expressed her intention to sell it.

Your directions to the trustees should ideally run along the following lines: the covenant to settle the proceeds of sale of the paintings was a contract to settle after-acquired monies. These monies did not exist at the time of the covenant and might never come into existence. The beneficiaries under the settlement had not been parties to the covenant and accordingly would not be permitted to sue at common law on it. Nor had the beneficiaries provided consideration for the covenant to settle (they did not fall within marriage consideration and had not provided valuable consideration in money or money's worth). So much for the common law. In the eyes of equity, the beneficiaries were mere volunteers and equity would not assist them. The beneficiaries were not entitled to require the trustees to enforce the covenant on their behalf. In fact, according to *Re Kay's Settlement* (see 5.4.1) the trustees should have been directed not to enforce the covenant even if they were minded to do so. These are essentially the same directions as those given by Buckley J in *Re Cook's Settlement Trusts*.

5.5 Assistance from Roman law

The Roman law of **donatio mortis causa** (a gift made because of death) plays a part in the modern law of England and Wales as a means by which a donee can claim a gift of certain property, where that gift has not been perfectly executed in accordance with the common law rules applicable to transfers of property of that type. The rule is almost invariably used to perfect absolute gifts, but there would appear to be no reason why it should not equally apply to perfect a trust where the gift is impressed with trust obligations (this would in any case be the inevitable result where, for example, a gift of land is made to two or more persons).

> **donatio mortis causa**
> A gift made inter vivos in expectation of the donor's imminent death, but which is not fully effective until the donor's death.

The Roman law doctrine of *donatio mortis causa* is often cited as a genuine exception to the maxim *equity will not assist a volunteer*. There is support for this view from the judgments of English courts, which tend to suggest that the doctrine is effective in English law through the use of an implied or constructive trust but in essence the doctrine is an anomalous wholesale importation of a Roman law doctrine into English law and is only English 'equity' in the loosest sense.

5.5.1 The Roman origins of the doctrine

Justinian, the Byzantine Roman Emperor between ad 527 and ad 565, oversaw the codification of Roman law. The result was the *Corpus Juris Civilis*, the main part of which was Justinian's *Digest*.

OUTSIDE THE BOX

Digest citation 39.6.3–6

It is permissible to make a gift *mortis causa* not only on grounds of weak health, but also on grounds of impending danger of death due to enemies or robbers or the cruelty or hatred of a powerful man or when about to undertake a sea voyage, or to travel through dangerous places, or when one is worn out by old age, since all these circumstances represent impending danger.

Andrew Borkowski observes in his *Textbook on Roman Law* (3rd edn, Oxford: Oxford University Press, 2005) that:

> [s]uch gifts were hybrid in character: they were made *inter vivos*, but did not take full effect until the contemplated death of the donor occurred. Ownership in the property normally passed to the donee on the making of the gift, but the gift was revocable before death. Automatic revocation occurred if the donee predeceased the donor, or if the latter became bankrupt.

Borkowski refers to citation 39.6.35.2 of the *Digest*.

OUTSIDE THE BOX

Digest citation 39.6.35.2

A gift *mortis causa* differs considerably from the true and absolute sort of gift which proceeds in such a way that it can in no circumstances be revoked. In that sort of case, of course, the donor wishes the recipient rather than himself to have the property. But the person who makes a gift *mortis causa* is thinking of himself and, loving life, prefers to receive rather than to give. This is why it is commonly said: 'He wishes himself rather than the recipient to have the property, but, that said, wishes the recipient rather than the heir to have it.'

5.5.2 The English formulation of the doctrine

The English law formulation of the doctrine is not very far removed from the Roman law conception, and has its roots firmly in that source. An early formulation of the English law can be found in *Cain v Moon* [1896] 2 QB 283, but more recently we have the decision of the Court of Appeal in *King v Dubrey*.

CASE CLOSE-UP

King v Dubrey (also known as King v Chiltern Dog Rescue) [2015] EWCA Civ 581, Court of Appeal

The requirements for a valid DMC in English law, as confirmed by the Court of Appeal (in paras [50]–[60]), are: (1) the donor 'should be contemplating his impending death', which means 'death in the near future for a specific reason'; (2) the form of the gift must be such that it 'will only take effect if and when his contemplated death occurs. Until then D has the right to revoke the gift' (in DMC the donor 'reserves the right to revoke the gift at will' and it will lapse automatically if the donor 'does not die soon enough' or if the donor 'recovers or survives'); (3) the donor should deliver 'dominion' over the subject matter. Jackson LJ, acknowledging that 'dominion' has been called 'amphibious' and 'slippery', concluded that it means 'physical possession of (a) the subject matter or (b) some means of accessing the subject matter (such as the key to a box) or (c) documents evidencing entitlement to possession of the subject matter'. (Followed in *Keeling* v *Keeling sub nom Re Exler (Deceased)* [2017] EWHC 1189 (Ch).)

 THINKING POINT

Bearing in mind the preceding criteria, do you think there was a valid *donatio mortis causa* on the following set of facts? A widow mortgaged a farm, in which she held a life interest, to her late husband's brother, A. After the widow's death he passed the deeds to the farm, apart from the mortgage deed, to the widow's executors (his nieces). It later transpired that A was dying of an incurable disease and so, in anticipation of his death, he passed a sealed envelope to his nieces which turned out to contain the mortgage deed. Some short time later A caught a chill and died of pneumonia. This action was brought by his executors, claiming that the mortgage was a subsisting security which could be enforced against the nieces.

The facts are taken from the case of *Wilkes* v *Allington* [1931] 2 Ch 104 where Lord Tomlin held that the mortgage could not be enforced. The otherwise imperfect gift of the mortgage to the nieces was made perfect by a valid *donatio mortis causa*, for it was clear that the gift was only to become binding on the donor's death (an intention could be implied that the property should be returned to him if he recovered). It was further held that it was not necessary for the donor to have died from the same disorder as that from which he had been suffering when contemplating death.

It was held in *Sen* v *Headley* [1991] Ch 425, Court of Appeal, that the doctrine could apply to gifts of title to land, a point which had until that decision been in doubt. Mrs Sen, who had lived with a man for several years in a house owned by him, was given a set of keys as he lay on his deathbed. The keys unlocked a box in which were held the deeds to the man's house. As he passed the keys to her, the dying man stated that the house was to be hers. It was held that passing possession of the deeds was sufficient to effect the *donatio*, as there had been 'a parting with dominion over the essential *indicia* of title'. The notion of ownership as 'dominion' is peculiarly Roman. Nourse LJ said: 'Let it be agreed that the doctrine is anomalous, anomalies do not justify anomalous exceptions . . . to make a distinction in the case of land would be to make just such an exception. A *donatio mortis causa* of land is neither more nor less anomalous than any other. Every such gift is a circumvention of the Wills Act 1837.'

Figure 5.2 Chapter summary

⟲ Summary

Figure 5.2 is intended to offer a summary of the main points covered in this chapter. However, the best way to learn is to design your own chart covering the salient issues.

Testamentary trusts: a valid will automatically constitutes any will trust incorporated within it, and that the trust thereby constituted is effective upon the death of the testator.

Inter vivos trusts: must comply with one of the two modes of constitution (*Milroy v Lord* (1862) 4 De G F & J 264):

- a declaration of self as trustee: where the settlor declares himself, or herself, to be a trustee for the benefit of the beneficiaries;

- a declaration of trust by transfer to trustees: where the settlor transfers the trust property to a trustee (or trustees) for the benefit of the beneficiaries.

- It is clear from the judgment of Turner LJ in *Milroy* v *Lord* that two equitable maxims underpin the rules on constitution of trusts:
  - *equity will not assist a volunteer* and
  - *there is no equity to perfect an imperfect gift.*

But we have seen that cases such as *Pennington* v *Waine* [2002] 1 WLR 2075, Court of Appeal, have relaxed the rules set down in *Milroy* v *Lord*.

The Common Law Assists in the Constitution of Trusts

The following persons are not mere volunteers, and can sue at common law for performance of the promise to set up the trust:

- persons who have provided money or money's worth in consideration of the promise;
- persons who are parties to a deed in which the promise was made.

We have seen that the common law rule in *Strong* v *Bird* can also perfect imperfect gifts (and constitute imperfectly constituted trusts).

Roman Law Assists in the Constitution of Trusts

For an effectual *donatio mortis causa* three things must combine:

- the gift or donation must have been in contemplation, though not necessarily in expectation, of death;
- there must have been delivery to the donee of the subject matter of the gift;
- the gift must be made under such circumstances as to show that the thing is to revert to the donor in case he should recover.

? | Summative assessment exercise

Herbert Chance, wishing to make future provision for his adult son, entered into the following covenant in a deed to which his friends Allan Smith and Clifford Overy were the only other parties: 'I promise to settle the sum of £100,000 in cash, or assets of equivalent value, for the benefit of my son for his life, to his issue in remainder. This bounty to be held on trust by Allan Smith and Clifford Overy in accordance with the terms of the settlement annexed hereto.'

Some years later Herbert fell grievously ill. As he lay on his deathbed, his friend Mr Overy reminded Herbert of the covenant he had made. The next day, when Mr Overy came to visit, Herbert passed to him a sealed envelope. 'In there', he said, 'are the share certificates for £100,000 of my shares in the family company. I want my son to have them in accordance with the terms of the settlement annexed to the covenant.' Herbert died minutes later.

Advise the son whether or not he will be able to claim any benefit under the settlement.

 Full specimen answers can be found at www.oxfordtextbooks.co.uk/orc/watt_directions5e/.

The bigger picture

The law of constitution of trusts seems to be peculiarly influenced by accidental factors. Two accidents feature prominently. First is the accidental timing of death. Would *Pennington* v *Waine* have been decided differently if the donor hadn't died? The answer is almost certainly 'yes'. It is hard to imagine, had the old lady lived, that the court would have insisted she complete the donation that she had commenced by making arrangements with her agent. Second is the fact that the appointment of an intended donee to be the donor's executor can have the accidental effect of perfecting the donation by transferring the subject matter of the donation to the donee (this is the basis of the so-called rule in *Strong* v *Bird*). Lawyers and law students tend to be suspicious of cases where the result seems to turn on accidental factors such as the timing of a death, but maybe we should appreciate that one of the great merits of the common law is its ability to respond to the accidental. A case-based system of law is by definition based on facts that happen to accidentally befall. (The word 'accident' and the word 'case' both derive from the Latin cadere 'to fall'.) Refer again to the *Quistclose* case (see 2.3.4.2) and ask yourself if this was not, in essence, a judicial response to the accidental timing of another death—the death (that is, the insolvency) of a company.

 Further reading

Barton, J.L. 'Trusts and Covenants' (1975) 91 LQR 236
an in-depth analysis of the relationship between covenants and the constitution of trusts

Borkowski, A. *Deathbed Gifts: The Law of Donatio Mortis Causa* (1999) Oxford: Blackstone Press
an engaging and detailed examination of the doctrine of *donatio mortis causa*

Garton, J. 'The Role of the Trust Mechanism in the Rule in *Re Rose*' (2003) 5 Conv 364
a case note on *Pennington* v *Waine*, focusing on the way it extends the rule in *Re Rose*

Jaconelli, J. 'Problems in the Rule in *Strong v Bird*' [2006] Conv 432
examines the principled basis of the rule in *Strong* v *Bird* and practical problems in its application which create a risk of professional negligence for the unwary

Ollikainen-Read, A. 'Assignments of Equitable Interests and the Origins of *Re Rose*' (2018) 63 Conv 63–73
argues that the so-called rule in *Re Rose* only applies to cases analogous to a trustee/beneficiary relationship, e.g. transfer of shares (a company owes duties to its shareholders that are similar to those of a trustee to beneficiaries), but that the rule should not apply in second order analogies, such as freehold land

Roberts, N. '*Donationes mortis causa* in a Dematerialised World' (2013) 2 Conv 113–28
questions whether *donatio mortis causa* is applicable to registered land

 For links to selected cases, statutes, academic papers and official reports mentioned in this chapter please visit the online resources at www.oup.com/uk/watt_directions6e/.

6 Public policy limitations on the formation of trusts

LEARNING OBJECTIVES

By the end of this chapter you should be able to:

- appreciate that private trusts may be unenforceable or void on grounds of public policy;

- prevent a breach of the rules against perpetuity and accumulations;

- detect an existing breach of the rules against perpetuity and accumulations;

- discern the situations in which a trust designed to shield assets from creditors will and will not be void;

- understand a number of other public policy limitations on the formation of trusts.

Introduction

You have had a great idea for a new board game based on the exciting world of equity. The players progress up a mountain according to the roll of dice, sliding down when they land on a 'stream of equity' and rising up when they land on a 'ladder of law'. The winner is the one who stays down to earth. You call it 'streams and ladders'. You plan to start a business to manufacture and sell the game to shops. Your next great idea is to transfer all your assets into the name of a close friend, to hold on trust for you 'in case the business venture fails'. If the game sells well, you will be rich; if it fails, your creditors will not be able to get their hands on your assets, because your friend will appear to own them. A cunning scheme, but it won't work. If you set up a trust to protect yourself from your creditors, the trust will be void. There are statutes governing the fair distribution of wealth when a person becomes insolvent (i.e. becomes unable to pay their debts when they fall due), and a trust is not permitted to undermine this statutory scheme. Public policy demands that public interests should not be defeated by private trusts.

A trust prejudicing one's creditors is just one example of a trust that is void on grounds of public policy. Other examples include trusts which tie up wealth for too long, trusts which restrain marriage and trusts which promote racial or sexual prejudice. We will see that the last example raises the controversial problem of drawing a line between acceptable private choice and unacceptable public discrimination.

6.1 The rules against perpetuities

 OUTSIDE THE BOX

Wall Street, **from the screenplay by Stanley Weiser and Oliver Stone**

GORDON GEKKO: 'The richest 1 per cent of this country owns half the country's wealth: five trillion dollars. One third of that comes from hard work, two thirds of it comes from inheritance, interest on interest accumulation to widows and idiot sons.'

The rules against perpetuity prevent the creation of trusts 'which tie up wealth for too long'. Such trusts are said to be void for perpetuity. The general point of the rules is to make sure that property subject to a trust does not remain subject to a trust for too long, but returns to its original state of being owned absolutely. The most commonly cited justifications for the rules against perpetuities are, first, the desire to keep wealth in the open market, where it can assist in financial enterprise to the greater public good; and, secondly, the perceived need to restrict particular families and other private institutions from becoming disproportionately wealthy over time.

There are three main rules. The first prevents gifts from vesting at too remote a time in the future. The second prevents capital from being tied up indefinitely. The third prevents income from being accumulated for too long a period.

THINKING POINT

Do these rules make sense in a world of corporations? Corporations do not die and therefore property owned by corporations can potentially be excluded from the open market in perpetuity.

The first rule is called 'the rule against remoteness of vesting'. It is a rule that renders void any gift to a *person* which may vest in that person at too remote a time in the future. To 'vest' here means to 'vest in interest', as opposed to 'vest in possession'.

types of interest These are: 'vested in interest', 'vested in possession' and 'contingent'. The difference between the two types of vested interest can be illustrated quite simply by taking the classic trust 'to A for life and B in remainder'. In such a trust, both A and B are entitled to an interest: their interests have both 'vested in interest'. However, only A can claim to be entitled to the present use and enjoyment of the trust property; B has to wait until A dies. So it is said that only A's interest has 'vested in possession'. Where an interest might never be acquired, as in the case of a gift that is dependent upon the happening of an uncertain event, e.g., 'to A when he qualifies as a barrister', A's interest is said to be 'contingent' and as such it has not 'vested' in either sense of the word.

The second rule is the rule against inalienability of capital. It is a rule which prevents capital, which has already vested in trustees, from being tied up for too long a period of time.

The third is the rule against accumulation of income. It is designed to prevent trust income from being accumulated for too long a time.

6.2 The rule against remoteness of vesting

OUTSIDE THE BOX

***Body Heat* (Warner Bros, 1981), starring William Hurt and Kathleen Turner**

Based on the film script by Lawrence Kasdan.

[This scene takes place in a legal firm's conference room, where a lawyer (Miles Hardin) is explaining the meaning of a will to the potential beneficiaries in the presence of, amongst others, Mr Racine—the lawyer who had made a fatal error in the drafting of the will.]

HARDIN: 'Everything's in order up to there. The problem comes in the language of the bequest to Heather. It's a technical matter. In writing the will, I'm afraid Mr Racine violated what is known as "the rule against perpetuities". It forbids an inheritance to be passed down indefinitely for generations. I knew that a probate judge in Miami would spot the mistake right away, so I thought I'd bring it up here to Okeelanta County—since Edmund had the residence here—and see if I could get lucky with a judge who didn't know the State law quite so well [dryly, he can't resist] perhaps find one with the same kind of legal training as Mr Racine.'

The rule against remoteness of vesting is concerned to prevent interests in property commencing (vesting in interest) at too remote a time in the future; as such it only applies to 'contingent' interests (see the earlier definition box). The rule is not concerned with the duration of interests after they have vested—the duration of capital retention and income accumulation is governed by the other perpetuity rules, considered later.

The modern rule against remoteness of vesting has its source in principles laid down by Heneage Finch, Lord Nottingham (Lord Chancellor between 1673 and 1682 and rightly called 'the father of equity'), in *The Duke of Norfolk's Case* (1681) 3 Chan Cas 1. (See A.W.B. Simpson, *An Introduction to the History of the Land Law*, 1979, at pp. 211, 212.) Lord Nottingham relied, in that case, upon two earlier authorities, the principal one being *Pells* v *Brown* (1620) Cro Jac 590. The judgment in *Pells* v *Brown* suggests that the historical motivation for the rule may not merely have been social concerns about family aggrandisement, economic stagnancy or the restrictive effect of dead men's wishes. There appears also to have been an ecclesiastical concern that to store up wealth is in some sense to deny the providence of God.

The reason we still study the rule is essentially threefold. First, to ensure that we never make the mistake of breaching the rule (the effect of failure to comply with the rules against perpetuity is to render the disposition, or other direction, void—as the extract from the film *Body Heat* shows). Secondly, because the rules present one of the most stimulating and demanding intellectual challenges that one can face in one's quest to understand law and the nature of legal reasoning. Thirdly, because the rules against perpetuities still impact in dramatic fashion in modern trust contexts. Take, for example, *Air Jamaica Ltd* v *Charlton* [1999] 1 WLR 1399, where, at first instance, a pension trust was held to be void under the rule against perpetuities with the result that the monies passed as *bona vacantia* (ownerless property) to the Crown. The Privy Council ultimately reversed this decision. Lord Millett held that the pension scheme would ordinarily be void for offending the rule against perpetuities, given that there was no applicable statutory exemption to the common law rule, but that a new settlement was created every time a new member joined the scheme. Each new settlement complied with the rules against perpetuities because every new member qualified as a 'life in being' in relation to the particular settlement. (Technical terms such as 'life in being' are explained shortly.)

The Perpetuities and Accumulations Act 2009 introduced the following main changes to the rule against remoteness of vesting:

- The rule against perpetuities is restricted in its application to successive estates and interests in property and to powers of appointment, thereby restoring it to its original function. It ceases to apply to rights over property such as options, rights of pre-emption and future easements. The rule will no longer apply to occupational pension schemes, personal pension schemes and public service pension schemes. (Sections 2(4), 20(4).)
- There is a single perpetuity period of 125 years and the principle of 'wait and see' applies to this period (which will apply regardless of any express provision to the contrary).

The good news is that all new trusts are subject to the simple 125-year period specified in the Act. The bad news is that for the time being we have three rules of remoteness of vesting running concurrently (common law, 1964 Act and 2009 Act).

According to s 12 of the Act, the trustees of *any trust created at any time* can execute an irrevocable deed to adopt a perpetuity period of 100 years if the trust specifies a perpetuity period by reference to lives in being and if the trustees express (in their deed) their belief 'that it is difficult or not reasonably practicable for them to ascertain whether the lives have ended'. Apart from trusts falling within s 12, the 2009 Act applies to all trusts taking effect on or after

6 April 2010, but not to any trusts effective before that date. Pre-2010 trusts not falling within s 12 of the 2009 are therefore still subject to the old law, under which there are essentially three different ways of calculating the perpetuity period applicable to a disposition:

- a special perpetuity period (up to a maximum of 80 years) can generally be expressly provided in the instrument by which the disposition was made (Perpetuities and Accumulations Act 1964, s 1(1));

- if no period has been specified in the instrument, the common law rules provide that the perpetuity period ends 21 years after the death of all 'lives in being' (see 6.3.1);

- the Perpetuities and Accumulations Act 1964 provides that the perpetuity period ends 21 years after the death of all the *statutory* lives in being (a list of these persons is provided in the statute).

Unless an express period is specified under s 1(1), a disposition can be valid under the 1964 Act *only* if it has already been shown to be void under the common law rules. This is most inconvenient, not least because (as we shall shortly see) the 1964 Act is far more generous in recognising the validity of dispositions than are the common law rules. To understand the context of the 2009 Act and to understand trusts not covered by the 2009 Act, it is necessary to outline the previous law.

6.2.1 **The common law rule**

The common law rule against remoteness of vesting provides that where an interest is disposed of in favour of X subject to a 'contingency' (a requirement which may or may not be met) it will be void for perpetuity from the date of the disposition unless the contingency will certainly be met (thus vesting the interest in the grantee)—if it is met at all—within the **perpetuity period**. Examples of such contingent gifts would include: 'to X upon his attaining a university degree'; to 'X upon his reaching the age of 25'; and 'to my grandchildren', where there are no grandchildren living at the effective date of the gift. The following definitions need to be noted:

> **perpetuity period**
> For the purpose of this rule this is the period ending 21 years after the death of all 'lives in being'.

If there are no **lives in being** at **the effective date of the disposition**, the perpetuity period will be a straightforward 21 years commencing at that effective date of the disposition. To summarise: 'no interest is good unless it must vest, if at all, not later than twenty-one years after some life in being at the creation of the interest' (J. Gray, *The Rule against Perpetuities*, 4th edn, Boston, 1915, para. 201). It is important to note that the rule is not that the interest must vest within the perpetuity period, but that it must vest within the perpetuity period *if it vests at all*. The whole nature of a contingent interest is that it might never vest!

---

lives in being Persons alive at the 'effective date' of the grant, or persons in their mother's womb at that time who are later born (see Re Wilmer's Trusts [1903] 2 Ch 411). However, for the purpose of the rule against remoteness of vesting 'lives in being' include only 'relevant' or 'measuring' lives in being. These descriptions usually correspond to those persons who are expressly or impliedly referred to in the instrument by which the disposition is effected. Thus the lives in being at the date of execution of an *inter vivos* gift to 'such of my grandchildren as qualify as lawyers' include not only the grandchildren, but also the settlor and any of his children who are then alive. The grandchildren were expressly referred to; the reference to the settlor and his children is implicit.

the 'effective date' of a disposition This varies according to whether the disposition was made *inter vivos* or by will. An *inter vivos* deed of gift or trust is effective at the date of its execution. A testamentary gift or trust is effective not at the date of execution of the will, but at the date of the testator's/testatrix's death.

6.2.1.1 **The lack of common sense in the common law rule**

At common law the rule has always been strictly applied, with the result that a gift will be declared void for perpetuity if there is the merest possibility that it might vest outside the perpetuity period, no matter how improbable the likelihood of it so doing. The common law rule against remoteness of vesting is said to be concerned with possibilities, not probabilities. The case of *Re Dawson* is a remarkable illustration of the lack of common sense in the common law rule.

Q CASE CLOSE-UP

Re Dawson (1888) 39 ChD 155

Facts: the testator, Dawson, left all his estate to trustees upon trust to pay an annuity to his daughter, M, for her life, directing that after his daughter's death the trustees should hold the estate for those of her children, and thereafter for those of her grandchildren, who should attain the age of 21 or (in the case of females) should marry under that age. The lives in being at the effective date of the gift (i.e. the date of Dawson's death) were M, who was then over 60 years of age, M's son and M's five daughters. There was a possibility, albeit extremely remote, that M would produce more children in the future (who would not, of course, have been 'lives in being' at Dawson's death). It followed that there was also a remote possibility that such later-born children of M might produce grandchildren of M outside the perpetuity period. It followed from this that there was also a remote possibility that certain of M's grandchildren would not satisfy the contingency until after the perpetuity period. In short, there was a remote possibility that the gift would vest outside the perpetuity period. (The perpetuity period was 21 years after the death of the last survivor of the lives in being.)

Held: on a strict application of the common law rules, the disposition was void on the basis that it *might* not vest until too remote a time. Evidence purporting to show that at Dawson's death M had passed the age of childbearing and was, as a result, highly unlikely to produce any further children was held to be inadmissible.

6.2.2 **Class gifts**

> **class** Persons who 'come within a certain category or description defined by a general or collective formula, and who, if they take at all, are to take one divisible subject in certain proportionate shares' (per Lord Selborne LC, Pearkes v Mosely (1880) 5 App Cas 714 at 723).

Gifts and trusts are often made to a **class**. An example would be a gift or trust 'to *all* my nephews who reach the age of 25'. The basic common law position is that the gift or trust will be void unless all potential members of the class *must* satisfy the contingency within the perpetuity period. Thus if (taking the example given at the beginning of this section and assuming that the gift has become effective today) there are three nephews in being and a fourth nephew is born a year from now, none of the nephews will take under the gift. The lives in being *might* all die tomorrow, in which event the fourth nephew will not reach 25 within the remaining 21 years of the perpetuity period.

The rule in *Andrews v Partington* (1791) 3 Bro CC 401 was created to address the clear hardship of the basic common law treatment of class gifts. The rule allows a member of the class to take his share if he has already satisfied the contingency at the effective date of the gift. The first beneficiary to meet the contingency will be given his share at that time. The size of this share is worked out by closing the class of potential beneficiaries to include all persons answering the class description (e.g. 'nephew') at the date when the first member of the class satisfies the contingency (e.g. reaches 25), and by effecting an equal division of the fund between the members of the closed class. Any persons answering the class description who are born after the class has been closed, and any persons who cannot possibly meet the contingency within the perpetuity period (e.g. because they cannot reach the age of 25 in time) will be excluded from taking any part of the fund.

THINKING POINT

Paragraph 5.26 of the Law Commission's Report No 251 observes that 'the class closing rules are rules of construction only and can be displaced by a sufficient expression of contrary intention, though this must be express'.

CASE CLOSE-UP

Re Clifford's Settlement Trusts [1981] 1 Ch 63

Facts: Clifford made an *inter vivos* settlement of a fund on trustees for the benefit of his son's children 'born in Clifford's lifetime or after his death who before the expiration of the period of 21 years from the death of the survivor of Clifford and the said son shall attain the age of 25 years and the other children of the said son living at the expiration of such period'. At the date of the settlement Clifford's son was 32 and had two children of his own (2½ years old and 2½ months old, respectively). At the date of the hearing of this case those two children had attained 25. However, since Clifford's death the son had fathered another two children who had not yet attained 25. (See Figure 6.1.) The question arising for consideration was whether A and B had each become entitled to a quarter share of the fund when they attained 25 or whether the whole class gift was void for perpetuity because further grandchildren (E, F, G, etc.) might be born who might not reach 25 until some time beyond the perpetuity period prescribed by the clause (i.e. 21 years after the death of Clifford's son).

Held: the rule in *Andrews v Partington* applied to save the gift of a quarter of the fund to A and B. C and D would also be entitled to a quarter share upon satisfying the contingency because they were alive when the eldest grandchild reached 25, and therefore came within the closed class. Any later born members of the class (E, F, G, etc.) would be excluded from the gift:

> Sir Robert Megarry V-C: 'it is well established that the rule [in *Andrews v Partington*] arises from an attempt by the court to reconcile two seemingly inconsistent directions of a settlor or testator. One is that the whole class of the children should be able to take, whenever born. The other is that a child who has reached the requisite age or satisfied the requisite condition should be able to take his share forthwith, without being forced to wait to see whether other children will be born whose claims may diminish the size of the shares to be taken.'

Figure 6.1 *Re Clifford's ST* [1981]

6.2.3 Age reducing provisions

Law of Property Act 1925, s 163 still applies in relation to gifts taking effect on or before 15 July 1964. That section provides that where the disposition of an interest is rendered wholly or partially void for remoteness because the vesting of the interest was made contingent upon the attainment of an age exceeding 21, that age requirement can be removed and replaced by a contingent age of 21, thus rendering the gift valid for perpetuity.

6.2.4 Summative chart on the common law rule of remoteness of vesting

Consider the summative chart set out in Figure 6.2.

6.2.5 The Perpetuities and Accumulations Act 1964

The 1964 Act has the effect of saving a number of gifts which would otherwise have been void for perpetuity under the strict common law rules. It applies only to gifts coming into effect after 15 July 1964. Unfortunately, the common law rules must be applied first, and only if a gift is void for perpetuity at common law will it be permissible to apply the more generous provisions of the Act. If the gift is valid at common law the gift will be subject to the common law rules, and not to the rules under the Act.

6.2.5.1 Express perpetuity period

A notable exception to the awkward 'double jurisdiction', whereby the common law rules must be applied before the 1964 Act, is the statutory perpetuity period contained in s 1 of the Act. Where a statutory period is specified in an instrument the common law perpetuity period will have no application. Section 1 provides that '[w]here the instrument by which any disposition is made so provides, the perpetuity period . . . shall be of a duration equal to such number of years not exceeding 80 as is specified . . . in the instrument'.

6.2.5.2 Fertility presumptions

We have seen that the common law rule is concerned with possibilities, not probabilities. This approach has thrown up some odd decisions. See *Re Dawson* (6.2.1.1).

Figure 6.2 Common law rule of remoteness of vesting

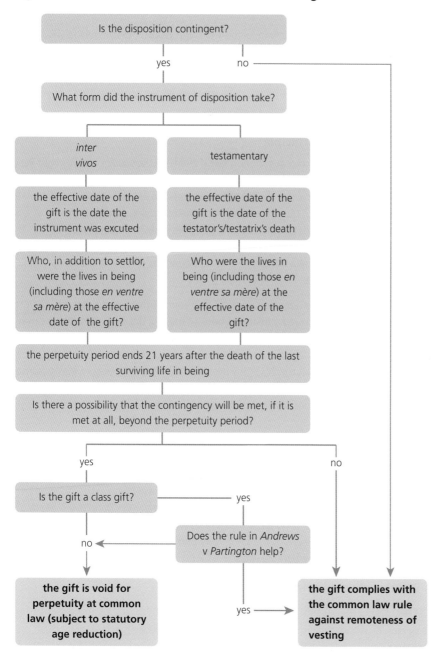

The 1964 Act has brought some common sense to this area. In relation to fertility, the Act raises a number of presumptions that can only be rebutted by clear contrary evidence. In other words, the Act is in this area concerned with probabilities, not remote possibilities.

Section 2(1)(a) of the Act provides that where a question of perpetuity turns on the ability of a person to have a child at some future time, then it shall be presumed that a male can have a child at the age of 14 years or over, but not under that age, and that a female can have a child at the age of 12 years or over, but not under that age or over the age of 55. Section 2(1)(b) adds that in the case of a living person evidence may be given to show that he or she will or will not be able to have a child at the time in question.

These provisions (except s 2(1)(b)) apply in relation to the possibility that a person will at any time have a child by adoption, legitimation or other means (s 2(4)).

It is important to note, especially in the light of scientific 'advances', that the fertility *presumptions* in the Act are just that. They are merely presumptions and may be rebutted by evidence to the contrary.

6.2.5.3 The 'wait and see' principle

Whereas a gift is automatically void at common law if there is a *possibility* that it might vest outside the perpetuity period, the Act treats the gift as valid until such time as it is clear that there is *no possibility* of it vesting within the perpetuity period. The Act will not save a gift where it is known that at the very end of the perpetuity period the contingency will not be met (if it is ever met at all) until some later date. However, the Act does allow the court, trustees, etc. to 'wait and see' whether or not the gift can vest within the perpetuity period. In most cases it vastly decreases the likelihood that a gift will be void for perpetuity. The 'wait and see' principle is enshrined within s 3 of the Act.

Section 3(1) provides that where a disposition would be void on the ground that the interest disposed of might not become vested until too remote a time, the disposition shall be treated, until such time as it becomes established that the vesting must occur (if it is to occur at all) after the end of the perpetuity period, as if the disposition were not subject to the common law rule against remoteness of vesting. Section 3(1) provides that dispositions by way of maintenance (see 13.1) and advancement (see 13.2) during the 'wait and see' period will be valid even if the interests of the beneficiaries do not vest within the perpetuity period.

6.2.5.4 Calculating the 'wait and see' period

Section 3(4) of the 1964 Act provides that where the 'wait and see' principle applies, and where the duration of the perpetuity period has not been expressed (see 6.3), the perpetuity period shall end 21 years after the death of the last surviving statutory life in being, unless the number of statutory lives is so large as to render it impracticable to ascertain the date of the death of the survivor. The statutory lives in being are those persons listed in s 3(5) who are 'in being and ascertainable at the commencement of the perpetuity period'. Where there are no statutory lives in being the period shall be a bare 21 years.

6.2.5.5 Statutory lives in being

The persons listed in s 3(5) as statutory lives in being are as follows:

- the person by whom the disposition was made, i.e. the settlor of an *inter vivos* trust;
- in the case of a disposition to a class of persons, any member or potential member of the class, and their parents and grandparents;
- in the case of an individual disposition to a person taking only on certain conditions being satisfied, any person who may in time satisfy all the conditions, and his parents and grandparents;
- in the case of a special power of appointment in favour of a class, any member or potential member of the class;
- any person on the failure or determination of whose prior interest the disposition is limited to take effect.

In each of the following tables a testamentary disposition is listed in the left-hand column and descriptions of certain people in the right-hand column. Tick the people who are 'lives in being' for the purpose of applying the rule against remoteness of vesting to the disposition in question.

Table 6.1 Statutory lives in being

To Mandy's first daughter to qualify as a doctor	Mandy
	All of Mandy's daughters alive at the date of the testator's death
	The father (or fathers) of every one of Mandy's daughters alive at the date of the testator's death
	The grandparents of every one of Mandy's daughters alive at the date of the testator's death
	The testator

Table 6.2 Statutory lives in being

To Laura for life, remainder to such of my grandchildren as attain the age of 30	The testator's grandchildren alive at his death (potential donees), their surviving parents and grandparents and Laura
	The testator's grandchildren in their mother's womb at his death, who are later born
	The father (or fathers) of everyone of Mandy's daughters alive at the date of the testator's death
	The parents of any of the testator's grandchildren alive at the testator's death or in their mother's womb at his death, who are later born
	The testator

In both cases the only person who should have no tick against them is the testator himself.

6.2.5.6 The class closing provisions

We have noted that the harshness of the common law rule in relation to class gifts is mitigated to some extent by the rule in *Andrews* v *Partington* (see 6.2.2). However, the effect of applying that rule is nevertheless to close the class so as to exclude any persons born after the class has closed, even though such persons might actually go on to satisfy the contingency within the perpetuity period.

The class closing provisions under the 1964 Act are more generous inasmuch as they operate in combination with the 'wait and see' principle. Section 4(4) provides that only such persons as will certainly fail to satisfy the contingency within the perpetuity period will be excluded. The trustees are accordingly permitted to wait until the end of the perpetuity period to see which members of the class have by that time satisfied the contingency. If one or more members of the class have failed to satisfy the contingency by the end of the perpetuity period, the class will be closed to exclude those members.

6.2.5.7 The age reducing provisions

We noted earlier that s 163 of the Law of Property Act 1925 operates to mitigate the harshness of the common law rule against remoteness of vesting in relation to gifts contingent upon achieving an age above 21 (see 6.2.3). The effect of s 163 is to replace the contingent age (e.g. 30) with the age of 21, if that will save the gift from remoteness. The effect of s 4 of the 1964 Act is similar, but rather more flexible. It also reduces the contingent ages specified in gifts, but only reduces the age to whatever extent is necessary in order to save the gift. Like s 163, the 1964 Act will not reduce an age to one below 21, but unlike s 163, the 1964 Act does not automatically reduce the age to 21. This is because the age reduction provisions in the 1964 Act operate in combination with the 'wait and see' principle. The trustees will be permitted to wait until the end of the perpetuity period and if at that time the potential beneficiary has not yet reached the contingent age, it is permissible to reduce the age requirement to whatever extent is necessary (but not below the age of 21) to save the gift.

6.3 The rule against excessive accumulation of income

> **accumulation of income** Instead of being spent or otherwise applied, trust income is sometimes retained by the trustees and accumulated. Accumulation of income is not the mere retention of income for administrative purposes. It is the process of adding income to capital. As Harman LJ put it in *Re the Earl of Berkeley* [1968] Ch 744 at 772: 'Accumulation to my mind involves the addition of income to capital, thus increasing the estate in favour of those entitled to capital and against the interests of those entitled to income.'

 OUTSIDE THE BOX

Douglas Adams, *The Hitchhiker's Guide to the Galaxy* (London: Pan Macmillan 1979)

The Restaurant at the End of the Universe is one of the most extraordinary ventures in the entire history of catering . . . All you have to do is deposit one penny in a savings account in your own era, and when you arrive at the End of Time the operation of compound interest means that the fabulous cost of your meal has been paid for. This, many claim, is not merely impossible but clearly insane, which is why the advertising executives of the star system of Bastablon came up with this slogan: 'If you've done six impossible things this morning, why not round it off with breakfast at Milliways, the Restaurant at the End of the Universe?'

Income cannot be accumulated for too long a period of time, and the reason for this is the fear that individuals might become disproportionately wealthy and by that means become a threat to the nation state. The rule has a colourful history, traceable back to the case of *Thellusson v Woodford*.

> **Q | CASE CLOSE-UP**
>
> **Thellusson v Woodford (1798) 4 Ves Jun 227**
>
> Facts: Thellusson had the bright idea of directing his trustees to accumulate income on a fund for the lives of all his sons, grandsons and great-grandsons living at the time of his death. On the death of the last survivor, the fund was directed to be divided between the three eldest male living descendants of his three sons. If there were no such descendants, the property was to pass to the Crown. In the event, the accumulation lasted for 70 years, but it could conceivably have gone on even longer.
>
> Held: Thellusson's direction was perfectly valid as the law then stood, and the House of Lords upheld it. Indeed, Lord Eldon pointed out that the accumulated capital was not being removed from circulation entirely, but merely locked away in land for a while. The land itself could, of course, be sold.

There was an outcry against Thellusson's will. A contemporary magazine suggested that if the accumulation continued for 120 years the fund would reach £140 million. Counsel for Thellusson's widow described the will as 'morally vicious . . . politically injurious . . . and by the time, when the accumulation shall end, it will have created a fund, the revenue of which will be greater than the civil list; and will therefore give its possessor the means of disturbing the whole economy of the country': (1805) 11 Ves 112 at 114. The resulting panic led to the enactment of the Accumulations Act 1800, or the so-called Thellusson Act (see P. Polden, 'Panic or Prudence? The Thellusson Act 1800 and Trusts for Accumulation' (1994) 45 NILQ 13). This Act was eventually repealed and replaced by s 164 of the Law of Property Act 1925.

6.3.1 **The modern rule**

As a result of s 13 of the Perpetuities and Accumulations Act 2009, there is no restriction on accumulations under non-charitable trusts created on or after 6 April 2010, which was the commencement date of the Act. (According to s 14 of the 2009 Act, charitable trusts remain a special case.) Statutory restrictions will, however, still apply to trusts taking effect before the commencement date of the 2009 Act, and so at the time of writing ss 164–5 of the Law of Property Act 1925 still apply to most trusts. According to s 164, Law of Property Act 1925, no person may settle or dispose of any property in such manner that the income thereof shall be accumulated for any longer period than one of the following:

- the life of the grantor or settlor;
- a term of 21 years from the death of the grantor, settlor or testator;
- the duration of the minority or respective minorities of any person or persons living or *en ventre sa mère* (in their mother's womb) at the death of the grantor, settlor or testator;
- the duration of the minority or respective minorities only of any person or persons who under the limitations of the instrument directing the accumulations would, for the time being, if of full age, be entitled to the income directed to be accumulated;
- added by the 1964 Act, s 13, and applicable to directions made after 15 July 1964: the period of 21 years from the date of making the disposition;
- added by the 1964 Act, s 13, and applicable to directions made after 15 July 1964: the duration of the minority or minorities of any person in being at the date of making an *inter vivos* disposition.

Any other directions to accumulate (except those within s 165, next) shall be void and the income on the property directed to be accumulated shall go to the person or persons who would have been entitled to it if the direction to accumulate had not been made.

6.3.2 **An exception to the modern rule on accumulations**

Section 165 of the Law of Property Act 1925 provides that where accumulations of surplus income are made during a *minority* under any statutory power or under the general law (see 13.1.2), the period for which such accumulations are made is not to be taken into account in determining the periods for which accumulations are permitted to be made by s 164. Therefore, according to s 165, an express trust for accumulation for any period not listed in s 164 shall not be void by reason only of accumulations having been made during a minority.

This is the major exception to s 164. There are also, if you will excuse the pun, certain *minor* exceptions such as accumulations to pay debts, to produce timber, and so on; consideration of these is left to more specialist texts.

6.4 The rule against inalienability of capital

A gift or trust will be void for perpetuity if it has the effect of rendering capital inalienable, i.e. indisposable, for a period longer than the perpetuity period. The perpetuity period here is the same as the common law period used in the rule against remoteness of vesting. However, whereas the rule against remoteness of vesting is concerned to prevent gifts from vesting in persons at too remote a time in the future, the rule against inalienability of capital is concerned to prevent trusts for non-charitable purposes from enduring until too remote a time into the future. It is important to note that the Perpetuities and Accumulations Act 1964 does not affect this rule (s 15(4)). When the Law Commission proposed the 2009 Act (discussed earlier) it did not propose any reform of the rule against inalienability of capital, preferring that reform of that rule should take place as part of a more comprehensive reform of the law relating to purpose trusts.

> **CROSS REFERENCE**
>
> The rule against inalienability of capital is considered further in Chapter 7.

This rule is most often invoked where property is given to a club or other unincorporated association subject to conditions, whether imposed by the terms of the gift or the rules of the club, which restrict its use to certain *purposes* and prevent it from being applied for the benefit of *legal persons* until too remote a time. An example would be a gift of £10,000 'to the Warwickshire Tennis Club to be used to replace the present clubhouse when it falls down'.

6.5 The rules against perpetuity and charities

The rule against remoteness of vesting applies to charities inasmuch as it requires that a disposition must vest in charity within the perpetuity period. However, once property has been devoted to charitable purposes, a gift over to another charity will be valid even if the gift over vests after the end of the perpetuity period. The rule against inalienability of capital has no application to capital that has been devoted to exclusively charitable purposes.

The leading case is the decision of the Court of Appeal in *Re Tyler* [1891] 3 Ch 252, a case which reads every bit like the backdrop to one of Sir Arthur Conan Doyle's adventures of Sherlock Holmes. The testator gave a fund to the trustees of the London Missionary Society and directed them to keep his family vault at Highgate Cemetery 'in good repair, and name legible, and to rebuild when it shall require'. If the trustees failed to comply with his request the monies were directed to pass to another charity, namely the Bluecoat School, Newgate Street, London. It was held that the condition for the maintenance and repair of the vault was valid and binding on the first charity; further, that the gift over to the second charity on failure to comply with the condition was good. It was held that the rule against perpetuities has no application to a transfer, on a certain event, of property from one charity to another.

The judgment refers generically to the 'rules against perpetuities' and does not distinguish one rule from another. Nevertheless, the gift to the London Missionary Society, *had the society been non-charitable*, would have been void for inalienability of capital, because the gift was by way of perpetual endowment (as is shown by the fact that the gift was determinable upon disrepair of the family tomb). In addition, the gift over to the Bluecoat School would have been void for remoteness of vesting. If you visit the grave of Karl Marx in Highgate Cemetery why not see if the inscription on the Tyler family tomb is still legible? The Bluecoat School in Newgate Street may be very interested to hear that you cannot read the name Tyler on any tomb in the cemetery!

Finally, it is worth noting that the rule against excessive accumulations applies to charities, but that charities appear to avoid the restrictions of the statutory rule by making extensive use of the administrative power that every trustee has to retain income on a temporary basis when it is in surfeit, in order to cover needs arising at leaner times. This is so-called 'administrative retention' (see *Re Earl of Berkeley* [1968] Ch 744).

6.6 Trusts created to prejudice the settlor's creditors are void

As we saw in the introduction to this chapter (when we considered the business to promote the game of 'streams and ladders'), it is illegal for a settlor to create a trust to protect himself from his own creditors. The leading case is the decision of the Court of Appeal in *Re Butterworth* (1882) 19 ChD 588, although the principle has since been enshrined in statute.

Q CASE CLOSE-UP

Re Butterworth (1882) 19 ChD 588

Facts: Butterworth (a baker) made a voluntary settlement of his assets in favour of his wife and children before embarking upon additional business as a grocer. ('Voluntary' means here that he received no legal consideration in return for making the settlement.) He continued in trade as a grocer for some years and then sold up. Shortly afterwards his bakery business became insolvent, his liabilities far exceeding his assets.

Held: the settlement was void as against the trustee in the liquidation (and therefore void against the creditors of Butterworth's bakery business). The settlement had clearly been executed with the intention of putting the settlor's property out of the reach of his creditors.

Sir George Jessel MR: 'the principle of *Mackay* v *Douglas* LR 14 Eq 106, and that line of cases, is this, that a man is not entitled to go into a hazardous business, and immediately before doing so settle all his property voluntarily, the object being this: "If I succeed in business, I make a fortune for myself. If I fail, I leave my creditors unpaid. They will bear the loss." That is the very thing which the statute of Elizabeth was meant to prevent. The object of the settlor was to put his property out of the reach of his future creditors. He contemplated engaging in this new trade and he wanted to preserve his property from his future creditors. That cannot be done by a voluntary settlement. That is, to my mind, a clear and satisfactory principle.

Now, as I understand the evidence in this case, the baker did very well as a baker, and probably he may not have recollected the old proverb *ne sutor ultra crepidam*. When he went into business as a grocer he was going into a business which it appears he did not understand, and it is obvious that the object was—(I am taking that as a fair inference)—to save his property for his wife and children in case the new business did not succeed. Well, that actually happened. The new business did not succeed; he lost money by it, and it probably brought him to bankruptcy.

His object was, as I have said, to make himself safe against that eventuality, and, if that was his object, then I think the principle of *Mackay* v *Douglas* applies, and that the deed was void also under the statute of Elizabeth. But, as I have said before, it is not really necessary to decide this point, because I am clearly of opinion that the deed is void under the 91st section of the Bankruptcy Act.'

THINKING POINT

Do commercial asset protection trusts offend the principle laid down by Sir George Jessel MR in *Re Butterworth*? Look back to 2.3.4 and 4.2.3, where we considered asset production trusts in detail.

A settlor is permitted to create a trust which will protect another person from the settlor's creditors. Far from being contrary to public policy, many of the commercial asset protection trusts considered in 2.3.4 were created for positively good reasons. The trust in *Re EVTR* was created for the purpose of sustaining failing companies, and the trust in *Barclays Bank* v *Quistclose* was upheld with the policy of protecting failing companies in mind. The trust in *Re Kayford Ltd (in liquidation)* [1975] 1 WLR 279 advanced the public interest in protecting mail order consumers.

A settlor is also permitted to create a protective trust to protect another person from that person's creditors (for 'protective trusts', see 2.3.2).

Although a trust set up to the prejudice of the *settlor's* own creditors will generally be void on public policy grounds, a trust set up to protect another person from *their* creditors will be valid if it complies with the statutory form of 'protective trust' (see 2.3.2). Protective trusts will often defeat the interests of the spendthrift's creditors, but that to some extent is also the purpose of the insolvency legislation itself. The statutory scheme for distribution of the insolvent person's estate is designed to satisfy the creditors as far as is reasonably possible but the statutory insolvency scheme is also designed to discharge the liabilities of the insolvent person so as to enable them to make a fresh start in due course.

The principle in *Re Butterworth* is now enshrined in s 423 of the Insolvency Act 1986. Under s 423(3)(a) the 'purpose' of the transaction is all important; thus in *Rubin v Dweck* [2012] BPIR 854 the transfer of the matrimonial home by a husband to his wife did not defraud his creditors where the facts showed that he intended the transaction to persuade his wife not to divorce him.

 STATUTE

Insolvency Act 1986

Section 423. Transactions defrauding creditors

(1) This section relates to transactions entered into at an undervalue, and a person enters into such a transaction with another person if—

    (a) he makes a gift to the other person or he otherwise enters into a transaction with the other on terms that provide for him to receive no consideration;

    (b) he enters into a transaction with the other in consideration of marriage; or

    (c) he enters into a transaction with the other for a consideration the value of which, in money or money's worth, is significantly less than the value, in money or money's worth, of the consideration provided by himself.

(2) Where a person has entered into such a transaction, the court may, if satisfied under the next subsection, make such order as it thinks fit for—

    (a) restoring the position to what it would have been if the transaction had not been entered into; and

    (b) protecting the interests of persons who are victims of the transaction.

(3) In the case of a person entering into such a transaction, an order shall only be made if the court is satisfied that it was entered into by him for the purpose—

    (a) of putting assets beyond the reach of a person who is making, or may at some time make, a claim against him; or

    (b) of otherwise prejudicing the interests of such a person in relation to the claim which he is making or may make.

(4) In this section 'the court' means the High Court or—

    (a) if the person entering into the transaction is an individual, any other court which would have jurisdiction in relation to a bankruptcy petition relating to him;

    (b) if that person is a body capable of being wound up . . . any other court having jurisdiction to wind it up.

(5) In relation to a transaction at an undervalue, references here and below to a victim of the transaction are to a person who is, or is capable of being, prejudiced by it; and in the following two sections the person entering into the transaction is referred to as 'the debtor'.

6.7 Gifts subject to conditions

If a trust required a beneficiary to rob a bank as a condition of receiving an interest in the fund, the trust would clearly fail on grounds of public policy. As the Law Commission has said: 'A condition in a trust inciting a beneficiary to do any act prohibited by law is void' ('Illegal Transactions: The Effect of Illegality on Contracts and Trusts', Law Commission Consultation Paper No 154, para. 3.1).

The position is less clear where the condition does not incite an illegal act, but merely relates to the nature of the beneficiary. It has never been doubted that a person can set up a trust in favour of whomsoever they wish. A trust for 'my daughters' is by its very nature discriminatory if the settlor has sons, but it does not fail for that reason. A trust for 'my black employees' is also discriminatory (assuming that the settlor has some non-black employees) but should it fail for this reason? Could this be an acceptable private choice as opposed to an unacceptable public discrimination? Racially discriminatory words constitute an offence under the Race Relations Act 1976 if they operate in the public sphere, e.g. if they are used in a job advertisement or such like, but the Act does not prohibit racial discrimination in purely private contexts.

Speaking with reference to a condition in a will trust, Lord Wilberforce once opined that '[d]iscrimination is not the same thing as choice: it operates over a larger and less personal area, and neither by express provision nor by implication has private selection yet become a matter of public policy' (*Blathwayt* v *Baron Cawley* [1976] AC 397, House of Lords). His Lordship was suggesting that the creation of a trust is a private matter (there is indeed no requirement to enter trusts on a public register or such like), so in theory a trust containing a discriminatory provision is not void per se, no matter how offensive. This is a fine sentiment (or a fine lack of sentiment) but even if certain discriminatory trusts are not void from the outset, it is nevertheless very difficult to imagine that a court would enforce a discriminatory trust or require the trustees to carry it out. It is quite likely that as a result of the Human Rights Act 1998 the court now has no power to enforce discriminatory clauses, but the point has yet to be judicially determined. It may be that discriminatory provisions in private trusts should be regarded as provisions that are valid if the trustees are willing to carry them out, but cannot be enforced against the wishes of the trustee.

6.7.1 Conditions as to marriage

▶ CROSS REFERENCE

Examples such as these should now be reassessed in the light of the Human Rights Act 1998.

According to Lord Mansfield, 'conditions in restraint of marriage are odious' (*Long* v *Dennis* (1767) 4 Burr 2052 at 2059). Despite this sentiment, a condition will not be void which restrains the *remarriage* of a beneficiary (*Jordan* v *Holkham* (1753) Amb 209), although, consistent with this, clauses which might encourage divorce or separation of husband and wife will be void. In *Re Johnson's WT* [1967] Ch 387 a clause was declared void which provided that the beneficiary would receive more income from the fund if she split up from her husband. The testator's intention had been to make greater provision in the event of such a breakdown of the marriage, it had not been his intention to promote divorce. The judge held nevertheless that the clause might operate as an incentive to divorce or separation, and that it must therefore be declared void. Nowadays it is quite likely that a clause operating to encourage the break-up of registered civil partnerships would suffer the same fate.

Despite the fact that conditions are void which operate in restraint of marriage *generally*, conditions which restrain marriage to *specific* individuals or classes of person will be legally valid.

Reported instances include conditions restraining marriage to a 'Papist' (*Duggan* v *Kelly* (1848) 10 I Eq R 473) and to a 'Scotchman' (*Perrin* v *Lyon* (1807) 9 East 170).

CASE CLOSE-UP

Blathwayt v Baron Cawley [1976] AC 397, House of Lords

Facts: a large estate (valued in 1975 at £2 million) was left in 1936 on various trusts, but such that any person who became entitled was to forfeit his interest if he should 'be or become a Roman Catholic' (or ceased to use the name and arms of Blathwayt). It was argued that with respect to the present children, the religious condition tended to restrain the carrying out of parental duties, and was therefore void on public policy grounds. It later transpired that a life tenant had indeed become a Roman Catholic. The judge at first instance held that his estate should be forfeit.

Held: the judgment of the judge at first instance was upheld by a 3:2 majority. The effect of the clause may have been to force the parents to choose between material and spiritual welfare for their offspring, but that this was not necessarily contrary to public policy. (Lords Wilberforce and Fraser of Tullybelton dissenting on the construction of the clause.)

Lord Wilberforce: 'finally, as to public policy. The argument under this heading was put in two alternative ways. First, it was said that the law of England was now set against discrimination on a number of grounds including religious grounds, and appeal was made to the Race Relations Act 1968 which does not refer to religion and to the European Convention on Human Rights of 1950 which refers to freedom of religion and to enjoyment of that freedom and other freedoms without discrimination on ground of religion. My Lords. I do not doubt that conceptions of public policy should move with the times and that widely accepted treaties and statutes may point the direction in which such conceptions, as applied by the courts, ought to move. It may well be that conditions such as this are, or at least are becoming, inconsistent with standards now widely accepted. But acceptance of this does not persuade me that we are justified, particularly in relation to a will which came into effect as long ago as 1936 and which has twice been the subject of judicial consideration, in introducing for the first time a rule of law which would go far beyond the mere avoidance of discrimination on religious grounds. To do so would bring about a substantial reduction of another freedom, firmly rooted in our law, namely that of testamentary disposition. Discrimination is not the same thing as choice: it operates over a larger and less personal area, and neither by express provision nor by implication has private selection yet become a matter of public policy.'

Lord Cross: 'it is true that it is widely thought nowadays that it is wrong for a government to treat some of its citizens less favourably than others because of differences in their religious beliefs; but it does not follow from that that it is against public policy for an adherent of one religion to distinguish in disposing of his property between adherents of his faith and those of another. So to hold would amount to saying that although it is in order for a man to have a mild preference for one religion as opposed to another it is disreputable for him to be convinced of the importance of holding true religious beliefs and of the fact that his religious beliefs are the true ones.'

6.8 Illegality and resulting trusts

The relationship between illegality and resulting trusts is very important, and is considered in depth in Chapter 16 (see 16.1.1.2).

6.9 Miscellaneous public policy restrictions

6.9.1 Use of the form of a trust to conceal true ownership is prohibited

The scope of this principle is debatable. It appears to be an application of the maxim that *equity looks to substance and not form*, yet that maxim would normally be applied in order to *recognise* the existence of a trust behind formal legal title. It is applied in this context, however, in order to *deny* the existence of a trust, where a *formal* trust has been used to conceal the true ownership position. As the judge stated in *Great Western Rly Co v Turner* (1872) 8 LR Ch App 149 at 154:

> There being no *bona fide* reason for the creation of any trust, the terms of the trust were gone through in order to conceal the true ownership of the property. That has been held to be in truth an abuse of the forms of trust for the purpose of creating a reputation of ownership, and placing the property within the order and disposition of another with the consent of the true owner of the property.

A blatant example of a so-called 'sham' trust appears from the facts of *Erlam v Rahman* [2016] EWHC 111. The husband's election as mayor of a London borough had been declared void for fraud and he was being pursued for the costs of the action that produced that declaration. To hide certain land from the claimants, his wife produced an unregistered form of declaration of trust which purported to show that she owned 74 per cent of the equitable interest in the land. The court dismissed this as a sham, holding that the declaration of trust had been 'prepared in order to be available, if needed'. The husband remained 100 per cent beneficial owner of the land.

Sometimes the parties genuinely intend to create a trust, so that it is not a sham as a such, but the court will nevertheless set it aside if the use of the trust form is 'illusory'. An express trust will fail as being illusory in its property aspect where there is no substantial split between legal and equitable ownership under the trust. A trust will also fail as being illusory in its obligation aspect where there is in substance no fiduciary obligation enforceable by the beneficiary against the trustee. The trust was set aside as being illusory in the New Zealand case *Harrison v Harrison* [2008] NZHC 2580, where a married couple put assets into a discretionary trust supervised by a trustee company that was controlled and removable by them. They also had power to appoint themselves as trustees, so that they could at will vest the trust assets in themselves absolutely. In *JSC Mezhdunarodniy Promyshlenniy Bank v Pugachev* [2017] EWHC 2426 (Ch), the High Court held that five discretionary trusts settled by 'Putin's banker' Sergei Pugachev (co-founder of the failed Russian bank Mezhprom Bank) were in fact bare trusts for his benefit. The judge did not find the language of 'sham' or 'illusory' trusts to be helpful, preferring to confine him-self to discovering 'The True Effect of the Trusts' (see also *Clayton v Clayton* [2016] NZSC 29, Supreme Court of New Zealand). In other words, the judge simply looked to substance instead of form. This is good news for claimants, because it is presumably easier to have an illusory trust set aside according to its effects than to have to overcome the additional hurdle of proving that the person or persons setting up the trusts intended a sham.

6.9.2 Fox hunting

It is interesting to speculate whether trusts for the purpose of fox hunting have also now joined the class of illegal trusts (see 7.2.3).

6.10 Consequences of failure

Where a trust fails *ab initio* for perpetuity or public policy reasons there will be a resulting trust to the settlor.

In the case of testamentary dispositions there will be a resulting trust to the residuary beneficiary of the testator's estate or to the deceased's next of kin in the event of intestacy. If there are no identifiable next of kin, the property will pass to the Crown as *bona vacantia*. However, the Perpetuities and Accumulations Act 1964, s 3(1) provides that if the trustees dispose of the trust property during the 'wait and see' period, by way of maintenance, advancement or otherwise, such dispositions will not be invalidated if it is later established that the interests of the benefi-ciaries to whom the dispositions were made cannot vest within the perpetuity period.

 Summary

- It is imperative to ensure that trust property returns within a reasonable time to the state of being owned absolutely. Thus:
  - a trust will be void (as infringing the rule against remoteness of vesting) if it postpones for too long a period the date at which the trust property will vest in ascertainable beneficiaries;
  - a trust will be void (as infringing the rule against inalienability of capital) if it requires capital to be tied up to provide an income for too long a period;
  - a trust will be void (as infringing the rule against accumulation of income) if it requires income to be accumulated for too long a period.
- We have seen that the rule against remoteness of vesting is very complicated. The common law rule must be applied first (see the summative chart on the common law rule of remoteness of vesting at 6.2.4). If a disposition infringes the common law rule (because there is a possibility, however unrealistic, that the gift might vest at too remote a time) it is then permitted (by the Perpetuities and Accumulations Act 1964) to wait until the end of the perpetuity period to allow the disposition the opportunity to vest in time.

- There is also the public policy against allowing the wishes of the dead donor to rule over the freedoms of the living donee. Nevertheless, donors still retain the power to choose the conditions on which they dispose of their property and, controversially, conditions which in a public context would be void for racism or sexism may be permitted (albeit unenforceable) if they are construed to be nothing more than expressions of private choice.

- It is not permitted to establish a trust to protect one's own wealth from one's creditors. It is, however, permitted to establish a trust to protect one's creditors from one's insolvency, and it is even permitted (by means of a protective trust) to protect another person from their creditors.

? Summative assessment exercise

Consider the validity of the following clauses in the will of X:

- clause one: 'I bequeath my stocks and shares to my trustees on trust for such of my grandchildren as shall attain the age of 30';

- clause two: 'To my son, Leonard, a life interest in the income earned from my country properties, to determine if the income of the fund becomes payable to another person. In the event of determination of the interest the income from the properties shall be held by my trustees on trust for such of my children and in such shares as my trustees shall in their absolute discretion think fit';

- clause three: 'In the event of any of the beneficiaries under this will marrying into Islam, the estate hereby limited to him or her shall cease and determine and be utterly void.'

Evidence has been produced to show that the testatrix was survived by a daughter aged 60, a son (Leonard) aged 50, a granddaughter aged 30 and two grandsons aged 25 and 23 respectively. The granddaughter wishes to convert to Islam in order to marry her Muslim boyfriend.

 Full specimen answers can be found at www.oxfordtextbooks.co.uk/orc/watt_directions5e/.

The bigger picture

As a matter of public policy, it is somewhat surprising that any State permits its citizens to create private trusts. The essence of a trust is that the apparent owner of trust property, the person with all the forms and powers of ownership, is not the true owner. A trust therefore creates an illusion in ownership that has the potential to prejudice trade creditors in the event of the trustee's insolvency and to deceive the State's tax collection agencies. In this chapter we have considered some safeguards that the law puts in place to reduce the adverse social effects of trust creation. So we have seen that there are rules in place to prohibit trusts which aim at such illegal outcomes as perpetuity, racial discrimination, restraint of marriage and the avoidance of statutory schemes governing the priorities of creditors' claims in insolvency. In Chapter 3 we also saw that formality requirements also assist by seeking to prevent fraud and the avoidance, or evasion, of tax. Still, we may not be surprised that some countries have decided that the Anglo-Saxon trust based on the division of property poses so great a danger to public policy that in their jurisdictions it should not be permitted to create trusts in that form at all. (See C. Raffenne, 'Why (Still) No Trust in French Law?' in A. Harding and E. Örücü (eds) *Comparative Law in the 21st Century* (London: Kluwer Law International, 2002), 75–100). More surprising, perhaps, is that several states of the USA have taken the liberalising step of removing the perpetuity rules so as to permit the creation of 'perpetual trusts' (see, for example, Max M. Schanzenbach and Robert H. Sitkoff, 'Perpetuities or Taxes? Explaining the Rise of the Perpetual Trust' (2006) 27 *Cardozo Law Review* 2465, 2472–81).

 ## Further reading

Grattan, S. 'Testamentary Conditions in Restraint of Religion' in E. Cooke (ed.), *Modern Studies in Property Law, Vol I: Property 2000* (2001) Oxford: Hart Publishing, 257–74

an excellent analysis of cases dealing with religious discrimination in trusts in Northern Ireland

Law Commission, 'The Law of Trusts: The Rules against Perpetuities and Excessive Accumulations', Report No 251 (1998)

contains a very clear summary of the existing law on remoteness of vesting and excessive accumulation of income

Law Commission, 'Illegal Transactions: The Effect of Illegality on Contracts and Trusts', Consultation Paper No 154 (1999)

contains a clear summary of the issues arising from the impact of illegality on trusts (note that as of March 2012 the government has declared that it intends not to adopt the Law Commission's proposed reforms)

Moss, C. 'A Sham Trust, and an Illusory Trust but Not in Those Terms; *Pugachev* Explained' (2018) 4 PCB 126–32

Examines *JSC Mezhdunarodniy Promyshlenniy Bank* v *Pugachev* [2017] EWHC 2426 (Ch), in which the High Court refused to recognise a form of trust which in substance had the effect of vesting absolute control in one person

Polden, P. 'Panic or Prudence? The Thellusson Act 1800 and Trusts for Accumulation' (1994) 45 Northern Ireland Law Quarterly 13

examines the panic arising from *Thellusson* v *Woodford*, which resulted in the Accumulations Act 1800

 For links to selected cases, statutes, academic papers and official reports mentioned in this chapter please visit the online resources at www.oup.com/uk/watt_directions6e/.

7 Purpose trusts

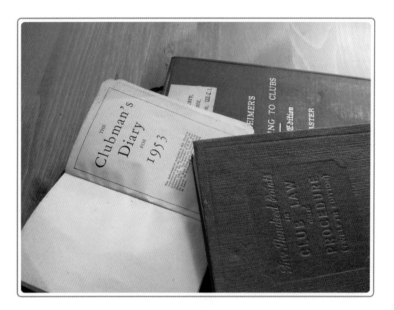

LEARNING OBJECTIVES

By the end of this chapter you should be able to:

- explain the reason why trusts for private purposes are generally void;
- list the anomalous exceptions to the general rule;
- employ the various devices for avoiding the prohibition against trusts for private purposes;
- elucidate the special problems raised by gifts to unincorporated associations;
- advise a donor as to the way in which they can achieve their intentions in making a gift to an unincorporated association.

Introduction

At the start of the previous chapter you invented a new board game called 'streams and ladders'. You now want to give £500 to your local golf club 'on trust' for the purpose of encouraging its members to play 'streams and ladders' in the club house. You hope to use their feedback to refine your game. It sounds like it should be the easiest thing in the world to create the trust, but a simple trust like this raises a number of problems. For one thing, the trust will be struck down from the outset if it is deemed to be capricious (this word is considered later—it means something along the lines of whimsical, quirky or foolish), and a trust to promote a board game in a golf club might well be considered capricious. If the trust overcomes this obstacle, it must still demonstrate that it is for the benefit of identifiable people—this is called the 'beneficiary principle'. The 'members of the golf club' will probably satisfy this requirement, but the court might conclude that the trust is not in fact beneficial to them. Or else the court might hold that the trust is for their benefit, but that it must fail for perpetuity because some future members might not benefit from the trust until, say, the year 2100. Worse still, the trust may be construed to be purely for a purpose, and not for a person at all, in which case the trust will fail unless the purpose is charitable. A trust to play 'streams and ladders' is unlikely to be considered beneficial to the public, and therefore it will not be charitable (see Chapter 8). It all looks quite bleak for our trust, but by the end of this chapter we will see that even where a trust cannot achieve the desired purpose, other legal devices might.

 THINKING POINT

We briefly encountered purpose trusts in earlier chapters. Can you remember where?

In Chapter 4 we observed that the object of an expressly created trust must be certain or capable of being rendered certain, and that the object of a trust can be a legal person (human or corporate), a public (i.e. charitable) purpose or a private purpose.

In this chapter we shall discover that trusts in the latter category, those for private purposes, are generally void. There are, however, a number of important exceptions to this general rule, where trusts for private purposes are valid—as, for instance, where the trust, though on one level expressed to be for a particular purpose (e.g. 'to build a swimming pool for my employees to swim in'), ought actually to be construed as a trust for particular persons (e.g. 'to build a swimming pool for my employees to swim in').

Where capital is tied up with a view to applying the income to certain non-charitable purposes, the rule against inalienability of capital naturally comes into play. A trust for private purposes often takes the form of a permanent endowment, thus potentially rendering the capital inalienable in perpetuity. A simple example of such a trust would be a trust 'to keep my collection of vintage cars intact and well maintained'. Although the income from the fund will be applied in carrying out the purpose of maintaining the collection, in order to ensure that income is always available it will be necessary to keep the capital subject to the trust obligations in perpetuity.

7.1 Trusts purely for private purposes

Trusts purely for private purposes are generally void because:

- being in nature 'private', a trust of this sort would not be subject to the *control* of the courts, nor of any department of State;

- following on from the preceding point, in order to bring the trust within the control of the court, there must always be someone in whose favour the court can decree performance, i.e. someone who will *enforce* the trust by, inter alia, bringing breaches of trust to the attention of the court. This is the so-called beneficiary principle (see *Leahy v A-G for New South Wales*, 7.4);

- trusts for private purposes must often be construed as perpetual endowments. Such endowments offend the rule against inalienability of capital (see 6.4);

- trusts for private purposes will fail the requirement of certainty of object if the purposes expressed are vague and indefinite, thus rendering them uncontrollable by the court. Roxburgh J made this point in *Re Astor* [1952] Ch 534, where he held that '[t]he purposes must be so defined that, if the trustees surrendered their discretion, the court could carry out the purposes declared, not a selection of them arrived at by eliminating those which are too uncertain to be carried out'. Note, however, that a purpose will only be *too* uncertain where the court cannot by a reasonable construction make it certain (*certum est quod certum reddi potest*—that is certain which can be rendered certain);

- trusts for private purposes will fail if they are capricious (see 7.2.1.3).

Whether or not there has been an attempt to create a trust purely for private purposes is a matter of construction.

 THINKING POINT

We noted earlier that a trust might be construed as being for a beneficiary, a charitable purpose or a private purpose. Into which category do you think a bequest to the Bishop of Durham for 'such objects of benevolence and liberality as the Bishop of Durham in his own discretion shall most approve' would fall?

> **CROSS REFERENCE**
>
> On the requirement that charities must be exclusively charitable, see 8.3.

This was the question for determination in the case of *Morice v Bishop of Durham* (1804) [1903–13] All ER Rep 451. Sir William Grant MR held that the words 'benevolence and liberality' were not charitable. Lord Eldon LC confirmed, on appeal, that those words could not be charitable because they were not exclusively so, with the result that the whole fund might be applied to non-charitable ends without there being a breach of the terms of the bequest.

Nor could the bequest be construed as a personal gift to the Bishop. The only other alternative would be to construe the bequest as a gift for purely private purposes, i.e. for 'objects of benevolence and liberality'. It was held that such objects were too ill defined to come under the court's control, and that the bequest for that reason failed. Accordingly, the Bishop took the bequest on a resulting trust for the residuary beneficiaries of the testatrix's estate.

Q | CASE CLOSE-UP

Re Astor [1952] Ch 534

Facts: non-charitable trusts were declared of substantially all the issued shares of 'The Observer Ltd' for purposes including the 'maintenance . . . of good understanding . . . between nations' and 'the preservation of the independence and integrity of newspapers'.

Held: the trusts were invalid because they were not for the benefit of individuals, but for a number of non-charitable purposes which no one could enforce. The trusts would, in any event, have been void for uncertainty.

Roxburgh J: 'The question on which I am giving this reserved judgment is whether the non-charitable trusts . . . are void. Counsel for the trustees of the 1951 settlement and for the Attorney-General have submitted that they are void on two grounds: (i) that they are not trusts for the benefit of individuals; (ii) that they are void for uncertainty. Lord Parker of Waddington dealt with [the second ground] in his speech in *Bowman* v *Secular Society Ltd* [1917] AC 406':

> A trust to be valid must be for the benefit of individuals, which this is certainly not, or must be in that class of gifts for the benefit of the public which the courts in this country recognise as charitable in the legal as opposed to the popular sense of that term . . . if the purposes are not charitable, great difficulties . . . arise both in theory and in practice. In theory, because, having regard to the historical origins of equity, it is difficult to visualise the growth of equitable obligations which nobody can enforce, and in practice, because it is not possible to contemplate with equanimity the creation of large funds devoted to non-charitable purposes which no court and no department of State can control, or, in the case of maladministration, reform. Therefore, Lord Parker's second proposition would *prima facie* appear to be well founded . . . no officer has ever been constituted to take, in the case of non-charitable purposes, the position held by the Attorney-General in connection with charitable purposes, and no case has been found in the reports in which the court has ever directly enforced a non-charitable purpose against a trustee. Indeed, where, as in the present case, the only beneficiaries are purposes and an at present unascertainable person, it is difficult to see who could initiate such proceedings. If the purposes are valid trusts, the settlors have retained no beneficial interest and could not initiate them. It was suggested that the trustees might proceed *ex parte* to enforce the trusts against themselves. I doubt that, but at any rate nobody could enforce the trusts against them.

Another disposition which was held to be void as a trust purely for private purposes was a non-charitable trust for purposes including the 'maintenance . . . of good understanding . . . between nations' and 'the preservation of the independence and integrity of newspapers' (*Re Astor* [1952] Ch 534). The trust fund comprised substantially all the issued shares of 'The Observer Ltd' (the newspaper company).

Perhaps the most famous dispositions held to be void as trusts purely for private purposes are those contained in the will of the playwright George Bernard Shaw (1856–1950). The trusts, which were declared on the income from his residuary estate, were established to ascertain the number of persons currently using the 26-letter English alphabet and to ascertain how much effort could be saved by replacing the 26-letter alphabet with a 40-letter phonetic 'British Alphabet' in which at least 14 letters are devoted to vowel sounds. When the case (*Re Shaw* [1957] 1 WLR 729) was heard, Harman J noted that 'an object cannot complain to the court, which therefore cannot control the trust'. He approved Lord Greene in *Re Diplock* [1941] Ch 253, who had said that 'in order for a trust to be properly constituted . . . the beneficiary must be ascertained or must be ascertainable'. Despite this, one of Shaw's plays was translated into his Shavian alphabet after his death. It is said of Shaw that he once observed, with typical haughtiness, that 'England and America are two countries separated by the same language'. It is somewhat ironic that it was only by virtue of Hollywood's adaptation of his play 'Pygmalion' (1916) into the musical film 'My Fair Lady' (1964) that there came to be sufficient funds in his estate to bring his 'alphabet' trusts to court!

7.2 Trusts of imperfect obligation

This class of trusts is anomalous, and will not be extended (*Re Endacott* [1960] Ch 232). They are trusts for purely private (non-charitable) purposes which are valid despite the lack of any ascertainable beneficiary. They include such purposes as looking after animals and the maintenance of tombs and monuments. There is no principled reason for their exceptional status, and it may be, as Sir Arthur Underhill suggested, that they are merely concessions to human weakness or sentiment (Underhill's *Law of Trusts and Trustees*, 10th edn, London: Butterworth's Law, p. 97). In *Re Endacott* [1960] Ch 232 Harman LJ described them as 'occasions when Homer has nodded', i.e. occasions where the usual logic of the law has lapsed. (Echoing the lament of Horace in his treatise on the art of poetry: *indignor quandoque bonus dormitat Homerus*: I am aggrieved when sometimes even the excellent Homer falls asleep ('nods').) Of course, modern readers will be familiar with another Homer who spends most of his time asleep, but that is another story.

They are classified as *trusts of imperfect obligation* because even though they are valid, there is no person in a position actively to enforce the trust obligations against the trustees. The practical, if not legal, result is that the trustees are not in fact bound to apply the trust fund in furtherance of the purposes stated, unless they undertake (whether voluntarily or by order of the court) to do so. The fact that the trust might not be fulfilled has led to the suggestion that trusts of imperfect obligation will only be recognised where they appear in a will which is drafted so as to make it clear that, if the fund is not expended on the non-charitable purpose, it will fall into the residue of the deceased's estate. (See *Re Thompson* [1934] Ch 342 at 344; *Re Astor's ST* [1952] Ch 534 at 546.)

Against this suggestion it has been pointed out that the residuary legatees of a will *or successors on intestacy* can always apply to the court to have the residue of the deceased's estate transferred to them whenever it appears that the trustees are not going to apply the fund in furtherance of the non-charitable purposes, and that there is no reason why the subject matter of the trust of imperfect obligation should not be the residue itself (Parker & Mellows, *The Modern Law of Trusts*, 6th edn, 1994, London: Sweet & Maxwell, p. 117).

In the following sections we shall consider the established categories of trusts of imperfect obligation.

7.2.1 The erection or maintenance of tombs or monuments

In *Re Hooper* [1932] 1 Ch 38 a testator made a bequest and declared that the income therefrom should be used for the care and upkeep of certain memorials in cemeteries and churchyards.

The memorials comprised graves (including that of his son in Shotley churchyard near Ipswich), a vault and certain monuments. In addition he declared that income from the bequest should be applied to the upkeep of a tablet and a window in St Matthias' Church at Ilsham.

Maugham J held that whereas the upkeep of the tablet and window were valid as charitable purposes, the trust for the upkeep of the other memorials would take effect as a trust of imperfect obligation, and be limited to take effect for 21 years after the testator's death. (For the meaning of 'charitable purposes', see Chapter 8.)

7.2.1.1 Uncertainty

It was primarily because of uncertainty that the Court of Appeal refused to recognise the trust in *Re Endacott* [1960] Ch 232. There the testator left his residuary estate to his local parish council 'for the purpose of providing some useful memorial to myself'. Harman LJ refused to extend the class of 'troublesome, anomalous and aberrant cases' to include Endacott's 'unspecified and unidentified memorial'.

7.2.1.2 Perpetuity

In *Mussett v Bingle* [1876] WN 170 a testator bequeathed (1) £300 to erect a monument to his wife's first husband and (2) £200, the income from which was to be used in the upkeep of the monument. The gift of £300 was upheld but the gift of £200 failed because it offended the rule against inalienability of capital.

7.2.1.3 Capriciousness

Any trust for purposes, whether charitable or not, may fail for capriciousness. A capricious trust is one characterised by the playful whim and fancy of the settlor. (The word derives ultimately from the Latin *caper*, meaning goat. A capricious settlor is one who is 'acting the goat'!) Such trusts fail because no trustee or court can reasonably be called upon to carry out a capricious trust. A good illustration of a capricious trust is provided by *Brown v Burdett* (1882) 21 ChD 667. There the expressed purpose of the trust was to block up the windows and doors of a house for 20 years! A trust for red-headed men is also liable to fail on the ground of capriciousness: see next.

 OUTSIDE THE BOX

Sir Arthur Conan Doyle, 'The Red-Headed League' from *The Adventures of Sherlock Holmes*

'the League was founded by an American millionaire, Ezekiah Hopkins, who was very peculiar in his ways. He was himself red-headed, and he had a great sympathy for all red-headed men; so, when he died, it was found that he had left his enormous fortune in the hands of trustees, with instructions to apply the interest to the providing of easy berths to men whose hair is of that colour.'

Capriciousness is perhaps raised most often as an objection in the context of trusts for the erection of tombs and monuments. Lord Kyllachy, in the Scottish case of *M'Caig v University of Glasgow* [1907] SC 231, had some strong words to say about the testamentary wishes of John Stuart M'Caig, who had provided in his will that the income from his estate should be applied to the erection of 'artistic towers' in his memory. On that occasion the court disallowed his testamentary directions on the ground of capriciousness (although he somehow got his way by another route, for 'M'Caig's Tower', a useless and not particularly scenic folly, now stands imperiously above the beautiful harbour in Oban on the west coast of Scotland). Lord Kyllachy thought that it 'ought to be unlawful, to dedicate by testamentary disposition, for all time, or for a length of time, the whole income of a large estate . . . to objects of no utility . . . and which have no other purpose or use than that of perpetuating at great cost, and in an absurd manner, the idiosyncracies of an eccentric testator'. To his Lordship's mind an equally useful variation on M'Caig's trust would be a trust to 'turn the income of the estate into money, and throw the money yearly into the sea'.

7.2.2 **The maintenance of specific animals**

In *Re Dean* (1889) 41 ChD 552 a testator set up a will trust for the maintenance of his horses and hounds for a period of 50 years. He declared that the trustees should not be bound to render any account of expenditure. It was held, by North J, that the trust was a valid trust of imperfect obligation. As a trust for the benefit of *specific* animals it could not be charitable, whereas another gift made by the testator (to the Royal Society for the Prevention of Cruelty to Animals) was held to be potentially charitable because it was a trust for the benefit of animals *generally* (see 8.2.13).

There was clearly no irony in 1889 in making simultaneous bequests for the benefit of hunting hounds and for the benefit of the RSPCA. However, the decision in *Re Dean* was in another respect highly ironic. For although North J had opined that a testator should limit his anomalous purposes to take effect within the perpetuity period, he omitted to strike down the present trust despite the fact that the trustee clearly intended the purposes to be met beyond the perpetuity period of 21 years after his death.

A will leaving benefits to cats for the duration of their lives provided the plot to the Disney film *The Aristocats* (1970) (although, as the film was set in Paris, it could not have involved an English-style trust).

7.2.3 **Fox hunting**

The testator in *Re Thompson* [1934] Ch 342 bequeathed a legacy to a friend to be applied by him as he should in his absolute discretion think fit towards the promotion and furtherance of fox hunting. The residuary legatee, a charity, objected to the bequest (for financial rather than ethical reasons, it is supposed). Rejecting the objection of the residuary legatee, Clauson J held that this was a valid trust of imperfect obligation.

THINKING POINT

Does it follow that these purpose trusts are void, now that hunting with hounds has been banned in England and Wales?

The ban on hunting wild mammals with dogs which was introduced by the Hunting Act 2004 does not render the 'fox hunting' category obsolete, since hunting is exempt from the statutory prohibition in certain circumstances, one of which is stalking and flushing out vermin to be shot: Hunting Act 2004, Schedule 1, para. 1(1).

7.2.4 **Saying private masses**

In *Re Hetherington* [1990] Ch 1 the testatrix left a legacy to 'the Roman Catholic Church Bishop of Westminster for the repose of the souls of my husband and my parents and my sisters and also myself when I die', and left the residue of her estate 'to the Roman Catholic Church St Edwards Golders Green for Masses for my soul'. It was held that the gifts were for charitable purposes. However, in reaching this decision the gifts were given a benignant construction, i.e. in order to validate the legacy as a gift for charitable purposes, the gift was construed to be for the purpose of saying masses *in public*. Had the gift been construed as a donation for the celebration of a mass in private, it would not have contained the element of public benefit necessary to charitable status, but it might nevertheless have been effective as a trust of imperfect obligation (*Bourne v Keane* [1919] AC 815 at 874–5).

7.3 Devices for avoiding the rule against trusts purely for private purposes

There are a number of devices that you might consider. One possibility would be to make a gift to a charity determinable in the event of failure (not necessarily failure by the charity itself) to carry out your desired purposes (see *Re Tyler* at 6.5). In the event of determination of the gift to the charity, you should provide a gift over in favour of another charity. As long as your desired purposes are not unlawful, this device will not only fulfil your purposes, it will also enable your purposes to be carried out in perpetuity. It is essential that failure of the private purpose is described as a *determining event*, for it will then operate informally by way of an incentive to the first charity. If fulfilment of your private purposes is described as being a *condition* attaching to the gift, the gift to the charity will fail. So, for example, in *Re Dalziel* [1943] Ch 277, where a legacy was left to the governors of St Bartholomew's Hospital 'upon and subject to the condition' that the income be used to maintain a mausoleum, the gift failed to take effect as a charitable gift because charitable trusts must exist for exclusively charitable purposes (see 8.3).

7.4 Purpose trusts with indirect human beneficiaries

It is in theory always a matter of construction whether or not a disposition is held to operate as an absolute gift, a gift subject to a mere moral obligation, a gift subject to a legal condition, a trust for private purposes, a trust for public purposes, a trust for persons or a mere power. We have already seen, however, that choosing the appropriate construction is an exercise in legal logic which appears often to be heavily influenced by pragmatic considerations (see 4.1.3). This section considers a number of cases where dispositions, which at first sight might appear to be trusts for private *purposes*, have in fact been construed to be dispositions in favour of the *persons* who would benefit from the carrying out of those purposes.

A simple example is provided by *Re Bowes* [1896] 1 Ch 507. There, the testator made a bequest of £5,000 'upon trust to expend the same in planting trees for shelter on the Wemergill estate being part of my settled estates'. The estate owners objected that this would be a very disadvantageous way of spending the money.

North J held that there was a trust to 'lay out' (apply) the £5,000, as opposed to a mere power to apply the fund. It was, however, a trust 'for the benefit of the estate, and the persons who, for the time being, are entitled to the estate', thus the expressed purpose of planting trees could be dismissed as being a mere motive for making the disposition in favour of the estate owners. The estate owners would be subject to no more than a moral obligation to use the monies to plant trees. In reaching this conclusion it appears that North J was mindful of the fact that the estate owners (the tenant for life and tenant in tail in remainder) were between them able to bring to an end the settlement of the estates if they so wished.

Consider a testamentary gift of freehold property 'upon trust for such order of nuns of the Catholic Church or the Christian Brothers as my executors and trustees shall select', the residue to be applied to build a new convent or to update existing buildings. This disposition was considered by the Privy Council in *Leahy v A-G for New South Wales* [1959] AC 457. It was held that the gift of residue was saved by a particular New South Wales statute. However, the principal gift was held to be invalid as a perpetual endowment in favour of a non-charitable body. (Due to the closed nature of some of the orders, the gift could not be charitable: see 8.2.4.3.) On the particular facts of *Leahy*, their Lordships refused to construe the principal gift as a gift to the members for the time being of the orders intended to take the benefit, a construction which would have saved the gift from the taint of perpetuity. However, their Lordships did accept, in principle, that in an appropriate case, where a gift is made to an association of persons 'for the general purposes of the association', those words can be disregarded and the gift can be sustained as an absolute gift to the individual members. It was in *Leahy* that Viscount Simonds gave the following exposition of the so-called 'beneficiary principle':

> A gift can be made to persons (including a corporation) but it cannot be made to a purpose or to an object; so, also, a trust may be created for the benefit of persons as *cestuis que trust*, but not for a purpose or object unless the purpose or object be charitable. For a purpose or object cannot sue, but, if it be charitable, the Attorney-General can sue to enforce it.

Q CASE CLOSE-UP

Re Denley's Trust Deed [1969] 1 Ch 373, Chancery Division

Facts: land was settled on trustees for use as a sports club 'primarily' for the benefit of the employees of a company, and 'secondarily' for the benefit of such other persons (if any) as the trustees may allow to use the same. The gift was limited to take effect within 21 years of the death of certain named persons.

Held: because of the private *nexus* between the potential beneficiaries of the trust and a particular company the trust was not sufficiently 'public' to be charitable. Prima facie, then, it would be void as a non-charitable purpose trust. However, though expressed to be for a purpose, the trust was indirectly for the benefit of the employees and did not fall foul of the beneficiary principle. Goff J was satisfied that, in contrast with the case of a pure purpose trust, there were persons here who would bring the matter to court if the trustees failed to meet their obligations. He did, however, acknowledge that practical difficulties might arise if some of the employees disagreed as to the purposes for which the sports club was to be used. This difficulty could be overcome, though, by the court giving its approval, on an order for directions, to a scheme drawn up by the employees.

Goff J: '[T]here may be a purpose or object trust, the carrying out of which would benefit an individual or individuals, where that benefit is so indirect or intangible or which is otherwise so framed as not to give those persons any *locus standi* to apply to the court to enforce the trust, in which case the beneficiary principle would, as it seems to me, apply to invalidate the trust, quite apart from any question of uncertainty or perpetuity. Such cases can be considered if and when they arise. The present is not, in my judgment, of that character . . .

Apart from this possible exception, in my judgment the beneficiary principle of *Re Astor*, which was approved in *Re Endacott (decd)* [1959] 3 All ER 562, see particularly by Harman LJ, is confined to purpose or object trusts which are abstract or impersonal. The objection is not that the trust is for a purpose or object per se, but that there is no beneficiary or *cestui que trust*. The rule is so expressed in *Lewin on Trusts* (16th edn.) p. 17, and in my judgment, with the possible exception which I have mentioned, rightly so. In *Re Wood, Barton v Chilcott* [1949] Ch 498, Harman J said:

> There has been an interesting argument on the question of perpetuity, but it seems to me, with all respect to that argument, that there is an earlier obstacle which is fatal to the validity of this bequest, namely, that a gift on trust must have a *cestui que trust*, and there being here no *cestui que trust* the gift must fail. Again, in *Leahy v A-G of New South Wales* [1959] AC 457, Viscount Simonds, delivering the judgment of the Privy Council, said: 'A gift can be made to persons (including a corporation) but it cannot be made to a purpose or to an object': so, also [and these are the important words] a trust may be created for the benefit of persons as *cestuis que trust* but not for a purpose or object unless the purpose or object be charitable. For a purpose or object cannot sue, but, if it be charitable, the Attorney-General can sue to enforce it. Where, then, the trust, though expressed as a purpose, is directly for the benefit of an individual or individuals, it seems to me that it is in general outside the mischief of the beneficiary principle.'

Leahy was followed by Goff J in the Chancery Division in *Re Denley's Trust Deed* [1969] 1 Ch 373. His Lordship's conclusion from *Leahy* was that 'where . . . the trust, though expressed as a purpose, is directly for the benefit of an individual or individuals . . . it is in general outside the mischief of the beneficiary principle'.

Goff J preferred to confine the rule against enforcing non-charitable purpose trusts to trusts which are abstract or impersonal.

 THINKING POINT

It is very important to note that the trust in *Re Denley* would have failed for inalienability of capital had it not been expressly limited to take effect within the perpetuity period!

7.5 Gifts to unincorporated non-profit associations

> **OUTSIDE THE BOX**
>
> **John Dewey, *Democracy and Education*, 1925: 'The Implications of Human Association'**
>
> Society is one word, but many things . . . Within every larger social organisation there are numerous minor groups: not only political subdivisions, but industrial, scientific, religious, associations. There are political parties with differing aims, social sets, cliques, gangs, corporations, partnerships, groups bound closely together by ties of blood, and so on in endless variety.

Quite complex problems arise in construing gratuitous dispositions in favour of unincorporated, non-charitable, non-profit associations, i.e. private clubs and societies. Speaking in very general terms, the law readily legislates for incorporated associations (e.g. limited liability companies) and profit-oriented **unincorporated associations** (i.e. partnerships), but it struggles to understand the essential nature of those unincorporated associations which do not exist primarily with a view to making financial profit (e.g. clubs and societies).

> **unincorporated association** 'My Lords, an unincorporated association is, as I have said, not a legal entity. It is a number of legal persons having mutual rights and duties in accordance with rules which constitute the contract under which they have agreed to be associated. The property of the association is owned by or on trust for the individual members and subject to the rules. The liability of the individual members for the debts incurred for the purposes of the association is governed by the ordinary law of contract and agency. The rights of the members, as against each other, to avail themselves of the common property and facilities are governed by their contract.' (*Eastbourne Town Radio Cars Association* v *Customs and Excise Commissioners* [2001] UKHL 19, para. [32]; [2001] 1 WLR 794, 803, HL, per Lord Hoffmann).

A corporation is a legal person, so it follows that a trust for the benefit of a corporation *ipso facto* satisfies the beneficiary principle. A club, on the other hand, has no legal personality of its own; it is not a separate legal person but a mere association of individuals. The question arises, therefore, whether a gratuitous disposition in favour of a club was intended to be a gift to the individual members of the association for the time being, or a trust to further the purposes of the club or a trust to benefit present and/or future members. In fact, gratuitous dispositions in favour of non-charitable, non-profit unincorporated associations can be construed in a number of different ways, as set out in Table 7.1 and considered in the following sections.

7.5.1 Absolute gift to the members as joint tenants

Cross J described this as 'a gift to the members of the association at the relevant date [the date of the gift] as joint tenants, so that any member can sever his share and claim it whether or not he continues to be a member' (*Neville Estates* v *Madden* [1962] Ch 832).

Table 7.1 Donations to associations

Gift	Trust	Mandate	Power
• as an absolute gift to the current members as joint tenants, so that any member can sever his or her individual share; or • as an absolute gift to the members for the time being with the intention that it should be held by them within the association according to the contractual rules of the association	• as a pure purpose trust, i.e. a trust for impersonal purposes; or • on trust for the benefit of the present members of the association; or • on trust for the benefit of the present and future members of the association	• as a mandate to the officers of the association to use the donation as instructed by the donor	• as the grant of a power to apply the donation for the purposes of the association • *[the courts are unlikely to favour this construction, but it is included here to show that the range of possible constructions is not closed]*

If a gift is made to a club only very rarely will a sensible construction allow it to be divided amongst the present members in individual shares. Whether this construction will be admitted will depend in large part upon the subject matter of the gift. Where a gift of land is made to a football club it is most unlikely that the donor intended the individual members to divide the land up physically and for each member to take allotments in it. However, if an aficionado made a gift of 12 bottles of wine 'to the Barchester string quartet' there is every likelihood that the donor intended the members to take three bottles each.

In *Re Grant's WT* (see 7.5.2) Vinelott J suggested that in any case where this construction is appropriate, 'the association is used in effect as a convenient label or definition of the class which it is intended to take: but the class being ascertained, each member takes as a joint tenant free from any contractual fetter'.

7.5.2 Absolute gifts to members subject to the contractual rules of the club

This construction was accepted *obiter* by Cross J in *Neville Estates Ltd* v *Madden* where it was framed as 'a gift to the existing members not as joint tenants, but subject to their respective contractual rights and liabilities towards one another as members of the association. In such a case a member cannot sever his share. It will accrue to the other members on his death or resignation, even though such members include persons who became members after the gift took effect.' This was followed by Brightman J in *Re Recher's WT* [1972] Ch 526.

In *Re Recher's WT* a testatrix left a share of her residuary estate to 'The London and Provincial Anti-Vivisection Society'. It was conceded that the gift was not for charitable purposes and the question therefore arose whether it could be construed in some other way so as to allow the wishes of the testatrix to be fulfilled. Brightman J started from the premise that '[i]t would astonish a layman to be told that there was a difficulty in his giving a legacy to an unincorporated non-charitable society which he had or could have supported without trouble during his life-time'. His Lordship held that the society's existing funds already formed the subject matter of a contract in accordance with which the members had bound themselves *inter se*, and that the testatrix's legacy should be construed as a gift to the *present* members of the society benefi-cially, as an accretion to the society's general funds. In short, this legacy was a gift to existing persons, not a trust for purposes. As such it did not breach the rule against inalienability of capital because if all the members agreed, they could decide to wind up the society and divide the net assets amongst themselves beneficially. The construction approved in *Re Recher's* was applied to the facts of *Re Grant's WT* [1980] 1 WLR 360.

🔍 CASE CLOSE-UP

Re Grant's WT [1980] 1 WLR 360

Facts: Grant, the testator, had been financial secretary of the Chertsey Constituency Labour Party, which had since become the Chertsey and Walton Constituency Labour Party. The new constituency party was subject to rules laid down by the National Executive Committee of the Labour Party and the national annual party conference. By his will, Grant devised and bequeathed all his real and personal estate (for the benefit of the Chertsey headquarters of the new constituency party) to the committee in charge of property at the headquarters.

Held: (*per* Vinelott J) 'the gift could not take effect as a gift to the current members of the new constituency party subject to their contractual rights and duties *inter se* because the members were not free, under the rules of their association, to dispose of the property in any way they thought fit. On the contrary, the rules made it plain that the decisions of the members of the local party were subject to the control of the national Labour Party. The gift must therefore fail for infringing of the rule against inalienability of capital.'

If the local branch, according to its own rules, could have seceded from the national organisa-tion and dissolved itself, the gift to the local branch would not have failed for inalienability of capital (see *News Group Newspapers Ltd* v *SOGAT 1982* [1986] ICR 716, Court of Appeal, which concerned a local branch of a trade union). Even where there is no rule providing for dissolution, the court might accept that the members could dissolve the association by unani-mous consent (see *Universe Tankships Inc of Monrovia* v *ITWF* [1983] 1 AC 366, HL).

In a case concerning an association called the Showmen's Guild the judge held that the primary contractual function of the association's rules was to set out the terms of the contracts be-tween an individual member and the remaining members collectively as 'the guild'. On that basis, the judge refused to allow an individual member to sue another individual member for breach of one of the contractual rules (*Anderton and Rowland (a firm)* v *Rowland* (1999) Times, 5 November).

7.5.3 Gift on trust for the abstract purposes of the association or club

A gift to an unincorporated association will rarely be construed in this way. An association is by definition a collection of individuals, and there is always likely to be someone in whose favour the court can decree performance and someone who will be in a position to supervise the proper discharge of the trust. In other words, there are usually ascertainable beneficiaries.

It is sometimes said that the devise in *Leahy* (see 7.4) 'upon trust for such order of nuns of the Catholic Church or the Christian Brothers as my executors and trustees shall select' failed because it was a trust purely for the abstract purposes of religious orders. In fact there is some ambiguity in Viscount Simonds' conclusion that the testator's intention was 'to create a trust not merely for the benefit of the existing members of the selected order but for its benefit as a continuing society and for the furtherance of its work'. His Lordship was not content to dismiss the devise as a pure purpose trust, but neither did he construe it to be a trust purely for present, nor indeed present and future, beneficiaries. The ambiguity did not affect the decision in that case because the devise would have failed *even as a gift on trust for human beneficiaries* due to the possibility that many of those beneficiaries would not be ascertainable until some time beyond the perpetuity period. When *Leahy* was followed in *Re Denley's Trust Deed* (1969) (see 7.4), Goff J preferred the view that the trust in *Leahy* had been a trust for beneficiaries, and not a trust for abstract, impersonal purposes.

7.5.4 Gifts on trust for the present members of the association or club

If a disposition can be construed to be a trust of this sort it will clearly comply with the rule against inalienability of capital, but only where the beneficiaries will certainly be able to appropriate the capital to their use and benefit within the perpetuity period.

In *Re Turkington* [1937] 4 All ER 501 the trust was held to be valid on this basis because the members of the association were both trustees and beneficiaries and able to vest the capital in themselves according to the rule in *Saunders* v *Vautier*. However, this construction will presumably not save a gift on trust to an association of infants (e.g. an association of Cub Scouts). An attempt to establish a church tennis club in *Re St Andrew's (Cheam) Lawn Tennis Club Trust (sub nom Philippe* v *Cameron)* [2012] EWHC 1040 (Ch); [2012] 3 All ER 746 failed because it represented 'an attempt to achieve the legally impossible: a perpetual trust for a non-charitable purpose' (*per* Arnold J at para. [45]).

7.5.5 Gifts on trust for the present and future members of the association or club

Whenever a gift is made expressly 'on trust' it must be either a trust for present members only (see 7.5.4) or a trust for the present and future members of the association. No other construction would accord with a straightforward reading of the words used by the settlor or testator. However it is not necessary that the words 'on trust' be used for the disposition to be construed as a trust. As Viscount Simonds stated in the Privy Council in *Re Leahy* [1959] AC 457 at 484:

> [I]f a gift is made to individuals, whether under their own names or in the name of their society, and the conclusion is reached that they are not intended to take beneficially, then they take as trustees. If so, it must be ascertained who are the beneficiaries. If at the death of the testator the class of beneficiaries is fixed and ascertained or ascertainable within the limit of the rule against perpetuities, all is well. If it is not so fixed and not so ascertainable the trust must fail.

Perhaps the best reported examples of dispositions which were construed to be gifts on trust for the present and future members of the association or club are those in *Re Leahy* itself (a gift on trust for certain religious orders) and *Re Denley's Trust Deed* [1969] 1 Ch 373 (a gift on trust for the employees of a company).

The trust in *Denley* succeeded because the trust had been expressly limited to take effect within 21 years. The trust in *Leahy* had not been limited in this way and would have failed had it not been saved by a particular New South Wales statute which validated the trust.

7.5.6 **Mandate to officers of the association**

Re Grant's WT (see 7.5.2) concerned a failed gift to a local Labour Party association. *Conservative and Unionist Central Office v Burrell* [1982] 1 WLR 522 concerned successful gifts to the central office of the Conservative Party. The Conservative and Unionist Central Office had been assessed to corporation tax on the ground that it was a 'company' within the meaning of s 526(5) of the Income and Corporation Taxes Act 1970. Included within the definition of 'company' were unincorporated associations of two or more persons bound together for common purposes (not being business purposes) by mutual undertakings and rules governing the holding and control of property. Appealing against the tax assessment, the central office contended that it was not an unincorporated association within this definition.

The Court of Appeal held that donations received by the central office were not held on behalf of an unincorporated association within the 1970 Act definition. It became necessary to consider, therefore, upon what basis donations *were* received by the central office. It was held *per curiam* ('by the court', for the sake of clarity) that when a contributor makes a donation to the treasurer, or other officer, of the central office, that officer receives the donation as an agent and subject to a **mandate** that it be used for the political purposes for which it was given. The law of agency, not of trusts, is applicable.

> **mandate**
> A binding instruction given to an agent.

Once the donation has been mixed with the general funds under the officer's control the mandate becomes irrevocable. In other words, it is then too late for the contributor to reclaim the donation. However, the contributor has a remedy against the officials to restrain or make good a misapplication of the mixed fund except where the contributor's donation can be shown, on normal accounting principles, to have been legitimately expended before the misapplication of the mixed fund.

Vinelott J stated that 'if someone invites subscriptions on the representation that he will use the fund subscribed for a particular purpose, he undertakes to use the fund for that purpose and for no other and to keep the subscribed fund and any accretions to it . . . separate from his own property'. His Lordship did acknowledge, however, that this mandate/agency construction could not be applied to donations made by will: 'in the case of a testamentary gift there is no room for the implication of any contract between the testator and the persons who are to receive the bequest.'

7.5.7 **Summative exercise**

In coming to your conclusion it is important to be aware that the principal aim of the Hull Judeans (Maccabi) Association was 'to promote the interest, and the active participation of Anglo-Jewish youth of both sexes, in amateur sports, in all forms of cultural, and in non-political, communal activities'.

THINKING POINT

Consider the following disposition, which arose for consideration in the case of *Re Lipinski* [1976] 1 Ch 235. Do you think it creates a valid trust or fails as a trust for private purposes?

> I give and devise the rest residue and remainder of my estate real and personal whatsoever and wheresoever unto my trustees upon trust to sell call in and convert into money the same with power to postpone such sale calling in and conversion and to hold the net proceeds of sale thereof and my ready money after payment thereout of my just debts and my funeral and testamentary expenses upon trust: –(a) as to one half thereof for the Hull Judeans (Maccabi) Association in memory of my late wife to be used solely in the work of constructing the new buildings for the association and or improvements to the said buildings.

Part (a) of the trust is clearly not charitable, because it produces insufficient benefit to the general public. The question, therefore, was whether it was void as a pure purpose trust (it being 'solely' for the erection and maintenance of buildings in memory of the testator's wife), or whether it was a valid trust in favour of the Hull Judeans (Maccabi) Association.

Oliver J gave three reasons for holding the disposition to be valid:

• because there was a trust indirectly for human beneficiaries (applying *Re Denley's Trust Deed* (see 7.4));

• because the gift should be construed as an outright gift to the members of the association, subject to the rules of the association (applying *Re Recher's WT* (see 7.5.2));

• because the members of the association were between them absolutely entitled to the fund, and thus able to vest the capital in themselves according to the rule in *Saunders* v *Vautier* (applying *Re Turkington* [1937] 4 All ER 501 (see 7.5.4)).

THINKING POINT

Do you agree that not one of the reasons given for the decision in *Re Lipinski* is particularly convincing? If you were appealing against the judgment of Oliver J, what arguments would you raise against each of his reasons? On a separate sheet of paper, attempt to draft your grounds of appeal. Compare your answer with the following points:

• against the judge's suggestion that *Re Denley's* should apply, it should be relatively easy to argue that the facts of *Re Lipinski* are distinguishable from those in *Re Denley's*. In *Re Denley's* the reference to building a sports ground had been construed as a mere motive for setting up the trust (applying *Re Bowes*, see 7.4). In other words, the purpose was ancillary to the ultimate human benefit. In *Re Lipinski* the trust was set up in memory of the testator's wife and was expressed to be 'solely' for the purpose of building. It is hard to dismiss such an imperative statement of purpose as an ancillary motive; the expressed purpose appears to be by its terms fundamental to the trust. Oliver J reasoned that the direction to build was not fundamental to the testator's intentions, but had been his attempt to second-guess the current needs, whatever they might be, of the ultimate human beneficiaries. A more compelling objection to the application of *Re Denley's* is that it should only apply where the trust is expressly limited to take effect during the perpetuity period. In the absence of any such provision, a trust will be void for potentially rendering the capital inalienable in perpetuity. The trust in *Re Lipinski* appears to fall foul of the rule against inalienability;

- the assumption underlying the judge's application of *Re Recher* to *Re Lipinski* was that an absolute gift had been made to the present members of the association. The difficulty with applying *Re Recher's* to *Re Lipinski* is that the benefiting class of persons in *Re Lipinski* are Jewish 'youth', the majority of whom would be precluded by their infancy from taking as an absolute gift that part of the residuary estate which comprised land;

- finally, the infancy of the beneficiaries means that the rule in *Saunders v Vautier*, and therefore the reasoning in *Re Turkington*, should not have been applied in *Re Lipinski*.

7.6 Distribution of surplus donations

When monies are given for a purpose or to an association, what happens if there are surplus funds after the purpose is fulfilled or the association dissolved? The answer depends in large part upon the way in which the original gift is construed. If the gift is construed to be a gift 'on trust' for a particular purpose, any surplus of the gift will generally be held on resulting trust for the original donor. If it was originally construed to be an absolute gift, any surplus of the gift will generally belong beneficially to the members in existence at the time of dissolution (in accordance, where relevant, with the association's rules).

7.6.1 *Bona vacantia*

Where a resulting trust or contractual solution is clearly inappropriate, the donation may pass to the Crown as *bona vacantia*.

 OUTSIDE THE BOX

William Black, *Prince Fortunatus*, 1905

Bona vacantia can't belong to anybody—therefore they belong to the king; that's a pretty piece of reasoning, isn't it? And if the crofter or the labourer says, '*Bona vacantia* can't belong to anybody—therefore they belong to me'—isn't the reasoning as good?

 CASE CLOSE-UP

***Cunnack v Edwards* (1896) 2 Ch 679**

Facts: the society had been established to raise a fund by members' subscriptions to provide annuities for the widows of deceased members. The last member died in 1879 and the last widow died in 1892, the society having then a surplus or unexpended fund of £1,250.

> Held: the widows, and not the members, were the beneficiaries of the society's funds; accordingly, there would be no resulting trust of the surplus in favour of the estates of the members of the society. The surplus went instead to the Crown as *bona vacantia*. As Smith LJ stated: 'as the member paid his money to the society, so he divested himself of all interest in this money for ever, with this one reservation, that if the member left a widow she was to be provided for during her widowhood.'

The *bona vacantia* solution will obviously be appropriate to a case like *Cunnack* v *Edwards*, where the association was utterly moribund and bereft of potential beneficiaries, but the courts will generally seek to avoid this solution. However, it will be the appropriate solution where the rules of the association do not permit a distribution according to the members' contract *inter se*, and where, in the case of a donation made on trust, a resulting trust solution is inappropriate because the donor clearly intended to part with the donation outright and for all time. This latter point, established in *Re West Sussex Constabulary's Widows, Children and Benevolent (1930) Fund Trusts* [1971] Ch 1 (see 7.6.3) was confirmed *obiter* by Lord Browne-Wilkinson in the House of Lords in the *Westdeutsche* case (see Chapter 16 Introduction and 16.1).

7.6.2 **Resulting trust**

The case of *Re Gillingham Bus Disaster Fund* [1958] Ch 300 involved the distribution of surplus donations to a disaster fund raised in response to one of the most heart-rending accidents it is possible to imagine, when (in the days before headlamps were compulsory) a coach ploughed into children taking part in a night walk, killing many. In that case Harman J stated the general principle (confirmed on appeal) that:

> where money is held on trust and the trusts declared do not exhaust the fund it will revert to the donor or settlor under what is called a resulting trust. The reasoning behind this is that the settlor or donor did not part with his money absolutely out and out, but only *sub modo* to the intent that his wishes, as declared by the declaration of trust, should be carried into effect. When, therefore, this has been done, any surplus still belongs to him.

Cunnack v *Edwards* was distinguished as being a case where the funds had been held subject to a contractual arrangement. Harman J was not impressed with the Crown's argument that the resulting trust solution should be avoided due to the impracticalities of identifying the anonymous donors. His Lordship was convinced that the resulting trust solution was appropriate to the named donors and saw no reason to suppose that the anonymous donor had any larger intention than the named donor as to the ultimate destination of their donation. In the event that the anonymous donors might not be found, the surplus should be held on the court's account, but should not pass as ownerless assets (*bona vacantia*) to the Crown. The preferred approach today (see 7.6.1) is to regard anonymous donations as out-and-out donations. The intention to make an outright disposition is said to rebut the presumption of a resulting trust (see 16.1.1).

7.6.3 **Contract**

In *Re West Sussex Constabulary's Widows, Children and Benevolent (1930) Fund Trusts* [1971] 1 Ch 1 a fund existed to provide for widows and orphans of deceased members of the West Sussex Constabulary, an unincorporated, non-charitable, non-profit association. When the constabulary amalgamated with other forces in 1968 the question arose as to how the funds should be distributed. Sources of the fund were: (1) members' subscriptions; (2) receipts from entertainments, raffles and sweepstakes; (3) collecting boxes; and (4) donations and legacies.

Goff J held that surplus of sources 1, 2 and 3 would pass to the Crown as *bona vacantia*, but that surplus of source 4 would be held on resulting trusts for the donors. He held, further, that equity would 'cut the Gordian knot' of accounting difficulties by dividing the surplus in proportion to the sources from which it had arisen. According to his Lordship, surplus of source 1 could not be the subject of a resulting trust because the members had received consideration for the payment of their subscriptions in the form of the benefits of membership. In other words, the members had already received everything they had bargained for. Surplus of source 2 could not be the subject of a resulting trust because, first, such payments had been made for consideration; and, secondly, they were not direct donations to the fund, but merely donations of net profits after payment out of prizes etc. Finally, surplus of source 3 would not be deemed subject to a resulting trust because donors to collecting boxes are presumed to have intended to part with their monies out and out.

 CASE CLOSE-UP

***Re West Sussex Constabulary's Widows, Children and Benevolent (1930) Fund Trusts* [1971] Ch 1**

Goff J (on the outside contributions): 'then counsel divided the outside monies into three categories, first, the proceeds of entertainments, raffles and sweepstakes; secondly, the proceeds of collecting-boxes; and thirdly, donations, including legacies if any, and he took particular objections to each. I agree that there cannot be any resulting trust with respect to the first category. I am not certain whether Harman J in *Re Gillingham Bus Disaster Fund* [1958] Ch 300 meant to decide otherwise. In starting the facts at p. 304 he referred to "street collections and so forth". In the further argument at p. 309 there is mention of whist drives and concerts but the judge himself did not speak of anything other than gifts. If, however, he did, I must respectfully decline to follow his judgment in that regard, for whatever may be the true position with regard to collecting-boxes, it appears to me to be impossible to apply the doctrine of resulting trust to the proceeds of entertainments and sweepstakes and such-like money-raising operations for two reasons: first, the relationship is one of contract and not of trust; the purchaser of a ticket may have the motive of aiding the cause or he may not; he may purchase a ticket merely because he wishes to attend the particular entertainment or to try for the prize, but whichever it be, he pays his money as the price of what is offered and what he receives; secondly, there is in such cases no direct contribution to the fund at all; it is only the profit, if any, which is ultimately received and there may even be none.'

The *Re West Sussex* case was distinguished (rather artificially) in *Re Bucks Constabulary Widows' and Orphans' Fund Friendly Society (No 2)* [1979] 1 WLR 936, on the basis that the former case involved a simple unincorporated association, whereas the latter involved a friendly society. The facts were that the society had been established to make provision for widows and orphans of deceased members of the Bucks Constabulary. In 1968 the Bucks Constabulary was amalgamated with other constabularies to form the Thames Valley Constabulary. The rules of the society did not make provision for the distribution of surplus assets on dissolution. The trustees therefore applied to court to determine: (1) whether the surplus assets should be distributed amongst the persons who were members of the society at the date of its dissolution or whether they should pass to the Crown as *bona vacantia*; and (2) if the assets were to be distributed amongst the members, whether they should be distributed in equal shares or pro rata the members' payment of subscriptions. Members' voluntary subscriptions had made up the majority of the fund.

Walton J held that, as there had been members in existence at the time of the dissolution, the surplus would be held for them according to a term that could be implied into the contract between the members. This would operate to the total exclusion of any claim on behalf of the Crown. As to the second issue, his Lordship held that where, as here, the contract between the members provided no other method of distribution, such funds were prima facie to be distributed amongst the surviving members in equal shares.

Walton J preferred the analysis of Brightman J in *Re Recher's WT* (see 7.5.2) to that of Goff J in *Re West Sussex*. Whereas Goff J had sought to draw a distinction between an association established for the benefit of its members and an association established for third parties or purposes, Walton J could 'see no reason for thinking that this analysis is any different whether the purpose for which the members of the association associate are a social club, a sporting club, to establish a widows' and orphans' fund, to obtain a separate Parliament for Cornwall, or to further the advance of alchemy. It matters not.'

7.7 When is an unincorporated association wound up?

In *Re GKN Bolts and Nuts Sports and Social Club* [1982] 1 WLR 774 Sir Robert Megarry V-C held that clubs do not automatically dissolve through mere inactivity unless the period of inactivity is such that the only reasonable inference was that the club had ceased to exist. As his Lordship put it: 'short inactivity coupled with strong circumstances, or long inactivity coupled with weaker circumstances may equally suffice. The question is whether, put together, the facts carry sufficient conviction that the society is at an end and not merely dormant.' The Vice-Chancellor (at 860) approved Brightman J in *Re William Denby & Sons Ltd Sick and Benevolent Fund* [1971] 2 All ER 1196, who classified four categories of case in which an unregistered friendly society or benevolent fund should be regarded as having been dissolved or terminated so that its assets become distributable:

> The first three categories of dissolution or termination were (1) in accordance with the rules, (2) by agreement of all persons interested, and (3) by order of the court in the exercise of its inherent jurisdiction. The fourth category was when the substratum on which the society or fund was founded had gone, so that the society or fund no longer had any effective purpose, and the assets became distributable without any order of the court.

In *Re GKN Bolts and Nuts Sports and Social Club* itself, it was held that the club had ceased to exist, but only by virtue of the positive resolution of the members to sell the club's sports ground. Sir Robert Megarry V-C's approach was essentially a pragmatic one. He observed (at 776) that 'in club cases, there are many obscurities and uncertainties, and some difficulty in the law. In such cases, the court usually has to take a broad sword to the problems, and eschew an unduly meticulous examination of the rules and regulations.' The same pragmatic approach was adopted in *Re Horley Town Football Club* [2006] EWHC 2386, Chancery Division, when the trustees of the club sought directions of the court as to whether they held club assets for 'temporary members' and 'Associate Members' as well as full members. It was held that beneficial ownership was held on bare trust for full members only, because they could either unanimously or at an AGM call for the assets to be transferred to them.

In *KD Hanchett-Stamford* v *H M Attorney-General* [2008] EWHC 330 (Chancery) it was held that even a sole surviving member of an association would take the association's assets. The judge (Lewison J) rejected the illogical alternative, which would be to say that if there are two members of an association with assets of, say, £2 million, 'they can by agreement divide those assets between them and pocket £1 million each, but if one of them dies before they have divided the assets, the whole pot goes to the Crown as *bona vacantia*'. His Lordship also thought that to deprive the sole survivor of his share might be a breach of article 1 of Protocol 1 of the European Convention on Human Rights and Fundamental Freedoms 1950, which guarantees the peaceful enjoyment of possessions.

Summary

- We 1have seen that trusts purely for private purposes are generally void for the following reasons:
  - being in nature 'private', a trust of this sort would not be subject to judicial *control*;
  - following on from the preceding point, in order to bring the trust within the control of the court, there must always be someone in whose favour the court can decree performance, i.e. someone who will *enforce* the trust by, inter alia, bringing breaches of trust to the attention of the court. This is the so-called 'beneficiary principle';
  - trusts for private purposes must often be construed as perpetual endowments. Such endowments offend the rule against inalienability of capital (see 6.4);
  - trusts for private purposes are liable to fail the requirement of certainty of object, since a purpose is never as definite as a person;
  - capriciousness.
- An exceptional class of trusts purely for private purposes, which are valid, are trusts of imperfect obligation (so called because the trustees are not obliged to discharge them—question: in that case are they properly described as *trusts* at all?). This class of 'trusts' is anomalous, and will not be extended (*Re Endacott* [1960] Ch 232). They include such purposes as looking after particular individual animals, the maintenance of tombs and monuments and the saying of masses in private.
- There are ways to avoid the rule against trusts purely for private purposes:
  - one possibility is to make a gift to a charity determinable in the event of failure (not necessarily failure by the charity itself) to carry out your desired purposes (see *Re Tyler* at 6.5);
  - another possibility is to make a gift to identifiable beneficiaries, but to express a purpose by way of motive for making the gift or by way of giving advice to the trustees;
  - another possibility is to make a gift to a company (incorporated entity);
  - another possibility is to make a gift to an unincorporated non-profit association (club/society).
- Gifts to unincorporated non-profit associations can be construed in a number of different ways:

Absolute Gift

- to the present members as joint tenants (with the intention that they should sever the joint tenancy and take their portion away); or

- to the present members subject to their contractual obligation (typically set out in the association's constitution) to hold assets for the purposes of the association and for the benefit of all members;

Trust

- as a pure purpose trust, i.e. a trust for impersonal purposes; or

- on trust for the benefit of the present members of the association; or

- on trust for the benefit of the present and future members of the association;

Mandate

- as a mandate to the officers of the association to use the donation as instructed by the donor;

Power

- as the grant of a power to apply the donation for the purposes of the association.

? Summative assessment exercise

The Whitestone Sportsclub is a largely autonomous body run by a committee elected by its members (who are employees of Whitestone Ltd). It manages a sports centre on land leased to trustees of the Club for a period of 21 years and is financed by subscriptions from members. The decisions of the committee are subject to veto by the board of directors of the company but the board has only rejected one decision, a proposal last year to charge a higher subscription to senior staff. The constitution of the Club provides that on its dissolution its assets shall belong to Whitestone Ltd. By his will, Mr White (a former director of Whitestone Ltd) left £100,000 to the Club to provide a cricket ground and modest pavilion for employees. The committee have voted to use the money not for a cricket ground, but for a football pitch.

Mr White's widow, his residuary legatee, claims the legacy.

Advise her.

 Full specimen answers can be found at www.oxfordtextbooks.co.uk/orc/watt_directions5e/.

☐ The bigger picture

Does it seem strange that the law struggles to understand something as socially straightforward as an unincorporated association? Does it surprise us that the law's default solution, when it comes to explaining the ways in which people gather socially into groups for non-profit purposes, is to look for the 'contract' that binds them together? Perhaps it shouldn't surprise us when we consider that since the Enlightenment (and the work of the French political philosopher Jean-Jacques Rousseau: see *Du contrat social ou Principes du droit politique*) the 'Social Contract' has been a preferred mode of understanding political community in western European States. Is it not, though, a little depressing to think that the diverse richness of human social association should have to be narrowed ('contracted') into one of the most simplistic legal formulas for human connection: the contractual bargain? The truth is that 'bargain' is very likely the last thing that brings and keeps the members of a social association together. As we have seen in this chapter (in a case like *Re Horley Town Football Club*), contract does not explain how or why social associations are made; for the most part it merely provides a scheme for distributing the association's assets in the pathological contexts of dispute and dissolution. This might be compared to the law's struggle to understand the complexity of cohabitation relationships in the event of their dissolution. The Law Commission of England and Wales has, quite rightly, given up in its attempt to achieve a comprehensive scheme for the definition and management of relationship breakdown in that context. See 'Cohabitation: The Financial Consequences of Relationship Breakdown' (Law Com No 307), 31 July 2007.

 ## Further reading

Baxendale-Walker, P. *Purpose Trusts for Commercial and Private Use* (1999) London: Butterworths
a practical guide to the creation and operation of purpose trusts

Matthews, P. 'Gifts to Unincorporated Associations' [1995] Conv 302
argues that the list of ways of construing gifts to unincorporated associations is not closed

Pawlowski, M. and Summers, J. 'Private purpose trusts—a reform proposal' [2007] Conv 440–55
proposes a new statute to enable valid private purpose trusts to be created which have no identifiable human beneficiary, along the lines of legislation found in numerous offshore jurisdictions

Stoljar, S.J. *Groups and Entities—An Inquiry into Corporate Theory* (1973) Sydney: Australian University Press
a theory on the nature of unincorporated entities—suggests that the group is defined by the fund it shares

Warburton, J. 'Holding of Property by Unincorporated Associations' [1985] Conv 318
argues that some gifts to unincorporated associations may be construed as trusts for present members

Warburton, J. *Unincorporated Associations: Law and Practice* (1992) London: Sweet & Maxwell
a practical guide to the operation of clubs, societies and other non-profit, unincorporated associations

 For links to selected cases, statutes, academic papers and official reports mentioned in this chapter please visit the online resources at www.oup.com/uk/watt_directions6e/.

8 Charitable trusts

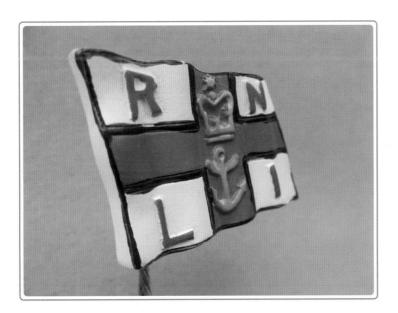

Introduction

At the start of every new chapter it is useful to pause to reflect. When it comes to a chapter on charity, it is more important than ever. Charity is a big idea; it has the potential to be the greatest of ideas. The UK public has supported a number of high-profile charitable fundraising initiatives over the years, including Live Aid in 1985 and Comic Relief's 'Red Nose Day' which has run every year since. It might surprise, therefore, to discover that we still lag far behind our American friends when it comes to charitable giving. The following extract is from an article on philanthropy written by Sir Philip Christopher Ondaatje, OC, CBE, a noted philanthropist. (An entire new wing of the National Portrait Gallery has been named after his family.)

 OUTSIDE THE BOX

Christopher Ondaatje, 'Giving It All Away', *New Statesman*, 15 January 2007

There are . . . enormous differences between how Americans and British people give: 77 per cent of all collection methods in the UK are spontaneous, looking for loose change. In the United States, there is a culture of "planned giving", which provides 61 per cent of the voluntary income of non-profit organisations. One critical factor is tax incentives. According to the biweekly US Chronicle of Philanthropy, 54 per cent of the richest US donors said that they give for the tax benefits. In Britain, the charity, rather than the individual, receives most of the refund under Gift Aid. As a result, many potential donors do not feel that the system gives them a tax break.

In addition, gifts of capital and assets in Britain do not attract an allowance similar to that on gifts of shares. A recent review published by the Treasury recommended a tax allowance to encourage getting more art into museums, but sadly nothing was done to implement this recommendation. When similar proposals were made by the Art Fund before the last Budget, they were apparently supported by Treasury officials, but then killed on the grounds that it was wrong to give tax benefits to the rich. Unfortunately, however, without obvious and understandable tax benefits, the rich in Britain are unlikely to put as much back into the community as Americans do.

8.1 The significance of charitable status

 THINKING POINT

In the following sections frequent reference is made to the 'privileges' of charitable status. We should acknowledge from the outset that the special treatment of charities established for the benefit of the public might be regarded as something they are justly entitled to rather than something that is granted to them by the government as an indulgence.

8.1.1 **The privileges of charitable status**

In 1955 the Radcliffe Commission on Taxation (Cmd 9474) recommended that when considering the validity of a charitable trust, the fiscal privileges attaching to such trusts should be considered separately from the general trust law privileges they enjoy. Approving this, Lord Cross has stated (in *Dingle* v *Turner* [1972] AC 601) that:

> [i]t is, of course, unfortunate that the recognition of any trust as a valid charitable trust should automatically attract fiscal privileges, for the question whether a trust to further some purpose is so little likely to benefit the public that it ought to be declared invalid and the question whether it is likely to confer such great benefits on the public that it should enjoy fiscal immunity are really two quite different questions. The logical solution would be to separate them and to say—as the Radcliffe Commission proposed—that only some charities should enjoy fiscal privileges.

For the purposes of the remainder of this section we will adopt the distinction between trust law and fiscal privileges.

8.1.1.1 **Trust law privileges**

Charitable trusts are not subject to the objections that are raised against *private* purpose trusts:

- although they are not public institutions, charities are subject to the constitutional *protection* of the Crown as *parens patriae* (acting through the Attorney-General), to the *supervision* of the Charity Commission and to judicial *control*;

- charities are not subject to the beneficiary principle; the Attorney-General represents the public as the person in whose favour the court can decree performance of a charitable trust, although he can be substituted as claimant for individuals: see *Hauxwell* v *Barton-on-Humber UDC* [1974] Ch 432;

- charitable trusts are not subject to the rule against inalienability of capital (6.4). This is because the public policy considerations which prohibit perpetual gifts and trusts should be no bar to the public benefits which charities bring about;

- charitable trusts will not fail for uncertainty of object. Provided that the trust was intended to be applied exclusively for charitable purposes it will not fail if those purposes are, or become, uncertain (see *cy près* at 8.4). It may be valid even if it is *impossible* to discharge the trust according to its strict terms. In *Chichester Diocesan Fund and Board of Finance* v *Simpson* [1944] AC 341 at 348, Viscount Simon LC held that charities are an exception to the fundamental principle that the testator must by the terms of his will determine the specific destination of the property with which the will proposes to deal.

Additional privileges of charitable status include:

- the more generous approach taken by the courts to the construction of charitable trusts. In *Weir* v *Crum-Brown* [1908] AC 162 at 167 Lord Loreburn stated that 'there is no better rule than that a benignant construction will be placed upon charitable bequests' and in *IRC* v *McMullen* Lord Hailsham of St Marylebone approved that *dictum* when he held that '[i]n construing trust deeds the intention of which is to set up a charitable trust, and in others too, where it can be claimed that there is ambiguity, a benignant construction should be given if possible';

- charities must be registered, registration bringing with it a conclusive presumption of charitable status for the period of registration.

8.1.1.2 **Tax law privileges**

Charitable trusts, and those who donate to them, enjoy a wide range of fiscal exemptions and privileges. They include exemptions for the charity from income tax, corporation tax and capital gains tax and exemptions for the donor from capital gains tax and inheritance tax. There are also exemptions from stamp duty on transfers and from non-domestic local rates. In addition, donors can reclaim income tax on one-off donations under the 'gift aid' scheme, and charities can reclaim income tax on annual covenants for more than three years.

The extent of these privileges has prompted some to call for a costs–benefit calculus as a prerequisite to the recognition of charitable status (see, for example, Lord Cross in *Dingle* v *Turner* [1972] AC 601). If it were to occur, it would undoubtedly involve a calculation of great complexity. It cannot be assumed, for instance, that gains made by charities due to fiscal privilege are equal in value to the losses made by the Inland Revenue as a result of that privilege. To use the economists' term, it is not a 'zero-sum game'. The fiscal privilege of charitable status may itself influence the size and frequency of donations made to the charity (at present, donors are entitled to a degree of tax relief on one-off donations of over £250 and donations covenanted to be made regularly for at least four years). The calculation is a complex one even before an attempt has been made to quantify the benefit in such abstract goods as research into a cure for cancer, education in the arts and the advancement of religion.

8.1.2 **The need for public benefit**

In theory, charities ought to enjoy certain advantages by right, but in practice they enjoy them by way of privileges granted by the political State. It will therefore come as no surprise to discover that a purpose will only be considered charitable if it is for the public benefit. This requirement has been strengthened by the Charities Act 2006. There is certainly merit in the idea that all charities should pass a threshold minimum public benefit requirement, but the difficulty will be to fix that threshold at the appropriate level. It is politically sensitive, economically complex and morally invidious to attempt to rate charities according to the degree to which they are beneficial to the public.

According to the Charity Commission's 2013 official guidance on public benefit, for a purpose to be 'for the public benefit' it must generally satisfy both the 'benefit' and 'public' aspects. The exception is if the purpose is to relieve or prevent poverty, where different rules apply (see later). The Commission explains that in order to satisfy the 'benefit aspect' of public benefit, the purpose must be 'beneficial' and 'any detriment or harm that results from the purpose must not outweigh the benefit'. To satisfy the 'public aspect' of public benefit, the purpose must 'benefit the public in general, or a sufficient section of the public' and 'not give rise to more than incidental personal benefit'. The Commission acknowledges that the 'benefit' and 'public' aspects can overlap, and warns that where a charity has more than one purpose, the public benefit of one purpose 'cannot be used to offset any lack of public benefit in another'. To satisfy the 'beneficial' requirement of the 'benefit aspect', the beneficial aspect must be identifiable and 'capable of being proved by evidence where necessary' and 'not based on personal views'. The Commission gives the example of emergency aid in response to natural disaster as one where the beneficial element is objectively self-evident and will not need to be proved. The artistic merit of paintings or the health benefits of a therapy, for example, are not objectively self-evident in that sense. Objective evidence of the detrimental effects of a purpose can outweigh its beneficial aspect, but where the benefit is clearly strong it will take especially strong evidence of detriment to outweigh it. In short, there seems to be a presumption in favour of supporting benefits in the face of possible detriment.

Under the 'public aspect' of public benefit, the requirement of benefit to the public in general is self-explanatory (it would include, for example, the benefit of protecting an endangered species), but the alternative requirement of benefiting 'a sufficient section of the public' (also called a 'public class' of people) requires more explanation. People in a certain area or belonging to a certain community will generally be a 'public class' of people. More controversially, so are categories of people defined by reference to a 'protected characteristic' under the Equality Act 2010. Thus a 'public class' may be identified by age, disability, sex, sexual orientation, gender reassignment, marriage and civil partnership, pregnancy and maternity, race or nationality (but not skin colour), religion or belief, 'provided the restriction of benefits to people having that characteristic is justified in relation to the purpose'. The question of what is and is not 'justified' promises to be hotly disputed in future cases.

A trust that excludes the poor from benefiting will not be for a 'sufficient section of the public'. Other trusts that will not be for a 'sufficient section of the public' will be determined on a case-by-case basis, but according to the Commission's guidance they will include the following: 'a purpose which is confined to a closed religious organisation'; 'a purpose where all the potential beneficiaries (now and in the future) are named, such as an individual or individuals or a fixed group of individuals'; 'a purpose where the number of people who can benefit (now and in the future) is numerically negligible (unless the purpose is for the relief, and in some cases the prevention, of poverty)'; 'a purpose which defines who can benefit in a manner which, when related to the purpose, is "capricious" (e.g. wholly irrelevant, irrational or without good reason)'; 'a purpose which benefits members of a mutual benefit society'; and, with the exception of a purpose for the relief, and in some cases the prevention, of poverty, 'a purpose which exists for the benefit of an organisation's members only unless: a sufficient section of the public can access those benefits by becoming members and the membership is a suitable way of carrying out the charity's purpose for the public benefit'. Finally, a charitable purpose may only confer personal benefits if these are 'incidental' to carrying out the purpose.

 CASE CLOSE-UP

***The Independent Schools Council v The Charity Commission for England and Wales* [2011] UKUT 421 (TCC)**

In response to issues referred by the Attorney-General under the Charities Act 1993, the UK's Upper Tribunal (Tax and Chancery Chamber) considered the law governing fee-paying schools.

Held: The 2006 Act 'makes little, if any, difference to the legal position of the independent schools sector', but it does 'bring into focus what it is that the pre-existing law already required', namely that a trust which 'excludes the poor from benefit cannot be a charity' and therefore a school which operates *solely* for the benefit of fee-paying students is not sufficiently for the public benefit even though it undoubtedly operates for the public benefit in the general sense of advancing the overall level of education in the population at large. It lies within the trustees' discretion to determine what level of provision (above the minimum necessary to secure charitable status) should be made for the poor to access the educational benefits arising from a fee-paying school. The Upper Tribunal suggested that the issue of the charitable status of fee-charging schools ought to be resolved by politicians rather than judges.

THINKING POINT

Do you think that the tribunal took an overly laissez-faire approach to the issue? (See next.)

 OUTSIDE THE BOX

'Charity that Begins at the School Gate' *The Guardian*, **Friday 11 July 2008**

(Extract from a letter submitted by members of the 'Education Reform Group')
'We are asking the Charity Commission to ensure . . . that [fee-charging] schools are made truly accountable to deliver public benefit, particularly to the 93% of children who do not attend them. State schools are made rigorously and publicly accountable for their performance. Charitable fee-charging schools should be equally accountable to the public, not just to fee-paying parents. We also call upon the Charity Commission to avoid approving public benefit activities that are in fact a disbenefit to the state sector: for example, bursaries—a reworking of the assisted places scheme that creams off the most able pupils; or the poaching of state school teachers in shortage subjects.'

NOTE: Throughout this chapter reference is made to the Charities Act 2011. This is a consolidating statute that brings the Charities Acts 1993 and 2006 and the Recreational Charities Act 1958 under one new title without changing the substance of the law in any significant way. Given the relatively recent date of this change and in the interests of ease of cross-referencing between this text and your study notes and other materials, references to the 2011 Act are sometimes still accompanied by references to corresponding provisions in the old 1993 and 2006 Acts.

8.1.3 **The management of charities**

8.1.3.1 **By a corporation**

Part VII of the Charities Act 1993 introduced a simplified scheme for the incorporation of charities. (See, now, Part 12 of the 2011 Act.) The increasing use of corporate status by charities should not be underestimated, but there is not the scope to consider that here. For present purposes, our attention will be confined to charitable trusts.

8.1.3.2 **By trustees**

The basic duties of charity trustees are the same as those of other trustees. There are, however, some additional duties peculiar to charity trustees. These include registration of the charity (most charities must be registered—see s 3 of the 1993 Act; ss 29–31 of the 2011 Act); seeking a *cy près* scheme (see 8.4) where the trust can no longer be discharged; avoiding needless accumulation of funds (1992 Charity Commissioners Report, p. 25); keeping accounts in the form appropriate to the size of the charity (Charities Act 1993, ss 41–43; Charities Act 2011, Part 8); and preparing an annual report (s 45). Charity trustees also have special duties in relation to the investment of the trust fund (see Chapter 14). If a problem should arise in the course of the administration of a charity, the trustees may, by written request, seek the advice of the Charity Commission (s 29).

Certain persons are disqualified from acting as trustees of charitable trusts (s 72). Examples include persons who have been convicted of dishonesty offences and persons subject to an undischarged bankruptcy. The maximum punishment for acting whilst disqualified is two years' imprisonment and a fine (s 73).

8.1.3.3 **By the court**

As a result of the Charities Act 1993 the role of the courts in deciding whether or not a body is charitable has been largely transferred to the Charity Commission. The court remains the forum of ultimate appeal. The court's jurisdiction to establish a scheme for the administration of a charity (matters such as the appointment of trustees, extending powers of investment, etc) is concurrent with that of the Charity Commission (as to which, see s 17 of the 1993 Act; Charities Act 2011, ss 69–75).

8.1.3.4 **By the Charity Commission**

The Charity Commission for England and Wales is a non-ministerial government department and part of the Civil Service. According to its website, the Commission is 'completely independent of Ministerial influence and also independent from the sector it regulates. It has a number of quasi-judicial functions where it uses powers similar to those of the High Court.' The Commission is required to report on its performance to Parliament annually.

The Charities Act 2006, s 7 (Charities Act 2011, Part 2) defines the objectives, functions and duties of the Charity Commission. Its *objectives* are as follows: its 'public confidence objective is to increase public trust and confidence in charities'; its 'public benefit objective is to promote awareness and understanding of the operation of the public benefit requirement'; its 'compliance objective is to promote compliance by charity trustees with their legal obligations in exercising control and management of the administration of their charities'; its 'charitable resources objective is to promote the effective use of charitable resources'; and its 'accountability objective is to enhance the accountability of charities to donors, beneficiaries and the general public'. The Commission's general *functions* include determining whether institutions are or are not charities; encouraging and facilitating the better administration of charities; identifying and investigating apparent misconduct or mismanagement in the administration of charities and taking remedial or protective action in connection with misconduct or mismanagement therein; determining whether public collections certificates should be issued, and remain in force, in respect of public charitable collections; obtaining, evaluating and disseminating information in connection with the performance of any of the Commission's functions or meeting any of its objectives (including the maintenance of an accurate and up-to-date register of charities); and giving information or advice, or making proposals, to any Minister of the Crown on matters relating to any of the Commission's functions or meeting any of its objectives. The Commission's general *duties* require it to act, so far as is reasonably practicable, in a way which is compatible with its objectives, and which it considers most appropriate for the purpose of meeting those objectives and so as to encourage all forms of charitable giving and voluntary participation in charity work.

8.2 The legal definition of charity

'Of all the words in the English language bearing a popular as well as a legal signification I am not sure that there is one which more unmistakably has a technical meaning in the strictest sense of term, that is a meaning clear and distinct, peculiar to the law as understood and administered in this country, and not depending upon or coterminous with the popular or vulgar use of the word' (*per* Lord Macnaghten, *Commissioners for Special Purpose of the Income Tax* v *Pemsel* [1891] AC 531).

'"Charity" and "charitable" are technical words in English law and must be so construed unless it can be seen from the wording of the will as a whole that they are used in some other than their technical sense' (*per* Lord Porter, *Chichester Diocesan Fund and Board of Finance v Simpson* [1944] AC 341 at 363).

 THINKING POINT

How would you have defined charity before you commenced your legal studies? How would you define charity now? Write down your definition and at the end of the chapter reflect upon how you would need to change your definition to make it legally accurate. Which of the pursuits listed at Table 8.1 would you regard as being charitable? Briefly write the reason for your choice under the relevant column and review your choices at the end of the chapter.

Table 8.1 Charity or not charity?

Purpose	Charitable	Non-charitable
Campaigning to end the Gulf War	☐	☐
Seeking a ban on vivisection	☐	☐
The provision of sporting facilities to the Royal Navy	☐	☐
Faith healing	☐	☐
Giving cash to a destitute nephew	☐	☐
The provision of a sanctuary for wild animals	☐	☐
The exhibition of watercolours by a little-known artist	☐	☐

Whilst we are playing the definition game, try to define the following concepts in your own words (again, it would be useful to write them down and review them at the end of the chapter to see if they need to be changed):

- poverty;
- education;
- art;
- sport;
- religion;
- political.

The presence of some of the words in the list might surprise you. Nevertheless, it has been the task of the courts down the years to attach useful meaning to some of these concepts and terms. As you work through this chapter reflect upon how the judges approach the problem of defining such large concepts as 'art' and 'religion'. Could you do any better?

8.2.1 **Statutory definitions**

The Charities Act 2006 attempted to provide a statutory definition of charity in the form of a list of charitable purposes. The only statutory precedent for such a list is the preamble to a statute of 1601, the so-called Statute of Elizabeth I. The preamble contains a list of contemporary charitable uses 'so varied and comprehensive that it became the practice of the court [of Chancery] to refer to it as a sort of index or chart' (Lord Macnaghten, *Commissioners for Special Purpose of the Income Tax* v *Pemsel* [1891] AC 531 at 581). Ironically, the statute itself was not at all concerned with the definition of charity.

 STATUTE

Statute of Charitable Uses (1601) 43 Eliz. I, c. 4

Preamble

Whereas Lands, Tenements, Rents, Annuities, Profits, Hereditaments, Goods, Chattels, Money and Stocks of Money, have been heretofore given, limited, appointed and assigned, as well as by the Queen's most excellent Majesty, and her most noble Progenitors, as by sundry other well disposed persons; some for Relief of aged, impotent and poor People, some for the Maintenance of sick and maimed Soldiers and Mariners, Schools of Learning, Free Schools, and Scholars in Universities, some for the Repair of Bridges, Ports, Havens, Causeways, Churches, Sea-Banks and Highways, some for the Education and Preferment of Orphans, some for or towards Relief, Stock or Maintenance for Houses of Correction, some for the Marriages of Poor Maids, some for Supportation, Aid and Help of young Tradesmen, Handicraftsmen and Persons decayed, and others for the Relief or Redemption of Prisoners or Captives, and for Aid or Ease of any poor Inhabitants concerning Payments of Fifteens [a tax on moveable property], setting out of Soldiers and other Taxes; which Lands, Tenements, Rents, Annuities, Profits, Hereditaments, Goods, Chattels, Money and Stocks of Money, nevertheless have not been employed according to charitable Intent of the givers and Founders thereof, by reason of Frauds, Breaches of Trust, and Negligence in those that should pay, deliver and employ the same: For Redress and Remedy whereof, Be it enacted . . .

 CASE CLOSE-UP

Morice v *Bishop of Durham* **(1804) 9 Ves 399, Court of Appeal**

Facts: a bequest was made to the Bishop upon trust for 'such objects of benevolence and liberality as the Bishop of Durham in his own discretion shall most approve'.

Sir William Grant MR: 'Is this a trust for charity? Do purposes of liberality and benevolence mean the same as objects of charity? That word in its widest sense denotes all the good affections men ought to have towards each other; in its most restricted and common sense relief of the poor. In neither of these senses is it employed in this court. Here its signification is derived chiefly from the statute 43 Eliz., c. 4 [relating to charitable gifts]. Those purposes are considered charitable which that statute enumerates or which by analogies are deemed within its spirit and intendment, and to some such purpose every bequest to charity generally shall be applied. But, it is clear, liberality and benevolence can find numberless objects not included in that statute in the largest construction of it. The use of the word 'charitable' seems to have been purposely avoided in this will in order to leave the bishop the most unrestrained discretion. Supposing the uncertainty of the trust no objection to its validity, could it be contended to be an abuse of the trust to employ this fund upon objects which all mankind would allow to be objects of liberality and benevolence though not to be said, in the language of this court, to be objects also of charity? But what rule of construction could it be said that all objects of liberality and benevolence are excluded which do not fall within the statute of Elizabeth? The question is not whether he may not apply it upon purposes strictly charitable, but whether he is bound so to apply it? I am not aware of any case in which the bequest has been held charitable where the testator has not either used that word to denote his general purpose or specified some particular purpose, which this court has determined to be charitable in its nature.'

All this talk of the 'spirit of the preamble' will understandably lead you to think that the legal definition of charity floats cloud-like above the judge's head. To decide whether or not a particular enterprise is charitable is indeed an invidious task, and the judges have generally preferred to avoid it by means of rules and precedent (see Gardner, *An Introduction to the Law of Trusts*, Oxford: Clarendon Press, 1990, pp. 105–6). This brings us to the next section.

8.2.2 **The heads of charity**

In *Commissioners for Special Purpose of the Income Tax* v *Pemsel* [1891] AC 531, Lord Macnaghten held that 'charity' in its legal sense comes under four principal heads:

- trusts for the relief of poverty;
- trusts for the advancement of education;
- trusts for the advancement of religion;
- trusts for other purposes beneficial to the community, not falling under any of the preceding heads.

In *Scottish Burial Reform and Cremation Society Ltd* v *Glasgow Corpn* [1968] AC 138 the appellant was a non-profit making company incorporated to promote cremation, which service it had carried out in Glasgow for many years. It provided opportunities for religious observance but had not been incorporated on any religious basis.

 THINKING POINT

Do you think that the business of the company fell within any of Lord Macnaghten's four heads of charity?

The House of Lords held that the objects of the company were for the benefit of the community and fell within the fourth of Lord Macnaghten's heads of charity. However, Lord Wilberforce asserted that the 'four heads' were a classification of convenience and not necessarily a comprehensive set of charitable classes, that Lord Macnaghten's words should not be given the force of statute and that the law of charity is a continually evolving subject. As mentioned earlier, the heads of charity have now been extended by statute. The list contained in s 3(1) of the Charities Act 2011 (s 2(2) of the Charities Act 2006) is as follows:

- the prevention or relief of poverty (para. a);
- the advancement of education (para. b);
- the advancement of religion (para. c);
- the advancement of health or the saving of lives (para. d);
- the advancement of citizenship or community development (para. e);
- the advancement of arts, culture, heritage or science (para. f);
- the advancement of amateur sport (para. g);
- the promotion of human rights, conflict resolution or reconciliation or the promotion of religious or racial harmony or equality and diversity (para. h);
- the advancement of environmental protection or improvement (para. i);
- the relief of those in need, by reason of youth, age, ill-health, disability, financial hardship or other disadvantage (para. j);
- the advancement of animal welfare (para. k);
- the promotion of the efficiency of the armed forces of the Crown or of the efficiency of the police, fire and rescue services or the ambulance services (para. l);
- [other existing charitable purposes or analogous charitable purposes. In essence, any other purpose intended to provide community benefit] (para. m).

In *Gilmour v Coats* [1949] AC 426 (subsequently followed by Cross J in *Neville Estates Ltd v Madden* [1962] Ch 832 at 853) Lord Simonds warned (at 449) that, in enlarging the compass of charity 'it is dangerous to reason by analogy from one head of charity to another'. In a similar vein, Lord Upjohn observed in *Scottish Burial Reform and Cremation Society Ltd v Glasgow Corpn* [1968] AC 138 that 'the authorities show that the "spirit and intendement" of the preamble to the Statute of Elizabeth have been stretched almost to breaking point' (at 153). The enlargement of the list of charitable 'heads' from four to 13 (and the inclusion within the 13 of a great many sub-heads) was a direct response to the fact that the four heads had been seriously overstretched with the effort of encompassing the range of modern charitable purposes. We can nevertheless expect new species of charity to be admitted in the future, by analogy to those listed in paras a–l. This is because the final head ('m') includes any purposes that may reasonably be regarded as analogous to, or within the spirit of, any purposes which have been recognised under charity law as falling within the other heads.

In the following sections *existing law* is arranged under each of the new heads of charity. The existing law remains valid apart from the very few cases in which the Charities Act 2006 expressly changed the meaning of charity.

8.2.3 The prevention or relief of poverty (head 'a')

8.2.3.1 The meaning of poverty

Does 'the relief of poverty' equate to 'the meeting of a material need'?

In *Re Gwyon* [1930] 1 Ch 255 the testator directed that the residue of his estate should be applied by his executor to establish the 'Gwyon's Boys Clothing Foundation'; a foundation to provide 'knickers' (a sort of trouser) for boys between the ages of 10 and 15 in a certain district. The boys could replace their old pair for a new pair, provided that the words 'Gwyon's Present' were still legible on the waistband of the old pair. The claim that the gift was a valid charitable trust for the relief of poverty failed. None of the conditions of the gift necessarily imported poverty. Eve J noted that the trustees would have no power to refuse a boy his gift on the ground merely that the boy was materially affluent. (In fact, a closer examination of the conditions attaching to the gift reveals that the gift was anything but charitable. According to its terms, no boy was eligible who was already receiving support from a charity or the local parish, and no 'black boy' was eligible!)

Does the 'relief of poverty' equate to 'the relief of the destitute'?

The *Oxford English Dictionary* defines 'destitute' in this sense as 'now, without the very necessaries of life or means of bare subsistence, in absolute want'. The attitude of the courts has always been that the destitute are always poor, but that the poor are not always destitute. In *Re Gardom* [1914] 1 Ch 662 at 668 Eve J held that 'there are degrees of poverty less acute than abject poverty or destitution, but poverty nevertheless'. In *Re Gardom* a trust for 'ladies of limited means' was held to be charitable, as was a trust for 'distressed gentlefolk' in *Re Young* [1951] Ch 344.

 OUTSIDE THE BOX

Institute for Fiscal Studies, Poverty and Inequality in the UK: 2011 (IFS Commentary C118)

Box 4.1. Poverty definitions and the reporting of poverty

Unless stated otherwise, we measure poverty by counting the number of individuals whose household income is below 60% of that of the median individual (the median individual is in the middle of the income distribution). The indicator is a 'relative' measure of poverty because the poverty line moves with median income each year. This definition of poverty as a relative concept is in common with those used in most of the rest of Europe but contrasts with, for example, the official measure of poverty used by the United States Census Bureau, which was initially based on the income required to purchase a fixed basket of food items and has since been uprated in line with price changes. Such measures are called 'absolute' measures of poverty—although this terminology is not intended to suggest that it measures a more severe state of poverty than relative poverty.

The relative nature of 'poverty' in charity law was made explicit by the Court of Appeal in *Re Coulthurst* [1951] Ch 622.

The testator, Coulthurst, directed that the income from his estate should be applied by his trustees 'to or for the benefit of such . . . of the . . . widows and orphaned children of deceased officers and deceased ex-officers' of a bank 'as the bank shall in its absolute discretion consider by reason of his, her or their financial circumstances to be most deserving of such assistance'.

This was held to be a valid charitable trust intended to benefit the poor, in accordance with the meaning of the preamble to the Act of 1601. The fact that the beneficiaries were chosen by reference to their employment with a particular bank did not defeat the charitable nature of a gift for the relief of poverty.

Evershed MR held that 'poverty does not mean destitution; it is a word of wide and somewhat indefinite import; it may not unfairly be paraphrased for present purposes as meaning persons who have to "go short in the ordinary acceptation of that term, due regard being had to their status in life, and so forth"'.

Are the 'working classes' poor?

It has long been accepted by the courts that 'the poor need not necessarily be poor of the class known as the working class, and many of the working class . . . are not poor' (*per* Lord Wrenbury in *Re Sutton* [1901] 2 Ch 640 at 646). Nevertheless, the question still came up for consideration in *Re Sanders' Will Trusts* [1954] Ch 265. There the testator had directed his trustees, by a codicil to his will, to 'apply one equal third part of my residuary trust fund in . . . providing dwellings for the working classes and their families resident in the area of Pembroke Dock, Pembrokeshire, Wales, or within a radius of five miles therefrom (with preference to actual dockworkers and their families employed at the said docks)'. Harman J held that the words 'working class' did not indicate a gift to the poor: 'These are not old persons; they are not widows, they are merely men working in the docks and their families, and, therefore, I cannot infer any element of poverty here.'

THINKING POINT

What if a testator provided that his residuary estate should be held upon trust to pay the capital and income to a local authority in a needy part of Cyprus 'on condition that the same shall be used for the purposes only of the construction of or as a contribution towards the cost of the construction of a working men's hostel'?

This disposition arose for consideration in *Re Niyazi's Will Trusts* [1978] 1 WLR 910. Megarry V-C held that this was a valid charitable trust for the relief of poverty. The judge described the case as 'desperately near the borderline', but concluded that only poor persons would be likely to live in a hostel. The word 'hostel', he said, was very different from the word 'dwelling' as used in *Re Sanders' WT* (see earlier in this section): the former suggested a poor inhabitant, the latter was appropriate to any house. The judge also took into account (1) the depressed nature of the area in which the hostel had been directed to be built, and (2) the fact that the relatively modest size of the fund made it unlikely that a 'grandiose building' would be erected.

8.2.3.2 **The public benefit requirement in poverty trusts**

As a result of the Charities Act 2006 (now Charities Act 2011), new trusts for the relief of poverty will only be awarded charitable status if they are for the public benefit. Prior to the Act it was not a requirement that poverty trusts should benefit the general public. However, in contrast to other charities, it is not necessary to demonstrate the 'sufficient section of the public' element of public benefit in the case of trusts for the relief (and in some cases for the prevention) of poverty (*AG* v *Charity Commission Upper Tribunal* (Tax and Chancery Chamber) FTC/84/2011 20 February 2012).

A trust to relieve the poverty of named or *identified* individuals has never been charitable, but trusts for the relief of poor members of a *private class of persons* (i.e. a class of people identified by reference to particular person or employer (such as the bank in *Re Coulthurst*, earlier in this section)) were charitable. This appears to be unchanged by the 2006 Act (*Her Majesty's Attorney General* et al. v *The Charity Commission Upper Tribunal* (Tax and Chancery Chamber)

(2012) WL 488349). In *Re Scarisbrick* [1951] Ch 622 a testatrix left one-half of her residuary estate upon ultimate trusts for such of the relations of her son and daughters as the survivor of her son and daughters shall deem to be 'in needy circumstances'. The Court of Appeal held that the disposition was a valid charitable trust for the relief of poverty because the gift was for a *class* of poor persons.

Re Scarisbrick was approved by the House of Lords in *Dingle v Turner* [1972] AC 601. There the testator gave his residuary estate to trustees upon trust for his wife for her life and thereafter to place £10,000 on trust 'to apply the income thereof in paying pensions to poor employees of E Dingle & Co Ltd' who were old or disabled. It was held that the terms of the will created a valid charitable trust for the relief of poverty, despite the personal nexus between the beneficiaries and the named company. In the case of trusts for the relief of 'poverty' the distinction between a public charitable trust and a private non-charitable trust depended upon whether, on a true construction of the gift, it was for the relief of poverty amongst a particular description of poor people or was merely a gift to particular poor persons.

Trusts for the benefit of 'poor relations' had been accepted as charitable for more than 200 years when the House of Lords heard *Dingle v Turner*, but trusts for 'poor employees' had only been recognised since around 1900 (*Re Gosling* (1900) 48 WR 300). It was suggested in argument that the poor relations cases were an established anomaly and should not be disturbed, but that trusts for poor employees should not be afforded the same respect. The House of Lords rejected this suggestion, as it would lead to 'illogical' distinctions between different types of poverty.

The requirement of public benefit introduced by the 2006 Act should in the future prevent trusts such as the one in *Re Segelman* from gaining charitable status. In *Re Segelman* [1996] 2 WLR 173 the court recognised the charitable status of a trust for the 'poor and needy' of a class comprising at the time of the hearing a mere 26 people related to the testator, a multi-millionaire. These 26 were for the most part 'comfortably off' (although the court accepted that they might need financial assistance to 'overcome an unforeseen crisis'). Chadwick J held that, although this case very nearly infringed the rule that relief should not be restricted to named individuals, it was saved by the inclusion within the class of after-born issue of the 26 identified beneficiaries, thereby raising the possibility of quite substantial numbers of additional beneficiaries who might themselves be, or become, poor.

8.2.4 The advancement of education (head 'b')

> I call . . . a complete and generous education that which fits a man to perform justly, skilfully and magnanimously all the offices both private and public, of peace and war.
>
> John Milton, *On Education*, 1673

Amongst the catalogue of charitable uses appearing in the preamble to the Statute of Elizabeth, reference is made to 'Schools of Learning and Scholars in Universities'. In fact the class of educational charitable trusts now includes museums, nursery schools, scholarly societies, trusts for industrial and technical training and trusts for the promotion of the arts.

 THINKING POINT

Can you think of any educational charities of which you are a beneficiary?

If you are a student at a university in the UK your institution will have charitable status (even private universities have charitable status). As a law student there is at least one further educational charity of which you are a beneficiary—provided that you read law reports! The House of Lords in *Incorporated Council of Law Reporting for England and Wales v A-G* [1972] Ch 73 agreed that the production and publication of Official Law Reports by the Incorporated Council of Law Reporting for England and Wales was a charitable activity. Their Lordships were unanimous in holding that the trust was charitable, with two of the five holding the primary purpose of the society to be the advancement of education. The suggestion that the law reports were merely a tool of the lawyer's trade was sharply dismissed as being as untenable as the suggestion that charitable trusts for the development of medicinal drugs exist only to promote the medical profession. Sachs LJ referred once again to the disjunction between the popular and the legal meaning of the word 'charity', stating that 'it is . . . necessary to eliminate from one's mind a natural allergy, stemming simply from the popular meaning of "charity", to the idea that law reporting might prove to be a charitable activity'. In reaching this conclusion their Lordships echoed the words of the Rt Hon Edmund Burke who in 1816 opined that 'to put an end to reports, is to put an end to the law of England'.

8.2.4.1 Educative value of research

George Bernard Shaw's trust for research into a new English alphabet failed as a charitable trust for the advancement of education (see 7.1). The judge held that 'if the object be merely the increase of knowledge, that is not in itself a charitable object unless it be combined with teaching or education'. Perhaps the judge had in mind the words of St Paul: 'knowledge puffeth up, but charity edifieth'. Shaw's trust was a trust for private purposes and therefore failed (see 7.1).

In contrast, the testamentary gift in *Re Hopkins* [1965] Ch 669 was held to be charitable because of the importance of the research that was being carried out. The testatrix had left a third of her residuary estate to the Francis Bacon Society, to be 'applied towards finding the Bacon–Shakespeare manuscripts and in the event of the same having been discovered by the date of my death then for the general purposes of the work and propaganda of the society'. The society, which was a registered charity under the Charities Act 1960, existed primarily to study the evidence for Francis Bacon's authorship of plays commonly ascribed to William Shakespeare. It was held that for a gift for research to be charitable it must be combined with teaching or education, albeit the education of the researchers themselves. Wilberforce J held that it did not matter that the charitable purposes might not fall neatly into any one only of the four heads of charity. He considered the possibility that the research might fall within the general head of charities 'beneficial to the community', and stressed that 'benefits' need not be material and would include intellectual or artistic benefits. According to virtually all Shakespearean scholars, the hypothesis that Francis Bacon wrote Shakespeare's plays borders on the ridiculous. One might ask whether such whimsical research should be charitable, but it is the fact that the law does not prejudge the merit of particular research (or particular religion) that makes the law of charity truly charitable in spirit.

The Amnesty International organisation set up a trust to administer those of its purposes which were considered to be charitable. Its aims included the release and humane treatment of prisoners of conscience, research into the observance of human rights and the dissemination of the results of such research. It applied to the Charity Commissioners for registration of the trust as a charity under s 4 of the Charities Act 1960. Registration was refused (*McGovern v Attorney-General* [1982] 1 Ch 321). On appeal to the High Court, Slade J confirmed the Commissioners' decision. The major part of the trust purposes was of a political, and therefore non-charitable, nature (see 8.2.17). However, had the provisions as to research stood alone they would have been charitable. The subject matter of the research was 'capable of adding usefully to the store of human knowledge'. His Lordship noted that human rights has become an accepted academic discipline, and stated that it should be benignly presumed that the trustees would not implement the research in a political manner.

8.2.4.2 The public benefit requirement in educational trusts

The key case is the decision of the House of Lords in *Oppenheim* v *Tobacco Securities Trust Co Ltd* [1951] AC 297. In that case a settlement directed trustees to apply the income from the trust fund 'in providing for . . . the education of children of employees or former employees of the British–American Tobacco Co Ltd . . . or any of its subsidiary or allied companies in such manner . . . as the acting trustees shall in their absolute discretion . . . think fit'. The employees referred to numbered more than 110,000. The issue was whether the class of potential beneficiaries constituted a sufficient section of the general public. It was held by the majority that, despite the huge number of potential beneficiaries, they were identified by the personal nexus between them and the employer company. Accordingly, the trust did not satisfy the requirement that it produce a benefit to a sufficient section of the community. The words 'section of the' community have no special meaning, but they indicate, first, that the possible beneficiaries must not be numerically negligible, and secondly, that they must not be distinguishable from other members of the public by reason of a relationship to a particular individual.

THINKING POINT

Would a trust to establish a school in a small mining village be charitable if the education it provided was limited to children of employees of the mining company?

According to the majority in *Oppenheim* it would not. Against this, Lord Cross of Chelsea had this to say in *Dingle* v *Turner* [1972] AC 601:

> That reasoning—based on the distinction between personal and impersonal relationships—has never seemed to me very satisfactory and I have always—if I may say so—felt the force of the criticism to which my noble and learned friend Lord MacDermott subjected it in his dissenting speech in the *Oppenheim* case. For my part I would prefer to approach the problem on far broader lines . . . with the bare contrast between 'public' and 'private' . . . One might say that . . . the employees in such concerns as ICI or GEC are just as much 'sections of the public' as the residents in some geographical area.

8.2.4.3 Preferences

THINKING POINT

Imagine that you are the Charity Commission. You have received an application to register a charitable trust in the following terms: 'for the promotion and furtherance of commercial education of persons of either sex who are British born subjects who are desirous of educating themselves or obtaining tuition for a higher commercial career, but whose means are insufficient or will not allow of their obtaining such education or tuition at their own expense; in selecting beneficiaries it is my wish that the charity trustees shall give a preference to any employees of J Co Ltd or any members of the families of such employees; failing a sufficient number of beneficiaries under such description then the persons eligible shall be any persons of British birth as the charity trustees may select. Provided that the total income to be available for benefiting the preferred beneficiaries shall not in any one year be more than seventy-five per cent of the total available income for such year.' Would you grant the application?

The facts set out in the thinking point reproduce almost exactly the trust that was considered in *Re Koettgen* [1954] Ch 252. Surprising as it may seem, Upjohn J held that the trust was a charitable one, despite the preference. His Lordship held that the primary class of beneficiaries was sufficiently large to satisfy the public benefit requirement for educational trusts and that the direction to prefer could not affect the validity of the primary trust given that it was not certain that the preferred class would exhaust 75 per cent of the fund in any year. However, if the direction to 'prefer' a class is made in absolute, imperative terms, so as to elevate the preferred class to the status of primary class of beneficiaries, the trust will only be charitable if the preferred class is itself large enough to constitute a sufficient section of the public. A trust for the education of 'deserving youths of the Islamic faith', which directed the trustees to grant an absolute priority to the settlor's family, failed as a charitable trust (*Caffoor v Commissioners of Income Tax* [1961] AC 584, PC). Crucial to the decision in *Re Koettgen* was the fact that it could not be said that the trustees would actually apply a full 75 per cent of the income in favour of the preferred class in any given year.

 THINKING POINT

Would it still be a charitable trust if the trustees did in fact exercise their power to favour the preferred class in this way?

This is what occurred in *IRC v Educational Grants Association Ltd* [1967] Ch 123. In that case the Inland Revenue successfully challenged an educational association which had very close links with a commercial company (the principal donor to the Association). Evidence showed that 76 to 85 per cent of the association's income had been applied to educate the children of persons connected with the commercial company. Despite this, the association had claimed a tax refund from the Inland Revenue. The Inland Revenue refused the refund, claiming that the association had failed to apply its funds to exclusively charitable ends. Pennycuick J criticised and distinguished *Re Koettgen* and decided in favour of the IRC. The Court of Appeal upheld his judgment, but without airing any opinion of *Re Koettgen*. The present status of *Re Koettgen* is therefore somewhat uncertain. The Charity Commissioners have followed *Re Koettgen* and registered similar trusts on a few occasions, but the Annual Report of the Charity Commissioners warned (in their 1978 report) that the 'application of too large a proportion of the income would constitute an application for non-charitable purposes'.

8.2.5 **The advancement of religion (head 'c')**

As you progress through this section it may be helpful to distinguish religious beliefs from religious practices. A belief may be religious but it will not be charitable unless it is backed up by practices which benefit the public.

8.2.5.1 **What is religion?**

> **some useful terms** 'Monotheism' is belief in one God; 'polytheism' is belief in more than one god; 'atheism' is belief in no god at all and 'agnosticism' is a belief that neither affirms nor denies the existence of a God or gods.

Before the Charities Act 2006 it was apparent that atheistic and agnostic beliefs were not to be considered religious. In *Barralet* v *Attorney-General (Re South Place Ethical Society)* Dillon J held that 'religion' is concerned with mankind's relations with God or gods, whereas ethics is concerned with relations between humans only. Without belief in a supernatural entity, faith could not properly be described as religious, no matter how sincerely held. The view held in America that a religion is any belief occupying in the life of the possessor a place parallel to that occupied by belief in God prompted the judge to remark that 'parallels, by definition, never meet'. The judge suggested, further, that worship of God or gods was essential to religion, and worship in that sense had no place between humans, and accordingly no place in a humanist ethical system of belief. According to the Charities Act 2006 (now the 2011 Act) the charity law meaning of 'religion' should now be taken to include not only monotheism and polytheism, but even some atheistic or, more properly, 'non-deistic', religions such as Buddhism. Express inclusion of 'non-deistic' religions brings the UK definition of religion more closely (but not exactly) in line with the US definition described earlier. Other requirements summarised by the Charity Commission are 'a relationship between the believer and the supreme being or entity by showing worship of, reverence for or veneration of the supreme being or entity'; 'a degree of cogency, cohesion, seriousness and importance' and 'an identifiable positive, beneficial, moral or ethical framework'. Applying these criteria, the Charity Commission decided on 21 September 2010 that 'The Druid Network' should be registered as an unincorporated association that exists for the purpose of advancing religion for the public benefit. According to its adherents, modern 'Druidry' is principally concerned with 'the spiritual interaction between an individual and the spirits of nature, including those of landscape and ancestry, together with the continuities of spiritual, literary and cultural heritage'. What isn't clear is where the line should be drawn (if indeed a line should be drawn) when taking account of 'literary and cultural heritage'. Consider the following 'thinking point'.

 THINKING POINT

Is Shakespearism a religion? It has a revered book (William Shakespeare's *Complete Works*), Stratford-upon-Avon is a focal point for international pilgrimage and the rituals of the religion are performed daily in dedicated temples around the globe (including the Globe itself). Dominic Dromgoole, the Artistic Director of the Globe Theatre, professes the faith in *Will & Me: How Shakespeare Took Over My Life* (Penguin, 2006): 'Stratford was electrifying . . . we went to his tomb and liked it so much we went back twice more . . . I was a Catholic in Rome, a Moslem in Mecca.'

George Bernard Shaw, whom we encountered under the previous head of charity, was a confirmed agnostic. In the preface to volume 2 of *Plays Pleasant and Unpleasant* (1898) he opined that 'there is only one religion, though there are a hundred versions of it'. Absent the cynicism, the courts have taken a similarly liberal approach to the recognition of religion (see next).

Thornton v Howe [1862] 31 Beav 14

Facts: the court considered a gift of land which had been made to assist in the promotion and publication of the 'sacred writings of the late Joanna Southcote'. She had claimed that she was with child by the Holy Spirit and would give birth to a Second Messiah.
Held: the Master of the Rolls described her as 'a foolish ignorant woman' but nevertheless held that the gift was a charitable gift for the advancement of religion.

Romilly MR: 'the Court of Chancery makes no distinction between one religion and another . . . [or] one sect and another . . . [unless] the tenets of a particular sect inculcate doctrines adverse to the very foundations of all religions and . . . subversive of all morality . . . If the tendency were not immoral and although this Court might consider the opinions sought to be propagated foolish or even devoid of foundation the trust would nevertheless be charitable. If the decision seems a surprising one, its context should be borne in mind. As a charitable gift of land, it failed under the Statute of Mortmain (now repealed) and passed to the donor's heir.'

Thornton v Howe was followed in *Re Watson* [1973] 1 WLR 1472. There the testatrix left her estate 'for the continuance of the work of God as it has been maintained by Mr HG Hobbs and myself since 1942 by God's enabling . . . in propagating the truth as given in the Holy Bible . . .' Hobbs (a retired builder) predeceased the testatrix but had written a number of religious tracts during his lifetime. His publications were regarded by experts as being unlikely to extend the knowledge of the Christian religion, but quite likely to confirm, in the group who had produced the publications, their own religious opinions. The trust was held to be a valid charitable trust for the advancement of religion.

It is clear from these judgments that all religions are regarded equally by the courts. Indeed, generally speaking courts do not profess to pass judgment on religious claims. (Although in *Khaira v Shergill* [2014] UKSC 33, where one of the questions was whether a person was 'holy' according to the Sikh religion, the Supreme Court confirmed that although 'courts do not adjudicate on the truth of religious beliefs or on the validity of particular rites', 'the judge may have to determine such religious issues as are capable of objective ascertainment' where a claimant asks the court to enforce private rights and obligations which depend on religious issues (para. [45])). It is also obvious that the courts regard any religion as better than none (if they did not, it would be difficult to justify their charitable status on public benefit grounds); indeed, Cross J said as much in *Neville Estates v Madden* [1962] Ch 832. What is not entirely clear is what belief systems count as 'religions'.

Is ancestor worship a religious practice? In *Yeap Cheah Neo v Ong Chen Neo* (1875) LR 6 PC 381 the Judicial Committee of the Privy Council held that it is not, giving two main reasons. First, worship of human ancestors did not involve the worship of a deity and could not therefore be described as being a religion. Secondly, on the terms of the particular trust there was no assurance that the worship would produce a sufficient public benefit (*Gilmour v Coats* [1949] AC 426 (see 8.2.5.2)).

Is faith healing a religious practice? In *Funnell v Stewart* [1996] *(Re Le Cren Clarke)* 1 WLR 288 it was held that faith healing could be charitable under either the category of advancement of religion or other purposes beneficial to the community. The private religious services of the group were ancillary to their work for the public benefit, and many of their services were open to the public.

8.2.5.2 The public benefit requirement in trusts for the advancement of religion

In *Gilmour* v *Coats* [1949] AC 426 £500 was settled upon trust for the purposes of the Carmelite Priory, a community of strictly cloistered nuns. The nuns devoted themselves to prayer, meditation, fasting, penance and self-sanctification. They conducted private religious services, but were not engaged in any good works outside of the convent. Do you think that the nuns' activities were for the benefit of the community? Your answer to this will probably depend upon whether you believe in the power of prayer! The House of Lords held that the trust for the purposes of the cloistered community did not satisfy the public benefit. Accordingly, this was not a valid charitable trust for the advancement of religion. The potential for religious edification of others through the example set by the nuns was said to be too vague. Nor did their Lordships accept the argument, made by analogy to educational trusts, that the public benefit requirement had been met through the fact that membership of the community was potentially open to any woman in the whole world. Lord Simonds made the following general observation: 'the law of charity . . . has been built up not logically but empirically . . . To argue by a method of syllogism or analogy from the category of education to that of religion ignores the historical processes of law.' *Gilmour* v *Coats* was distinguished in *Neville Estates Ltd* v *Madden* [1962] Ch 832.

 CASE CLOSE-UP

***Neville Estates Ltd* v *Madden* [1962] Ch 832**

Facts: the company claimed specific performance of a contract for the sale of land owned by a synagogue. The trustees of the synagogue claimed that the synagogue existed for charitable purposes and that the consent of the Charity Commissioners would be required before the sale could proceed.

Held: the synagogue's purposes were charitable.

Cross J: 'the trust with which I am concerned resembles that in *Gilmour* v *Coats* [1949] AC 426 in this, that the persons immediately benefited by it are not a section of the public but the members of a private body. All persons of the Jewish faith living in or about Catford might well constitute a section of the public, but the members for the time being of the Catford Synagogue are no more a section of the public than the members for the time being of a Carmelite priory. The two cases, however, differ from one another in that the members of the Catford Synagogue spend their lives in the world, whereas the members of a Carmelite priory live secluded from the world. If once one refuses to pay any regard—as the courts refused to pay any regard—to the influence which these nuns living in seclusion might have on the outside world, then it must follow that no public benefit is involved in a trust to support a Carmelite priory. As Lord Greene MR said in the Court of Appeal: "Having regard to the way in which the lives of the members were spent, the benefit was a purely private one". But the court is, I think, entitled to assume that some benefit accrues to the public from the attendance at places of worship of persons who live in this world and mix with their fellow citizens. As between different religions the law stands neutral, but it assumes that any religion is at least likely to be better than none.

But then it is said—and it is this part of the argument that has caused me the greatest difficulty: But this is a case of self help. Suppose that a body of persons, being dissatisfied with the facilities for the education of small children provided in their district, form an association for the education of the children of members . . .

I feel the force of this analogy; but, as Lord Simonds pointed out in *Gilmour v Coats*, it is dangerous to reason by analogy from one head of charity to another.'

In the *Pemsel* case, mentioned earlier, Lord Bramwell cast doubt on a trust to **proselytise**: 'What of a trust for the conversion of the Jews? Is that a charitable purpose? If so, what of a trust for their reconversion?' He concluded that this was not a charitable purpose. Lord Herschell in the same case observed, somewhat cynically, that 'You may desire to convert the richest people, and very often do . . . A religious object is not necessarily a charitable object.'

> **proselytise** 'To convert or attempt to convert (someone) from one religion, belief, or opinion to another' (The Oxford Dictionary of English, 2nd edn, Oxford: Oxford University Press, 2003).

8.2.5.3 Churches and churchyards

The preamble to the Statute of Elizabeth 1601 lists amongst charitable uses 'Repair of Bridges, Ports, Havens, Causeways, Churches'. Inspired by this, the courts have recognised as charitable trusts for the maintenance of a churchyard (*Re Douglas* [1905] 1 Ch 279) and for the erection, to the memory of the testatrix and her relations, of a stained glass window in a parish church (*Re King* [1923] 1 Ch 243).

8.2.6 The advancement of health or the saving of lives (head 'd')

The advancement of health includes the prevention or relief of sickness, disease or human suffering. A gift for the purposes of a hospital is prima facie a good charitable gift under this head, but the presumption could be rebutted if evidence showed that the hospital was carried on commercially for the benefit of private individuals. In *Resch's Will Trusts* [1969] 1 AC 514 the testator left his residuary estate (then valued at around eight million Australian dollars) to trustees upon trust to pay two-thirds of the income 'to the Sisters of Charity for a period of 200 years so long as they shall conduct the St Vincent's Private Hospital'. The hospital did not seek to make a commercial profit, but its charges for treatment, whilst not necessarily excluding the poor, were not low. The Privy Council held that it was a valid charitable trust for purposes beneficial to the community. The requisite public benefit had been satisfied because evidence showed that the public needed accommodation and treatment of the type provided by the hospital. Other purposes falling under this head include charities that provide 'complementary' or 'alternative' medical treatment or health-related services such as research and hospital radio, and even (according to the Charity Commission website) self-defence classes.

> ❯ CROSS REFERENCE
> A trust for the maintenance of a particular tomb or grave is not charitable, although it could take effect as a trust of imperfect obligation (*Re Hooper* [1932] 1 Ch 38 (see 7.2.1)).

8.2.7 The advancement of citizenship or community development (head 'e')

Head 'c' having effectively defined religion out of existence, head 'e' threatens to replace it with a new secular cult of 'citizenship'. Organisations which promote belief in citizenship will henceforth attract charitable support. It hardly seems to matter that individual and 'community' notions of citizenship vary according to individual beliefs and the nature of communities, and still less that in the UK we are not merely citizens, but also (primarily) subjects of the Crown. However, one suspects that the labels 'citizenship' and 'community development' may be nothing more than political rhetoric. The Act itself equates it with such mundane aims as 'rural or urban regeneration' and 'the promotion of civic responsibility, volunteering, the voluntary sector or the effectiveness or efficiency of charities'.

8.2.8 The advancement of arts, culture, heritage or science (head 'f')

When Lord Greene MR held that the Royal Choral Society is charitable, he opined that 'the education of artistic taste is one of the most important things in the development of a civilised human being' (*Royal Choral Society* v *IRC* [1943] 2 All ER 101 at 104). If by 'artistic taste' the Master of the Rolls was referring to 'critical appreciation', there can be little doubt that the cultivation of critical appreciation is as beneficial in the field of art as it is in the fields of science or law. However, if by 'artistic taste' the Master of the Rolls meant 'artistic *good* taste' the concept becomes a highly subjective one, and hardly the proper subject matter for determination by a court.

 CASE CLOSE-UP

Re Pinion [1965] Ch 85, Court of Appeal

Facts: the testator left his freehold studio, together with his paintings and some antique furniture, silver, china, etc, to be offered to the National Trust to be kept together as a collection. The income from his residuary estate was left to be used for the maintenance of the collection. In the eveant that the National Trust might decline the gift, his executors were directed to keep the collection as a museum.

Held: that this was not a valid trust for the advancement of education.

Harman LJ: 'For myself a reading of the will leads me rather to the view that the testator's object was not to educate anyone . . . there is a strong body of evidence here that as a means of education this collection is worthless. The testator's own paintings, of which there are over fifty, are said by competent persons to be in an academic style and 'atrociously bad' and the other pictures without exception to be worthless . . . Indeed one of the experts expresses his surprise that so voracious a collector should not by hazard have picked up even one meritorious object. The most that a skilful cross-examination extracted from the expert witnesses was that there were a dozen chairs which might perhaps be acceptable to a minor provincial museum and perhaps another dozen not altogether worthless, but two dozen chairs do not make a museum and they must, to accord with the will, be exhibited stifled by a large number of absolutely worthless pictures and objects.

It was said that this is a matter of taste, and *de gustibus non est disputandum* [an opinion cannot be disputed], but here I agree with the judge that there is an accepted canon of taste on which the court must rely, for it has itself no judicial knowledge of such matters, and the unanimous verdict of the experts is as I have stated. The learned judge with great hesitation concluded that there was that scintilla of merit which was sufficient to save the rest. I find myself on the other side of the line. I can conceive of no useful object to be served in foisting on the public this mass of junk. It has neither public utility nor educative value. I would hold that the testator's project ought not to be carried into effect and that his next-of-kin is entitled to the residue of his estate.'

In *Re Delius*, the widow of Frederick Delius, the composer, left her residuary estate to trustees upon trust to apply the income therefrom 'for or towards the advancement . . . of the musical works of my late husband under conditions in which the making of profit is not the object to be attained . . . by means of the recording upon the gramophone or other instrument for the mechanical reproduction of music of those works . . . the publication and issue of a uniform edition of the whole body of the works . . . and . . . the performance in public of the works'. Roxburgh J held that the trusts were valid charitable trusts for the advancement of education. The court did not have to make a value judgment in this case because counsel on both sides were unanimous in their view that the standard of Delius's work was very high. The judge did not consider what he might have decided had the works been of an 'inadequate composer'; he mused that 'perhaps I should have no option but to give effect even to such a trust', although later in his judgment he did state, *obiter*, that 'if it is charitable to promote music in general it must be charitable to promote music of a particular composer, presupposing . . . that the composer is one whose music is worth appreciating!'

The fact that the trust would incidentally enhance the reputation of Delius and bring pleasure to listeners was not a reason for denying the charitable nature of the trust. It was, however, crucial to the success of the case that the residuary legatee was held to have no possibility of profiting personally from the trusts.

In *Re Pinion* the court was able to avoid the need to form a purely subjective value judgment on the merits of the art by the admission of expert evidence. In that case the experts concluded that the collection had no value as a means of education.

8.2.9 The advancement of amateur sport (head 'g')

In this context, 'sport' must involve physical or mental skill or exertion. Sports such as chess may also be charitable if they are educational (e.g. *Re Dupree's Deed Trusts* [1945] Ch 16) or 'promote health by involving . . . mental skill or exertion' (Charities Act 2006 s 2(3)(d)). School sports, such as football trusts, are also better considered under the educational head (e.g. *IRC v McMullen* [1981] AC 1, which concerned the FA Youth Trust created by the Football Association in 1972). The word 'sport' is derived from the word 'disport', which is itself derived from the French *porter*, 'to carry'. Literally, sport is that which carries one off, that which acts as a diversion from work and the mundane, so when for amusement we read about 'sport' on the back pages of our daily newspapers and watch it on our televisions it is we, and not the professionals whom we observe, who are the ones engaged in sport! Clearly the professional pursuit of 'sport' for personal profit will not be charitable. George Orwell once famously wrote that 'serious sport has nothing to do with fair play. It is bound up with hatred, jealousy, boastfulness, and disregard of all the rules' (*Shooting an Elephant* (1950)). Amateur sport, in contrast, is bound up with health, teamwork and fair play. Community Amateur Sports Clubs (CASCs) enjoy special tax status under Schedule 18 of the Finance Act 2002.

8.2.10 The promotion of human rights, conflict resolution or reconciliation or the promotion of religious or racial harmony or equality and diversity (head 'h')

 THINKING POINT

This set of aims is laudable, but does it look more like a political manifesto than a charitable category? Will it fall foul of the general prohibition on political charities (see 8.2.17)? Might the promotion of certain human rights and the promotion of religious harmony conflict with each other? (Consider, for example, the case of Roman Catholic adoption agencies and adoption by homosexual couples.)

8.2.11 The advancement of environmental protection or improvement (head 'i')

This is another laudable purpose, but again one which is potentially highly political and liable to irritate the government. There are also problems of definition. If a woodland is replaced by a thousand new homes equipped with solar panels, charities such as the Woodland Trust will no doubt object but charities promoting solar power might approve.

8.2.12 The relief of those in need, by reason of youth, age, ill-health, disability, financial hardship or other disadvantage (head 'j')

The preamble to the Statute of Elizabeth I 1601 refers to the relief of 'the aged, the impotent and poor'. In *Pemsel* Lord Macnaghten read this phrase disjunctively when he isolated the relief of poverty within the first of his four heads of charity. However, a trust under this head may not be charitable if it *excludes* the poor (*Re MacDuff* [1896] 2 Ch 446). After all, we would not expect a trust for the relief of aged millionaires to be charitable! On the other hand, an incidental financial benefit might be permitted. *Joseph Rowntree Memorial Trust Housing Association Ltd* v *Attorney-General* [1983] 2 WLR 284 concerned a charitable housing association which desired to build individual dwellings for sale to elderly people on long leases in consideration of a capital payment. On the tenant's death the lease would be assigned to the tenant's spouse or a family member, provided that person was also elderly. Failing such an assignment the lease would revert to the association, who would pay to the tenant's estate 70 per cent of the then current market value of the lease. The Charity Commissioners objected to the scheme on the grounds, inter alia, that it operated by way of contract, benefited private individuals rather than a charitable class and could produce a financial profit for those individuals. In the *Joseph Rowntree* case it was held that the scheme was a valid charitable scheme for the relief of the aged notwithstanding the objections of the Charity Commissioners.

Also falling under this head, according to the Charity Commission website, are such purposes as 'children's care homes'; 'apprenticing'; 'senior citizens' drop-in centres'; 'the relief of disability' and the 'provision of housing'.

8.2.13 The advancement of animal welfare (head 'k')

Trusts for specific animals must be distinguished from trusts for animals generally. A trust for animals *generally* may be charitable: examples include a trust to establish a home for lost dogs (*Re Douglas* (1887) 35 ChD 472) and a trust for animal welfare (*Re Wedgwood* [1915] 1 Ch 113). However, a bequest to the faithful dog Fido will not be charitable. It might, though, take effect as a private purpose trust of imperfect obligation (see, for example, *Re Dean* at 7.2.2).

The reason for recognising the charitable status of trusts for the benefit of animals generally was said by Swinfen-Eady LJ in *Re Wedgwood* [1915] 1 Ch 113 at 122 to be that the trust would 'tend to promote and encourage kindness towards [animals], and to ameliorate the condition of the brute creation, and thus to stimulate humane and generous sentiments in man towards the lower animals, and by this means to promote feelings of humanity and thus elevate the human race'.

A trust to provide an animal sanctuary where wild animals could thrive without the intrusion of people failed because it did not appear to prevent cruelty to animals or in any other way provide an elevating lesson to mankind; on the contrary, the wild animals would be free to molest each other (*Re Grove-Grady* [1929] 1 Ch 557). It may be that the Court of Appeal also harboured an objection to the fact that all the officials of the society had to be anti-vivisectionists and opponents of all blood sports (including angling).

 THINKING POINT

Do you think that an anti-vivisection society should have charitable status under this head of charity?

This was the issue before the House of Lords in *National Anti-Vivisection Society v IRC* [1948] AC 31. The society had claimed to be exempt from income tax as being 'a body of persons established for charitable purposes only'. It was held that the society was not charitable because it failed the overriding test of charitable status, i.e. whether the purposes of the organisation existed for the public benefit. It was held that, on balance, the object of the society was detrimental to the public benefit (Lord Porter dissenting). Further, a prime object of the society was political, namely, to secure the repeal of the Cruelty to Animals Act 1876 and to see it replaced by an enactment absolutely prohibiting vivisection. The court could not award charitable status to a trust for a political purpose (see 8.2.17).

The front page of the *Daily Telegraph* on 7 February 1998 carried the headline: 'RSPCA drops animal rights after threat to charity status.' In the article the reporter noted that the RSPCA had withdrawn a key policy statement declaring support for 'animal rights' following warnings from the Charity Commissioners that it breached the society's charitable status. Another borderline case is the Wolf Trust, which seeks to promote the reintroduction of wolves into the Highlands of Scotland, which at present is generally prohibited under the s 14(1) of the Wildlife and Countryside Act 1981 (it may be licensed by the Secretary of State for Scotland). Is such a trust charitable, as being for the public benefit? Does it infringe the prohibition on charities established for political objects? (See 8.2.17.) The Charity Commissioners for England and Wales refused to register the trust on the ground that it was political (30 January 2003), but the trust has since been registered as a charity in Scotland (SC 035926).

8.2.14 The promotion of the efficiency of the armed forces of the Crown or of the efficiency of the police, fire and rescue services or the ambulance services (head 'l')

The preamble to the Statute of Elizabeth refers to 'Maintenance of sick and maimed Soldiers and Mariners' and to the 'setting out of Soldiers and other Taxes'. In the *Pemsel* case Lord Macnaghten cited 'support for a lifeboat' as an example of a charitable purpose. It would now fall under this head. It has also long been recognised as charitable to promote the well-being of the fire service (*Re Wokingham Fire Brigade Trusts* [1951] Ch 373) and the police force (*IRC v City of Glasgow Police Athletic Association* [1953] AC 380), although now that the police have more armed officers and coercive powers than ever before it has become politically expedient to refer to the police force as the 'police service'. The phrase 'fire and rescue services' under the new head 'l' means services provided by fire and rescue authorities under Part 2 of the Fire and Rescue Services Act 2004 (c. 21).

8.2.15 Other existing charitable purposes or analogous charitable purposes (head 'm')

Not every trust purpose which is beneficial to the community will fall within this residual category and thereby qualify as a charitable purpose. Every purpose within this head must still fall within the 'spirit and intendment' of the preamble to the Statute of Elizabeth (*per* Sir William Grant MR in *Morice v Bishop of Durham* (1804) 9 Ves 399 at 405). Russell LJ in *Incorporated Council of Law Reporting v A-G* [1972] Ch 73 at 88 described this as 'a line of retreat . . . in case [the courts] are faced with a purpose (e.g. a political purpose) which could not have been within the contemplation of the Statute even if the then legislators had been endowed with the gift of foresight into the circumstances of later centuries'.

In later centuries it has indeed become clear that not all that is beneficial to the public is charitable. In 1976 the Goodman Committee stated that 'many things which are far removed from charity may benefit the community. For instance, a highly successful commercial venture, generating exports and providing massive employment is of immense benefit to the community but it is not charitable.' Lord Macnaghten in *Pemsel* stated, in similar vein, that 'A layman would probably be amused if he were told that a gift to the Chancellor of the Exchequer for the benefit of the nation was a charity' (para. 27).

 THINKING POINT

Could it be that those activities recognised by the courts to be for the public benefit are activities which the State would have to finance were they not supported from private funds? Take, for example, the provision of cremation services (see *Scottish Burial Reform and Cremation Society Ltd v Glasgow Corpn* at 8.2.2), private hospitals (see 8.2.6) and 'retraining and assistance to the unemployed' (*IRC v Oldham Training and Enterprise Council* [1996] STC 1218).

8.2.16 **Recreational charities**

The Recreational Charities Act 1958 was a response to the decision of the House of Lords in *IRC v Baddeley* [1955] AC 572. In that case, land, including a mission church, lecture room and store, was given to trustees on trust to permit the leaders of the mission to promote thereon 'the religious, social and physical well-being of persons resident in the county boroughs of West Ham and Leyton . . . by the provision of facilities for religious services and instruction and for the social and physical training and recreation of such aforementioned persons who for the time being are in the opinion [of the leaders of the mission] members of or likely to become members of the Methodist Church'.

The House of Lords held that the trust was not for the relief of poverty, for 'relief' implied the meeting of a need or quasi-necessity, such as the provision of a dwelling. Nor could the trust be charitable as being for a purpose beneficial to the community. The trust did not benefit a sufficient section of the public because the beneficiaries had been selected not only by reference to a particular geographical area, but by the further condition that they share a particular creed. Further, promotion of 'religious, social and physical well-being' was too wide a statement of the trust's objects, and accordingly the trust would be void for potentially including non-charitable purposes.

 STATUTE

Charities Act 2011, s 5 (replacing the Recreational Charities Act 1958)

5. Recreational and similar trusts, etc.

(1) It is charitable (and is to be treated as always having been charitable) to provide, or assist in the provision of, facilities for—

(a) recreation, or

(b) other leisure-time occupation,

if the facilities are provided in the interests of social welfare.

(2) The requirement that the facilities are provided in the interests of social welfare cannot be satisfied if the basic conditions are not met.

(3) The basic conditions are—

(a) that the facilities are provided with the object of improving the conditions of life for the persons for whom the facilities are primarily intended, and

(b) that—

(i) those persons have need of the facilities because of their youth, age, infirmity or disability, poverty, or social and economic circumstances, or

(ii) the facilities are to be available to members of the public at large or to male, or to female, members of the public at large.

(4) Subsection (1) applies in particular to—

(a) the provision of facilities at village halls, community centres and women's institutes, and

(b) the provision and maintenance of grounds and buildings to be used for purposes of recreation or leisure-time occupation, and extends to the provision of facilities for those purposes by the organising of any activity.

> But this is subject to the requirement that the facilities are provided in the interests of social welfare.
>
> **(5)** Nothing in this section is to be treated as derogating from the public benefit requirement.

Charities Act 2011, s 5 (replacing the Recreational Charities Act 1958) recognises as charitable the provision of (or assistance in the provision of) facilities for recreation or other leisure time occupation if the facilities are provided in the interests of social welfare. This requirement can be established by one of two routes (see Table 8.2).

Table 8.2 Recreational charities

Route one	Route two
The provision of facilities for persons in need due to youth, age, infirmity or disability, poverty or social and economic circumstances	The provision of facilities available to the members or female, or male, members of the public at large
With the object of improving the conditions of life for the persons for whom the facilities are primarily intended	With the object of improving the conditions of life for the persons for whom the facilities are primarily intended
And for the public benefit	And for the public benefit

The trust in *Baddeley* might have been valid under route one, to the extent that it provided facilities for persons in need due to their youth, were it not for the inclusion of other, potentially non-charitable objects. In *Re Guild* [1992] 2 AC 310, a testator left the residue of his estate 'to the town council of North Berwick for the use in connection with the sports centre in North Berwick or some similar purpose in connection with sport'. Do you think that this was a charitable purpose? The IRC claimed that the transfer of value was liable to capital transfer tax. The executor appealed, claiming that the gift was for charitable purposes and therefore exempt from the tax. The House of Lords held that, on a proper construction of s 1(2)(a) of the Recreational Charities Act 1958, a gift for the provision of recreational facilities could be charitable notwithstanding the fact that the intended beneficiaries were not in a position of social disadvantage and did not suffer from any particular deprivation. Accordingly, the gift in the present case was a charitable one, the facilities having been provided in the interests of social welfare. In construing the second part of the gift, 'or some similar purpose in connection with sport', it should be presumed that the testator had intended those other purposes to share the aspects of social welfare provision and public benefit which had been present in the first part of the gift. Such a benignant construction should be applied to deeds whose wording was ambiguous and susceptible to two constructions, one of which would render the trust void, the other of which would render it a valid charitable trust.

8.2.16.1 Reform of the 1958 Act

The Charities Act 2006 amended ss 1 and 2 of the 1958 Act, to bring it in line with the European Convention on Human Rights. Section 5(2) of the 2006 Act amended s 1(2) of the 1958 Act so that facilities made available to men only are to be regarded as charitable on the same basis as facilities made available to the public as a whole or to women only. Section 5(3) repealed s 2 of the 1958 Act. The effect of this is that miners' welfare organisations that can show that they are charitable under the definition of charity contained in Recreational Charities Act 1958, s 1 (now Charities Act 2011, s 5) will retain their charitable status. Other miners' welfare organisations will not retain their charitable status.

8.2.17 Trusts for political purposes

Trusts for the promotion of one political party (*Bonar Law Memorial Trust* v *IRC* (1933) 49 TLR 220) and trusts for the promotion of a particular political doctrine (*Re Bushnell* [1975] 1 WLR 1596) are not charitable, but neither are trusts for purposes which might be considered 'political' in the sense that they seek a change in the law. In *Bowman* v *Secular Society Ltd* [1917] AC 406 Lord Parker stated that 'a trust for the attainment of political objects has always been held invalid, not because it is illegal . . . but because the court has no means of judging whether a proposed change in the law will or will not be for the public benefit'. The prime reason for refusing charitable status to trusts for political purposes is that courts, whose role it is to enforce the law of Parliament, cannot sanction organisations whose role it is to change the law of Parliament (see *National Anti-Vivisection Society* v *IRC* [1948] AC 31).

For these reasons Amnesty International was denied charitable status in *McGovern* v *Attorney-General* [1982] 1 Ch 321. Slade J held that a trust for the relief of human suffering was capable of being charitable, but not where a direct and main object of the trust was to secure such relief through attempting to change the laws of a foreign country. Such a trust would be a trust for a political purpose and as such would not be capable of being a valid charitable trust. The judge stated that an English court has 'no adequate means of judging whether a proposed change in the law of a foreign country will or will not be for the public benefit' of the foreign community. The judge also pointed out the risk of prejudicing relations between the United Kingdom and foreign states if English courts passed judgment on foreign regimes. The judge did acknowledge, however, that if the main objects of a charitable trust are non-political it will not cease to be charitable if the trustees have the power to use political means to achieve those non-political ends.

In its response to the decision in that case, the Charity Commissioners gave, amongst others, the following (somewhat depressing) guidelines to charity trustees:

The Annual Report of the Charity Commissioners, 1981

'To avoid doubt being cast on the claim of the institution to be a charity, its governing instrument should not include power to exert political pressure except in a way that is ancillary to a charitable purpose . . . In general, what is ancillary is that which furthers the work of the institution, not something that will procure the performance of similar work by, for example, the government of the day' (para. 54(ii)).

'Charities, whether they operate in this country or overseas, must avoid . . . seeking to eliminate social, economic, political or other injustice' (para. 54(vii)).

In 1995 the Charity Commissioners issued a circular summarising the law in relation to charities and politics. The Commissioners draw a fundamental distinction between political purposes and political activities. A charitable organisation may be involved in the latter, but can never be established to achieve the former.

Political Activities and Campaigning by Charities, Leaflet CC 9, July 1995

'Any political activity undertaken by trustees must be in furtherance of, and ancillary to, the charity's stated objects and within its powers' (para. 8).

'To be ancillary, activities must serve and be subordinate to the charity's purposes. They cannot, therefore, be undertaken as an end in themselves and must not be allowed to dominate the activities which the charity undertakes to carry out its charitable purposes directly. The trustees must be able to show that there is a reasonable expectation that the activities will further the purposes of the charity, and so benefit its beneficiaries to an extent justified by the resources devoted to those activities' (para. 9).

 THINKING POINT

Is it really possible to reconcile the prohibition on political proposes with the supposed charitable status of such purposes as 'the resolution of national or international conflicts', 'promoting equality and diversity by the elimination of discrimination on the grounds of age, sex or sexual orientation' and 'enabling people of one faith to understand the religious beliefs of others'—all of which, according to the Charity Commission, are said to promote human rights? (Charity Commission, 'The Promotion of Human Rights', Review of the Register RR12.)

It is also clear that the courts will not recognise the charitable status of a political trust merely because it is masquerading as a trust for education or some other charitable purpose (see *Re Hopkinson* [1949] 1 Ch 346, where the testator gave his residuary estate to four well-known members of the Labour Party), but see *Re Koeppler* [1986] Ch 423, next.

 CASE CLOSE-UP

Re Koeppler **[1986] Ch 423, Court of Appeal**

Facts: the testator, Koeppler, came to England from Germany in 1933. After World War II he ran conferences, known collectively as the 'Wilton Park' project, for politicians, academics, civil servants, industrialists and journalists. By his will he left a large part of his estate to the Wilton Park project for 'as long as Wilton Park remains a British contribution to the formation of an informed international public opinion and to the promotion of greater cooperation in Europe and the West in general'. The will provided that, in the event of Wilton Park ceasing to exist, there should be a gift over to a named Oxford college. The Wilton Park conferences were private, unofficial and not intended to follow any party political line. In fact, the law had never acknowledged Wilton Park to be an entity; rather, it was a sort of movement or body of thought. Accordingly the gift was bound to fail outright unless it could be shown to be a gift for a charitable purpose. The judge at first instance decided that the gift must fail for vagueness of purpose. The Attorney-General appealed.

Held: because Wilton Park was not a legal entity, Koeppler's gift must have been intended to be for *purposes* of one sort or another. Those purposes must be taken to be the purposes of the Wilton Park project, namely for the advancement of education through the provision of conferences. It followed that this was a valid charitable gift for the advancement of education. The persons attending the conferences would benefit themselves and pass on the benefits of their education to the general public. So far as the conferences touched upon political matters they were merely genuine attempts objectively to ascertain and disseminate truth. The trust was entitled to a 'benignant construction'. In other words, it should be assumed that the trustees would act in accordance with their duties, and would not use the funds to propagate tendentious political opinions.

8.2.17.1 Student unions

In *Webb* v *O'Doherty* (1991) Times, 11 February a student union, being an educational charity, was not permitted to make donations to a national student campaign to stop the Gulf War. Following Scott J in *A-G* v *Ross* [1986] 1 WLR 252, Hoffmann J held that discussion of political issues was undoubtedly included within the union's charitable educational purposes, but:

> There is . . . a clear distinction between the discussion of political matters, or the acquisition of information which may have a political content, and a campaign on a political issue. There is no doubt that campaigning, in the sense of seeking to influence public opinion on political matters, is not a charitable activity. It is, of course, something which students are, like the rest of the population, perfectly at liberty to do in their private capacities, but it is not a proper object of the expenditure of charitable money.

8.3 The exclusivity requirement

The purposes of a charitable trust must be exclusively charitable (Charities Act 2001, s 1(1)(a)). In the following sections we will consider what 'exclusively' means in this context. First, it should be noted that if a trust established for a certain class of people does not specify any purpose the courts may construe it to be for purely charitable purposes. This occurred in *Re Harding* [2008] Ch 235, where Lewison J held that a trust 'for the black community of Hackney, Haringey, Islington and Tower Hamlets' was held to be charitable. The judge was content for the precise purposes to which the money should be applied to be determined by a charitable scheme settled on by the trustees. (Incidentally, the limitation in favour of the 'black community' was struck out as being in breach of s 34(1) of the Race Relations Act 1976.)

8.3.1 Purposes ancillary to, incidental to, or *de minimis* in comparison with, the charitable purposes

In *Re Coxen* [1948] Ch 747 the testator gave the residue of his estate, some £200,000, to the Court of Aldermen of the City of London upon certain trusts. In Table 8.3 tick the ones you think are charitable.

All the trusts were valid charitable trusts. It was held that the provisions in favour of the aldermen personally were made to ensure the better administration of the main charitable trusts. In any event, even if those provisions had not themselves been charitable, the sums involved were so insignificant in comparison with that part of the fund devoted to the medical charities that the provisions for the benefit of the aldermen personally could be seen as merely ancillary to the principal trust and would take effect on that basis. In cases where the non-charitable allocation was so significant as not to be 'ancillary' the whole trust must fail, unless the non-charitable part could be precisely quantified, in which case only that part would fail.

8.3.2 Non-charitable purposes compounded with charitable purposes

In *Re Best* [1904] 2 Ch 354 a bequest of residue was made to such 'charitable and benevolent institutions' as the trustees shall in their discretion determine. The gift was construed to be exclusively charitable. The use of the conjunction 'and' meant that there was no possibility of an institution benefiting which was benevolent but not charitable.

8.3.3 Non-charitable purposes severable from the charitable purposes as a matter of construction

In *Salusbury* v *Denton* (1857) 3 K & J 529 a testator left a fund to his widow for life and directed that after her death she should leave a part of the fund to certain charities and the remainder to his relatives. The widow died having failed to make the relevant appointments. The Vice-Chancellor, Sir W. Page Wood, held that the wording of the trust permitted a severance of the non-charitable from the charitable objects, because the will clearly bound the trustees to apply an unspecified moiety (part) of the estate to charity. In accordance with the maxim *equality is equity* the court applied half of the fund towards the charitable purposes and the other half to the testator's relatives.

Table 8.3 The trusts in *Re Coxen*

(1)	Spend £100 towards an annual dinner for the aldermen upon their meeting together upon trust business
(2)	Pay one guinea to each alderman who attended the whole of a committee meeting in connection with the trust
(3)	To apply the remainder for the benefit of certain medical charities

8.3.4 Validation under the Charitable Trusts (Validation) Act 1954

A trust provision which could properly be construed as being for exclusively charitable purposes, but which could nevertheless be used for non-charitable purposes, is validated as a charitable trust by s 1 of this Act. However, the Act only applies where the trust provision is contained in an instrument which took effect before 16 December 1952. The effect of the Act on a relevant trust provision is to render it *exclusively* charitable for the period before the commencement of the Act. For the period after the commencement of the Act any relevant trust provision will be construed as valid only *to the extent* that it authorised the use of trust property for charitable purposes.

8.3.5 Where non-charitable purposes are alternatives to the charitable purposes

If on a proper construction of the gift it is clear that the non-charitable purposes are alternatives to the charitable purposes, the trust will not be a valid charitable trust. In *Chichester Diocesan Fund and Board of Finance* v *Simpson* [1944] AC 341 Caleb Diplock left the residue of his estate on trust 'for such charitable institution or institutions or other charitable or benevolent object or objects as his executors might in their absolute discretion select'. The residue was distributed amongst several charities. After the distribution the testator's statutory next of kin claimed that the residuary gift was not a valid charitable bequest because the words 'charitable or benevolent' had rendered the gift uncertain.

The House of Lords held that, upon a true construction of the clause, the conjunction 'or' indicated that 'benevolent' was intended to be an alternative to 'charitable', rather than merely descriptive of it. 'Or' was used in this disposition as it is used in the phrase 'House of Commons or House of Lords' and not as it is used in the phrase 'House of Lords or Upper Chamber'. Accordingly, the gift was void for uncertainty, though it was surely never as uncertain as Lord Porter's 'explanation' of the law, to quote: 'the word "charitable" to be exegetical of "benevolent", should follow and not precede it. The wording should be "benevolent" or "charitable" meaning "benevolent, i.e. charitable" not charitable or benevolent meaning "charitable, i.e. benevolent".'

The decision in that case meant, of course, that the statutory next of kin had to try and recover the misapplied property—for that stage of the court proceedings see *Re Diplock* [1948] 1 Ch 465 (see 18.3.3.3). It may be true to say that if Viscount Simon had held the gift to be charitable, English law would have been denied, in the form of *Re Diplock*, the leading case in the modern law of tracing and restitution.

8.4 *Cy près*

Where a private trust fails, the property usually returns to the settlor or testator's estate under a resulting trust (see 16.1.2.1). However, where money has been successfully dedicated to charity, rarely will it result to the settlor or testator's estate in this way. For where a charitable trust cannot be carried out, or is fulfilled leaving a surplus of charitable funds, the doctrine of *cy près* may enable an application of the funds to charitable purposes as near as possible in type to those intended by the settlor.

> **cy près**
> Old law French for the 'the nearest thing', literally 'that which is near' (pronounced 'sea-pray').

Property can only be applied *cy près* at the direction of the court or the Charity Commission, the trustees having a duty under s 13(5) of the Charities Act 1993 (s 61 of the Charities Act 2011) to make the appropriate application to court wherever circumstances deem it necessary.

Different considerations apply to the operation of the doctrine according to whether or not the gift fails *ab initio* or at some later date.

8.4.1 Initial failure

Where a gift fails from the outset the *cy près* doctrine will only save the gift where the donor, in making the gift, had a *general* or *paramount* charitable intent. The question to be asked is: did the donor desire a charitable outcome by whatever means, or was the means specified essential to the donor's intention in making the charitable gift? If the donor's intention is restricted to making a gift for a particular purpose (albeit a charitable purpose) in a particular way, the gift will fail and the subject matter of the gift will result to the donor. An example of failure *ab initio* without general charitable intent occurred in *Kings* v *Bultitude* [2010] EWHC 1795 (Ch) (when the last surviving priest of a church denomination died, the church was deemed to have 'died' with her). In each of the following cases there was an initial failure of the gift. Consider the cases and tick the ones in which you think the donor has displayed a general charitable intention in making the gift.

A testatrix left £200 to 'Mrs Bailey's Charity, Rotherhithe'. The charity, founded in 1756 for the benefit of poor widows of Rotherhithe, had, by the date of the gift, been *amalgamated* in 1905 with other charities in the area of Rotherhithe (see *Re Faraker* [1912] 2 Ch 488). Consider the 'thinking point' next.

THINKING POINT

Do you think that there was an initial failure of the gift?

In this case the Court of Appeal held that the amalgamated charities would be entitled to the legacy. However there had been no initial failure, and this was not a case for the application of the doctrine of *cy près*. The amalgamated charities were entitled to receive the legacy because the original charity continued to exist in a slightly modified form.

8.4.2 The modern law of *cy près*

Prior to the Charities Act of 1960 the *cy près* doctrine would only be applied where the charitable objects of the trust were *impossible* or *impracticable* to fulfil. Section 13 of the 1960 Act relaxed these limitations on the application of *cy près*. That law is now consolidated in s 62 of the Charities Act 2011. Before proceeding it is absolutely crucial to note that s 62 does not affect the need to show a general or paramount charitable intent before the doctrine of *cy près* will apply in cases of initial failure (see 8.4.1). This was confirmed by the Court of Appeal in *Varsani* v *Jesani* [1999] Ch 219 (in relation to the precursor to the Charities Act 2011). See Table 8.4 for an exercise.

How do your conclusions compare with the outcomes presented in Table 8.5?

Table 8.4 Initial failure exercise—case facts. What do you think was decided in the following cases?

Case 1
A testator left £5,000 'to the rector for the time being of St Thomas' Seminary for the education of priests in the diocese of Westminster'. Reference was made in the gift to the choice of particular candidates. At the date of the will the seminary still existed, but it had ceased to exist at the date of the testator's death (i.e. at the effective date of the gift).

Case 2
A testator left money to pay the salary of a school master. He was to teach at a specified school according to a syllabus of the testator's design. In the event the school was never built.

Case 3
A testatrix settled the net residue of her estate on the Royal College of Surgeons as trustee for the charitable purposes of the college. Conditions attaching to the gift excluded women, Jews and Roman Catholics from partaking of a studentship funded by the gift. The college threatened to disclaim the trusteeship unless those conditions were removed from the gift.

Case 4
A testatrix left £200 to the Wisbech Peace Society, Cambridge and £300 to the Peace Society of Belfast. The former had ceased to exist before the date of the testatrix's death, whilst the latter had never existed at all.

Case 5
A testatrix left gifts to the National Radium Commission, an unincorporated association, and to the National Council for Maternity and Child Welfare, an incorporated company.

Table 8.5 Initial failure exercise—case outcomes

Case 1
In *Re Rymer* [1895] 1 Ch 19, on the question whether the £5,000 could be applied *cy près* it was held, instead, that the gift lapsed and resulted to the testator's residuary estate. Chitty J held that this was a gift for the particular seminary, and *not a general gift* for the education of the priests in the diocese of Westminster. It was plain from the language used, which referred to the saying of masses and the choice of candidates, that the choice of the seminary was not mere 'machinery' for the carrying out of a general charitable intent, but went to the very substance of the testator's gift.

Case 2
In *Re Wilson* [1913] 1 Ch 314, it was held that there was an initial failure but that the doctrine of *cy près* would not apply to save the gift because the fine details of the testator's gift were not consistent with a general charitable intent.

Case 3
In *Re Lysaght* [1966] 1 Ch 191, the court removed the conditions, stating that the gift would otherwise fail. The court was able to find (perhaps artificially) a general charitable intention by making these 'peripheral' alterations to the donor's expressed intentions.

Case 4
In *Re Harwood* [1936] Ch 285, it was held that the gift of £200 to the Wisbech Peace Society failed and would not be applied *cy près* as the testatrix had lacked a general charitable intention in making that gift. As regards the gift of £300, it was held that the testatrix had shown a general charitable intention to benefit any society connected with Belfast which existed for the promotion of peace. The gift of £300 was applied *cy près*.

Case 5
In *Re Finger's WT* [1972] 1 Ch 286, it was held that the gift to the former institution was valid as a trust for general charitable purposes, whereas the gift to the company was prima facie void as being for a particular legal person which had ceased to exist (see *Re Harwood*, Case 4). However, Goff J thought the present case to be a special one and distinguished *Re Harwood* on the basis that here the major part of the estate, including the residue, had been specifically devoted to charitable purposes. Accordingly, the gift to the corporation was validated by the operation of the *cy près* doctrine.

STATUTE

Charities Act 2011, s 62 (replacing Charities Act 1993, s 13)

(1) Subject to subsection (3), the circumstances in which the original purposes of a charitable gift can be altered to allow the property given or part of it to be applied cy-près are—

  (a) where the original purposes, in whole or in part—

    (i) have been as far as may be fulfilled, or

    (ii) cannot be carried out, or not according to the directions given and to the spirit of the gift,

  (b) where the original purposes provide a use for part only of the property available by virtue of the gift,

  (c) where—

    (i) the property available by virtue of the gift, and

    (ii) other property applicable for similar purposes,

    can be more effectively used in conjunction, and to that end can suitably, regard being had to the appropriate considerations, be made applicable to common purposes,

  (d) where the original purposes were laid down by reference to—

    (i) an area which then was but has since ceased to be a unit for some other purpose, or

    (ii) a class of persons or an area which has for any reason since ceased to be suitable, regard being had to the appropriate considerations, or to be practical in administering the gift, or

  (e) where the original purposes, in whole or in part, have, since they were laid down—

    (i) been adequately provided for by other means,

    (ii) ceased, as being useless or harmful to the community or for other reasons, to be in law charitable, or

    (iii) ceased in any other way to provide a suitable and effective method of using the property available by virtue of the gift, regard being had to the appropriate considerations.

(2) In subsection (1) 'the appropriate considerations' means—

  (a) (on the one hand) the spirit of the gift concerned, and

  (b) (on the other) the social and economic circumstances prevailing at the time of the proposed alteration of the original purposes.

(3) Subsection (1) does not affect the conditions which must be satisfied in order that property given for charitable purposes may be applied cy-près except in so far as those conditions require a failure of the original purposes.

(4) References in subsections (1) to (3) to the original purposes of a gift are to be read, where the application of the property given has been altered or regulated by a scheme or otherwise, as referring to the purposes for which the property is for the time being applicable.

The circumstances in which the original purposes of a charitable gift can be altered to allow the property given or part of it to be applied *cy près* are as follows (references are to subsections of Charities Act 1993, s 13 and Charities Act 2011, s 62):

- *impossibility*: where the original purposes, in whole or in part, have been as far as may be fulfilled (s (1)(a)(i)) or cannot be carried out, or cannot be carried out in accordance with the letter and spirit of the gift (s (1)(a)(ii));

- *surplus property*: where the original purposes provide a use for part only of the property available by virtue of the gift (s (1)(b));

- *common investment*: where the property available by virtue of the gift and other property applicable for similar purposes can be more effectively used in conjunction for common purposes, regard being had to the spirit of the gift (s (1)(c));

- *unsuitability or impracticality of benefiting persons or area*: where the original purposes were laid down . . . by reference to a class of persons or to an area which has for any reason ceased to be suitable (regard being had to the spirit of the gift) or to be practical (s (1)(d));

- *unsuitability and ineffectiveness*: where the original purposes, in whole or in part, have, since they were laid down, been adequately provided for by other means (s (1)(e)(i)) or ceased, as being useless or harmful to the community or for other reasons, to be in law charitable (s (1)(e)(ii)) or ceased in any other way to provide a suitable and effective method of using the property available by virtue of the gift, regard being had to the spirit of the gift (s (1)(e)(iii)).

THINKING POINT

Examine the Charities Act 2011, s 62 set out earlier. In what circumstances will the doctrine of *cy près* apply today?

The Charity Commissioners referred to some of the uses to which s (1)(e) had been put in para. 43 of their Annual Report for 1970:

> [W]e have made schemes for a number of charities established for the repair of roads and bridges, substituting for those purposes other general purposes for the benefit of local inhabitants which could include, for instance, the promotion of the arts, the provision of seats and shelters, the preservation of old buildings, or the improvement of local amenities.

8.4.3 **Subsequent failure**

In *National Anti-Vivisection Society v IRC* Lord Simonds stated *obiter* that the concept of what is charitable may change from age to age, and that a trust which was once held to be charitable might one day cease to be so, in which case the trust fund should be applied *cy près*.

The crucial point to grasp is that in cases of subsequent impossibility the property can be applied *cy près* without the need to show a general or paramount charitable intention.

In *Re King* [1923] 1 Ch 243 the testatrix left the residue of her estate to provide for the erection, to the memory of the testatrix and her relations, of a stained glass window in a parish church. This was held to be a valid charitable trust of the whole fund, so that any surplus remaining after the erection of the stained glass window should be applied *cy près*, with the consent of the Attorney-General, towards the provision of a further stained glass window or windows in the same church. Romer J stated (at 246): 'in the case of a legacy to a charitable institution that exists at the death of the testator, but ceases to exist after his death and before the legacy is paid over, the legacy is applied *cy près*, even in the absence of a general charitable intention: see *Re Slevin* [1891] 2 Ch 236.' This example brings us to our next topic.

8.4.4 The disposal of surplus donations

Prior to the Charities Act 1960 *cy près* would only apply to cases of this type where the donors had shown a general or paramount charitable intent, the practical (or impractical) consequence of this being that all other surplus donations resulted to the donors, many of whom (being anonymous) could not be found. In response to this unsatisfactory state of affairs, ss 63–66 of the Charities Act 2011 (Charities Act 2011, s 14) provide that surplus monies donated to collecting boxes, raffles, entertainments and so on may be applied *cy près* without having to obtain the donors' consent. As regards other donations, the trustees must advertise and take steps to find the donors and, if they are found, return the donation to them or obtain in writing a waiver of the donors' claims to the donation. However, this advertising and inquiry process can be dispensed with by order of the court where it appears to the court either that it would be 'unreasonable, having regard to the amounts likely to be returned to the donors, to incur expense with a view to returning the property' (Charities Act 2011, s 64(2)(a); Charities Act 1993, s 4(4)(a)) or that it would be 'unreasonable, having regard to the nature, circumstances and amounts of the gifts, and to the lapse of time since the gifts were made, for the donors to expect the property to be returned' (Charities Act 2011, s 64(2)(b); Charities Act 1993, s 4(4)(b)). The Charities Act 2006 extended this power of the court to the Charity Commission. The Act also inserted a (very poorly drafted) s 14A after s 14 of the Charities Act 1993. The essential import of the new s 14A (now consolidated as Charities Act 2011, s 65) is that, if a donation for a specific charitable purpose is solicited from the donor with the assurance that it will be applied *cy près* if that specific purpose fails, the donor can declare, at the time he makes the donation, that he would like to be offered the return of his donation. The section sets out the steps that the trustees are required to take to inform the donor that the specific purpose has failed and the steps that the donor must then take to secure the return of his donation. A further clause of the 1993 Act inserts a new s 14B (now consolidated as Charities Act 2011, s 67), which provides that where property is applicable *cy près*, the court or the Commission may make a scheme providing for the property to be applied as appropriate in the light of the spirit of the original gift, the desirability of securing that the property is applied for charitable purposes which are close to the original purposes and the need for the benefiting charity to have purposes which are suitable and effective in the light of current social and economic circumstances. Concern that charitable trusts should be 'suitable' to 'current social . . . circumstances' means that if a charitable trust cannot be carried out because of a racist or otherwise discriminatory provision, the court will be justified in applying the fund *cy près* to similar charitable purposes, but with the offensive limitation removed (this has long been the law. See, for example, *Re Lysaght* [1966] 1 Ch 191).

Summary

- We have distinguished the legal notion of charity from the everyday notion that charity connotes altruism and benevolence. We have seen that a purpose is only charitable in law when it is beneficial to the public. The Charities Act 2006 as consolidated in the Charities Act 2011 groups the main categories of charity under 13 heads.

- The fact that charitable trusts are beneficial to the public explains the many privileges they enjoy. These include:
  - exemption from the requirement that a trust must have an ascertainable object;
  - exemption from the beneficiary principle (i.e. the usual requirement that a trust must have a beneficiary interested in enforcing the trust);
  - exemption from the rule against inalienability of capital;
  - a wide range of fiscal (tax) exemptions and privileges.

- Where a charitable trust cannot be carried out, or is fulfilled leaving a surplus of charitable funds, the doctrine of *cy près* may enable an application of the funds to charitable purposes of a type 'as near as possible to' those intended by the settlor. We have seen that different considerations apply to the operation of the doctrine according to whether or not the gift fails *ab initio* or at some later date.

? **Summative assessment exercise**

Reginald died recently. Consider which of the following provisions in his will might be a valid charitable legacy:

- £100,000 to my trustees on trust to provide temporary shelter for Old Etonians who have fallen on hard times. Preference to be given to my old classmates;

- £10,000 to my trustees to support research into the likely consequences for political and public life of a legal ban on the Society of Free and Accepted Masons;

- £5,000 to my trustees to promote the playing of card games by deprived youth as an alternative to watching television;

- £5,000 to my psychotherapist, Doctor F. Reud, to buy a new couch for the greater comfort of his many grateful patients.

 Full specimen answers can be found at www.oxfordtextbooks.co.uk/orc/watt_directions5e/.

 The bigger picture

This chapter has focused on the challenge of knowing what to do with donations, but this question will only arise if people are willing to part with their wealth to begin with. Nothing will discourage charitable giving more than the sense that charities are administered negligently or fraudulently. Following a number of scandals concerning charities that are alleged to have used bullying tactics in seeking donations from elderly and other vulnerable persons, Parliament has passed the Charities (Protection and Social Investment) Act 2016. The 2016 statute creates a new regime designed to ensure '(a) public confidence in charities, (b) the level of charitable donations, and (c) people's willingness to volunteer' (s 16). The regime includes potential for official warnings by the Charity Commission (s 1), investigations and power to suspend or remove trustees (ss 2, 4–5), power to direct specified action not to be taken (s 6), power to direct winding up of the charity (s 7), power to direct property to be applied to another charity (s 8) and a requirement that there will be no fundraising by professionals unless they agree to protect vulnerable people and other members of the public from 'unreasonable intrusion', 'unreasonably persistent approaches for the purpose of soliciting or otherwise procuring money or other property' and 'undue pressure . . . to give money'.

 Further reading

Charity Commission, *Decision of the Charity Commissioners for England & Wales: Application for Registration as a Charity by the Church of Scientology (England and Wales)* 17 November 1999
an interesting case study on the refusal to recognise the Church of Scientology as religious in charity law (but contrast this with the Supreme Court's decision to recognise scientology as a religion in the context of wedding ceremonies: *R (on the application of Hodkin)* v *Registrar General of Births, Deaths and Marriages* [2013] UKSC 77; [2014] AC 610)

Clune, S. 'Maintaining a social conscience' (2014) 158(48) Solicitors' Journal 33–4
examines proposed powers under the new Charities (Protection and Social Investment) Bill 2015 including the ability to remove a disqualified trustee, to issue official warnings and to disqualify a person from acting as a trustee

Edge, P. 'Charitable Status for the Advancement of Religion: An Abolitionist's View' (1995–6) 3 *Charity Law and Practice Review* 29–35
an article which argues that to treat all religions equally one should remove charitable status from all

Garton, J. *Public Benefit in Charity Law* (2013) Oxford: Oxford University Press
argues that it is possible to identify four elements within the assessment of public benefit: the public benefit inherent in the categories ('heads') of charity; the extent to which individual would-be charities can demonstrate sufficient direct and tangible benefit; the extent to which those benefits are open to a sufficient section of the community; and the restriction of private benefits to those that are merely incidental

Luxton, P. *The Law of Charities* (2001) Oxford: Oxford University Press
a general detailed text on the subject of charities

Matthew Mills, 'The Development of the Public Benefit Requirements for Charitable Trusts in the Nineteenth Century' (2016) 37(3) J Leg Hist 269–302
historical study of the public benefit requirement in charity law

National Council for Voluntary Organisations, *For the Public Benefit? A Consultation Document on Charity Law Reform* (2001)
the original inspiration for the 2006 Act

The Charity Commission for England and Wales, *Trust in Charities* (2018)

This report considers how the public views charities, what this means for the sector, and how trust can be increased

Synge, M. *'New' Public Benefit Requirement: Making Sense of Charity Law?* (2015) Oxford: Hart

this book examines the public benefit requirement under the Charities Act 2006. The author asks whether the public benefit requirement, as recently enacted and interpreted, has brought sense to charity law

Synge, M. 'Charitable Status: Not a Negligible Matter' (2016) 132 LQR 303–17

calls for reconsideration of the requirement (*Oppenheim v Tobacco Securities Trust Co Ltd*) that in a charitable trust the potential beneficiaries should 'not be numerically negligible' and should form a 'sufficient section of the public'

Warburton, J. 'Charitable Trusts—Unique?' [1999] Conv 20

an accessible article examining the distinction between charitable trusts and other trusts

 For links to selected cases, statutes, academic papers and official reports mentioned in this chapter please visit the online resources at www.oup.com/uk/watt_directions6e/.

9 Variation of trusts

LEARNING OBJECTIVES

By the end of this chapter you should be able to:

- explain the possible reasons for varying the terms of a trust;
- detail the numerous modes of varying trusts;
- distinguish administrative variations from variations in beneficial interests;
- manage an application to the court for a variation under the Variation of Trusts Act 1958;
- advise as to when a variation will be for the benefit of the beneficiaries;
- judge the extent to which courts take the settlor's intentions into account when considering a variation.

Introduction

Suppose that you are the beneficiary of a trust and that your younger brother (aged ten) and your parents are the only other beneficiaries of the trust. The person who set up the trust provided that each of the beneficiaries (you, your brother and your parents) should have a quarter share in the fund. Suppose now that there has been a change in the tax laws which makes it far more beneficial in the long term for your parents to have mere life interests in the fund now, and for you and your brother to enjoy nothing now but to postpone the vesting of your interests until after your parents have died. It is possible that the court will approve a variation of your trust, even though this involves a departure from the expressed intentions of the original settlor.

Crucially, though, '[a] court will not re-write a trust' (*Re Downshire Settled Estates* [1953] Ch 218 at 248, *per* Lord Evershed MR). This quote demonstrates what Professor Harris called the court's general 'fidelity' to the settlor's intentions. Nevertheless, the fact cannot be escaped (as Professor Harris demonstrated in his book *Variation of Trusts* (London: Sweet & Maxwell, 1975)) that the court must weigh in the balance the equitable property rights of the persons beneficially entitled under the trust against the wishes of the person who set up the trust in the first place. The latter may, of course, already be dead.

In most reported cases the motive for seeking a variation is to achieve a financial benefit for the beneficiaries, and in the majority of these cases the financial benefit is a fiscal one. Tax laws change every year. If the terms and structures of trusts were fixed once and for all by the settlor, trusts would be 'sitting ducks' for the guns of the Inland Revenue. The court's power to vary trusts is a valuable means of dodging the shot! To the extent that variation of trusts can be seen to be a tax avoidance measure we must question the assumption that variation necessarily conflicts with the settlor's intentions. In most trusts the settlor would surely wish their trust to respond flexibly to changes in fiscal regulation. Indeed, the Inland Revenue expressly allows adult beneficiaries of a will to agree by a 'Deed of Variation' to vary their benefits under the will within two years of the testator's death (for the example of one famous family, see next).

 OUTSIDE THE BOX

Ian Jack, 'Journalists in Glass Houses Target Ed Miliband' (*The Guardian*, 9 October 2010)

Marxist academic Ralph Miliband owned a house in Edis Street, Primrose Hill. At some point after he died in 1994, his widow and two sons signed a 'deed of variation' to his will that gave Ed and David each a 20% share in the house, which meant that on their mother's death they would pay inheritance tax only on the remaining 60%.

To the extent that the courts' jurisdiction to vary trusts is a tax avoidance facility, it is a facility which reduces the amount of revenue available to the Treasury. It might be asked whether the jurisdiction to vary trusts is giving the average taxpayer value for their money. How many of us will ever need to vary a trust? There is nothing illegal in arranging one's affairs so as to avoid attracting a tax liability (although it is illegal to evade a tax liability once it has arisen), but even though tax avoidance is not illegal, is it something that the courts should actively assist in? The courts have turned a blind eye to this question and have been content to make the best interests of the beneficiary their 'moral' imperative. This contrasts sharply with the courts' insistence upon a guarantee of public benefit prior to any grant of fiscal privilege through the recognition of charitable status, which we considered in the previous chapter.

However, not every variation is made to achieve tax advantages. Sometimes there is undoubtedly a public interest in the variation of a trust, as where a settlor has included a clause in the trust which promotes racial or religious prejudice. We shall consider some cases in this category later.

9.1   Modes of varying trusts

We will discover in the following sections that some variations involve a variation of the beneficial interests under the trust, whereas others involve a variation in the way in which the trust is administered.

9.1.1   The rule in *Saunders v Vautier*

According to the rule in *Saunders* v *Vautier* (1841) 10 LJ Ch 354 an adult beneficiary who is solely entitled to the trust property may deal with his equitable interest as he wishes. (Note that the rule has no application where potential beneficiaries (e.g. grandchildren) do not yet exist, no matter how remote their interests might be or however unlikely it might be that they will ever come into existence: *Thorpe* v *Revenue and Customs Commissioners* [2009] EWHC 611 (Ch).) The trustee will hold the trust property on what is called a 'bare trust' for the sole beneficiary. Beyond this, and perhaps more remarkable, is the aspect of the rule which applies where there are several beneficiaries. If they are all *sui juris* and together absolutely entitled to the trust property, they may unanimously agree to terminate the trust and may demand that the trust property be handed over to them.

> **sui juris**
> Adult and of sound mind (pronounced 'soo-ee your-is').

There are, however, some limitations on the application of the rule designed to protect trustee discretions. The rule was considered in detail in *Stephenson (Inspector of Taxes)* v *Barclays Bank Trust Co Ltd* [1975] 1 All ER 625. There Walton J stated some 'elementary principles' of the application of the rule: (1) where persons, being *sui juris*, between them hold the entirety of the beneficial interest under a trust, they can direct the trustees as to how to deal with the trust property; (2) but they cannot thereby override the existing trusts and at the same time keep them in existence; (3) so, for instance, they cannot require the current trustees to make particular investments; (4) nor can they deny the trustees' basic right to be indemnified out of the trust fund for any expenses incurred by them in carrying out the trust.

In *Saunders* v *Vautier* itself the testator left property on trust for Vautier with a direction that interest should be accumulated until he reached 25. On reaching 25, he was to become entitled to claim the capital and all the accumulated income. When Vautier reached the age of majority (21 in those days) he claimed the whole of the fund. The then Master of the Rolls and the then Vice-Chancellor decided that Vautier's interest had vested absolutely upon his attaining majority, and he was entitled to claim the property now, notwithstanding the settlor's obvious intention that Vautier's enjoyment of the property should be postponed until he reached the age of 25.

This is an extreme instance of the variation of a trust, and it is in many ways the conceptual precedent for the Variation of Trusts Act 1958 (see 9.3). Having said that, the rule in *Saunders* v *Vautier* is concerned more with revocation than with variation. *Saunders* v *Vautier* is *not* authority for allowing the adult beneficiaries to instruct the trustees to act as they are told. So, under the rule, the beneficiaries are not permitted to direct the trustees to make investments chosen by the beneficiaries. Either the beneficiaries keep the old trusts 'on foot', in which case they must not interfere with the trustees' management of the trust, or the beneficiaries must bring the old trust to an end and divide the trust property between them, or resettle it on new trusts. It is the latter possibility that illustrates how the rule in *Saunders* v *Vautier* might be utilised to effect a genuine variation of a trust, as opposed to a mere revocation of it. A genuine variation might also be achieved if the beneficiaries being *sui juris* and between them absolutely entitled to the fund wish to vary the terms of the trust and the trustees *agree* to act on the trusts in their varied form.

9.1.2 **Variation of Trusts Act 1958**

This is examined in great detail at 9.2.

9.1.3 **Trustee Act 1925, s 57**

 STATUTE

Trustee Act 1925, s 57 *Power of court to authorise dealings with trust property*

(1) Where in the management or administration of any property vested in trustees, any sale, lease, mortgage, surrender, release, or other disposition, or any purchase, investment, acquisition, expenditure, or other transaction, is in the opinion of the court expedient, but the same cannot be effected by reason of the absence of any power for that purpose vested in the trustees by the trust instrument, if any, or by law, the court may by order confer upon the trustees, either generally or in any particular instance, the necessary power for the purpose, on such terms, and subject to such provisions and conditions, if any, as the court may think fit and may direct in what manner any money authorised to be expended, and the costs of any transaction, are to be paid or borne as between capital and income.

(2) The court may, from time to time, rescind or vary any order made under this section, or may make any new or further order.

(3) An application to the court under this section may be made by the trustees, or by any of them, or by any person beneficially interested under the trust.

(4) This section does not apply to trustees of a settlement for the purposes of the Settled Land Act 1925.

 THINKING POINT

Imagine a trust under which ten beneficiaries are entitled to an equal share in the fund. Could the Trustee Act 1925, s 57 be used to vary the trust so as to permit an arrangement which (to achieve a tax saving for every beneficiary) would remove the requirement of equal division?

No, it could not. Section 57 permits variations in the way that the trust is managed (see, for example, *Gelber v Sunderland Foundation* [2018] EWHC 2344 (Ch)), but does not authorise remoulding of beneficial interests. Having said that, it does permit merely 'incidental' variation of beneficial interests arising from administrative changes; thus in *Southgate v Sutton* [2011] EWCA Civ 637, the Court of Appeal made an order under s 57 to create a sub-trust for the benefit of US-resident beneficiaries. (*Southgate* was followed in *Re English & American Insurance Co Ltd* [2013] EWHC 3360 (Ch); [2014] WTLR 57.) In the words of the section, it allows the court to authorise the trustees to carry out any transaction 'in the management or administration' of the trust property where such transaction is 'expedient'. It was suggested in *Re Downshire SE* [1952] 2 All ER 603 that the section would permit 'specific dealings' with the trust property, which the court might not otherwise be authorised to permit under its inherent jurisdiction (see 9.1.5). So, for example, variation of investment powers should normally be sought under this section (*Anker-Petersen v Anker-Petersen* (1991) 16 LS Gaz 32). According to *Re Mair* [1935] Ch 562, s 57 operates by inserting an 'overriding power' in the trust instrument so as to permit the trustees to act in accordance with the variation ordered by the court.

9.1.4 Trustee Act 1925, s 53

Under this section the trust may be varied for the maintenance, education or benefit of an infant beneficiary. The variation is effected by making a conveyance on sale of the beneficiary's interest. The capital proceeds of the sale and income made thereon are then 'applied' for the maintenance of the infant. This power is most useful where the beneficiary has an interest only in capital under the trust, and in other situations where the trustees will not have the usual power to maintain the beneficiary (see Chapter 13).

9.1.5 Variation under the courts' inherent jurisdiction

The courts have always had an inherent jurisdiction to vary the manner in which a trust is administered, although the courts prefer that such variations be sought under s 57 wherever appropriate. This inherent jurisdiction of the courts is limited to cases of 'salvage' and 'emergency'. What do these terms mean?

Q | **CASE CLOSE-UP**

***Re New* [1901] 2 Ch 534, Chancery Division**

Facts: the trustees wished to approve a proposal to reorganise a limited company in which the trust owned shares, but they had no power to do so. The beneficiaries could not approve the reorganisation because they were not all *sui juris*, but the reorganisation would certainly have been to their benefit. Accordingly the trustees applied to the court for a variation under the court's inherent jurisdiction.

Held: the court could approve the variation under its inherent jurisdiction to alter the administration of a trust in cases of 'emergency', where circumstances have arisen which the settlor of the trust had not foreseen and had not made provision for. Such variations would be approved only where the variation was desirable in the best interests of the beneficiaries.

Romer LJ: 'as a rule, the Court has no jurisdiction to give, and will not give, its sanction to the performance by trustees of acts with reference to the trust estate which are not, on the face of the instrument creating the trust, authorised by its terms . . . But in the management

of a trust estate, and especially where that estate consists of a business or shares in a mer-
cantile company, it not infrequently happens that some peculiar state of circumstances arises
for which provision is not expressly made by the trust instrument, and which renders it most
desirable, and it may be even essential, for the benefit of the estate and in the interest of all
the *cestuis que trust*, that certain acts should be done by the trustees which in ordinary circumstances they would have no power to do. In a case of this kind, which may reasonably
be supposed to be one not foreseen or anticipated by the author of the trust, where the
trustees are embarrassed by the emergency that has arisen and the duty cast upon them to
do what is best for the estate, and the consent of all the beneficiaries cannot be obtained
by reason of some of them not being *sui juris* or in existence, then it may be right for the
Court, and the Court in a proper case would have jurisdiction, to sanction on behalf of all
concerned such acts on behalf of the trustees as we have above referred to . . .

Of course, the jurisdiction is one to be exercised with great caution, and the Court will take
care not to strain its powers. It is impossible, and no attempt ought to be made, to state
or define all the circumstances under which, or the extent to which, the Court will exercise
the jurisdiction; but it need scarcely be said that the Court will not be justified in sanctioning every act desired by trustees and beneficiaries merely because it may appear beneficial
to the estate; and certainly the Court will not be disposed to sanction transactions of a
speculative or risky character. But each case brought before the Court must be considered
and dealt with according to its special circumstances.'

'Salvage' cases almost exclusively involve infants. In such cases the administration of the trust
may be varied in the interests of the infant beneficiary, but only in situations of absolute necessity. An example might be where one part of the property is mortgaged to raise monies to
prevent another part of the property from becoming valueless—as where Greenacre is mortgaged to prevent Green Mansion from falling down.

Trusts may be varied in situations of 'emergency' without having to show that the variation is
absolutely necessary. 'Emergency' refers to situations which the settlor had not foreseen. A
variation under this heading can therefore be made entirely in keeping with the settlor's presumed intention for the trust.

Re New has been described as the high-water mark because there were suggestions in the
judgment that the court could vary the administration of the trust under its inherent jurisdiction in cases where the variation would be desirable, even if it was not in fact essential.
However, Romer LJ did state that the court will not be justified in sanctioning every act desired
by the trustees and beneficiaries 'merely because it may appear beneficial to the estate'.

9.1.6 Matrimonial jurisdiction

Section 24 of the Matrimonial Causes Act 1973 (now the Family Law Act 1996, s 15, Sch. 2,
para. 6) grants to the courts a wide power to vary the beneficial interests under trusts to achieve
a fair distribution of property upon the pronouncement of a decree of divorce or nullity of marriage. The breadth of the judge's discretion was confirmed in *P* v *P* [2015] EWCA Civ 447.

9.1.7 Mental Capacity Act jurisdiction

The Mental Capacity Act 2005 grants the court the jurisdiction to create a trust of property of
a person lacking mental capacity (ss 16, 18(1)(h)). Supplementary provisions in Sch. 2 of the Act

provide that these trusts can be varied later if there is a significant change of circumstances: for example, if the patient ceases to be of unsound mind.

9.1.8 Inherent jurisdiction to maintain

Even where a trust orders that income should be accumulated, which would normally be taken as evidence of the settlor's intention to exclude the statutory power to maintain beneficiaries out of that income, the court has an inherent jurisdiction to maintain beneficiaries where there are no other monies out of which they could be maintained (see *Re Walker* [1901] 1 Ch 879). The statutory power of maintenance is restricted to infant beneficiaries (see Chapter 13) but the court's inherent jurisdiction to maintain is not so limited. Nor is this jurisdiction restricted to cases of absolute necessity or emergency. The assumption is that the settlor would not have intended that the beneficiaries should want for life's basic necessities.

9.1.9 Rectification of wills

⏩ CROSS-REFERENCE
On rectification of wills see 20.2.5.2.

According to the Administration of Justice Act 1982, s 20(1), if a court is satisfied that a will is so expressed that it fails to carry out the testator's intentions, in consequence of a clerical error or a failure to understand his instructions, it may order that the will may be rectified so as to carry out his intentions.

9.1.10 Compromise of disputes—a dubious jurisdiction to 'vary' trusts

It is a truism to say that the courts have an inherent jurisdiction to compromise disputes. If a dispute arises as to the proper construction to be given to the words of a trust instrument, it goes without saying that the courts are the most expert arbiters of it. In the past, beneficiaries would seek to vary the terms of their trusts by recourse to the courts' inherent jurisdiction to resolve disputes in relation to the meaning of trusts. This procedure became a popular way to effect a variation of the beneficial interests under the trust, in relation to variations which could otherwise be achieved only by bringing the trust to an end under the rule in *Saunders* v *Vautier*. However, the courts began to consider cases where there was no real dispute at all. The 'disputing' parties would agree a 'compromise' in terms favourable to the beneficiaries, and the court would sanction the sham compromise by court order. This practice continued until it was brought to an end by the House of Lords in *Chapman* v *Chapman* [1954] AC 429 (Lord Cohen dissenting) after which it was decided that the courts would be able to vary trusts under this jurisdiction only in cases of genuine dispute. After *Chapman* v *Chapman* the Law Reform Committee noted that the House of Lords had deprived the courts of a very flexible and, as they saw it, necessary jurisdiction to vary trusts. It approved Lord Cohen's view that a compromise did involve a genuine variation. The Variation of Trusts Act 1958 was passed in response to the recommendations of the Law Reform Committee.

9.1.11 Summative exercise

The table at Table 9.1 lists the main modes by which a trust may be varied. Against each mode place a tick according to whether the method can vary beneficial interests under the trust or only vary administration of the trust.

The solution is that the first mode varies beneficial interests only—by bringing the trust to an end. The courts' inherent jurisdiction and ss 53 and 57 of the Trustee Act 1925 vary administration only (although incidental minor variations to beneficial interests may be tolerated). The remaining modes vary beneficial interest and administration.

Table 9.1 Summative exercise

Mode of variation	Varies beneficial interests only	Varies administration only	Varies beneficial interests and administration
The rule in *Saunders* v *Vautier*			
Variation of Trusts Act 1958			
Trustee Act 1925, s 57			
Trustee Act 1925, s 53			
Variation under the court's inherent jurisdiction			
Matrimonial jurisdiction			
Mental Health Act jurisdiction			

9.2 Variation of Trusts Act 1958

If all the beneficiaries are *sui juris* and between them absolutely entitled to the trust fund, they can take advantage of the rule in *Saunders* v *Vautier* (see 9.1.1). Other beneficiaries, e.g. infants and the unborn, cannot take advantage of that rule. The essence of the 1958 Act is that it authorises the Chancery Division of the High Court to approve, on behalf of beneficiaries in these (and certain other) categories, an arrangement varying or revoking all or any of the trust. The consent of beneficiaries who do not fall within the relevant categories must be given by them personally (i.e. cannot be given by the court) if the proposed arrangement is to go ahead.

 STATUTE

Variation of Trusts Act 1958

1. Jurisdiction of courts to vary trusts

   (1) Where property, whether real or personal, is held on trusts arising, whether before or after the passing of this Act, under any will, settlement or other disposition, the court may if it thinks fit by order approve on behalf of—

> **(a)** any person having, directly or indirectly, an interest, whether vested or contingent, under the trusts who by reason of infancy or other incapacity is incapable of assenting, or
>
> **(b)** any person (whether ascertained or not) who may become entitled, directly or indirectly, to an interest under the trusts as being at a future date or on the happening of a future event a person of any specified description or a member of any specified class of persons, so however that this paragraph shall not include any person who would be of that description, or a member of that class, as the case may be, if the said date had fallen or the said event had happened at the date of the application to the court, or
>
> **(c)** any person unborn, or
>
> **(d)** any person in respect of any discretionary interest of his under protective trusts where the interest of the principal beneficiary has not failed or deter-mined, any arrangement (by whomsoever proposed, and whether or not there is any other person beneficially interested who is capable of assenting thereto) varying or revoking all or any of the trusts, or enlarging the powers of the trustees of managing or administering any of the property subject to the trusts:
>
> Provided that except by virtue of paragraph (d) of this subsection the court shall not approve an arrangement on behalf of any person unless the carrying out thereof would be for the benefit of that person.

Unlike s 57 of the Trustee Act 1925 (see 9.1.3), which is restricted to variations in the manage-ment of the trust, the Variation of Trusts Act 1958 enables the remoulding of beneficial interests under trusts as well as permitting incidental changes to the administration of the trust. For example, in *Bathurst v Bathurst* [2016] EWHC 3033, the High Court authorised a variation under the 1958 Act which gave the power of trustee appointment to the principal beneficiary instead of the settlor on the basis that making a change in the arrangement would not be de-parting radically from the structure the settlor first created. The reference in s 1 to powers of 'administering' trust property does not supersede the Trustee Act 1925, s 57. Where *all* that is being requested is an administrative variation an order should still be sought by making an ap-plication under s 57.

You should note that the Act merely authorises the court to approve the arrangement; the court is never obliged to vary a trust under the Act. In the words of s 1, the 'court may *if it thinks fit* by order approve . . . any arrangement (by whomsoever proposed, and whether or not there is any other person beneficially interested who is capable of assenting thereto) varying or revoking all or any of the trusts, or enlarging the powers of the trustees of managing or administering any of the property subject to the trusts' (emphasis added).

For judicial consideration of the ideological underpinning of the 1958 Act see *Goulding v James* [1997] 2 All ER 239 (see 9.5).

9.2.1 Applications under the Act—who should be the parties?

Section 1 states that the court has authority to approve an arrangement 'by whomsoever pro-posed'. In fact, applications should be made by adult beneficiaries under the trust. According to *Re Druce's ST* [1962] 1 WLR 363 the trustees should not make the application themselves unless they believe, first, that the variation would be for the benefit of the beneficiaries and, secondly, that there is no adult beneficiary willing to make the application for a variation. In fact, far from being claimants under the application, the trustees should be joined as defendants, for it is they who have the fiduciary duty to protect the interests of all the beneficiaries under the trust and they who should raise objections if the proposed variation appears to benefit some but not all of the beneficiaries. Indeed, the right to a fair trial under Art 6 of the European Convention on Human Rights requires that trustees should be joined as parties to an application to vary a trust, without which no order would be binding on them (*M v H* [2016] EWHC 572 (Fam); [2016] 4 WLR 78). If the beneficiaries are not unanimous in making the application the non-claimant beneficiaries should be joined as additional defendants. The settlor should be joined as a defendant where variation of an *inter vivos* trust is proposed and the settlor is still alive. The form of the application is an originating summons exhibiting a draft scheme of arrangement.

9.2.2 How does the variation occur?

Megarry J stated in *Re Holt's Settlement* [1969] 1 Ch 100 that:

> [a]ny variation owes its authority not to anything in the initial settlement but to the statute and the consent of the adults coming, as it were, *ab extra*. This certainly seems to be so in any case not within the Act where a variation or resettlement is made under the doctrine of *Saunders* v *Vautier* . . . by all the adults joining together, and I cannot see any real difference in principle in a case where the court exercises its jurisdiction on behalf of the infants under the Act of 1958.

On the further question whether the variation involved a disposition of equitable interests by the beneficiaries who had consented to the variation, the learned judge decided that it did. However, he yielded reluctantly to counsel's submission that this disposition should be treated as an exception to s 53(1)(c) of the Law of Property Act 1925, and need not be formalised by signed writing. Thus, the beneficiaries were saved from a liability to stamp duty which then attached to dispositions of equitable interests by signed writing. This appears to be yet another instance of the courts granting the beneficiaries a fiscal advantage in this area. Megarry J was persuaded to recognise this exception to s 53(1)(c) because it accorded with the practice which had been accepted by the Inland Revenue and by the courts for many years 'in some thousands of cases'.

9.2.3 Consents given by the court

We have seen that a variation under the Act will be approved only if all the beneficiaries give their consent to it. We have also noted that the court may itself consent on behalf of certain beneficiaries, but that all other beneficiaries must give their own consent. Hearings are normally in public. In a case where the parties are concerned that a public hearing will prejudice the parties (for example by publicising the wealth of a private company or revealing the identities of wealthy infant beneficiaries), reporting restrictions may be imposed and the judgment may be anonymised (*V v T* [2014] EWHC 3432 (Ch); [2014] All ER (D) 293 (Oct)).

9.2.3.1 Persons under legal disability (s 1(1)(a))

This class includes minors (infants) and any other persons who are incapable of assenting to the arrangement varying the trusts. Included in this category would be persons of unsound mind and persons suffering from a severe (and relevant) physical disability. It may seem rather surprising that the consent of persons aged, say, 16 and 17 should be treated in the same manner as the consent of persons of unsound mind. However, in practice the court will take into account the expressed wishes of persons approaching majority, although their lack of actual consent is, at the end of the day, not a conclusive consideration. An arrangement will be approved if the court believes that it is in the interest of the infant beneficiary, even if the infant does not share that view. If the infant is still under parental influence there is the very real possibility that the parents would try to influence the exercise of their child's consent in order to achieve their own ends. By giving the court the power to consent on the infant's behalf this potential abuse is prevented to some degree.

9.2.3.2 **Persons with mere expectations (s 1(1)(b))**

This class of persons on whose behalf the court may give consent is by far the most difficult to comprehend. However, a series of cases has helped to isolate those persons who do and those persons who do not fall within this class. Section 1(1)(b) is transcribed next, with certain key words emphasised. These key words have received particular attention in those cases where the courts have considered s 1(1)(b).

According to s 1(1)(b) the court may, if it thinks fit, approve a variation on behalf of:

> any person (whether ascertained or not) who *may* become entitled, *directly or indirectly*, to an interest under the trusts as being at a future date or on the happening of *a future event* a person of any specified description or *a member of any specified class of persons, so however* that this paragraph shall not include any person who *would be* of that description or a *member of that class*, as the case may be, if the said date had fallen or the *said event had happened at the date of the application to the court* (emphasis added).

Re Suffert's Settlement [1960] 3 All ER 561 demonstrates the operation of the section. Miss Suffert was a 61-year-old spinster who had no children and her only ascertainable relations were three adult first cousins. The court held that it could give its consent on behalf of any persons unascertained as they would fall within s 1(1)(b) and it could consent on behalf of any persons unborn as they would fall within s 1(1)(c). The stumbling block was the consent of the three cousins. One of them had expressly joined Miss Suffert in making the application to the court, but that still left two adult cousins who had not given their consent to the arrangement. Could the court consent on their behalf? In other words, did those two cousins fall within s 1(1)(b)?

Under the terms of the original trusts, if Miss Suffert died without issue, and in default of her having exercised a power of appointment to other persons, the fund would pass in trust to her statutory next of kin. The three cousins were her statutory next of kin. Let us, then, apply the wording of s 1(1)(b) to the case, as did the court.

First, were the cousins persons who 'may become entitled . . . as being . . . on the happening of a future event . . . member[s] of any specified class of persons'? Yes they were! They could be ('may be') the next of kin ('specified class of persons') on Miss Suffert's death ('a future event'). Because 'next of kin' is a class of persons the constitution of which can change continually, it is possible to say only that the cousins 'may be' next of kin.

So, the cousins also fall within s 1(1)(b), and is the court able to consent on their behalf? Not necessarily! We should be careful not to jump to a premature conclusion. There is more to s 1(1)(b).

Secondly, we must take into account the important proviso to s 1(1)(b). This is the part of the paragraph which begins with the words 'so however'. It goes on to say that s 1(1)(b) does not include 'any person who *would be* . . . a member of that class . . . if the . . . said event had happened *at the date of the application to the court*' (emphasis added).

THINKING POINT

Do the cousins fall within this exception to s 1(1)(b)?

Yes they do! If the said event (Miss Suffert's death) had happened 'at the date of the application to the court' (taken to be the date of the court hearing) the cousins *would be* immediately entitled as next of kin to an interest under the trust. In effect, on account of the proviso, the court asks itself at the date of the court hearing of the application, 'What would be the cousins' entitlement if Miss Suffert died *today*?' By asking itself this question the court is able to ignore the theoretical possibility that the class of 'next of kin' might change at some time in the future. In the case of *Re Suffert's Settlement* the court decided that if Miss Suffert had died on the date of the court hearing the cousins would then have had a definite entitlement as her next of kin. They would therefore have fallen within the proviso to s 1(1)(b), and the court accordingly refused to consent to the arrangement on their behalf. No matter that the court may have been of the view that the cousins would have willingly consented to the application; the cousins had to be sought out and their own consent procured before the court would approve the arrangement.

The reasoning in *Re Suffert's Settlement* was followed in the case of *Re Moncrieff's ST* [1962] 3 All ER 838, which was reported a year later. The decision in *Re Moncrieff's ST* was different because of a subtle difference in the facts of the two cases. In *Re Moncrieff's ST* the primary beneficiary, Mrs Joan Parkin, applied to court for an order approving an arrangement to vary the trusts under which she was entitled. Mrs Parkin had an adopted son, Alan. If she survived Alan, her next of kin would be the four infant grandchildren of her maternal aunt.

The judge in *Re Moncrieff's ST* was able to provide the consent of Alan because he was still an infant and therefore fell within s 1(1)(a) of the Act. However, the consent of the four infant grandchildren could not be provided in the same way. Section 1(1)(a) could not apply to them because that section applies only to persons 'having' an interest under the trust. Because the class of 'next of kin' can change continually it would be possible to say only that the infant grandchildren 'may' have an interest under the trust. Because s 1(1)(a) did not apply to them the crucial question in the case was whether they fell within s 1(1)(b). Let us try to answer that question.

First, were the four infant grandchildren of her maternal aunt persons who 'may become entitled . . . as being . . . on the happening of a future event . . . member[s] of any specified class of persons'? Yes they were! They could be ('may be') the next of kin ('specified class of persons') on the death of Mrs Joan Parkin ('a future event').

THINKING POINT

Would the four infants have been 'next of kin' if Mrs Parkin had died on the date of the application to the court?

However, as we already know, this is not the end of the story. Secondly, we must take into account the important proviso to s 1(1)(b), which states that s 1(1)(b) does not include 'any person who *would be* . . . a member of that class . . . if the . . . said event had happened *at the date of the application to the court*' (emphasis added).

The answer is, of course, 'no'. Alan, Mrs Parkin's adopted son, would have been her statutory next of kin if she had died at the date of the application to the court. The infant grandchildren did not fall within the proviso to s 1(1)(b) and so their own consent was not required before approval could be given for the arrangement varying the trusts. The court in *Re Moncrieff's ST* was itself able to consent on behalf of the four infants.

As Buckley J stated: 'Their interests can be looked after by the trustees, and they are persons who may never fall within the class of beneficiaries because they may predecease the settlor or the first respondent [Alan] may survive the settlor.' He went on to approve the arrangement as proposed by Mrs Parkin.

In summary, when considering whether a person will fall within s 1(1)(b) it might be useful to ask, 'how many events must happen before this person is entitled under the trust?' If the answer is 'one event', they will probably fall within the proviso to s 1(1)(b) and will have to give their own consent to an arrangement before the arrangement can be approved. If the answer is 'two events', they will probably not fall within the proviso, with the result that the court can consent on their behalf.

CASE CLOSE-UP

Knocker v *Youle* [1986] 2 All ER 914, ChD

Facts: under the original terms of the settlement in question, the primary beneficiary, the settlor's daughter, had a life interest in income under the trust. The remainder of the fund would pass to persons appointed by the primary beneficiary in her will. If she made no appointment the remainder interest would pass to the following persons or classes of person in the following strict order:

- the settlor's son; or if he were dead to
- the settlor's sisters; or if they were dead to
- their issue at the age of 21.

The settlor's daughter and son applied to court for an order approving a variation of the trusts. The settlor's sisters had all died. The question arose whether the sisters' issue had to give their consent to the arrangement, or whether the court was able to consent on their behalf under s 1(1)(b). The court concluded that the sisters' issue were not persons who 'may' be entitled upon the happening of a certain event etc. They must give their own consent to the arrangement. Although their interests were very remote, they nevertheless had more than a mere expectation that they would acquire an interest under the trusts; they had an interest directly conferred by the settlement.

Warner J: 'what counsel invited me to do was in effect to interpret the word "interest" in s. 1(1) loosely, as a layman might, so as not to include an interest that was remote. I was referred to two authorities: *Re Moncrieff's Settlement Trusts* [1962] 3 All ER 838 and the earlier case of *Re Suffert's Settlement, Suffert* v *Martyn-Linnington* [1960] 3 All ER 561. In both those cases, however, the class in question was a class of prospective next of kin, and, of course it is trite law that the prospective or presumptive next of kin of a living person do not have an interest. They have only a *spes successionis*, a hope of succeeding, and quite certainly they are the typical category of persons who fall within s. 1(1)(b). Another familiar example of a person falling within that provision is a potential future spouse. It seems

> to me, however, that a person who has an actual interest directly conferred on him or her by a settlement, albeit a remote interest, cannot properly be described as one who "may become" entitled to an interest . . .
>
> Otherwise, the words 'whether vested or contingent' in s. 1(1)(a) would be out of place . . . the distinction between an expectation and an interest is one which I do not think that I am entitled to blur.'

Warner J went on to state that even if the applicants had been able to argue a way around the importance that he had attached to the word 'may', the sisters' issue would still have been required to give their own consent to the arrangement because they would have been in the same position as the cousins in *Re Suffert's Settlement*, being persons within the proviso to s 1(1)(b).

9.2.3.3 **The spectral spouse**

Suppose an unmarried primary beneficiary applies to the court for an order approving an arrangement varying or revoking the trusts under which they are presently entitled. A potential future spouse whom they might marry could fall within the ambit of s 1(1)(b). This potential future spouse has been given the eerie title of 'spectral spouse'. In the case of *Re Steed's WT* [1960] 1 Ch 407 (see further 9.5) the court refused to consent to a proposed arrangement on behalf of the spectral spouse because it was thought that the proposed arrangement would not be for his benefit. This was despite the fact that the primary beneficiary was aged 53, had never married, and did not consider it at all likely that she would ever marry. The Master of the Rolls took a more romantic view, observing that 'many have said that before and subsequent events have proved them wrong'.

CROSS REFERENCE

Refer back to 2.3.2 where we considered the nature of 'protective trusts'.

9.2.3.4 **The unborn (s 1(1)(c))**

The court may consent to an arrangement on behalf of any person unborn. This class is not restricted to persons in the womb. It would include 'the children of X', even if X were an avowed celibate (presumably by extension of the reasoning that 'many have said that before and subsequent events have proved them wrong' (see 9.2.3.3)). It is uncertain whether the presumptions of fertility and infertility established by the Perpetuities and Accumulations Act 1964 (see 6.2.5.2) would apply by analogy to this context. Consider, for example, a trust 'to Ms A for life and to her issue in remainder in equal shares absolutely'. If Ms A is a childless octogenarian who makes an application to court for the revocation of the trust under which she holds her life interest, would the court be required to consent on behalf of her non-existent issue before approving the arrangement? Would her 'potential' issue be 'unborn' within s 1(1)(c)? The fertility presumptions in the 1964 Act would respond with a resounding 'no'! In any event, fertility presumptions are nothing new to the administration of estates. Traditionally the court has been happy to distribute estates on the basis that a woman will pass her child-bearing age in her mid- to late fifties.

9.2.3.5 **Protective trusts (s 1(1)(d))**

Where there is a protective trust the court may provide the consent of any person who would have an interest under a discretionary trust springing up on the determination of the life interest. To make any sense of this section it is necessary first of all to have a basic acquaintance with the concept of a protective trust.

THINKING POINT

Having familiarised yourself with the idea of a 'protective trust', can you identify the persons in the following scenario who would fall within s 1(1)(d)?

S has settled a trust upon trustees for P for life and R in remainder. By the terms of the trust P's interest will determine in the event of P being declared bankrupt. Upon the determination of P's interest the trust fund will be held by the trustees upon a new trust, with the duty to distribute the fund as they, in their absolute discretion, think fit, amongst a range of potential beneficiaries. P is one of those potential beneficiaries; others include Q and R, P's brothers.

No doubt you have worked out that P, Q and R are all technically within s 1(1)(d) and their consent will not be required to an arrangement varying or revoking all or any of the trusts. In practice P is an exception to this, because as well as falling within s 1(1)(d), P is also the primary beneficiary under the protective trust and in this capacity, always assuming that P's interest has not yet determined, P's own consent will be needed before the court will approve of the arrangement.

9.2.4 **The benefit requirement**

> If you apply yourself to our intents,/Which towards you are most gentle,/You shall find a benefit in this change.
>
> William Shakespeare, *Antony and Cleopatra*, Act V, scene 2

Where the court provides the consent of any person under s 1(1)(a), (b) or (c) it may not approve the arrangement varying the trusts unless the carrying out thereof would be for the benefit of that person. Section 1(1)(d) is expressly excluded from this benefit requirement. The consent of a person falling within para. (d) may be given even if the arrangement would not be for their benefit (see *Re Turner's WT* [1960] 1 Ch 122). The 1958 Act gives no indication as to what may constitute a 'benefit', nor how benefit and detriment are to be weighed, but the cases provide some guidance.

9.2.4.1 **Financial benefits**

In the great majority of cases, the benefit provided by the Act is a tax planning advantage, and so, ultimately, a financial one. In *Re Duke of Norfolk's WT* (1966) Times, 23 March the beneficiaries saved £550,000 in taxes because of the variation.

This case illustrates how the jurisdiction to vary trusts under the Act appears to serve the financially more privileged members of society, at the 'expense' of the ordinary taxpayer. Of course, persons benefiting from variations in cases like *Re Norfolk's WT* would no doubt argue that they are extraordinary taxpayers attempting merely to retain ownership of their own property and that ordinary taxpayers would be well advised to do the same wherever possible. Tax savings and the possibility of cheaper life insurance justified a 1958 Act variation in *Re RGST* [2007] EWHC 2666 (Ch).

Less controversial, one assumes, would be a variation designed to shield from taxation a damages award held in trust to maintain a person who had been seriously injured in a road traffic accident.

THINKING POINT

Do you think it could benefit the children of a settlor for the trust to be varied to grant the settlor's spouse a life interest on the settlor's death?

In *Ridgwell* v *Ridgwell* [2007] EWHC 2666 (Ch) the court held that such a variation would benefit the children of the settlor and his spouse. In terms of direct financial benefits, it is hard to see how the surviving spouse could gain a benefit without the children suffering a corresponding financial loss, and yet the court held that the arrangement was to the financial benefit of the children. It might have been more convincing to acknowledge that this is an area in which financial benefits should sometimes give way to the broader benefit of familial harmony.

9.2.4.2 Social and moral benefits

In *Re Holt's Settlement* [1969] 1 Ch 100 Megarry J held that benefit is 'not confined to financial benefit, but may extend to social or moral benefit'. Hence in *Re Weston's Settlements* [1969] 1 Ch 223 the Court of Appeal refused to approve an arrangement which would have provided a tax planning advantage, and thus a financial benefit, to the beneficiaries. The applicant in the case, Mr Stanley Weston, applied for an order approving an arrangement under which the trust would be exported to Jersey from England. Because Jersey is a 'tax haven' the trust would stand to save £163,000 in capital gains tax if the trust could be exported. However, the family had been resident in Jersey for only three months and it was highly likely that they would not stay there after the exportation of the trust. Lord Denning MR laid emphasis on the moral and social benefits of being brought up in England, which, for him, outweighed the financial benefits that tax avoidance would bring: 'There are many things in life more worthwhile than money. One of these things is to be brought up in this our England which is still "the envy of less happier lands".'

It might surprise us that Jersey was deemed to fall within the class of less happy lands! In fact, Lord Denning had other reasons for reaching the conclusion he did. He seemed impressed by the need for stability in a young beneficiary's life: 'Are they to be wanderers over the face of the earth, moving from this country to that, according to where they can best avoid tax? I cannot believe that to be right. Children are like trees: they grow stronger with firm roots.'

The benefits of stability, coupled with the perceived benefits of an English upbringing, were deemed to be more important in this case than the financial proceeds of a tax avoidance scheme. However, Lord Denning did not doubt that tax avoidance was a quite proper use of the courts' jurisdiction to vary trusts: 'the exodus of this family to Jersey is done to avoid British taxation. Having made great wealth here, they want to quit without paying the taxes and duties which are imposed on those who stay. So be it. If it really be for the benefit of the children, let it be done.'

9.2.4.3 Benefit by deferral

In *Re Holt's Settlement* it was seen to be a benefit to the beneficiaries to defer the vesting of the gift until they were reasonably advanced in a career and settled in life. This involved a deferral of the contingent age from 21 to 30. Megarry J stated that he did not require evidence of special immaturity or irresponsibility. In *Re T's Settlement* [1963] 3 All ER 759 it was likewise seen to be a benefit to the beneficiary to defer the vesting of a gift until she was more mature and responsible, thereby protecting her from creditors, exploitation and her own folly. Of course, it cannot be presumed beneficial to defer the coming into possession of a valuable interest under a trust. In *Wright* v *Gater* [2011] EWHC 2881 an application to postpone from age 18 to age 30 was rejected on the ground that no benefit had been shown, and because the variation would come close to being a resettlement (see 9.3).

9.2.4.4 The benefit of familial harmony

In some cases applicants for a variation have sought to set the benefit of familial harmony against the reduced financial benefits which would flow from the new arrangement. They have had varying degrees of success.

In *Re Tinker's Settlement* [1960] 1 WLR 1011, a fund was held on trust for the settlor's son and daughter in equal shares. The daughter's share was contingent upon her attaining the age of 30, failing which it would pass to her issue or to her brother if she died without issue. The brother's share was given upon a similar contingency but with no gift over to his issue should he fail to attain the age of 30; instead his share would pass to his sister. This crucial difference between the two gifts was quite reasonably presumed to have resulted from an inadvertent omission in the drafting of the settlement. By applying to court for an order approving an arrangement varying the trusts it was hoped to rectify the error so as to allow the brother's children to take if he died before the age of 30. The application failed and approval was refused. The court had to be satisfied that the new arrangement would be for the benefit of unborn beneficiaries within s 1(1)(c) of the Variation of Trusts Act 1958. The daughter's unborn children could not possibly benefit financially from the arrangement, as they had a financial advantage over their unborn cousins under the original settlement. The variation would remove that advantage. Russell J was not persuaded that the advantage of familial harmony would outweigh the financial advantage. There are even suggestions in Russell J's judgment that only financial benefits would be a valid consideration, but we have seen that this cannot be correct after *Re Weston's* and *Re Holt's Settlement*.

By way of contrast to *Re Tinker's Settlement* we will now turn to *Re Remnant's ST* [1970] 1 Ch 560, where the testator left a fund ultimately upon trust to the issue of his two daughters. However, he provided that any child who, on the death of its mother, was 'practising Roman Catholicism' (which included being married to a Roman Catholic) should forfeit any interest. The forfeited share was directed to be passed to the issue of the other sister. One of the daughters had become a Roman Catholic, and it was likely that her children would forfeit their interests under the terms of the will. Both daughters disliked the forfeiture clause and they applied, within less than two years of their father's death, for a variation of the trusts which would cut out the forfeiture clauses. Additionally, the new arrangement, if approved, would accelerate the interests of the sisters' children in £10,000 of the fund which would be set aside for that purpose.

Pennycuik J took into account the fact that the forfeiture clause might 'operate as a deterrent to each of the . . . children in the selection of a husband when the time comes' and 'might well cause very serious dissension between the families of the two sisters'. These considerations, together with the fact that each of the sisters' issue had an accelerated financial entitlement, persuaded the judge to approve the arrangement. As he said: 'I have not found this an easy point, but I think that I am entitled to take a broad view of what is meant by "benefit", and so taking it, I think this arrangement can fairly be said to be for their benefit.'

So, are we able to explain the different decisions in *Re Tinker's Settlement* and *Re Remnant's ST*? It has been suggested that the distinction lies in the fact that in *Re Remnant's ST* both sides of the family could benefit from the freedom to marry without financial penalty which the new arrangement secured.

There may be a better distinction. *Re Tinker's Settlement* involved the granting of a beneficial interest to a beneficiary who would have had nothing under the original settlement. On the other hand, the variation in *Re Remnant's ST* did not give any beneficiary anything that they did not already have, but simply removed a forfeiture provision which could have stripped them of their entitlement and accelerated their entitlement to part of the fund. *Re Tinker's Settlement* involved the creation of an equitable entitlement; *Re Remnant's ST* involved the protection of an existing equitable entitlement. The judge in *Re Remnant's ST* acknowledged that the new arrangement 'defeats the settlor's intention', but that had to be set against the fact that 'forfeiture provisions are undesirable in themselves'.

9.2.4.5 **Risks of detriment?**

What if the arrangement which has been put forward for approval would, in the normal course of events, be for the benefit of all the beneficiaries, but carries a risk that certain potential beneficiaries might in certain possible circumstances suffer a detriment rather than a benefit? How much weight should be attached to the potential that such a beneficiary might someday suffer the detriment? The question is of particular relevance when the court comes to consider whether the arrangement would be for the benefit of unborn beneficiaries under s 1(1)(c). In *Re Cohen's Will Trusts* [1959] 1 WLR 865 Danckwerts J held that in exercising the jurisdiction under the Act the court must, on behalf of those persons for whom it was approving the arrangement, take the sort of risk which an adult would be prepared to take on their own behalf. In the similarly named case of *Re Cohen's Settlement Trusts* [1965] 1 WLR 1229 approval for an arrangement was refused because the prospects for one unborn person under the arrangement would have been hopeless whatever events might actually have happened to pass.

In *Re Holt's Settlement* there was a risk that one of the unborn beneficiaries would receive no interest under the trust if their mother died during or shortly after childbirth. However, this risk had to be balanced against the possibility that the mother might survive for a reasonable, or indeed substantial, period after the birth, whereupon the infant would undoubtedly receive a benefit under the new arrangement. In *Re Holt's Settlement* Megarry J concluded that the risk was one which an adult would be prepared to take in order to secure the benefit. Accordingly, he gave approval for the new arrangement.

There is authority to show, however, that if the proposed arrangement involves risks as to whether or not a financial benefit would accrue to a beneficiary, the court will require that the trustees take out insurance against that risk, even at the expense of that beneficiary's income (*Re Robinson* [1976] 3 All ER 61). If the insurance premiums would involve an excessive drain on the income, insurance would not be required. The arrangement taken as a whole must, after all, be for the benefit of the beneficiary.

The hypothesis that an adult would have taken the sort of risk that the court took on behalf of the unborn beneficiary in *Re Holt's Settlement* involves the court in mental gymnastics. The court in *Re CL* [1968] 1 All ER 1104 carried out a similar exercise. There the court provided the consent of a mentally unsound beneficiary, under s 1(1)(a), on the basis that the beneficiary would have given their own consent had they been in a position to do so. This was despite the fact that the new arrangement resulted in the removal of the beneficiary's interest under the trust. Cotterell (1971) 34 MLR 98 has observed in relation to this case that 'it is hard to avoid the conclusion that benefit and the measure of it is simply what the court says it is'. Certainly the lack of a sta e for judicial intervention.

9.3 Resettlement or variation?

The Act, as we have seen, permits the court to approve any arrangement 'varying or revoking all or any of the trusts'. However, does there come a point at which a trust has been so varied that it cannot be said to be a variant of the original trust at all, but is, in truth, a wholly different settlement? Does the Variation of Trusts Act 1958 permit resettlements or must arrangements be genuine variations?

We have already considered (at 9.2.4.3) the case of *Re T's Settlement* [1963] 3 All ER 759. You should recall that in that case a mother wished to avoid the effect of her immature and irresponsible daughter becoming entitled to the capital at the age of 21. She applied for an order approving an arrangement under which her daughter's share would be transferred to a new trust under which the fund would be held on a protective trust for the daughter's life, with remainder to her issue. Approval for the arrangement was refused. Wilberforce J stated that where the arrangement 'is in truth a complete new settlement' it will not be approved.

In *Allfrey v Allfrey* [2015] EWHC 1717 (Ch), the court approved a variation under the VTA 1958 extending the perpetuity period of a trust to 125 years. HMRC agreed that this did not amount to a resettlement of the trust for capital gains tax purposes. In *Re Ball's Settlement* [1968] 1 WLR 899 Megarry J laid down a test for distinguishing resettlements which would be void from variations which would be valid. Megarry J's test has been referred to as the 'substratum test'. He said; 'if an arrangement, while leaving the substratum, effectuates the purpose of the original trust by other means, it may still be possible to regard the arrangement as merely varying the original trusts, even though the means employed are wholly different and even though the form is completely changed.'

This analysis is in accordance with the general maxim that *equity looks to substance, not form*. In *Re Ball's Settlement* the settlor's life interest was removed, and so the form of the trust had undoubtedly changed but the remaining trusts were held to be 'still in essence trusts of half of the fund for each of the two named sons and their families'. However, it must be queried whether the removal of a life interest is merely a change of form. It does appear to be a fairly substantial alteration. Indeed, the whole distinction between extensive variation and total resettlements looks like a rather artificial one. A.J. Oakley (Parker and Mellows, *The Modern Law of Trusts*, 6th edn, London: Sweet & Maxwell, 1994, p. 553) suggests that 'a pedantic distinction has grown up between variation and resettlement for which there appears to be no sanction in the words of the Act, nor any practical justification'.

9.4 Exporting the trust

This is a form of varying a trust which involves the wholesale removal of the administration of a trust to a foreign jurisdiction. We have considered some of the factors which a court will take into account when considering whether an export will be for the benefit of the beneficiaries (see *Re Weston's Settlements* at 9.2.4.2). In this section it is intended to show that if there is a benefit to the beneficiaries in exporting the trust, for example smoother administration, without any outweighing disadvantages, the court will generally give its approval. (We will consider the appointment of foreign trustees at 10.1.2.2.)

In *Re Seale's Marriage Settlement* [1961] 3 WLR 262 the beneficiaries under the original settlement had emigrated to Canada a number of years before the date on which their application was heard. They had taken Canadian citizenship and intended to live there permanently. This case was clearly different from *Re Weston's*, where the children were at risk of being uprooted during crucial developing years. Further, the financial advantage of exporting the trust in *Re Seale's Marriage Settlement* was primarily the saving that would be made on administration costs. The primary aim of the export was not to secure a short-term tax advantage.

In *Re Windeatt's WT* [1969] 2 All ER 324 the contrast with *Re Weston's* is even more dramatic, as both cases involved applications for an export to Jersey. The judge in *Re Windeatt's* did not take Lord Denning's view that Jersey was 'a less happy land' than 'this our England'. In fact, the export of the trust to Jersey was permitted. Again the facts were quite different from those in *Re Weston's* because here the family had lived in Jersey for 19 years and were clearly settled there.

9.5 The settlor's intentions

 OUTSIDE THE BOX

John Locke, *An Essay Concerning Human Understanding*

[T]hat a man may have one self-same single idea a long time alone in his mind, without any variation at all, I think, in matter of fact . . . is not possible. For which (not knowing how the ideas of our minds are framed, of what materials they are made, whence they have their light, and how they come to make their appearances) I can give no other reason but experience: and I would have any one try, whether he can keep one unvaried single idea in his mind, without any other, for any considerable time together.

The settlor's intentions belonged to the moment he wrote the trust. Who knows how his actual intentions might have changed thereafter, and what form his intentions would take today? The testator's intentions, and apparent departure from them, should be regarded as a 'serious but by no means conclusive consideration' (*Re Remnant's ST* (see 9.2.4.4)). Cases in which the courts have insisted upon the paramountcy of the settlor's expressed intentions are rare (a good example of such a case is *Re Steed's WT* [1960] 1 Ch 407).

 THINKING POINT

How serious a consideration was the settlor's intent in *Goulding* v *James* [1997] 2 All ER 239, next?

 CASE CLOSE-UP

***Goulding* v *James* [1997] 2 All ER 239, Court of Appeal**

Facts: the testatrix, Mrs Froud, made a will in 1992 whereby she directed that her estate was to be divided into two parts to be given to her daughter June and June's husband, Kenneth. She further provided that their interest was to pass to their son, Marcus, contingent upon his attaining the age of 40 if either June or Kenneth predeceased the testatrix.

This will was revoked in 1994 and replaced with a new will which created a trust under which June had a life interest in possession of the residuary estate, subject to which Marcus was to take absolutely provided he reached the age of 40. The new will further provided that if Marcus failed to attain the age of 40 or died before June, then Marcus's children would take the estate absolutely. After the death of the testatrix, June and Marcus applied to court for a variation of the trust contained in the will under s 1(1)(c) of the Variation of Trusts Act 1958. The variation sought was for 45 per cent of the estate to be held for June, 45 per cent for Marcus and the remaining 10 per cent for Marcus's children. Laddie J at first instance declined to approve the arrangement as it was contrary to the testatrix's wishes.

Mummery LJ: 'the effect of Megarry J's observation in [*Re Holt's Settlement, Wilson v Holt* [1968] 1 All ER 470 at 479, *Re Ball's Settlement Trusts* [1968] 2 All ER 438 at 442 and *Spens v IRC, Hunt v IRC* [1970] 3 All ER 294 at 301] is this. First, what varies the trust is not the court, but the agreement or consensus of the beneficiaries. Secondly, there is no real difference in principle in the rearrangement of the trusts between the case where the court is exercising its jurisdiction on behalf of the specified class under the 1958 Act and the case where the resettlement is made by virtue of the doctrine in *Saunders v Vautier* (1841) 4 Beav 115 and by all the adult beneficiaries joining together. Thirdly, the court is merely contributing on behalf of infants and unborn and unascertained persons the binding assents to the arrangement which they, unlike an adult beneficiary, cannot give. The 1958 Act has thus been viewed by the courts as a statutory extension of the consent principle embodied in the rule in *Saunders v Vautier*. The principle recognises the rights of beneficiaries, who are *sui juris* and together absolutely entitled to the trust property, to exercise their proprietary rights to overbear and defeat the intention of a testator or settlor to subject property to the continuing trusts, powers and limitations of a will or trust instrument.'

The answer is, not a great deal! The Court of Appeal held that in deciding whether or not to grant the approval under that section, its only concern was to ensure that the arrangement was 'beneficial' to those for whom its consent was sought. The purpose of the section was merely to enable a *Saunders v Vautier* type of arrangement to take place where it would otherwise be precluded because there were beneficiaries who could not give their own consent. The court approved the arrangement.

9.6 Return of procedural trickery?

The 1958 statutory jurisdiction to vary trusts replaced an earlier judicial device under which trusts were varied through the pretended compromise of fake disputes. It seems that judges are nowadays willing to remove practical obstacles to variation under the 1958 statutory jurisdiction by approving similarly dubious procedural tricks.

CASE CLOSE-UP

A v B [2016] EWHC 340 (Ch)

Facts: trustees had a power of appointment that might potentially benefit a very wide class of potential beneficiaries. To remove the need to seek their consent to the proposed arrangement varying the trusts, the trustees proposed to execute deeds by which their power of appointment would be released immediately prior to seeking the court's approval for the variation and reinstated immediately after the variation had been approved.

Held: such an exercise of the trustees' fiduciary powers was in the interests not only of the core beneficiaries but also of the class of remoter beneficiaries, and the artificial process of release and reinstatement did not amount to a fraud on the fiduciary power of appointment.

Summary

- We have seen that the allocation of beneficial interests under trusts can be varied, even in spite of the settlor's intentions. Where all the potential beneficiaries are adult and between them absolutely entitled to the trust fund, they can bring the trust to an end and re-allocate their beneficial interests as they wish under the rule in *Saunders* v *Vautier*. Where the beneficiaries are not competent to consent on their own behalf, the court can in certain circumstances consent on their behalf to an arrangement varying the trusts under the Variation of Trusts Act 1958.

- The wide power of the courts to vary beneficial interests under trusts produces dilemmas: one is the difficulty in weighing the settlor's intentions against the interests of the persons entitled to the fund. The courts appear to have resolved this dilemma in favour of the beneficiaries. Another dilemma, in regard of which you must come to your own conclusion, is one which we anticipated in the introduction—namely, the need to balance, against the provision of a tax avoidance facility for beneficiaries, the interests of the general taxpayer.

- A variation of the trustee's administrative power which does not impact, or has a merely incidental impact, upon the allocation of the beneficial interests under the trusts should be sought under the Trustee Act 1925, s 57.

Summative assessment exercise

By his will Abdul provided that £500,000 should be held on trust for his wife, Fatima, for life, with remainder to such of their children as should attain the age of 21 absolutely. Abdul died in 2002 leaving two sons, Bashir and Dan, aged 7 and 5 respectively. The trustees of the fund are experienced businessmen, and due to their efforts the fund is now worth £700,000.

Fatima feels that the income from the fund is more than sufficient to meet her needs, and wishes to surrender her interest in one half of the income of the fund in favour of Bashir and Dan. Additionally, she is worried about the effect of inherited wealth on Bashir and Dan, and would like to postpone their interests until they are 35 years old. In the meantime she would like the income on their respective shares to be accumulated until they attain 30 or die.

Fatima wishes to settle in Guernsey where she has friends. Bashir and Dan attend Harrchester School in England and it is proposed that they should complete their education in England. Fatima believes that the trust could be administered more easily in Guernsey, but the trustees do not agree.

Advise Fatima.

 Full specimen answers can be found at www.oxfordtextbooks.co.uk/orc/watt_directions5e/.

The bigger picture

The approach to the variation of trusts in the jurisdiction of England and Wales should be contrasted with the approach taken in the USA. There the rule is that no trust may be terminated or modified by the beneficiaries if it would defeat a 'material purpose' of the settlor or testator (*Claflin* v *Claflin* (1889) 20 NE 454; American Law Institute, Restatement of the Law of Trusts (3rd) §65(1), and Uniform Trust Code (2000), s 411(b)). Gregory S. Alexander observes that '[t]he *Claflin* doctrine . . . immunized private trusts from attempts by beneficiaries to destroy them through premature termination' ('The Dead Hand and the Law of Trusts in the Nineteenth Century' (1984–1985) 37 Stan L Rev 1189, 1191).

Further reading

Cotterrell, R.B.M. 'The Requirement of Benefit under the Variation of Trusts Act' (1971) 34 MLR 96
a lucid scholarly discussion of the crucial 'benefit' requirement under the 1958 Act

Harris, J.W. *Variation of Trusts* (1975) London: Sweet & Maxwell
still the only book dedicated solely to the subject of variation of trusts

Law Reform Committee's Sixth Report, 'Court's Power to Sanction Variation of Trusts' (1957) Cmnd 310, para. 13
the report which preceded and led to the Variation of Trusts Act 1958

Luxton, P. 'Variation of Trusts: Settlors' Intentions and the Consent Principle in *Saunders v Vautier*' (1997) 60 MLR 719
a note on *Goulding v James* which gives a useful overview of developments since the 1958 Act came into force

Watkins, D., 'The (Literal) Death of the Author and the Silencing of the Testator's Voice' (2012) 24(1) *Law & Literature* 59
this essay considers the seemingly inconsistent way in which the underlying intention of the testator is frequently acknowledged by courts but nevertheless abandoned in an overly literal or formalistic textual reading

 For links to selected cases, statutes, academic papers and official reports mentioned in this chapter please visit the online resources at www.oup.com/uk/watt_directions6e/.

10 Trustee appointments

LEARNING OBJECTIVES

By the end of this chapter, you should be able to:

- apply the principle that a trust does not fail for want of a trustee;
- identify the persons able to appoint trustees and the persons able to act as trustees;
- organise the matters to which a trustee should attend upon their appointment;
- advise a trustee as to how they may disclaim the trust;
- identify the modes by which a trustee might retire, or be removed, from the trust.

Introduction

If the reader wonders why a whole chapter, albeit a short one, has been devoted to the topic of trustee appointments, the answer is simple. If you make a mistake in this practical aspect of trusts law, the consequences can be disastrous. The case of *Jasmine Trustees v Wells & Hinds* [2007] EWHC 38 (Ch) illustrates this as well as any. The case, which was a professional negligence action brought against various solicitors' firms, arose from a 1982 deed of appointment and retirement of trustees which appointed a Mr Thornton and a trust company to act as new trustees. The new trustees were based in the Isle of Man and that was the problem. In 1982 trustees could retire provided the trustees they left behind them were at least two humans or one trust corporation (s 37(1)(c) of the Trustee Act 1925: see 10.3.2.1). Unfortunately, in this case the retiring trustees left behind one human and one trust company which (because it was incorporated outside the EU) could not be regarded as a trust corporation. The retirement of the trustees had been invalid and the retired trustees continued to be liable for trust matters. (Section 37(1)(c) has since been amended, so this particular case would not have arisen had the deed of appointment and retirement been made today: see 10.3.2.1.) The knock-on effect of the new trustees being unaware of the fact that the trust was now invalid in the UK was to render subsequent trustees' appointments void. The trustees would hope that would get them off the hook, but even though they were not true trustees they would still be liable to the trust (as 'trusteeship *de son tort'*, see 19.4) and liable to pay trust tax (which is why the *Jasmine* case was brought). They could also, conceivably, have been required to account for two decades of wrongfully received remuneration, plus compound interest and without any hope of relief from liability.

10.1 The mechanics of appointing trustees

The maximum number of trustees permitted in a private trust of land is four (in charitable trusts and trusts of pure personalty there may be many more). In the case of land it is useful to have at least two trustees or a trust corporation (to enable **overreaching**). In any case where there are two or more trustees they will hold the legal title as joint tenants and upon the death of any of them the legal title remains vested in the surviving trustees by 'right of survivorship'. But what happens when a trustee (perhaps the last, or only, trustee) dies or for some other reason ceases to act? It is said that 'a trust does not fail for want of a trustee', but who is able to appoint new trustees, and who should be appointed?

> **overreaching** This process enables a purchaser of land to take free of the beneficiaries' interests provided he pays all the trustees and the trustees are at least two in number or a trust corporation.

This chapter will provide answers to these questions, but it must be admitted that the answers are often to be found in a number of somewhat dry statutory provisions, so the reader will discover that this chapter includes a number of interactive exercises to make the process of grappling with the statutory wording more engaging.

STATUTE

Trustee Act 1925

36. Power of appointing new or additional trustees

(1) Where a trustee, either original or substituted, and whether appointed by a court or otherwise, is dead, or remains out of the United Kingdom for more than twelve months, or desires to be discharged from all or any of the trusts or powers reposed in or conferred on him, or refuses or is unfit to act therein, or is incapable of acting therein, or is an infant, then, subject to the restrictions imposed by this Act on the number of trustees,—

   (a) the person or persons nominated for the purpose of appointing new trustees by the instrument, if any, creating the trust; or

   (b) if there is no such person, or no such person able and willing to act, then the surviving or continuing trustees for the time being, or the personal representatives of the last surviving or continuing trustee;

   may, by writing, appoint one or more other persons (whether or not being the persons exercising the power) to be a trustee or trustees in the place of the trustee so deceased, remaining out of the United Kingdom, desiring to be discharged, refusing, or being unfit or being incapable, or being an infant, as aforesaid.

(2) Where a trustee has been removed under a power contained in the instrument creating the trust, a new trustee or new trustees may be appointed in the place of the trustee who is removed, as if he were dead, or, in the case of a corporation, as if the corporation desired to be discharged from the trust, and the provisions of this section shall apply accordingly, but subject to the restrictions imposed by this Act on the number of trustees.

(3) . . .

(4) The power of appointment given by subsection (1) of this section or any similar previous enactment to the personal representatives of a last surviving or continuing trustee shall be and shall be deemed always to have been exercisable by the executors for the time being (whether original or by representation) of such surviving or continuing trustee who have proved the will of their testator or by the administrators for the time being of such trustee without the concurrence of any executor who has renounced or has not proved.

(5) . . .

(6) Where a sole trustee, other than a trust corporation, is or has been originally appointed to act in a trust, or where, in the case of any trust, there are not more than three trustees (none of them being a trust corporation) either original or substituted and whether appointed by the court or otherwise, then and in any such case—

   (a) the person or persons nominated for the purpose of appointing new trustees by the instrument, if any, creating the trust; or

   (b) if there is no such person, or no such person able and willing to act, then the trustee or trustees for the time being;

may, by writing appoint another person or other persons to be an additional trustee or additional trustees, but it shall not be obligatory to appoint any additional trustee, unless the instrument, if any, creating the trust, or any statutory enactment provides to the contrary, nor shall the number of trustees be increased beyond four by virtue of any such appointment.

(7) Every new trustee appointed under this section as well before as after all the trust property becomes by law, or by assurance, or otherwise, vested in him, shall have the same powers, authorities, and discretions, and may in all respects act as if he had been originally appointed a trustee by the instrument, if any, creating the trust.

(8) The provisions of this section relating to a trustee who is dead include the case of a person nominated trustee in a will but dying before the testator, and those relative to a continuing trustee include a refusing or retiring trustee, if willing to act in the execution of the provisions of this section.

(9) Where a trustee is incapable, by reason of mental disorder within the meaning of the Mental Health Act 1983, of exercising his functions as trustee and is also entitled in possession to some beneficial interest in the trust property, no appointment of a new trustee in his place shall be made by virtue of paragraph (b) of subsection (1) of this section unless leave to make the appointment has been given by the authority having jurisdiction under Part VII of the Mental Health Act 1983.

 STATUTE

Trusts of Land and Appointment of Trustees Act 1996 (as amended by the Mental Capacity Act 2005)

19. Appointment and retirement of trustee at instance of beneficiaries

(1) This section applies in the case of a trust where—

(a) there is no person nominated for the purpose of appointing new trustees by the instrument, if any, creating the trust, and

(b) the beneficiaries under the trust are of full age and capacity and (taken together) are absolutely entitled to the property subject to the trust.

(2) The beneficiaries may give a direction or directions of either or both of the following descriptions—

(a) a written direction to a trustee or trustees to retire from the trust, and

(b) a written direction to the trustees or trustee for the time being (or, if there are none, to the personal representative of the last person who was a trustee) to appoint by writing to be a trustee or trustees the person or persons specified in the direction.

(3) Where—

(a) a trustee has been given a direction under subsection (2)(a),

(b) reasonable arrangements have been made for the protection of any rights of his in connection with the trust,

    (c)   after he has retired there will be either a trust corporation or at least two persons to act as trustees to perform the trust, and

    (d)   either another person is to be appointed to be a new trustee on his retirement (whether in compliance with a direction under subsection (2)(b) or otherwise) or the continuing trustees by deed consent to his retirement, he shall make a deed declaring his retirement and shall be deemed to have retired and be discharged from the trust.

(4)   Where a trustee retires under subsection (3) he and the continuing trustees (together with any new trustee) shall (subject to any arrangements for the protection of his rights) do anything necessary to vest the trust property in the continuing trustees (or the continuing and new trustees).

(5)   This section has effect subject to the restrictions imposed by the Trustee Act 1925 on the number of trustees.

10.1.1 Who can appoint trustees?

Familiarise yourself with the following extracts from the Trustee Act 1925, s 36, and the Trusts of Land and Appointment of Trustees Act 1996, ss 19–20. These sections are crucial to the law on the appointment of trustees.

You will see from s 36(1) that one or more new trustees may be appointed, in writing, whenever an existing trustee dies, remains abroad for more than a year, retires, refuses to act, is unfit to act, is incapable of acting or is an infant. The person empowered to make the appointment is the person named in the trust deed to carry out that particular function. Only if nobody is so named is the power to appoint given to the existing trustees or, if they have all died, to the personal representatives of the last trustee to have died. In fact, when a sole trustee dies that trustee's personal representatives will become the trustees for the time being if they accept the trusts (Administration of Estates Act 1925, s 1(2)), but they can be ousted by the appointment of other trustees by a person nominated in the trust instrument to appoint trustees.

Since 1 January 1997 ss 19 and 20 of the Trusts of Land etc Act 1996 apply *where there is no person nominated under the trust instrument to appoint new trustees* to allow the beneficiaries to appoint new trustees in certain circumstances (see 10.1.1.2).

 STATUTE

Trusts of Land and Appointment of Trustees Act 1996 (as amended by the Mental Capacity Act 2005)

Appointment of substitute for trustee who lacks capacity

20. Appointment of substitute for incapable trustee

    (1) This section applies where—

        (a) a trustee lacks capacity (within the meaning of the Mental Capacity Act 2005) to exercise his functions as trustee,

        (b) there is no person who is both entitled and willing and able to appoint a trustee in place of him under section 36(1) of the Trustee Act 1925, and

> (c) the beneficiaries under the trust are of full age and capacity and (taken together) are absolutely entitled to the property subject to the trust.
>
> (2) The beneficiaries may give to—
>
> (a) a deputy appointed for the trustee by the Court of Protection,
>
> (b) an attorney acting for him under the authority of an enduring power of attorney or lasting power of attorney registered under the Mental Capacity Act 2005, or
>
> (c) a person authorised for the purpose by the Court of Protection, a written direction to appoint by writing the person or persons specified in the direction to be a trustee or trustees in place of the incapable trustee.

10.1.1.1 **Person nominated**

Occasionally a settlor or testator will include in the trust instrument a clause nominating a person able to appoint replacement or additional trustees, although such clauses are usually found only in large institutional trusts such as pension fund trusts and charitable trusts. However, if the clause says something like 'I nominate X as the person able to appoint trustees in the event of the death of any of the current trustees', the obvious question arises: did the settlor intend X to be treated as the person referred to in s 36(1) as having the power to appoint trustees in the numerous circumstances listed in s 36(1), or is X limited to making appointments only in the event of the *death* of the current trustees? Following *Re Wheeler* [1896] 1 Ch 315, and the judgment of Kekewich J, the answer is that X's power is limited to the event expressly mentioned in the trust instrument and does not extend to all the events listed in s 36(1).

Let us now consider another problem with nominated appointors.

Andrew is permitted to appoint some other person to the fourth post but he should not appoint himself. There is a very good reason for this. The settlor clearly knew of Andrew's existence and availability, but nevertheless decided not to appoint him as the fourth trustee. (*Re Power's Settlement Trusts* [1951] 1 Ch 1074.)

An infant (any person under the age of 18) cannot act as a trustee. However, you may be surprised to discover that an infant can be nominated to exercise the power of appointing new trustees. Nevertheless, an appointment made by an infant is liable to be set aside if the appointment is prejudicial to the infant or could affect his interest under the trust or is in some other way imprudent. See *Re Parsons* [1940] 1 Ch 973.

10.1.1.2 **The beneficiaries**

Sections 19 and 20 of the Trusts of Land etc Act 1996 have applied since 1 January 1997. Section 19 applies where all the beneficiaries under the trust are of full age and capacity and are together absolutely entitled to the trust property. Section 19(2)(b) provides that, *apart from where there is a person nominated under the trust instrument to appoint new trustees* (see 10.1.1.1), the beneficiaries may in writing direct the existing trustees (or, if there are none, the personal representatives of the last surviving trustee) to appoint by writing such person or persons as may be specified in the direction to be a trustee or trustees.

Section 20 is also notable in that it provides that where a trustee lacks capacity (within the meaning of the Mental Capacity Act 2005), the beneficiaries (if they are of full age and capacity and together absolutely entitled to the trust property) may in writing direct the receiver or attorney of the trustee to appoint by writing such person or persons as may be specified in the direction to be a trustee or trustees. Section 20 applies only where there is no person entitled, able and willing to make the appointment under s 36(1).

10.1.1.3 **The court**

> **THINKING POINT**
>
> Read s 41 of the Trustee Act 1925. According to this section, when will the court appoint new trustees?

> **STATUTE**
>
> **Trustee Act 1925**
>
> 41. Power of court to appoint new trustees
>
> (1) The court may, whenever it is expedient to appoint a new trustee or new trustees, and it is found inexpedient, difficult or impracticable so to do without the assistance of the court, make an order appointing a new trustee or new trustees either in substitution for or in addition to any existing trustee or trustees, or although there is no existing trustee . . .
>
> (4) Nothing in this section gives power to appoint an executor or administrator.

You should note that this section does not say that the court can appoint a trustee whenever it is expedient to do so. It says that the court will appoint a new trustee whenever it is expedient to appoint a new trustee *and* inexpedient, difficult or impractical to do so without the court's assistance. In one case (*Re May's Will Trusts* [1941] Ch 109) where a trustee was trapped in territory occupied by the Germans during the Second World War, the court would not certify that the persons empowered by s 36 to appoint trustees were, within the wording of s 36, able to appoint a new trustee in these circumstances. It was therefore inexpedient to appoint without the court's assistance and so the court made the appointment. In another case the person empowered by s 36 to appoint new trustees had become incapable through age and infirmity of being able to exercise the power and the court intervened to appoint new trustees (*Re Lemann's Trusts* (1883) 22 ChD 633).

A trustee appointed by the court may act in every respect just as if they were one of the original trustees (s 43, Trustee Act 1925).

10.1.2 **Who can be appointed as trustees?**

Nowadays it is quite common for professional trustees to be appointed, such as a solicitor or trust corporation. However, the factors which we are about to consider, though of general application, are perhaps of most relevance to the appointment of private persons as trustees.

10.1.2.1 **Persons unfit, unwilling or lacking capacity to act**

It would be quite wrong to attempt to appoint persons who are bankrupt, who have convictions for offences involving dishonesty or who are otherwise unfit for the office of trustee or unwilling to act as a trustee. Nor should persons be appointed who lack capacity to act by reason of mental disorder, ill health or some other relevant disability. (Note: when the new Mental Capacity Act 2005 came into force on 1 October 2007 the phrase 'incapable of' which appears in s 41 was replaced by 'lacks capacity to' (Sch. 6, para. 3(3)).)

10.1.2.2 **Persons resident abroad**

In *Re Whitehead's WT* [1971] 1 WLR 833 Pennycuick V-C said that, 'apart from exceptional circumstances, it is not proper to make such an appointment . . . The most obvious exceptional circumstances are those in which the beneficiaries have settled permanently in some country outside the United Kingdom and what is proposed to be done is to appoint new trustees in that country.' In *Richard* v *The Hon A.B. Mackay* (14 March 1987, unreported) Millett J suggested that 'the language of Sir John Pennycuick, which is narrowly drawn, is too restrictive for the circumstances of the present day if, at least, it is intended to lay down any rule of practice'. In that case, Millett J approved the trustees' request for a declaration that transfer of part of the trust fund to new trustees in Bermuda would be valid. In coming to this decision his Lordship placed some weight on the fact that the trustees had already decided that the export of the fund would be for the benefit of the beneficiaries, and were merely seeking the court's approval of that course. His Lordship suggested that where the court is being asked to exercise an original discretion of its own (for example, under s 41 of the Trustee Act 1925 or under the Variation of Trusts Act 1958 (see 9.2)) the applicants must make out a positive case to show that the scheme gives the beneficiaries more than a mere tax advantage.

10.1.2.3 **Factors which the court considers**

> **THINKING POINT**
>
> Read the following extract from *Re Tempest* (1866) LR 1 Ch App 485 and underline the factors which guide the exercise of the court's discretion when appointing new trustees. What other factors do you think should influence appointments by the court?

> **CASE CLOSE-UP**
>
> **Re Tempest (1866) LR 1 Ch App 485, Court of Appeal**
>
> The will of Sir C.R. Tempest, Bart appointed Stonor and Fleming as trustees of certain real estates. A codicil to the will appointed Stonor, Fleming and Lord Camoys as trustees of certain charitable trusts. Stonor predeceased the testator. Fleming and one Arthur Tempest, the testator's uncle, were empowered by the will to appoint new trustees of the real estates, but they could not agree upon a replacement trustee. Most of the beneficiaries concurred with Arthur Tempest's choice, but Fleming opposed it on the ground that the proposed trustee was connected with a branch of the family with whom the testator had not been on friendly terms. The surviving trustees of the charitable trusts were, on the other hand, able to agree to a replacement trustee of those

trusts. It was held that the trustee proposed by Arthur Tempest should not be appointed to the trusts.

Sir G.J. Turner LJ: 'the following rules and principles may, I think, safely be laid down as applying to all cases of appointments by the Court of new trustees.

First, the Court will have regard to the wishes of the persons by whom the trust has been created, if expressed in the instrument creating the trust, or clearly to be collected from it . . .

Another rule which may, I think, safely be laid down is this—that the Court will not appoint a person to be trustee with a view to the interest of some of the persons interested under the trust, in opposition either to the wishes of the testator or to the interests of others of the *cestuis que trusts*. I think so for this reason, that it is of the essence of the duty of every trustee to hold an even hand between the parties interested under the trust. Every trustee is in duty bound to look to the interests of all, and not of any particular member or class of members of his *cestuis que trusts*.

A third rule which, I think, may safely be laid down, is, that the Court in appointing a trustee will have regard to the question, whether his appointment will promote or impede the execution of the trust, for the very purpose of the appointment is that the trust may be better carried into execution . . . but, on the other hand, if the continuing or surviving trustee refuses to act with a trustee who may be proposed to be appointed . . . I think it would be going too far to say that the Court ought, on that ground alone, to refuse to appoint the proposed trustee; for this would, as suggested in the argument, be to give the continuing or surviving trustee a veto upon the appointment of the new trustee. In such a case, I think it must be the duty of the Court to inquire and ascertain whether the objection of the surviving or continuing trustee is well founded or not, and to act or refuse to act upon it accordingly. If the surviving or continuing trustee has improperly refused to act with the proposed trustee, it might be a ground for removing him from the trust.'

In addition to the guidance in *Re Tempest*, the court will never appoint a person to be a sole trustee of a valuable fund (*per* Bennet J in *Re Parsons* [1940] 1 Ch 973) and the court inclines against appointing a beneficiary or a beneficiary's spouse to be a trustee (*Re Kemp's Settled Estate* (1883) 24 ChD 485, CA).

10.1.3 Actions of the trustee upon appointment

> Here art thou in appointment fresh and fair,/Anticipating time with starting courage.
>
> William Shakespeare, *Troilus and Cressida*, Act IV, scene 5

It is a courageous person who accepts appointment as a trustee. In the game of cricket the person who has just come in to bat is generally more vulnerable than the person who is comfortable and has already scored a few runs. The same is true of trustees. A new trustee is vulnerable and more likely than an established trustee to commit an honest breach of trust. A new trustee should make careful enquiries as to the nature of the trust and must be sure to carry out their initial duties diligently and without unreasonable delay. They should also examine all previous trustee appointments (and retirements) in the light of the law then applicable to ensure that they have been validly appointed.

> **⬤ CROSS REFERENCE**
>
> At this point you should refer back to *Jasmine Trustees v Wells & Hinds* [2007] EWHC 38, Ch: see Introduction at the start of this chapter.

10.1.3.1 **Ascertaining the terms of the trust**

> **THINKING POINT**
>
> List the sorts of things a trustee might try to ascertain from the trust instrument and other trust documentation, and compare your answer to the following.

The first action that a trustee must carry out upon accepting an appointment is to check that they have been validly appointed. They should acquaint themselves with the trust instrument and other trust documentation.

From an examination of the documents the trustee will discover the identity of the beneficiaries and the extent of their equitable entitlements. Further, memoranda on the trust instrument will inform the trustee whether the beneficiaries have sold or otherwise dealt with their interests under the trust. (The beneficiaries must inform the trustees, by notice, of dealings with their equitable interest.) The trustee will also discover the nature of the trust property. This raises issues which are dealt with in the next section.

10.1.3.2 **Transfer of trust property**

The legal title to the trust property must be transferred into the names of the new and continuing trustees. Where a new trustee is appointed by deed the legal title to most forms of land, chattels and choses in action will vest automatically in the names of the new and continuing trustees as joint tenants. This is in accordance with s 40 of the Trustee Act 1925, although in the case of registered land the register must be amended to reflect the new proprietorship (s 47, Land Registration Act 1925). However, apart from some technical exceptions (as to which you may wish to read the section in detail), s 40 is not effective to transfer mortgages, land held under leases or stocks and shares. If the subject matter of the trust consists of any property of this kind it is the duty of the trustees actively to 'get it in'. See *Re Brogden* (1888) 38 ChD 546.

10.1.3.3 **Duty to act on suspicions**

This duty makes the new trustee sound like a private detective. In fact, it is not like that at all. The new trustee is under no obligation to search for suspicious circumstances. The duty is simply to take action to recover the trust fund if, having acquainted himself with the trust, it appears that the previous trustees have committed a breach of trust which has resulted in a depletion of the fund. If the new trustee fails to act upon a suspicion, that failure to act might in itself constitute a breach of trust unless the new trustee reasonably considers that taking action would be fruitless.

10.1.4 **Summative exercises on trustee appointments**

The following exercise is designed to answer the question: 'who can appoint a new trustee to an existing trust, and in what order of priority?' Having revised the relevant statutory sections (Trustee Act 1925, ss 36 and 41; Trusts of Land and Appointment of Trustees Act 1996, s 19), try to arrange the following persons into a list according to their right to appoint new trustees, the person with the first right to appoint trustees coming first:

- the surviving or continuing trustees (choice A);

- beneficiaries of the trust who are of full age and capacity and together entitled to the entirety of the fund (choice B);
- the court (choice C);
- a person nominated in the trust instrument (choice D);
- the settlor of the trust (choice E);
- personal representatives of the last trustee to die (choice F);
- where nominated will trustees die before the testator, their personal representatives (choice G).

The next exercise is designed to identify those persons whose appointment as a trustee would generally be invalid under ss 36(1) and 41 of the Trustee Act 1925. Place a tick next to the persons whose appointment would be invalid:

- an undischarged bankrupt (choice A);
- a person with whom the current trustees will unreasonably refuse to co-operate (choice B);
- a person resident abroad (choice C);
- the spouse of a beneficiary (choice D);
- a person approved of by some beneficiaries but not others (choice E);
- the person nominated in the trust instrument to appoint trustees (choice F).

The next exercise (see Table 10.1) lists in the left-hand column some of the tasks that trustees should attend to upon their appointment and in the right-hand column the objectives of (or qualifications to) the various tasks. Draw a line from the task to its appropriate partner.

In the first exercise, the correct order is DBAFC. Did you spot that choices G and E were red herrings? People described in categories G and E have no power to appoint new trustees. In the second exercise, you should have ticked ACDE. In the final exercise, the answers are A6, B5, C1, D4, E3 and F2.

Table 10.1 Actions on appointment

Take action against past or present trustees for suspected breaches of trust (choice A)	because such property will not vest in the new trustee automatically under s 40 of the Trustee Act 1925 (choice 1)
Examine memoranda annexed to the trust instrument (choice B)	to determine the identity and entitlements of the beneficiaries (choice 2)
Actively 'get in' trust property which comprises mortgages, leases, stocks and shares (choice C)	to ascertain the current make-up of the trust fund (choice 3)
Check that they (the new trustees) have been validly appointed (including checking that previous appointments were valid) (choice D)	in order to establish whether the trust property has vested in the new trustees (choice 4)
Examine the trust instrument and the trust accounts (choice E)	to ascertain whether the beneficiaries have sold or otherwise dealt with their equitable interests (choice 5)
Ascertain the terms of the trust instrument (choice F)	if there are reasons for suspicion and if there is no reasonable ground for believing that such action would be fruitless (choice 6)

10.2 Disclaimer of the trust

10.2.1 The general law

A person appointed as trustee of an express trust may decide to decline the appointment, in which event they should do so by a disclaimer, usually in the form of a deed. But if the trustee acts in performance of the trust it will then be too late to disclaim.

10.2.2 No partial disclaimer

In *Re Lord and Fullerton's Contract* [1896] 1 Ch 228 the question arose whether a trustee of real and personal property, some existing in England and some abroad, could disclaim the trust except as to the property abroad. The Court of Appeal decided against partial disclaimer in any circumstances. Lindley LJ did not think that a trustee could 'accept the office as to some part of the estate and not accept it as to the rest'. One reason for this decision was the undesirable consequences of partial disclaimer for a purchaser from the trustee who would be uncertain as to the trustee's power to sell particular property.

10.2.3 Trust void because of disclaimer

In certain limited situations a trust will fail because the potential 'trustee' disclaims the trustee-ship.

> **THINKING POINT**
>
> Is there a conflict here with the principle that a trust does not fail for want of a trustee?

There appears to be a conflict at first sight, but it can be resolved. In those rare situations where disclaimer causes a trust to fail it is because the trust is treated as never having come into being. It is said to have been void *ab initio*. The rule that a trust does not fail for want of a trustee only applies to existing trusts and so it has no application to trusts which are made void by disclaimer.

10.2.3.1 Trusts which require specific trustees

It is prerequisite to the existence of some trusts that only a specific, named trustee shall hold the office. As Buckley J said in *Re Lysaght* [1966] 1 Ch 191, 'If it is of the essence of a trust that the trustees selected by the settlor and no one else shall act as the trustees of it and if those trustees cannot or will not undertake the office, the trust must fail.'

10.2.3.2 *Inter vivos* trusts disclaimed before constitution

You should recall from 5.3 that, apart from cases where a settlor declares himself to be a trustee, an *inter vivos* trust is not fully constituted until the trust property has been transferred to the trustees. (A will trust, on the other hand, is perfectly constituted by the death of the testator.) It should follow that an *inter vivos* trust is void *ab initio* if the trustees disclaim the trust before the trust property is transferred to them. On the basis of this analysis one jurist (P. Matthews [1981] Conv 141) has argued that the decision in *Mallott v Wilson* [1903] 2 Ch 494 was wrong. In that case the trustee disclaimed the trust 'as soon as he heard of it' and the trust property was never transferred to the trustee. Despite this the judge decided that the trust was not void *ab initio*, but valid until the disclaimer.

10.3 Retirement from the trust

In Jane Austen's novel *Emma*, the eponymous 'heroine' (famously described as 'handsome, clever, and rich') boasted that she 'had no fear of retirement'. A trustee, on the other hand, *should* fear retirement—no matter how clever or rich (or handsome) they might be—since trustee liability continues after retirement if the retirement was technically ineffective for any reason.

10.3.1 General

In *Re Chetwynd's Settlement* [1902] 1 Ch 692 Farwell J stated that '[n]o trustee accepts the responsibility for the term of his natural life, or for more than a reasonable period'. It is important to note, however, that a trustee cannot retire on a whim and in some circumstances their retirement will not be valid unless a new trustee is appointed in their place.

10.3.2 Modes of retirement

Trustees may retire whenever the trust instrument entitles them to do so and, as a last resort, whenever the court approves an application for retirement. Apart from these instances the Trustee Act 1925 details two modes of retirement.

10.3.2.1 Retirement under the Trustee Act 1925, s 36

You will recall that this section provides, inter alia, for the appointment of a new trustee, or trustees, 'in the place of' a trustee 'desiring to be discharged'. The crucial point to note is that a retirement purported to be carried out in pursuance of this section will only be valid to discharge the trustee if at least one new trustee has been appointed in their place. Subject to the trust instrument providing to the contrary, s 36 does not authorise the appointment of a sole trustee, not being a trust corporation, where the trustee, when appointed, would not be able to give valid receipts for all capital money arising under the trust (s 37, Trustee Act 1925). In practice this means that where the only trustee of the trust retires, he must be replaced by two trustees or a trust corporation (*see Adam & Co International Trustees Ltd* v *Theodore Goddard (a firm)* (2000) 97(13) LSG 44).

Section 37(1) of the Trustee Act 1925 contains supplemental provisions as to appointment of trustees, including:

- the possibility of increasing the number of trustees on any appointment;
- the possibility of appointing a separate set of trustees, not exceeding four, for any part of the trust property held on trusts distinct from those relating to any other part or parts of the trust property;
- it shall not be obligatory to appoint more than one new trustee where only one trustee was originally appointed but a retiring trustee shall not be discharged from his trust unless he leaves behind a trust corporation or at least two persons to act as trustees to perform the trust (the word 'persons' was substituted for 'individuals' by the Trusts of Land and Appointment of Trustees Act 1996, s 25(1), so whereas previously a retiring trustee would need to leave two humans behind, he can now leave a human and a company or other 'person').

10.3.2.2 Retirement under the Trustee Act 1925, s 39

The essential difference between s 39 and s 36 is that s 39 permits retirement of a trustee without the appointment of a replacement trustee.

THINKING POINT

Read s 39, set out next, and underline the conditions which must be satisfied before a trustee may retire under this section.

STATUTE

Trustee Act 1925

39. Retirement of trustee without a new appointment

(1) Where a trustee is desirous of being discharged from the trust, and after his discharge there will be either a trust corporation or at least two individuals to act as trustees to perform the trust, then, if such trustee as aforesaid by deed declares that he is desirous of being discharged from the trust, and if his co-trustees and such other person, if any, as is empowered to appoint trustees, by deed consent to the discharge of the trustee, and to the vesting in the co-trustees alone of the trust property, the trustee desirous of being discharged shall be deemed to have retired from the trust, and shall, by the deed, be discharged there from under this Act, without any new trustee being appointed in his place.

(2) Any assurance or thing requisite for vesting the trust property in the continuing trustees alone shall be executed or done.

The conditions are as follows:

- the trustee must retire by deed;
- the trustee must obtain the consent of the other trustees and any person who is empowered to appoint new trustees;
- such consent must be given by deed and must approve of the retirement and of the vesting of the trust property in the remaining trustees alone;
- the retirement will only be valid if two trustees remain or a trust corporation remains after the retirement.

If any one of these conditions is not met the retirement will not be effective to discharge the trustee from their obligations under the trust.

10.3.2.3 Retirement under the Trusts of Land etc Act 1996, s 19

As was indicated earlier (see 10.1.1.2), s 19 of the Trusts of Land etc Act 1996 applies where all the beneficiaries under the trust are *sui juris* and together absolutely entitled, unless there is someone nominated under the trust instrument to appoint new trustees. In relation to retirement, s 19(2)(a) provides that the beneficiaries may in writing direct a trustee to retire from the trust. Before the retiring trustee declares his retirement (which he must do by deed), arrangements must be made to ensure that the trustee's rights in connection with the trust have been protected and to ensure that upon retirement at least two trustees (or a trust corporation) will remain. Further, if no other trustee is to be appointed in the place of the retiring trustee, the continuing trustees must consent to the retirement by deed.

 THINKING POINT

Attempt the following exercise which is designed to test your grasp of the statutory technicalities of retirement. Table 10.2 contains a list of prerequisites to retirement. Some requirements are statutory, some are red herrings. All you have to do is to place a tick in the appropriate column corresponding to each requirement.

Table 10.2 Modes of retirement

Prerequisites to retirement	Retirement under the Trustee Act 1925, s 39	Retirement under the Trustee Act 1925, s 36(1)	Retirement under the Trusts of Land etc Act 1996, s 19	Red herrings
All the beneficiaries under the trust are *sui juris* and together absolutely entitled to the fund (choice A)				
Trustee must retire by deed (choice B)				
There is nobody nominated under the trust instrument to appoint new trustees (choice C)				
According to this section persons may be nominated for the purpose of deciding when a trustee may retire (choice D)				
Remaining trustees must consent by deed and must approve of property vesting in them alone (choice E)				
Two trustees or a trust corporation must remain after retirement (choice F)				
At least one new trustee must be appointed in writing in the place of the retiring trustee (choice G)				
According to this section the trustee must express by written notice to the other trustees his or her desire to be discharged (choice H)				
Trustee must obtain the consent of the other trustees and those nominated to appoint trustees (choice I)				
According to this section retirement is only possible where two trustees or a trust corporation are appointed to replace the retiring trustees (choice J)				

The solution is as follows:

- retirement under s 39: BIFE;
- retirement under s 36(1): G;
- retirement under the Trusts of Land etc Act 1996, s 19: AC;
- red herrings: DHJ.

10.3.3 **Liability after retirement**

A trustee continues to be liable for breaches of trust which occur after they have attempted to retire if their 'retirement' was technically defective, but what if the retirement was technically valid? The general rule here is that a trustee will only be liable for breaches of trust which occurred when they were a trustee.

 THINKING POINT

According to *Head* v *Gould* (see next), in what exceptional circumstance might a trustee be liable even after retirement?

 CASE CLOSE-UP

Head v Gould [1898] 2 Ch 250, ChD

Kekewich J: 'it is the duty of trustees to protect the funds entrusted to their care, and to distribute those funds themselves or hand them over to their successors intact, that is, properly invested and without diminution, according to the terms of the mandate contained in the instrument of trust. This duty is imposed on them as long as they remain trustees and must be their guide in every act done by them as trustees. On retiring from the trust and passing on the trust estate to their successors—and this whether they appoint those successors or merely assign the property to the nominees of those who have the power of appointment—they are acting as trustees, and it is equally incumbent on them in this ultimate act of office to fulfil the duty imposed on them as at any other time. If therefore they neglect that duty and part with the property without due regard to it, they remain liable and will be held by the Court responsible for the consequences properly traceable to that neglect. This explanation will, I think, be found consistent with all judicial utterances on the subject, and haply aid to make them consistent with themselves.'

10.4 Removal of trustees

10.4.1 **General**

In certain circumstances trustees may be removed from office against their will. Removal is effected by persons nominated for that task by the terms of the trust instrument, or (in the absence of a nominee) by persons authorised under s 36 of the Trustee Act 1925, or under s 19 of the Trusts of Land etc Act 1996 (see 10.3.2.3), or by the court. The court may carry out such removal under its inherent jurisdiction or when appointing substitute trustees under s 41 of the Trustee Act 1925. Where the trustees are removed under a power contained in the trust instrument they can be replaced under s 36 as if they had died.

10.4.2 Removal under the Trustee Act 1925, s 36(1)

The grounds for removal include absence abroad for more than a year, refusal to act, unfitness to act and incapacity. The persons empowered by s 36 to appoint new trustees are similarly the persons empowered to remove the current trustees (see 10.1.1).

10.4.3 Removal under the court's inherent jurisdiction

In *Letterstedt* v *Broers* (1884) 9 App Cas 371 Lord Blackburn said that '[i]n exercising so delicate a jurisdiction as that of removing trustees, their Lordships do not venture to lay down any general rule beyond the very broad principle . . . that their main guide must be the welfare of the beneficiaries'. In *Re Wrightson* [1908] 1 Ch 798 Warrington J expanded upon this by adding that trustees will be removed if the court thinks that the trust property is endangered by their continuing in office. Thus in *Jones* v *Firkin-Flood* [2008] EWHC 2417 (Ch), in which a millionaire had left the vast majority of his wealth to his youngest son whom he had also appointed to act as a trustee, the testator's daughter and eldest son succeeded in having their brother and two other of the four trustees removed because of 'total abdication of their duties'. While courts look at the circumstances of each case separately, the cases do provide limited guidelines. Thus it has been held that a trustee will not be removed simply because he has interests in conflict with the trust, provided the trust can function properly without him ever having to choose between the trust and his private interests (*Public Trustee* v *Cooper* [2001] WTLR 901), and it has been held that the occasional error by a trustee is not of itself a ground for removal (*Isaac* v *Isaac* [2005] EWHC 435, ChD, para. 73). In one case a trustee who had wrongfully assumed that she was beneficially entitled to the trust property was permitted to continue in office once the court had pointed out her error (*Rafferty* v *Philp* [2011] EWHC 709, (Ch)). The following sections set out further points of general guidance.

10.4.3.1 Hostility

In *Letterstedt* Lord Blackburn said that hostility between trustees and beneficiaries was 'not of itself a reason for the removal of the trustees' but should not be disregarded. In that case several factors, including hostility between the trustees and the beneficiaries, had the cumulative effect of leading to the removal of the trustees. Hostility between trustees can also be a ground for removal, as in *Re E A Scott (1991 Children's Settlement N1)*; *Scott* v *Scott* [2012] EWHC 2397 (Ch).

10.4.3.2 Trustees' dishonesty

In *Letterstedt* Lord Blackburn approved the removal of trustees whose acts or omissions 'show a want of honesty, or a want of proper capacity to execute the duties, or a want of reasonable fidelity'. In *Re Wrightson* Warrington J approved this approach, saying that it was ancillary to the court's principal duty to see that the trusts are properly performed.

10.4.3.3 The expense of removal

There are indications in *Re Wrightson* that the court is sometimes reluctant to remove trustees because of the administrative expense to the trust fund of doing so. This may mean that the courts will be more reluctant to remove trustees from trusts with smaller funds.

10.4.4 **Removal under the Trustee Act 1925, s 41**

In *Re Lemann's Trust* (1883) 22 ChD 633 an aged trustee was removed because, 'through old age and consequent bodily and mental infirmity', she was incapable of executing any documents. In *Re Henderson* [1940] Ch 764 a trustee was removed because she initially stated her wish to retire from the trust but at a later date insisted that she would not retire unless certain conditions were met. In *Re Tempest* (1866) LR 1 Ch App 485 it was stated that, if an existing trustee unreasonably refuses to co-operate with a new trustee whom the court has appointed, this might be a ground for removing the *existing* trustee from office.

10.5 What if nobody is willing to act as trustee?

The maxim states that *no trust will fail for want of a trustee*. If nobody can be found who is willing to accept the appointment, the court will in certain circumstances appoint the Public Trustee or a judicial trustee to discharge the trust. As a last resort, the court can even act as trustee itself on an ad hoc basis. As Lord Eldon LC acknowledged long ago in *Morice v Bishop of Durham* (1805) 10 Ves 539: 'As it is a maxim, that the execution of a trust shall be under the control of the court . . . if the trustee dies, the court itself can execute the trust.'

Judicial trustees are appointed where the ordinary trustees of the trust have failed in their administration of the trust. Their appointment under the Judicial Trustees Act 1896 is designed to avoid the expense of the court itself discharging the administrative obligations of the trustee. They have all the powers of ordinary trustees, but, as officers of the court, they also have ready access to the court's directions as to administration of the trust. The remuneration of a judicial trustee must be justified, reasonable and proportionate and is generally limited to 15 per cent of the capital value of the trust property (Judicial Trustees Rules 1983, r 11(1)(a), see Practice Direction [2003] All ER (D) 93 (Jul)).

The office of Public Trustee was established by s 1 of the Public Trustee Act 1906. The role of the Public Trustee is to administer trusts (typically private, non-business trusts), no matter how small, for whom no other trustee can be found. Although the court will take into account the wishes of the settlor when choosing new trustees, the settlor cannot exclude appointment of the Public Trustee in an appropriate case (*Re Duxbury's Settlement Trusts* [1995] 1 WLR 425).

It is in the office of the Public Trustee that the maxim *a trust will never fail for want of a trustee* finds its fullest expression.

⟳ Summary

- We have seen that a trust does not fail for want of a trustee. According to s 36(1) of the Trustee Act 1925, one or more new trustees may be appointed, in writing, whenever an existing trustee dies, remains abroad for more than a year, retires, refuses to act, is unfit to act, is incapable of acting or is an infant.

- We have identified the persons able to appoint trustees and the persons able to act as trustees:
  - the person empowered to make the appointment is the person named in the trust deed to carry out that particular function;
  - if nobody is so named, adult beneficiaries can direct retirements and appointments. Otherwise the power to appoint is given to the existing trustees, or, if they have all died, to the personal representatives of the last trustee to have died;
  - when a sole trustee dies that trustee's personal representatives will become the trustees for the time being if they accept the trust (Administration of Estates Act 1925, s 1(2)) but they can be ousted by the appointment of other trustees by a person nominated in the trust instrument to appoint trustees.
- We have identified the matters to which a trustee should attend upon taking up an appointment, including:
  - ascertaining the terms of the trust;
  - 'getting in' the trust property;
  - acting on suspicions, bringing a claim against current and former trustees if necessary.
- We can advise a trustee as to how they may disclaim the trust:
  - a person appointed as trustee of an express trust may decide to decline the appointment, in which event they should do so by a disclaimer, usually in the form of a deed. But if the trustee acts in performance of the trust it will then be too late to disclaim;
  - in certain limited situations a trust will fail because the potential 'trustee' disclaims the trusteeship: trusts which require specific trustees and *inter vivos* trusts disclaimed before constitution.
- We know the methods by which a trustee might retire, or be removed, from the trust:
  - retirement at the direction of all the beneficiaries, if they are competent adults;
  - retirement under the Trustee Act 1925, s 36: this section provides, inter alia, for the appointment of a new trustee, or trustees, 'in the place of' a trustee 'desiring to be discharged';
  - retirement under the Trustee Act 1925, s 39: the essential difference between s 39 and s 36 is that s 39 permits retirement of a trustee without the appointment of a replacement trustee;
  - removal under the Trustee Act 1925, s 36(1): the grounds for removal include absence abroad for more than a year, refusal to act, unfitness to act and incapacity. The persons empowered by s 36 to appoint new trustees are similarly the persons empowered to remove the current trustees;
  - where the facts which constitute the grounds for removal are not disputed, the court may remove trustees under s 41 of the Trustee Act 1925 when appointing one or more replacement trustees under that section. In any other case the court may remove a trustee under its inherent jurisdiction;
  - removal under the court's inherent jurisdiction: possible grounds include hostility between trustees and beneficiaries, and trustees' dishonesty.

? Summative assessment exercise

The following scenario has been devised to raise several of the matters considered in this chapter. When you have attempted the question relating to the scenario you should compare your answer to the guideline answer provided. Then look back at the objectives listed at the beginning of this chapter. If you are satisfied that you have met the objectives proceed to the next chapter.

Sarah settled an *inter vivos* trust. The deed appointed Tom, Tracy, Tim, Terry and Tarquin to be trustees and Albert, who was then 17, to be the person able to appoint new trustees. The trust property consisted of two freehold houses, directed to be held upon trust for certain infant beneficiaries as joint tenants in equity. Immediately upon hearing of the trust the named trustees executed a 'deed of disclaimer'. Without delay Albert told a friend, Tabitha, that she could be a trustee and sometime afterwards he appointed himself as a trustee. A short while later Tabitha expressed a desire to be discharged from the trust. Albert agreed to release her.

Who are the current trustees, if any, of the trust?

 Full specimen answers can be found at www.oxfordtextbooks.co.uk/orc/watt_directions5e/.

▢ The bigger picture

Would you act as a trustee? Perhaps the answer will come down to the usual motivations of 'love' or 'money'. Simon Gardner, in his *Introduction to the Law of Trusts* (Oxford: Clarendon Press, 1990) observes (at p. 165) that 'human goodwill and the profit motive between them can be relied upon to produce a supply of people *prima facie* willing to be trustees'. This finds support in a 1988 survey of 'a group of solicitors in Lancashire and Cumbria who did trust work on a regular basis'. The author of the survey notes that:

> [t]he solicitors' survey showed that despite the onerous nature of the office of trustee, getting suitable private individuals to agree to become trustees is not a major problem. Friendship for the settlor/testator or a sense of duty arising from the fact that the settlor/testator is a relative are the main reasons for private individuals agreeing to act as trustees. However, knowledge of the beneficiaries and a desire to help them was also highlighted in the solicitors' survey as a factor. It is interesting to note that private individuals who agree to act as trustees usually regard it as an honour and not a chore. (C. Bell, 'Some Reflections on Choosing Trustees' (1988) 8 *Trust Law & Practice* 86–8)

☰ Further reading

Bell, C. 'Some Reflections on Choosing Trustees' (1988) 8 *Trust Law & Practice* 86
practical observations on the challenge of choosing trustees, including some empirical statistics

Kirkland, K. 'Recruiting, Selecting and Inducing Charity Trustees' (2002) 4 *Private Client Business* 253 considers special issues concerning the appointment of trustees in the charity context (see www.charity-commission.gov.uk for more guidance)

Morris J. and O'Sullivan C. 'Jasmine Trustees: Tangles in the trusteeship chain: Parts 1 and 2' (2007) 5 *Private Client Business* 347; 6 *Private Client Business* 442
comments on the trust law and tax consequences of an invalid appointment of trustees

Consult the website of the Pensions Regulator (www.thepensionregulator.gov.uk/trustees) for guidance on the appointment of pension trustees, and useful forms

 For links to selected cases, statutes, academic papers and official reports mentioned in this chapter please visit the online resources at www.oup.com/uk/watt_directions6e/.

11 The nature of trusteeship

Introduction

If there is one thing you should learn in the course of studying the law of trusts, it is that it is a high-risk occupation to accept appointment as a trustee. Of course it is an honour, and you will feel morally bound to accept. Of course, you also have a little legal knowledge that will come in handy. But don't be fooled. In this chapter we will see that trusteeship requires the proper discharge of a number of fundamental duties. The first is the duty of undivided loyalty (the fiduciary duty), the second is the duty of care for the trust fund (the duty of care), and within this there are a number of more defined duties, such as the duty to exercise a sound discretion. In future chapters we will consider particular trustee duties in more depth, but in this chapter you should contemplate the general nature of trusteeship and ask yourself whether it is a job you would accept! Trustees have all the powers of an absolute owner, but remember what we learned from Spiderman in Chapter 2: 'with great power comes great responsibility'!

11.1 Terminology

 THINKING POINT

What do you think the terms 'trustee' and *cestui que trust* mean? What do the definitions tell you about trusteeship?

'Trustee' means 'one who is trusted', and *cestui que trust* literally means 'the one who trusts'. Although nowadays we invariably refer to the *cestuis que trust* as the 'beneficiaries', the message is still clear: the trustee must act in the interests of the beneficiaries and not out of self-interest. This does not mean that a trustee must obey the wishes of the beneficiaries. The trustee must serve the beneficiaries, but within their larger obligation to serve the trust in accordance with the terms of the trust instrument and the general law. The trustees must, it is said, discharge the trust that is placed in them, for in one sense the settlor is 'the one who trusts'!

Trustees might be held personally liable to the beneficiaries for breaches of their trust, whether arising out of their acts or omissions. In particular you should be aware that trustees can breach their trust by inactivity. Trustees must act, but they must act carefully. (We consider the standard of care at 11.3.) Trustees must also act loyally—we consider that duty next.

11.2 Fiduciary office

We have already noted that the trustee's relationship to the beneficiary of the trust is a fiduciary one.

 THINKING POINT

Can you think of other relationships which the law generally regards to be fiduciary?

You might have chosen the relationship between:

- an agent and their principal (e.g. solicitor and client);
- a director and their company;
- a doctor and their patient.

The first party to each of these relationships is in some sense in a position of trust and certain consequences flow from this. For example, a solicitor is not permitted to place their own money and clients' money in the same bank account. Likewise, a company director 'on appointment to that office, assumes the duties of a trustee in relation to the company's property' (*per* Chadwick LJ in *JJ Harrison (Properties) Ltd* v *Harrison* [2002] 1 BCLC 162). It is important to appreciate, however, that not every duty of a person in a fiduciary office is necessarily a fiduciary duty (*New Zealand Netherlands Society* v *Kuys* [1973] 1 WLR 1126, PC, *per* Lord Wilberforce at 1130).

Who is and who is not a fiduciary is a question which has taxed the minds of leading judges and academics for many years. For a flavour of the difficulties involved see Professor Paul Finn's chapter, 'Fiduciary Law', in McKendrick (ed.), *Commercial Aspects of Trusts and Fiduciary Obligations* (Oxford: Oxford University Press, 1992). Professor Finn's illuminating work was at the forefront of the thinking of Millett LJ in *Bristol and West Building Society* v *Mothew* [1998] Ch 1, where his Lordship said (at 18):

CROSS REFERENCE

The duty not to profit from a position of trust is one facet of the fiduciary duty. See Chapter 12 and the case of *Boardman* v *Phipps* (see 12.1.2.2 and 16.3.1.2).

A fiduciary is someone who has undertaken to act for or on behalf of another in a p articular matter in circumstances which give rise to a relationship of trust and confidence. The distinguishing obligation of a fiduciary is the obligation of loyalty. The principal is entitled to the single-minded loyalty of his fiduciary. This core liability has several facets. A fiduciary must act in good faith: he must not make a profit out of his trust; he must not place himself in a position where his duty and his interest may conflict; he may not act for his own benefit or the benefit of a third person without the informed consent of his principal. This is not intended to be an exhaustive list, but it is sufficient to indicate the nature of fiduciary obligations. They are the defining characteristics of the fiduciary. As Dr Finn pointed out in his classic work *Fiduciary Obligations* (1977, p. 2), he is not subject to fiduciary obligations because he is a fiduciary; it is because he is subject to them that he is a fiduciary.

The trustee–beneficiary relationship is the fiduciary relationship par excellence. Transactions carried out by the trustee will be scrutinised. As the Privy Council stated in *Williams* v *Scott* [1900] AC 499: 'the burden of proof that the transaction is a righteous one rests upon the trustee.' But, what is more, the law will not permit trustees so much as to put themselves in a position where there *might be* (a) a conflict between their duty to the trust and their self-interest or (b) a conflict between their duty to the trust and their duty to others.

It may be legitimate to suggest a distinction between two basic forms of breach of fiduciary duty. The first, 'positional' breach, occurs when the fiduciary puts himself in a position of potential conflict of interest and duty. The second, 'transactional' breach, occurs when the potential conflict is actualised by some transaction, e.g. the purchase of trust property from the trust (see self-dealing at 11.2.1.1). In *Bristol and West BS* v *Mothew* (earlier) Millett LJ (now Lord Millett) stated that a fiduciary must take special care to avoid not only *potential* conflict, but what his Lordship described as a position of 'actual conflict'. This, in his Lordship's words, is a position where he 'cannot fulfil his obligations to one principal without failing in his obligations to the other . . . if he does, he may have no alternative but to cease to act for at least one and preferably both'. In such a case the inevitability of the transactional breach creates a positional breach, even where the fiduciary finds himself in the position of conflict through no fault of his own.

11.2.1 Conflict of interest and duty

On fiduciary conflicts in the context of company law, see section entitled 'The bigger picture' near the end of this chapter. For present purposes, we are concerned with cases of conflict between trustees' duty to the trust and their duty to others *and* cases where the conflict is between the trustees' duty to the trust and their self-interest.

THINKING POINT

Read the following extract from the decision of the Court of Appeal *in Sargeant* v *National Westminster Bank plc* (1990) 61 P & CR 518. In that case the trustees were in a position of potential conflict between their self-interest and their duties to the beneficiaries, but they were not in breach of trust. Why?

CASE CLOSE-UP

Sargeant v National Westminster Bank plc (1990) 61 P & CR 518, Court of Appeal

A testator let a number of farms to his children which they worked as a partnership. He then appointed his children to be executors and trustees under his will. When one of the children (Charles) died, the surviving children exercised an option to purchase the deceased child's share of the partnership. Later they revealed plans to purchase the freehold of one of the farms of which they were tenants, and to sell the other freeholds. The administrators of the estate of the deceased child objected to these plans and argued that the surviving children would be in breach of their trust were they to sell, to themselves, the trust-owned freeholds of which they were trustees and under which they were tenants. The trustees sought a declaration that they would be entitled to sell the freeholds. This declaration was granted. The administrators appealed.

Nourse LJ: 'what then happened on the death of Charles? He necessarily ceased to be a trustee of the will. His estate retained his beneficial interest in the farms, subject to the tenancies. The arrangements between the children might have been such that his estate retained his interest in the tenancies as well. No doubt for a short period it did. But under the provisions of the partnership deed, to which Charles himself had been a party, the trustees acquired his share in the partnership, including his share in the tenancies. Thenceforth each of the trustees continued to have the rights of a tenant and a beneficiary. But Charles' estate only had the rights of a beneficiary.

It cannot be doubted that the trustees have ever since been in a position where their interests as tenants may conflict with their duties as trustees to the estate of Charles. But the conclusive objection to the application of the absolute rule on which Mr Romer relies is that it is not they who have put themselves in that position. They have been put there mainly by the testator's grant of the tenancies and by the provisions of his will and partly by contractual arrangements to which Charles himself was a party and of which his representatives cannot complain. The administrators cannot therefore complain of the trustees' continued assertion of their rights as tenants.'

If the trustees had *put themselves* in the position of potential conflict of interest and duty that would indeed have constituted a breach of trust. However, the trustees in *Sargeant* were not liable because it was the testator who had placed the trustees in the position of conflict. In the absence of evidence that the trustees had failed, or would fail, to discharge their duty to the beneficiaries there was no breach of trust. The trustees were able to exercise their pre-existing right, as tenants, to purchase the trust-owned freeholds from themselves! There had been no 'positional' breach of trust, and provided that the trustees obtained the best price reasonably obtainable for these freeholds (subject to the tenancies) there would be no 'transactional' breach of trust. Compare *Newman* v *Clarke* [2016] EWHC 2959 (Ch); [2017] 4 WLR 26, where a tenant was entitled to exercise his right of enfranchisement (the right to purchase the freehold under the Leasehold Reform Act 1967) even though the freehold was part of an estate of which the tenant was trustee. Crucially, the tenant was already a tenant of the lease at the date of his appointment as trustee.

In *Re Mulholland's WT* [1949] 1 All ER 460, Wynn-Parry J stated that 'the existence of the fiduciary relationship creates an inability in the trustee to contract in regard to the trust property [but] does not touch the position arising where the contract in question has been brought into existence before the fiduciary relationship'. *Mulholland* was not referred to in *Sargeant* but the consequence of these cases when read together seems to be that, to some degree at least, the beneficiaries must take the trustees as they find them, despite the existence of prior, potentially conflicting, interests.

 THINKING POINT

Read the following extract from the judgment of Millett LJ (as he then was) in the Court of Appeal in *Bristol and West Building Society* v *Mothew*. In what circumstances is a trust beneficiary (or the 'beneficiary' of a fiduciary duty) entitled to complain of conflict of interest even though the conflict pre-existed the trust or was otherwise authorised?

 CASE CLOSE-UP

Bristol and West Building Society v Mothew [1998] Ch 1

Millett LJ: 'even if a fiduciary is properly acting for two principals with potentially conflicting interests he must act in good faith in the interests of each and must not act with the intention of furthering the interests of one principal to the prejudice of those of the other (see Finn, p. 48). I shall call this "the duty of good faith". But it goes further than this. He must not allow the performance of his obligations to one principal to be influenced by his relationship with the other. He must serve each as faithfully and loyally as if he were his only principal. Conduct which is in breach of this duty need not be dishonest but it must be intentional. An unconscious omission which happens to benefit one principal at the expense of the other does not constitute a breach of fiduciary duty, though it may constitute a breach of the duty of skill and care. This is because the principle which is in play is that the fiduciary must not be inhibited by the existence of his other employment from serving the interests of his principal as faithfully and effectively as if he were the only employer. I shall call this "the no inhibition principle". Unless the fiduciary is inhibited or believes (whether rightly or wrongly) that he is inhibited in the performance of his duties to one

> principal by reason of his employment by the other, his failure to act is not attributable to the double employment. Finally, the fiduciary must take care not to find himself in a position where there is an *actual* conflict of duty so that he cannot fulfil his obligations to one principal without failing in his obligations to the other: see *Moody v Cox* [1917] 2 Ch 71 and *Commonwealth Bank of Australia v Smith* (1991) 102 ALR 453. If he does, he may have no alternative but to cease to act for at least one and preferably both. The fact that he cannot fulfil his obligations to one principal without being in breach of his obligations to the other will not absolve him from liability. I shall call this "the actual conflict rule".'

We have already observed that, as a general rule, the inquiry according to which one determines whether there is a conflict of interest is to ask 'not what was done, but what *might* be done' (*per* Viscount Dunedin in *Wright v Morgan* [1926] AC 788 (emphasis added)). A number of cases have been decided as exceptions to this general rule. One is *Holder v Holder* [1968] Ch 353, where Harman LJ held in favour of a trustee having acknowledged that 'there must never be a conflict of duty and interest but in fact there *was none* here' (emphasis added). Another exception appears from *Re Drexel Burnham Lambert UK Pension Plan* [1995] 1 WLR 32. Here a scheme to distribute surplus assets in a pension fund was approved, even though it had been proposed by trustees who were beneficiaries under the scheme. Lindsay J recognised that there were many exceptions to the general rule and that the trustees in this case had doubtless been selected as persons able to exercise their discretion properly.

In *University of London v Prag* [2014] EWHC 3564 the university successfully defended a claim that it had breached its fiduciary duty to avoid conflict of interest. The claim alleged that the university had acted inappropriately in the way it allocated central resources between the university as a whole and an institute of which the university was trustee. The court rejected the claim on the basis that when the trust was established it must have been intended that the institute would be funded as part of the university, so that any conflict was to that extent authorised.

11.2.1.1 The self-dealing rule and fair-dealing rule

Chapter 12 examines the specific duties of trustees arising from the general nature of trusteeship. However, it is convenient to mention here the self-dealing and fair-dealing rules, the principal rationale of which is that trustees must not let their duty and interest conflict.

 THINKING POINT

Analyse the passage from *Re Thompson's Settlement* [1985] 2 All ER 720 set out next. Try to define in your own words the distinction between self-dealing and fair-dealing.

 CASE CLOSE-UP

Re Thompson's Settlement [1985] 2 All ER 720

Vinelott J: 'it is clear that the self-dealing rule is an application of the wider principle that a man must not put himself in a position where duty and interest conflict or where his duty to one conflicts with his duty to another: see in particular the opinion of Lord Dunedin in

Wright v *Morgan* [1926] AC 788 which I have cited. The principle is applied stringently in cases where a trustee concurs in a transaction which cannot be carried into effect without his concurrence and who also has an interest in or owes a fiduciary duty to another in relation to the same transaction. The transaction cannot stand if challenged by a beneficiary because in the absence of an express provision in the trust instrument the beneficiaries are entitled to require that the trustees act unanimously and that each brings to bear a mind unclouded by any contrary interest or duty in deciding whether it is in the interest of the beneficiaries that the trustees concur in it.

The same principle also applies, but less stringently, in a case within the fair-dealing rule, such as the purchase by a trustee of a beneficiary's beneficial interest. There, there are genuinely two parties to the transaction and it will be allowed to stand if freely entered into and if the trustee took no advantage from his position or from any knowledge acquired from it.

In the instant case the concurrence of the trustees of the grandchildren's settlement was required if the leases were to be assigned to or new tenancies created in favour of the new company and the partnership. The beneficiaries were entitled to ask that the trustees should give unprejudiced consideration to the question whether they should refuse to concur in the assignments in the expectation that a surrender of the leases might be negotiated from the old company and the estates sold or let on the open market.'

In *Re Thompson's*, Vinelott J followed the authority of *Tito* v *Waddell (No 2)* [1977] 3 All ER 129, in which he had appeared as counsel and had successfully advanced the orthodox view that the self-dealing and fair-dealing rules were different rules and not merely separate limbs of the same rule. The self-dealing rule is that 'if a trustee sells the trust property to himself the sale is voidable by any beneficiary *ex debito justitiae*, however fair the transaction'. The fair-dealing rule, on the other hand, is that 'if a trustee purchases the beneficial interest of any of his beneficiaries, the transaction is not voidable *ex debito justitiae* but can be set aside by the beneficiary unless the trustee can show that he has taken no advantage of his position and has made full disclosure to the beneficiary, and that the transaction is fair and honest'. (*Ex debito justitiae* means, literally, 'out of a debt to justice'.)

In *Re Thompson's* Vinelott J stated that the principle that a trustee must not put himself in a position where his duty and interest may conflict applies less stringently in a case of fair-dealing as compared with a case of self-dealing, because the former can involve a genuine contract between two independent parties.

 THINKING POINT

Attempt the following exercise (see Table 11.1), which is designed to test whether or not you have grasped the distinction between self-dealing and fair-dealing. The table has three columns. The first column contains descriptions of each of the rules. The other two columns name the two rules at the top. For each of the descriptions appearing in the first column, place a tick in one of the other columns to indicate the rule to which the description refers. There are four descriptions to each rule.

Table 11.1 Self-dealing and fair-dealing

	Self-dealing	Fair-dealing
This transaction must be set aside at the instance of any beneficiary (choice A)	☐	☐
This transaction need not be set aside provided a fair price was paid (choice B)	☐	☐
The beneficiaries' right to avoid such a transaction is effective against any subsequent purchaser from the trustee who has no notice of the trustee's breach (choice C)	☐	☐
This transaction cannot be validated by the trustee's honesty or the fact that he paid a good price (choice D)	☐	☐
This transaction is voidable *ex debito justitiae* (out of a debt to justice) (choice E)	☐	☐
This is where a trustee purchases trust property from adult beneficiaries with competent independent advice (choice F)	☐	☐
It is a defence for the trustee to show that he has taken no advantage of his position (choice G)	☐	☐
To participate in the transaction the trustee must make full disclosure of all the facts known to him relating to the trust property (choice H)	☐	☐

The solution is as follows: self-dealing (CAED); fair-dealing (FHBG).

11.2.1.2 The effect of retirement

In *Re Boles* [1902] 1 Ch 244 the purchase of trust property by the trustee 12 years after his retirement was held not to infringe the rule that trustees must not put themselves in a position where their interest and duty might conflict. According to Buckley J a retired trustee can purchase trust property if 'there is nothing to show that at the time of retirement there was any idea of a sale'. This will be hard to prove unless a very long period of time has gone by (although a span of 12 years is unlikely to be required in the majority of cases). The court will certainly regard with suspicion a purchase of trust property occurring shortly after retirement. In any event, do not forget that the burden is on the trustee to show that the transaction is a 'righteous' one!

11.3 Trustees' standard of care

We have already observed that trustees must *act* in service of the trust; they cannot stand idly by. It follows that they should act carefully, but just how careful must they be?

The answer to that question is clearer since the Trustee Act 2000 came into force on 1 February 2001.

11.3.1 **The law before the Trustee Act 2000**

Before the Act it was sometimes hard to identify the standard of care appropriate to particular trustees in particular circumstances. It was fairly clear that the standard of care varied according to whether the trustees were amateur or professional and according to whether or not they were remunerated. However, it was difficult to discern from the cases the relative weight attached by the courts to the factors of 'professionalism' and 'remuneration'. Whilst it was apparently of some significance that trustees were remunerated (e.g. *Bartlett* v *Barclays Bank (Nos 1 and 2)* [1980] 1 All ER 139; *Re Waterman's WT* [1952] 2 All ER 1054), others did not consider remuneration in itself to be a factor that should lead to a higher standard of care (*Jobson* v *Palmer* [1893] 1 Ch 71). Those cases in which the standard was raised on account of trustees' professed expertise usually involved trust corporations, so it was no easy task to determine how a human trustee professing particular expertise should be judged.

Absent any special factors such as remuneration and professionalism, the standard of care generally applied to trustees in the performance of their duties is the standard of the ordinary prudent person of business. Jessel MR in *Speight* v *Gaunt* (1883) 22 ChD 727 expressed that duty thus: 'a trustee ought to conduct the business of the trust in the same manner that an ordinary prudent man of business would conduct his own.'

In the Court of Appeal in *Re Whiteley* (1886) ChD 347 (later approved in the House of Lords), Lindley LJ enlarged upon the *Speight* test:

> The duty of the trustee is to take such care as an ordinary prudent man of business would take if he were minded to make an investment for the benefit of *other people* for whom he felt morally obliged to provide. That is the kind of business the ordinary prudent man is supposed to be engaged in (emphasis added).

THINKING POINT

Do you think that such a high standard of care is fair? (You might want to list the arguments for and against it.)

At first sight it does not seem fair, but the courts often have the invidious task of trying to establish where loss to the trust should fall as between the honest trustee in breach and the innocent beneficiary. Why should they not prefer the innocent beneficiary, as long as the office of trustee is not made so onerous that honest people will be reluctant to undertake it?

Perhaps the strongest argument in *favour* of a high standard of care is that the trustees have undertaken their office voluntarily and the beneficiaries rely upon them. This argument is all the more compelling where the trustee is a paid professional. As Harman J put it in *Re Waterman's WT* [1952] 2 All ER 1054: 'I do not forget that a paid trustee is expected to exercise a higher standard of diligence and knowledge than an unpaid trustee, and that a bank which advertises itself largely in the public press as taking charge of administration is under a special duty' (followed in *Bartlett* v *Barclays Bank (Nos 1 and 2)* [1980] 1 All ER 139). Conversely, in one case the court appears to have been persuaded, by the fact that the particular trustee was an unpaid non-professional ('a missionary ignorant of business affairs' is how he was described), to judge that trustee by a subjective standard of care. That case was *Re Vickery* [1931] 1 Ch 572. The facts were similar to those in *Speight* v *Gaunt* (1883) 22 ChD 727, in that the loss was caused to the trust fund by a third party who had been appointed as an agent by the trustee. Both cases were similar in their result, the court deciding that the loss caused by the third party should fall upon the trust fund and not upon the trustees personally, but whereas in *Speight* an objective standard was applied, in *Re Vickery* the trustee was held not to have breached his trust because he had not been subjectively conscious of any wrongdoing. The reasoning in *Re Vickery* has been much criticised because it appears to protect 'honest fools', but even its most determined critic (G.H. Jones (1959) 22 MLR 388) admits that 'in the result' the case may have been correctly decided. The authors of *Parker and Mellows* (6th edn) also express the view that the result in the case was arguably 'desirable', despite the fact that it was 'technically incorrect'.

THINKING POINT

Read the following brief quotation from 'The Trustee's Duty of Skill and Care' (1973) 37 Conv 48. For which types of trustee does the author recommend a subjective standard of care?

Dennis R. Paling, 'The Trustee's Duty of Skill and Care' (1973) 37 Conv 48

[I]t is preferable to distinguish between the standards imposed upon paid and unpaid trustees, because the status of paid and unpaid trustees is different. The paid trustee is frequently a banker or actuary who advertises for business and has no personal relationship with the settlor. The unpaid trustee is frequently a personal friend of the settlor . . . if the standard of skill and care expected of an unpaid trustee is that of an ordinary prudent man in the conduct of his own affairs, the higher standard to be imposed upon a paid trustee must be oppressively high. This may make the trustee excessively cautious, and because he chooses the safest investments the income produced will often be relatively less. Moreover, unless the court is prepared to examine the adequacy of the payment, it may enable the settlor to impose the higher standard of liability by making a token payment.

The distinction between paid and unpaid trustees could however be retained and these unfortunate consequences could be avoided if the standard of skill and care demanded of an unpaid trustee were to be that which he is accustomed to exercise with regard to his own private affairs, whilst the standard of skill and care demanded of a paid trustee was henceforth that which the ordinary prudent man would exercise in the management of his own affairs if he were regardful of the pecuniary interests in the future of those having claims upon him.

Dr Paling suggested a subjective standard of care for unremunerated trustees precisely because they are, typically, also amateurs. He contrasts them with the usual paid trustee, who is 'frequently a banker or actuary who advertises his services for business and has no personal relationship with the settlor'.

STATUTE

Trustee Act 2000

2. —(1) Whenever the duty under this subsection applies to a trustee, he must exercise such care and skill as is reasonable in the circumstances, having regard in particular—

(a) to any special knowledge or experience that he has or holds himself out as having, and

(b) if he acts as trustee in the course of a business or profession, to any special knowledge or experience that it is reasonable to expect of a person acting in the course of that kind of business or profession.

(2) In this Act the duty under subsection (1) is called 'the duty of care'.

11.3.2 **The law after the Trustee Act 2000**

The new standard of care is as follows:

According to Schedule 1 of the Act the duty of care applies to a trustee (a) when exercising the general power of investment or a power of investment conferred on him by the trust instrument and (b) when carrying out statutory duties relating to the exercise of a power of investment or to the review of investments.

According to the notes accompanying the Act the duty applies to trustees not only 'when carrying out their functions under the Act' but also when carrying out 'equivalent functions under the trust instrument'. The notes add that 'the phrase "duty of care" signifies a duty to take care to avoid causing injury or loss'. The duty is intended to take effect in addition to such fundamental duties of trustees as acting in the best interests of the beneficiaries and complying with the terms of the trust *but* 'will exclude any common law duty of care which might otherwise have applied'. The Act is not intended to alter the orthodox rule of trust law which prohibits beneficiaries from suing their trustees for negligence at common law. If one were suspicious that the reason for this was because the statutory duty of care is merely a version of the common law duty of care in negligence applied to a trust (equitable) context, the notes accompanying the Act seek to allay those suspicions. They provide (at note 12) that:

> [i]n relation to the investment of trust funds the new duty makes statutorily explicit the present common law duty which measures the behaviour of the trustees against that expected of the ordinary prudent man of business.

The statutory duty of care is intended to enact, and not to discredit, the standard of care which was formerly set out in such cases as *Speight* v *Gaunt* and *Re Whiteley* (the Court of Appeal confirmed in *Richards* v *Wood* [2014] EWCA Civ 327 that the 2000 Act has not 'materially altered' the ordinary trustee standard of care as set out in the Victorian cases). The standard remains a high one, akin to the care that might be expected from a prudent family provider. However, the new duty of care resolves the uncertainties of the old cases. There can now be no doubt that *Re Vickery* is bad law, that trustees should never be judged according to their own subjective *opinions* as to what constitutes prudent behaviour. Having said that, the statutory 'duty of care', whilst objective, is nevertheless one which is variable according to the subjective *characteristics* of the trustee. Factors which might lead to a stricter standard would include the trustee's experience and expertise (professed or real). Hence, according to note 13 of the explanatory notes accompanying the Act:

> in relation to the purchase of stocks and shares, a higher standard may be expected of a trustee who is an investment banker, specialising in equities, than of a trustee who is a beekeeper, particularly if the investment banker is acting as a trustee in the course of his or her investment banking business.

According to s 1(1) the appropriate level of the new standard of care is to be determined according to whatever is reasonable 'in the circumstances'. It could be raised (e.g. if the trustee professed a relevant expertise) or perhaps even lowered (e.g. in the case of a trainee professional). The circumstances appearing in para. 1(1)(a) and (b) (set out at the start of this section) will be of particular relevance to the determination of the appropriate standard. Other circumstances which might be taken into account include the nature, composition and purposes of the trust.

It is notable that s 1(1) makes no express reference to remuneration, which may be because the 2000 Act introduces a presumption that all professional trustees will be remunerated (see 12.1). Yet despite this omission one imagines that an especially high level of remuneration would be a factor in favour of raising the standard of care required of a trustee, although equally one expects that the courts will wish to avoid as far as possible passing judgment on the highly subjective and sensitive question of what constitutes normal remuneration. It should be noted that, even if remuneration is not relevant to the identification of the appropriate standard of care, it will be relevant to determining whether a trustee ought to be relieved of liability for a breach of trust. A paid trustee is less likely to be relieved of liability under s 61 of the Trustee Act 1925 than an unpaid trustee (see 15.3.4).

Schedule I to the Act lists the circumstances in which the statutory duty of care will apply (Trustee Act 2000, s 2). They include the exercise of general investment powers, 'however conferred' (Sch. I, para. 1: see Chapter 14); the exercise of any power, 'however conferred', to acquire land (Sch. I, para. 2: see Chapter 14); the appointment of agents, nominees and custodians (Sch. I, para. 3) and the insurance of trust property (Sch. I, para. 5). But '[t]he duty of care does not apply to powers conferred by a trust instrument if or in so far as it appears from the trust instrument that the duty is not meant to apply' (Sch. I, para. 7).

11.3.3 **Exemption clauses**

Having seen that the general law applies a high standard to certain professional trustees, it may come as a surprise to discover that in practice professional trustees are less likely than their amateur and unpaid counterparts to be held liable for breach of trust. In such cases we might as well say to the professional trustee: 'I trust I may not trust thee, for thy word/Is but the vain breath of a common man' (William Shakespeare, *The Life and Death of King John*, Act III, scene 1). The reason for this bizarre state of affairs is that a professional trustee is more likely than an amateur trustee to insist upon the inclusion in the trust instrument of carefully drafted exemption clauses designed to limit his liability.

Exemption clauses must be fairly construed without any presumption in favour of one party or the other, but if there remains a doubt whether the matter complained of came within the scope of the exemption clause it must be regarded as falling outside it (*Bogg v Raper* (1998) Times, 22 April, *per* Millett LJ). In other words, if there is any ambiguity in the meaning of the clause it will be construed *contra proferentem* (against the benefit of) the trustee who is seeking to rely upon the clause. See, further, *Wight v Olswang (No 1)* (1999) Times, 18 May, where a settlement contained two exemption clauses: a general one protecting all trustees, and one which specifically did not apply to paid trustees. The Court of Appeal held that the paid trustees could not even rely upon the general clause.

 THINKING POINT

Which of the following exemption clauses would be legally effective, do you think?

- a clause relieving one of the trustees of any responsibility or duty in relation to a particular class of beneficiaries;
- a clause providing that the trustees shall not be liable for errors, omissions or neglect of diligence;
- a clause purporting to excuse the trustees from all liability apart from that which arises from their own actual fraud;
- a clause purporting to excuse the trustees from liability for losses caused by their gross negligence;
- a clause purporting to excuse the trustees from liability for deliberate wrongdoing.

You may be surprised to discover that only the final clause is certainly invalid. In *Rae v Meek* (1889) 14 App Cas 558, a decision of the House of Lords under Scottish law, Lord Herschell approved the view that a trustee exemption clause 'is ineffectual to protect a trustee against the consequences of *culpa lata*, or gross negligence on his part, or of any conduct which is inconsistent with *bona fides*', but when the English Court of Appeal considered a clause in a trust instrument which purported to excuse the trustees from all liability apart from that which might arise from their own actual fraud, Millett LJ (as he then was) held that the clause was effective to exclude liability no matter how indolent, imprudent, lacking in diligence, negligent or wilful the trustees may have been, so long as they had not acted dishonestly (*Armitage v Nurse* [1997] 3 WLR 1046). It was held that the clause was not void for repugnancy or contrary to public policy. The beneficiaries in *Armitage* did not allege dishonesty, therefore the trustees were not liable for any breach of trust.

The meaning of dishonesty was considered in *Walker v Stones* (2000) Independent, 27 July, Court of Appeal. The judge at first instance had held ([2000] 1 WTLR 79) that the deliberate commission of a breach of trust was dishonest only where the trustee committing that breach acted in the knowledge that it was contrary to the interests of the beneficiary or was recklessly indifferent thereto. A trustee's conduct in breach of trust could not be categorised as dishonest where he acted in a genuine, if misguided, belief that his actions were for the benefit of the beneficiary. The Court of Appeal disagreed. In allowing the appeal, it was held that an individual could act dishonestly, in the ordinary sense of the word, even where they genuinely believed their actions to be morally justified. The distinction between dishonesty (or '*mala fides*') and gross negligence is also a hard one to define, but in English law the distinction certainly exists. Thus in *Spread Trustee Company Ltd v Hutcheson* [2011] UKPC 13, the Privy Council approved the observation made by Lord Denman CJ *in Goodman v Harvey* (1836) 4 A & E 870 that in English law '[g]ross negligence may be evidence of *mala fides* but is not the same thing'. Lord Kerr in the *Spread Trustee* case (at para. [180]) added his voice to those who have argued that trustees should not be able to exclude liability for gross negligence:

> If . . . placing of reliance on a responsible person to manage property so as to promote the interests of the beneficiaries of a trust is central to the concept of trusteeship, denying trustees the opportunity to avoid liability for their gross negligence seems to be entirely in keeping with that essential aim.

🔍 CASE CLOSE-UP

Armitage v *Nurse* [1997] 3 WLR 1046, Court of Appeal

By a settlement made on 11 October 1984 the plaintiff, who was then aged 17, became entitled in remainder to settled agricultural land of which her mother was tenant for life. Her portion was to be held on certain trusts until she reached the age of 40. Clause 15 of the settlement provided that no trustee should be liable for any loss or damage to the plaintiff's fund or the income thereof at any time or from any case unless it was caused by his own actual fraud. It was held by Millett LJ that there was 'no question of the clause being repugnant to the trust'.

Millett LJ: 'there is an irreducible core of obligations owed by the trustees to the beneficiaries and enforceable by them which is fundamental to the concept of a trust. If the beneficiaries have no rights enforceable against the trustees there are no trusts. But I do not accept . . . that these core obligations include the duties of skill and care, prudence and diligence. The duty of the trustees to perform the trusts honestly and in good faith for the benefit of the beneficiaries is the minimum necessary to give substance to the trusts, but in my opinion it is sufficient . . . a trustee who relied on the presence of a trustee exemption clause to justify what he proposed to do would thereby lose its protection: he would be acting recklessly in the proper sense of the term . . .

The submission that it is contrary to public policy to exclude the liability of a trustee for gross negligence is not supported by any English or Scottish authority . . .

At the same time, it must be acknowledged that the view is widely held that these clauses have gone too far, and that trustees who charge for their services and who, as professional men, would not dream of excluding liability for ordinary professional negligence should not be able to rely on a trustee exemption clause excluding liability for gross negligence. Jersey introduced a law in 1989 which denies effect to a trustee exemption clause which purports to absolve a trustee from liability for his own "fraud, wilful misconduct or gross negligence." The subject is presently under consideration in this country by the Trust Law Committee under the chairmanship of Sir John Vinelott. If clauses such as clause 15 of the settlement are to be denied effect, then in my opinion this should be done by Parliament, which will have the advantage of wide consultation with interested bodies and the advice of the Trust Law Committee.'

Note: in *Bristol and West* v *Mothew* [1998] 1 Ch 1 at 17 his Lordship drew a similar distinction between breach of fiduciary duty (i.e. breach of the fiduciary duties of loyalty, honesty and good faith) and the obligation to use proper skill and care in the discharge of his duties.

Bonham v *David Fishwick* [2008] EWCA Civ 373, CA suggests that trustees who follow legal advice will be able to rely on a clause exempting them from liability for wilful default. The honesty of a trustee's conduct is judged according to what an objective trustee, looking on, would make of it—it is not judged subjectively according to the trustee's own beliefs (*Barnes v Tomlinson* [2006] EWHC 3115, [2007] WTLR 377).

11.3.3.1 Reform of the law relating to trustee exemption clauses

On 19 July 2006 the Law Commission for England and Wales published a report (No 301) containing its recommendations for the reform of the law governing trustee exemption clauses. The recommended reform takes the form of a rule to be adopted by regulatory and professional bodies to the effect that '[a]ny paid trustee who causes a settlor to include a clause in a trust instrument which has the effect of excluding or limiting liability for negligence must before the creation of the trust take such steps as are reasonable to ensure that the settlor is aware of the meaning and effect of the clause'. The Law Commission expects that this will ensure that exemption clauses will in future 'represent a proper and fully informed expression of the terms on which settlors are willing to dispose of their property on trust' (para. 1.19). The report follows a consultation paper on the same subject ('Trustee Exemption Clauses' (2003) Law Commission Consultation Paper No 171).

11.4 Trustee decision making

THINKING POINT

On the basis of what you have already learned about trustees draw up a list of the sort of issues you think trustees have to make decisions on.

You will be able to add many items to your list by the end of this book. Trustees must, for example, decide whom to appoint as new trustees should the need arise, as well as how to invest the trust fund, and we have already seen that in 'discretionary trusts' they must appoint the beneficiaries of the trust and decide how to divide the trust fund amongst them. Although trustees are obliged to exercise their own discretion, they are permitted to ask the court to confirm any proposed course of action. The court will give its guidance by way of an order for directions or declaratory relief.

11.4.1 The exercise of discretion

Trustees' discretions are classified as being either 'dispositive' or 'administrative'. According to the orthodox view, dispositive discretions relate to the disposition of the trust property and administrative discretions relate to the management of the trust. Examples of 'dispositive discretions' include the distribution of income and capital under discretionary trusts (see 4.4.2) whereas the class of 'administrative discretions' includes the trustees' choice as to how best to invest the trust property (see Chapter 14). The detail of these specific examples is to be found in other chapters and our aim here is to attempt to distil from the cases general principles which should inform the exercise by trustees of their discretions. In particular, trustees should be aware of the degree to which their decisions will be subject to review by the courts.

The first thing to note is that where the trustees have a power and the trust instrument gives them the discretion to exercise it or not, the new duty of care (Trustee Act 2000, s 1) governs the manner of the exercise of that power should the trustee choose to exercise it. However, the notes to the Act make it clear that the duty of care 'will not apply to a decision by the trustees as to whether to exercise that discretionary power in the first place'.

Gisborne v *Gisborne* (1877) 2 App Cas 300 was a case involving a dispositive discretion. A will trust granted the trustees an absolute discretion and 'uncontrollable authority' over a fund. Lord Cairns, the Lord Chancellor, stated:

> [l]arger words than these, it appears to me, it would be impossible to introduce into a will. The trustees are not merely to have a discretion, but they are to have 'uncontrollable', that is, 'uncontrolled', authority. Their discretion and authority, always supposing that there is no *mala fides* with regard to its exercise, is to be without check or control from any superior tribunal.

For the Lord Chancellor 'the question . . . must really come back to the construction of the will'.

The trustees in *Re Locker's Settlement* [1977] 1 WLR 1323 had an 'absolute and uncontrolled' dispositive discretion, according to the terms of the settlement. Goulding J, following *Gisborne* v *Gisborne*, acknowledged that this prevented interference by the court in a *bona fide* exercise of that discretion but held that it did not prevent the court's intervention in a case where the trustees had totally failed to act. However, if the trustees, as in *Re Locker's ST*, wished to exercise their discretion *late*, the court would normally encourage them to do so, as Goulding J acknowledged:

> A tardy distribution at the discretion of the trustees is . . . nearer to . . . what the settlor intended, than tardy distribution by the trustees at the discretion of someone else.

In *Re Locker's ST* the beneficiaries' best interests required that the court did intervene to exercise the discretion.

These cases illustrate the courts' general reluctance to interfere in the exercise of trust discretions. They should be contrasted with the case of *Re Roper's Trust* (1879) 9 ChD 272, where the testator's will required the trustees to pay income to his niece, Fanny Keech, for her to hold upon trust for her children and 'to be by her applied for their benefit at her discretion'. Fry J said: 'I think that Fanny Keech has not exercised a sound discretion, and that where the court finds such to be the case, though the income is by the words of the will left to the discretion of a given person, the court has power to control that discretion and to deal with the income.' It is notable that in *Re Roper's Trust* the discretion had not been expressly described in the trust instrument as being 'absolute' or 'uncontrolled' and it must be doubted that Fry J would have set aside the exercise of a trustee's discretion in the face of such wording.

It is one thing for the court to set aside the exercise of a discretion because it does not approve of the result (as in *Re Roper's Trust*); it is another thing to set aside a decision on the ground that the mode of its exercise was fundamentally flawed. A trustee's purported exercise of discretion, whether qualified as 'uncontrollable' or not, will be liable to be set aside if there has been no real exercise of discretion at all. To this we now turn.

 CASE CLOSE-UP

Sieff v Fox [2005] EWHC 1312, ChD

Lloyd LJ (sitting as a judge of the Chancery Division) (para. 38):

'There are several different categories of case where an exercise by trustees of a discretionary power may be held to be invalid.

i) There may be a formal or procedural defect, such as the failure to use the stipulated form of document . . . or to obtain a necessary prior consent.

ii) The power may have been exercised in a way which it does not authorise, for example with an unauthorised delegation, or by the inclusion of beneficiaries who are not objects of the power.

iii) The exercise may infringe some rule of the general law, such as the rule against perpetuities.

iv) The trustees may have exercised the power for an improper purpose, in cases known as fraud on the power. *Cloutte* v *Storey* [1911] 1 Ch 18, among the cases cited to me, is an example of this, where the power was exercised in favour of one of the objects, but under a private arrangement whereby he passed the benefit back to his parents, who had made the appointment . . . an exercise which is not in good faith is, or at any rate includes, a case where the exercise is a fraud on the power.

v) The trustees may have been unaware that they had any discretion to exercise: see *Turner* v *Turner* [1984] Ch 100, an extreme and highly unusual case on the facts, which has been described as equitable *non est factum*.

vi) To these categories, of which the first four are clear and well-established, the rule or principle in *Re Hastings-Bass* is said to add a further class of case.'

11.4.1.1 **The so-called rule in *Re Hastings-Bass***

The so-called rule in *Re Hastings-Bass* is pragmatic. It provides that a trustee's decision, even if it was based on unsound reasoning, should not be reviewed by the courts or sent back to the trustees for reconsideration if, were the trustees to reconsider the issue on a sound basis, they might simply confirm their original decision. (Note that the rule allows the court to set aside a trustee's discretionary judgment in a particular case, but does not allow the court to replace the trustee's decision with a decision of its own.)

In *Re Hastings-Bass* [1975] Ch 25 itself, the Court of Appeal refused to interfere with the trustees' decision to exercise their power of advancement (see 13.2) by means of a sub-settlement which they had not appreciated would be void for perpetuity. Lord Walker retained the description 'the rule in *Hastings-Bass*' in his speech in the Supreme Court in *Futter* v *HMRC Commissioners; Pitt* v *HMRC Commissioners* [2013] UKSC 26, but his Lordship acknowledged (at para. [1]) that the description is a misnomer and that, if anything, the rule should be named after *Mettoy Pension Trustees Ltd* v *Evans* [1991] 2 All ER 513. In *Mettoy*, Warner J had suggested that the rule requires the court to ask three questions: (1) What were the trustees under a duty to consider? (2) Did they fail to consider it? (3) If so, what would they have done if they had considered it? Sir Robert Walker, as he then was, has suggested extrajudicially that the rule promotes practical certainty and gives trustees confidence to make decisions without fear of constant challenge ('Trust principles in the pension context', in A.J. Oakley (ed.), *Trends in Contemporary Trust Law* (Oxford: Oxford University Press, 1997) at 129).

Lord Walker of Gestingthorpe, as indicated earlier, has recently re-examined the 'rule' in the Supreme Court in the twin appeals in *Futter* v *HMRC Commissioners* and *Pitt* v *HMRC Commissioners*. See next.

> ### 🔍 CASE CLOSE-UP
>
> **Futter v HMRC Commissioners; Pitt v HMRC Commissioners [2013] UKSC 26; [2013] 2 WLR 1200, UK Supreme Court**
>
> Facts: The facts of *Futter* concern incorrect advice given by solicitors as to the capital gains tax implications of gains realised by non-resident trustees. In particular, they failed to give correct advice concerning the Taxation of Chargeable Gains Act 1992, s 87. The facts of *Pitt* concerned the failure of Frenkel Topping, a firm of financial advisers professing to specialise in personal injury trusts, to take account of the inheritance tax implications of a settlement designed to hold funds for a man who, as a result of an accident, had been rendered incapable of caring for himself.
>
> Held: That when trustees, acting within their powers, obtain and act on apparently competent professional advice on relevant matters they cannot have their decision set aside just because the advice later turns out to have been wrong. Lord Walker was seeking to address and bring an end to what he called 'a striking feature of the development of the *Hastings-Bass* rule', namely that it had led to 'trustees asserting and relying on their own failings, or those of their advisers, in seeking the assistance of the court' (para. [69]).
>
> Lord Walker held that the court should not interfere with a trustee's decision except where the outcome is unauthorised by the power conferred upon the trustee (para. [26]). In so deciding, his Lordship approved the judgment of Lightman J in *Abacus Trust Co (Isle of Man) v Barr* [2003] Ch 409, where Lightman J had made the following observation: 'If the trustee has in accordance with his duty identified the relevant considerations and used all proper care and diligence in obtaining the relevant information and advice relating to those considerations, the trustee can be in no breach of duty and its decision cannot be impugned merely because in fact that information turns out to be partial or incorrect.'
>
> Lord Walker also approved Lloyd LJ in *Sieff v Fox* [2005] EWHC 1312 (Ch). Lloyd LJ, who had sat in that case as a judge of the Chancery Division, had drawn a 'very important distinction' between a trustee's error in going beyond the scope of a power (so-called excessive execution) and a trustee's error in failing to give proper consideration to relevant matters in making a decision within the scope of the relevant power (so-called inadequate deliberation). Lord Walker added that 'a fraudulent appointment (that is, one shown to have been made for a positively improper purpose) may need a separate pigeonhole somewhere between the categories of excessive execution and inadequate deliberation' (para. [62]).

On the question whether a trustee's decision is void or voidable if it falls foul of the rule in *Hastings-Bass*, Lord Walker expressed his agreement with the following part of Lloyd LJ's judgment in *Sieff v Fox*:

> [I]f an exercise by trustees of a discretionary power is within the terms of the power, but the trustees have in some way breached their duties in respect of that exercise, then (unless it is a case of a fraud on the power) the trustees' act is not void but it may be voidable at the instance of a beneficiary who is adversely affected.

A settlor who is 'adversely affected' can also apply to have a settlement set aside if it was made on erroneous grounds (*Freedman v Freedman* [2015] EWHC 1457 (Ch)). Following *Futter v HMRC Commissioners*, the Royal Court of Guernsey held in *Re Abacus Global Approved Managed Pension Trust* (2016) 18 ITELR 753 that where the member of a Guernsey pension fund received a lump-sum distribution out of the fund on the basis of mistaken advice that the payment would not be subject to UK tax, the transaction would not be set aside on the grounds of equitable mistake. The test was whether it would be unconscionable for the recipient to retain the distribution in light of the mistake, which in this case it would not be. The recipient was the only one who suffered as a result of the tax consequences of the distribution.

11.4.1.2 **The exercise of discretion by the court**

In very exceptional cases the court will actually exercise a discretion for the trustee, if the trustee encounters a particular problem in its exercise. The case of *Mettoy Pension Trustees* v *Evans* [1991] 2 All ER 513 is an example of this. There, as you may recall (see 2.2.3), the liquidator of an insolvent company had to exercise a discretion as to the proper destination of a pension fund surplus. However, the liquidator had conflicting fiduciary obligations: on the one hand to safeguard the interest of the company (the liquidator was trustee of the insolvent company's estate and affairs); on the other to exercise the fiduciary power to allocate the surplus fairly as between the company and the employees entitled to the pension fund. Faced with this dilemma, Warner J intervened to exercise the fiduciary power on behalf of the liquidator. For another instance of a court exercising a trust discretion, see the Privy Council in *Marley* v *Mutual Security Merchant Bank & Trust Co Ltd* [1991] 3 All ER 198. In that case it was stressed that the court will only be able to exercise the discretion if it is in possession of all the necessary information.

11.4.2 **Reasons for decisions**

Trustees need not give reasons for their decisions (*Re Londonderry's Settlement* [1965] Ch 918). In *Re Beloved Wilkes' Charity* (1851) 3 Mac & Cr 440 the Lord Chancellor suggested that trustees would be 'most prudent and judicious' simply to state 'that they have met and considered and come to a conclusion'.

11.4.2.1 **Disclosure of trust documentation**

The court has a jurisdiction to order disclosure within the course of litigation under the Civil Procedure Rules, Part 31, but it also has a number of common law powers to order disclosure of trust documentation in other contexts. In *Ong* v *Ping* [2015] EWHC 3258 (Ch) 14 these powers were confirmed (at para. [14]) to be as follows:

- 'power to order a trustee to give disclosure to a beneficiary (including a discretionary beneficiary under a discretionary trust) of trust documents' (*Schmidt* v *Rosewood Trust* [2003] 2 AC 709);
- 'power to order disclosure for the purpose of ascertaining the whereabouts of trust property or its traceable proceeds where there is an allegation that a person is in possession of the trust property or its traceable proceeds' (*Bankers Trust Co* v *Shapira* [1980] 1 WLR 1274);
- 'power to make an order, ancillary to a freezing order, requiring disclosure either under s. 37 of the Senior Courts Act 1981 or the court's inherent jurisdiction' (on 'freezing orders', see Chapter 20);
- 'power to order disclosure which is ancillary to the intended execution of a judgment of the court' (*Maclaine Watson* v *International Tin Council (No 2)* [1989] Ch 286).

The Privy Council held in *Schmidt* v *Rosewood Trust* [2003] 2 AC 709 that trust beneficiaries are not entitled to disclosure of trust documents, but that disclosure may be ordered on a case-by-case basis as part of the courts' inherent jurisdiction to ensure the proper administration of trusts (*Schmidt* v *Rosewood Trust Ltd* [2003] 2 AC 709). It follows that a person must normally 'establish as a *prima facie* case that he is a beneficiary' before the court will consider ordering disclosure (*Birdseye v Roythorne* [2015] EWHC 1003 (Ch); WLR (D) 169, at para. [24]). The approach advanced by the Privy Council in *Schmidt* is in practice preferable to an approach which presumes beneficiaries to have a right to disclosure. The later approach inevitably conflicts with the fact that trustees are under no duty to disclose reasons for their decisions on trust matters.

Q CASE CLOSE-UP

Breakspear v Ackland [2008] EWHC 220; [2008] 3 WLR 698, Chancery Division

Facts: A settlor set up a discretionary trust for the benefit of himself and his children. By a non-binding 'wish letter' which was contemporaneous with the settlement, the settlor requested that the trustees take stated matters into account when exercising their dispositive powers. The claimants, three of the beneficiaries, asked for disclosure of the wish letter in order to evaluate their future expectations under the trust.

Held: allowing the claim for disclosure, that the basis on which trustees and the court should approach a request for disclosure of a wish letter was one calling for the exercise of discretion rather than the adjudication upon a proprietary right of beneficiaries to see trust documents, but here the risk of family division occasioned by disclosure was outweighed by the requirement to give the claimants a proper opportunity to ask the court to sanction a scheme of distribution of the trust fund; and that, accordingly, disclosure of the wish letter to the claimants would be ordered.

Briggs J: 'The defining characteristic of a wish letter is that it contains material which the settlor desires that the trustees should take into account when exercising their (usually dispositive) discretionary powers. It is therefore brought into existence for the sole purpose of serving and facilitating an inherently confidential process. It seems to me axiomatic that a document brought into existence for the sole or predominant purpose of being used in furtherance of an inherently confidential process is itself properly to be regarded as confidential, to substantially the same extent and effect as the process which it is intended to serve.'

11.4.3 Summary of factors influencing the courts' willingness to review trustee decisions

The following factors present themselves:

- the courts never interfere with trustee discretions which the trust instrument describes as being 'absolute', 'uncontrolled' or 'uncontrollable';

- the courts are more willing to review decision making on purely administrative/ministerial matters, e.g. how to invest the trust fund, and less willing to review decisions relating to the disposition of the trust fund, e.g. decisions relating to maintenance, advancement and the appointment of beneficiaries to discretionary trusts;

- the courts are more willing to review decision making where the decision is one which is common to all trustees, and are less willing to review the exercise of discretions which the settlor has expressly granted to the trustees;

- the courts are more willing to review decision making where there is some norm or established paradigm/standard against which the decision can be judged, e.g. investment, and are less willing to review decisions for which there is no norm, e.g. the decision whether or not it would benefit Miss X to pay her income from the fund.

THINKING POINT

Before reading the summary which follows, why not try and write up your own list—after all, that's the best way to learn.

11.4.4 **Unanimity**

Trustees must act unanimously in exercising any of their powers under a trust, including their decision making. There can be 'sleeping partners' in business ventures who take no active role in the management of the business, but there is no such thing as a 'sleeping trustee'. All the trustees must be unanimous in the exercise of their discretions. There are, however, some exceptions to this rule. The Charities Act 1993 provides, for example, that in small trusts a two-thirds majority of the trustees is competent to pass resolutions authorising the transfer of the entirety of the trust property to other charities (s 74) and the expenditure of trust capital as well as income (s 75). Furthermore, it is quite usual for the trust instruments of charitable trusts and pension fund trusts to reserve the exercise of administrative discretions to a core group of managing trustees.

 ## Summary

- In this chapter we have seen that a trustee owes a fiduciary duty to the beneficiaries of the trust as part of a broader duty to serve the trust. Trustees must never put themselves in a position where their duties to the trust might conflict with their self-interest or their duty to others.

- A trustee should conduct the business of the trust in the same manner as an ordinary prudent business person would conduct their own. However, this standard might be raised or lowered according to the characteristics of the particular trustee, so trust corporations and professional trustees will be judged according to higher standards. In Chapter 12 we will see that such trustees are presumed to be entitled to remuneration.

- In this chapter we considered that the level of remuneration might be a factor relevant to the identification of the standard of care to which such trustees should be subject. However, even if remuneration is not relevant to the identification of the appropriate standard of care, it will be relevant to determining whether a trustee ought to be relieved of liability for a breach of trust. A paid trustee is less likely to be relieved of liability under the Trustee Act 1925, s 61 than an unpaid trustee (see 15.3.4).

- We have seen, however, that the practical significance of this may be limited, since in practice most corporate and professional trustees insist upon the inclusion in the trust deed of exculpatory clauses. Such clauses are capable of excluding liability for all breaches of trust, apart from those tainted by the trustee's dishonesty.

- According to the notes which accompany the Trustee Act 2000 it is intended that the statutory standard of care will act as a safeguard for beneficiaries sufficient to off-set the increased risks which will attend the wider powers of investment and delegation introduced by the Act. However, it may prove to be a weak safeguard in practice due to the widespread use by professional trustees of exculpatory clauses.

- Finally, in this chapter we examined the factors which a trustee should consider in exercising a trust discretion. We noted that courts are reluctant to review the exercise of trustee discretions (especially dispositive discretions) unless the trustee has acted fraudulently, capriciously or has failed to exercise a proper discretion in accordance with the rule in *Re Hastings-Bass*.

? Summative assessment exercise

Albert settled a trust on Beryl and Charlie as trustees for certain beneficiaries. The fund consisted of freehold properties of which Beryl and Charlie were tenants, and cash. The trust instrument granted the trustees the power to invest in such investments as they in their absolute discretion and uncontrolled authority should think fit. The trust instrument also included a charging clause which permitted the trustees to be handsomely remunerated out of the fund. In the event, the trustees invested trust monies in shares in Y Co, a company with which they had no connection. Some time later the trustees purchased the freehold properties at market value by exercising options to purchase which they had been granted at the commencement of their leases. They also bought the shares in Y Co from the trust for what was a very fair and even generous price, believing that the price of those shares was about to rise. In the event those shares did increase in value, but only very slightly. The trustees made fresh investments of the trust fund in Z Co, whose trading record they had taken no steps to investigate. The value of the shares in that company has now plummeted dramatically.

Advise the trustees, who are concerned that the beneficiaries might have grounds to take action against them for breach of their trust.

 Full specimen answers can be found at www.oxfordtextbooks.co.uk/orc/watt_directions5e/.

☐ The bigger picture

In the Court of Appeal in *Towers v Premier Waste Ltd* [2011] EWCA Civ 923; [2012] 1 BCLC 67 Mummery LJ described the rules against conflict of interest and duty as 'simple, strict and salutary' (para. [2]). That case concerned company directors' fiduciary duties. The rules in the company context differ in their details from those in the trust context. The Companies Act 2006 requires that there should be full disclosure of the directors' interests (ss 177, 182), and it imposes a duty to avoid actual or potential conflicts between the directors' interests and those of the company (s 175), but s 175 does not apply to directors' transactions with the company and in relation to other transactions it permits directors of private companies to authorise conflicts with the interests of the company unless the company's constitution expressly prohibits the activity in question. The fiduciary rules in the trust context are more strict, for in the case of a potential conflict between the trust and the trustee's private interests the trustee will not be permitted to stay in post without the court being first satisfied that the trustee can discharge his duties to the trust without ever having to choose between the conflicting interests (*Public Trustee v Cooper* [2001] WTLR 901).

Further reading

Ashdown, M. *Trustee Decision Making: The Rule in* Re Hastings-Bass (2015) Oxford: Oxford University Press
examines recent developments in 'the rule'

Conaglen, M. 'The nature and function of fiduciary loyalty' (2005) 121 LQR 452 and 'Fiduciary regulation of conflicts between duties' (2009) 125 LQR 111
two articles arguing that the function of fiduciary duties is *to protect the proper performance of non-fiduciary duties*

Hayton, D. 'The future of the Anglo-Saxon trust in the age of transparency' (2015) 29(1) Tru LI 30–8
notes that in Jersey and Bermuda, for example, statutes have been introduced to preserve the old rule in *Hastings-Bass* to enable trustee decisions still to be set aside where the trustees took qualified advice but that advice was erroneous

Langbein, J.H. 'Questioning the trust law duty of loyalty: sole interest or best interest?' (2005) 114 Yale LJ 929
argues that the technique of avoiding all possible conflicts sometimes obstructs the aim of serving the beneficiaries' best interest

 For links to selected cases, statutes, academic papers and official reports mentioned in this chapter please visit the online resources at www.oup.com/uk/watt_directions6e/.

12 Trustees' duties

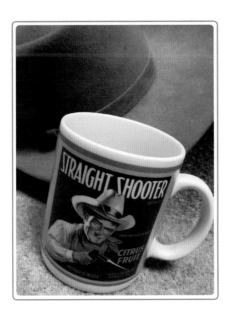

Introduction

Chapter 11 considered the general fiduciary nature of the office of trustee. This chapter analyses some specific duties to which trustees are subject.

Breach of trustees' duties can result in personal liability for the trustee concerned (Chapter 15 considers the consequences of breach of trust). Indeed, as a general rule the trustees have all the duties and burdens, whilst the beneficiaries have all the rights and benefits. So, why would anybody agree to be a trustee? As we progress through this chapter we will see that the courts are involved in an on-going attempt to balance the strict enforcement of the trustees' duties with the need to ensure that there are always persons willing to act as trustees. In carrying out this balancing act the courts have as their ultimate goal the best administration of the trust in the interest of the beneficiaries. We will also see that the Trustee Act 2000 has made trusteeship more attractive to trust corporations and professional trustees than it used to be. The Act grants them improved powers of delegation and raises a presumption in favour of their remuneration, but without prejudice to the potential of trust instruments to make even more generous provision by express terms.

12.1 Trustee profits

The first point to make is that the law distinguishes trustees' profits from their expenses. 'A trustee is entitled to be reimbursed from the trust funds, or may pay out of the trust funds, expenses properly incurred by him when acting on behalf of the trust' (s 31(1) of the Trustee Act 2000, replacing the provision to like effect in s 30(2) of the Trustee Act 1925). Where the expenses (and this includes on-going contractual liability) have not been incurred 'properly' there is no indemnity and the trustee will be personally liable to any third party to whom he owes a debt or other contractual obligation.

The courts' approach to trustees' expenses should be contrasted with their approach to trustees' profits. The general rule is that fiduciaries (trustees included) must not profit from their trust, and, according to Lord Herschell in *Bray v Ford* [1896] AC 44, this rule is an 'inflexible' one (although his Lordship did allow for trustees to make a profit where the trust instrument so provides).

Now, according to Part V of the Trustee Act 2000, certain types of trustee (broadly speaking 'professional' trustees) are presumed to be *entitled* to remuneration unless the trust instrument provides to the contrary. Trustees who do not have the benefit of this statutory right to remuneration (broadly speaking 'non-professional' trustees) are still subject to the old rule as expressed by Russell J in *Williams v Barton* [1927] 2 Ch 9: '[o]n the same principle [that a trustee may not profit from their trust] a trustee has no right to charge for his time and trouble.' If 'non-professional' trustees desire unauthorised remuneration or improved remuneration in respect of the services they provide to the trust, they will have to apply to the court for it. We can summarise the position as regards trustee remuneration as follows:

- the proper construction of the terms of the trust instrument prima facie determines whether or not trustees are entitled to remuneration;
- if the trust instrument makes no express provision, the general position (except in the case of professional trustees to whom the Trustee Act 2000 applies) is that trustees must act gratuitously;

- the courts have an inherent jurisdiction to grant or to increase remuneration if it is in the interests of the beneficiaries on the facts of the particular case.

We will now consider the various aspects of fiduciary profits, including trustee remuneration, in turn.

12.1.1 Unauthorised fiduciary gains

It is no defence to a breach of the 'inflexible rule' against unauthorised fiduciary profits for the fiduciary to establish that the profit was made without loss to the trust (see *Keech* v *Sandford* at 12.1.2.2), nor even to point out that the transaction which yielded the profit to the fiduciary also yielded a profit for the trust (see *Boardman* v *Phipps* [1966] 3 All ER 827, HL at 12.1.2.2).

12.1.2 Award of fiduciary profit by the court under its inherent jurisdiction

We have seen that a lay trustee may not be remunerated out of the trust fund unless remuneration is permitted by the trust instrument or is in the interests of the beneficiaries as furthering the good administration of the trust. Having said that, this section considers cases where the courts seem to approve the remuneration of trustees more on account of their exemplary *past* performance than on account of the future good administration of the trust. The trustee or fiduciary may be awarded remuneration by way of **quantum meruit**.

> **quantum meruit** The literal translation of this Latin phrase is 'as much as he has deserved'. It is, according to The Oxford Dictionary of English, 'a reasonable sum of money to be paid for services rendered or work done when the amount due is not stipulated in a legally enforceable contract' (2nd edn, Oxford: Oxford University Press, 2003).

It is often very hard to see how such awards can be made in the interests of the beneficiaries of the particular trust, although one might argue that potential beneficiaries everywhere will derive an indirect benefit, in the form of willing trustees, from the fact that the courts are seen to treat trustees fairly. Nevertheless, it is in the case of an award by way of *quantum meruit* that the inflexible rule seems to bend almost to breaking point.

> **CROSS REFERENCE**
> On bribes and secret commissions see *FHR European Ventures LLP* v *Cedar Capital Partners LLC* [2014] UKSC 45, Chapter 16.

In *Boardman* v *Phipps* [1966] 3 All ER 827 a bare majority of the House of Lords held that a solicitor who had used information gained from his fiduciary role in relation to a trust (of which he was not in fact a trustee) had to account for all profits he had made for himself by virtue of his fiduciary position. This was despite the fact that his activity had also resulted in substantial benefits for the trust and had been carried out openly and honestly. However, whilst deciding that the fiduciary had breached the inflexible rule, their Lordships held that he should be paid for the work he had done to the great profit of the trust, and 'that payment should be on a liberal scale' (for more detail, see 16.3.1.2). The result was that their Lordships in *Boardman* modified the strict rule of fiduciary propriety by whispering *inter partes* justice beneath the shout of the inflexible fiduciary rule. Judicial willingness to do this in cases of unauthorised gains made from inherently harmless opportunities should be contrasted with the strict approach taken in cases of gains made in the forms of bribes and secret commissions.

In *O'Sullivan* v *Management Agency and Music Ltd* [1985] 3 All ER 351, a case where a musician's agent was held to have profited from a position of undue influence over an inexperienced pop star (Gilbert O'Sullivan), the recording contracts were set aside and the agent was ordered to account for all profits made on them. However, Dunn LJ stated that 'in taking the account the defendants are entitled to an allowance . . . for reasonable remuneration, *including a profit element*, for all work done in promoting and exploiting O'Sullivan and his compositions' (emphasis added). He stated that 'although equity looks at the advantage gained by the wrongdoer rather than the loss to the victim, the cases show that in assessing the advantage gained the court will look at the whole situation in the round'. He approved the defendants' counsel's submission that the maxim *he who seeks equity must do equity* should be applied (see 1.3.7). Mr O'Sullivan had sought the assistance of equity to recover monies from the agency, and he would have to allow the agency reasonable remuneration for its work. It should also be emphasised, of course, that the judgment did not go so far as to approve 'profit sharing' as such (*O'Sullivan* was applied to very similar facts in *Badfinger Music v Evans* (2001) 2 WTLR 1).

The maxim *he who seeks equity must do equity* was applied again in *Re Berkeley Applegate Ltd* [1989] Ch 32. There Edward Nugee QC stated that:

> [t]he authorities establish, in my judgment, a general principle that where a person seeks to enforce a claim to an equitable interest in property, the court has a discretion to require as a condition of giving effect to that equitable interest that an allowance be made for costs incurred *and skill and labour expended* in connection with the administration of the property. (emphasis added)

The orthodox view is that the fiduciaries have all the obligations and their principals have all the rights, but modern applications of the maxim *he who seeks equity must do equity* represent a pragmatic shift away from this orthodox position. Decisions such as *O'Sullivan* and *Re Berkeley* suggest that equity will not recognise the principal's claim without ensuring that the fiduciary is also dealt with equitably, even if this does involve allowing him to profit from his trust. In *O'Sullivan* the claimant was seeking the exercise of equitable *discretion* in his favour. The maxim will not apply where a beneficiary of an orthodox trust is bringing a claim against their trustee on the basis of an equitable *entitlement*. However, in such cases the courts have attempted to achieve justice between the parties on another basis, that of 'unjust enrichment'. Thus, in *Foster v Spencer* [1996] 2 All ER 672, the judge made an award of remuneration to trustees for their past services to the trust. Refusal of the award, he said, would 'result in the beneficiaries being unjustly enriched at the expense of the trustees'. However, unless one assumes that the trustees had a pre-existing right to remuneration it is hard to see in what way the receipt of the trustees' services can constitute an enrichment of the beneficiaries, still less how it can be said to have been gained unjustly, and still less how it can be said to have been gained at the trustees' expense. On the contrary, if regarded as an incident of the beneficiaries' equitable entitlement, any 'windfall' there might have been must have been entirely 'just' enrichment. See *Foskett v McKeown* (see 18.3.3.5), where, albeit on very different facts, the House of Lords rejected a submission that a windfall received by beneficiaries had enriched them unjustly. In *Crown Dilmun v Sutton* [2004] 1 BCLC 468, ChD, Peter Smith J did not rule out the possibility that the fiduciary's liability to account may be reduced where it would otherwise unjustly enrich his principal, but noted that in this area 'the law favours conferring benefits on the wronged even though that is at the expense of the wrongdoer' and stressed that where the fiduciary has acted dishonestly there can be no question of reducing his liability to account.

In *Paul v Preston* (12 December 1996, unreported) Robert Walker J approved Walton J in *Re Duke of Norfolk*, who had doubted that remuneration should be awarded where the trustees' claim comes a long time after the date of their appointment. Robert Walker J distinguished *Foster v Spencer*, where the trustees (of a cricket club) had been awarded past remuneration a very long time after their appointment on the 'unusual facts' of that case (there were no funds against which to claim remuneration until the sale of the cricket field some time after the trustees' appointment).

It is important to note that a *quantum meruit* award will be restricted to those cases where it cannot have the effect of encouraging trustees or fiduciaries in any way to 'put themselves in a position where their interests conflict with their duties as trustees', *per* Lord Goff in *Guinness plc* v *Saunders* [1990] 2 AC 663, HL.

12.1.2.1 The causal connection

The inflexible rule is that a person in a fiduciary position is not entitled to make an unauthorised profit 'by virtue' of that position. There is no rule preventing a fiduciary from obtaining a profit by other means where there could be no possible conflict with the interests of the beneficiaries. In *Boardman* v *Phipps* [1967] 2 AC 46 (where a solicitor made a personal profit on shares in a private company by virtue of information gained in his fiduciary capacity), Lord Cohen stated that 'had the company been a public company and had the appellants bought the shares on the market, they would not, I think, have been accountable'. It was the fact that the profit had been made *by virtue of* the fiduciary office that gave rise to liability in *Boardman* v *Phipps*. *Boardman* v *Phipps* followed *Regal (Hastings) Ltd* v *Gulliver* [1967] 2 AC 134, where Viscount Sankey had reached a similar conclusion:

> In the result I am of the opinion that the directors standing in a fiduciary relationship to Regal in regard to the exercise of their powers as directors, and having obtained these shares *by reason and only by reason* of the fact that they were directors of Regal and in the course of the execution of that office, are accountable for the profits which they have made out of them.

The preceding *dicta* are hard to reconcile with the judgment of Morritt LJ in the Court of Appeal in *United Pan-Europe Communications NV* v *Deutsche Bank AG* [2000] 2 BCLC 461, where his Lordship said:

> If there is a fiduciary duty of loyalty and if the conduct complained of falls within the scope of that fiduciary duty . . . then I see no justification for any further requirement that the profit shall have been obtained by the fiduciary by virtue of his position.

The implication of this judgment is that a solicitor such as Mr Boardman should sometimes be disqualified from purchasing shares even if they are quoted on the public stock exchange, and that directors such as those in *Regal* should sometimes be accountable for profits made on shares even if they might have been acquired independently of their fiduciary position. (In *United Pan-Europe* itself, the defendant had received documents from the claimant in confidence and, on the basis of information contained within the documents, had proceeded to purchase shares in competition with the claimant.) However, Morritt LJ does not remove considerations of causation entirely. He still requires that the conduct complained of must 'fall within the scope of' the fiduciary duty. There must, in other words, be a basic factual connection between the particular gains and the defendant's lack of authority to retain such gains. His Lordship's point is that the duty to account should arise directly when profits are made in breach of fiduciary duty without any additional requirement to prove that such profits arise from a fiduciary position as such. Read in this way, his Lordship's *dictum* can be seen as an inevitable next step in the movement (started by Millett LJ in the *Mothew* case) towards describing remedies against fiduciaries in terms of the fiduciary's duty as opposed to the fiduciary's 'status' or 'relationship' or 'position'. Since a fiduciary duty can arise independently of any traditional category of fiduciary position (solicitor, agent, director, etc) it follows that there is no need to prove that an unauthorised profit was made by virtue of a fiduciary position in order to establish a fiduciary duty to account for it. In fact, the explanation for Morritt LJ's *dictum* may be even more straightforward than this. It is arguably nothing more than a restatement of the principle that the burden of proof in fiduciary transactions rests heavily upon the fiduciary. If this analysis of his Lordship's *dictum* is correct it is significant in at least two respects. First, it explains why the claimant is under no obligation to prove causation as an element of his cause of action. Secondly, it leaves open the possibility that the defendant will be able to raise the absence of basic factual causation as a *defence*.

An approach similar to that adopted in the *United Pan-Europe* case was adopted by the court in *Crown Dilmun* v *Sutton* [2004] 1 BCLC 468. The case concerned an action against a former employee of the claimant company. The claimant was successful in preventing the defendant from taking the benefit on his own account of a business opportunity which he had acquired in the course of his employment and had declined to pursue on the company's account. It was no defence for the defendant to show that he could have acquired the information independently of his fiduciary position. Peter Smith J held that '[w]hether or not the information is confidential, if the opportunity that arises by reason of the acquisition of the information puts the fiduciary in a position of conflict, he cannot take that opportunity' (para. 187). The disputed business opportunity in this case concerned the commercial development of Craven Cottage, the home ground of Fulham FC.

12.1.2.2 Is the rule against fiduciary profits too strict?

In *Keech* v *Sandford* (1726) Sel Cas Ch 61 a trustee had taken advantage of an opportunity to renew a lease in circumstances where the landlord had made it clear that he would not have permitted the beneficiary to enjoy the same privilege. The trustee's gain could in no way have been to the detriment of the trust, although it was gained by virtue of the trustee's fiduciary office. Lord King LC said: 'This may seem harsh that the trustee is the only person of all mankind who might not have the lease; but it is very proper that the rule should be strictly pursued, and not in the least relaxed.' In the Court of Appeal in *Wrexham Association Football Club Ltd* v *Crucialmove Ltd* [2006] EWCA Civ 237 Sir Peter Gibson confirmed that any relaxation of the strict equitable principle must be left to the House of Lords.

> **THINKING POINT**
>
> Should fiduciaries be held strictly to account in order to set an example to others?

Lord Upjohn attempted, but failed, to relax the rule in his dissenting speech in *Boardman* v *Phipps* [1967] 2 AC 46. He preferred to restrict the trustee's liability to cases where there was 'a real and sensible possibility of conflict'. Professor Peter Birks has objected that in cases like *Boardman* v *Phipps* the strict rule produces 'windfalls to rather sharp plaintiffs at the expense of honest and industrious defendants' (*Butterworth Lecture* 1990, p. 55 at 97).

Whatever the arguments may be in relation to fiduciaries like the solicitor in *Boardman* v *Phipps*, in the case of trustees of express trusts there are arguably good reasons for maintaining a strict presumption of gratuitous service. First, the settlor is always free to make express provision for remuneration in the trust instrument. Secondly, the trustee is always entitled to refuse to accept the terms of a trust if they do not provide for remuneration. Thirdly, if trustees were automatically entitled to remuneration out of the trust fund (which might involve them paying cheques to themselves), the opportunity for fraud would surely increase. Fourthly, even if there was no such obvious fraud, the risk that fee-paying work might be generated unnecessarily would surely increase. Fifthly, retaining gratuitous service in small family trusts might ensure the continued appointment of trustees who are close family members or friends, who might be expected to work more conscientiously on behalf of the trust than a 'hired hand'. It is arguable that insufficient weight was attached to considerations such as these when the Law Commission made the recommendations which now appear in Part V of the Trustee Act 2000.

Professor Gareth Jones once observed that 'there are cases where the innocent fiduciary must suffer, like Admiral Byng. Policy may demand a public sacrifice of the fiduciary's profit.' John Byng was an English Admiral sent in 1756 to relieve Minorca from the French. He failed and was unfairly court martialled for dereliction of duty. Having been found guilty he was executed on the quarterdeck of his own ship, leading the French satirist and philosopher Voltaire to suggest that in England it is deemed beneficial to kill an Admiral from time to time 'pour encourager les autres'.

 OUTSIDE THE BOX

Voltaire, *Candide*, Chapter 23 (*translated*)

As they were chatting together they arrived at Portsmouth. The shore on each side of the harbour was lined with a multitude of people, whose eyes were steadfastly fixed on a robust man who was kneeling down on the deck of one of the men-of-war, with his eyes bandaged. Opposite to this person stood four soldiers, each of whom shot three bullets into his skull, with all possible composure; and when it was done, the whole company went away perfectly well satisfied.

'What the devil is all this for?' said Candide, 'and what demon, or foe of mankind, lords it thus tyrannically over the world?' He then asked who was that robust man who had been sent out of the world so ceremonially. When he received for answer, that it was an admiral. 'And pray why do you put your admiral to death?'

'Because he did not put a sufficient number of his fellow creatures to death. You must know, he had an engagement with a French admiral, and it has been proved against him that he was not near enough to his antagonist.'

'But,' replied Candide, 'the French admiral must have been as far from him.'

'There is no doubt of that; but in this country it is deemed beneficial, now and then, to put an admiral to death, in order to encourage the others' *(dans ce pays-ci il est bon de tuer de temps en temps un amiral pour encourager les autres).*

12.1.3 Trustee remuneration under the trust instrument

A trust instrument can provide for remuneration directly (i.e. by way of a 'charging clause') or indirectly (e.g. by permitting the trustee to hold a remunerated post in a trust-owned company). Jenkins J in *Re Llewellin's WT* [1949] 1 Ch 225 allowed a clause in a trust instrument its 'ordinary construction' even though this meant that the trustees would be able to appoint themselves to be directors of a company whose shares they held on trust. As directors they would be empowered to award themselves remuneration at a level they themselves could fix. The result appears to be a very real conflict between the interests of the director-trustees and the beneficiaries and a breach of the rule that a trustee must not profit from their trust. However, it was held that on the 'ordinary construction' of the trust instrument such remuneration had obviously been authorised by the testator, and therefore the 'inflexible' rule had not been breached.

THINKING POINT

Consider the clause: 'I direct that my executor and trustee "EC" shall be the solicitor to my trust property and shall be allowed all professional and other charges for his time and trouble notwithstanding his being such executor and trustee.' Does this clause allow 'EC' to charge for business he could have carried out in his private capacity, as opposed to in his professional capacity, even though it was business a solicitor would have charged an ordinary client for?

In *Re Chalinder and Herrington* [1907] 1 ChD 58 it was held that, according to the strict construction of the clause, the trustee could not charge for this business. *Re Chalinder* illustrated how the courts construe remuneration clauses and other terms of trust instruments *contra proferentem*, that is, against the trustee who is seeking to rely on them. *Re Chalinder* has now been superseded by s 28(2) of the Trustee Act 2000. This section would allow EC to charge for the services outlined in the preceding clause, but on condition that the majority of the other trustees agree that he should be paid for such services. So-called charging clauses will be construed against the trustees, which is to say that the trustees, as the accounting party, have the onus of establishing the reasonableness of the remuneration charged. Having said that, a clause allowing professional trustees to charge for their services will authorise payment of such charges as are usual in that profession (be it accountant, lawyer, banker or so forth). In *Pullan* v *Wilson* [2014] EWHC 126 (Ch), senior solicitors were permitted to charge nearly £400 per hour.

Trustee Act 2000, s 28(2) confirms that where the trust instrument provides for the remuneration of a trust corporation, or a trustee acting in a professional capacity, the trustee will be entitled to that remuneration even when it is claimed in relation to services which a lay trustee could have provided. In the case of a charitable trust, this right only applies to a 'non-trust corporation' trustee if there are other trustees, and only then 'to the extent that a majority of the other trustees have agreed that it should apply to him' (s 28(3)).

12.1.4 Trustee remuneration under general law

Outside the context of professional trustee remuneration, the rule against unauthorised fiduciary profits remains strict. The Trustee Act 2000, s 29 provides that, apart from in the case of charitable trusts, and subject to contrary provision in the trust instrument, a trust corporation is entitled to receive reasonable remuneration out of the trust fund for services provided to the trust (s 29(1)), and a trustee acting in a professional capacity (e.g. a solicitor) is similarly entitled, provided that the trustee receiving the remuneration is not a sole trustee and provided also that every other trustee has agreed to the remuneration in writing (s 29(2)). It doesn't matter that a lay trustee would be capable of providing the services charged for (s 29(4)). 'Reasonable remuneration' means such remuneration as is reasonable in the circumstances for the provision of the services. Expressly included are reasonable banking charges levied by trustees who are authorised institutions (typically, banks) under the Banking Act 1987. For the purpose of Part V of the Act a trustee 'acts in a professional capacity' if he acts in the course of a profession or business that consists of or includes the provision of services connected with trust administration or management. A person 'acts as a lay trustee' if he is not a trust corporation and does not act in a professional capacity. However, the general right to remuneration provided by s 29 will not apply in every case. Section 29(5) excludes it in any case where there is express provision regarding remuneration in other legislation or in the trust instrument itself.

12.1.5 Award of trustee remuneration by the court under its inherent jurisdiction

Courts have an inherent jurisdiction to grant or to increase remuneration to trustees (whether corporate, professional or lay) if it is in the interests of the beneficiaries on the facts of a particular case (*Re Duke of Norfolk's ST* [1981] 3 All ER 220 (CA), *per* Fox LJ). Such an award is usually prospective, with a view to ensuring the sound administration of the trust. Remuneration can be awarded retrospectively (see the *'quantum meruit'* exception, discussed earlier), but the fate of the amateur trustee in *Brudenell-Bruce v Moore* [2014] EWHC 3679 (Ch) shows that retrospective remuneration is highly exceptional and the consequences for the trustee can be serious. In this case, the trustee mistakenly thought that he was entitled to fees he had taken from the fund to compensate him for his efforts on behalf of the trust, but the court refused to authorise those payments and ordered him to repay them as well as removing him from office.

> **THINKING POINT**
>
> Do you think that the court should have jurisdiction to award remuneration where the trust instrument does not award any?

Keith Hodkinson ((1982) 46 Conv 231) has written approvingly of the Court of Appeal's decision to make such an award in *Re Duke of Norfolk's ST*:

> One can . . . see with some force [the] view that as a matter of policy the court should not exercise its jurisdiction to bail out professional trustees who have made a bad bargain. But given that a trustee may retire and that there is no means of compelling him to continue in office, the fact must be faced that there will often be a stark choice between increasing remuneration of a skilled trustee familiar with the trust property and being forced to look for new trustees who may well not undertake the office without the inducement of higher fees.

12.1.6 Summative exercises

Reacquaint yourself with Part V of the Trustee Act 2000, which relates to remuneration. Then attempt to match the trustees described in the left column of Table 12.1 to the extent of their authority to receive remuneration as listed in the right column.

Having noted that the rule against fiduciary profits is still a strict one, we have nevertheless discovered a number of respects in which the so-called inflexible rule has been bent. Which of the following are genuine exceptions to the rule (place a tick against your choices)?

- where a trust instrument allows the trustees to appoint themselves to remunerated directorships of trust-owned companies;
- remuneration for trust corporations and professional trustees;
- trustees are permitted to make unauthorised profits where they openly and honestly declare the profit in advance of making it;
- where the trustee has produced a profit for the trust, the court may award a sum of money to the trustee in acknowledgement of the trustee's past service to the trust;
- under its inherent jurisdiction to safeguard the proper administration of the trust, the court may increase trustees' remuneration beyond that authorised by the trust instrument and authorise the future remuneration of trustees where there is no charging clause in the trust instrument.

Table 12.1 Trustee Act 2000 Part V

The trustee of a charitable trust (Trustee 1)	is entitled to such reasonable remuneration out of the trust funds for service as the trustee may determine provided he is engaged on terms entitling him to be remunerated for those services (Trustee Act 2000, s 32) (Choice A)
A solicitor acting in his professional capacity as the sole trustee of a non-charitable trust (Trustee 2)	subject to contrary expression in the trust instrument the trustee is to be treated as being entitled to receive reasonable payment in respect of services even if they are capable of being provided by a lay trustee (Trustee Act 2000, s 28) (Choice B)
A nominee of the trustees (Trustee 3)	Section 29(2) of the Trustee Act 2000 states that such a trustee is not entitled to remuneration, unless the trust instrument or the court provide to the contrary. The key word is 'sole' trustee in s 29(2)(b) (Choice C)
A 'non-professional' trustee who desires remuneration or improved remuneration in respect of the services they provide to the trust (Trustee 4)	such a trustee will only be entitled to remuneration if the trust instrument or the court so provide (Choice D)
In the trust instrument of a non-charitable trust there is a provision entitling the trustee (who is a trust corporation or otherwise acting in a professional capacity) to receive payment out of the trust funds (Trustee 5)	is entitled to such remuneration as the Secretary of State by regulation might provide (Trustee Act 2000, s 30(1)) (Choice E)

The solution to the Table 12.1 exercise is as follows: 1E; 2C; 3A; 4D; 5B. In the other exercise you should have ticked all the choices, apart from the middle one.

12.2 The duty of personal service

Trustees who take on themselves the management of property for the benefit of others have no right to shift their duty on other persons; and if they employ an agent, they remain subject to responsibility towards their *cestui que trust*, for whom they have undertaken the duty.

Turner v Corbey (1841) 5 Beav 515 at 517, *per* Lord Langdale MR

> **delegatus non potest delegare** This is the classic maxim which summarises the trustees' duty of personal service. It means 'the delegate has no power to delegate'.

The main advantage of a rule against delegation, particularly in more traditional family trusts, is that it goes some way towards ensuring personal proximity in the relationship between the original parties to the trust (settlor, trustee, beneficiary). This proximity facilitates mutual supervision and a sense of moral accountability. The sentiment of the rule may have its roots in the biblical observation that, unlike the good shepherd, the hired hand does not care for the sheep (John 10: 12–13).

The trustee's duty to provide personal service and not to delegate cannot be strictly applied in the modern world. In the seminal text *Farwell on Powers* (3rd edn, 1916) the learned authors asserted that, strictly speaking, the rule only ever prohibited the delegation of trustees' *fiduciary* powers, and does not prohibit the delegation by them of 'powers to do acts merely ministerial' (p. 498). In relation to the delegation of fiduciary powers and duties, the position was summarised by Viscount Radcliffe in the House of Lords in *Pilkington* v *IRC* [1964] AC 612: 'The law is not that a trustee cannot delegate: it is that trustees cannot delegate unless they have authority to do so.' In the following sections we shall be considering the sources and extent of trustees' authority to delegate. We shall also consider the standard of care which trustees must exercise in appointing and supervising their agents.

12.2.1 **Authority to delegate**

As in the case of remuneration, one must look first to the trust instrument. The trust instrument can enlarge upon the trustees' powers of delegation as authorised by the general law, but it can also restrict or exclude them (Trustee Act 2000, s 26(b)). Subject to what is said in the trust instrument, one should then turn to consider the trustees' authority to delegate as provided by the general law. Such authority is to be found in a number of statutes and statutory provisions. It should also be borne in mind that the court has the power, on an application under s 57 of the Trustee Act 1925, to vary the powers of delegation authorised by a particular trust (see 9.1.3).

12.2.1.1 **Statutory authority**

The major statutory provisions regarding the delegation of trustees' functions are now to be found in Part IV of the Trustee Act 2000 (ss 11–27).

According to Part IV of the Trustee Act 2000 a trustee function is delegable unless it appears in the list of *non-delegable* functions set out in s 11(2). In the case of charitable trusts, however, a trustee function is non-delegable unless it appears on the list of *delegable* functions set out in s 11(3). In Table 12.2 place a tick against the trustee functions according to whether they are delegable or not.

Table 12.2 Trustee Act 2000 s 11

	Delegable function	Non-delegable function
The appointment of a trustee to a non-charitable trust	☐	☐
The purchase of shares by a stockbroker on the trustees' instructions	☐	☐
Implementing an advertising campaign on behalf of a charity	☐	☐
Appointing persons to benefit from a discretionary trust	☐	☐
Deciding to pay tax out of trust capital	☐	☐
Appointing a person to appoint agents to assist with trust administration	☐	☐

Subject to any express provision to the contrary appearing in the trust instrument itself, only functions (b) and (c) are delegable. Section 11(2) provides that in the case of non-charitable trusts, all functions are delegable apart from the distribution of trust assets (e.g. under a discretionary trust), the choice between income or capital as the source of a payment (such as payment of tax due) and the appointment of a trustee, agent, nominee or custodian. Section 11(3) provides that in the case of a charitable trust, the only delegable functions are those which involve the carrying out (administration) of decisions the trustees have made—for example, investing trust assets and managing trust-owned land. Also, most forms of fundraising activity can be delegated, and any other function can be delegated if the Secretary of State makes an order authorising the delegation.

The Trustee Act 2000 repeals the Trustee Act 1925, s 23. Section 23(1) permitted trustees to appoint an agent 'to transact any business or do any act required to be transacted or done in the execution of the trust'. Section 25(1) of the 1925 Act, according to which a trustee was permitted to delegate by power of attorney 'for a period not exceeding twelve months the execution or exercise of all or any of the trusts, powers and discretions vested in him as trustee either alone or jointly with any other person or persons', has been replaced with a new s 25(1) (by s 5 of the Trustee Delegation Act 1999). The new s 25(1) introduces more procedural safeguards into this potentially very risky form of delegation. The safeguards include such things as giving notice to the other trustees that a trustee has appointed a person to act as his attorney, and requiring the actual appointment of the attorney to be made by means of a standard form. However, delegation under this section is not attractive, not least because trustees remain liable for the acts and defaults of their delegate as if they were the trustees' own acts and defaults (Trustee Delegation Act 1999, s 5(7), which reproduces the wording of, and repeals, Trustee Act 1925, s 25(5)).

12.2.1.2 Restrictions on the terms of an agency

Section 14 of the 2000 Act provides that trustees may authorise agents to act on such terms as they may determine, even in regard to remuneration. However, unless the trust instrument otherwise provides (see s 26(b)), there are certain terms which trustees are not permitted to include 'unless it is reasonably necessary for them to do so' (s 14(2)). The terms in question are those which would permit agents to appoint substitutes (s 14(3)(a)), restrict the agent's liability (s 14(3)(b)) or permit the agent to act in circumstances capable of giving rise to a conflict of interest (s 14(3)(c)). There is obviously good sense in restricting terms of this kind, but regrettably one suspects that trustees will not struggle to satisfy the requirement of 'reasonable necessity' with regard to their use. The spectre of well-paid sub-agents with limited liability in positions of conflict will send shivers down the spines of beneficiaries everywhere.

12.2.1.3 Special restrictions on the delegation of asset management

Trustees are not permitted to authorise an agent to exercise asset management functions except by an agreement evidenced in writing in which the agent agrees to comply with a 'policy statement' which the trustees are obliged to provide as a guide to the exercise of asset management functions in the best interests of the trust (s 15(1), Trustee Act 2000). The agent must agree to be bound by any revisions of the policy statement made under s 22 of the Act (s 15(2)(b)(ii)). The policy statement (and presumably any revisions of it) must be in writing or evidenced in writing (s 15(4)).

According to s 15(5), 'asset management functions' are those functions which relate to the investment of assets subject to the trust (s 15(5)(a)), the acquisition of property which is to be subject to the trust (s 15(5)(b)) and the management of property subject to the trust, including the creation or disposition of interests in such property (s 15(5)(c)).

12.2.2 Choice of agent

12.2.2.1 Trustees must choose prudently

In *Fry* v *Tapson* (1884) 28 ChD 268 Kay J said: 'I am most reluctant to visit trustees acting *bona fide* with the consequences of a want of due caution, but . . . they most incautiously employed the mortgagor's agent . . . although he was a London surveyor, and it was most important to obtain the opinion of some experienced local surveyor.' The principle laid down in this case is still good law, namely that a trustee (even an honest one) will be liable for losses caused to the fund by an agent who was appointed to perform a task outside that agent's field of expertise. According to s 23(1)(a) of the Trustee Act 2000, trustees may be liable if they fail to exercise the standard of care set out in s 1(1) of the Act when appointing agents, nominees and custodians.

12.2.2.2 Persons who may be appointed

Subject to what was said in 12.2.2.1, trustees may even appoint one or more of their own number to act as agents to the trust (Trustee Act 2000, s 12(1)) but no two (or more) agents may be appointed to exercise a function unless they are to exercise it jointly (s 12(2)). Beneficiaries may not be appointed to act as agents to the trust, even if they are also trustees (s 12(3)).

12.2.3 Supervision of agents

12.2.3.1 Trustees must supervise prudently

According to the Trustee Act 2000, s 23(1)(b), even where a trustee has validly appointed an agent, the trustee will still be subject to the standard of care as laid down in s 1(1) of the 2000 Act.

Consider *Re Lucking's WT* [1968] 1 WLR 866 where the claimant was one of the beneficiaries under a will trust. L, the son of the testatrix, was the sole trustee of the trust and a beneficiary under it. Part of the trust property was a majority holding in a private company. To secure the profitable running of the company, L appointed D to be a director. Over time, a practice was established whereby D sent blank cheques to L to be signed (two signatures were needed to authorise drawings on the company's account) to cover D's expenses. It became apparent to L that D was making withdrawals for his own ends but L took no action to prevent this, and continued to sign D's blank cheques. The company's gross profits had increased under D's management, but so had its overdraft. D's personal indebtedness to the company eventually reached such a level that he was dismissed from his directorship. He was declared bankrupt whilst still owing £15,890 to the company. It was held that L had failed adequately to supervise D's financial activities. He should have exercised the care of an ordinary prudent man of business. This would have meant ensuring that he had been represented on the board of the company. Having failed to do so he was liable to the other beneficiaries for the devaluation in the shares owned by the trust. Nowadays, L would be liable under s 23(1)(b) of the Trustee Act 2000.

Law Commission Report No 260, 'Trustees' Powers and Duties' (1999), recommended that trustees should, so long as delegation continues, keep under review the arrangements relating to it and the manner in which those arrangements are implemented (para. 4.10). This recommendation is enacted in ss 21–23 of the Trustee Act 2000. These sections also provide that trustees must, where appropriate, exercise any power of intervention they have to protect the trust (s 22(1)(c)).

Trustees must also keep under review any policy statement made for the purposes of s 15 of the Act (see 12.2.1.3) in relation to delegated asset management functions.

12.2.3.2 **Restrictions on the exercise of delegated functions**

Given that trustees must supervise their agents it makes sense that they should be aware of the restrictions to which the agents are subject in the exercise of the delegated functions. The trust instrument may impose certain restrictions, such as requiring that an agent must report to the trustees at given intervals. However, even if there are no restrictions apparent from the trust instrument, s 13 of the Trustee Act 2000 makes it clear that agents do not have a totally free hand with regard to the manner in which they exercise the functions delegated to them. That, however, is the only thing that is very clear about s 13. The section is set out in rather convoluted fashion, but the gist of it is that agents are subject to any restrictions specific to the particular function that they are carrying out. So, for example, if a person is authorised to *invest* on behalf of the trust, they are subject to statutory restrictions relating to *investment*, such as those appearing in s 4 of the 2000 Act (see Chapter 14).

Under s 11 of the 2000 Act a person authorised 'to exercise any function relating to land subject to the trust' is not required to consult competent adult beneficiaries and give effect to their wishes. Other delegates exercising functions relating to trusts of land *are* so required (unless the general interests of the trust suggest otherwise—s 11(1) of the Trusts of Land and Appointment of Trustees Act 1996), and the trustees may not authorise such delegates to carry out their delegated functions on terms which would prevent them from complying with that duty.

12.2.4 **Appointment of nominees and custodians**

Sections 16–20 of the 2000 Act relate to the appointment of nominees and custodians to trusts other than trusts already having custodian trustees (the latter include charitable trusts where the assets are vested in the official custodian for charities). A nominee is a person in whose name trust assets are vested. A custodian is a person who 'undertakes the safe custody of the assets or of any documents or records concerning the assets' (s 17(2)).

According to s 16, the appointment of a nominee must be in writing or evidenced in writing and may relate to such assets as the trustees may determine. The section authorises trustees to take such steps as are necessary to vest the relevant assets in the nominee. Likewise, the appointment of a custodian must be in writing or evidenced in writing (s 17).

Unless the trust instrument (or legislation) provides to the contrary, the appointment of a custodian is a *requirement* whenever the trust holds 'bearer securities' (securities payable to the bearer) (s 18).

A person cannot be appointed to act as nominee or custodian unless one of the following conditions is satisfied. They are: (a) the person's business includes acting as a nominee or custodian, (b) the person is a body corporate controlled by the trustees (to be determined in accordance with s 840 of the Income and Corporation Taxes Act 1988) or (c) the person is a body corporate recognised under s 9 of the Administration of Justice Act 1985 (Trustee Act 2000, s 19).

Subject to this, trustees may appoint one of their number to act as a nominee or custodian, or two (or more) of their number to act jointly in that capacity, and may appoint the same person(s) to be nominee(s), custodian(s) and agent(s). However, nominees and custodians are subject to the same restrictions as those we considered at 12.2.1.2 in relation to agents (Trustee Act 2000, s 20). Sections 21–23, concerning the supervision, review and intervention of agents (see 12.2.3.1), also apply to nominees and custodians.

Section 23 is most significant because it provides that a trustee will not be liable for the defaults of any agent, nominee or custodian unless he failed to meet the requisite standard of care (see 11.3) in appointing the delegate or supervising the delegate as required by s 22. Similarly, the trustee is not liable for the defaults of any person acting as substitute for an agent, nominee or custodian unless the trustee failed to meet the requisite standard of care (see 11.3) in giving the agent, nominee or custodian the power to appoint a substitute, or in supervising the performance of the agent, nominee or custodian in relation to the substitute.

12.2.5 Summative exercise

The exercise in Table 12.3 is intended to test a number of aspects of the law relating to the delegation of trustees' functions. Assume in each of the situations described that the trust instrument makes no reference to the trustees' powers of delegation, so that the general law applies. Against each of the following transactions place a cross if the trustees have breached their trust and a tick if there has been a valid delegation:

Table 12.3 Delegation—summative exercise

(a) A two-thirds majority of the trustees of a small charitable trust appointed Mr Brownfield, an expert valuer, to carry out the conveyance of trust-owned land to another charity	☐
(b) The trustees placed trust-owned land in the name of a nominee with a view to sale, but with the direction that the nominee must not consult any of the beneficiaries of the trust at any time. The beneficiaries are all adult and competent	☐
(c) The trustees appointed an expert tax solicitor to choose whether a payment to the Inland Revenue of tax due from the trust should be made out of trust income or capital	☐
(d) The trustees appointed a leading firm of solicitors to evict squatters from trust-owned land, but having paid sums on account to cover the solicitors' fees, the trustees took no further steps to ensure that the squatters had been evicted. In the event the squatters completed 12 years of adverse possession and have now been registered as proprietors of the fee simple estate	☐
(e) The trustees of a charitable trust appoint a stockbroker to decide upon an ethical investment policy that would be both financially profitable and in accordance with the charities' aims	☐

Did you realise that the trustees breached their trust in every case? In (a) it was because, even if the two-thirds majority were entitled to pass a resolution to sell the land, the agent was not qualified to discharge that delegated function, and an estate agent or solicitor should have been appointed (see 12.2.2.1). In (b) it was because, apart from a person authorised (under s 11 of the 2000 Act) 'to exercise any function relating to land subject to the trust', delegates are required to consult competent adult beneficiaries and give effect to their wishes and the trustees may not authorise such delegates to carry out their delegated functions on terms which would prevent them from complying with that duty. In (c) it was because this was a non-delegable function. A solicitor can be appointed to advise on such a matter, but not to make the choice (see s 11(2), Trustee Act 2000). In (d) it was because the trustees must exercise prudence, not only in relation to the appointment of the trustees, but also in relation to their supervision (see 12.2.3). In (e) it was because this was a non-delegable function. A stockbroker can be appointed to advise on such a matter, but not to decide upon the investment policy (see s 11(3), Trustee Act 2000).

12.3 Miscellaneous duties

We have focused on the duty to act gratuitously and the duty to provide personal service, and the correlating rules that trustees may not profit from their trust and must not delegate their trust. This section briefly considers some of the other duties to which trustees are subject in the execution of their office.

12.3.1 The duty to act impartially

Where a trust instrument gives a trustee the power to choose between persons with competing claims on the fund (e.g. in a discretionary trust: see 4.4.2) that dispositive discretion will almost inevitably mean that, in the appointment of beneficiaries, some persons will be preferred to others, and as between beneficiaries some will get more than others (see 2.2.3). However, even in such a case, the trustee must not be swayed by a subjective personal preference for one beneficiary or class of beneficiaries. Similarly, in a traditional settlement trust (e.g. to A for life, to B in remainder), where A and B have *competing* claims to the fund (the traditional view is that A wants more income and B wants more capital, but see 14.1.1 and 14.1.3.2), the trustee's duty is to consider fairly their competing claims and to exercise its administrative investment discretion even-handedly. Fairness, however, need not import 'equality' (*per* Hoffmann J in *Nestle* v *National Westminster Bank plc* (1996) 10 TLI 112 at 115).

 THINKING POINT

Suppose that Terry has just been appointed trustee of the residue of a will trust under which Libby is the life beneficiary and Ronnie the remainderman. Upon his appointment Terry discovers that the whole of the fund is invested in crates of fine pink champagne. Is there a potential breach of the duty to act impartially?

The crates of champagne are wasting assets—their value decreases the more the champagne is consumed—with the possibility that the investment may be worthless before Ronnie's interest vests in possession. In contrast, Libby, during her life, would have been in receipt of the benefits of the consumption of the champagne.

In such a case the trustee may be obliged to sell the champagne and re-invest in property which will more fairly meet the beneficiaries' respective claims (*Howe* v *Earl of Dartmouth* (1802) 7 Ves 137—note that the rule in this case applies only to residuary estates of personalty). However, as a result of the Trusts (Capital and Income) Act 2013 this apportionment rule and others like it are no longer law as regards trusts coming into effect after 31 January 2013. The other reform of interest to students of trusts law is the proposal to make total-return investment more easily accessible to charitable trusts with a permanent endowment. This means that charities will not be required to keep all their investments tied up in capital whilst making distributions out of income, but, within a framework determined by the Charity Commission, will be permitted to invest with a view to producing 'total returns' (that is, returns that make no rigid distinction between capital and income).

Trustees' expenses, like trust investments, must be apportioned appropriately, but here the general rule (unchanged by the 2013 Act) is that expenses incurred for the benefit of both the income and capital beneficiaries should be charged against capital. It is only expenses incurred exclusively for the benefit of the income beneficiaries that may be charged against income (*Commissioners for HM Revenue & Customs* v *Trustees of the Peter Clay Discretionary Trust* [2008] EWCA Civ 1441).

12.3.2 The duty to keep accounts and to give information

Trustees have a duty to keep a diary-like record of the administration of the trust for production to new trustees (*Tiger* v *Barclays Bank Ltd* [1951] 2 KB 556, CA).

> ⟫ CROSS REFERENCE
>
> On the law governing disclosure of trust documentation, see *Schmidt* v *Rosewood Trust* [2003] 2 AC 709, Privy Council, and 11.4.2.1.

⟳ Summary

This chapter concluded with consideration of the trustees' duty to act impartially and to account to the beneficiaries for the state of the trust fund, but the greater part of this chapter has been concerned with two other trust duties: the duties of 'gratuitous' and 'personal' service, or in other words, the rule which prohibits trustees from taking unauthorised profits or payment from the trust fund and the rule that a trustee must not delegate their functions unless authorised to do so. We have seen that the relevant 'authority' to depart from these rules can come from the trust instrument or in some circumstances from the general law. So, for example, the general law (since the Trustee Act 2000) now authorises professional trustees to take reasonable payment from the trust and the Trustee Act has also liberalised the rules on trustee delegation so as to allow more matters to be delegated to nominees and custodians. The reforms may not have a significant impact in cases where trust deeds are drawn up by professionals, but when it proposed the reforms the Law Commission envisaged that they would have an impact where trusts arise in 'home-made' wills. Trusts arising in this way will sometimes include no remuneration clause in favour of the trustees, and are unlikely to permit delegation of investment decisions and the appointment of nominees and custodians, and will almost certainly fail to allow investment in the full range of modern financial products (on investment, see Chapter 14).

? Summative assessment exercise

Trudy has been appointed trustee. The trust deed contains the following clause:

The trustees shall be entitled to all professional charges incurred in the execution of the trust and shall be entitled to delegate all or any of their duties in accordance with the general law.

Trudy has accepted the trust, even though she is a total amateur and rather ignorant of business affairs. She purchases a large quantity of office equipment and stationery to facilitate the smooth running of her tasks but still finds that the job is too complicated. After putting in several months of work in service of the trust she eventually enlists the assistance of a friend who, having run his own betting office for many years, is more at ease with commercial matters. She transfers the trust fund into the friend's bank account with the instruction that he should invest it wisely for the benefit of the trust. In fact the friend 'invests' the money on Lucky Laddie, the favourite to win a greyhound race. Lucky Laddie loses the race and the trust fund is lost.

Is Trudy liable for breach of her trust, and why? If she is liable, will she be required to reinstate the full value of the fund, or can she claim remuneration and or expenses?

 Full specimen answers can be found at www.oxfordtextbooks.co.uk/orc/watt_directions5e/.

 ## The bigger picture

Fiduciary law is intensely practical and significant in a wide range of contemporary commercial contexts, but it depends upon deep and perennial philosophical assumptions that have far-reaching implications beyond the immediate context of the cases in which fiduciary principles are applied. A.S. Gold and P.B. Miller have gathered together a collection of essays on some of these broader perspectives on fiduciary law (see *Philosophical Foundations of Fiduciary Law* (Oxford: Oxford University Press, 2014)). Even if your library doesn't have a copy you might find it stimulating to think around some of the titles in the collection, for example 'Fiduciary Loyalty as Kantian Virtue' (by Irit Samet), 'Is Loyalty a Virtue, and Even if It Is, Does It Really Help Explain Fiduciary Liability?' (by James E. Penner) and 'Can We Be Obliged to Be Selfless?' (by Lionel D. Smith).

 ## Further reading

Birks, P. 'The Content of Fiduciary Obligation' (2002) 16(1) Tru LI 34
considers the implications for trustees of trends extending fiduciary duties to the law of torts and the role of morality and levels of obligatory altruism

Conaglen, M. 'The Nature and Function of Fiduciary Loyalty' (2005) 121 LQR 452
argues that the function of fiduciary duties is to ensure the proper performance of non-fiduciary duties

Griffiths, G.Ll.H. 'Antipodean Revelations? The Beneficiary's Right to Information after *Rosewood*' [2005] Conv 93
examines a New Zealand High Court ruling on the extent of the trustee's duty to disclose information about the trust to the beneficiaries

Jones, G.H. 'Delegation by Trustees: A Reappraisal' (1959) 22 MLR 388
argues that the provisions in the Trustee Act 1925 relating to delegation should be reappraised in the light of the law existing prior to that statute. The detail is somewhat out of date, but the methodology is informative

Langbein, J.H. 'Questioning the Trust Law Duty of Loyalty: Sole Interest or Best Interest?' (2005) 114 Yale LJ 929, 987–90
argues that the sole interest rule, which currently requires no conflict of interest between trustee and trust, should be reformulated to emphasise that the beneficiary's best interests are paramount

Reynolds, F.M.B. 'Solicitors and Conflicts of Duties' (1991) 107 LQR 536
considers how fiduciary conflict rules apply in the particular context of solicitors' practice

Simpson, E. 'Conflicts in Breach of Trust' in P. Birks and A. Pretto (eds), *Breach of Trust* (2002) Oxford: Hart Publishing 75–94
a lucid scholarly overview of fiduciary conflicts of interest as it applies to trustees

 For links to selected cases, statutes, academic papers and official reports mentioned in this chapter please visit the online resources at www.oup.com/uk/watt_directions6e/.

13 Maintenance and advancement

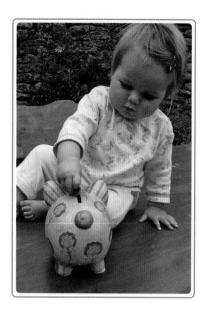

LEARNING OBJECTIVES

By the end of this chapter you should be able to:

- advise a settlor as to the extent of the statutory powers of maintenance and advancement;

- advise a settlor how to exclude or modify the statutory powers by the express terms of the settlement;

- identify a valid exercise of the powers of maintenance and advancement.

Introduction

Take a typical trust, 'To A for life, to B in remainder'. The settlor has expressed an intention as regards the extent of the beneficial entitlements under the trust. The two beneficiaries are to have vested interests. A will have an interest vested in possession now and B's entitlement will be vested 'in interest' until A's death, when it will vest in possession.

But does the settlor's intention end there? Suppose that A is an infant so not yet absolutely entitled to the income of the trust, and is currently in urgent need of financial assistance. Or suppose that B desperately requires capital during A's lifetime. Surely it is natural to presume that the settlor's general motivation for setting up the trust in the first place will extend to providing for the beneficiaries in these circumstances.

It has long been the practice to insert clauses in trusts to deal with the situations outlined and Parliament confirmed this practice in the Trustee Act 1925. The Act implies into every trust a power in the hands of the trustees to make payments out of the trust income for the maintenance of infant beneficiaries (s 31) and a power to make payments out of trust capital for the advancement and benefit of infant and adult beneficiaries (s 32). However, these provisions can be excluded or modified by the express terms of the trust instrument.

13.1 Maintenance

> **OUTSIDE THE BOX**
>
> **Jane Austen, *Emma*, 1815**
>
> She proved to be the daughter of a tradesman, rich enough to afford her the comfortable maintenance which had ever been hers.

Section 31 of the Trustee Act 1925 provides that trustees may 'at their sole discretion' apply the whole or any part of the income of the trust property for 'the **maintenance**, education or benefit' of an infant beneficiary. (An 'infant' is any person under the age of 18—Family Law Reform Act 1969, s 1.)

> **maintenance** A statutory power granted to trustees (which may be altered, enlarged or removed by the trust instrument) under which the trustee can apply trust income for the benefit of infant beneficiaries of the trust.

The power is crucial because unmarried infant beneficiaries, unlike married or adult beneficiaries, cannot give a valid receipt for income (Law of Property Act 1925, s 21). This means that, even where the infant's interest has vested 'in possession', the trustees cannot safely pay income to the infant. If they do so, the beneficiary could demand the money *again* upon attaining majority.

THINKING POINT

Read s 31(1) of the Trustee Act 1925, set out next. Although the power is exercised in the trustees' 'sole discretion', there are numerous factors which the trustee must take into account. Underline those factors as they appear in the following extract, before moving on.

STATUTE

Trustee Act 1925, s 31

As amended (in relation to trusts coming into effect on or after 1 October 2014) by the Inheritance and Trustees' Powers Act 2014, s 8.

(1) Where any property is held by trustees in trust for any person . . . then, subject to any prior interests or charges affecting the property—

   (i) during the infancy of any such person, if his interest so long continues, the trustees may, at their sole discretion, pay to his parent or guardian, if any, or otherwise apply for or towards his maintenance, education or benefit, the whole or such part, if any, of the income of that property as the trustees may think fit. **[Note that prior to the 2014 reform, payments had to be reasonable in all the circumstances.]**

   (ii) if such person on attaining the age of eighteen years has not a vested interest in such income, the trustees shall thenceforth pay the income of that property and of any accretion thereto under subsection (2) of this section to him, until he either attains a vested interest therein or dies, or until failure of his interest.

Did you identify the following points?

- the trustees' power to maintain is subject to the rights of persons with prior interests. So, if the trust provides for A for life and for B in remainder, the income should not be applied to maintain B because A is absolutely entitled to all the income on the fund;

- when income is applied to maintain an infant beneficiary the income should not actually be paid to the infant. Payment should be made to the infant's parent or guardian or paid directly to address the particular financial need. So, for example, if the payment of income is intended to pay for the infant's school fees, the trustees should make the payment to the child's guardian or to the school direct;

- in relation to trust interests created or arising before 1 October 2014 (i.e. before the Inheritance and Trustees' Powers Act 2014 came into force), trustees who have notice that more than one fund is available to meet the infant's particular financial need should maintain the beneficiary from the trust income in proportion to contributions from other sources where practicable.

13.1.1 Gifts carrying intermediate income

Section 31(3) states that the power of maintenance contained in s 31(1) will not apply to every interest under a trust:

This section applies in the case of a contingent interest only if the limitation or trust carries the **intermediate income** of the property, but it applies to a future or contingent legacy by the parent of, or a person standing *in loco parentis* to, the legatee.

We shall consider contingent legacies later (13.1.1.2). First we shall scrutinise other forms of gift to discover which carry the **intermediate income**.

> **intermediate income** Income arising from a gift, including a trust, during the period between the effective date of the trust (e.g. the date of the testator's death, in the case of a trust made by will) and the date that the beneficiary's interest vests in possession.

13.1.1.1 Testamentary gifts

The Law of Property Act 1925, s 175 applies to **devises** and **bequests** in post-1925 wills.

> **bequest** A gift of personalty made by will. Personalty means personal property, so the term includes all forms of property apart from land. The one exception is leases, which for historical reasons are treated as personalty.

> **devise**
> A gift or trust of realty made by will. Realty means real property, so the term would include land apart from leases.

 STATUTE

Law of Property Act 1925, s 175

Contingent and future testamentary gifts to carry the intermediate income

(1) A contingent or future specific devise or bequest of property, whether real or personal, and a contingent residuary devise of freehold land, and a specific or re-siduary devise of freehold land to trustees upon trust for persons whose interests are contingent or executory shall, subject to the statutory provisions relating to accumu-lations, carry the intermediate income of that property from the death of the testa-tor, except so far as such income, or any part thereof, may be otherwise expressly disposed of.

(2) This section applies only to wills coming into operation after the commencement of this Act.

The section does not cover legacies, which are gifts of cash made by will. Devises, bequests and legacies may be specific or residual. If T leaves Blackacre (freehold property) to S and the rest of his realty to R, S is said to have a specific devise and R is said to have been given a residuary devise. Do not forget that leases are classed as personalty, even though they are interests in land!

Finally, it is worth being reminded of the distinction between a contingent and a deferred (or 'future' gift). A contingent gift is one which might never take effect, for example, 'To A when she qualifies as a doctor'. A deferred gift is one which will take effect at some time in the future; the gift is vested 'in interest' now, but actual beneficial enjoyment of the property (the vesting 'in possession') is deferred, for example, 'To A when X dies'. X will certainly die at some point and A will take the gift 'in possession' at that date. If A has already died by the date that A's interest vests in possession, A's beneficial interest will pass to those entitled under A's will or, if there is no will, to those entitled under the intestacy rules.

With these definitions in mind you should be able to carry out the exercise set out at Table 13.1.

Table 13.1 Intermediate income on testamentary gifts

Testamentary gift	Tick if the gift carries the intermediate income
'£1,000 to B, Whiteacre (leasehold) to A at 25, residue to C' (Gift A)	
'Greenacre (freehold) to A on 1 January 2000' (Gift B)	
'Greenacre (freehold) to B, the rest of my freehold property to A upon his attaining 21 or graduating from university, whichever is the earlier' (Gift C)	

The answers are as follows:

- (Gift A) This is a contingent specific bequest of personalty. It does carry the intermediate income, as would a contingent specific devise of realty.
- (Gift B) This is a deferred ('future') specific devise of realty. It carries the intermediate income. A deferred ('future') specific bequest of personalty also carries the intermediate income.
- (Gift C) This is a contingent residuary devise of freehold land. It also carries the intermediate income.
- The wording of s 175 omits several types of gift. One important omission is the 'pecuniary legacy', which is dealt with in 13.1.1.3. Certain other gifts not included in s 175 are considered in the next section.

13.1.1.2 Some gifts not included in s 175

Immediate vested gifts

An example of an immediate vested gift *to A* would be a clause in a will or an *inter vivos* settlement stating: 'I instruct my trustees to hold everything I own for the benefit of A and B in equal shares absolutely.' As has already been indicated, 'immediate' vested gifts of any property, whether made by will or *inter vivos*, will carry the income arising on the property unless there is a contrary intention in the trust instrument.

Inter vivos contingent gift

An example of an *inter vivos* contingent gift would be a settlement on trustees, effective during the lifetime of the settlor, under which the beneficiary would be entitled to the trust fund upon graduating from law school. Section 175 only applies to *testamentary* dispositions. Generally, *inter vivos* contingent gifts will carry the intermediate income.

Contingent residuary bequests of personalty

Such gifts carry the intermediate income not otherwise disposed of. *Re Adams* [1893] 1 Ch 329 concerned a bequest of residue to such of a class of children who shall attain 21 or, being daughters, marry. North J asked 'How does the matter stand as to the income?' and concluded 'I think it is fallacious to say that they take an interest in the income, *qua* income of the capital they have an interest in. But it is undisposed of income, and as such becomes part of the residue . . . the income belongs contingently to the children, in the same way as the capital belongs contingently to them.' In other words, undisposed income results to the residue of the testator's estate, so contingent residual bequests carry the intermediate income by default!

Deferred residuary bequests of personalty

According to Jenkins J in *Re Oliver* [1947] 2 All ER 162, the general rule is that 'a gift expressly limited to take effect on a future date does not carry the intermediate income'. Deferred residuary bequests follow this general rule and do not carry the intermediate income. An example of such a gift *to A* would be the following clause in a will: 'I leave my car to B and the residue of my personal estate to A on B's death or on 1 January 2010, whichever is the later.'

Deferred residuary devises

In *Re McGeorge* [1963] Ch 544 Cross J accepted the general rule that an expressly deferred gift will not carry the intermediate income, and interpreted s 175 of the Law of Property Act 1925 as providing that because the income had not been otherwise disposed of, the devise would carry the intermediate income. Whether or not that was a correct construction of the section, he went on to hold that the mere fact that the gift technically carried the intermediate income would not lead him to hold that the beneficiary should be maintained out of that income. He held that to maintain the infant would defeat the testator's intention, for to do so would establish her as the only beneficiary entitled to the income, effectively granting her an interest in possession in the income on the devise during the lifetime of the testator's wife. To permit the interest in the income from the land to vest in possession now would be inconsistent with the testator's expressed intention to defer the vesting in possession of the interest in the land itself.

Deferred contingent bequests of residuary personalty

An example of such a gift, *to A*, would be a gift of 'My Rolls-Royce to B and the rest of my personalty to A'. In *Re Geering* [1964] 3 All ER 1043 it was held that a deferred contingent residuary bequest does not carry the intermediate income. In this case, as in *Re McGeorge* [1963] Ch 544, Cross J drew a clear distinction between contingent gifts which are immediate and contingent gifts which are deferred: 'The very fact that a testator defers a gift of residue to a future date is itself *prima facie* an indication that he does not intend the legatee to have the income of residue accruing before that date.'

Deferred contingent devises of residuary realty

An example of such a gift, *to A*, would be a gift of Greenacre (freehold) to B, with a gift of the rest of the testator's realty to A on 1 January 2000 upon condition that A had married by that date. If A marries he will be entitled to the residuary realty, but will have to wait until the year 2000 for the gift to vest in possession. Due to the omission of this category of gift from the wording of s 175 it is debatable whether it will or will not carry the intermediate income. No case has been decided on the point. There are, however, good reasons to suppose that it will not.

First, one of the prime aims of the 1925 legislation, and of the Law of Property Act in particular, was to assimilate as far as possible the legal treatment of real property to the legal treatment of personal property, in order to make land easier to sell. Section 175 was drafted with this very aim in mind (according to Cross J in *Re McGeorge* [1963] Ch 544). As there is authority to show that deferred contingent gifts of residuary personalty do not carry the intermediate income (*Re Geering*) it would surely be inconsistent to permit deferred contingent gifts of residuary realty to carry the intermediate income.

Secondly, it is quite clear from the wording of s 175 that vested deferred devises of residuary realty do not carry the intermediate income and this has been confirmed in numerous cases since (see, for example, *Re McGeorge*). If vested forms of the gift do not carry the intermediate income there can be no sensible reason for supposing that contingent forms of the gifts will, or should.

Contingent pecuniary legacies

This important class of gifts is dealt with in the next section.

13.1.1.3 Contingent pecuniary legacy

The general rule, established not long after s 175 came into being, is that such a gift will not carry the intermediate income (*Re Raine* [1929] 1 Ch 716). This was because s 175 refers only to 'bequests' and 'devises'. However, there are exceptions to the general rule (see B.S. Ker, 'Trustees' Powers of Maintenance' (1953) 17 Conv 273).

The main exceptions are as follows:

- a contingent (or, indeed, a deferred) pecuniary legacy will carry the intermediate income if the testator was the parent of, or was a person standing *in loco parentis* to, the legatee (see s 31(3)). This exception is based on the presumed intention of the testator and can be rebutted by evidence that the testator has provided another fund out of which the infant is to be maintained. It is sometimes suggested that this exception will not apply if the contingency attached to the pecuniary legacy is the attaining of an age greater than the age of majority (now 18). The reasoning goes, once again, to the presumed intention of the testator: the testator, in choosing the higher contingency age, clearly did not intend his gift to meet the beneficiary's needs as an infant. The courts will not presume that the testator intended the contingent pecuniary legacy to carry the intermediate income for the purpose of maintaining the infant beneficiary;

- even where the testator was not a parent or person *in loco parentis* the contingent pecuniary legacy will carry the intermediate income if the testator has shown an intention to maintain the beneficiary. For instance, in *Re Churchill* [1909] 2 Ch 431 the testatrix empowered her trustees to apply 'the share to which any beneficiary . . . may be contingently entitled in or towards the advancement in life or otherwise for the benefit of such beneficiary'. This clause was construed as authorising maintenance of an infant beneficiary (the beneficiary was entitled to a pecuniary legacy upon his attaining 21);

- finally, the case of *Re Medlock* (1886) 54 LT 828 is authority for another exception to the general rule. In this case it was held that a contingent pecuniary legacy would carry the intermediate income if the testator had separated the legacy from the rest of his estate. In *Re Medlock* the legacy was held by trustees on separate trusts.

13.1.1.4 Conceptual rationale

THINKING POINT

Can you suggest a possible conceptual rationale which could give principled justification for the distinctions which are drawn in the statutes and cases between gifts which carry the intermediate income and gifts which do not?

The underlying rationale, which we keep coming back to, is the presumed intention of the person who made the gift. The only contingent gift which does not automatically carry the intermediate income is the pecuniary legacy; it is an exception that is hard to justify. Easier to rationalise is the general rule that deferred gifts do not carry intermediate income. A deferred gift, unlike a contingent gift, has been deliberately put back in time. The only deferred gift that does carry the intermediate income is a gift of a specific item of property.

13.1.1.5 Summative chart

The law governing the carrying of intermediate income is summarised in Figure 13.1.

Figure 13.1 Does the gift carry the 'intermediate income'?

Note: All 'yes' answers are subject to express contrary intention apparent from the terms of the trust (s. 69(2), LPA 1925).

13.1.2 During infancy

The trustees do not have a *duty* to maintain if the gift carries the intermediate income: they have a *power* to do so. Accordingly, it may be that in certain cases the intermediate income is not applied to maintain the beneficiary, perhaps because the beneficiary has no financial needs, or because those needs are being fully met from other sources (e.g. parents).

What happens to the unapplied income in these circumstances? According to s 31(2) of the Trustee Act 1925 this 'residue' of the income should be accumulated annually by investing it. These accumulations may be applied in future years to maintain the infant beneficiary.

If a beneficiary dies during infancy the accumulations on that beneficiary's share are added to the capital of the trust as a whole, and not just to that beneficiary's share. The accumulations will not, therefore, devolve on the estate of the deceased infant. This is so even though the infant had a vested interest in the income during their life (*Re Delamere's ST* [1984] 1 WLR 813).

13.1.3 Attaining majority

When the infant beneficiary attains majority (reaches the age of 18), or marries under that age, the trustees must add the accumulations to the main capital from which the accumulated income arose. There are two exceptions to this rule. When either of those exceptions applies the trustees will not add the accumulations to the main capital, but will hold them on trust for the beneficiary absolutely, so that the accumulations may be paid to the beneficiary and the beneficiary's receipt will discharge the trustee.

The exceptions are to be found in s 31(2) of the Trustee Act 1925. The first covers cases where the beneficiary already had a vested interest in the income *before* they attained majority (or earlier marriage or civil partnership). The second exception is where the beneficiary's contingent interest in the income vests *at the date* that they attain majority (or earlier marriage or civil partnership). The latter exception operates where the beneficiary 'becomes entitled to the property from which such income arose in fee simple, absolute or determinable, or absolutely, or for an entailed interest' (s 31(2)(i)(b)).

> **THINKING POINT**
>
> Benny has just reached the age of 18. According to the terms of a late friend's will, he will be entitled to 'Whiteacre' (freehold) upon his attaining the age of 21. He was not maintained from the income during his infancy. Is Benny entitled to the accumulations now?

No, he is not. Benny does not fall within either of the exceptions, so the accumulations will be added to his capital entitlement to 'Whiteacre'. He will be able to claim the capital and the accumulations when he reaches the age of 21.

What if Benny needs (or wants) financial assistance now that he is 18? He cannot be maintained because he is not an infant (unless there is an express provision for maintenance of adult beneficiaries in the will the court will not maintain adult beneficiaries under its inherent jurisdiction) and the trustees are unable to pay him the accumulations made during his infancy. Is Benny entitled to anything now? Section 31(1)(ii) of the Trustee Act 1925 reflects what would probably have been the testator's intention for such a situation. It provides that beneficiaries in Benny's position will be absolutely entitled *now* to the income which is currently being earned on the combined fund of capital and accumulations.

13.1.4 **Class gifts**

If there is a gift to a class contingent upon its members attaining the age of 21, or some other age, the class will close provisionally (for the purpose of maintenance) when the first person attains that age (the class will include all members living at the date the class closed). The trustees may then maintain that beneficiary out of the income attributable to their notional share. If a new beneficiary is born later the class is re-closed, again on a provisional basis, and a fresh allocation of notional shares made. This re-allocation occurs every time a member of the class attains the contingent age or a new member is born.

13.1.5 **Tax considerations**

During the minority of a beneficiary to whom the power of maintenance applies the trust is charged income tax on all income. If the beneficiary receives the accumulations upon attaining majority the accumulations will be treated as capital and therefore inheritance tax will be charged on all capital above a fixed-value threshold (currently £300,000). If the beneficiary is not entitled to the accumulations upon attaining majority they will be entitled to the income under s 31(1)(ii) and they will have to pay income tax on it. The level at which the beneficiary will pay income tax depends upon the level of their total income from this and other sources.

These fiscal considerations will influence the exercise of a trustee's discretion whether or not to maintain the infant beneficiary.

13.1.6 **Perpetuities**

 THINKING POINT

Look back to the rule against excessive accumulations (see 6.3) and attempt the following question.

Tina left certain shares to Belinda in her will, and directed that dividends on the shares should be accumulated until Belinda reached the age of 25. At the date of Tina's death Belinda was aged five. Is the gift void for excessive accumulation? Would the answer be any different if Belinda had been two at the date of Tina's death?

If Belinda was five, the answer is that the gift is not void for perpetuity; this is because the ac-cumulation will come to an end within 21 years of the testator's death. If Belinda was two, the result would be different. The direction to accumulate would infringe the rule against excessive accumulations. Having said that, the gift as a whole will not be void for perpetuity. Only the accumulations made beyond the authorised period will be disallowed. The whole gift would only be void for perpetuity if the direction to accumulate might extend the period of accumula-tion beyond the common law 'perpetuity period'.

13.2 Advancement

Trustee Act 1925, s 32 provides that trustees may apply trust capital for the **advancement** or benefit of a beneficiary, regardless of whether that beneficiary is an infant or an adult.

advancement A statutory power granted to trustees (which may be altered, enlarged or removed by the trust instrument) under which the trustee can apply trust capital for the benefit of beneficiaries even though the beneficiaries are not yet strictly entitled to it.

 STATUTE

Trustee Act 1925, s 32 (as amended by Inheritance and Trustees' Powers Act 2014, s 9)

(1) Trustees may at any time or times pay or apply any capital money subject to a trust, or transfer or apply any other property forming part of the capital of the trust prop-erty, for the advancement or benefit, in such manner as they may, in their absolute

discretion, think fit, of any person entitled to the capital of the trust property or of any share thereof, whether absolutely or contingently on his attaining any specified age or on the occurrence of any other event, or subject to a gift over on his death under any specified age or on the occurrence of any other event, and whether in possession or in remainder or reversion, and such payment or application may be made notwithstanding that the interest of such person is liable to be defeated by the exercise of a power of appointment or revocation, or to be diminished by the increase of the class to which he belongs:

Provided that—

(a) property (including any money) so paid, transferred or applied for the advancement or benefit of any person must not, altogether, represent more than the presumptive or vested share or interest of that person in the trust property; and

(b) if that person is or becomes absolutely and indefeasibly entitled to a share in the trust property the money or other property so paid, transferred or applied shall be brought into account as part of such share; and

(c) no such payment, transfer or application shall be made so as to prejudice any person entitled to any prior life or other interest, whether vested or contingent, in the money or other property paid, transferred or applied unless such person is in existence and of full age and consents in writing to such payment, transfer or application.

(1A) In exercise of the foregoing power trustees may pay, transfer or apply money or other property on the basis (express or implied) that it shall be treated as a proportionate part of the capital out of which it was paid, transferred or applied, for the purpose of bringing it into account in accordance with proviso (b) to subsection (1) of this section.

(2) This section does not apply to capital money arising under the Settled Land Act 1925

(3) This section does not apply to trusts constituted or created before the commencement of this Act.

In trusts coming into effect prior to 1 October 2014 (when the relevant provisions of the Inheritance and Trustees' Powers Act 2014 came into force), the old statutory power of advancement applies, and this was limited to payment of one-half of the beneficiary's presumptive share in the trust. However, even before the 2014 Act it was accepted that the courts have power under the Variation of Trusts Act 1958 (see Chapter 9) to approve an arrangement removing or relaxing that limitation. In *CD (a minor) v O* [2004] All ER (D) 413 the one-half limit was exceeded in favour of a child (indeed it was held that the child's entire presumptive share could be used) in order to pay her school fees. The judge was fortified by the fact that the beneficiary in this case was solely entitled to the fund and would, but for her age, have been entitled to bring the trust to an end.

13.2.1 Capital money

Although s 32 states that maintenance must be made out of capital *money* it has been held that trustees may apply capital *assets* for the advancement of the beneficiary. This happened in *Re Collard's Will Trusts* [1961] 1 All ER 821. The capital asset in that case was a farm to which the beneficiary was entitled under a will. Buckley J observed that the trustees would have the power to advance £20,000 in capital monies to the beneficiary and then to sell the farm to the beneficiary at that price. The judge concluded, therefore, that the farm could be given to the beneficiary directly. R.E. Megarry described this as the 'healthy realism' of equity ((1961) 77 LQR 161 at 163). That healthy realism has now been incorporated into statute. Inheritance and Trustees' Powers Act 2014, s 9 amends the statutory power of advancement to confirm that trustees are able to transfer or apply property and not just cash in the exercise of the statutory power of advancement.

13.2.2 The meaning of 'advancement'

Read the short section of Viscount Radcliffe's speech in *Pilkington* v *IRC* [1964] AC 612 (next). How does his Lordship define 'advancement', and what examples does he give of payments which would be for the 'advancement' of the beneficiary?

 CASE CLOSE-UP

Pilkington v *IRC* [1964] AC 612

Viscount Radcliffe: 'the word "advancement" itself meant in this context the establishment in life of the beneficiary who was the object of the power or at any rate some step that would contribute to the furtherance of his establishment. Thus it was found in such phrases as "preferment or advancement" (*Lowther* v *Bentinck* (1874) LR 19 Eq 166), "business, profession, or employment" or . . . "advancement or preferment in the world" (*Roper-Curzon* v *Roper-Curzon* (1871) LR 11 Eq 452) and "placing out or advancement in life" (*Re Breeds' Will* (1875) 1 ChD 226). Typical instances of expenditure for such purposes under the social conditions of the nineteenth century were an apprenticeship or the purchase of a commission in the army or of an interest in business. In the case of a girl there could be advancement on marriage (*Lloyd* v *Cocker* (1860) 27 Beav 645). Advancement had, however, to some extent a limited range of meaning, since it was thought to convey the idea of some step in life of permanent significance, and accordingly, to prevent uncertainties about the permitted range of objects for which monies could be raised and made available, such words as "or otherwise for his or her benefit" were often added to the word "advancement". It was always recognised that these added words were "large words" (see Jessel MR in *Re Breeds' Will*) and indeed in another case (*Lowther* v *Bentinck*) the same judge spoke of preferment and advancement as being "both large words" but of "benefit" as being the "largest of all". So, too, Kay J in *Re Brittlebank* (1881) 30 WR 99. Recent judges have spoken in the same terms—see Farwell J in *Re Halsted's Will Trusts* [1937] 2 All ER 570 and Danckwerts J in *Re Moxon's Will Trusts* [1958] 1 WLR 165. This wide construction of the range of the power, which evidently did not stand upon niceties of distinction provided that the proposed application could fairly be regarded as for the benefit of the beneficiary who was the object of the power, must have been carried into the statutory power created by s. 32, since it adopts without qualification the accustomed wording "for the advancement or benefit in such manner as they may in their absolute discretion think fit".'

His Lordship defines 'advancement' as 'the establishment in life of the beneficiary who was the object of the power or at any rate some step that would contribute to the furtherance of his establishment'. It is a common semantic error to think of advancements as payments 'in advance', in the sense of 'early' payment. It is true that payments of capital under s 32 are often made early, in anticipation of the beneficiary's interest vesting in possession, but the technical meaning of 'advancement' in this context is 'getting on in life'.

The historical examples given by his Lordship are payment to support an apprenticeship, to purchase a commission in the army or an interest in a business, or to provide a dowry on the marriage of a girl. Later in his speech he gives the further examples of paying off the beneficiary's debts or setting up the beneficiary's spouse in business. More modern examples have included the purchase of a house for the beneficiary to live in and to use as a doctor's surgery and enabling a beneficiary to purchase shares in a family company for which he worked. In *Pilkington* v *IRC* itself, applying capital monies to reduce the tax liability of the beneficiary was considered to be a valid advancement.

Additionally, there are suggestions in some of the cases that 'advancement', historically at least, is understood to take place in the 'early period' of the beneficiary's life. It is a process for 'getting them started'.

 OUTSIDE THE BOX

Jane Austen, *Pride and Prejudice*, 1813

My excellent father died about five years ago; and his attachment to Mr Wickham was to the last so steady, that in his will he particularly recommended it to me, to promote his advancement in the best manner that his profession might allow—and if he took [religious] orders, desired that a valuable family living might be his as soon as it became vacant. There was also a legacy of one thousand pounds. His own father did not long survive mine, and within half a year from these events, Mr Wickham wrote to inform me that, having finally resolved against taking orders, he hoped I should not think it unreasonable for him to expect some more immediate pecuniary advantage, in lieu of the preferment, by which he could not be benefited. He had some intention, he added, of studying law, and I must be aware that the interest of one thousand pounds would be a very insufficient support therein. I rather wished, than believed him to be sincere; but, at any rate, was perfectly ready to accede to his proposal. I knew that Mr Wickham ought not to be a clergyman.

13.2.3 The meaning of 'benefit'

 OUTSIDE THE BOX

Plato, *Laws*

For I consider that the true lawgiver, like an archer, aims only at that on which some eternal beauty is always attending, and dismisses everything else, whether wealth or any other benefit, when separated from virtue.

Traditionally, the power to make a payment for the advancement of a beneficiary had to be exercised so as to contribute a major step in the furtherance of the beneficiary. Section 32, however, provides that capital money may be applied for the advancement or 'benefit' of the beneficiary. Benefit has a much wider meaning than advancement. *Re Clore's ST* [1966] 1 WLR 955 illustrates just how broad the concept of benefit can be. The beneficiary's father had established a charitable foundation to which the beneficiary felt morally obliged to contribute. It would be more tax efficient for the donation to be made by the trustees out of the trust capital than out of the beneficiary's private funds. At one level, then, the benefit was nothing more remarkable than the receipt of a tax saving, but at another level the benefit to the beneficiary was being relieved of a moral obligation in the most tax efficient way. *Re Clore's ST* was applied in *X* v *A* [2006] 1 WLR 741. In *X* v *A*, trustees of a marriage settlement had exercised their power of advancement to give the life tenant (the wife of the settlor) £350,000 in 1996 and £500,000 in 2000, which sums she had given to charity in accordance with her Christian beliefs. The trustees now applied for direction as to whether it was open to them to give her a very substantial part of the remaining trust capital for the purpose of enabling her to devote it to charitable causes. The judge refused to authorise the advancement on the ground that the sums proposed to be released were too large a proportion of the whole.

 CASE CLOSE-UP

X v *A* [2006] 1 WLR 741

Hart J: [having considered *Re Clore's ST*] 'how, as Mr Le Poidevin asked rhetorically, can the court assess the validity and nature of a moral obligation otherwise than by reference to the beneficiary's own views on the subject? That is certainly not a question to with the court can give an abstract answer, whether by reference to the Bible or to Bentham, to Kant or the Koran. The answer has to be found in the concrete examples provided by the decided cases and the reliance placed in them on generally accepted norms applicable in the context of dealings with settled wealth. No such case goes anywhere near recognising the existence of a moral obligation of the extent in question here. For those reasons I do not think that I can conclude that it is open to the trustees to make the proposed advance. In saying that I should not be taken as casting any doubt on the propriety of the earlier advances which were made to the wife in 1996 and 2000.'

The case is especially interesting for the first-hand account it contains of the settlor's reasons for setting up the trust in the first place and the settlor's opinions on inherited wealth. The settlor's account provides a rare insight into the human dimension of real life at the fringes of a trust:

 CASE CLOSE-UP

X v *A* [2006] 1 WLR 741

I created the settlement understanding from the advice I received that the trustees' discretionary powers included the power to advance to my wife up to the whole of the capital; that the conditions in which they might do so were not defined; and that no potential beneficiary had a claim on the settlement as of right and could therefore challenge such a decision of the trustees.

In our experience inherited wealth is liable to have many adverse consequences. It is likely to undermine the incentive to work and to gain qualifications for work; to result in hasty and unwise decisions; to affect the relationship between a husband and wife adversely where one partner has power and possessions which the other does not have. It may cause bad relationships between neighbours. We have experienced these and other adverse consequences of inherited wealth in our own family.

Inherited wealth may also be a cause of bad relationships within families, as it is becoming increasingly difficult today to define who is a member of the family, and for grandparents to define who are their grandchildren. While [B] was married to [J's father] [J] . . . was our step grandchild. Now that marriage has ended, he has ceased to be our step grandchild. But he has grown up regarding us as grandparents and he continues to be a regular visitor to [B]'s home.

It is therefore not only in light of the pressing needs of the world today, but also of what we believe to be in their own best interests, that we wish that the provision made for our grandchildren should not exceed three-fifths of the value of what we have termed an 'average house'.

 THINKING POINT

Betty's beneficial interest under a trust is contingent upon her attaining the age of 25. The trustees are proposing to apply capital monies for her advancement by resettling her beneficial interest on new trusts under which her interest will vest when she reaches the age of 30. Could this possibly be for her benefit?

These facts are similar to the facts of *Re T's Settlement Trusts* [1963] 3 All ER 759, which were considered in Chapter 9 on variation of trusts. In that case it was held that a postponement of the beneficiary's entitlement could be for their benefit where the evidence suggests that the beneficiary is immature, reckless or a spendthrift. Similar reasoning might be applied in the context of making an advancement.

13.2.4 Incidental beneficiaries

We have already seen that it will be a valid exercise of the power in s 32 to apply capital monies to pay off the beneficiary's debts and, in another case, to set the beneficiary's spouse up in business. In these cases it is clear that the beneficiary's creditors and spouse are benefiting from the exercise of the trustees' power. This, however, does not make the exercise of the power invalid. As Viscount Radcliffe stated in *Pilkington v IRC* [1964] AC 612: 'It is no objection to the exercise of the power that other persons benefit incidentally from the exercise of the power.' Miss Pilkington was the object of the power of advancement. The trustees had proposed to advance her by resettling capital monies for her benefit. Her children would have received nothing under the original trust, but under the resettlement they would benefit if she died under the age of 30 leaving surviving issue. The children were the 'incidental beneficiaries'.

13.2.5 Hotchpot under Trustee Act 1925, s 32(1)(b)

This section provides that if a beneficiary becomes absolutely and indefeasibly entitled to a share in the trust property, the money they have already received by way of advancement must be brought into account as part of their share. This process is called 'hotchpot'. It is illustrated in the following 'thinking point'.

> **THINKING POINT**
>
> A and B are the beneficiaries of a trust under which they will become entitled to an equal share of the fund upon their attaining the age of 21. The trustees paid £10,000 to A to finance A's time as a student at university. A is 21 today, and the fund is today valued at £100,000. How much is A entitled to?

A is entitled to £45,000. The whole fund is £110,000, of which A's share is £55,000, but A must bring into 'hotchpot' the £10,000 that has already been received.

13.2.6 Prior interests under Trustee Act 1925, s 32(1)(c)

According to this section the trustees will not be permitted to make a payment by way of advancement if to do so would prejudice any person with a prior interest in the fund, unless the person with the prior interest gives their consent in writing to the advancement.

If a trust provides for A for life and for B in remainder, the trustees will not be permitted to apply any capital money for the advancement or benefit of B unless A has given consent in writing because A has a definite interest in income earned on the capital of the trust. If A had been the potential object of a discretionary trust his consent would not be required because such a beneficiary has merely a 'hope' that he will receive an interest in the trust (see *Re Beckett's Settlement* [1940] Ch 279).

The written consent of a person with a prior interest will still be required despite a clause in the trust instrument dispensing with the requirement. This is a rare instance of the settlor being unable to oust the provisions of the general law by the express terms of the trust instrument. The case which decided the point, *Henley* v *Wardell* (1988) Times, 29 January, involved a clause in a will which purported to remove the requirement for consent. The caption to the *Times Law Report* carried a witty summary of the decision: 'Will Power Doesn't Override Consent'.

13.2.7 Advancement by resettlement

> 'Tis somewhat indirectly, I confess: But there is much advancement in the world, that comes in indirectly.
>
> John Webster, *The Devil's Law Case*, 1623

There is nothing wrong in principle with making an advancement by way of resettlement, but the basic rule is that '[t]rustees cannot under the guise of making an advancement create new trusts merely because they think they can devise better trusts than those which the settlor has chosen to declare. They must honestly have in mind some particular circumstances making it right to apply funds for the benefit of an object or objects of the power' (*Re Wills* [1959] Ch 1 at 14, *per* Upjohn J). The resettlement will be invalid if it is not made for the benefit of the advancee, if it is void for perpetuity or if it involves the unauthorised delegation of a basic discretion. We have already considered the 'benefit' factor (see 13.2.3) and the rule against perpetuities has been considered at length in Chapter 6. The factor which requires further attention here is the risk that the resettlement will involve the delegation of a basic discretion.

In *Pilkington* v *IRC* [1964] AC 612 Viscount Radcliffe stated that 'the law is not that a trustee may not delegate; it is that trustees may not delegate unless they have authority to do so' (see 12.2). Upjohn J in *Re Wills* [1959] Ch 1 stated that 'unless upon its proper construction the power of advancement permits delegation of powers and discretion, a settlement created in exercise of the power of advancement cannot in general delegate any powers or discretion, at any rate in relation to beneficial interests'. The final reference to discretions involving beneficial interests suggests that the learned judge had the so-called dispositive discretions in mind (see 11.4.1). According to the Court of Appeal in *Southgate* v *Sutton* [2011] EWCA Civ 637, an advancement by way of resettlement is more likely to be permitted where it varies the trusts applicable to *part* only of the beneficial interests in the trust property.

13.2.8 Exercise of discretion

What are the factors which should be taken into account when exercising the discretion to make an advancement? Some relevant factors are considered in the following sections.

13.2.8.1 Benefit

The most important question that the trustees should ask themselves when considering an exercise of their power under s 32 is 'will the application of capital monies be for the benefit of the beneficiary?' As Danckwerts J stated in *Re Moxon's WT* [1958] 1 All ER 386: '"Benefit" is the widest possible word one could have and . . . it must include a payment direct to the beneficiary; but that does not absolve the trustees from making up their minds whether the payment in the particular manner which they contemplate is for the benefit of the beneficiary.' What will and will not constitute 'benefit' was discussed earlier (see 13.2.3).

13.2.8.2 Trustees as incidental beneficiaries

What if one of the *trustees* exercising the power of advancement stands to profit from the exercise of that power? In *Molyneux* v *Fletcher* [1898] 1 QBD 648 the trust instrument granted the trustees the power to make payments for the 'advancement in life' of the beneficiary. It was held to be an invalid exercise of the trustees' discretion to pay monies to the beneficiary with the knowledge that the sums would be used by the beneficiary's spouse to repay a debt due to one of the trustees.

13.2.8.3 The fiduciary aspect

The power to make an advancement is a fiduciary power. Therefore the trustees must weigh against the benefit to the advancee the interests of other persons entitled under the trust (*Re Pauling's Settlement Trusts* [1963] 3 All ER 1). They must also ensure that the capital monies paid to the advancee are used by the advancee for the use intended by the trustees. As Wilmer LJ stated in *Re Pauling's ST* in the Court of Appeal: 'They [the trustees] cannot . . . prescribe a particular purpose, and then raise and pay the money over to the advancee leaving him or her entirely free, legally and morally, to apply it for that purpose or to spend it in any way he or she chooses, without any responsibility on the trustees even to inquire as to its application.' The trustees (a bank) in *Re Pauling's ST* had been advised by counsel that they could pay trust monies over to the adult advancees, and what they did with them thereafter was their concern. Clearly, the Court of Appeal came to a different view.

As stated, the power of advancement is a fiduciary power; the trustees cannot simply pay over the capital monies and then wash their hands of the affair. They have a duty to make enquiries as to how the monies are actually spent. If the monies are not used for the prescribed purpose, and the trustees receive notice of this fact, they will be under a duty not to make further advances in the future without first satisfying themselves that the money will be properly applied.

13.3 Contrary intention

The statutory powers of maintenance and advancement apply only in so far as a contrary intention is not expressed in the trust instrument (Trustee Act 1925, s 69(2)). In *IRC* v *Bernstein* [1961]
1 Ch 399 the settlor had directed that the income on his trusts should be accumulated during
his lifetime and this was held to be evidence of an intention to exclude the statutory power to
make an advancement of capital monies. The court found that the settlor had clearly intended
that capital should not be distributed until his death. The direction to accumulate would, of
course, be evidence of an intention to exclude the power of maintenance also!

In *Re Ransome* [1957] 1 All ER 690 a similar direction to accumulate income was held to amount
to an intention to exclude the trustees' duty to pay income on accumulations under s 31(1)(ii)
(see 13.1.3). This was in spite of the fact that the direction to accumulate was held to be void
for perpetuity. The beneficiary in this case got the worst of both worlds! They did not receive
the accumulations which the settlor had intended should be made for their benefit, but neither
did they receive the income released when the direction to accumulate was declared void. *Re
Ransome* looks like a case where the settlor's 'true' intentions for the beneficiary have been
denied because of the strict application of the settlor's presumed 'contrary intention' under s
69(2). (See J.G. Riddall's imaginative article, '*Re Ransome* Revisited or "First The Good News"'
(1979) 43 Conv 423.)

13.3.1 Express powers of maintenance and advancement

Before this chapter concludes, it is worth reiterating that the statutory powers of maintenance and advancement may be extended, or otherwise varied, by express provision in the
trust instrument.

13.3.2 The court's inherent jurisdiction

Even where a trust instrument excludes the statutory powers of maintenance and advancement, and does not contain any such provisions of its own, the court retains an inherent jurisdiction to maintain infant beneficiaries out of income and capital and to advance infant
beneficiaries out of capital.

 Summary

- We have seen in this chapter that the law reads between the lines of a gift. The settlor
  or testator has a general intention to benefit the beneficiary—that much is obvious
  from the fact that they have made a gift at all. The statutory powers of maintenance
  and advancement are an acknowledgement that the intentions of most 'gift-makers'
  will go beyond the express terms of the gift; thus, where a gift of antique furniture is
  made to an infant, it is natural to assume that the trustees will have power to sell the
  furniture and use the capital proceeds for the advancement of the beneficiary, or else
  maintain the beneficiary out of income (in this case interest) arising from the proceeds
  of sale. Few 'gift-makers', if asked, would want the infant's education or health to suffer by insisting upon the retention of an old table and some chairs.

- We have examined both the statutory power of maintaining infants out of trust income and the statutory power, applicable to infant and adult beneficiaries, of advancement out of capital monies.

- We have seen that if a settlor or testator objects to the statutory powers of maintenance and advancement they have the power to exclude them by the express terms of their gift. Conversely, if they feel that the statutory powers are not extensive enough, the 'gift-makers' are at liberty to make more generous provision of their own.

? Summative assessment exercise

Wilhelm, who died in 2013, left the residue of his estate in trust for his grandchildren, Betty and Andrew, at the age of 25, in equal shares absolutely. The trustees have invested the fund and accumulated all the income on it. The capital value of the fund is now £20,000. Betty is 19 years old; Andrew is 12.

The trustees have received the following requests:

- first, they have been asked to transfer £4,000 into a trust fund set up by the children's uncle in 1985 under which the fund trustees may, in their sole discretion, pay income or capital to any of his nephews or nieces who are students at university, and any capital remaining after a period of 21 years will be divided equally between all his nephews and nieces. At present the fund is valued at £6,000 and Betty is the only eligible beneficiary;

- secondly, Andrew's parents have asked the trustees to pay all the income of the fund to them for ten years to enable them to meet the initial running costs of a riding school which they propose to establish at their home. Andrew is interested in riding and supports the proposal.

Advise whether the trustees may comply with these requests.

 Full specimen answers can be found at www.oxfordtextbooks.co.uk/orc/watt_directions5e/.

☐ The bigger picture

You will recall that in the case of *X* v *A*, the judge declined to entertain the possibility that, in ascertaining the nature of moral obligation in relation to dealings with settled wealth, the court might find guidance by making reference to 'the Bible or to Bentham, to Kant or the Koran'. Presumably, though, the judge would have admitted guidance from medical experts in matters of medical law. Judges typically respect scientific opinion on scientific matters, so why not respect religious and philosophical opinion on the morality of wealth? It seems that modern judges have forgotten that, along with medics or physicians, the authority of philosophers and poets is to be 'heard and respected'. These are not my words, but a translation of the words of Thomas Littleton, who was one of the first great authorities of English property law (in the original, he wrote '*authoritates philosophorum, medicorum et poetarum sunt in causis allegandae et tenendae*': see Sir Edward Coke, *Commentary on Littleton* (1628) 264a).

Further reading

Goldsworth, J. 'The Power of Advancement and Charitable Donations' (2007) 13(3) *Trusts & Trustees* 99
a brief but useful note on *X* v *A* [2006] 1 WLR 741

Hassall, N. 'Powers of Advancement: How Far Can Pilkington Be Stretched' (2007) 4 PCB 282
considers the extent to which trustees can use the power of advancement to resettle a trust so as to adapt it to revised inheritance tax rules under the Finance Act 2006

Ker, B.S. 'Trustees' Powers of Maintenance' (1953) 17 Conv 273
a clear exposition of the issues, especially regarding the carrying of intermediate income

Riddall, J.G. '*Re Ransome* Revisited or "First The Good News"' (1979) 43 Conv 423
a very entertaining and informative guide to the complexities caused by the fact that the trustees' power of maintenance is subject to express contrary intention. It imagines the beneficiary's reaction to the decision in *Re Ransome* in the form of a scripted dialogue between the beneficiary and his counsel

 For links to selected cases, statutes, academic papers and official reports mentioned in this chapter please visit the online resources at www.oup.com/uk/watt_directions6e/.

14 Investment

Introduction

Imagine that you have been appointed to act as trustee of a small fund of money to be held on trust for very young infant beneficiaries until they are old enough to bring the trust to an end and take the money absolutely. What will you do with the money in the meantime? Will you 'speculate to accumulate' by giving the money to a friend of yours who has just watched the BBC programme 'Dragons' Den' and has been inspired to start a new business called 'The Cat's Whiskers' which sells cosmetics for pet cats (tested on humans)? Or perhaps you will put the money under your mattress, confident that it will lie totally undisturbed for the next ten years. Or perhaps you will place it in a diverse portfolio of international stocks, shares and gilt-edged securities. If you do any of these things you will almost certainly have breached your trust, and by the end of this chapter you will know why. The first broad question to ask is whether a particular *type* of investment is unauthorised for trustees—we will see that there are very few types of investment prohibited by the general law (although any particular trust instrument may expressly prohibit any particular type of investment). The second broad question to ask is whether it is prudent to invest the trust fund in this particular investment as an example of its type (e.g. you know you may invest in companies, but is it prudent to invest in this particular company?). The third broad question to ask is whether it is prudent to invest in this way (e.g. is it prudent to invest in this particular company without taking advice and without investing in other companies so as to 'spread the risk'?).

Previously the general law would not allow trustees to participate in the market as if they were absolute owners of the fund. That could only be achieved by the terms of the trust instrument or, in an exceptional case, by a special order of the court enlarging the trustees' investment powers. Now, as a result of Part II of the Trustee Act 2000, every trustee 'may make any kind of investment that he could make if he were absolutely entitled to the assets of the trust' (Trustee Act 2000, s 3(1)). This power 'will enable trustees to hold investments jointly or in common with other persons' (note 20 accompanying the Act). In fact, the only type of investment which still requires express authorisation in the trust instrument is investment in interests in land other than mortgages (s 3(3)), and freeholds and leaseholds (s 8).

Note, however, that the provisions of Part II of the Act do not apply to occupational pension schemes and authorised unit trusts, or to certain schemes under the Charities Act 1993. These special forms of trust are subject to their own statutory rules (which, in the case of pension trustees, grant investment powers as wide as those provided by the 2000 Act. See the Pensions Act 1995, s 34(1)). For 'normal' trustees the Trustee Act 2000 repeals the old scheme for investment laid down by the Trustee Investments Act 1961. It did this because (as note 6 to the 2000 Act puts it):

> [T]he law governing the powers and duties of trustees, particularly the relevant provisions of the Trustee Act 1925 and the Trustee Investments Act 1961, has not kept pace with the evolving social and economic role which trusts now fulfil. This discrepancy has been brought into sharp focus by the fundamental changes in the conduct of investment business during the last ten years such as the introduction of the **CREST** system on the London Stock Exchange. The situation is now so serious that the view is widely held that it is very difficult for such trustees acting under the terms of trust instruments which make no specific provisions as to investment powers, to satisfy their paramount duty to act in the best interests of the beneficiaries of the trust.

> **CREST** An electronic share settlement and securities depository system introduced to the UK Stock Exchange in 1996. Since 2002 it has been administered by a company called Euroclear.

14.1 The meaning of 'investment'

> **Investment**
> The process by which assets are applied with the intention of producing income and/or capital growth over the medium to long term.

Before s 3 of the Trustee Act 2000 introduced 'the general power of investment', an **investment** to be valid, had to be of an authorised type and had to be an appropriate investment of that type. Now (with the exception of some minor interests in land) there are no unauthorised *types* of investment. The crucial question becomes whether the type of investment chosen was appropriate to the trust in the light of the 'standard investment criteria' (s 4(2)). We will consider these criteria at 14.1.4 but a preliminary issue needs to be addressed at this point. It stems from the fact that s 3 authorises any kind of 'investment'. The question is whether 'investment' is a term that is apt to describe some purchases, assets and financial products, but not others. The simple answer to that question is 'yes'. It stretches the language too far to describe such things as insurance cover, lottery tickets and personal services as 'investments'. An investment is something that is acquired in the expectation that it will produce profit in the form of direct financial returns. The acquisition of insurance cover is not intended to produce a financial return (all being well); the payment of agents, custodians, nominees and delegates of every kind is sometimes intended to produce financial returns, but only indirectly; and we would not describe the acquisition of a lottery ticket as an investment, because there is no realistic expectation of any return. These examples would suggest that it is not particularly difficult to identify forms of financial outlay which do *not* qualify as investments, but the courts have sometimes found it hard to identify the boundary between investments and non-investments.

14.1.1 The historical need for income production

Before the 2000 Act, the law identified the boundary between investments and non-investments by holding that an acquisition made on behalf of a trust would only qualify as an 'investment' if it produced direct financial benefits in the form of *income*. As Buckley J put it in *Re Peczenik's Settlement* [1964] 1 WLR 720: 'property which is acquired merely for use and enjoyment is not an investment.' In a similar vein, Jenkins J held (in *Re Power* [1947] Ch 572) that an investment must produce income of a financial nature and that the appreciation of benefits-in-kind is not sufficient:

> [T]here is a distinction between purchasing freehold property for the income one is going to get from it and purchasing freehold property for the sake of occupying it.

The requirement that a trust investment must be income-producing arises from the strict distinction that has traditionally been drawn between the entitlements of life beneficiaries and remainder beneficiaries under settlement trusts. It was always assumed that life beneficiaries are interested only in income and that remainder beneficiaries are interested only in capital, therefore both could be satisfied by the deposit of monies in bank accounts or by the purchase of assets such as gilts and bonds, which are income-producing but have more or less stable capital values.

14.1.2 A new approach: capital gains as investment returns

In *Cowan* v *Scargill* [1985] Ch 270 at 287 Megarry V-C acknowledged that the return on an investment can include capital appreciation, but he was reluctant to acknowledge that an investment need not produce income. His Lordship stated that the trustees' investment power 'must be exercised so as to yield the best return for the beneficiaries, judged in relation to the risks of the investment in question, and the prospects of the yield of income and capital appreciation; both have to be considered in judging the return from the investment'. Nicholls V-C seemed to accept that income production and capital growth can be *alternative* bases for assessing the success of an investment. In *Harries* v *Church Commissioners* [1992] 1 WLR 1241 at 1246 his Lordship stated that:

> *prima facie* the purposes of the trust will be best served by the trustees seeking to obtain therefrom the maximum return, whether by way of income or capital growth, which is consistent with commercial prudence.

THINKING POINT

Can it be said that 'investment' under the new 'general investment power' (Trustee Act 2000, s 3) should now be taken to include financial outlay which is expected to realise returns in the form of capital growth alone?

There is nothing expressly to that effect anywhere in Part II of the Trustee Act 2000, but the 'general investment power' in s 3 implies that 'investment' should now be given the meaning that an absolute owner would attach to the word. An absolute owner will generally be far less concerned than trust beneficiaries to ensure that an investment maintains a balance between income and capital returns. This is borne out by consideration of one of the most common forms of investments made by absolute owners: houses. A house is acquired for its day-to-day usefulness, but also because of its investment potential. For most owners the anticipated investment returns will not take the form of income, but that of long-term *capital* growth.

The explanatory notes which accompany the Act also suggest that capital growth will be just as acceptable a form of return as income production (note 22: see 14.1.3.2).

It used to be the rule that income beneficiaries were entitled only to that part of the trust income that accrued during their period of entitlement (Apportionment Act 1870, s 2). Another rule protected income beneficiaries against the trustees' decision to retain investments in capital form (the rule in *Re Earl of Chesterfield's Trusts* (1883) 24 Ch D 643) and another rule (the rule in *Allhusen* v *Whittell* (1867) LR 4 Eq 295) required liabilities falling to be paid out of the residuary estate to be apportioned between capital and income residuary beneficiaries. Such formal rules on the apportionment of capital and income have now been abolished by the Trusts (Capital and Income) Act 2013 for new trusts coming into force after the commencement of the Act (on 31 January 2013).

14.1.3 Modern portfolio theory

According to Hoffmann J in *Nestle* v *National Westminster Bank plc* (1988) (reported in (1996) 10 TLI 112):

> Modern trustees acting within their investment powers are entitled to be judged by the standards of current portfolio theory which emphasises the risk level of the entire portfolio rather than the risk attaching to each investment in isolation.

Viewed in isolation, any investment in shares in a private company will look prohibitively risky. Investment in any particular share will expose the fund to specific risks, such as the failure of the company in question and the collapse of the share price. The major insight offered by modern portfolio theory is that such specific risks can be reduced through diversification. Crudely, the investor is able to offset the risk that stock in X Co will decrease, against the chance that stock in Y Co will increase. To come close to eliminating such specific risk entirely the investor would need to invest in every available equity in proportion to the size of the company; holding the shares of just a few different companies will offset the greater part of the risk. Nevertheless, there remains the problem of the market in shares as a whole suffering loss, perhaps in the form of a 'stock market crash'. This 'systemic' or 'non-diversifiable' risk remains a real one.

Prior to the Trustee Act 2000 there were a number of obstacles to modern portfolio theory woven into the fabric of the English law of trusts. The Trustee Act removes them all, either directly or indirectly. The explanatory notes which accompany the Act expressly state that the 'standard investment criteria' (suitability and diversity) are intended to accord with modern portfolio theory (note 25).

14.1.3.1 Obstacle one: a restrictive range of investment options

The Trustee Act 2000 removes this obstacle by repealing the Trustee Investments Act 1961. The preamble to the 1961 Act introduced it as 'an Act to make fresh provision with respect to investment by trustees'. In 1961 its provisions were indeed 'fresh'. The general law had previously restricted trustees' investments to a limited class of ultra-secure investments such as stocks issued or guaranteed by the British government. The Act broadened the range of investments permitted under the general law considerably by permitting investment in companies listed on the London Stock Exchange. However, even such companies had to be very secure. According to Part IV of the First Schedule to the 1961 Act, they had to have a paid-up capital of £1 million and had to have declared a dividend on all shares in each of the last five years. Furthermore, trustees were only permitted to invest in fully paid-up shares in these secure public limited companies. In the year 2001 £1 million is not as significant a restriction as it was in 1961, but the other conditions would still be very restrictive had they not been repealed. They would, for instance, prohibit the purchase by trustees of shares in newly privatised utilities and demutualised building societies. What is more, according to s 2 of the Trustee Investments Act 1961 a maximum of 50 per cent of the fund could be devoted to such investments, and the other 50 per cent had to be devoted to ultra-secure investments (although the greater profitability of shares tended over time, along with other factors, to reduce the proportion of the fund held in ultra-secure investments). Not until 1996 was the 50–50 rule modified to allow three-quarters of the fund to be devoted to investment in shares in quoted companies and other 'risky' investments (SI 1996/845). The Trustee Act 2000 has now removed such restrictions entirely.

There were two ironic aspects to the timing of the relaxation of the investment rule. The first was that the stock market suffered a major collapse (from which it has still not recovered) almost immediately after the Trustee Act 2000 liberated trustees to invest in it as they wished. The second was that the Treasury report which preceded the 2000 Act was published in 1996, just months after Barings, England's oldest merchant bank, had been bankrupted as a direct result of a single employee trading on the bank's behalf on the Far East derivatives market. The bank's collapse was caused by the employee's fraudulent trading, but it was also to a great extent attributable to the fact that the employee was investing in sophisticated innovative futures contracts and the bank's officers didn't fully understand these new investment devices. If the officers of a bank are not sufficiently expert to supervise their own employees with regard to innovative investment products, what hope, it might be asked, do trustees have of knowing whether or not their agents are investing appropriately on behalf of the fund? The Law Commission is currently considering whether the way in which the law of fiduciary duties applies to investment intermediaries works in the interests of the ultimate beneficiaries. (Law Commission Report No 350, 'Fiduciary Duties of Investment Intermediaries', June 2014).

14.1.3.2 Obstacle two: the rule that trust investments must yield an income

This rule unduly limits the range of possible trust investments, and reduces the possibility for investment in a balanced portfolio. (See E.M. David, 'Principal and Income—Obsolete Concepts' (1972) 43 *Penn Bar Association Quarterly* 247.) We have already considered the possible impact of the 2000 Act on this rule (see 14.1.1). The explanatory notes which accompany the Act anticipate that the general power of investment will permit trustees to invest assets with a view to income *or* capital return (note 22).

14.1.3.3 Obstacle three: the standard of care

Prior to the Trustee Act 2000 the standard of care expected of trustees in relation to the exercise of their investment powers did not allow them to make risky or speculative investments, but the Trustee Act 2000 now authorises trustees to invest as if they were absolute beneficial owners of the fund, and it is consistent with this that they should be permitted to select a portfolio that is prudent overall, even if it includes some individual investments of a more or less speculative nature. The modern equities (shares) market is said to be 'efficient' in the sense that new information relating to shares is immediately reflected in current share prices. This means that investors have little hope of finding undervalued shares, and consequently the only way to increase returns is to increase risk. What is needed is to produce a portfolio in which the risks inherent in investment X are hedged against risks inherent in investment Y. In this modern investment environment trustees will still be judged by an objective standard of prudence, but prudence should be assessed in relation to the choice and management of the portfolio (which includes appropriate recourse to proper expert advice), and should not be presumed automatically to exclude 'risky investments' per se. (See, generally, Bevis Longstreth, *Modern Investment Management and the Prudent Man Rule*, Oxford: Oxford University Press, 1986 and 14.1.3.)

14.1.3.4 Obstacle four: the 'anti-netting' rule

This is the rule that insists that trustees may not set off gains made in one breach of trust (e.g. investment in a speculative investment) against losses made in another breach of trust (see, generally, 15.3.1). The Trustee Act 2000 doesn't abolish that rule as such, but there will be no breach of trust under the 2000 Act unless the trustee is imprudent in the choice of portfolio; individual investments will not be judged in isolation.

14.1.4 The standard investment criteria

According to s 4(1) of the 2000 Act: 'In exercising any power of investment . . . a trustee must have regard to the standard investment criteria.' The standard investment criteria require that investments should be suitable and diversified. The suitability and diversity of the investments must be subjected to periodic review and proper advice should be taken in deciding whether or not to vary the portfolio as a result of the review.

STATUTE

Trustee Act 2000

Part II Investment

Section 3 General power of investment

(1) Subject to the provisions of this Part, a trustee may make any kind of investment that he could make if he were absolutely entitled to the assets of the trust.

(2) In this Act the power under subsection (1) is called 'the general power of investment'.

(3) The general power of investment does not permit a trustee to make investments in land other than in loans secured on land (but see also section 8).

[subsections (4), (5) and (6) have been omitted to save space]

Section 4 Standard investment criteria

(1) In exercising any power of investment, whether arising under this Part or otherwise, a trustee must have regard to the standard investment criteria.

(2) A trustee must from time to time review the investments of the trust and consider whether, having regard to the standard investment criteria, they should be varied.

(3) The standard investment criteria, in relation to a trust, are—

   (a) the suitability to the trust of investments of the same kind as any particular investment proposed to be made or retained and of that particular investment as an investment of that kind, and

   (b) the need for diversification of investments of the trust, in so far as is appropriate to the circumstances of the trust.

Section 5 Advice

(1) Before exercising any power of investment, whether arising under this Part or otherwise, a trustee must (unless the exception applies) obtain and consider proper advice about the way in which, having regard to the standard investment criteria, the power should be exercised.

(2) When reviewing the investments of the trust, a trustee must (unless the exception applies) obtain and consider proper advice about whether, having regard to the standard investment criteria, the investments should be varied.

(3) The exception is that a trustee need not obtain such advice if he reasonably concludes that in all the circumstances it is unnecessary or inappropriate to do so.

(4) Proper advice is the advice of a person who is reasonably believed by the trustee to be qualified to give it by his ability in and practical experience of financial and other matters relating to the proposed investment.

The provision as to periodic reviews enacts the previous wisdom of the judges: 'a trustee with a power of investment must undertake periodic reviews of the investments held by the trust': *Nestle v National Westminster Bank plc (No 2)* [1993] 1 WLR 1260 at 1282G, *per* Leggatt LJ. However, in *Nestle* itself the bank escaped liability despite a deplorable failure to review the trustee investments. The Court of Appeal held that the claimant had failed to prove that the bank's omission to carry out periodic reviews had caused a loss to her (see 14.2.4). It is notoriously difficult to establish that a loss has been caused by omissions, especially in the investment context, and one imagines that the mere statutory enactment of the requirement to conduct reviews will do nothing to assist claimants to prove such loss.

14.1.4.1 Suitability and diversity of investments

The standard investment criteria, which require that investments should be suitable and diverse, are not new. Section 6(1) of the Trustee Investments Act 1961 provided that, in the exercise of their powers of investment, trustees should have regard to:

- 'the need for diversification of investments of the trust, in so far as is appropriate to the circumstances of the trust';
- 'the suitability to the trust of investments of the description of investment proposed and of the investment proposed as an investment of that description'.

Now, according to s 4(3)(a) of the Trustee Act 2000, trustees are required, when investing the trust fund, to consider the suitability to the trust of investments of the type proposed (the trustee must ask, for example, '*in general*, are private company shares suitable for the trust?'). And they must also consider the suitability to the trust of the *particular* investment as an investment of that kind (the trustee must ask, for example, 'are these *particular* private company shares suitable to the trust?').

Prior to the 2000 Act the suitability of a particular investment was judged in isolation, according to the strict investment standard of prudence. The standard investment criteria haven't changed in any material way, but the liberalisation of the duty of care should now permit trustees to invest, as a private investor would, in accordance with modern portfolio theory (see 14.1.3). It is likely that the courts will from now on judge the *suitability* of particular investments in the light of the overall portfolio of investments. Having said that, factors such as the size and risk of the investment and the need to produce an appropriate balance between income and capital growth (see 12.3.1) and even 'ethical considerations' (see 14.2.1) will be relevant in judging whether the portfolio is a suitable one (these factors are suggested by note 23 of the explanatory notes accompanying the Act).

Like the old Trustee Investments Act 1961, the Trustee Act 2000, s 6(1)(a) provides that trustees should have regard to 'the need for diversification of investments of the trust, in so far as is appropriate to the circumstances of the trust' (s 4(3)(b)).

THINKING POINT

What do you think is meant by 'the *circumstances* of the trust'?

In *Cowan* v *Scargill* Megarry V-C stated that:

> the reference to 'circumstances of the trust' plainly includes matters such as the size of the trust funds: the degree of diversification that is practicable and desirable for a large fund may plainly be impracticable or undesirable (or both) in the case of a small fund.

The requirement that investments should be diversified is based on the idea that it would be imprudent to place all the eggs in the same basket, but Andrew Carnegie, the American industrialist, had a different view: 'Put your eggs in one basket. And watch the basket. That's the way to make money.' There are transaction costs involved in building a portfolio and in smaller trusts these might offset the risk-spreading benefits of diversification.

Another 'circumstance of the trust' which might be relevant is the presence of successive interests under the trust, e.g. a life interest followed by an interest in remainder. In these circumstances the trustees' duty to act fairly between the beneficiaries may necessitate a certain degree of diversification so as to include investments the capital value of which is likely to be maintained for the benefit of the remainderman.

 CASE CLOSE-UP

Nestle v National Westminster Bank plc (1996) 10(4) TLI 112, ChD

Hoffmann J: 'the preservation of the monetary value of the capital requires no skill or luck. The trustees can discharge their duties, as they often did until 1961, by investing the whole fund in gilt-edged securities. Preservation of real values can be no more than an aspiration which some trustees may have the good fortune to achieve. Plainly they must have regard to the interests of those entitled in the future to capital and such regard will require them to take into consideration the potential effects of inflation, but a rule that real capital values must be maintained would be unfair to both income beneficiaries and trustees.

. . . the trustee must act fairly in making investment decisions which may have different consequences for different classes of beneficiaries. There are two reasons why I prefer this formulation to the traditional image of holding the scales equally between tenant for life and remainderman. The first is that the image of the scales suggests a weighing of known quantities whereas investment decisions are concerned with predictions of the future. Investments will carry current expectations of their future income yield and capital appreciation and these expectations will be reflected in their current market price, but there is always a greater or lesser risk that the outcome will deviate from those expectations. A judgment on the fairness of the choices made by the trustees must have regard to these imponderables. The second reason is that the image of the scales suggests a more mechanistic process than I believe the law requires. The trustees have in my judgment a wide discretion. They are for example entitled to take into account the income needs of the tenant for life or the fact that the tenant for life was a person known to the settlor and a primary object of the trust whereas the remainderman is a remoter relative or a stranger. Of course these cannot be allowed to become the overriding considerations but the concept of fairness between classes of beneficiaries does not require them to be excluded. It would be an inhuman law which required trustees to adhere to some mechanical rule for preserving the real value of the capital when the tenant for life was the testator's widow who had fallen upon hard times and the remainderman was young and well off.'

14.1.4.2 Periodic review

The Trustee Act 2000, s 4(2) provides that '[a] trustee must from time to time review the investments of the trust and consider whether, having regard to the standard investment criteria, they should be varied'.

14.1.5 **The need to take proper advice**

In relation to the exercise of any power of investment and the carrying out of a periodic review of investments, trustees must 'obtain and consider proper advice about whether, having regard to the standard investment criteria, the power should be exercised' or 'the investments . . . varied' (s 5(1) and (2)). Obviously 'obtain and consider' (which was also the wording of the old Trustee Investments Act 1961, s 6) does not mean 'follow', but trustees depart from expert advice at their peril. In *Cowan* v *Scargill* Megarry V-C stated that the duty to take advice was part of a trustee's general duty of care, and this has now been put on a statutory footing by the Trustee Act 2000. Accordingly, a trustee who imprudently fails to follow proper advice risks liability for breach of trust.

Section 5(4) defines 'proper advice' as 'the advice of a person who is reasonably believed by the trustee to be qualified by his ability in and practical experience of financial and other matters relating to the proposed investment'. There is no requirement that the advice be given or confirmed in writing, but 'to do so will no doubt be regarded as best practice in many circumstances, and may be necessary for trustees to show compliance with the general duty of care in section 1' (note 28 accompanying the Act). If one of the trustees is qualified to give advice the trustees are together entitled to rely on the advice of the 'expert' trustee.

There is, however, an important exception to the duty to obtain and consider advice. According to s 5(4) 'a trustee need not obtain such advice if he reasonably concludes that in all the circumstances it is unnecessary or inappropriate to do so'. However, unless trustees have a personal expertise upon which they are confident to rely, it is hard to imagine them being prepared to risk investment without considering proper advice.

 THINKING POINT

Can you imagine any other case in which it would be reasonable for a trustee to conclude that it would not be appropriate to seek advice?

The explanatory notes accompanying the Act suggest that if the proposed investment is *small*, the cost of obtaining advice might be disproportionate to the benefit to be gained from doing so; in such a case it would therefore be reasonable not to seek the advice (note 26).

Arguably, the move to portfolio-based investment has made it necessary to take advice even in relation to investment in bank accounts and ultra-secure bonds and gilt-edged securities. Ultimately, the propriety of the trustees' decision whether or not to obtain and consider advice will be judged, as will be their decision whether or not to follow proper advice, according to the general standard of prudence required of trustees by s 1 of the 2000 Act.

14.1.6 **Particular types of investment**

There may now be very few types of investment which are prohibited by the general law, but certain types of investment still call for special consideration.

14.1.6.1 **Investment in land**

Buy land, they aren't making it anymore.

Mark Twain (attributed)

We have seen that 'the general power of investment does not permit a trustee to make investments in land other than in loans secured on land' (i.e. mortgages), but a very significant exception appears in s 8 of the Trustee Act 2000. That section provides that a trustee may acquire 'freehold or leasehold land in the United Kingdom . . . as an investment . . . for occupation by a beneficiary' or 'for any other reason'.

Previously, investment in freehold land was not permitted unless expressly authorised by the trust instrument; that state of affairs has now been reversed. The power to invest in legal estates is general (apart from in cases of settled land and university land), but the trust instrument can exclude or restrict that power (Trustee Act 2000, s 9).

14.1.6.2 Investments on personal security

In *Khoo Tek Keon* v *Ch'ng Joo Tuan Neoh* [1934] AC 529, Lord Russell of Killowen stated that 'loans on no security beyond the liability of the borrower to repay . . . are not investments'. Buckley J in *Re Peczenik's Settlement* also doubted investments 'merely upon personal security', although there is authority to show that a trustee will be permitted to 'invest' on personal security if the trust expressly and precisely authorises such an investment (in *Re Laing's Settlement* [1899] 1 Ch 593 the instrument authorised investment 'upon such personal credit without security as the trustees . . . think fit'). If Lord Russell was correct, investments on personal security are not really investments at all, and they will therefore remain unauthorised despite the general investment power provided by the Trustee Act 2000. However, a better approach under the 2000 Act may be to allow this *type* of investment, but to *presume* that such investments will not satisfy the standard investment criterion of 'suitability' unless specifically authorised by the trust instrument.

14.1.6.3 Investment in limited companies

The bank in *Bartlett* v *Barclays Bank Trust Co Ltd (Nos 1 and 2)* [1980] Ch 515 had breached its trust because it had failed adequately to supervise one of the trust investments, namely a limited company in which the trust had a 99.8 per cent shareholding. Brightman J said this about the trustees' duty to supervise investment in a limited company:

> What the prudent man of business will *not* do is to content himself with the receipt of such information on the affairs of the company as a shareholder ordinarily receives at annual general meetings. Since he has the power to do so, he will go further and see that he has sufficient information to enable him to make a responsible decision from time to time either to let matters proceed as they are proceeding, or to intervene if he is dissatisfied.

His Lordship pointed to a number of 'convenient' methods of securing 'sufficient' information. These included the appointment of a director or nominee to the board of directors who would act on behalf of the trust, or even 'receipt of the copies of the agenda and minutes of board meetings if regularly held'. His Lordship did not wish to lay down a general rule and stated that the prudent approach would vary according to the facts of each case.

14.1.6.4 Mortgages

According to the Trustee Act 1925, s 8, a trustee should take expert advice as to the value of land which is to be security for a loan. If a trustee, acting on that advice, advances a loan which does not exceed two-thirds of the expert's valuation, the trustee will not be liable if the land is subsequently shown to be inadequate security. According to s 8, the trustee in the preceding question is liable for a breach of trust in making an improper investment. However, according to the Trustee Act 1925, s 9, a loan of £180,000 would be treated as a proper investment (being two-thirds of £270,000), and the trustee will be liable to make good only the £20,000 difference between the proper loan and the improper loan, plus interest.

Note that trustees do not have to abide by the value restrictions laid down in s 8, but it is prudent that they do so. They will be liable for loss arising out of their failure to abide by the valuation guidelines, as such failure will be treated as prima facie evidence of imprudence (*Palmer v Emerson* [1911] 1 Ch 758).

Note that ss 8 and 9 only affect loans and investments made before the coming into force of the Trustee Act 2000.

14.2 Investment policy

In general, a trustee is required to invest with a view to achieving the *maximum financial return* consistent with prudence. However, this requirement has been considered in a number of cases where trustees have wanted to invest in accordance with policies which do not have financial considerations as their only goal.

In *Cowan v Scargill* [1985] Ch 270 one half of the management committee of the National Coal Board's pension fund trust sued the other half, which comprised Mr Arthur Scargill and four other officials of the National Union of Mineworkers (NUM). The complaint was that the NUM trustees had refused to invest the pension fund in certain overseas industries. The NUM trustees objected to the fact that the overseas industries were competitors of the British mining industry. They defended their refusal to invest as being in the beneficiaries' best interests. The beneficiaries were, of course, retired British mineworkers.

 THINKING POINT

Read the following extract from *Cowan v Scargill*. Were the NUM trustees in breach of trust in refusing to invest in the overseas industries?

 CASE CLOSE-UP

Cowan v Scargill [1985] Ch 270, ChD

Sir Robert Megarry V-C: 'in considering what investments to make trustees must put on one side their own personal views. Trustees may have strongly held social or political views. They may be firmly opposed to any investment in South Africa or other countries, or they may object to any form of investment in companies concerned with alcohol, tobacco, armaments or many other things. In the conduct of their own affairs, of course, they are free to abstain from making any such investments. Yet under a trust, if investments of this type would be more beneficial to the beneficiaries than other investments, the trustees must not refrain from making the investments by reason of the views that they hold.

. . . I should say that I am not asserting that the benefit of the beneficiaries which a trustee must make his paramount concern inevitably and solely means their financial benefit, even if the only object of the trust is to provide financial benefits. Thus if the only actual or potential beneficiaries of a trust are all adults with very strict views on moral and social matters, condemning all forms of alcohol, tobacco and popular entertainment, as well as armaments, I can well understand that it might not be for the 'benefit' of such beneficiaries to know that they are obtaining rather larger financial returns under the trust by reason of investments in those activities than they would have received if the trustees had invested the trust funds in other investments. The beneficiaries might well consider that it was far better to receive less than to receive more money from what they consider to be evil and tainted sources. 'Benefit' is a word with a very wide meaning . . . But I would emphasise that such cases are likely to be very rare, and in any case I think that under a trust for the provision of financial benefits the burden would rest, and rest heavy, on him who asserts that it is for the benefit of the beneficiaries as a whole to receive less by reason of the exclusion of some of the possibly more profitable forms of investment. Plainly the present case is not one of this rare type of case.'

Yes they were! Sir Robert Megarry V-C also went on to hold that:

[i]n considering what investments to make trustees must put on one side their own personal interests and views . . . [and] . . . the broad economic arguments of the defendants provide no justification for the restrictions that they wish to impose. Any possible benefits from imposing the restrictions under the scheme . . . are far too speculative and remote.

The political arguments of the NUM trustees were disallowed, and the financial benefits they hoped to secure for retired British miners (by preventing investment in overseas competitors to the British coal trade) were held to be too indirect.

A pension fund trust has as its purpose the provision of financial benefits to the pensioners, so it is not surprising that the NUM trustees were required to invest with a view to obtaining the best financial returns to the exclusion of other considerations, but what if the trust had existed to achieve other purposes? This question brings us to the next section.

14.2.1 **Ethical investment**

The explanatory notes which accompany the Trustee Act 2000 suggest that the appropriateness of a proposed investment is to be judged partly according to ethical considerations (note 23). This is very encouraging, but there is no such reference in the Act itself, and it may prove as difficult as ever to persuade judges that trustees should, in certain cases, be permitted to prefer ethical considerations over financial considerations.

In *Cowan* v *Scargill* [1985] 1 Ch 270 the Vice-Chancellor had acknowledged that '"benefit" is a word with a very wide meaning, and there are circumstances in which arrangements which work to the financial disadvantage of the beneficiary may yet be for his "benefit"'. However, his Lordship emphasised that such cases would be very rare and that the onus would rest heavily upon the trustee to show that non-financial benefits were a valid investment criterion in the particular case. It is assumed, however, that ethical considerations will be permissible to determine a choice between two investments of equal financial merit. (In support of that view see Lord Nicholls of Birkenhead, 'Trustees and Their broader community: where duty, morality and ethics converge' (1995) 9(3) TLI 71.)

 THINKING POINT

Look at the extract from *Cowan* v *Scargill* again. List some of the situations which the Vice-Chancellor acknowledged might justify investment with a view to non-financial benefits. Try to think of some examples yourself and add them to the list.

The Vice-Chancellor gives, amongst others, the examples of trusts in which all the beneficiaries have strong views against tobacco and alcohol. He acknowledges that such beneficiaries might prefer to receive smaller financial returns from investments which avoid the industries to which they strongly object. Applying this, the trustees of a cancer research trust will not be in breach of their investment duties for refusing to invest in the tobacco industry!

An important limitation on the Vice-Chancellor's concession to allow investments with non-financial benefits is that the actual or potential beneficiaries must all be adults who share the same strict views. Problems arise where the beneficiaries of a trust are likely to have differing views on particular investments, some objecting to them, others approving of them. What should happen here?

In *Harries v Church Commissioners for England* [1992] 1 WLR 1241 the Bishop of Oxford, Richard Harries, sought a declaration from the court requiring the Church Commissioners to invest according to Christian ethics. The Church Commissioners are trustees of a charitable trust, and the Bishop of Oxford was himself one of the trustees.

 CASE CLOSE-UP

***Harries v Church Commissioners for England* [1992] 1 WLR 1241**

Sir Donald Davidson V-C: 'in most cases the best interests of the charity require that the trustees' choice of investments should be made solely on the basis of well-established criteria, having taken expert advice where appropriate and having due regard to such matters as the need to diversify, the need to balance income against capital growth, and the need to balance risk against return.

In a minority of cases the position will not be so straightforward. There will be some cases, I suspect comparatively rare, when the objects of the charity are such that investments of a particular type would conflict with the aims of the charity. Much-cited examples are those of cancer research companies and tobacco shares, trustees of temperance charities and brewery and distillery shares, and trustees of charities of the Society of Friends and shares in companies engaged in production of armaments. If, as would be likely in those examples, trustees were satisfied that investing in a company engaged in a particular type of business would conflict with the very objects their charity is seeking to achieve, they should not so invest . . . [however, it] is not easy to think of an instance where in practice the exclusion for this reason of one or more companies or sectors from the whole range of investments open to trustees would be likely to leave them without an adequately wide range of investments from which to choose a properly diversified portfolio.

There will also be some cases, again I suspect comparatively rare, when trustees' holdings of particular investments might hamper a charity's work either by making potential recipients of aid unwilling to be helped because of the source of the charity's money, or by alienating some of those who support the charity financially. In these cases the trustees will need to balance the difficulties they would encounter, or likely financial loss they would sustain, if they were to hold the investments against the risk of financial detriment if those investments were excluded from their portfolio. The greater the risk of financial detriment, the more certain the trustees should be of countervailing disadvantages to the charity before they incur that risk. Another circumstance where trustees would be entitled, or even required, to take into account non-financial criteria would be where the trust deed so provides.'

THINKING POINT

The Bishop failed to obtain the declaration. What do you think might have been the court's reasons for refusing it?

First, the court noted that it was not possible to say with any certainty that all the beneficiaries would agree with the Bishop's investment policy. Sir Donald Davidson V-C stated that 'different minds within the Church of England, applying the highest moral standards, will reach different conclusions' as to the merits of a particular investment. It must be acknowledged that in an institution as large and inclusive as the Church of England opinions will vary on a range of ethical issues. If the beneficiaries do not have a completely unanimous approach to a particular ethical issue, a trustee should be wary of investing along those ethical lines. The court may take the view, as they did in *Cowan* v *Scargill*, that the trustees were simply putting their own ethical opinions before the interests of the beneficiaries.

Secondly, the court in *Harries* noted that the Church Commissioners' existing investment policy already excluded investment in 13 per cent (by value) of listed UK companies, and they were concerned to note that the Bishop's proposals would have excluded a further 24 per cent of that important investment market. (See 14.2.3 in relation to diversification.)

On the particular facts of *Harries* the court rejected the argument that potential *donors* to the charity would be discouraged from making donations unless the Church Commissioners' current investment policy were extended. However, the court did acknowledge that where there is a real risk of financial detriment due to reduced donations this should be taken into account, and weighed against the financial benefits of retaining ethically 'unsound' investments. In a similar vein it was acknowledged that it might be possible to argue that a particular ethical investment policy should be pursued if otherwise potential *donees* of the charitable fund would refuse to accept donations.

THINKING POINT

Do you agree with the Vice-Chancellor's conclusions in *Harries*? How might they be criticised?

Richard Nobles makes the point that charity trustees are permitted to *give away* trust property to meet the charitable purposes of the trust, and so logically they should be permitted a wider discretion to *invest* with a view to meeting the charitable purposes ('Charities and Ethical Investment' (1992) 56 Conv 115). In response to this kind of concern, the Charities (Protection and Social Investment) Act 2016 s 15 adds new sections to the Charities Act 2011. The proposed new Section 292B provides a general power to make social investments provided it does not use or apply (or put at risk of use or application) the charity's 'permanent endowment' in a manner that is expected to contravene a restriction with respect to expenditure of the permanent endowment. The general power is subject to the express terms of the trust.

THINKING POINT

This question incorporates several of the points covered in this section. Take some time to try to identify all the issues. Certain of the trustees of a charitable trust 'for the promotion of health education and compassion through vegetarianism' wish to invest in a highly profitable British public limited company, one subsidiary business of which is to export live veal calves. Two of the trustees object to such an investment. Advise them.

Your advice should take into account the following points:

- the burden on the objecting trustees to justify a restriction on the investment options is a heavy one. The other trustees are not proposing to invest in the veal trade per se, but to invest in a large British company with a subsidiary interest in the veal trade. Trustees must not exclude too large a section of top UK-listed companies. A factor which will have an important bearing on your advice is whether the trustees already pursue an ethical investment policy, and the restrictions which the current policy places on the investment market;

- it is not clear that the potential beneficiaries of the 'health education' would object to the export of live calves. When the potential beneficiaries cannot be presumed to be unanimous in their ethical views the trustees may be in breach of trust if they prefer a less profitable/more ethical investment over a more profitable/less ethical investment;

- a more pertinent consideration for charity trustees than the last one may be whether the proposed investment would accord with the charitable purposes of the trust. How the trustees answer this question will depend upon the range of charitable purposes and the degree to which a proposed investment conflicts with those charitable purposes;

- this might be a case in which potential patrons of the charity will refuse to make donations if the charity invests, albeit indirectly, in the export of live veal calves. This would probably be the strongest ground on which to object to the proposed investment;

- a quite radical (and risky) piece of advice would simply be to encourage the trustees to prefer ethical investments (without, of course, advising them to volunteer the fact that they have done so) in the secure knowledge that it is notoriously difficult to prove that a 'less ethical' investment would *in fact* have been more profitable (see 14.2.4).

14.2.2 The trust instrument

It should not be forgotten that the application of the general law may be excluded or modified by the express terms of the trust instrument. Even the general investment power introduced by the Trustee Act 2000 is subject to any other provision appearing in the trust instrument (s 6(1)(b)), provided the trust instrument was not made before 3 August 1961 (s 7(2)). In the same vein, the trust instrument can authorise preference for ethical benefits over financial ones. As Sir Donald Nicholls V-C acknowledged in *Harries*, 'trustees would be entitled, or even required, to take into account non-financial criteria . . . where the trust deed so provides'. *Re Harari's ST* [1949] 1 All ER 430 confirms that clauses in trust instruments should be given their plain meaning.

THINKING POINT

What if the settlor of a trust executed on 10 April 1997 included the clause: 'My trustees' powers of investment are those currently permitted by the general law.' Are the trustees of that trust restricted to the general law as at 10 April 1997, or can they take advantage of the wider investment powers introduced by the 2000 Act?

The answer is that, according to the Trustee Act 2000, s 7(3)(a), the trustees would be able to take advantage of the new general power of investment. The explanatory note for this provision explains that it 'ensures that an intention of a settlor to provide ample powers of investment is not frustrated by this liberalisation of the general law'.

THINKING POINT

What if the settlor of a trust executed on 10 April 1997 included the clause: 'My trustees are permitted to invest in nothing other than government bonds.' Are the trustees of that trust bound by that restriction, or can they take advantage of the wider investment powers introduced by the 2000 Act?

This question is taken from the explanatory notes to the 2000 Act. The answer is that a clause of this nature, because it was created after 2 August 1961, is effective to exclude the general power provided by the 2000 Act.

THINKING POINT

What if the settlor of a trust executed on 10 April 1997 included the clause: 'My trustees are permitted to invest in shares quoted on the London Stock Exchange, but not in shares of X plc.' Can the trustees take advantage of the general investment power provided by the 2000 Act?

A version of this example appears in the explanatory notes to the Act. The answer is that the trustees would have the benefit of the general power of investment, but subject to the prohibition against investment in X plc (Trustee Act 2000, s 6(1)).

14.2.3 **Extension of investment powers**

Prior to the Trustee Act 2000, despite widespread use of express investment clauses, many trusts were still subject to restrictive powers of investment. Consequently, trustees sometimes sought the courts' approval for an extension to these powers. Such extensions were authorised by the Trustee Investments Act 1961, s 15. The approach of the courts to requests for extensions evolved dramatically during the years after the 1961 Act. In 1961

Cross J stated that 'the powers given by the Act must, I think, be taken to be *prima facie* sufficient and ought only to be extended if, on the particular facts, a special case for extending them can be made out' (*Re Kolb's WT* [1962] 1 Ch 531). The fact that all the beneficiaries in this case were *sui juris* and could have agreed between them to confer wider powers on the trustees seems also to have influenced the judge's decision. The principle in *Re Kolb's WT* was followed in 1983 in *Mason v Farbrother* [1983] 2 All ER 1078, but in that case the trustees' application for an extension was granted. Blackett-Ord V-C noted that *Re Kolb's WT* permitted extensions if 'special circumstances' could be shown in the particular case. The 'special circumstances' were 'inflation since 1961' and also the fact that the trust was not 'a private or family trust but a pension fund with perhaps something of a public element in it'. But are these circumstances truly 'special' at all? Later in the same year Sir Robert Megarry V-C, in *Trustees of the British Museum v Attorney-General* [1984] 1 All ER 337, said:

> I would hesitate to describe inflation since 1961 as amounting to 'special circumstances'; it is, unhappily, a very general circumstance. With all respect, I can see little virtue (judicial comity and humility apart) in seeking to preserve the rule [in *Re Kolb's WT*] and yet establishing universal special circumstances which will engulf the rule.

Megarry V-C held that 'the principle laid down in the line of cases started by *Re Kolb's WT*' should no longer be followed because conditions had changed greatly since 1961. In future, each application for an extension of the trustees' investment powers should be judged on its own merits, 'without being constrained by the provisions of the 1961 Act'.

In *Steel v Wellcome Custodian Trustees Ltd* [1988] 1 WLR 167 the trustees sought an extension of their powers to permit them to invest as if they were beneficial owners of the fund! They succeeded because:

- investment practice had changed in the preceding 20 years. For example, inflation had caused a general move away from long-term investment in fixed-interest securities and into equities and property ('equities' here is the investors' term for shares);
- the fund was very large, suggesting a greater need for a diverse portfolio of investments and investment flexibility;
- the trustees would be in receipt of specialist advice from a number of professional fund managers.

Ironically, the stock market crashed shortly after this wide extension had been granted.

The Trustee Act 2000 now authorises all trustees to invest as if they were absolute beneficial owners of the trust fund. It might be thought that there will no longer be any need to apply to court for an extension of investment powers. For the most part that is true, but it should not be forgotten that the Trustee Act 2000 still excludes certain types of investment in land, and there may be a question mark over investments on merely personal security. If trustees ever thought it desirable to make investments of that sort, they should be advised (in the absence of express authorisation in the trust instrument or the unanimous consent of the beneficiaries) to apply to court for an extension to their investment powers. Any such application would probably be brought under s 57 of the Trustee Act 1925 (s 15 of the Trustee Act 1961 having been repealed).

14.2.4 Overcautious investment?

Trustees have to act prudently, but it is possible to be *too* cautious.

OUTSIDE THE BOX

The Gospel of St Matthew, **Chapter 25, verses 14–30 (New International Version)** ***The Parable of the Talents***

The kingdom of heaven will be like a man going on a journey, who called his servants and entrusted his property to them. To one he gave five talents of money, to another two talents, and to another one talent, each according to his ability. Then he went on his journey. The man who had received the five talents went at once and put his money to work and gained five more. So also, the one with the two talents gained two more. But the man who had received the one talent went off, dug a hole in the ground and hid his master's money. After a long time the master of those servants returned and settled accounts with them. The man who had received the five talents brought the other five. 'Master,' he said, 'you entrusted me with five talents. See, I have gained five more.' His master replied, 'Well done, good and faithful servant! You have been faithful with a few things; I will put you in charge of many things. Come and share your master's happiness!' The man with the two talents also came. 'Master,' he said, 'you entrusted me with two talents; see, I have gained two more.' His master replied, 'Well done, good and faithful servant! You have been faithful with a few things; I will put you in charge of many things. Come and share your master's happiness!' Then the man who had received the one talent came. 'Master,' he said, 'I knew that you are a hard man, harvesting where you have not sown and gathering where you have not scattered seed. So I was afraid and went out and hid your talent in the ground. See, here is what belongs to you.' His master replied, 'You wicked, lazy servant! So you knew that I harvest where I have not sown and gather where I have not scattered seed? Well then, you should have put my money on deposit with the bankers, so that when I returned I would have received it back with interest.'

[Note: a talent was a very valuable unit of currency. A single talent was worth several times the annual wage of a typical worker.]

The preceding parable is a metaphorical lesson in spiritual wealth and not literally a lesson in financial investment. Nevertheless, it does contain some sound investment advice to trustees: namely that money must be 'put to work' and not left idle. The purchasing power of money decreases over time due to increases in the price of standard goods (this increase is called 'inflation'), so the best way to maintain the real value of money (i.e. to maintain its purchasing power) is to expose it to some risks. Money that is invested in business or such like might realise a return (think of the BBC series 'Dragons' Den'). Money buried in the ground or hidden under the bed has no such hope. Figure 14.1 illustrates how the purchasing power of the UK's pound sterling decreased dramatically between 1750 and 1998.

Inflation has been relatively low since 1998, and is currently virtually non-existent, but it is usually significant enough to make it imprudent to leave money 'in the ground' for a long period. The other advice in the parable is that money should be deposited with a bank as a last resort. This is also true. Depositing money with a high street bank is virtually risk-free, but because there is very little risk there is also very little return. In fact, at the time of writing, one can hardly find a bank deposit account that will pay interest higher than a few percentage points. Thus the real value (the real 'purchasing power') of money will usually decrease over time, even when the money is deposited with a bank.

Figure 14.1 Value of the pound 1750–1998

Source: R. Twigger, 'Inflation: The Value of the Pound 1750–1998', Research paper 99/20, 23 February 1999 (Economic Policy and Statistics Section, House of Commons Library) (www.parliament.uk/commons/lib/research/rp99/rp99-020.pdf)

Jesse Dukeminier and James E. Krier, 'The Rise of the Perpetual Trust' (2003) 50 UCLA L Rev 1303, 1335

'How do you make a small fortune? Give a bank a large one to manage in trust.'

No case illustrates the truth of this statement better than *Nestle* v *National Westminster Bank plc* [1993] 1 WLR 1260. (Note that the name Nestle does not have an acute accent over the last 'e'—the family is not connected to the famous chocolate company founded in Switzerland by Henri Nestlé.) Far from seeking wider investment powers in this case, the trustees were cautious to the point of 'incompetence or idleness' (*per* Staughton LJ). When the claimant (the remainder beneficiary) became absolutely entitled to the trust fund in 1986 the fund was valued at £270,000. She claimed that with proper investment it should have been worth nearly £2 million. The fund was initially (in 1922) valued at £53,963, which in real terms would be equivalent to about £1 million in 1986. The First World War produced the worst inflationary period since records began (the period 1915–20 inclusive saw successive annual inflation rates of 12.5 per cent, 18.1 per cent, 25.2 per cent, 22.0 per cent, 10.1 per cent and 15.4 per cent) but even that is run close by the late '*Nestle* v *Nat West*' period 1974–81, which saw successive annual inflation rates of 17.2 per cent, 24.2 per cent, 16.5 per cent, 15.8 per cent, 8.3 per cent, 13.4 per cent, 18.0 per cent and 11.9 per cent (source: R. Twigger, 'Inflation: The Value of the Pound 1750–1998', Research paper 99/20, 23 February 1999, Economic Policy and Statistics Section, House of Commons Library).

The Court of Appeal held that the claimant had to prove a loss, and although it was conceded that loss *could* include making a gain less than that which would have been made by prudent investment, Staughton LJ found there was no proof that a prudent trustee would *in fact* have acted differently from the bank. This was despite the finding that the bank had misconstrued the terms of the trust and had mistakenly believed that it could invest only within the provisions of the Trustee Investments Act 1961. Leggatt LJ stated that:

> it does not follow from the fact that a wider power of investment was available to the bank than it realised, that it would have been exercised or that, if it had been, the exercise of it would have produced a result more beneficial . . . than was actually produced. Loss cannot be presumed, if none would necessarily have resulted.

🔍 CASE CLOSE-UP

Nestle v National Westminster Bank plc No 2 [1993] 1 WLR 1260, Court of Appeal

Leggatt LJ: 'a breach of duty will not be actionable, and therefore will be immaterial, if it does not cause loss. In this context I would endorse the concession of Mr Nugee for the bank that "loss" will be incurred by a trust fund when it makes a gain less than would have been made by a prudent businessman. A claimant will therefore fail who cannot prove a loss in this sense caused by breach of duty. So here in order to make a case for an inquiry, the plaintiff must show that loss was caused by breach of duty on the part of the bank . . . it does not follow from the fact that a wider power of investment was available to the bank than it realised either that it would have been exercised or that, if it had been, the exercise of it would have produced a result more beneficial to the bank than actually was produced. Loss cannot be presumed, if none would necessarily have resulted. Until it was proved that there was a loss, no attempt could be made to assess the amount of it . . .

No testator, in the light of this example, would choose this bank for the effective management of his investment. But the bank's engagement was as a trustee; and as such, it is to be judged not so much by success as by absence of proven default. The importance of preservation of a trust fund will always outweigh success in its advancement. Inevitably, a trustee in the bank's position wears a complacent air, because the virtue of safety will in practice put a premium on inactivity. Until the 1950s active management of the portfolio might have been seen as speculative, and even in these days such dealing would have to be notably successful before the expense would be justified. The very process of attempting to achieve a balance, or (if that be old-fashioned) fairness, as between the interests of life-tenants and those of a remainderman inevitably means that each can complain of being less well served than he or she ought to have been. But by the undemanding standard of prudence the bank is not shown to have committed any breach of trust resulting in loss.'

Gerard McCormack has observed ('Liability of Trustees for Negligent Investment Decisions' (1997) 13(2) Professional Negligence 45) that:

> [s]ome people might see it as remarkable that the bank incurred no liability notwithstanding the fact that they plainly misconstrued the scope of their investment powers especially since the trustee was a paid professional who supposedly owes higher duties of care.

As was suggested at 11.4.1.1, the decision in *Nestle* appears to have been an erroneous application of *Hasting-Bass*-type reasoning to a form of discretion to which that type of reasoning is inappropriate. This analysis would explain why the court felt constrained to deny the claimant's claim on the basis that the investment choices the bank had made were such that a prudent, correctly advised trustee *might* also have made. The better approach, it is submitted, is not to ask the three questions in *Re Hastings-Bass*, but to ask the questions suggested by Brightman J in *Bartlett v Barclays Bank Trust Co Ltd (Nos 1 and 2)* [1980] 1 All ER 139:

> (1) what was the duty of the bank . . . ? (2) was the bank in breach of duty in any and if so what respect? (3) if so, did that breach of duty cause the loss which was suffered by the trust estate? (4) if so, to what extent is the bank liable to make good that loss?

If these questions had been asked in *Nestle* it must be doubted that the bank would have escaped liability. (1) The bank in *Nestle* had a duty to acquaint itself with its investment powers, and to review the appropriateness of its investments periodically. (2) The bank was clearly in breach of that duty. (3) In *Nestle* their Lordships held that no loss had necessarily been caused. What, it might be asked, does *necessarily* have to do with it? The causal inquiry should be a straightforward question of fact, informed by the best available evidence (from share indices etc) and designed to establish how the shares would *probably* (not *necessarily*) have behaved if the trustee had retained them instead of selling them because it thought it had no authority to keep them. (4) The trustee in *Nestle* should have been liable on the civil standard of proof (the balance of probabilities) to the full extent of the loss it had *probably* caused, subject only to the possibility of defences and relief.

The approach taken by the court in the New Zealand case of *Re Mulligan (deceased)* [1998] 1 NZLR 481 is to be preferred. (The court distinguished *Nestle*.) In *Re Mulligan* the testator died in 1949 leaving his widow a substantial legacy and a life interest in a farm. The widow was one of the trustees of the estate. The farm was sold in 1965 and the estate invested in fixed-interest securities until the widow died in 1990. The other trustee had, between 1965 and 1990, tried to persuade the widow to invest in shares to counter inflation but she adamantly refused to do so. That trustee (a trust corporation) was held to be in breach of trust because it had appreciated the corrosive effect of inflation on the estate capital (which was held to be reliable evidence of the standard of prudence in the industry at the time), but had nevertheless deferred to the widow's wishes.

The court in *Re Mulligan* should be commended for its (successful) attempt to identify objective contemporary indicia of trustee prudence against which to measure the prudence of the defendant trust corporation. However, the English courts still appear reluctant to take that course, preferring instead to relieve a trustee of liability where there is a possibility that *one prudent trustee* (somewhere out there) might have acted as the defendant trustee did, even in the face of evidence that the *particular* defendant trustee *probably* failed to discharge his duties prudently. The problem with the *one prudent trustee* approach is that it puts an almost impossible burden on the claimant to prove, as the judges put it, that 'no prudent trustee' would have acted in the way the particular defendant trustee acted.

CROSS REFERENCE
See, further, Chapter 15 and G. Watt and M. Stauch, 'Is There Liability for Imprudent Trustee Investment?' (1998) 62 Conv 352.

Summary

- The Trustee Act 2000 has introduced a new general power of investment, but the exercise of this power is still subject to the trustees' usual duty of care or prudence. It is also required that trustees should have regard to the standard investment criteria and from time to time review the investments of the trust and consider whether, having regard to the standard investment criteria, they should be varied. The standard investment criteria are:

- the suitability to the trust of investments of the same kind as any particular investment proposed to be made or retained and of that particular investment as an investment of that kind; and

- the need for diversification of investments of the trust, in so far as is appropriate to the circumstances of the trust.

- In *Nestle* v *National Westminster Bank plc* [1993] 1 WLR 1260 Leggatt LJ stated that 'the importance of preservation of a trust fund will always outweigh success in its advancement'. The bias of the law is towards caution, or prudence. If the motto of the private investor is 'speculate to accumulate', the motto of the trustee investor is 'select to protect'.

- It is probable that the prudence of the trustees' choice will from now on be judged according to whether an investment is suitable to the portfolio as a whole, in accordance with modern portfolio theory. Individual investments will not be judged in isolation.

- Whereas it may be straightforward enough to prove that the trust has suffered a loss on account of an unauthorised or imprudent *exercise* of investment powers, the *Nestle* case shows that it is an altogether more difficult task to establish that an imprudent *omission* to exercise investment powers or sell investments has caused a loss to the fund.

? Summative assessment exercise

Steve and Jane are trustees of a £300,000 cash fund for the benefit of their sister Joanne for her life, remainder to her sons Mark and Peter. Joanne is a widow and her only source of income is the trust.

The trust instrument, dated 1 March 2008, states that the trustees are 'subject to the default powers of investment for the time being permitted by the general law'.

Steve and Jane propose to purchase freehold premises for Joanne to live in. The freehold is valued at £50,000. They also propose to put aside £10,000 for investment in Chelsea porcelain figurines because Jane collects these, and the remainder is to be put in a bank account.

Advise Steve and Jane as to the validity of the proposed investments.

 Full specimen answers can be found at www.oxfordtextbooks.co.uk/orc/watt_directions5e/.

☐ The bigger picture

We should not expect the courts to abandon lightly their long-held assumption that beneficiaries' best interests are their best financial interests. Lord Nicholls has described ethical investment as '*an example* par excellence *of an instance where, if social conditions today are thought by some to dictate a need for a change in the law, the change ought to be made by the legislature*' (Lord Nicholls of Birkenhead, 'Trustees and Their broader community: where duty, morality and ethics converge' (1995) 9(3) TLI 71 at 75). Nevertheless, we know that the paradigm of prudence shifts in line with trends in good investment practice and it may be that one day the hypothetical 'prudent investor' will also be an ethical investor. The 1997 Social Investment Forum (SIF) Report on Responsible Investing Trends in the USA found that 10 per cent of all managed funds were managed in some consciously socially responsible way (see J.H. Langbein and R. Posner, 'Social investing and the law of trusts' [1980] 79 Michigan LR 72), and around that time evidence in the UK suggested that ethical portfolios may be a financially strong alternative to comparable, but less ethical, portfolios, especially over the long term ('A good environmental record May Be a sign of long-Term potential', *The Ethical Investor*, EIRIS November/December 1999). A survey carried out by the Ethical Investment Research Service (EIRIS) in February 1999 found that 73 per cent of the UK adult population would like to have pension funds run on ethical lines and almost a third of those questioned would have been prepared to accept some reduction in their pension benefits as a result (*The Independent*, 10 March 1999). However, nearly two decades later one can perhaps detect a more cynical or cautious attitude to the merits of investment 'products' such as pension funds that hold themselves out as 'ethical' (see, for example, John Plender, 'Ethical investment Can Be surprisingly unethical', *Financial Times*, 11 October 2015).

Further reading

Docking, P. and Pittaway, I. 'Social Investment by English Pension Funds: Can It Be Done?' [1990] Trust Law and Practice 25
this article addresses the apparent prohibition on investing pension trust funds to achieve non-financial ends

Ford, E. 'Trustee investment and modern portfolio theory' (1996) 10(4) TLI 102
an excellent succinct introduction to the economics of diversifying investment in the trust context

Lord Nicholls of Birkenhead, 'Trustees and Their broader community: where duty, morality and ethics converge' (1995) 9(3) TLI 71
this article seeks to make clear that trustees may invest ethically provided it is financially no worse than a less ethical alternative

 For links to selected cases, statutes, academic papers and official reports mentioned in this chapter please visit the online resources at www.oup.com/uk/watt_directions6e/.

15 Breach of trust: defences and relief

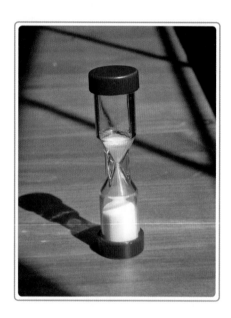

Introduction

No trustee can dispute the fact that he should be liable, and liable to the utmost, for a dishonest breach of trust, but what about the trustee who commits a breach of trust that is not dishonest? In previous chapters we have seen that not every breach of trust is deliberate, let alone dishonest. A trustee may be liable for lack of care and for other inadvertent breaches of trust and may even be liable for an essentially 'technical' or 'formal' breach of fiduciary duty even where he acted honestly and carefully (you should recall *Keech* v *Sandford* and *Boardman* v *Phipps* in this regard: see 12.1). Thus a trustee may be liable if he inadvertently fails to 'get in' trust property upon appointment to the office of trustee or if he makes a technically unauthorised investment or if he takes advantage of an opportunity acquired in the course of his trusteeship, even if the trust itself could not have benefited from that opportunity. In this chapter we are concerned with the extent of trustees' civil liability for breach of trust. We will consider whether there might be a valid defence to a breach of trust and whether, if there is no defence, a trustee's liability ought to be reduced by some form of relief.

Imagine you are the trustee in the following scenario. What should be your liability, do you think? Be kind to yourself. You are a lawyer, if only a student lawyer, so you can expect to be offered a trusteeship at some point!

While undertaking a summer vacation scheme with a local solicitors' firm, one of the partners of the firm arranged for you to be appointed as a second trustee to a trust of which the partner was, immediately prior to your appointment, the sole surviving trustee. The partner assured you that the appointment would be temporary and was merely to assist in the sale of trust-owned land. The only adult beneficiary of the trust was in the office with you at the time and gave you a verbal assurance that she was entirely happy with your appointment and with the proposed sale. The sale went ahead, but the next day the partner failed to turn up for work. It turned out that he had probably run away with the sale proceeds, and with the adult beneficiary of the trust. It turns out that the sale was carried out in breach of trust because a clause of the trust prohibited sale of the land without the consent of named persons whose consent was required by the trust instrument and because the sale was carried out without expert advice as to the value of the land. Do you think you have any defence to liability for breach of trust? Should you be relieved of some or all of your liability for breach of trust? See if your views have changed by the end of this chapter.

15.1 Beneficiaries' remedies

The basic right of a beneficiary is to have the trust duly administered in accordance with the provisions of the trust instrument, if any, and the general law (*per* Lord Browne-Wilkinson in *Target Holdings Ltd* v *Redferns* [1996] AC 421 at 434).

<table>
<tr><td>

Q **CASE CLOSE-UP**

</td></tr>
</table>

Target Holdings Ltd v Redferns [1996] AC 421

Lord Browne-Wilkinson: 'the equitable rules of compensation for breach of trust have been largely developed in relation to such traditional trusts, where the only way in which all the beneficiaries' rights can be protected is to restore to the trust fund what ought to be there. In such a case the basic rule is that a trustee in breach of trust must restore or pay to the trust estate either the assets which have been lost to the estate by reason of the breach or compensation for such loss. Courts of Equity did not award damages but, acting *in per-sonam*, ordered the defaulting trustee to restore the trust estate . . . If specific restitution of the trust property is not possible, then the liability of the trustee is to pay sufficient compensation to the trust estate to put it back to what it would have been had the breach not been committed . . . Even if the immediate cause of the loss is the dishonesty or failure of a third party, the trustee is liable to make good that loss to the trust estate if, but for the breach, such loss would not have occurred . . . Thus the common law rules of remoteness of damage and causation do not apply. However, there does have to be some causal connection between the breach of trust and the loss to the trust estate for which compensation is recoverable, *viz* the fact that the loss would not have occurred but for the breach . . .

Hitherto I have been considering the rights of beneficiaries under traditional trusts where the trusts are still subsisting and therefore the right of each beneficiary, and his only right, is to have the trust fund reconstituted as it should be. But what if at the time of the action claiming compensation for breach of trust those trusts have come to an end? . . . in the ordinary case where a beneficiary becomes absolutely entitled to the trust fund the court orders, not restitution to the trust estate, but the payment of compensation directly to the beneficiary. The measure of such compensation is the same, i.e. the difference between what the beneficiary has in fact received and the amount he would have received but for the breach of trust.'

Certain breaches of trust can be remedied by the acts of the trustees. So, for example, if they have failed to 'get in' trust property, they can get it in late. In such a case the court can order that the appropriate remedial action be taken. In many situations, however, the breach will not be susceptible of such straightforward rectification; examples include the situation where an unauthorised investment has been made and the investment has proved worthless, resulting in a loss to the fund, and the situation where a trustee has obtained an unauthorised personal profit by virtue of their fiduciary position. It is the trustees' liability to compensate for financial losses caused to the trust and their duty to disgorge unauthorised benefits that will be our main concern in this chapter.

The first step in determining trustee liability will usually be for the beneficiary to seek the remedy of account: this is a procedure and a remedy. It involves the production of the trust's financial accounts and requires the trustee to give an account of his dealings with the trust property. (For a further analysis of the remedy of account see Robert Chambers, 'Liability', in Birks and Pretto (eds), *Breach of Trust*, Oxford: Hart, 2002, p. 1.) It requires the trustee to account personally to the trust for any trust property or money which, according to the procedure, is or ought to be in the trustee's possession or under his control. The beneficiary can 'falsify' any unauthorised transactions and 'surcharge' the account for any shortfall: (*Ultraframe (UK) Ltd* v *Fielding* [2005] EWHC 1638 (Ch) at para. [1513]; *Pullan* v *Wilson* [2014] EWHC 126 (Ch) at para. [27]; *AIB Group (UK) Plc* v *Mark Redler & Co Solicitors* [2014] UKSC 58; [2015] AC 1503 (SC) at paras [52]–[54], [90]). An account is in essence a procedure leading to the following forms of compensation:

- compensation to the trust estate for loss caused to the trust (or, in the case of a bare trust, direct compensation to the beneficiary);
- restitution of specific items of property due to the trust.

Rather confusingly, the word 'account' can also be used to describe situations which have nothing to do with compensating the trust's losses and have everything to do with disgorgement of the trustee's personal gains. We saw in Chapter 12 that a trustee is not permitted to retain an unauthorised personal profit acquired by reason of the trusteeship (see 12.1).

A beneficiary may seek compensation, specific restitution and an account of unauthorised profits *all at the same time*. If, for example, a trustee has misappropriated property belonging to the trust he will be liable to make immediate restitution to the trust fund of the specific property. If that property has been, let us say, destroyed, the trustee will be liable to compensate the trust for the loss of that property. Further, suppose that the trustee has been paid to destroy the trust property—he would then be liable to account to the trust fund for the unauthorised profit he had made. Where the remedies available to the claimant are inconsistent, the claimant must elect between them before final judgment is entered in his favour, as the next section explains.

15.1.1 Election between inconsistent remedies

Where a claimant has the right to claim for both compensation *and* an account of profits, the claimant has to elect which remedy he wishes to pursue, so affirmed the Judicial Committee of the Privy Council in *Tang Man Sit (deceased) (personal representative)* v *Capacious Investments Ltd* [1996] 1 All ER 193. Their Lordships held that the claimant company's action for an account of profits was incompatible with its action for an award of compensation for loss. The two remedies were alternative, not cumulative.

 THINKING POINT

Applying your common sense, can you see why the actions for compensation and an account are inconsistent with each other when claimed in respect of the same breach?

The facts of *Tang Man Sit* were briefly that Tang, the owner of land, was party to a joint venture for the building of houses on the land. He agreed to assign some of the houses to the claimant after completion of the building works. No assignment was made. Instead, Tang let out the houses as homes for the elderly without the claimant's knowledge or approval. The presence of the tenants in the flats produced rents but it reduced the letting value of the flats; their presence therefore produced a gain and caused a loss. Accordingly, the claimant sought, on the one hand, an account of unauthorised profits and compensation for breach of trust, and, on the other hand, damages for loss of use and occupation and diminution of the value of the property due to wrongful use and occupation. Lord Nicholls held that the two sides of the claimant's claim were mutually exclusive and that the claimant would have to elect between the two remedies, the basic rule being that election between remedies must be made before judgment is finally entered against the defendant. His Lordship cited, with approval, Lord Wilberforce in *Johnson* v *Agnew* [1979] 2 WLR 487 who had held that '[e]lection, though the subject of much learning and refinement, is in the end a doctrine based on simple considerations of common sense and equity'.

Lord Nicholls described this as the 'classic example' of alternative, inconsistent remedies. The reason they are incompatible, he explained, is because 'the former is measured by the wrong-doer's gain, the latter by the injured party's loss'. You might be thinking that the wrongdoer's gain will be the same as the injured party's loss. In fact, one can think of many cases where this will not be so.

> ### THINKING POINT
>
> Try to think of a fact situation in which you, the beneficiary of a trust, would bring an action against your trustee for compensation rather than for an account of profits.

The obvious example is where the trustee has destroyed or dissipated the trust property and any profits made from it. There is no point seeking an action for an account in such circumstances. However, there are more sophisticated examples. Suppose that I am the beneficiary of a trust in which the trust property is a rare matching pair of Chippendale chairs. If my trustee sells one of them for cash he will gain, let us say, £2,000. I, on the other hand, will have lost more than £2,000 because there is added value in holding a *pair* of matching antiques. Each chair might be worth only £2,000 as a single piece, but a pair might be worth £5,000. Let us take another example. Suppose that I am the beneficiary of a controlling interest in a private company (the trust owns 80 per cent of the shares in the company and I am the sole beneficiary of the trust). If my trustee sells half the shares and misappropriates the profits to himself, his gain will not be as large as my loss. I have lost more than a mere 40 per cent of the shares in the company; I have also lost *control* of the company, and that has an added value!

It may be that the trustee has misappropriated the trust fund to his own use, but has put it to work and produced a vast profit from it. In such a case you will not be content to recover merely that which you have lost; you will also want to recover that which the wrongdoer has gained! (Sometimes even innocent fiduciaries find themselves on the wrong end of such an action: see *Boardman* v *Phipps* at 16.3.1.2.)

We nowadays hold it to be self-evident that compensation and an account for profits are incompatible, hence the need to elect between them. However, the late Professor Stoljar argued that where the defendant makes a profit this is a profit that the claimant could have made, so it is a profit made at the defendant's expense. Thus the account for profit becomes a form of compensation for loss (S. Stoljar, 'Restitutionary Relief for Breach of Contract' (1989) 2 JCL 1). One problem with that view is that it will not always be the case that the claimant *could* have made the profit. Indeed, sometimes it would have been practically impossible for the claimant to have made the profit (see, for example, *Keech* v *Sandford* at 16.3.1.1).

15.1.2 **Comparison with common law remedies**

Brightman J in *Bartlett v Barclays Bank (Nos 1 and 2)* [1980] Ch 515 stated that 'the obligation of a trustee who is held liable for a breach of trust is fundamentally different from the obligation of a contractual or tortious wrongdoer'. There were *dicta* in *Target* to suggest that cases of bare trusts in commercial contexts (e.g. where a solicitor or accountant holds funds for a client) are considered to be analogous to cases in which the common law tort of negligence is alleged, which is why an analogous common-sense test should be applied to determine whether the defendant's wrongdoing had caused harm. However, their Lordships in *AIB Group (UK) Plc v Mark Redler & Co Solicitors* [2014] UKSC 58; [2015] AC 1503 (SC) made the point of stressing that, however apparent and appealing the analogy might be, equitable reasoning is quite different to common law reasoning: 'It follows that the liability of a trustee for breach of trust, even where the trust arises in the context of a commercial transaction which is otherwise regulated by contract, is not generally the same as a liability in damages for tort or breach of contract' (para. [136]).

Broadly speaking, the aim of contractual damages is to put the injured party in the position that they would have been in had the contract been properly performed, while the aim of tortious damages is to place the injured party, as near as possible, in the position that they were in before they suffered the tortious wrong. In both cases the remedies focus upon the personal circumstances of the injured party; damages are awarded because 'damage' has been suffered. As a general rule, it is incorrect to refer to an equitable award of 'damages', although Brightman J in *Bartlett v Barclays Bank Trust Co Ltd (Nos 1 and 2)* [1980] Ch 515 stated that in reality compensation for breach of trust is 'not readily distinguishable from damages except with the aid of a powerful legal microscope'. In situations where the trust fund has suffered a loss due to the breach of trust, the trustee's obligations are similar, but not identical, to those of the contractual or tortious wrongdoer. If specific restitution of the trust property is not possible, then the liability of the trustee is to pay sufficient compensation to the trust estate to put it back to what it would have been had the breach not been committed. However, in determining the proper level of the equitable award the courts prefer to risk overcompensating beneficiaries than to risk the possibility that a trustee might profit from their wrong. Rather than focusing exclusively upon the personal circumstances of the injured party, which is the focus of a common law award of damages, the focus in an award for breach of trust is to a greater extent upon the wrongdoer.

This peculiar focus of an equitable award influences the answers that a court will give to the following questions, when considering the appropriate level of the award:

- How much capital must be repaid to the trust?
- is interest payable, and if so, how much?
- must the trustee who has paid tax on the sums claimed by the beneficiaries pay the full amount or only the amount net of tax?

The following sections attempt to answer these questions.

15.1.3 **Capital repayment**

15.1.3.1 **In an award of compensation**

Compensation is an equitable monetary remedy to recover for loss caused by the defendant. It seeks to restore to the claimant that which has been lost through the breach of trust. The level of compensation should be equivalent to the claimant's actual loss, assessed at the date of the court hearing with the full benefit of hindsight. It was held in *Re Dawson* [1966] 2 NSWR 211 that equitable compensation 'is not limited to common law principles governing remoteness of damage', but the leading English case in this area suggests a growing judicial acceptance of common law reasoning (or language).

 THINKING POINT

Read the extract from *Target Holdings* v *Redferns* (see 15.1). In your own words, briefly state why the trustee was not liable to compensate the beneficiary in that case.

There was no liability to compensate the beneficiary in that case because on a common-sense reading of the facts the trustee's breach had not *caused* the beneficiary's loss. The beneficiary would have suffered to the same degree even if there had not been a breach.

The facts of *Target* were as follows. The defendants were a firm of solicitors acting on behalf of a mortgagor (an established client) and a mortgagee on the creation of a mortgage. The defendants held the loan monies on trust for the mortgagee but paid them over to the mortgagor before the mortgage had been completed. This was in breach of trust. The mortgagee sued the firm of solicitors. In their defence the solicitors argued that they had only committed a technical breach of trust and that the claimant had not suffered any loss because the solicitors had acquired the mortgage to which the claimants were entitled. It was held in the Court of Appeal that when the trustees (solicitors) paid away the trust monies to a stranger they came under an immediate duty to reinstate the trust fund, and that an inquiry into whether the breach of trust actually caused loss to the trust fund was unnecessary, the causal connection being obvious.

The House of Lords reversed this, holding that a common-sense view of causation should be applied, with the full benefit of hindsight. Applying this test the defendants were not liable because the claimant would have suffered the same loss without the defendant's breach of trust. (See, generally, D. Capper, 'Compensation for Breach of Trusts' (1997) 61 Conv 14.) *Target* was followed by the Supreme Court in the *AIB Group* case.

 CASE CLOSE-UP

***AIB Group (UK) Plc v Mark Redler & Co Solicitors* [2014] UKSC 58; [2015] AC 1503, Supreme Court**

Facts: The claimant bank sought to recover compensation from a firm of solicitors that had acted negligently in a remortgage transaction. AIB had loaned £3.3m to Mr and Mrs Sondhi to enable them to remortgage a house then worth £4.25m. The house was subject to a first charge in favour of Barclays Bank plc. The charge secured a total debt of £1.5m owed by the Sondhis and recorded in two different accounts at the bank. AIB made the loan on condition that Barclays' prior mortgage would first be paid off and that AIB would take a first charge over the house. Mark Redler solicitors agreed to carry out the instructions, but mistakenly paid off only one of the Barclays debt accounts. Realising their mistake, they used AIB's money to pay off the second account, in the sum of £309,000, but because of the mistake AIB's charge did not have priority to secure that part of the debt. The Sondhis subsequently defaulted on their repayments and Barclays repossessed the house and sold it for £1.2m. AIB received the first slice of proceeds (£867,697), but they claimed that the solicitors had caused their entire loss (which now stood at about £2.5m). The solicitors admitted the breach of trust but argued, relying on *Target*, that they should be liable to compensate only for such losses as were caused by their failure to register a first charge to secure the £309,000 (which in retrospect could now be seen to have caused a loss of about £275,000). The solicitors argued that they should not be responsible for losses they did not cause, including losses caused by the general decline in the market value of land and (possibly fraudulent) overvaluing of the Sondhis' land.

Held: A key difference between this case and *Target* was that in *Target* the solicitors did what they were meant to do, only late, whereas in *AIB Group* the solicitors never did register a first charge to secure the £309,000 (in fact they tried to keep their error secret). Despite these differences, the Supreme Court held that the solicitors should not be turned into insurers against market risk, but should only compensate for losses which would not have occurred but for their breach. Their Lordships confirmed that the 'the basic *right* of a beneficiary is to have the trust duly administered in accordance with the provisions of the trust instrument, if any, and the general law' and clarified that where there has been a breach of that duty 'the basic *purpose* of any remedy will be either to put the beneficiary in the same position as if the breach had not occurred or to vest in the beneficiary any profit which the trustee may have made by reason of the breach' (para. [64]) (emphasis added). In the same paragraph their Lordships made the following broader conceptual observation which is very interesting in terms of the nature of the strict rules that apply to trustees:

> Placing the beneficiary in the same position as he would have been in but for the breach may involve restoring the value of something lost by the breach or making good financial damage caused by the breach. But a monetary award which reflected neither loss caused nor profit gained by the wrongdoer would be penal.

Hence their Lordships decided that AIB's recovery should be limited to the sum that the solicitor's breach had actually caused, which at the date of judgment was around £275,000, plus interest from 2011, which was the date of sale of the house and the commencement of the proceedings. The interest in such a case will be simple, not compound. (This distinction is discussed later in this chapter.)

The trust in *Target Holdings v Redferns* was a bare trust which had arisen in a commercial setting. Lord Browne-Wilkinson indicated that the level of capital repayment in a traditional trust (of the generic type 'to A for life and B in remainder') should be assessed on a different basis—at least where the life beneficiary is still alive. (When the life beneficiary dies the settlement comes to an end and the trust between trustee and remainder beneficiary should then be treated as a bare trust of the *Target Holdings* type; see, for example, *Hulbert v Avens* (2003) WTLR 387.) It is not that commercial contexts automatically call for different rules governing remedies for breach of trust, but that commercial contexts more often give rise to the sort of bare trusts that call for remedies different to the remedies that apply to settlement type trusts. Traditional family trusts are more likely to have trusts of the settlement type. (In the *AIB Group* case, the Supreme Court sought to dampen enthusiasm for the suggestion that legal doctrinal analysis should be different according to whether the trust context is 'commercial' or 'traditional'.)

Figure 15.1 What is loss?

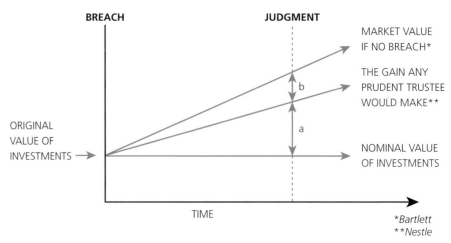

Target provides a very clear and helpful rule of causation to be applied when attempting to fix the appropriate level of an award of equitable compensation for loss. However, it is no panacea. It is a rule that only applies to bare trusts (or settlement trusts that have come to an end), and it does not answer the more basic question: *what is loss? Target* informs us that loss is to be calculated at the date of judgment, with the full benefit of hindsight, but as Figure 15.1 is intended to illustrate, in the context of trustee investments loss can mean either one of two things. Is loss represented by arrow 'a' alone or does it also include arrow 'b'?

Lord Millett, writing extrajudicially, has been strongly critical of the reasoning in *Target Holdings* and critical of the Supreme Court in *Redler* for following *Target*, especially when the Supreme Court in *Redler*:

> confirmed the distinction between cases where the trust is still continuing and cases where it has come to an end on the distribution of the trust fund; the notion that equitable compensation is compensation for loss; and the consequent introduction of a causation requirement. These are all heretical. But the underlying error lies in categorising the remedy as compensatory when it is not. Although the case was decided as a question of causation, it is really a case about remedies. ((2018) *Trust Law International* 44)

Lord Millett went on to list the 'principal remedies which equity makes available for breach of an equitable obligation' as being (i) rescission, (ii) specific performance, (iii) account and orders to make good any deficit and (iv) equitable compensation. His Lordship points out that the 'first three are primary remedies' whereas the fourth 'is a secondary remedy, granted when it would be impractical or unjust, particularly to third parties, to grant the primary remedy'. It follows that, in his Lordship's opinion, the Supreme Court was wrong in *Target* and *Redler* to resort to equitable compensation as a primary remedy. Lord Millett writes, further, that the 'primary remedy for breach of trust is not equitable compensation but account, and the orders which follow the taking of the account are not compensatory but restorative'. It will be interesting to see if the Supreme Court takes the next opportunity to respond to these fundamental criticisms of the current approach.

15.1.3.2 In an account of profits

A trustee is not permitted to profit from his trust; consequently, the rule is that a trustee must reinstate the original capital and account for all profits made on it.

15.1.3.3 In an action for specific restitution

Occasionally, the beneficiaries will wish to recover specific trust property which trustees have misappropriated. So, for example, in *Re Massingberd's Settlement* (1890) 63 LT 296, CA, the trustees had sold an authorised investment and had invested the proceeds in breach of trust in an unauthorised investment. The beneficiaries were entitled to recover the proceeds of sale of the authorised investment but took the alternative option to recover the original investments *in specie* because their value had now increased beyond the level of the original sale proceeds.

Note, however, that in *Re Bell's Indenture* [1980] 1 WLR 1217, Vinelott J held that the decision in *Re Massingberd's* (that the date for valuing assets sold in breach of trust was the date of issue of the writ) was reached *per incuriam* and the correct date should be the date of judgment (which is, of course, in line with *Target*).

15.1.4 Interest on the judgment

By virtue of s 3(1) of the Law Reform (Miscellaneous Provisions) Act 1934 only **simple interest** may be awarded on common law damages. Equity, on the other hand, allows an award of **compound interest** where a person has improperly profited from their fiduciary position (see *Wallersteiner* v *Moir (No 2)* [1975] 1 QB 373).

> **simple interest**
> Interest calculated, usually on an annual basis, on the capital monies due from the trustee to the trust.

> **compound interest** Interest calculated annually by adding to the capital the simple interest which has arisen during the previous year. Compound interest for the following year is calculated on the compound sum of capital and simple interest. The following year accumulated compound interest is added to capital, and the process repeated. It is, essentially, interest on interest.

THINKING POINT

> Here is a question of interest: what do you think is the purpose of awarding compound interest against a trustee? To punish the trustee or merely to ensure that the trustee does not retain profits gained through the unauthorised use of trust monies for the trustee's own purposes?

The answer is that the purpose of awarding compound interest on an account of profits is to ensure that the defendant is not permitted to retain any profits he might have made on misappropriated funds. The award of compound interest is intended to prevent unjust enrichment at the expense of the trust. Compound interest should not be awarded as a punishment.

In *Westdeutsche Landesbank Girozentrale* v *Islington London Borough Council* [1996] 2 WLR 802 the parties had entered a ten-year interest swap agreement based on a notional sum of £25 million. (Under such an agreement one party pays a fixed rate of interest on the sum and the other party pays a variable rate of interest on the sum.) Ancillary to the agreement the bank paid £2.5 million to the council. The council paid 'interest' to the bank under the interest swap agreement. Subsequently it was established (in another case) that interest swap agreements were *ultra vires* the authority of councils. The council in the instant case therefore made no further payments under the agreement. The bank brought this action to recover the balance of the £2.5 million, plus interest. The judge at first instance awarded judgment to the bank for the principal sum plus compound interest. The Court of Appeal dismissed the council's appeal. It brought a further appeal against the award of compound interest.

It was held that in the absence of fraud (or the possibility that a fiduciary might have misapplied property so as to give rise to a personal profit) equity would not award compound interest. The recipient of monies under a contract subsequently rendered void for mistake or as being *ultra vires* did not hold those monies on a resulting trust (see 16.1). As the council was not a trustee or other fiduciary of the monies, the proper award was of simple interest only. This rule has since been relaxed. In *Sempra Metals Ltd (formerly Metallgesellschaft Ltd) v IRC* [2007] UKHL 34 it was held by a bare majority of the House of Lords that the court has power to make an award of compound interest in a claim for restitution where such an award was necessary to achieve full justice for the claimant. As a result of a decision of the Court of Justice of the European Communities which had held certain UK tax provisions to be in contravention of Art 52 (now Art 43) of the EC Treaty, numerous taxpayers sought restitution of tax paid. It was held that the detriment suffered by a taxpayer by the premature payment of tax was loss of use of the money for the period of prematurity and such loss included interest paid on borrowing substitute money during that period. Alternatively, if the taxpayer's reparation claim was framed in restitution, the Inland Revenue had been unjustly enriched by the tax and by interest earned on it. Accordingly, an award of compound interest 'was necessary to achieve full restitution and, hence, a just result'.

We have seen that the *type* of interest awarded is in the discretion of the court, and the same is true of the *rate* of interest. Thus in *Wallersteiner* v *Moir (No 2)* the interest was fixed at 1 per cent above the minimum bank lending rate. In *West* v *West* [2003] All ER (D) 17 (Jun) it was fixed (in order adequately to compensate the beneficiaries for their losses caused by a breach of trust) at 1 per cent over the special account rate. In *Bartlett* v *Barclays Bank (Nos 1 and 2)* [1980] Ch 515 it was fixed at the rate from time to time allowed on the court's short-term investment account.

15.1.5 Is liability net of tax?

When trustees reinstate the trust 'net of tax' this means that they have reduced their repayment to the trust by the amount of tax that the trust has been relieved from having to pay by reason of the breach of trust. The trustees may, for instance, have already paid tax on their improper profits during the time that those profits had been in their hands. This was the situation in *O'Sullivan* v *MAM Ltd* [1985] QB 428. In that case the fiduciary was given credit for the tax which it had already paid on the improper profits, and which it would be unable to reclaim from the Inland Revenue. Clearly there could be no question of the fiduciary profiting from this reduction in its liability to account!

The result in *Bartlett* v *Barclays Trust (Nos 1 and 2)* [1980] Ch 515 was less generous. There the defendant trustee contended that by reason of its breach the sums repayable to the claimant beneficiaries would not, or may not, have been taxable in their hands, whereas they would probably have been taxable had the breach not occurred. The defendant claimed that compensation should not exceed the amount which the claimant would have been left with after taxation. Rejecting that submission, Brightman LJ stated that 'the tax liabilit[ies] of individual beneficiaries . . . do not enter into the picture because they arise not at the point of restitution to the trust estate but at the point of distribution of capital or income out of the trust estate. These are different stages.' The judge accepted the fact that this may place a heavier burden on fiduciary wrongdoers as compared with contractual or tortious wrongdoers.

THINKING POINT

Brightman LJ was considering a traditional type of trust in that case. Do you think that he would have come to the same conclusion if he had been considering a bare trust in a commercial context?

Probably not! After *Target Holdings* v *Redferns* [1996] AC 421 the tax liabilities of 'individual beneficiaries' would be considered. In such a case the courts can be expected to take a common-sense view of the extent of trustees' liability, taking all the facts into account, with the benefit of hindsight.

15.2 Defences

15.2.1 Limitation Act 1980

15.2.1.1 The general time limit

According to s 21(3) of the Act 'an action by a beneficiary to recover trust property or in respect of any breach of trust . . . shall not be brought after the expiration of *six years* from the date on which the right of action accrued'.

The right of action may accrue to different beneficiaries at different times. Consider a typical trust under which A has a life interest and B will take in remainder. A's interest is vested in possession, but B's interest is currently vested in interest only. B's interest will not vest in possession until A's death. If the trustees commit a breach of trust during the currency of A's life interest (that is, during A's life) A will have six years within which to bring an action for breach of trust. However, time does not begin to run against B until B's interest falls into possession on A's death.

THINKING POINT

Lindsey, an adult beneficiary, has a life interest under a trust of which Roger is remainderman. Eleven years ago the trustees of the settlement had placed the trust fund in unauthorised investments. Lindsey died four years ago, having never got around to suing the trustees for their breach. Advise Roger, who now wishes to sue.

Even though the breach of trust occurred 11 years ago, Roger has only been able to sue for the past four years. He is still able to bring an action against the trustees, as long as he does so within two years.

15.2.1.2 Disability

If the person to whom a right of action has accrued was under a disability at the date when the right accrued, they may bring their action within six years from the date that they ceased to be under the disability (s 28, Limitation Act 1980). This applies even if they cease to be under the disability by reason of their death—in which case their personal representatives may bring the action on behalf of their estate.

Infants and persons of unsound mind are treated as being under a disability for the purposes of the Act.

THINKING POINT

Laura, an adult beneficiary, has a life interest under a trust of which Richard is remainder-man. Sixteen years ago the trustees of the settlement placed the trust fund in unauthorised investments. Laura died nine years ago, never having got around to suing the trustees for their breach. Advise Richard, aged 20, who now wishes to sue.

Even though the breach of trust occurred 16 years ago, and Richard's interest vested in possession seven years ago, he has only been absolutely entitled and able to sue for the last two years—before then he had been an infant. He is therefore still able to bring an action against the trustees, as long as he does so within four years.

15.2.1.3 **Concealment**

If any fact relevant to the right of action against the trustee has been deliberately concealed by the defendant, the period of limitation will not begin to run until the claimant becomes aware of the concealment (s 32(1), Limitation Act 1980). The words 'deliberately concealed' received a rather creative interpretation in *Liverpool Roman Catholic Archdiocese Trustees Inc* v *Goldberg* (2000) Times, 18 July, where the judge held that 'concealment' need not be a deliberate concealment of a fact, but could be a deliberate breach of duty of a sort which was not likely to be discovered for some time. The words 'by the defendant' also require further consideration, as *Thorne* v *Heard* [1895] AC 495 illustrates.

The claimant's action was time-barred in *Thorne* v *Heard* because, even though the claimant's cause of action had been concealed, the defendant had not been responsible for the concealment. The defendant in that case was the first mortgagee of a property. The claimants were second mortgagees of the property. The property had been sold and the solicitor employed by the first mortgagee paid off the first mortgage from the proceeds of sale of the property. The solicitor should also have accounted to the second mortgagee. Instead, he kept that part of the proceeds of sale to himself but kept paying off the second mortgage in his dual capacity as solicitor to the mortgagor. The second mortgagee had a right of action against the first mortgagee because the agent of the first mortgagee (the solicitor) had failed to hand over the proceeds of sale, but this right of action had been concealed by the solicitor's actions.

Because of the solicitor's continued repayments of the second mortgage, the second mortgagee had had no reason to think that anything was amiss. By the time they realised the true state of affairs they were too late to bring an action against the first mortgagee. They could not rely upon s 32 to achieve an extension of time because their right of action had been concealed by the solicitor, and not by the defendant.

15.2.2 **Situations to which the Act does not apply**

The Limitation Act 1980 has no application where a beneficiary brings an action for a fraudulent breach of trust, nor where the trustee still holds trust property in breach of trust. Certain crucial sections of the Act will not apply to an action brought by the Attorney-General against the trustees of a charitable trust.

15.2.2.1 **Fraud**

Section 21(1)(a) states that no period of limitation prescribed by the Act shall apply to an action brought by a beneficiary 'in respect of any fraud or fraudulent breach of trust to which the trustee was a party or privy'. Fraud includes 'dishonesty' for this purpose, as where a trustee dishonestly conceals the fact that he has a personal interest in a transaction carried out on behalf of the trust (*Gwembe Valley Development Co Ltd* v *Koshy* [2003] EWCA Civ 1478). 'For a breach of trust to be fraudulent it is not enough to show that it was deliberate. There must also be an absence of honesty or good faith. This can include being reckless as to the consequences of the action complained of' (*First Subsea Ltd* v *Balltec Ltd* [2017] EWCA Civ 186, Court of Appeal, per Patten LJ at para. [64]). This subsection removes the statutory six-year time limit on actions brought by beneficiaries not only against trustees, but also against third parties who were parties to the breach and certain third parties who have received trust property (see Chapters 18 and 19).

15.2.2.2 **Still holding property**

Section 21(1)(b) states that no period of limitation under the Act shall apply to actions 'to recover from the trustee trust property or the proceeds of trust property in the possession of the trustee, or previously received by the trustee and converted to his use'. In *Wassell* v *Leggatt* [1896] 1 Ch 554 a husband who held his wife's property as a trustee was unable to use the Limitation Act as a defence to her action due to his continuing breach of trust in failing to account to her for property that was still in his hands. As Romer J said, 'He was her trustee at first, and never ceased to be her trustee'. In a sense, therefore, a fresh duty to account arose each day and a corresponding cause of action accrued to the beneficiary on a daily basis. The Limitation Act could have no sensible application to this sort of situation, hence its express exclusion by s 21(1)(b).

Contrast *Re Howlett* [1949] 2 All ER 490, where the property was 'notional'. It did not really exist! The father (trustee) was liable to account to his son (beneficiary) for an 'occupation rent' which the father should have been paying by virtue of his occupation of freehold trust property belonging, in equity, to his son. The trustee had been occupying the premises for his own benefit, and because he could not be permitted to profit from his position he was deemed to owe rent to the trust. Accordingly, the son's action for breach of trust would not be barred by the Act because the trustee still had trust property (notional rent) in his possession.

Although s 21(1)(b) excludes the Limitation Act as a defence, s 21(2) places a limit on trustees' liability for actions brought under s 21(1)(b): a claim brought after the limitation period has expired against a trustee who is also a beneficiary under the trust, is limited to property in excess of that trustee's proper share under the trust. Note also that s 21 applies to company directors by analogy so that where misappropriated trust property remains legally and beneficially owned by a corporate vehicle, s 21(1)(b) catches the directors because they are treated as being in possession of it from the outset by virtue of being the fiduciary stewards of it (*Burnden Holdings (UK) Ltd* v *Fielding* [2018] UKSC 14; [2018] 2 WLR 885, Supreme Court, at paras [16–19]). In *Martin* v *Myers* [2004] EWHC 1947 (Ch) the issue was whether a surviving cohabitee who remained in the home she had shared with her deceased partner had become a constructive trustee for their children (who were entitled on her partner's intestacy) so as to be barred under s 21(1)(b) from relying on the Limitation Act 1980 to claim title to the house by long possession. It was held that the surviving cohabitee never became a constructive trustee for her children because her conscience was never affected by knowledge of any entitlement her children might have in the house.

15.2.2.3 **Breaches of mere fiduciary duty/'nominal' trust**

In *Paragon Finance plc* v *DB Thakerar & Co (a firm)* [1999] 1 All ER 400, Court of Appeal, Millett LJ (as he then was) considered *obiter* a defendant who was 'entitled to pay receipts into his own account, mix them with his own money, use them for his own cash flow, deduct his own commission, and account for the balance to the plaintiff only at the end of the year'. His Lordship held that such a defendant will not be a constructive trustee in the event of failure to account, even if he is in a fiduciary relationship (e.g. solicitor/client) with the person to whom he must account. As his Lordship stated:

> It is fundamental to the existence of a trust that the trustee is bound to keep the trust property separate from his own and apply it exclusively for the benefit of his beneficiary. Any right on the part of the defendant to mix the money which he received with his own and use it for his own cash flow would be inconsistent with the existence of a trust. So would a liability to account annually, for a trustee is obliged to account to his beneficiary and pay over the trust property on demand. The fact that the defendant was a fiduciary was irrelevant if he had no fiduciary or trust obligations in regard to the money. If this was the position, then the defendant was a fiduciary and subject to an equitable duty to account, but he was not a constructive trustee.

Of course the significance of this decision for present purposes is that a trustee who is still holding trust property cannot claim the time-bar defence under the Limitation Act 1980, whereas a time limit of six years would apply in the case of a mere fiduciary duty to account. The time limit will also apply to persons liable for dishonestly assisting in the misapplication of trust funds by the trustees, or for knowingly receiving trust funds in breach of trust, for they are not true trustees (*Williams* v *Central Bank of Nigeria* [2014] UKSC 10, Supreme Court; see, further, Chapter 19).

🔍   CASE CLOSE-UP

First Subsea Ltd v *Balltec Ltd* [2017] EWCA Civ 186, Court of Appeal

Facts: the defendant company director resigned and set up a rival company which competed for tenders against the director's former company.

Held: the defendant director had not breached an existing trust of any assets held by him for the claimant. He only became a nominal or formulaic 'constructive trustee' of gains acquired after his breach of fiduciary duty. The judge at first instance had properly held that s 21(1)(b) did not operate to exclude the limitation period, but by reason of his fraud the defendant should be barred from claiming that the limitation period had passed (applying s 21(1)(a)). Their Lordships noted that, following the decision of the Supreme Court in *FHR European Ventures LLP* v *Cedar Capital Partners LLC* [2014] UKSC 45 (see Chapter 19), a person who makes an unauthorised gain in breach of fiduciary duty is deemed to hold the gain on constructive trust for his principal and therefore cannot claim that the limitation period has expired.

15.2.2.4 **Charitable trusts**

In *Attorney-General* v *Cocke* [1988] Ch 414 Harman J held that the Limitation Act could be no bar to an action for an account brought by the Attorney-General against the trustees of a charitable trust because the only possible 'beneficiary' of a charitable trust, to whom a cause of action could accrue, would be 'the public at large'. Accordingly, as it could not sensibly be said in such a case that an action had accrued, the action could not be said to have been barred by the Limitation Act 1980.

15.2.3 **Time bars by analogy to the Act**

According to *Knox* v *Gye* (1872) 5 App Cas 656 at 674, where equity exercises a concurrent jurisdiction (giving the same or corresponding relief) as the common law, the exercise of such equitable jurisdiction will be time-barred by analogy to the time bar under the Act in relation to the comparable common law jurisdiction. In *Coulthard* v *Disco Mix Club Ltd* [1999] 2 All ER 457 an equitable claim based on breaches of fiduciary duty by way of deliberate and dishonest underaccounting, arising from the same facts as a common law fraud, were held to be subject to the Limitation Act 'by analogy'.

The Limitation Act 1980, s 36(1) states that the time limits under the Act may be 'applied by the court by analogy' to bar *equitable* relief of a sort which would have been time-barred under the Act in comparable legal proceedings. In *P&O Nedlloyd BV* v *Arab Metals Co* [2006] EWCA Civ 1717 the Court of Appeal concluded that in claims for specific performance it is never appropriate to apply a limitation period in equity by analogy to the common law because specific performance has no common law counterpart. Where trust monies have been improperly paid away by a trustee, the situation may be sufficiently analogous to a claim at common law for a fixed sum of money, so that the expression 'liquidated pecuniary claim' in s 29(5)(a) of the 1980 Act might in some cases include a claim against a trustee for the recovery of such monies or for compensation in respect of other trust assets wrongly misapplied (stated *obiter* in *Barnett* v *Creggy* [2016] EWCA Civ 1004; [2017] 2 WLR 1054; Court of Appeal. Noted Whayman (2017) 2 Conv 139–46).

15.2.4 *Laches*

The doctrine of *laches* bars an action by reason of the 'staleness' of the claim. (The word *laches* has its root in the Latin *laxus*, meaning 'loose'. Even in everyday speech we might describe as 'lax' a person who acts in a tardy manner.) But this defence can be resorted to only in situations where the Act does not apply either expressly or by analogy. According to Lindley LJ in *Re Sharpe* [1892] 1 Ch 154, 'A defence based on the staleness of demand renders it necessary to consider the time which has elapsed and the balance of justice or injustice in affording or refusing relief'. The modern approach to the doctrine of *laches* does not entail slavish adherence to formulae derived from earlier cases. Each case is decided on its facts applying a broad approach directed to ascertaining whether, in all the circumstances, it would be unconscionable for a party to be permitted to exercise his beneficial right (*Frawley* v *Neill* [2000] CP Rep 20, Court of Appeal; followed in *Patel* v *Shah* [2005] EWCA Civ 157, Court of Appeal). However, as well as seeking justice between the parties, the courts are also conscious of the public interest in seeing an end to litigation (G. Watt, 'Laches Estoppel and Election', in Birks and Pretto (eds), *Breach of Trust*, Oxford: Hart Publishing Ltd, 2002, p. 353).

The following *dictum* of Lord Camden in *Smith* v *Clay* (1767) Ambl 645, 3 Bro CC 639n expounds the relationship between *laches* and 'time-bars by analogy' (see 15.2.3):

> A Court of Equity, which is never active in relief against conscience or public convenience, has always refused its aid to stale demands, where the party has slept upon his right and acquiesced for a great length of time . . . But, as the Court has no legislative authority, it

could not properly define the time-bar by a positive rule to an hour, a minute or a year; it was governed by circumstances. But so often as Parliament had limited the time of actions and remedies to a certain period in legal proceedings, the Court of Chancery adopted that rule and applied [it] to similar cases in equity. For when the legislature had fixed the time at law it would have been preposterous for equity (which by its own proper authority always maintained a limitation) to countenance laches beyond the period that law had been confined to by Parliament.

It may be surprising to learn that *laches* can apply as a defence in a case of fraud. The position in equity on this matter was set out as long ago as *Bulli Coal Mining v Osborne* [1899] AC 351 at 363: 'It has always been a principle of equity that no length of time is a bar to relief in a case of fraud, in the absence of laches on the part of the person defrauded.'

15.2.5 Beneficiary's instigation of or consent to the breach

It will be a defence to show that a beneficiary has instigated or consented to a breach of trust, but the trustee may raise this defence only to the particular beneficiary who requested or instigated the breach, and only then if the beneficiary was *sui juris* and not subject to any undue influence. The claims of other beneficiaries will not be prejudiced.

A beneficiary can only be said to have instigated or consented to a breach of trust if they have knowledge of all the facts constituting the breach of trust. However, it is not necessary for the trustee to show that the beneficiary was aware that these facts amounted to a breach of trust to raise a successful defence.

 CASE CLOSE-UP

Somerset v Earl Poullett [1894] 1 ChD 231, Court of Appeal

Facts: trustees of a settlement committed an innocent breach of trust when they invested in an undersecured mortgage. One of the beneficiaries had consented in writing to investing by way of mortgage; the question therefore arose whether the trustees should for that reason be indemnified by the beneficiaries for the consequences of their breach. It was held that the trustees would be liable in full.

Lindley LJ: 'if a *cestui que trust* instigates, requests, or consents in writing to an investment not in terms authorised by the power of investment, he clearly falls within the section; and in such a case his ignorance or forgetfulness of the terms of the power would not, I think, protect him—at all events, not unless he could give some good reason why it should, e.g. that it was caused by the trustee. But if all that a *cestui que trust* does is to instigate, request, or consent in writing to an investment which is authorised by the terms of the power, the case is, I think, very different. He has a right to expect that the trustees will act with proper care in making the investment, and if they do not they cannot throw the consequences on him unless they can show that he instigated, requested, or consented in writing to their non-performance of their duty in this respect.'

A beneficiary who has instigated or consented to the breach of trust may have to relieve the trustees from liability in actions taken by the other beneficiaries (see the discussion on impounding at 15.3.5).

15.2.6 **Beneficiary's acquiescence in breach**

If the breach has already occurred a beneficiary might release the trustee from liability by either a formal release or by acquiescing in the breach by words or conduct. As for instigation or consent, **acquiescence** must be fully informed and the beneficiary must be *sui juris*. In *Holder v Holder* [1968] 1 All ER 665 a trustee bought trust property in a manner which was voidable at the instance of the beneficiary. The beneficiary did not take advantage of his right to avoid the sale but was held not to have acquiesced because they had not been aware of their right to avoid the sale.

The Court of Appeal in *Holder* v *Holder* approved the following *dictum* of Wilberforce J in *Re Pauling's ST* [1963] 3 All ER 1:

> The court has to consider all the circumstances in which the concurrence of the *cestui que trust* was given with a view to seeing whether it is fair and equitable that, having given his concurrence, he should afterwards turn around and sue the trustees: that, subject to this, it is not necessary that he should know that what he is concurring in is a breach of trust, provided that he fully understands what he is concurring in, and that it is not necessary that he should himself have directly benefited by the breach of trust.

> **acquiescence**
> The decision by an injured party not to take action in response to the wrong done. Acquiescence may be a ground for barring a claim.

15.2.7 **Summative exercise on the defences of instigation, consent and acquiescence**

Your task is to place each of the following three factors in the appropriate place in the Venn diagram at Figure 15.2:

- even where this defence is good against beneficiaries complicit in the breach of trust, it is not good against other beneficiaries;
- this defence will only succeed against beneficiaries who have knowledge of all the facts constituting the breach of trust;
- this defence is based upon the beneficiaries' words or conduct after the breach of trust occurred.

Figure 15.2 Summative exercise Venn diagram

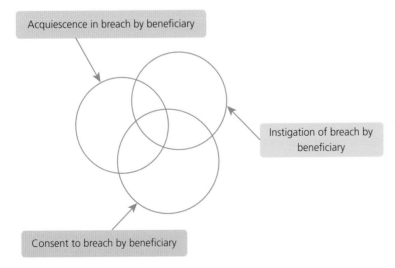

Acquiescence in breach by beneficiary

Instigation of breach by beneficiary

Consent to breach by beneficiary

With one exception, all three factors need to be proved in every case and should therefore have been placed in the central segment of the Venn diagram. The exception is the third factor in the list, which should have been placed in the acquiescence circle only.

15.3 Relief from liability

If trustees are unable to raise a defence to a breach of trust, or if the defence can only be raised against some of the beneficiaries, trustees may nevertheless be relieved from all or some of their liability.

15.3.1 **Set-off**

The general rule is that if a trustee makes a gain in one breach of trust he cannot set off that gain against a loss arising out of another breach of trust. However, in the modern commercial environment, investments are often made on a 'portfolio' basis. A number of apparently separate investments may be treated as part and parcel of a single transaction.

 THINKING POINT

In *Bartlett* v *Barclays Trust (Nos 1 and 2)* [1980] 1 All ER 139 a property development company, which was almost wholly owned by the trust corporation (the bank), made a loss on one speculative property investment and made a gain on another. What was the result of that case? Did the result infringe the general rule against set-off of one breach against another?

The court treated both investments, the successful investment in Guildford and the failed investment in London, as part of the same wrongful course of conduct. Gains made in Guildford were set off against the losses made in London. However, the result in the case did not infringe the general rule against set-off between breaches of trust because both investment transactions could easily be seen as forming part of the same breach of trust, i.e. the same failure to supervise the trust-owned company. It is interesting to speculate whether the set-off would have been permitted if the trustee, and not the trust-owned company, had entered into the two transactions.

15.3.2 **Contribution**

A trustee who is liable for a breach of trust may recover a contribution from any other person (usually another trustee) who is liable for the same damage.

Trustees are, of course, liable only for their own defaults; they will not be held vicariously liable for breaches committed by their co-trustees. The trustees will, however, be jointly and severally liable for breaches to which they have together been parties and because trustees are required to exercise their powers unanimously, they will be liable for losses that were caused by their own imprudence in failing to supervise the activities of their co-trustees. In *Bahin* v *Hughes* (1886) 31 ChD 390, a trustee was unable to escape liability merely by showing that they had taken a passive role in the execution of the trust. It was held that they had been in a position to supervise the activities of their co-trustees and to prevent the breach. This liability for omissions goes beyond that which is found in the law of torts. In *Styles* v *Guy* (1849) 1 Mac & G 422, executors were held to be in the same position as trustees in so far as having a duty to supervise their co-executors. One executor owed money to the estate and the other executors took no effective steps to bring the money into the estate. The first executor eventually went bankrupt and his co-executors were required to make up the losses to the fund.

Where such breaches occur after 1978, the Civil Liability (Contributions) Act 1978 applies. Under this Act the court may apportion liability between trustees who are 'jointly and severally liable' for the same breach of trust, according to whatever is 'just and equitable'. Apportionment is effected by requiring one trustee to make a financial contribution to another trustee in reduction of the latter's liability to the trust. Section 6(1) of the Act confirms that a person is liable to contribute under the Act whether his liability is based in 'tort, breach of contract, breach of trust or otherwise'. A person who is liable for knowing receipt of property misapplied in breach of trust (see Chapter 19) is also liable to contribute under the Act (*Charter plc v City Index Ltd (Gawler, Part 20 defendants)* [2008] EWCA Civ 1382; [2008] 2 WLR 950 (noted G. Virgo, 'Contribution Revisited' (2008) 67 CLJ 254). Carnwath LJ observed that:

> [w]hen the recipient has retained the receipts or profited from them it would be just and equitable for the recipient's liability to be met from the retained money or profits rather than to expect any other defendant to make a contribution, however the knowing recipient should be able to claim a contribution from another party if that party is liable to the claimant for a distinct wrong such as tort.

15.3.3 Indemnity

A trustee who is liable to the beneficiaries for a breach of trust may claim an indemnity from a co-trustee if that co-trustee:

- is a solicitor-trustee whose controlling influence over the other trustees resulted in the breach (see 15.3.3.2); or
- committed the breach fraudulently; or
- exclusively benefited from the breach.

15.3.3.1 The trustee beneficiary

Where a trustee who has exclusively benefited from a breach of trust is also a beneficiary under the trust, he will be liable to indemnify his co-trustees up to the extent of his beneficial interest under the trust. This is because a beneficiary cannot complain of a breach to which they were a party. The judge in *Chillingworth* v *Chambers* [1896] 1 Ch 685 described this as the co-trustee's 'lien'.

As a general rule defaulting trustees cannot claim any beneficial entitlement in a trust estate until they have made good their default, as they are deemed to have received their share already.

This rule did not apply in *Re Towndrow* [1911] 1 Ch 662 because the trustee was entitled only to a specific legacy under the trust whereas his breach had caused a loss to the residue of the testator's estate. Because the legacy and the residue were held upon distinct trusts the trustee beneficiary was not liable to indemnify out of the legacy.

15.3.3.2 **Trustees with controlling influence**

In *Re Partington* (1887) 57 LT 654 a solicitor-trustee had a controlling influence over the other trustee, the testator's widow. The widow made an unauthorised investment in breach of trust. The court held that the solicitor-trustee had misled the widow into making the investment. He would therefore have to indemnify the widow against her liability to the trust. However, it will not be *presumed* that a solicitor has a controlling influence (*Head* v *Gould* [1898] 2 Ch 250).

15.3.4 **Trustee Act 1925, s 61**

Under this section the courts may relieve a trustee who has acted *honestly* and *reasonably* and *ought fairly to be excused*. As long as these three requirements are met the award of relief is in the discretion of the court, and consequently appellate courts have shown some reluctance to overturn the decisions of judges at first instance (see *Marsden* v *Regan* [1954] 1 WLR 423).

Before awarding relief under this section, all three requirements must be met. The honesty requirement is straightforward enough; the other two require further analysis.

15.3.4.1 **'Reasonably'**

Section 61 of the Trustee Act 1925 seems to introduce a tort-like test of reasonableness by the back door. An 'imprudent' trustee will be liable for a breach of trust, but the same trustee, if he has acted reasonably (and the other conditions of s 61 are satisfied), might be relieved from some or all of their liability. (See A.M. Kenny, 'The Reasonable Trustee' (1982) 126 Sol Jo 631.)

There are numerous reported cases in which trustees have sought to rely upon s 61 or its statutory precursors. While they have almost invariably satisfied the honesty requirement, many of them have failed to show that they have acted reasonably.

Occasionally trustees, especially non-professional trustees, do succeed in relying on s 61 on the basis that they committed a 'reasonable' error of judgment (for example, in *Re Evans* [1999] 2 All ER 777). The section assisted trustees of land used by a tennis club who omitted to charge rent because they (erroneously) believed that the land was held on charitable trusts for the benefit of the club members (*Re St Andrew's (Cheam) Lawn Tennis Club Trust (sub nom Philippe* v *Cameron*) [2012] EWHC 1040 (Ch); [2012] 3 All ER 746). Trustees who do their reasonable best by following expert investment advice may be relieved of liability under s 61 for loss caused by the investment (*Daniel* v *Tee* [2016] EWHC 1538 (Ch)). However, professional trustees who inadvertently handed trust money to a fraudster could not rely upon s 61, because even a single error could undermine the regime to protect beneficiaries from risk (*Santander UK Plc* v *RA Legal Solicitors* [2014] EWCA Civ 183).

15.3.4.2 **'Ought fairly to be excused'**

In *Marsden* v *Regan* [1954] 1 WLR 423 the claimant complained that the defendant executrix had paid off all the business creditors of a trust-owned business before the business had eventually been wound up, but had not paid him. Given that the claimant had been the landlord of the premises from which the business had been run, the claimant argued that it would not be fair to relieve the defendant of her liability to account to him. It is interesting that the claimant had relied upon evidence of the defendant's treatment of others as a basis for showing that the defendant should not be relieved from her particular liability to him.

The judge at first instance decided that the defendant had acted honestly and reasonably and ought fairly to be excused. In the Court of Appeal Denning LJ doubted that the defendant ought fairly to be excused, but he felt that it would not be proper to interfere in the fully in-formed exercise of the judge's discretion at first instance.

In the same case Evershed MR made it clear that it will not be sufficient, by itself, for a trustee seeking relief from liability to say 'I acted throughout on a solicitor's advice'.

15.3.5 Impounding the beneficiary's interest

The court has the power to impound a beneficiary's interest under the trust in certain circum-stances. That impounded interest can then be used, in whole or in part, to relieve a trustee from their liability to the other trustees.

15.3.5.1 Impounding under the court's inherent jurisdiction

Under its inherent jurisdiction the court can impound if the beneficiary:

- *instigated* or *requested* the breach *with the intention of obtaining a personal benefit*; or
- *consented* to the breach and *actually benefited* from it.

15.3.5.2 Impounding under s 62

Under this section the court can impound if the beneficiary:

- *instigated* or *requested* the breach; or
- *consented in writing* to the breach.

15.3.6 Contributory fault

Suppose that the sole adult beneficiary of a bare trust instructs his trustee to invest the fund by making a loan to a high-risk borrower on a specified date, but through carelessness the trustee makes the loan early and by the specified date the borrower is already bankrupt. Or suppose that a competent adult beneficiary strongly encourages his trustee to invest in a particular asset, the asset being of an authorised type, but one which would have been discovered on reason-able inquiry by the trustee or beneficiary to be an inappropriately high-risk example of its type. In both of these cases the trustee breaches his trust when he makes the investment, and he is presumed liable to account to the beneficiary for the full extent of any loss that would not have occurred but for the breach. Common law liability for negligence can be reduced to take ac-count of the claimant's contributory fault, but in *Nationwide Building Society* v *Various Solicitors (No 3)* [1999] PNLR 606, Blackburne J held that a trustee's liability should not be reduced to take account of the trust beneficiary's contributory fault, but arguably contributory fault should be recognised as a ground of apportioning trustee liability for breach of the duty of care in the context of bare trusts. In bare trusts the trustee's duty is not to compensate the beneficiary in-directly by accounting to the trust fund, but to compensate the beneficiary directly; accordingly there is no fundamental difference in a bare trust between the trustee's duty to compensate for losses caused by breach of the trustee's duty of care and common law liability to compensate an injured party for negligently caused harm, as I have argued in G. Watt, 'Contributory fault and breach of trust' (2005) 5(2) OUCLJ 205. In that article I also noted the theoretical possibility that the Trustee Act 1925, s 61 (see earlier) might be used to reduce a bare trustee's liability to take account of a beneficiary's negligence, but the courts have shown reluctance to extend the section in that direction when Parliament could have done so expressly (*Lloyds TSB Bank Plc* v *Markandan & Uddin (A Firm)* [2010] EWHC 2840 (Ch)).

15.4 Exemption from liability

We have considered trustees' exemption clauses in some detail in the context of trustees' standard of care (see the case of *Armitage* v *Nurse* at 11.3). We have seen that liability for breach of trust may be excluded by a clause to that effect, although liability for a dishonest breach of trust cannot be excluded. We also noted that professional trustees are more likely than lay trustees to include such a clause in their trust, with the perverse result that professional trustees are subject to a higher standard of care than common trustees, but a lower likelihood of liability for breach of that standard of care. Thankfully, the Law Commission is currently proposing a new scheme for regulating such clauses to ensure that they are only relied upon where reasonable (see 11.3.3).

 Summary

The liability of trustees for breach of trust can be extensive. They may even be liable where they have acted reasonably, although their reasonableness is one of the factors relevant to whether or not the court will relieve them from their liability:

- The basic duty of a trustee is to account for the assets entrusted to him. The trustee will be liable to make up any shortfall by compensating the fund ('accounting to the fund' may be a better description), but only where the fund is still being managed for the benefit of several beneficiaries. Where there is only one beneficiary, the trustee will be required to compensate that beneficiary directly by the payment of damages (called 'equitable compensation' to distinguish it from common law damages). The trustee might also be required to make specific restitution of particular assets (e.g. an heirloom) which ought to have been retained in the fund and was wrongfully misapplied.

- Beyond the basic duty to account for losses, the trustee must also account for unauthorised gains, and on top of any liability there may be additional liability to pay interest (which in the case of a breach of fiduciary duty or fraud may be compound interest).

- On the positive side for the trustee, there are a number of defences he can turn to. They include:

  - time bar under the Limitation Act 1980 (but this does not apply to cases of fraudulent breaches of trust and cases where the trustee is still holding the trust property);

  - time bars by analogy to the Act (time limits under the Act may be 'applied by the court by analogy' to bar equitable relief of a sort which would have been time-barred under the Act in comparable legal proceedings);

  - *laches*;

  - a beneficiary's instigation of or consent to the breach.

- A trustee in breach might also seek to be relieved of some or all of his liability; in an appropriate case this can be achieved by any of the following methods:

  - contribution from other (more blameworthy) trustees;

  - indemnity from a co-trustee if that co-trustee is a solicitor-trustee whose controlling influence over the other trustees resulted in the breach (see 15.3.3.2), or committed the breach fraudulently, or exclusively benefited;

  - impounding the interest of any beneficiary who instigated or consented to the breach.

Often, the choice is stark: either the courts visit the trustee with liability or they allow the loss to remain with the beneficiaries. Where the choice is between an honest and reasonable, but imprudent, trustee on the one hand, and wholly innocent beneficiaries on the other, the trustee will never win.

? Summative assessment exercise

Theresa died in 2013. By her will she settled a trust of £20,000 cash on trustees for the benefit of her nephew Bill and her niece Barbara, 'in equal shares upon their attaining the age of 21'. At the date of Theresa's death Bill was 13 and Barbara was 15. Theresa had also made a gift in her will of £10,000 to another nephew, Barry. The trustees are Tricia, Tracy and Barry. Tricia is a solicitor.

In January 2014, Tricia urged Tracy and Barry to join her in investing in a private limited company which, she said, promised to be a very profitable investment. She explained to the trustees that although the investment was 'technically unauthorised' (the trust instrument prohibited investment in private companies) it was perfectly sound. In the event the trustees went ahead with the investment in the company, having first obtained the consent of Bill and Barbara, who had been told that the investment was a 'safe one'.

Shortly after making the investment the shares rose in value and yielded large dividends to the trust, but later they fell in value and today they are practically worthless. It is now April 2019 and Bill and Barbara have issued proceedings against the trustees.

Advise the trustees as to the possible extent of their liability to the trust and any defences which might be open to them.

 Full specimen answers can be found at www.oxfordtextbooks.co.uk/orc/watt_ directions5e/.

The bigger picture

In this chapter we have been considering trustees' liability for breach of a duty owed to the trust or to a beneficiary, but as an endnote to this chapter it is worth clarifying that a trustee will be able to raise an absolute defence to a beneficiary's claim if by the express terms of the trust the trustee has no duty to that beneficiary.

Where the trust excludes a duty there can be no question of liability arising if that duty has not been executed, or if it has been executed without appropriate care. As was stated in *Hayim v Citibank* [1987] 1 AC 730:

> It is of course unusual for a testator to relieve the trustee of his will of any responsibility or duty in respect of the trust property, but a testator may do as he pleases.

In that case, a particular clause of the will had relieved the trustee of any 'responsibility or duty' to the beneficiaries with respect to certain property owned by the trust. It appears to follow from this decision that, whereas a trustee may not disclaim a trust in part (by accepting the trust as regards some property and disclaiming the trust as regards other property (see 10.2.2)), a similar 'partial trusteeship' may be achieved by virtue of the express terms of the trust.

Further reading

Birks, P. and Pretto, A. (eds), *Breach of Trust* (2002) Oxford: Hart Publishing
a collection of essays on various aspects of breach of trust

Conaglen, M.D.J. 'Equitable Compensation for Breach of Fiduciary Dealing Rules' (2003) 119 LQR 246
an overview of the law governing the types of conduct and losses that must be proved to establish a right to equitable compensation

Davies, P.S. 'Remedies for breach of trust' (2015) 78(4) MLR 681–94
commenting on the *AIB Group* case, the author considers whether traditional trusts should be distinguished from commercial trusts

Davies, P.S. 'Section 61 of the Trustee Act 1925: Deus Ex Machina?' (2015) 5 Conv 379–94
reviews the case law permitting courts to relieve trustees of personal liability for breach of trust under the Trustee Act 1925, s 61

Degeling, S. and Varuhas, J.N.E. (eds) *Equitable Compensation and Disgorgement of Profit* (2017) Oxford: Hart Publishing
a collection of essays on equitable compensation and disgorgement of profit

Hayton, D. 'The Irreducable Core Content of Trusteeship' in A.J. Oakley (ed.), *Trends in Contemporary Trust Law* (1996) Oxford: Oxford University Press 47
an article that questions the extent to which general trustee duties and general liability for breach of trustee duties can be removed by the particular terms of a trust instrument

Lord Millett, 'Case Comment on *AIB* v *Redler*', Supreme Court [2018] Trust Law International 44
a strong critique of *Target Holdings* as followed in *AIB* v *Redler*, arguing that 'the primary remedy for breach of trust is not equitable compensation but account, and the orders which follow the taking of the account are not compensatory but restorative'.

Oakley, A.J. 'The Liberalising Nature of Remedies for Breach of Trust' in A.J. Oakley (ed.), *Trends in Contemporary Trust Law* (1996) Oxford: Oxford University Press 217
an article considering the general trend towards allowing trustees to act as freely as possible

Paling, D.R. 'The Trustee's Duty of Skill and Care' (1973) 37 Conv 48
an article examining the potential to judge trustee conduct by a subjective standard of care

Worthington, S. 'Fiduciary Duties and Proprietary Remedies: Addressing the Failure of Equitable Formulae' (2013) 72(3) CLJ 720–52
advances a systematic framework for assessing the availability of proprietary remedies for breach of the fiduciary duty of loyalty

 For links to selected cases, statutes, academic papers and official reports mentioned in this chapter please visit the online resources at www.oup.com/uk/watt_directions6e/.

16 Resulting and constructive trusts

Introduction

If you are a ballet aficionado, you will be familiar with all sorts of sauts, which are balletic leaps of various types. If the circus is your preferred entertainment, you will be familiar with the somersaults of the trapeze artist. Both words have their root in the Latin saltus, meaning 'a jump'. The resulting in 'resulting trust' has the same derivation. Resulting trusts are jumping trusts. Whereas an express trust is a form of disposition under which the beneficial interest in the trust assets leaves the settlor, a resulting trust describes the trust under which, in certain circumstances, the beneficial interest is said to jump back to the settlor.

The etymology can be highly informative. Take the simple case where A delivers an asset to a stranger, B, in circumstances where B gives nothing in return and there is no available evidence of A's intentions in making the transfer. We cannot tell to whom the asset belongs. Equity is said to 'abhor' such a vacuum in beneficial ownership and therefore presumes that the asset, although held by B, has 'jumped back' to A under a resulting trust. Until the asset is transferred back to A, B will remain legal owner by virtue of his possession, but A will be the owner of the benefit in equity. Now imagine the simple case where A delivers an asset to B, to be held on trust by B for a specific purpose. If that trust fails for some reason, perhaps because the purpose has become impossible to perform, who, in equity, will own the asset? Again, equity sees a resulting trust as the solution to the vacuum in beneficial ownership, and regards B to be a trustee for A. A simple example of a resulting trust is where someone pays money into the bank account of a company that no longer exists (see, for example, *Omojole v HSBC Bank Plc* [2012] EWHC 3102 (Comm)). The money cannot belong to the company. If no other recipient is entitled to the money under a contract or such like, this leaves two possibilities. Either the money belongs to nobody, in which case it will pass to the Crown as '*bona vacantia*' ('ownerless assets'), or it will return to the original owner under a resulting trust. Judges know that the former outcome is the last that any donor would intend, so the latter outcome is preferred—not only on the basis of the donor's intention, but because as a matter of policy private property should be kept in private ownership where possible. One way to imagine the mechanism of the resulting trust is to picture the benefit of the asset as a bouncy ball that is thrown to a person who does not exist. The law is most reluctant for the benefit to be deemed ownerless, so the court erects a notional barrier to prevent the wealth from passing into Crown ownership. The bouncy ball of benefit having missed the intended donee, it hits the barrier raised to prevent *bona vacantia* and bounces straight back to the person who put the benefit in to begin with.

We will see that resulting trusts arise *in accordance with* the presumed intention of the settlor or donor. In relation to constructive trusts, the trust is enforced *against* the personal wishes of the constructive trustee. As Lord Browne-Wilkinson stated in *Westdeutsche Landesbank Girozentrale v Islington London Borough Council* [1996] 2 WLR 802 at 828–9: 'A resulting trust is not imposed by law against the intentions of the trustee (as a constructive trust) but gives effect to his presumed intention.'

In previous chapters we have mainly been concerned with the creation and operation of express trusts. Such trusts are characterised by the settlor's expressed intention to create a trust, whether or not the word 'trust' is actually used. Resulting and constructive trusts, which are the subject of the present chapter, are united by the fact that they are not based on any express intention. They are also united by the fact that they are not subject to statutory formality. The Law of Property Act 1925, s 53(2) provides that 'the creation or operation of resulting, implied or constructive trusts' is not subject to any written formality. This is a particularly important provision in relation to the creation of trusts of land, as we shall witness in the next chapter. (Note that the 2007 decision of the House of Lords in *Stack* v *Dowden* (see 17.2.1) creates a significant exception to the orthodox law of resulting trusts so far as it concerns land shared as a home by cohabitants who are not married or in a civil partnership.)

16.1 Resulting trusts

A sensible starting point for any attempt to classify **resulting trusts** is the speech of Lord Browne-Wilkinson in *Westdeutsche Landesbank Girozentrale* v *Islington London Borough Council* [1996] 2 WLR 802. The case concerned a dispute over the type of interest (compound or simple) appropriate to a restitutionary award (see 15.1.4) so his Lordship's comments on resulting trusts are strictly speaking *obiter dicta*, but his Lordship sought to summarise the law in this area.

> **THINKING POINT**
>
> Consider the following extract from his Lordship's speech. He classified all resulting trusts as falling within one of two main categories. What were they?

 CASE CLOSE-UP

Westdeutsche Landesbank Girozentrale v Islington London Borough Council [1996] 2 WLR 802, House of Lords

Lord Browne-Wilkinson: 'under existing law a resulting trust arises in two sets of circumstances: (A) where A makes a voluntary payment to B or pays (wholly or in part) for the purchase of property which is vested either in B alone or in the joint names of A and B, there is a presumption that A did not intend to make a gift to B: the money or property is held on trust for A (if he is the sole provider of the money) or in the case of a joint purchase by A and B in shares proportionate to their contributions. It is important to stress that this is only a presumption, which presumption is easily rebutted either by the counter-presumption of advancement or by direct evidence of A's intention to make an outright transfer: see Underhill and Hayton, *Law of Trusts and Trustees*, pp. 317 *et seq.*; *Vandervell* v *IRC* [1967] 2 AC 291, 312 *et seq.*; *Re Vandervell's Trusts (No 2)* [1974] Ch 269, 288 *et seq.* (B) Where A transfers property to B on express trusts, but the trusts declared do not exhaust the whole beneficial interest: *ibid.* and *Quistclose Investment Ltd* v *Rolls Razor Ltd (in liquidation)* [1970] AC 567. Both types of resulting trust are traditionally regarded as examples of trusts giving effect to the common intention of the parties. A resulting trust is not imposed by law against the intentions of the trustee (as is a constructive trust) but gives effect to his presumed intention. Megarry J in *Re Vandervell's Trusts (No 2)* suggests that a

> resulting trust of type (B) does not depend on intention but operates automatically. I am not convinced that this is right. If the settlor has expressly, or by necessary implication, abandoned any beneficial interest in the trust property, there is in my view no resulting trust: the undisposed-of equitable interest vests in the Crown as *bona vacantia*: see *Re West Sussex Constabulary's Widows, Children and Benevolent (1930) Fund Trusts*, Re [1971] Ch 1.'

His Lordship held that resulting trusts arise in two sets of circumstances, which he labelled (A) and (B) as follows:

(A) where A makes a voluntary payment to B or pays (wholly or in part) for the purchase of property which is vested either in B alone or in the joint names of A and B, there is a presumption that A did not intend to make a gift to B: the money or property is held on trust for A (if he is the sole provider of the money) or in the case of a joint purchase by A and B in shares proportionate to their contributions . . .

(B) Where A transfers property on express trusts, but the trusts declared do not exhaust the whole of the beneficial interest.

We will now turn to consider each of Lord Browne-Wilkinson's categories in turn, under their orthodox denomination 'presumed resulting trusts', and will consider whether, contrary to his Lordship's view, there exists an additional category of 'automatic resulting trusts'. However, before proceeding, it is important to note that resulting trusts will only be presumed where the settlor has made no express provision to the contrary. The settlor's intentions cannot be *presumed* to be one thing, when he or she has *expressly* intended another. As Harman J stated in *Re Cochrane's Settlement Trusts* [1955] 1 All ER 222: 'A resulting trust is the last resort to which the law has recourse when the draftsman has made a blunder or failed to dispose of that which he has set out to dispose of.'

Figure 16.1 illustrates the general circumstance in which a failed intention will give rise to a resulting trust.

Figure 16.1 The resulting trust

16.1.1 Presumed resulting trusts on a voluntary transfer

This is Lord Browne-Wilkinson's category (A). Under this category a resulting trust is presumed to arise where property is transferred to another person for no consideration in circumstances in which no gift was intended. The presumption of the resulting trust is based upon the transferor's presumed intention to recover the transferred wealth. According to *Dyer* v *Dyer* (1788) 2 Cox Eq Cas 92, this category of resulting trust will apply whether the trust property is real or personal. An interesting contemporary example of the latter appears from *Abrahams* v *Trustee in Bankruptcy of Abrahams* [1999] BPIR 637. A wife paid £1.00 each week into a National Lottery syndicate under the name of the husband, from whom she had separated. The syndicate won. The court held that the right to winnings had the character of a property right, and that this right, though in the husband's name, was presumed to be the wife's under a resulting trust because she had contributed the winning £1.00.

Some of the best examples of resulting trusts within this category are to be found in the purchase of land. Those cases will be considered in Chapter 17. This chapter confines itself, in the main, to resulting trusts of personalty, in relation to which one of the leading cases is *Fowkes* v *Pascoe* (1875) 10 Ch App 343 (which is discussed in the next section).

16.1.1.1 Rebutting the presumption of a resulting trust

A presumption may be an unwelcome prejudice in life, but it is a convenient prejudice in law. It produces factual and legal certainty so long as real facts are uncertain, but is rebutted as and when real facts turn out to be different from those presumed. The presumption of a resulting trust is not a strong one. Indeed, it 'is rebutted by evidence of *any* intention inconsistent with such a trust', *per* Lord Browne-Wilkinson in *Westdeutsche* (emphasis added). His Lordship approved the analysis put forward by William Swadling in 'A New Role for Resulting Trusts', 16 *Legal Studies* 110 and rejected that put forward by Professor Peter Birks in S. Goldstein (ed.), *Equity and Contemporary Legal Developments* (Jerusalem: Sacher Institute Hebrew University, 1992). The conclusion of Mr Swadling's paper was that:

> it boils down to a debate as to the types of evidence which will rebut the presumption of resulting trust in the case of a gratuitous transfer outside any relationship of advancement [see 16.1.1.3]. For Professor Birks, only one type of evidence will do, *viz*, evidence of a positive intention to give. My argument has been that the presumed intention resulting trust which arises in the case of a gratuitous transfer is a presumption of actual intent and therefore *any* evidence that the parties intended something other than a transfer on trust will suffice. Evidence of a mistaken intent to give will therefore rebut the presumption of a resulting trust.

 THINKING POINT

Can you think of any examples of an actual intention in the transferor that would be inconsistent with the presumption of a resulting trust?

One possibility is that the transferor might have intended to make an outright gift; another is that a loan might have been intended. In *Vajpeyi* v *Yusaf* [2003] All ER (D) 128 (Sep) (approved judgment) the claimant, who had given the defendant money to buy a house, failed in her claim to recover the house under a resulting trust. The court held that the money had been given as a loan and the defendant's obligation to the claimant was completely discharged by repayment of the loan.

In *Fowkes* v *Pascoe* (1875) 10 Ch App 343 Mrs B purchased certain stock in the joint names of herself and P, the son of her daughter-in-law. On the same day she purchased more of the same stock in the joint names of herself and a lady companion. Mrs B's will left the residue of her estate to the daughter-in-law for life, thereafter for P and his sister equally. The Court of Appeal held that the presumption of a resulting trust had been rebutted by evidence that a gift had been intended. Mellish LJ could think of no other reason why Mrs B, who already owned £5,000 worth of the stock in her own name, should invest £250 in the joint names of herself and P on the same day as investing £250 in the joint names of herself and her companion. The facts were not consistent with an intention to subject the stock to a trust. Contrast the outcome in that case with the outcome in *Re Vinogradoff* [1935] WN 68. There Mrs V placed £800 worth of stock into the joint names of herself and her granddaughter. On the question whether the property belonged to the granddaughter after Mrs V's death, it was held that it did not. The presumption of resulting trust applied and so the stock belonged to Mrs V's estate.

 THINKING POINT

The most common situation in which property is transferred is where it is transferred under a contractual obligation. Having bought your morning paper you cannot return in the evening to reclaim the purchase monies under a resulting trust. It is not that the presumption of a resulting trust is rebutted, rather that it doesn't even arise in the first place. Why doesn't it arise?

The answer is that the presumption of a resulting trust within Lord Browne-Wilkinson's category (A) will only arise in the case of a voluntary transfer, i.e. a transfer made for no consideration. A legal contract is, by definition, made for consideration.

16.1.1.2 Illegality and the presumption of a resulting trust

Suppose there is a transaction between two parties involving the legal transfer of wealth and suppose that the transaction has been carried out to further some illegal scheme between the parties which is never actually carried out. If the recipient of the wealth seeks to deny the transferor's legal right to recover the wealth, we naturally object to the idea that the court should assist the transferor in light of the parties' illegal plan. However, the alternative—of leaving the wealth with the recipient—is surely just as objectionable. We might ask, first, why the recipient should be enriched at the transferor's expense given that they were both parties to the same illegal scheme. We might ask, second, whether it is accurate to say that the court is specifically assisting the transferor to recover their wealth—isn't it more accurate to say that the transferor is recovering wealth under the legal rules (contract, property, etc) by which the law assists all transferors in general?

 CASE CLOSE-UP

Patel v Mirza [2016] UKSC 42; [2016] 3 WLR 399, UK Supreme Court

Facts: Mr Patel transferred £620,000 to Mr Mirza to bet it on the price of Royal Bank of Scotland shares as part of an illegal insider dealing scheme, but when the scheme failed to materialise Mr Mirza refused to repay the money. Mr Patel brought a claim for unjust enrichment, but Mr Mirza argued that any such claim was barred by illegality according to the principle *ex turpi causa non oritur action* (no claim may arise from an illegal act).

Held: A panel of nine Justices unanimously agreed that Mr Patel should recover his money, but only a bare majority of five, led by Lord Toulson, posited an agreed analysis of the situation. Their preference was to allow the recovery of wealth according to contractual and proprietary entitlement unless there were specific policy reasons against such recovery. Lord Toulson opined that 'one cannot judge whether allowing a claim which is in some way tainted by illegality would be contrary to the public interest, because it would be harmful to the integrity of the legal system, without a) considering the underlying purpose of the prohibition which has been transgressed, b) considering conversely any other relevant public policies which may be rendered ineffective or less effective by denial of the claim, and c) keeping in mind the possibility of overkill unless the law is applied with a due sense of proportionality. We are, after all, in the area of public policy. That trio of necessary considerations can be found in the case law' (at para. [101]). Lord Toulson also opined that the '*Bowmaker* rule' or 'reliance on illegality' test laid down in the House of Lords in *Tinsley* v *Milligan* [1994] 1 AC 340, HL should no longer be taken to represent the law. (In *Tinsley* v *Milligan* the House of Lords held that a claimant could recover transferred wealth under a resulting trust only where they could prove the facts of the transfer without alluding to the fact that the transfer had been in furtherance of an illegal transaction.)

THINKING POINT

After *Patel* v *Mirza*, it seems that reliance on the fact of an illegal (or attempted illegal) transaction will be irrelevant to the recovery of wealth. Only some other overriding policy consideration will bar recovery. What do you think might count as an overriding policy consideration? Might recovery be denied if, for example, the transaction might enable a party to profit from fraud? (Lord Toulson stressed in *Patel* v *Mirza* that the claimant in that case was 'seeking to unwind the arrangement, not to profit from it'.)

16.1.1.3 The presumption of advancement

Where a voluntary conveyance is made to the wife, fiancée or child of the transferor, or where the transferor is *in loco parentis* ('in the position of parent') to the transferee, there is a presumption that the transferor has made a gift for the advancement of the transferee. This presumption rebuts the presumption of a resulting trust. However, the presumption of advancement can itself be rebutted if there is evidence that the transferor did not in fact intend to make a gift to the volunteer transferee. Nowadays the presumption of advancement is relatively easy to rebut. The decision of the Court of Appeal in *McGrath* v *Wallis* [1995] 2 FLR 114 is a good illustration of this. The facts were, briefly, that a father bought a house subject to a mortgage, but placed both the house and the mortgage in the name of the son. Nourse LJ held that the presumption of advancement had been rebutted by evidence (that the son was unemployed and could not have bought a house in his own name) which showed that the father had not intended to make an outright gift to the son, but to make provision only until the son could afford to purchase a house in his own right. See, also, *Sekhon* v *Alissa* [1989] 2 FLR 94. *Obiter dicta* in *Laskar* v *Laskar* emphasise the weakness of the presumption in gifts from parent to child, especially where the child is adult ([2008] EWCA Civ 347 at para. [20]). In *Lavelle* v *Lavelle*

[2004] EWCA Civ 223 (CA), the presumption of advancement from father to daughter was rebutted by evidence that the transfer of land into the daughter's name had been made with the intention of avoiding inheritance tax. (*Lavelle* was followed in *Kyriakides* v *Pippas* [2004] EWHC 646.)

THINKING POINT

When s 199 of the Equality Act 2010 becomes law (it has not come into force at the time of writing) the presumption of advancement will be abolished, except as regards existing transactions. What grounds might there be for abolishing the presumption? (The anti-discrimination provisions under the Human Rights Act 1998 should give you a clue!)

16.1.2 Presumed resulting trusts where express trusts do not exhaust the whole of the beneficial interest

16.1.2.1 General

The simplest example is where A settles property 'on trust for B for life', but makes no provision as to what should be the destination of the capital fund on the death of B. Equity abhors a vacuum in beneficial ownership, so insists that somebody must be entitled to the fund at all times. Accordingly, equity presumes that a resulting trust had been intended, and that the capital jumps back (results) to A (or A's estate if A has died) upon the death of B.

Examples of this category of trust can be found in less traditional contexts. Indeed, Lord Browne-Wilkinson places the *Quistclose* trust (see 2.3.4.2) in this category.

16.1.2.2 Automatic resulting trusts

Suppose that A intends to give away all his beneficial interest in a piece of property and thinks he has done so, but by some mistake or accident or failure to comply with the requirements of the law, he has failed to do so. A simple example is the case of a person who pays money into the bank account of a company that no longer exists (*Omojole* v *HSBC Bank Plc* [2012] EWHC 3102 (Comm)). A rather more complicated series of cases are those in the Vandervell saga, discussed next.

Vandervell v IRC [1967] 2 AC 291

Guy Anthony Vandervell was an English industrialist and founder of the 'Vanwall' Formula One Racing Team (part of Vandervell Products Ltd—hereinafter 'VP Ltd'). In 1958 V was the controlling director and shareholder of VP Ltd. He decided to give 100,000 shares in VP Ltd to the Royal College of Surgeons (RCS) to found a chair in pharmacology. The shares were currently held by V's bank under a bare trust for V. Accordingly, V directed the bank to transfer 100,000 shares to the RCS. It was intended that the RCS should keep the shares for a limited period only, and should relinquish them after receiving £150,000 income on the shares by way of dividends. To ensure that the RCS did not keep the shares forever, upon receipt of the shares, it executed an option in favour of a trustee company set up by V. The terms of the option provided that the RCS must transfer the shares to the trustee company upon the future receipt of a payment of £5,000 from the trustee company. By 1961 the RCS had received over £150,000 in dividends from the shares and so the trustee company exercised the option to repurchase the shares for £5,000. The present action was brought by the Inland Revenue Commissioners to recover tax from V which had been assessed on the dividends for the period between 1958 and 1961. The question therefore arose whether V had owned the shares during the period in which the dividends were declared. The Revenue argued that V, in directing the bank to transfer the shares to the RCS, had purported to dispose of his equitable interest in the shares but had failed to do so because the disposition had not been made in writing (s 53(1)(c), LPA 1925).

The House of Lords held that s 53(1)(c) did not apply to these facts. However, the decision in the present case ultimately went in favour of the Revenue for other reasons. Three out of the five Lords of Appeal in Ordinary held that the option had been held by the trustee company upon unspecified trusts. In accordance with the maxim *equity abhors a vacuum in beneficial ownership*, the option could not be permitted merely to remain 'in the air'. Their Lordships held that the benefit of the option must have been held by the trustee company under a resulting trust for V. In failing to specify trusts of the option, V had failed to divest himself of his equitable interest in the option. It followed that he had also failed fully to divest himself of his equitable interest in the shares which were the subject of the option. As a result, V was liable to pay tax on the dividends declared on the shares.

Re Vandervell's Trusts (No 2) *[1974] 1 All ER 47*

As a result of the Inland Revenue's claim against him personally, V executed a deed in 1965 under which he transferred to his trustee company all or any right, title or interest which he *might* have in the option (see *Vandervell v IRC*) to be held by it on trust for V's children according to the terms of an existing settlement. V died in 1967. His executors brought the present action against the trustee company, claiming that V had owned the shares for the period between 1961 and 1965. The Inland Revenue was joined to the action and sought to recover tax from V's estate for the period between 1961 (when the option was exercised) and 1965 (when V executed the deed divesting himself entirely of his equitable interest). The trustee company claimed that the shares should be treated as belonging to the children's settlement.

Megarry J identified two main issues in this stage of the Vandervell saga: first, to determine whether the defendant trustee company had taken the option beneficially or on trust; secondly, what those trusts were. Having decided that the trustee company held the option on trust, his Lordship then asked: 'was the option held on a resulting trust or other trust for Mr Vandervell, or was it held on the trusts of the children's settlement?'

Megarry J concluded that a resulting trust in favour of Mr Vandervell had arisen automatically:

> I cannot see how an intention not to get the shares back can negative a resulting trust if in the event he made no effective disposition of his beneficial interest in them and the operation of equity brought them back to him in ways never considered by him. Whatever may be the position under a presumed resulting trust, I do not see how the donor's intention not to have the beneficial interest can prevail where the resulting trust is automatic.

Re Vandervell's Trusts (No 2) *[1974] 3 All ER 205, Court of Appeal*

It was held, on appeal from Megarry J, that as a result of the exercise of the option by the trustee company in 1961, the trustee company thereafter held the shares on the trusts of the children's settlement. This was because it had been the intention of V and the trustee company that the shares should be thereafter held for the benefit of the children's settlement, and the £5,000 used to exercise the option had actually been taken from the fund of the children's settlement. It followed that, after the exercise of the option, the shares did not form part of V's estate and his estate could not be taxed for the period 1961 to 1965. Lord Denning MR stated that when the option was exercised the 'gap in the beneficial ownership' came to an end. The resulting trust under which the shares had previously been held for the benefit of V ceased to exist upon the exercise of the option and the registration of the shares in the name of the trustee company. Applying *Milroy v Lord* (see 5.3.1), V and the trustee company had, after the exercise of the option, 'done everything which needed to be done to make the settlement of these shares binding upon them'.

Figure 16.2 summarises the facts of the Vandervell saga.

Figure 16.2   The facts of the Vandervell saga (events numbered chronologically)

Lord Denning MR stated, further, that even if V had retained an equitable interest in the shares after the exercise of the option he would have been estopped from asserting his entitlement to those shares as against his children. He could not claim to own the shares after having done everything possible to give them away to the trustees of the children's settlement.

THINKING POINT

Can you see any inconsistency between the judgment of Lord Denning MR and the speeches of their Lordships in *Vandervell v IRC*?

There are arguably several points of inconsistency. For example, Lord Denning MR held that in 1961 V intended to, and did indeed, divest himself of his equitable interest in the shares, despite the fact that V apparently did not realise until much later that he might have any equitable interest in the shares! (He waited until 1965 to disclaim his beneficial interest in them by transferring his interest to the trust company to be held on the trusts of the children's settlement.)

The most significant of the Vandervell cases as regards 'automatic' resulting trusts is *Re Vandervell (No 2)* [1974] 3 All ER 205. In that case, as you will recall, Megarry J held that 'the option was granted to the defendant company on trust, but that no effective trusts were ever established and so the defendant company held the option on a resulting trust for Mr Vandervell'. As to the type of resulting trust, Megarry J concluded that the resulting trust was automatic, rather than presumed: 'Whatever may be the position under a presumed resulting trust, I do not see how the donor's intention not to have the beneficial interest can prevail where the resulting trust is automatic.' His Lordship was of the view that 'there are branches of the law of resulting trusts where the proof of an intention carries one a very little distance'.

Megarry J's view can claim some support from Lord Upjohn in *Vandervell v IRC* [1967] 1 All ER 1, who held that:

> [i]f A intends to give away all his beneficial interest in a piece of property and thinks he has done so but by some mistake or accident or failure to comply with the requirements of the law, he has failed to do so, either wholly or partially, there will, by operation of law, be a resulting trust for him of the beneficial interest of which he had failed effectually to dispose.

However, in *Westdeutsche* Lord Browne-Wilkinson observed that:

> Megarry J in *Re Vandervell's Trusts (No 2)* suggests that a resulting trust of type (B) does not depend on intention but operates automatically. I am not convinced that this is right. If the settlor has expressly, or by necessary implication, abandoned any beneficial interest in the trust property, there is in my view no resulting trust.

THINKING POINT

What was Lord Browne-Wilkinson's preferred solution to any case where the donor had clearly intended to part outright with property and that intention had failed in some unforeseen way? (See the extract appearing earlier in this chapter.)

His Lordship held that the undisposed-of equitable interest in such a case vests in the Crown as *bona vacantia* (ownerless property). In support of this view he cited *Re West Sussex Constabulary's Widows, Children and Benevolent (1930) Fund Trusts* [1971] Ch 1 (see 7.6.3). This analysis has a greater conceptual appeal than Megarry J's distinction between automatic and resulting trusts, but is surely apt to create injustice in some cases. Why, it might be asked, should the Crown receive a windfall where, for instance, the vacuum in beneficial ownership arose because of the settlor's reasonable mistake in his understanding of the legal effect of a particular disposition?

THINKING POINT

Do you see any possible conflict between Lord Browne-Wilkinson's statement: 'If the settlor has expressly, or by necessary implication, abandoned any beneficial interest in the trust property, there is in my view no resulting trust', and his 'uncontroversial' fundamental propositions of trust law? (For which, see Chapter 16 Introduction.)

One of Lord Browne-Wilkinson's fundamental propositions was that '[i]n the case of a trust, the conscience of the legal owner requires him to carry out the purposes for which the property was vested in him'. Here 'the legal owner' must be a reference to the trustee rather than the settlor, for the trustee is the one who has had property 'vested in him'. This suggests, in apparent contradiction to Lord Browne-Wilkinson's analysis of *Vandervell*, that where a resulting trust arises (whether because of failure of the trust or a surplus of funds) it is the trustee's state of mind (and not that of the settlor) that is relevant to determination of the ultimate destination of the funds. Yet, to add further confusion, Lord Browne-Wilkinson, immediately after outlining his two categories of resulting trust, suggested that '[b]oth types of resulting trust are traditionally regarded as examples of trusts giving effect to the *common* intention of the parties' (emphasis added).

It is submitted that the correct analysis is that the trustee's conscience will be affected by his knowledge of the purposes for which the settlor vested the property in him, and that this is the only extent to which the settlor's intentions are relevant once the trust has been established. It follows that *only if the trustee knew that the settlor wished to part with the property outright* will the trustee be justified in surrendering the property to the Crown as *bona vacantia*. In other cases one can see the force in Megarry J's opinion that the funds should be returned to the settlor.

An example is *Re Gillingham Bus Disaster* [1958] 1 All ER 37. The facts were tragic. A bus careered into a column of Royal Marine cadets who were marching along a road in Gillingham, Kent. Twenty-four were killed and others were injured. A memorial fund was set up for the purpose of meeting funeral expenses, caring for the disabled and other worthy causes. It was held that the surplus should be held on resulting trust for the donors. Harman J held that:

> [t]his doctrine does not rest . . . on any evidence of the state of mind of the settlor, for in the vast majority of cases no doubt he does not expect to see his money back; he has created a trust which, as far as he can see, will absorb the whole of it. The resulting trust arises where that expectation is, for some unforeseen reason, cheated of fruition, and is an inference of law based on after-knowledge of the event.

The problem with Megarry J's distinction between presumed and automatic trusts is that it is hard to justify analytically and even harder to apply in practice. To say that the resulting trust arises automatically is to make an assertion without any conceptual foundation. It explains merely that such a trust does not arise according to the settlor's presumed intention; it does *not* explain, for example, why, when a settlor clearly intended to make an outright disposition of his property, the surplus does not pass 'automatically' to the Crown as *bona vacantia*. On the other hand, the problem with Lord Browne-Wilkinson's analysis is that it provides no solution to a case like *Vandervell v IRC*, where Vandervell clearly did not intend to retain the benefit of the shares, but even more clearly did not intend that they should pass to the Crown as *bona vacantia*.

A new approach is needed to the destination of surpluses when express trusts fail or are fulfilled early. Lord Browne-Wilkinson's taxonomy is conceptually rigorous, but has the potential to produce an unjust windfall for the Crown. Megarry J's analysis tends to produce practical justice in most cases, but can operate in the face of a sensible view of the parties' intentions, and has no real conceptual underpinning.

One alternative would be to remove Megarry J's automatic trust from the category of resulting trust, and to regard it as *sui juris*. This would have the merit of removing the conflict with Lord Browne-Wilkinson's taxonomy. However, it would not solve the more fundamental question: 'on what conceptual basis can one justify the recognition of such a trust?' Perhaps, like Harman J (*Re Gillingham*, earlier), we will be forced to recognise that the court's response is pragmatic, not dogmatic.

The controversy received fresh impetus in the Privy Council case of *Air Jamaica v Charlton* [1999] 1 WLR 1399 (see 2.3.3). There Lord Millett held that:

> [l]ike a constructive trust, a resulting trust arises by operation of law, though unlike a constructive trust it gives effect to intention. But it arises whether or not the transferor intended to retain a beneficial interest –he almost always does not –since it responds to the absence of any intention on his part to pass a beneficial interest to the recipient. It may arise even when the transferor positively wished to part with the beneficial interest.

Charles Harpum, commenting on the *Air Jamaica* case, has suggested that Lord Millett's analysis might herald a swing of the pendulum back in favour of Megarry J's 'automatic resulting trust' (Harpum [2000] Conv 170). If Lord Millett's analysis is correct, says Harpum, it is doubtful that a resulting trust arising where *express* trusts do not exhaust the whole of the beneficial interest can ever be rebutted. That which cannot be rebutted should not be described as 'presumed'; hence Megarry's preference for describing such trusts as 'automatic'.

Of course, the best (perhaps the only satisfactory) remedy to the problem of automatic resulting trusts lies in prevention rather than cure. An appropriately worded trust ought to leave no doubt as to the settlor's intentions in the event of failure of his primary intention. A clearly worded trust would prevent a vacancy from arising in the beneficial ownership of the fund or any part of it, and pre-empt the fund from passing *bona vacantia* to the Crown. Such a prophylactic approach would have assisted in all the reported category (B) cases, e.g. *Quistclose* (see 2.3.4.2). But in many cases, practically speaking, it is simply never going to happen (see, e.g. the collection box donations in *Re Gillingham*).

16.2 Constructive trusts

> **constructive trust** A trust imposed by the court on the legal owner of an asset to prevent that person asserting beneficial ownership of the asset in bad conscience to the prejudice of the true beneficial owner.

In the *Westdeutsche* case, Lord Browne-Wilkinson characterised **constructive trusts** as trusts *imposed against* the legal owner of the trust assets on account of the legal owner's unconscionability. We will take this to be the hallmark of true constructive trusts, but it must be admitted that in some of the situations said to give rise to a 'constructive trust', the trust appears to have been at the very least intended by the settlor and willingly accepted by the trustee (see, e.g., secret trusts, 3.2.3). The judgment of Millett LJ in *Paragon Finance plc v DB Thakerar & Co (a firm)* [1999] 1 All ER 400 takes this into account.

CASE CLOSE-UP

***Paragon Finance plc v DB Thakerar & Co (a firm)* [1999] 1 All ER 400, Court of Appeal**

Having stated that a constructive trust arises by operation of law whenever the circumstances are such that it would be unconscionable for the owner of property (usually but not necessarily the legal estate) to assert his own beneficial interest in the property and deny the beneficial interest of another, Millett LJ proceeded to identify two classes of constructive trust:

> In the first class of case . . . the constructive trustee really is a trustee. He does not receive the trust property in his own right but by a transaction by which both parties intend to create a trust from the outset and which is not impugned by the plaintiff. His possession of the property is coloured from the first by the trust and confidence by means of which he obtained it, and his subsequent appropriation of the property to his own use is a breach of that trust . . . The second class of case is different. It arises when the defendant is implicated in a fraud. Equity has always given relief against fraud by making any person

> sufficiently implicated in the fraud accountable in equity. In such a case he is traditionally though I think unfortunately described as a constructive trustee and said to be 'liable to account as constructive trustee'. Such a person is not in fact a trustee at all, even though he may be liable to account as if he were. He never assumes the position of a trustee, and if he receives the trust property at all it is adversely to the plaintiff by an unlawful transaction which is impugned by the plaintiff. In such a case the expressions 'constructive trust' and 'constructive trustee' are misleading, for there is no trust and usually no possibility of a proprietary remedy; they are 'nothing more than a formula for equitable relief': *Selangor United Rubber Estates Ltd v Cradock (No 3)* [1968] 2 All ER 1073.

▶ CROSS REFERENCE

For the *Selangor* breed of false or 'formulaic' constructive trust, see Chapter 19.

Millett LJ's analysis is a welcome diversion from the on-going judicial and academic inquiry into whether beneficial interests under constructive trusts are *created* by the courts (remedially) or merely *recognised* by the courts (as equitable rights arising institutionally—that is, predictably—from particular fact situations). The conflict between the 'remedial' and 'institutional' approaches to constructive trusts is considered next.

16.2.1 Constructive trust: property-based or free-standing remedy?

There is no English authority binding *against* the remedial constructive trust, but 'an English Court will be very slow indeed to adopt the US and Canadian model' (*London Allied Holdings Ltd v Lee* [2007] EWHC 2061 (Ch) *per* Etherton J at para. [274]).

16.2.1.1 The US approach

This is how Professor A.W. Scott ((1955) 71 LQR 39 at 41) described the US approach:

> The court does not give relief because a constructive trust has been created; but the court gives relief because otherwise the defendant would be unjustly enriched; and because the court gives this relief it declares that the defendant is chargeable as a constructive trustee.

> Amongst American jurists there is a history of enthusiasm for the remedial constructive trust. Judge Cardozo opined that the constructive trust 'is the formula through which the conscience of equity finds expression' (*Beatty v Guggenheim Exploration Co.* (1919) 225 NY 380 at 386).

16.2.1.2 The English approach

In contrast with the US position, English law does not as yet recognise a remedial constructive trust and some English jurists are far from enthusiastic about the idea. Sir Peter Millett once called it 'a counsel of despair which too readily concedes the impossibility of propounding a general rationale for the availability of a proprietary remedy' ('Remedies: The Error in *Lister v. Stubbs*', in P. Birks (ed.), *The Frontiers of Liability* (Oxford: Oxford University Press, 1994, p. 51)). There are, however, occasional indications that the courts might one day accept the idea. Lord Browne-Wilkinson in *Westdeutsche* (see 16.2) stated that:

> [t]he court may by way of remedy impose a constructive trust on a defendant who knowingly retains the property of which the plaintiff has been unjustly deprived. Since the remedy can be tailored to the circumstances of the particular case, innocent third parties would not be prejudiced and restitutionary defences, such as change of position, are capable of being given effect.

(As to the change of position defence, see 18.2.2.) His Lordship concluded, however, that whether English law should adopt this remedy would have to be decided in a future case when the point was directly in issue.

It seems clear from this *dictum* that even if English courts eventually recognise a constructive trust on the basis of unjust enrichment, it will only be where the enrichment of the defendant had been at the claimant's expense (so-called 'subtractive unjust enrichment'). In *Halifax Building Society* v *Thomas* [1995] 4 All ER 673 a mortgagee, after its loan had been fully repaid, claimed the surplus proceeds of sale of the mortgagor's property. The claim was brought on the basis of a constructive trust arising because the mortgage loan had been obtained by fraud. The Court of Appeal rejected the mortgagee's claim because the fraudulent borrower had not been unjustly enriched *at the mortgagee's expense*.

In the light of *Westdeutsche* and *Halifax* v *Thomas* it may only be a matter of time before the English courts remedy subtractive unjust enrichment by means of a constructive trust. However, at present English law does not go this far, and only recognises constructive trusts where they are asserted to vindicate a pre-existing proprietary right.

In *Re Sharpe (a bankrupt)* [1980] 1 WLR 219, Browne-Wilkinson J (as he then was) recognised the claimant's constructive trust interest, but refused to regard the imposition of a constructive trust as a mere remedy which the court could impose to address injustice: 'it cannot be that the interest in property arises for the first time when the court declares it to exist. The right must have arisen at the time of the transaction in order for the plaintiff to have any right the breach of which can be remedied.'

 THINKING POINT

Read the extract from *Re Sharpe* next. Do you agree that the claimant in that case had a pre-existing proprietary right, or do you think that this was a case of remedial constructive trust in all but name?

Mr S, Mrs S and the claimant, Mrs Johnson (an elderly aunt), lived together in leasehold premises which were held in the name of Mr S. The claimant had contributed the majority of the purchase price of the lease. In providing the money, she had been told that she would be permitted to reside in the premises for as long as she wished. Upon Mr S being declared bankrupt, the trustee in bankruptcy took out a summons for possession of the premises. The court dismissed the summons. His Lordship held that the claimant did not have an interest in the land under a *resulting trust* because she had given her money by way of loan. The terms of the loan gave her a mere contractual right to reside in the premises until the loan had been repaid, and such a right would not bind the trustee in bankruptcy.

 CASE CLOSE-UP

Re Sharpe (a bankrupt) [1980] 1 WLR 219, ChD

Browne-Wilkinson J: 'even if it be right to say that the courts can impose a constructive trust as a remedy in certain cases—which to my mind is a novel concept in English law—in order to provide a remedy the court must first find a right which has been infringed . . . in cases such as this, it cannot be that the interest in property arises for the first time when the court declares it to exist. The right must have arisen at the time of the transaction in order for the plaintiff to have any right the breach of which can be remedied.

> Accordingly, if I am right in holding that as between the debtor and Mrs Johnson she had an irrevocable licence to remain in the property, authority compels me to hold that that gave her an interest in the property before the bankruptcy and the trustee takes the property subject to that interest. In my judgment the mere intervention of the bankruptcy by itself cannot alter Mrs Johnson's property interest. If she is to be deprived of her interest as against the trustee in bankruptcy, it must be because of some conduct of hers which precludes her from enforcing her rights, that is to say, the ordinary principles of acquiescence and laches which apply to all beneficiaries seeking to enforce their rights apply to this case.
>
> [His Lordship held that Mrs Johnson had not acquiesced in the breach: see, generally, 15.2.6.]
>
> Accordingly, I hold that Mrs Johnson is entitled as against the trustee in bankruptcy to remain in the property until she is repaid the sums she advanced. I reach this conclusion with some hesitation since I find the present state of the law very confused and difficult to fit in with established equitable principles. I express the hope that in the near future the whole question can receive full consideration in the Court of Appeal, so that, in order to do justice to the many thousands of people who never come into court at all but who wish to know with certainty what their proprietary rights are, the extent to which these irrevocable licences bind third parties may be defined with certainty. Doing justice to the litigant who actually appears in the court by the invention of new principles of law ought not to involve injustice to the other persons who are not litigants before the court but whose rights are fundamentally affected by the new principles.'

There are echoes of the *Re Sharpe* approach in *Chase Manhattan Bank NA v Israel-British Bank (London) Ltd* [1981] Ch 105. This was another case, on a larger scale, in which the claimant needed to establish a proprietary claim to recover its funds from the estate of an insolvent defendant. The claimant had mistakenly made two payments of $2 million to the defendant bank, when it had only intended to make one. Goulding J held that the claimant bank could trace its property in equity into the hands of the defendant bank, and that the defendant would be a constructive trustee of those funds until it made restitution to the claimant. In reaching this judgment his Lordship emphasised the need to show a pre-existing proprietary right in the fund: 'a person who pays money to another under a factual mistake retains an equitable property in it and the conscience of that other is subjected to a fiduciary duty to respect his proprietary right.'

Sir Peter Millett, writing extrajudicially, has affirmed the restrictive approach to recognising constructive trusts: 'there is neither room nor need for the remedial constructive trust. In my view it is a counsel of despair which too readily concedes the impossibility of propounding a general rationale for the availability of proprietary remedies' ((1995) 9 TLI 35 at 40). Professor Andrew Burrows (*The Law of Restitution*, Oxford: Oxford University Press, 1993 at p. 37) has suggested that 'even if one puts to one side the difficulty in describing the constructive trust as a remedy, there is an immediate obstacle to justifying it, within a restitutionary framework, in a case of unjust enrichment by subtraction in a case like *Chase Manhattan*'. One difficulty pointed out by Professor Burrows is that straightforward restitution would insist upon the return of $2 million plus interest, whereas a constructive trust solution would entitle the claimant to $2 million *plus any profits* made by the trustee through the use of that $2 million, plus interest on the total. (The remedial constructive trust was once again dismissed by the Court of Appeal in *Re Polly Peck International plc (No 2)* [1998] 3 All ER 812.)

16.2.1.3 **Commonwealth approaches**

Having considered the approach taken in the United States, as summarised by Professor Scott (see 16.2.1.1), let us make the short journey north to Canada. In that jurisdiction the constructive trust has been used widely as a remedial device for the reversal of unjust enrichment (see Simon Gardner, 'Rethinking Family Property' (1993) 109 LQR 263 at 269–74). The leading case is *Pettkus* v *Becker* (1980) 117 DLR (3d) 257. The facts were that Miss Becker had worked for 14 years on a honey farm owned by her cohabitee, Mr Pettkus. The Supreme Court of Canada, led by Dixon J, granted her a half-share in Mr Pettkus's property under a constructive trust in order to remedy his unjust enrichment at her expense. According to the judge, this 'unjust enrichment' arises where there is 'an enrichment, a corresponding deprivation and absence of any juristic reason for the enrichment'. As Gardner points out in his article, the first and third elements are problematic: the first because, apart from to the extent that it has yielded an obvious financial benefit, the defendant can simply deny that he has been enriched by the claimant's services; the third because it is never easy to show that an enrichment has been unjustly received when it was consensually conferred. Untroubled by this, Dixon J held that:

> where one person in a relationship tantamount to spousal prejudices herself in the reasonable expectation of receiving an interest in property and the other person in the relationship freely accepts benefits conferred by the first person in circumstances where he knows or ought to have known of that reasonable expectation, it would be unjust to allow the recipient of the benefit to retain it.

In Australia constructive trusts have been granted to remedy the 'unconscionability' of the legal owner, a concept even more nebulous than 'unjust enrichment'. This modern trend has its origins in the judgment of Deane J in *Muschinski* v *Dodds* (1985) 160 CLR 583. In that case Mrs Muschinski met the entire purchase price of property which had been purchased in the joint names of Mrs Muschinski and Mr Dodds, with whom she had embarked upon a commercial joint venture. She did so in the expectation that he would pay half the cost in due course. He never did, and so the court imposed a constructive trust on his half-share of the property to repay her contributions to the extent that they exceeded his. Deane J held (at 451) that 'the constructive trust can properly be described as a remedial institution which equity imposes regardless of actual or presumed intention . . . to preclude the retention or assertion of beneficial ownership of property to the extent that such retention or assertion would be contrary to equitable principle', or, as he later stated, 'to the extent that it would be unconscionable' (455).

The constructive trust in *Muschinski* is a free-standing remedy. It is not based on the vindication of any pre-existing proprietary right. On the contrary, it operates from the date of the court order granting it. This was confirmed in the leading Australian case *Baumgartner* v *Baumgartner* (1987) 164 CLR 137, in which Deane J appeared again, but this time with Wilson J and Mason CJ in the High Court of Australia.

The facts of *Baumgartner* were typical of the sorts of cases which will form the focus of the next chapter. The Baumgartners, an unmarried couple, had both contributed to a house which had been purchased in the man's name alone. Their Lordships held that the woman was entitled to a share in the house under a constructive trust, and that the size of that share should be roughly equivalent to the value of her contributions. The judgment of the majority of the High Court in *Baumgartner* was that:

> [his] assertion, after the relationship had failed, that the . . . property, which was financed in part through the pooled funds, is his sole property, is his property beneficially, to the exclusion of any interest at all on [her part], amounts to unconscionable conduct, which attracts the intervention of equity and the imposition of a constructive trust.

Simon Gardner has observed (*op. cit.* at 275) that the judgment 'gives no very definite account of the parameters of unconscionability. It implicitly rejects the idea of resting the doctrine merely on idiosyncratic notions of what is fair and just, but then invokes these very notions.' Weight is added to this criticism by the definition provided by Deane J in *Commonwealth v Verwayen* (1990) 170 CLR 394 at 441: '"Unconscionable" should be understood in the sense of referring to what one party "ought not in conscience, as between [the parties] be allowed to do".'

Lord Nicholls has stated: 'unconscionable is not a word in everyday use by non-lawyers. If it is to be used . . . it is essential to be clear on what, in this context, unconscionable means' (*Royal Brunei v Tan* [1995] 3 WLR 64, Privy Council). Lord Nicholls is a forward-thinking judge, but his conservatism in this respect no doubt stems from the fear that the elevation of 'unconscionability' to the status of free-standing cause of action will not herald a positive movement 'from an era of strict law to one which gives greater emphasis to equity and natural law' (Mason CJ (1994) 110 LQR 238 at 259), but will be retrograde. The fear is that it might put back the clock of English jurisprudence to the days when equitable intervention was based on the bare notion of fraud. One doesn't have to go back too far (relative, that is, to the long history of equity) to discover aberrant cases such as *Chattock v Muller* (1878) 8 Ch 177. And, of course, one could go back still further—to the days when equity was said to vary according to the length of the Chancellor's foot (see 1.1.1.2).

 THINKING POINT

Despite this criticism, can you imagine that there would be any advantage in granting constructive trusts as a free-standing equitable remedy, rather than as a means of vindicating pre-existing proprietary rights?

The great advantage of a true remedial constructive trust is that it would not be awarded if to do so would be inequitable in all the circumstances. This means that remedial constructive trusts would not be awarded if to do so would prejudice the interests of innocent third parties. This is of particular relevance where the defendant is insolvent, because in such circumstances the award of a constructive trust in favour of the claimant would, because it is a proprietary award, reduce the funds available to satisfy the defendants' general creditors. As Mummery LJ observed in *Re Polly Peck International plc (No 2)* [1998] 3 All ER 812: 'The insolvency road is blocked off to remedial constructive trusts, at least when judge driven in a vehicle of discretion.' In this respect the great *dis*advantage of the institutional constructive trust is that it is designed to vindicate a pre-existing proprietary right. The court is left, in theory at least, with no discretion as to whether or not to award the remedy, no discretion as to the nature of the remedy, and only a limited discretion as to its *quantum*. Because the claimant's institutional constructive trust will take priority in the event of the defendant's insolvency, the potential prejudice to the defendant's innocent third party creditors is obvious.

16.2.2 The obligations of a constructive trustee

'It is a mistake to suppose that in every situation in which a constructive trust arises the legal owner is necessarily subject to all the fiduciary obligations and disabilities of an express trustee', *per* Millett J in *Lonrho plc v Fayed (No 2)* [1992] 4 All ER 961.

The facts of *Lonrho* were as follows. The claimant, a large shareholder in ACo, had given an undertaking to the Secretary of State for Trade and Industry that it would not acquire more than

30 per cent of the shares in ACo. It sold its shares in ACo to BCo, thereby hoping to be released from its undertaking, to enable a future takeover of ACo. However, having received the shares in ACo, BCo went on to acquire more than 50 per cent of the shares in ACo. The claimant *was* subsequently released from its undertaking, but by then it was too late to acquire a majority shareholding in ACo. The claimant claimed inter alia that BCo held the shares in ACo on trust for the claimant because they had been acquired by the fraud of BCo.

Millett J held that a contract obtained by fraudulent misrepresentation is voidable, not void, even in equity. The representee (the claimant) may elect to avoid it, but until he does so no fiduciary relationship arises and the representor (BCo) cannot be a constructive trustee of the property transferred pursuant to the contract. In the present case there was no constructive trust because the claimant had demonstrated only that the majority shareholding in ACo might have been acquired by fraud; it had not shown that it would be unconscionable for its interest to be denied.

It follows from the fact that many constructive trustees do not know that they are trustees until the court determines that they are, that they are not subject to the full rigours of the general law in relation to express trusts. They do not, for example, have to invest the trust fund prudently within the terms of the Trustee Investments Act 1961.

16.3 Types of constructive trust

The following catalogue of situations in which constructive trusts have been recognised illustrates how diverse are the circumstances in which the constructive trust has been employed, and how difficult it is to establish any underlying unifying concept that can be applied with theoretical rigour to new cases.

16.3.1 Constructive trustee of unauthorised profits

For more general consideration of the principle that fiduciaries must not profit from their position without authorisation, see 12.1.

At this juncture the author's intention is a limited one: namely, to distinguish the *proprietary* claim against *a constructive trustee of unauthorised profits* from the *personal* claim against *a fiduciary for an account of unauthorised profits*. When one considers that a fiduciary often *is a trustee* to his principal of whatever property he holds in his fiduciary capacity, the distinction may appear to be a somewhat slight one. Whether the conceptual distinction is or is not artificial we will consider in a moment, but what cannot be doubted are the potentially serious practical implications of the distinction, especially in the context of the defendant's insolvency. If a mere fiduciary becomes insolvent the claim of the principal against the fiduciary's estate will rank with other unsecured personal claims against the fiduciary. If, on the other hand, a trustee becomes insolvent, the claim of the beneficiary ranks ahead of the claims of general creditors. It is for this reason that it is frequently objected that constructive trusts disturb the normal priority of claims in insolvency, and should not readily be recognised in insolvent contexts. A.J. Oakley objects to constructive trusts in commerce because general trade creditors cannot discover them in the usual course of their business (A.J. Oakley (1995) 54(2) CLJ 377 at 381). He is right, of course. But, as we have seen, the same is true of many *express* trusts in commercial contexts (see 2.3.4).

16.3.1.1 Claims against a constructive trustee of unauthorised profits

The reports provide numerous examples of cases in which successful claims have been brought to recover unauthorised profits on the basis of a constructive trust. An early example is provided by *Keech* v *Sandford* (1726) Sel Cas Ch 61. There the trustee held a lease in trust for an infant beneficiary. The landlord was unwilling to renew the lease for the benefit of the trust, but did renew it in favour of the trustee personally. King LC adjudged that the trustee held the renewed lease, and any profits made from it, on constructive trust in favour of the infant beneficiary: '[t]his may seem hard, that the trustee is the only person of all mankind who might not have the lease; but it is very proper that rule should be strictly pursued.' The Lord Chancellor was confirmed in his judgment by the 'very obvious' risk that unscrupulous trustees might take advantage of their position, if the legal rule were in any way relaxed. *Keech* v *Sandford* has been extended to the case where a fiduciary purchases the freehold reversion of his principal's lease (*Protheroe* v *Protheroe* [1968] 1 WLR 519 and *Thompson's Trustee* v *Heaton* [1974] 1 WLR 605).

16.3.1.2 Claims against a fiduciary for an account of unauthorised profits

Boardman v *Phipps* [1967] 2 AC 46 is an important case. Boardman, the solicitor to a trust, attended the AGM of a company in which the trust had a substantial shareholding. Unhappy with the state of the company, he (together with one of the beneficiaries under the trust) decided to launch a personal takeover bid for those shares in the company which were not already trust-owned. Insider knowledge of the company gained in his capacity as solicitor to the trust enabled the solicitor to make the takeover bid. Boardman wrote to the beneficiaries outlining his plans to take a personal interest in the company, giving them an opportunity to raise any objections they might have to his so doing. No objectors having come forward, Boardman proceeded with the takeover. In the event the takeover was very successful and the value of all the shares in the company increased in value. The trust had profited from the takeover, and so had the solicitor. So, was everybody happy? Not quite.

The present action was brought by Phipps, a beneficiary under the trust, for an account of profits made by Boardman in his fiduciary capacity as solicitor to the trust. The trial judge found as a fact that Phipps had not been fully informed by Boardman as to the precise nature of his plans. A bare majority of their Lordships (Viscount Dilhorne and Lord Upjohn dissenting) held that Boardman had placed himself in a fiduciary position in relation to the trust and would be accountable for the profits that he had made on information obtained in his fiduciary capacity. However, it was held that he had acted honestly and openly throughout and because his actions had yielded profits for the trust he was awarded generous remuneration as reward for his work and skill (see 12.1.3).

 THINKING POINT

Do you think that Boardman's insider information might fall within the legal definition of property?

The majority of their Lordships rejected this suggestion. Lord Cohen stated that information was 'not property in the strictest sense of that word'. However, Lord Guest and Lord Hodson regarded the information obtained by Boardman to be property of the trust and held him liable to account as a constructive trustee for profits he had made thereon.

It was suggested that Boardman should be treated as a constructive trustee 'by reason of the fiduciary position in which [he] stood' (applying the *dictum* of Lord Selborne in *Barnes* v *Addy* [1874] 9 Ch App 244 (see Chapter 19)).

In response to this, Professor Birks has suggested ((1988) LMCLQ 128) that the use of constructive trust language was as inappropriate to the facts of *Boardman* v *Phipps* as it was to the facts of *Barnes* v *Addy*. Birks feels that *Boardman* v *Phipps* was a case which should have been disposed of as a straightforward personal claim against the principal, and that in essence, despite the occasional unconvincing reference to constructive trusteeship, this is how the case *was* disposed of. It is true that the House of Lords made no order requiring that the defendants should transfer the shares to the claimant. Against this Professor Andrew Burrows points out that a declaration that the defendant held the shares on constructive trust *was* made at first instance, and (that judgment having been upheld) 'it must follow that the plaintiffs would have been entitled to proprietary remedies, affording priority, had the defendants been insolvent' (*The Law of Restitution* (1993), p. 413).

16.3.1.3 Controversy between the fiduciary account and the constructive trust–the case of wrongful fiduciary gains

In view of the extra benefits attached to a proprietary remedy in the event of the defendant's insolvency it has been argued that such remedies should only be awarded in favour of claimants who can show that a pre-existing proprietary right has been prejudiced, hence the debate in *Boardman* as to whether the information was itself 'property'. This would be in keeping with the orthodox English law conception of the constructive trust as an institution which vindicates a pre-existing proprietary right.

In *A-G for Hong Kong* v *Reid* [1994] 1 All ER 1, the Privy Council held that whenever a fiduciary receives property of his principal in breach of his fiduciary duty, he is a constructive trustee of it, and of any traceable profit from and proceeds of it (as to tracing, see Chapter 18). Mr Reid was acting Director of Public Prosecutions in Hong Kong. In breach of his fiduciary duty to the Crown he received substantial bribes in consideration of which he obstructed the prosecution of certain criminals. The Crown was able to trace the bribe monies through to three freehold properties in New Zealand, and to assert a restitutionary claim to them under a constructive trust. Mr Reid failed in his assertion that the Crown should be limited to its claim against him personally, and that the personal claim should be limited to the value of the initial bribe. Lord Templeman held: 'Equity considers as done that which ought to be done. As soon as the bribe was received, whether in cash or in kind, the false fiduciary held the bribe on a constructive trust for the person injured.'

The decision of the Privy Council in *Reid* has now been approved by the Supreme Court in *FHR European Ventures LLP* v *Cedar Capital Partners LLC* [2014] UKSC 45. FHR purchased a Monte Carlo hotel company for €211.5 million. Cedar was FHR's agent in the negotiation, but Cedar had secretly entered into a brokerage agreement with the vendor under which it received €10m. FHR argued that any unauthorised benefit (such as a bribe or secret commission) that is received by an agent by reason of his agency and in breach of fiduciary duty should be held on constructive trust for the principal. Lord Neuberger approved FHR's argument as having 'the merit of simplicity' (para. [35]) and the Supreme Court confirmed the High Court's decision that Cedar held the €10m subject to a constructive trust in favour of FHR.

The decision has the merit of ensuring that a fiduciary must disgorge any unauthorised gains in full. The most radical element of the decision is to regard the fiduciary as a constructive trustee of the principal's equitable property even though the principal had no prior proprietary interest in the 'bribe' (on this point their Lordships overruled the Court of Appeal in *Sinclair Investments (UK) Ltd v Versailles Trade Finance Ltd (In Administration)* [2011] EWCA Civ 347). The decision means that when a bribed fiduciary becomes insolvent, the fiduciary will be permitted to go to the front of the queue to claim its property right in the bribe under a constructive trust while ordinary trade creditors of the fiduciary will have to fight between themselves over the remnants of the insolvent fiduciary's personal estate. Professor J.W. Harris doubted the justice of this. He asked: 'Why should the principal take a windfall in priority to those to whom the fiduciary owes purchased obligations?' (*Property and Justice* (Oxford: Clarendon Press, 1996) at 338). The answer given in *FHR* is that to remove wealth in the form of bribes and secret commissions does not reduce the insolvent fiduciary's estate because such assets should never have been considered part of that estate.

Even before *FHR*, imposing a constructive trust on a bribe received by a fiduciary was relatively unproblematic where the bribe itself was or had been beneficially the property of the fiduciary's principal. It was on this basis that a constructive trust was imposed on the facts of *Daraydan Holdings Ltd v Solland Interiors Ltd* ([2004] EWHC 622 (Ch)). The facts of that case were that the claimant principal had a prior proprietary interest in the bribe claimed from his dishonest fiduciary (a director of the principal company), because the price paid by the claimant to a third party under a contract had been artificially inflated by the defendant to allow the third party to pay a bribe to the defendant. In *FHR*, their Lordships held, by extending this type of reasoning (in a more causally relaxed way), that the bribe or commission would probably have reduced the benefit received by the principal and that it should therefore be considered to be part of his property.

NOTE: It is also a criminal offence for a person in a 'position of trust' to give or receive a bribe (Bribery Act 2010, s 3(5)).

 THINKING POINT

Suppose that a sergeant in the British Army had been bribed to accompany civilian lorries through security checkpoints in Egypt in order to assist the transport of contraband goods. In the light of what you have learned so far, do you think that these facts would give rise to a constructive trust or mere personal liability to account?

These facts are taken from *Reading v Attorney-General* [1951] AC 507. It was held that Sgt Reading owed a fiduciary obligation to the Crown not to use his position against the interests of the Crown and that he had to account for any profits made through a breach of those obligations. The fact that a fiduciary relationship was acknowledged at all was, on these facts, fairly exceptional in itself (in the Court of Appeal Asquith LJ acknowledged that he was applying a very 'loose' concept of fiduciary ([1949] 2 KB 232)). The fact is that the Crown needed *some* legal basis on which it could require Reading to disgorge his ill-gotten gains (£19,000 was found in his possession).

16.3.2 Constructive trust to prevent fraudulent or unconscionable assertion of legal rights in land

More general examples of this will be considered in the next chapter. Here, we will focus on the issues raised by the peculiar case of *Lyus v Prowsa Developments* [1982] 1 WLR 1044.

Mr and Mrs Lyus contracted to purchase a house from property developers who in fact became insolvent before the house could be built. Unfortunately, Mr and Mrs Lyus had not placed a notice of their estate contract against the developers' registered title to the land. The Lyus' bank was under no obligation to build the house, and instead sold the vacant plot to the defendants, but expressly subject to the Lyus' contract to have a house built. Dillon J held that the Lyus' contract was itself a property right (an estate contract) and that the defendants took subject to it. This was despite the fact that, according to the Land Registration Act 1925, the defendants had taken the land free from any unprotected estate contracts (ss 20(1) and 59(6)). Because they had expressly agreed to take the land subject to the estate contract, the contract would be enforced against them. Dillon J held that a constructive trust had arisen when the defendants purchased the land, to prevent the defendants from unconscionably or fraudulently denying their promise and relying upon their rights under the Land Registration Act 1925.

Charles Harpum, a former Law Commissioner for property and trusts, has suggested ([1983] CLJ 54) that:

> [t]he *Lyus* constructive trust looks to be 'remedial' rather than 'substantive' and as such without much precedent in English law, which has tended to treat constructive trusts as part of the law of property, preferring to develop the remedial possibilities of estoppel instead [see 17.6]. It remains to be seen whether the *Lyus* constructive trust is a one-case mutant or the progenitor of a new species.

In the years since *Lyus* there has been no further evidence of a new species of constructive trust. It appears to be an anomaly (or in Harpum's language a 'mutant'). The real objection to the anomalous case of *Lyus* v *Prowsa* is not that it proceeded from an unorthodox application of equitable principles, but rather that equitable reasoning was employed to the unorthodox end of thwarting the policy of purchaser protection which underlies the statutory scheme of land registration.

16.3.3 **Vendor–purchaser trust**

Suppose that A is the absolute legal owner of a parcel of land which he intends to sell to B. Some time later A and B enter into a valid legal contract for the sale of the land from A to B. Finally A and B execute a legal deed under which the land is conveyed at law from A to B, thus completing the sale.

 THINKING POINT

We know that A was the owner at the beginning, and that B is the owner at the end. But who was the owner from the creation of the contract until the execution of the deed?

The answer is that A and B were both owners during that period. A was the legal owner at law because a deed is necessary to transfer legal ownership (Law of Property Act 1925, s 52) and one had not been executed. B was the owner in equity because equity regards A's contractual promise as binding on A's conscience from the moment the promise is made in legally binding form (as to the form, see the Law of Property (Miscellaneous Provisions) Act 1989, s 2), in accordance with the maxim *equity sees as done that which ought to be done* (see *Walsh* v *Lonsdale* at 1.2.4). From the moment of contract, A is said to hold his legal title on trust for B.

Because the trust arises against the intentions of the vendor it is said to be a constructive trust. However, it is somewhat misleading to describe the vendor–purchaser trust as a constructive trust. For one thing, its existence depends upon a formal contract, whereas most constructive trusts do not depend upon any written formality. For another, the constructive trust is co-existent with the award of specific performance, a remedy which in theory the court awards in its discretion (although normally it is awarded as a matter of course). This lends this 'constructive trust' an unorthodox remedial flavour. As we have seen, the orthodox view is that constructive trusts are awarded to vindicate pre-existing proprietary rights. M.P. Thompson has contended that '[w]hile it is too late to argue against the view that some sort of trust arises, it is contended that it is misleading to describe it as a constructive trust and that it is better to regard it as *sui generis*' ('Must a Purchaser Buy a Charred Ruin?' (1984) 48 Conv 43).

16.3.4 **Mutual wills**

See 3.2.2.1, where mutual wills are considered in detail.

16.3.5 **The equitable liability of strangers**

Third party 'strangers' who are liable in equity for knowing receipt of misapplied trust property or for dishonest assistance in a breach of trust have sometimes been described as 'constructive trustees', but this is something of a misnomer (see 15.2.2.3 and 19.6).

16.3.6 **Secret trusts**

See 3.2.3, where secret trusts are considered in detail.

16.3.7 **'New model' constructive trusts**

This is the appellation attached to a remedial form of constructive trust developed by Lord Denning MR in the 1970s as an attempt to achieve a just distribution of property between cohabitees.

See 17.4.4, where this approach is considered in more detail.

16.3.8 **Joint venture constructive trusts**

Banner Homes Group plc v Luff Developments Ltd (No 1) [2000] Ch 372 illustrates the commercial utility of the constructive trust in relation to an agreement to acquire a site by joint venture.

Luff agreed *in principle* with Banner that they would create a new joint venture company to purchase a commercial site. They agreed to take equal shares in the new company. On that understanding, Luff purchased S Ltd (a new company) for use in the joint venture. Later, Luff began to have doubts about the proposed joint venture and started looking for a new partner. It did not tell Banner, fearing that Banner might put in an independent bid for the commercial site. Banner continued to act on the footing that the joint venture would proceed, always anticipating that Banner and Luff would enter into a formal agreement setting out the terms of the joint venture. S Ltd eventually acquired the site with funds provided by Luff, and only then did Luff inform Banner that the proposed joint venture would not be going ahead.

Banner contended, inter alia, that it was entitled to half the shares in S Ltd under a constructive trust. At first instance, the judge rejected this contention. He held that equity could not transform the agreement, which was implicitly qualified by the right of either side to withdraw, into a binding arrangement. He also held that Banner had suffered no detriment, inasmuch as he refused to accept that Banner might have made an independent bid for the land if it had been aware of Luff's intention to abandon the proposed joint venture.

The Court of Appeal overturned that judgment. It was held that an equity arose because it would have been inequitable to allow Luff to claim, outright, a site which it had acquired in furtherance of the non-contractual, pre-acquisition understanding that it would be held for the joint benefit of Luff and Banner. The court would have held otherwise if Luff had informed Banner soon enough to avoid advantage to Luff and detriment to Banner. Their Lordships held that in many cases the advantage/detriment would be found, as in this case, in the undertaking of the non-acquiring party (Banner in this case) not to make an independent bid for the site. Their Lordships did stress, however, that it was not necessary that there should be both an advantage and a detriment, although the two would normally go hand in hand. The advantage to Luff in the instant case was not merely the knowledge that Banner would not make an independent bid, but the comfort of knowing that Banner would support Luff in acquiring a site which Luff had originally been wary of purchasing at its sole risk. (*Pallant* v *Morgan* [1952] 2 All ER 951 was applied.)

Perhaps the most controversial aspect of this decision is that Luff's 'conscience' was held to be bound in equity by Banner's *detrimental* reliance on the parties' informal understanding. It is hard to see how Banner's lost opportunity to make an independent bid can be described as a detriment without evidence being pleaded to suggest that Banner would probably have made such an independent bid in the absence of the understanding with Luff.

 CASE CLOSE-UP

Crossco No 4 Unlimited v Jolan Ltd [2011] EWCA Civ 1619, Court of Appeal

Facts: The parties had entered a 'joint venture' agreement to divide a large commercial group into two halves of roughly equal value. It was agreed, in brief, that one side would take the land and the other side would take the trade. Part of the agreement was for the trade side to take a lease to which the other side would be landlord, but the trade side did not realise that the lease contained a break clause. Having carried out the division of assets as agreed, the landlord exercised the break clause to bring the lease to an end and the party on the trade side naturally sought to resist this. The latter claimed that it would be unconscionable for the landlord to exercise its right in light of the parties' overall intention to divide the assets equally.

Held: No *Pallant* v *Morgan* equity arose to protect the trade side against the landlord. Their Lordships differed in their understanding of the conceptual basis of the equity. The majority, following *Banner* v *Luff*, held that the equity arises to prevent unconscionability in a manner comparable to the operation in domestic cohabitation contexts of so-called 'common intention constructive trusts' (constructive trusts arising from a shared understanding between the parties). The majority did not feel free to depart from the binding decision of the Court of Appeal in *Banner* v *Luff*. Etherington LJ, dissenting, thought that the law had progressed since *Banner* v *Luff*. His Lordship took the view that the close relationship between proprietary estoppel and the *Pallant* v *Morgan* equity that had been assumed by Chadwick LJ in *Banner Homes* was now in some doubt as a result of distinctions drawn by the House of Lords between proprietary estoppel in commercial and domestic contexts (the relevant cases, *Yeoman's Row Management Ltd* v *Cobbe* and *Thorner* v *Major*, are discussed later in Chapter 17) and distinctions drawn by the House of Lords between common intention constructive trusts in commercial and domestic contexts (the relevant cases, *Stack* v *Dowden* and *Jones* v *Kernott*, are discussed in Chapter 17). Etherington LJ made the point that, unlike domestic cohabitants, commercial parties 'do not expect the Court to determine their respective property rights and interests by the imputation of intentions which they did not have but which the Court considers they would have had if they had acted justly and reasonably and thought about the point' (para. [87]). On the contrary, commercial parties expect to be bound by the terms of their agreement made at a certain time and to suffer the consequences of failing to take legal advice or failing to formalise the terms of their agreement.

It follows from the decision to base the *Pallant* v *Morgan* equity on the restraint of unconscionability that the equity will not arise unless the defendant's conscience is affected by knowledge that a binding agreement was intended (*Herbert* v *Doyle* [2010] EWCA Civ 1095). The equity depends upon an intention that the claimant would acquire a proprietary interest in the disputed assets, but it is not necessary that the nature of the intended proprietary interest should be specified precisely in advance (*Kearns Brothers Ltd* v *Hova Developments Ltd* [2012] EWHC 2968 (Ch)). The *Pallant* v *Morgan* equity can apply even where negotiations between the parties were expressly 'subject to contract' (*Generator Developments LLP* v *Lidl UK GmbH* [2016] EWHC 814 (Ch)).

Summary

This chapter has considered the creation and operation of two special types of trusts which are not based on any express intention:

- We have seen that resulting trusts arise *in accordance* with the presumed intention of the settlor. Where an attempt is made by the owner of an asset to dispose of the beneficial ownership of the asset, the benefit will return to the donor under a resulting trust whenever the attempt is for any reason unsuccessful, unless it is clear that the owner intended to abandon the entirety of his interest in the asset.

- Whereas a resulting trust is enforced to fulfil the intentions of the original owner, a constructive trust is enforced to thwart the wrongful ('unconscionable') intentions of the original owner. Sir Robert Megarry once observed that '"Constructive" is, of course, an unhappy word in the law . . . "Constructive" seems to mean "It isn't, but has to be treated as if it were", and the less of this there is in the law, the better' ('Historical Development' in *Special Lectures of the Law Society of Upper Canada 1990 (Fiduciary Duties* (1991) p. 1 at 5)). However, we have seen that all law is an attempt to achieve a balance between general regulation through formality and certainty, and justice in the individual case. Constructive trusts lie on the latter side of the balance, and it may be that the more of this there is in the law, the better. It is still the case, however, that the English constructive trust is not remedial. Rather, it vindicates pre-existing beneficial entitlement. Hence the glossary to this book defines the 'constructive trust' as a 'trust imposed by the court on the legal owner of an asset to prevent that person asserting beneficial ownership of the asset in bad conscience to the prejudice of the true beneficial owner'.

? Summative assessment exercise

In his book *Property and Justice* (Oxford: Clarendon Press, 1996), Professor J.W. Harris observed that the strict rule that a fiduciary must account for unauthorised profit 'confers the windfall constituted by the fiduciary's profit, not on the community, but on his principal', with the result that the principal is entitled to claim it in preference to the fiduciary's creditors. Professor Harris asks: 'Why should the principal take a windfall in priority to those to whom the fiduciary owes purchased obligations?'

Outline the reasons why English law takes this approach, and state why, in your opinion, this is (or is not) the correct approach for the law to take.

 Full specimen answers can be found at www.oxfordtextbooks.co.uk/orc/watt_directions5e/.

▢ The bigger picture

The Law Commission has recommended that the 'reliance principle' should be abolished and replaced with a broad judicial discretion to decide on a case-by-case basis whether illegality should displace the application of general trust principles, (*Illegal Transactions: The Effect of Illegality on Contracts and Trusts*, Law Commission Consultation Paper No 154, January 1999). In its final report ('The Illegality Defence', Law Com No 320, 2010) the Law Commission proposed a draft Trusts (Concealment of Interests) Bill that would apply where a trust has been created or continued in order to conceal the beneficiary's interest for a criminal purpose and which, in exceptional circumstances, would give the court discretion to deny the beneficiary their usual property right in the light of such factors as the conduct of the parties, the value of the interest, whether refusing the claim would act as a deterrent and the interests of third parties, but in March 2012 the government declared that it intends not to adopt the Law Commission's proposed reforms. This does not mean that reform is not needed. The Supreme Court has since made the point that this is an area in urgent need of clarification (*Les Laboratoires Servier & Anor* v *Apotex Inc* [2014] UKSC 55 at para. [64]). Their Lordships have acknowledged the on-going doubt about the *Tinsley* v *Milligan* 'reliance principle' in cases in illegality, but have taken the view that it is a matter for the Supreme Court to consider with a panel of at least seven and 'conceivably nine' Justices (*Jetivia SA* v *Bilta (UK) Ltd (in liquidation)* [2015] UKSC 23 at paras [15]–[17]).

☰ Further reading

Andrews, G. 'The Presumption of Advancement: Equity, Equality and Human Rights' [2007] Conv 340
considers the grounds for abolition of the presumption of advancement under the Human Rights Act 1998

Chambers, R. *Resulting Trusts* (1997) Oxford: Clarendon Press
a book which argues that resulting trusts reverse unjust enrichment

Glister, J. 'Section 199 of the Equality Act 2010: How Not to Abolish the Presumption of Advancement' (2010) 73(5) MLR 807
an article arguing that the Equality Act 2010 does not go far enough in its proposal to abolish the presumption of advancement

Grower, J.A.W. 'Explaining the "*Pallant* v *Morgan* Equity"' (2016) 6 Conv 434–52
argues that the so-called *Pallant* v *Morgan* equity is not a distinct category, but an orthodox instance of a fiduciary agent's liability to account as a constructive trustee

Hopkins, N. 'The *Pallant* v *Morgan* Equity?' [2002] Conv 35
an article casting doubt on the utility of the '*Pallant* v *Morgan*' equity

Liew, Ying K. *Rationalising Constructive Trusts* (2017) Oxford: Hart Publishing
An attempt to impose a logical structural scheme upon the diverse categories of constructive trust

McFarlane, B. 'Constructive Trusts Arising on a Receipt of Property *Sub Conditione*' (2004) 120 LQR 667
an article examining the problems arising where constructive trusts arise in response to contractual conditions

Oakley, A.J. *Constructive Trusts* (1997) London: Sweet & Maxwell
a detailed survey of constructive trusts

Swadling, W. 'Explaining Resulting Trusts' (2008) 124 LQR 72
a scholarly overview of the subject

 For links to selected cases, statutes, academic papers and official reports mentioned in this chapter please visit the online resources at www.oup.com/uk/watt_directions6e/.

17 Informal trusts of land

LEARNING OBJECTIVES

By the end of this chapter you should be able to:

- understand the social reasons why informal trusts of land are recognised;
- distinguish the varieties of informal trusts of land;
- advise as to whether facts give rise to a resulting trust or a constructive trust;
- explain the practical significance of the distinction between constructive and resulting trusts of land;
- appreciate the relationship between proprietary estoppel and constructive trust;
- set out some of the problems addressed by, and caused by, the operation of informal trusts in the context of cohabitation.

Introduction

This chapter should be of universal interest, and not just to students of equity and trusts. One day it is likely that many of us will share the ownership of land with another person. Even if we do not, it is likely that many of us have parents who share ownership of land. Some statistics suggest that more and more of us are living alone, but against this there is a trend of people home-sharing because it is the only way to afford to purchase a house at today's prices. Even if we live alone for normal residential purposes, it is possible that we own land in a *business* partnership. Sharing land is what we do, especially on this small island, and in the part that is England and Wales co-ownership of land always exists under a trust in which legal title is held by the trustees as beneficial joint tenants.

> **beneficial joint tenants** Where legal title to land is in the joint names of two or more persons who are also joint owners in equity, the co-owners are said to be beneficial joint tenants. Husband and wife will often be beneficial joint tenants.

Suppose you live alone and one day meet your dream lover. You were solely entitled to your land, but you now have the option of transferring the land into joint names and declaring a trust to make you joint owners. Even if you don't do this, you might find that the court can 'construct' a trust from your informal behaviour together—although the court will never presume shared ownership just because people share a home.

The trusts issues raised by the preceding scenario lie at the intersection of the law of real property and the law governing the family, so it may be that you are familiar with some of the material from studying land law or family law earlier in your course. That can help you, so long as you keep in mind that we are studying informal trusts of land in the wider context of trusts law. You should especially bear in mind that the trust law which applies to family land might not apply to other types of land. Resulting trusts are a particular cause for concern. The doctrines of resulting trust have long been settled in the law of trusts, but this chapter will reveal that they have lately been seriously unsettled in the context of the family home.

17.1 The problem of informality

▶ **CROSS REFERENCE**

For more detail on statutory formalities governing trusts, see Chapter 3.

A declaration of an *express* trust of land, or of any interest therein, must be formally 'manifested and proved by some writing signed by some person who is able to declare such trust or by his will' (Law of Property Act 1925, s 53(1)(b)). This is the usual formality rule, but it does not apply to 'the creation or operation of resulting, implied or constructive trusts' (s 53(2)). It is these 'informal trusts' that we will focus on in this chapter.

The exemption from the formality rule which applies to 'resulting, implied or constructive trusts' has proved especially useful in the context of home-sharing or 'cohabitation'. This is because cohabitation, if it is not within the bounds of a marriage or a **civil partnership**, is always essentially informal in the eyes of the law. Cohabitation is not a category defined *in law*; it is a spectrum of ways in which a home may be shared *in fact*. If property law had no means to recognise informal trusts within this range, all cohabitation outside of a marriage or a civil partnership would be left to survive without the law of property.

civil partnership
A registered relationship between two people 'of the same sex' (Civil Partnership Act 2004).

17.1.1 Preventing problems—the use of an express trust

The more informal the cohabitation, the harder it is for the law to determine the proper allocation of property between the parties if and when the relationship breaks down, but potential disputes as to proprietary entitlement could be avoided by the simple expedient of placing title to the shared home into the cohabitants' joint names subject to a formal express declaration of trust. The trust would specify that they hold the land as joint tenants in equity, or that they hold certain shares as equitable tenants in common. Since 1 April 1998, the standard Land Registry Form for the transfer of land (form TR1) asks joint transferees to express whether the beneficial (equitable) interest in the land will be held by them jointly under a beneficial joint tenancy or in shares under a tenancy in common. If the latter, the form asks them to express the shares in the equitable interest to be held. If the form is completed and signed it will constitute an express trust. Unfortunately it isn't compulsory to complete the form in most cases, and even when it is completed, evidence suggests that cohabitants frequently fail to appreciate its significance and effect.

17.1.2 Curing problems—why informal cohabitants have it especially tough

Unfortunately, not every cohabiting couple takes the simple precautionary step of drawing up an express trust, and if cohabitees do not take that simple step to prevent property disputes, they will find to their cost that the law does not provide a simple cure. Where a property dispute arises between *married* parties in the context of proceedings for divorce or judicial separation, the court has wide powers to apportion proprietary entitlement according to what is fair in all the circumstances (see the Matrimonial Causes Act 1973, s 24), and similar assistance is extended to registered civil partners, but other shades of cohabitee have no such help.

In *Hammond* v *Mitchell* [1991] 1 WLR 1127 at 1129 Waite J summarised the particular property law difficulties facing informal cohabitees when their relationship breaks down. Commenting on the couple in that case ('a married man of 40 separated from his wife' and 'a Bunny Girl employed at a high salary by the Playboy Club in Mayfair') his Lordship observed:

> Had they been married, the issue of ownership would scarcely have been relevant, because the law these days when dealing with the financial consequences of divorce adopts a forward-looking perspective in which questions of ownership yield to the higher demands of . . . the needs of each, the first consideration given to the welfare of children. Since the couple did not marry, none of that flexibility is available to them, except a limited power to direct capital provision for their children. In general, their financial rights have to be worked out according to their strict entitlements in equity, a process which is anything but forward-looking and involves, on the contrary, a painfully detailed retrospect.

His Lordship paints a bleak scene, and after his promotion to the Court of Appeal, he added one or two more clouds to the picture when he noted that 'the rights of married occupiers can be equally problematic . . . when the claims of third parties such as creditors or mortgagees become involved' (*Midland Bank plc* v *Cooke* [1995] 4 All ER 562).

> ### 🔍 CASE CLOSE-UP
>
> **Midland Bank plc v Cooke [1995] 4 All ER 562, Court of Appeal**
>
> Waite LJ: 'equity has traditionally been a system which matches established principle to the demands of social change. The mass diffusion of home ownership has been one of the most striking social changes of our own time. The present case is typical of hundreds, perhaps even thousands, of others. When people, especially young people, agree to share their lives in joint homes they do so on a basis of mutual trust and in the expectation that their relationship will endure. Despite the efforts that have been made by many responsible bodies to counsel prospective cohabitants as to the risks of taking shared interests in property without legal advice, it is unrealistic to expect that advice to be followed on a universal scale. For a couple embarking on a serious relationship, discussion of the terms to apply at parting is almost a contradiction of the shared hopes that have brought them together. There will inevitably be numerous couples, married or unmarried, who have no discussion about ownership and who, perhaps advisedly, make no agreement about it. It would be anomalous, against that background, to create a range of home-buyers who were beyond the pale of equity's assistance in formulating a fair presumed basis for the sharing of beneficial title, simply because they had been honest enough to admit that they never gave ownership a thought or reached any agreement about it.'

17.2　Varieties of informal trust

The Law of Property Act 1925, s 53(2) exempts 'resulting, implied or constructive trusts' from the usual formality associated with the creation of an enforceable express trust of land, but the courts have very rarely talked of 'implied' trusts, and they have sometimes treated resulting and constructive trusts as if they were the same thing. We have noted the observation made by Waite LJ that the financial rights of cohabitants have to be worked out 'according to their strict entitlements in equity' (*Midland Bank v Cooke*), but that is true only to the extent that equity is 'strict'. In fact, equity's treatment of non-married cohabitation has tended to waiver historically between times where doctrine has been quite strictly adhered to and times when the strictures of doctrine have been almost utterly thrown off (see Lord Denning at 17.4.4). Judges have sometimes been especially ill-disciplined in keeping resulting trusts distinct from constructive trusts and constructive trusts distinct from proprietary estoppel. In *Drake v Whipp* [1996] 1 FLR 826 Peter Gibson LJ called for clearer use of terminology in cases where one cohabitee asserts a beneficial ownership claim against property vested in the name of another cohabitee. He pointed out that resulting trusts operate according to the presumed intention of the contributing party, in the absence of rebutting evidence of actual intention, whereas constructive trusts operate to give effect to the actual or inferred common intention of both parties. In the following section we will see that his Lordship's call for a clear distinction between resulting trusts and constructive trusts in cohabitation contexts has been resoundingly answered by the House of Lords.

17.2.1　The decision of the House of Lords in *Stack v Dowden*

Now we must turn to the highly significant decision of the House of Lords in *Stack v Dowden* [2007] UKHL 17, [2007] 2 AC 432. Mr Stack and Ms Dowden began cohabiting in the early

1980s in a house which was in Ms Dowden's sole name. Mr Stack may have contributed to the deposit on that house, but the deposit was paid out of Ms Dowden's account and she provided the balance by means of a mortgage loan which she repaid. They had four children and in 1993 moved into a new home. Title to that house was registered in their joint names. There was a new mortgage on that house under which both Stack and Dowden were liable and under which they both made repayments. Ms Dowden paid all the domestic bills. They separated in 2002 and Mr Stack brought proceedings to establish a beneficial share in the house. He was awarded a half-share at first instance, but the Court of Appeal reduced that to a third (35 per cent in fact) and that was upheld by the House of Lords. It is interesting to observe that in the end the value of the family home was divided between them in almost exactly the same proportions in which, at the end of their relationship, Mr Stack and Ms Dowden had been bringing income into the 'family finances' (Ms Dowden, 'the most highly qualified woman electrical engineer in the London area', earned a £42,000 salary representing 63 per cent of the whole of their income; Mr Stack earned £24,000, representing 37 per cent). Baroness Hale of Richmond (who is, of course, the most highly qualified woman judge in the London area) delivered the leading speech for the majority, with the concurrence of Lords Hoffmann, Walker and Hope. Lord Neuberger agreed in the result, but on a more traditional resulting trust basis.

The case presented the House of Lords with its first opportunity to consider a property dispute arising from the breakdown of the relationship between a non-married couple. It also provided the first opportunity for the House of Lords to scrutinise a purchase in the joint names of co-habiting parties where they had failed to declare the size of their respective beneficial interests. It is important to note that their Lordships did not consider the situation, still very common in practice, where legal title is in the *sole name* of one of the cohabitants. It follows that nothing said in *Stack* v *Dowden* is binding in that situation. The Supreme Court has confirmed 'that the starting point for analysis is different' in sole-owner and in joint-owner situations (*Jones* v *Kernott* [2011] UKSC 53; [2011] 3 WLR 1121 at para. [16]), although elements of their Lordships' reasoning in *Stack* will inevitably be highly persuasive even in the context of sole ownership. Where property is purchased or held in the name of a sole legal owner that person will prima facie be the sole beneficial owner as well. In *Stack* v *Dowden* their Lordships held that there is a similar strong presumption where a shared home is purchased or held in joint names that the parties will be joint owners in equity. 'The presumption will be that equity follows the law' (*per* Lord Walker at para. [33]). Furthermore, 'cases in which the joint legal owners are to be taken to have intended that their beneficial interests should be different from their legal interests will be very unusual' (*per* Baroness Hale at para. [69]). (The strong presumption in favour of joint beneficial ownership, where land is held in joint names, was applied in *Fowler v Barron* [2008] EWCA Civ 377; [2008] 2 FLR 831.)

Despite this, their Lordships held on the facts of *Stack* v *Dowden* that the strong presumption in favour of equality had been rebutted, with the result that a larger share went to the party who had made the biggest financial contribution. But apart from the different monetary contributions, it is hard to identify any factor which would justify the discrepancy in the shares awarded to the parties—and can different financial contributions really make a case 'very unusual'?

Leaving those concerns aside, the case confirms that the best way to establish a trust of any land is to use an *express* trust setting out all the rights and entitlements of the parties having an interest in the land. As Baroness Hale said, '[n]o-one now doubts that such an express declaration of trust is conclusive unless varied by subsequent agreement or affected by proprietary estoppel' (at para. [49], approving *Goodman* v *Gallant* [1986] Fam 106). Ideally, an express trust will deal with such matters as whether the equitable interest in the land is owned jointly or in shares (remember that the *legal* title to co-owned land is always, as with all forms of property held on trust, held by the trustees jointly). If the express trust declares that the co-owners own distinct equitable shares in the land, the trust should also express the size of the parties' distinct shares. The problem is that not everyone takes the sensible precaution of drawing up an express trust. In this respect, the parties in *Stack v Dowden* are typical. All they did was to sign a conveyance which provided that the survivor could 'give a valid receipt for capital money arising on a disposition of the land'. It was held that this mere form of words did not constitute an express declaration of trust.

Before *Stack v Dowden* a party claiming an interest under an informal trust of the family home was allowed two bites at the cherry. She could argue that she had an interest under a resulting trust, or, in the alternative, an interest under a constructive trust. Following the decision of the House of Lords in *Stack v Dowden* it would appear that the resulting trust alternative is now no longer available to the claimant where the land is in joint names. That alternative died when the House of Lords held that where land is in joint names it is presumed that beneficial ownership is also joint and that the presumption of joint ownership is not rebutted by the mere fact of unequal contributions to the purchase price. (Before *Stack v Dowden*, unequal contributions to the purchase gave rise, as we have seen, to the presumption of a resulting trust in proportion to contributions, even where land was transferred into joint names.)

To reduce the influence of resulting trusts in land acquisition is at first sight a welcome innovation, as there never was a case of disputed ownership of the family home disposed of on the basis of resulting trust which could not have been as fairly disposed of by constructive trust. The decision is also consistent with a general trend, traceable back to the Law of Property Act 1925, s 60(3), to reduce the presumption of resulting trusts in land law contexts. (Section 60(3) provides that the presumption of a resulting trust should no longer apply on a *voluntary conveyance* of land: see later.)

However, even if a constructive trust can do the job of a resulting trust, it can't do it anywhere nearly as efficiently. The presumption of a resulting trust is based on the single factor of financial contributions to the initial purchase price, whereas *Stack v Dowden* (as we will shortly see) requires the court to consider a wide range of factors. Another criticism of the decision in *Stack v Dowden* is that it proceeds on the assumption that there is a fundamental and clear distinction between the family home and other sorts of property, including other sorts of land. In an age when the family home is often used as a place of work and frequently serves as mortgage security for business loans, it is not clear that the assumed distinctiveness of the family home is altogether an appropriate one. When a family home is re-mortgaged it may be done to raise cash for purposes wholly unrelated to enhancing the house as a shared home, in which event the home is being used as a commercial resource. Yet according to *Stack v Dowden*, and despite concerns raised by Lord Neuberger, the presumption of joint tenancy will apply just as much to re-mortgage situations as to home acquisition. This is despite the fact that a transfer into joint names on re-mortgage is in no way intended to express the parties' understanding as to their relative entitlement, but is an artificial step inserted merely to placate the lender.

A more general difficulty with the decision in *Stack v Dowden* is that in one fell swoop it has made the application of the settled property doctrine of resulting trust turn upon such relatively ill-defined concepts as 'family' and 'shared home'. And yet, after the majority of their Lordships pushed resulting trust doctrine to one side, their Lordships decided that on the particular facts of *Stack v Dowden* the strong presumption in favour of equality had been overcome and that the parties should have interests in the property proportionate to their financial contributions to acquisition—precisely the same outcome that would have been reached on a resulting trust approach!

For a summary of the general position after *Stack v Dowden*, see Figure 17.1.

Figure 17.1 Trusts of the shared home after *Stack v Dowden*

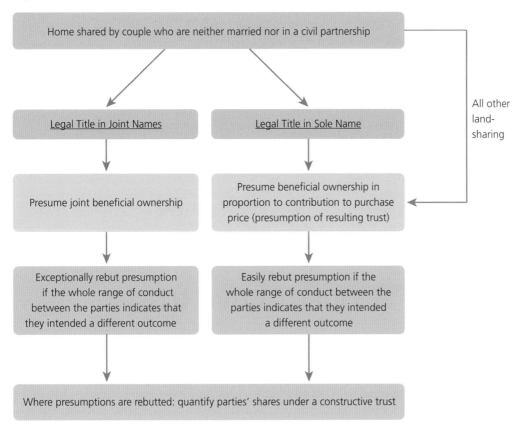

17.3 Resulting trusts

Under a resulting trust, a contribution towards the acquisition of land gives the contributor a beneficial share in the land proportionate to their contribution; hence it is sometimes referred to as a 'purchase money resulting trust' (see, for example, *Curley v Parkes* [2004] EWCA Civ 1515 (CA)). You should recall that '*re-sult*' is Latin for 'jump back'.

Since *Stack v Dowden*, the presumption of resulting trust no longer applies to land acquired by 'romantic' cohabitants in their joint names, but the resulting trust will still be of relevance to other land, including shared homes having a sole legal owner. In *Laskar v Laskar* [2008] EWCA Civ 347; [2008] 1 WLR 2695, *Stack* was distinguished on the basis that the normal presumption of resulting trust applies where land is acquired for a commercial venture, even as between family members. In *Prest v Petrodel* [2013] UKSC 34, Lord Sumption advised (at para. [52]) that where cohabitees reside in a home held in the name of a company controlled by one of them, judges should suspect that the cohabitee who controls the company intends to retain beneficial ownership of the land.

In *Stack v Dowden* Lord Neuberger of Abbotsbury, dissenting from the majority analysis, preferred the orthodoxy under which unequal contributions to purchase in joint names were presumed to give the owners beneficial shares under a resulting trust in direct proportion to their contributions. This orthodox approach was confirmed in the House of Lords as recently as 1996

CROSS REFERENCE

To remind yourself of the basics of resulting trusts, see Chapter 16, Introduction.

(see the italicised portion of the following quote, which was cited with approval by Lord Neuberger of Abbotsbury in *Stack* v *Dowden*) and after *Stack* it remains the orthodox position unless the purchased land happens to be purchased for cohabitation by a couple who are neither married nor in a civil partnership.

CASE CLOSE-UP

***Westdeutsche Landesbank Girozentrale* v *Islington London Borough Council* [1996] 2 WLR 802, House of Lords**

Lord Browne-Wilkinson: 'where A makes a voluntary payment to B or pays (wholly or in part) for the purchase of property which is vested either in B alone or in the joint names of A and B, there is a presumption that A did not intend to make a gift to B: the money or property is held on trust for A (if he is the sole provider of the money) or in *the case of a joint purchase by A and B in shares proportionate to their contributions.*'

17.4 Constructive trusts

The facts of the leading House of Lords case *Lloyds Bank plc* v *Rosset* [1991] 1 AC 107 are fairly typical. Mr Rosset had received a loan to buy a derelict house on the understanding that the house should be in his name alone. Mrs Rosset did a limited amount of work towards the renovation of the house; in particular, she helped with the interior decorations. However, the vast bulk of the work was carried out by contractors employed and paid for by the husband. Following matrimonial problems, the husband left home, leaving his wife and children in the premises. The loan which the husband had taken out was not, in the event, repaid. Consequently, the bank brought proceedings for possession. The husband raised no defence to that action, but the wife did resist. She claimed to have a beneficial interest in the house under a trust. The House of Lords held that, to succeed, Mrs Rosset would have to show that there had been some 'agreement' (evidenced by express discussions between herself and her husband) that they were to share the property beneficially in equity. In the absence of evidence of such an agreement, a trust would not arise in her favour unless she had made *direct* contributions to the purchase price or mortgage repayments.

Note that direct contributions to the purchase price are preferable to contributions by way of mortgage instalments, because the payment of mortgage instalments can be ambiguous in the absence of an agreement expressly relating to that type of payment. Payment of mortgage instalments could, for instance, be construed to be merely a payment made instead of rent: see *Barrett* v *Barrett* [2008] EWHC 1061 (Ch) and *Carlton* v *Goodman* [2002] EWCA Civ 545; 2 FLR 259. The court is more likely to infer a common intention to share the beneficial interest in the land if the legal owner would have had difficulty meeting the mortgage payments without the claimant's contribution (*Le Foe* v *Le Foe* ([2001] 2 FLR 970 *per* Nicholas Mostyn QC at 982 at para. [50]); as confirmed in the Privy Council in *Abbott* v *Abbott* [2007] UKPC 53 and *obiter* in *Stack* v *Dowden*.

The key part of Lord Bridge's speech in *Rosset* is the distinction he draws between two very different bases on which A might successfully claim a beneficial interest against the legal owner, B. Lord Bridge had very little to say about purchase money resulting trusts (i.e. those within Lord Browne-Wilkinson's category (A)). Instead, Lord Bridge seemed content to use constructive trusts (and maybe proprietary estoppel) to satisfy the beneficial ownership claims of non-owning cohabitees.

Lloyds Bank plc v Rosset [1991] 1 AC 107, House of Lords

Lord Bridge of Harwich: 'the first and fundamental question which must always be resolved is whether, independently of any inference to be drawn from the conduct of the parties in the course of sharing the house as their home and managing their joint affairs, there has at any time prior to acquisition, or exceptionally at some later date, been any agreement, arrangement or understanding reached between them that the property is to be shared beneficially. The finding of an agreement or arrangement to share in this sense can only, I think, be based on evidence of express discussions between the partners, however imperfectly remembered and however imprecise their terms may have been. Once a finding to this effect is made it will only be necessary for the partner asserting a claim to a beneficial interest against the partner entitled to the legal estate to show that he or she acted to his or her detriment or significantly altered his or her position in reliance on the agreement in order to give rise to a constructive trust or a proprietary estoppel.

In sharp contrast with this situation is the very different one where there is no evidence to support a finding of an agreement or arrangement to share, however reasonable it might have been for the parties to reach such an arrangement if they had applied their minds to the question, and where the court must rely entirely on the conduct of the parties both as the basis from which to infer a common intention to share the property beneficially and as the conduct relied on to give rise to a constructive trust. In this situation direct contributions to the purchase price by the partner who is not the legal owner, whether initially or by payment of mortgage instalments, will readily justify the inference necessary to the creation of a constructive trust. But, as I read the authorities, it is at least extremely doubtful whether anything less will do.

The leading cases in your lordships' House are *Pettitt v Pettitt* [1970] AC 777 and *Gissing v Gissing* [1971] AC 866. Both demonstrate situations in the second category to which I have referred and their Lordships discuss at great length the difficulties to which these situations give rise.'

In *Stack v Dowden* [2007] 2 AC 432 Lord Neuberger cautioned against inferring a constructive trust of the shared home based only on the way the cohabitants manage their finances and share their other property ([113] and [132]). A majority of their Lordships in *Stack v Dowden* agreed upon the following list of factors which will be amongst those a court might consider when seeking to determine the parties' intentions regarding ownership of the shared home (taken mostly from the speech of Baroness Hale of Richmond at paras [69]–[70]):

- the parties' financial contributions to the acquisition of the property. (In *Burton v Liden* ([2016] EWCA Civ 275; [2017] 1 FLR 310) a cohabitee who made monthly payments 'towards the house' successfully established an equitable interest because these were understood to be payments 'towards ownership of the house');
- any advice or discussions at the time of the transfer which cast light upon their intentions then;
- the reasons why the home was acquired in their joint names;
- the reasons why (if it be the case) the survivor was authorised to give a receipt for the capital monies;

- the purpose for which the home was acquired;
- the nature of the parties' relationship;
- whether they had children for whom they both had responsibility to provide a home;
- how the purchase was financed, both initially and subsequently;
- how the parties arranged their finances, whether separately or together or a bit of both;
- how they discharged the outgoings on the property and their other household expenses;
- the parties' individual characters and personalities;
- the fact that one party has financed (or constructed himself) an extension or substantial improvement to the property, so that what they have now is significantly different from what they had initially [note: this factor is of course very significant given that few people can now afford to move to bigger houses, and therefore prefer to extend their existing house];
- any other factors which indicate that the parties' intentions have changed over time.

Baroness Hale emphasised that this list is not exhaustive, and she made the general observation that '[i]n the cohabitation context, mercenary considerations may be more to the fore than they would be in marriage, but it should not be assumed that they always take pride of place over natural love and affection'. Her Ladyship also confirmed that the court must not seek 'the result which the court itself considers fair', but rather, the result which the parties 'must, in the light of their conduct, be taken to have intended'.

The cohabitants in *Jones* v *Kernott* [2011] UKSC 53 expressly agreed, when their relationship broke down and Mr Kernott left the family home in 1993, that they were at that time beneficial joint owners in equity. Thereafter Ms Jones remained in occupation and met all future expenses and outgoings of maintaining the premises and paying off the mortgage. Some years later, Mr Kernott purported to sever and recover his half-share of the land, but the County Court judge awarded Ms Jones 90 per cent of the value of the land on the basis that this was 'fair and just'. That decision was upheld in the High Court. The Court of Appeal allowed Mr Kernott's appeal by a majority of two to one ([2010] EWCA Civ 578; [2010] 3 All ER 423). Their Lordships emphasised that (following *Stack* v *Dowden*) the judges in the lower courts ought to have respected the parties' agreement to share equally in the event of sale and, in the absence of compelling evidence that the parties' intentions had changed, that initial agreement should stand. However, when the matter came before the UK Supreme Court in 2011, their Lordships held that the parties' intentions *had* changed during the period of Mr Kernott's absence from the shared home and, allowing the appeal, upheld the decision of the County Court judge. Their Lordships favoured fair maintenance of the current occupants (the woman and the children of her cohabitation with Kernott) over a strict allocation on the basis of initial financial contribution to purchase, or to put it in the legal terms they adopted, their Lordships held that purchase money resulting trusts do not determine the outcome of cohabitation cases and that the court should look instead to fulfil the parties' actual intentions by means of a constructive trust. In other words, they confirmed what had been said by the House of Lords in *Stack* v *Dowden*. This approach might work justice in some cases, but it is equally liable to work injustice, for the parties' 'intentions' can only ever be that which the court finds them to be 'on the balance of probabilities'. The outcome of any given 'cohabitation case' is as unpredictable as ever as a result of *Jones* v *Kernott*, and it is fair to say that judicial discretion in this area is now so wide that courts are not far off the broad approach to allocation that is required by statute when married cohabitants divorce, but which Parliament has so far not seen fit to grant to unmarried cohabitants.

CASE CLOSE-UP

Jones v *Kernott* [2011] UKSC 53, UK Supreme Court

Lord Walker and Lady Hale (at para. [51]):

'In summary, therefore, the following are the principles applicable in a case such as this, where a family home is bought in the joint names of a cohabiting couple who are both responsible for any mortgage, but without any express declaration of their beneficial interests.

(1) The starting point is that equity follows the law and they are joint tenants both in law and in equity [note: despite making the maxim 'equity follows the law' the first point in their conclusion, in para. [19] of their judgment their Lordships call it a 'mantra' and, rather unconvincingly, attempt to downplay its importance].

(2) That presumption can be displaced by showing (a) that the parties had a different common intention at the time when they acquired the home, or (b) that they later formed the common intention that their respective shares would change.

(3) Their common intention is to be deduced objectively from their conduct: "the relevant intention of each party is the intention which was reasonably understood by the other party to be manifested by that party's words and conduct notwithstanding that he did not consciously formulate that intention in his own mind or even acted with some different intention which he did not communicate to the other party" (Lord Diplock in *Gissing* v *Gissing* [1971] AC 886, 906). Examples of the sort of evidence which might be relevant to drawing such inferences are given in *Stack* v *Dowden*, at para. 69.

(4) In those cases where it is clear either (a) that the parties did not intend joint tenancy at the outset, or (b) had changed their original intention, but it is not possible to ascertain by direct evidence or by inference what their actual intention was as to the shares in which they would own the property, "the answer is that each is entitled to that share which the court considers fair having regard to the whole course of dealing between them in relation to the property": Chadwick LJ in *Oxley* v *Hiscock* [2005] Fam 211, para. 69. In our judgment, 'the whole course of dealing . . . in relation to the property' should be given a broad meaning, enabling a similar range of factors to be taken into account as may be relevant to ascertaining the parties' actual intentions.

(5) Each case will turn on its own facts. Financial contributions are relevant but there are many other factors which may enable the court to decide what shares were either intended (as in case (3)) or fair (as in case (4)).'

THINKING POINT

Their Lordships in *Stack* (and to some extent in *Jones* v *Kernott* also, but see the preceding extract from that case) placed emphasis on the maxim 'equity follows the law'. This maxim raises a presumption that a sole legal owner is the sole beneficial owner and this would make it harder to claim a beneficial interest against a sole legal owner under *Stack* than under *Rosset*. Is that an outcome that their Lordships would expect and want the maxim to produce?

17.4.1 **Express agreement plus detrimental reliance**

In Chapter 4 we noted that the courts are, in theory, reluctant to hold that an express trust has been created on the basis of 'loose conversations' (see *Jones* v *Lock* at 4.2.2). Cases where the courts have recognised express trusts on the basis of such conversations are exceptional (see, for example, *Paul* v *Constance* at 4.2.2). It might come as something of a surprise to discover that Lord Bridge is prepared to recognise a constructive trust on the basis of 'any agreement, arrangement or understanding . . . that the property is to be shared beneficially . . . based on evidence of express discussions between the partners, however imperfectly remembered and however imprecise their terms may have been'.

 THINKING POINT

Do you think Lord Bridge is being overgenerous?

The criteria laid down by Lord Bridge for the recognition of trusts of this sort are not particularly stringent and the danger is that they will encourage the fanciful recollection of discussions that never in fact existed. However, the potential for injustice to a bank, such as Lloyds, may not be statistically significant. Even where there has been an agreement between the cohabitees, it will only bind the bank where the agreement was concluded before the bank took the mortgage. And before taking the mortgage the bank, like any purchaser, should have carried out a prudent search for evidence of any such pre-existing agreement by making an inquiry into the rights of all occupiers of the land.

In short, Lord Bridge's first basis for a constructive trust appears to have the twin merits of conceptual clarity and practical utility. However, before we ascribe the status and force of statute to this 'new orthodoxy', we should look at the defining ingredients more closely.

17.4.1.1 **'Express'**

The problem is that an agreement is only relevant if it is expressed. Too many couples don't give their own account of the relationship until it is too late.

In *Springette* v *Defoe* [1992] 2 FCR 561 (CA) Dillon LJ confirmed that '[i]t is not enough to establish a common intention which is sufficient to found an implied or constructive trust of land that each of them happened at the same time to have been thinking on the same lines in his or her uncommunicated thoughts'.

In *Grant* v *Edwards* [1986] Ch 638 the defendant explained that if he were to place the claimant's name on the legal title, it would prejudice matrimonial proceedings pending between her and her estranged husband. (Compare *Williamson* v *Sheikh* [2008] EWCA Civ 990 (CA), where a constructive trust was found despite the parties' deliberate choice not to make it express; the man was held to the terms of the formal trust on the ground that the only reason he had not executed it had been an expression of informal trust between the parties.)

In *Eves* v *Eves* [1975] 1 WLR 1338 the defendant told the claimant that the only reason why the property was to be acquired in his name alone was because she was under 21 and that, but for her age, he would have had the house put into their joint names. Lord Bridge (in *Rosset*) held that *Grant* v *Edwards* and *Eves* v *Eves* were cases decided on the basis of an express agreement plus detrimental reliance thereon.

The case of *Grant v Edwards* is particularly intriguing because in that case the only *expressed* intention was the defendant's intention *not* to give the claimant any interest in the property! To get from these words to an understanding that the claimant should have an interest in the property could only have been achieved by *inferring* that those words had an actual meaning contrary to their apparent meaning. As Nourse LJ put it in *Grant v Edwards*: 'these facts raise a clear inference that there was an understanding . . . otherwise no excuse for not putting her name onto the title would have been needed.'

Simon Gardner has criticised this type of reasoning. He says: '[i]f I give an excuse for rejecting an invitation to what I expect to be [a] dull party, it does not mean that I thereby agree to come: on the contrary, it means that I do not agree to come, but for one reason or another I find it hard to say outright' ('Rethinking Family Property' (1993) 109 LQR 263 at 265). Such 'excuses' will sometimes protect the legal owner. In *Curran v Collins* ([2015] EWCA Civ 404), which was a classic case of relationship breakdown between long-term unmarried cohabitees, the man expressly told the woman that he would remain sole owner of all the properties owned in his sole name. Arden LJ confirmed that this 'was sufficient to negate any reasonable belief in any common intention' (para. [3]). However, a question arose in relation to one property because the man, the woman claimed, had given an 'excuse' for not adding the woman's name to the title. The excuse was that it would mean an increase in life insurance premiums. The judge at first instance found as a fact that the man 'had made the statement to avoid any embarrass-ment' over his refusal to add the woman to the title. On this basis the judge rejected the woman's claim that there was a common intention that she should have an interest in the man's property. On appeal, Arden LJ declined, in the absence of evidence that the judge had made a mistake, to interfere with the judge's finding of fact as to the man's intent in offering the 'ex-cuse'. In further support of the judge's finding was the fact that the parties did not commence cohabitation until many years after the alleged 'excuse' was spoken.

Rowe v Prance [1999] 2 FLR 787 illustrates how different can be the law's response to trusts of personal property. On facts otherwise reminiscent of *Grant v Edwards*, the cohabitees bought a boat to live on. The man paid for it but frequently stated that the boat belonged to them both. His explanation ('excuse') for not registering the woman as joint owner was that she did not possess 'a relevant certificate'. The court held that he had constituted himself an express trustee of the boat for himself and the woman in equal shares. Surely *Grant v Edwards* would likewise have been disposed of as a case of express trust had it not been for the fact that the parties' failure to comply with statutory formality requirements would have rendered an express trust of *land* unenforceable.

17.4.1.2 'Agreement'

Lord Bridge described it as an 'agreement, arrangement or understanding reached between them that the property is to be shared beneficially'. Lord Diplock in *Gissing v Gissing* [1971] AC 866 called it a 'transaction between the trustee and the *cestui que trust*'. For the agreement, arrangement or understanding to found a constructive trust it must be an agreement, arrange-ment or understanding that the non-legal owner should get a beneficial interest in the land. In one case a husband and wife contributed their common fund of money to the purchase of a house for the husband's mother. When the husband's mother died, the wife (then divorced) sought to claim a share in the house. She failed because, although the husband and wife would *together* have been entitled to a beneficial interest in the house, it was perfectly consistent with the nature of their joint venture for the husband to get the entire beneficial *ownership* of his mother's house and for the wife merely to get the *use* of the house (*Buggs v Buggs* [2003] EWHC 1538, Ch). However, it is not necessary that the agreement should contain a consensus as to the size of the parties' respective shares under the trust (*per* Peter Gibson LJ in *Drake* v *Whipp* [1996] 1 FLR 826). Nor is it necessary for there to have been an actual *subjective* agreement, as cases such as *Grant* v *Edwards* and *Eves* v *Eves* show.

The date of the agreement will usually be prior to or concurrent with the financial outlay of the claimant, but Fox LJ in *Burns* v *Burns* held that even where 'initially, there was no intention that the claimant should have any interest in the property, circumstances may subsequently arise from which the intention to confer an equitable interest upon the claimant may arise (e.g. the discharge of a mortgage or the effecting of capital improvements to the house at his or her expense)'. Lord Bridge in *Rosset* also accepted that the agreement between the parties need not be established prior to acquisition, but may occur 'exceptionally at some later date'.

The discovery of an agreement between the parties can appear to be somewhat convenient. It may also be value-laden. Simon Gardner (*op. cit.*) has described the law regarding the discovery of a common understanding as being 'very far from neutral'. He continues:

> Its basic proclivity is towards finding an understanding and so a trust, because its approach is not very literal: the necessary understanding can be inferred on the basis of quite remotely extrinsic material. But this proclivity extends only to cases where the woman's input has been essentially financial; otherwise, she is left unaided.

It only takes one more small step for the cynic to ask why agreement should create trusts at all! It is, after all, rather unorthodox to make consensus prerequisite to the creation of a trust. Trusts are generally created in accordance with the unilateral intentions of one party and constructive trusts are typically imposed by courts *against* the intentions of the legal owner.

 THINKING POINT

Why have the courts deemed it necessary to prove a common understanding to establish a constructive trust?

The answer is, of course, that proof of agreement is proof that B's conscience is affected, and it is because B's conscience is affected by A's claim that B is made a constructive trustee for the benefit of A.

17.4.1.3 'Detrimental reliance'

In *Grant* v *Edwards* [1986] Ch 638 Browne-Wilkinson V-C approved the decision in *Midland* v *Dobson* [1986] 1 FLR 171 that 'mere common intention is not by itself enough: the claimant has also to prove that she has acted to her detriment in the reasonable belief by so acting she was acquiring a beneficial interest'.

 THINKING POINT

Imagine that you are a woman who has lived for 15 years with the legal owner of your quasi-matrimonial home. You have borne him two children and given up a promising career to bring them up, on the express understanding that you would have a half beneficial share in the house. Can you see any difficulties you might face in showing that you have relied to your detriment upon your common understanding?

There are two main obstacles. The first is showing that you have suffered any detriment at all as a consequence of the arrangement. On one (deliberately overstated) view you have been liberated from the need to work, you have benefited from the joys of children and you have lived rent-free for 15 years in someone else's house. The second obstacle you will face, assuming you can show that you have suffered a detriment, is to prove that the detriment was suffered as a result of (i.e. was causally connected to) the arrangement.

In *Grant* v *Edwards* the Vice-Chancellor was alert to these obstacles when he held that 'setting up house together, having a baby and making payments to general housekeeping expenses . . . may all be referable to the mutual love and affection of the parties and not specifically referable to the claimant's belief that she has an interest in the house'. However, in granting the claimant a half interest in the house in that case their Lordships decided that Mrs Grant had acted to her detriment. In so holding, Nourse LJ described detrimental reliance as 'conduct on which the woman could not reasonably be expected to embark unless she was to have an interest in the home'.

> **THINKING POINT**
>
> In *Smith* v *Bottomley* [2013] EWCA Civ 953, the Court of Appeal declined to decide whether accepting an offer of marriage might amount to a detriment. (Perhaps it was reluctant to undermine the public interest in promoting stable long-term relationships.) What would you have decided on this point?

17.4.2 Direct financial contributions

This is Lord Bridge's second basis for acknowledging a cohabitation constructive trust. It exists in stark contrast to the first basis (i.e. express agreement plus detrimental reliance) because it proceeds on the assumption that there is no evidence of any express agreement whatsoever. In other words, in establishing a constructive trust on the second basis the court must infer a common intention on the basis of the *conduct* of the parties and nothing more.

> **THINKING POINT**
>
> Imagine that you are a woman who has lived for 15 years with the legal owner of your quasi-matrimonial home. You have borne him two children and you gave up work to bring them up. There was no express agreement of any sort in relation to your ownership of the house. Do you think that an agreement should be inferred from your conduct?

No doubt you think that it should, and yet the courts have been happy to explain such behaviour on other grounds ('mutual love and affection' etc). In *Rosset* Lord Bridge held that:

> direct contributions to the purchase price by the partner who is not the legal owner, whether initially or by payment of mortgage instalments, will readily justify the inference necessary to the creation of a constructive trust. But, as I read the authorities, it is at least extremely doubtful whether anything less will do.

Lord Bridge cited *Grant* v *Edwards* as a case in which the woman's conduct would not have been sufficient to create a constructive trust in her favour. (Mrs Grant contributed to general household expenses, provided housekeeping and brought up the children.)

17.4.2.1 Direct financial contributions to purchase price

It is uncontroversial that direct financial contributions to the purchase price of the land, whether made *initially* (by way of deposit at the contract stage or money provided on completion of the purchase) or *subsequently* by payment of mortgage instalments, will 'readily justify the inference necessary to the creation of a constructive trust' (Lord Bridge in *Rosset*).

Paying mortgage instalments is presumed to give rise to an interest, but only if the mortgage was an acquisition mortgage (in *McKenzie* v *McKenzie* [2003] EWHC 601 (Ch), Mr McKenzie re-mortgaged his land but his son, who helped pay off the instalments, failed to acquire a beneficial share in it). In *James* v *Thomas* [2007] All ER (D) 373 it was held that courts should be especially slow to impose a trust on land which had been acquired before the relationship between the cohabitants began. Undertaking joint and several liability for mortgage repayments in reliance upon an understanding that one will acquire a share of the secured land will generally render the reliance 'detrimental' and give rise to an interest under a constructive trust. In fact, it suggests a beneficial joint tenancy of the land (*Crossley* v *Crossley* [2005] EWCA Civ 1581, CA (Civil Division)).

17.4.2.2 Subsequent expenditure on improving the land

In the case of married couples, s 37 of the Matrimonial Proceedings and Property Act 1970 applies. That section provides that where a spouse makes a substantial contribution in money or money's worth to the improvement of property in which either or both have a beneficial interest, the spouse will get a share or enlarged share in the property unless there is any express *or implied* agreement to the contrary. The share will be that which has been agreed or, in the absence of agreement, whatever would be fair. (This provision applies to engaged couples by virtue of s 2(1), Law Reform (Miscellaneous Provisions) Act 1970.) Lord Denning MR was also of the view that s 37 was declaratory of the previous law, and should therefore extend to cover engaged couples (*Davis* v *Vale* [1971] 2 All ER 1021). It is arguable that *Stack* v *Dowden* has now extended this approach to all non-married couples (see 17.4).

Where there is evidence of a special agreement that calculation of the parties' respective beneficial shares should be left until such time as the property ceased to be theirs, substantial improvements carried out by the parties will be relevant to the *quantification* of their interests (*Passee* v *Passee* [1988] 1 FLR 263 (CA)). As to quantification generally, see 17.5.

17.4.3 Indirect financial contributions

Lord Bridge, in *Rosset*, thought it extremely doubtful that such contributions would suffice to raise the inference of a common understanding to grant a beneficial interest. In *Stack* v *Dowden* this issue did not fall to be determined, but it was suggested *obiter* that making improvements that added significant value to the property should be sufficient to generate an interest. Lord Walker opined that 'the law has moved on [since *Rosset*], and your Lordships should move it a little more in the same direction', at para. [27] (since approved by Baroness Hale in the Privy Council in *Abbott* v *Abbott* [2007] UKPC 53).

There were similarly generous *dicta* in cases preceding *Rosset*:

CASE CLOSE-UP

Gissing v Gissing [1971] AC 866, House of Lords

Lord Diplock: 'it may be no more than a matter of convenience which spouse pays particular household accounts, particularly when both are earning, and if the wife goes out to work and devotes part of her earnings or uses her private income to meet joint expenses of the household which would otherwise be met by the husband, so as to enable him to pay the mortgage instalments out of his monies, this would be consistent with and might be corroborative of an original common intention that she should share in the beneficial interest in the matrimonial home and that her payments of other household expenses were intended by both spouses to be treated as including a contribution by the wife to the purchase price of the matrimonial home . . .

Where in any of the circumstances described above contributions, direct or indirect, have been made to the mortgage instalments by the spouse into whose name the matrimonial home has not been conveyed, and the court can infer from their conduct a common intention that the contributing spouse should be entitled to *some* beneficial interest in the matrimonial home, what effect is to be given to that intention if there is no evidence that they in fact reached any express agreement as to what the respective share of each spouse should be?

. . . In such a case the court must first do its best to discover from the conduct of the spouses whether any inference can reasonably be drawn as to the probable common understanding about the amount of the share of the contributing spouse on which each must have acted in doing what each did, even though that understanding was never expressly stated by one spouse to the other or even consciously formulated in words by either of them independently. It is only if no such inference can be drawn that the court is driven to apply as a rule of law, and not as an inference of fact, the maxim *equality is equity*, and to hold that the beneficial interest belongs to the spouses in equal shares.'

(Note, however, that the influence of *Gissing* v *Gissing* is somewhat weakened by the fact that it was a case involving the divorce of a married couple before the Matrimonial Causes Act 1973. The case might have been decided differently after the Act.)

Whatever the status of indirect financial contributions to the acquisition of the land may be, it is clear that any financial and labour contributions to domestic life which are unrelated to acquisition of the land are no ground for inferring a common intention to share beneficial ownership of the land.

17.4.4 Non-financial contributions

Should it be possible to establish an interest in land on the basis of non-financial contributions such as labour? Is the legal owner of a house unjustly enriched if he accepts the benefit of labour and services provided by the person with whom he shares his home, so that it would be unconscionable for him to deny a share in the home? The following passage challenges any such notion.

J.W. Harris, 'Doctrine, Justice, and Home-Sharing' (1999) 19(3) *Oxford Journal of Legal Studies* **421**

We are here in the realm of metaphor. It seems that a person with money in her pocket is to be taken as carrying around with her both so much cash and a fixed quantity of labour-power. She 'owns' both. She may transfer some portion of the one or of the other, so that there will be 'subtraction' or 'deprivation' from the total sum (of money or labour-power). Restitution theory, in this respect, comes in august company. Karl Marx founded his critique of capitalist production and its appropriation of surplus values on the assumption that every service contract represents a conveyance, for the contract's duration, of the worker's entire labour-power to the employer . . . The metaphor may be readily unravelled. When I work I may be said to 'expend' physical or mental energy and I may, perhaps, feel in some way depleted. But it is not the case, as with spending money, that I cease to own some resource which formerly I did own. I have maintained that arguments for property-distribution based on labour-ownership, or the connected notion of self-ownership, are spurious. *Quantum meruit* claims were, in law, once founded on the fiction of promise. Are we better off if we erect claims arising from labour on the metaphor of depletion and transfer?

 THINKING POINT

The preceding passage concluded with a question—how would you answer it? Consider the answer provided by the Court of Appeal in *Burns* v *Burns*, next.

 CASE CLOSE-UP

Burns v *Burns* **[1984] Ch 317, Court of Appeal,** *per* **May LJ at 344**

Where . . . the house is bought with the aid of a mortgage, then the court has to assess each party's respective contributions in a broad sense; nevertheless, the court is only entitled to look at the financial contributions, or their real and substantial equivalent, to the acquisition of the house; that the husband may spend his weekends redecorating or laying a patio is neither here nor there, nor is the fact that the woman has spent so much of her time looking after the house, doing the cooking and bringing up the family.

In the light of doubt that has been cast upon indirect *financial* contributions by *Rosset*, one would have thought it virtually impossible to infer the requisite common intention from *non-financial* contributions. Not so! *Stack* v *Dowden* presumes that where land is in joint names, it is jointly owned in equity—the lack of direct financial contributions might rebut the presumption, but only exceptionally. Of course *Stack* v *Dowden* does not touch the case of land in the sole name of one owner, so the hurdle of making financial contributions will remain as high as ever in that context. If their Lordships had gone so far as to presume equality of beneficial ownership in such a case they would, in effect, have introduced community of property into English law. English law has always rejected any presumption that property shared in fact must be deemed to be shared in equity, and only Parliament can relax that rule. This is not to say that some judges haven't tried, and no modern judge tried harder than Lord Denning MR.

In *Hussey* v *Palmer* [1972] 3 All ER 744 Lord Denning held that the cohabitation constructive trust 'is a trust imposed by the law whenever justice and good conscience require it. It is a liberal process, founded on large principles of equity, to be applied in cases where the defendant cannot conscientiously keep the property for himself alone but ought to allow another to have the property or a share in it.'

In *Cooke* v *Head* [1972] 2 All ER 38 the house was in the name of the man, and he paid the deposit, but the woman contributed to mortgage repayments and helped physically to demolish old buildings (the court held that she 'did quite an unusual amount of work for a woman'). She was held to have a one-third interest in the property, her work having been taken into account. Had only her direct financial contribution been taken into account, she would have been entitled to only one-twelfth of the value of the property under the constructive trust.

It is clear from these decisions, and the facts of *Cooke* v *Head* in particular, that Lord Denning's so-called 'new model' constructive trust represented a radical innovation in the law. For a few years at least, English law inferred the common intention necessary to establish a constructive trust on the basis of indirect non-financial contributions. The only higher 'authority' for this approach is the following *dictum* taken from the speech of Lord Diplock in *Gissing*:

> A resulting, implied or constructive trust—and it is unnecessary for present purposes to distinguish between these three classes of trusts—is created whenever the trustee has so conducted himself that it would be inequitable to deny the *cestui que trust* a beneficial interest in the land acquired. And he will be held so to have conducted himself if by his words or conduct he has induced the *cestui que trust* to act to his own detriment in the belief that by so acting he was acquiring a beneficial interest in the land.

Lord Denning MR relied upon this *dictum* when formulating his 'new model' constructive trust in *Eves* v *Eves* [1975] 3 All ER 768. The woman in that case had moved in with a married man and took his name but never married him. The reason he gave for leaving her name off the title deeds was the fact that she was under the age of 21. She did not make a financial contribution but she did housework and gardening and looked after him and their children. Lord Denning held that 'a few years ago . . . equity would not have helped her. But things have altered now. Equity is not past the age of child bearing. One of her latest progeny is a constructive trust of a new model. Lord Diplock brought it into the world and we have nourished it.'

 THINKING POINT

Remind yourself of the content of Lord Diplock's speech in *Gissing* v *Gissing*. Is it entirely consistent with Lord Denning's new formulation?

It would appear not. As we have already noted, Lord Diplock made it fairly clear that direct or indirect contributions must be financial. He refers repeatedly to contributions 'to the mortgage instalments'. Certainly he provides no example of a situation in which non-financial contributions might suffice.

The reasoning underlying Lord Denning's new model was not followed by the differently constituted Court of Appeal in *Burns* v *Burns* [1984] 1 All ER 244. Their Lordships' judgments in *Burns* v *Burns* displayed a return to *Gissing* v *Gissing* orthodoxy. While Fox LJ accepted that the 'basis of such a claim . . . is that it would be inequitable for the holder of the legal estate to deny the claimant's right to a beneficial interest', his Lordship went on to say that, in the absence of either an express declaration of trust, an express agreement to share or a direct financial contribution, it is necessary to infer that the parties had the requisite common intention:

> In determining whether such common intention exists it is, normally, the intention of the parties when the property was purchased that is important . . . it seems to me that at the time of the acquisition of the house nothing occurred between the parties to raise an equity which would prevent the defendant denying the plaintiff's claim. She provided no money for the purchase; she assumed no liability in respect of the mortgage; there was no understanding or arrangement that the plaintiff would go out to work to assist with the family finances; the defendant did nothing to lead her to change her position in the belief that she would have an interest in the house. It is true that she contemplated living with the defendant in the house and, no doubt, that she would do housekeeping and look after the children. But those facts do not carry with them any implication of a common intention that the plaintiff should have any interest in the house.

The Court of Appeal in *Burns* v *Burns* [1984] Ch 317 confirmed that indirect financial contributions will suffice if 'referable to the acquisition of property'. *Burns* v *Burns* was strongly endorsed by the House of Lords in *Winkworth* v *Edward Baron Development* [1987] 1 All ER 114.

The move away from Lord Denning's liberal approach is now pretty much complete. In *Springette* v *Defoe* in 1992, Dillon LJ stated that 'the court does not, as yet, sit under a palm tree to exercise a general discretion to do what the man in the street, on a general overview of the case, might regard as fair'. Having said that, Lord Denning did much to develop another broad equitable concept, that of proprietary estoppel. His judgments in relation to that concept continue to exert great influence (see 17.6.1).

 THINKING POINT

As a man or woman in the street, do you think that the orthodox rules on 'qualifying contributions' are fair, or apt to create injustice?

Simon Gardner, in *An Introduction to the Law of Trusts* (Oxford: Clarendon Press, 1990), suggests, at p. 238, that 'the position of the law regarding the discovery of a common understanding—and so of the constructive trust itself—is very far from neutral'. He argues that there are two major concerns to counter the social imbalance against women in respect to ownership of family assets. The first is based on the idea of the family as a communal entity: 'The argument is that it is adventitious that the man undertakes the income-generating work which enables him to acquire assets, while she undertakes domestic functions; both roles are equally essential to the success of the family as a whole.' The second is based on an unjust enrichment which should be addressed: in that *where the woman is earning money herself*, 'her earnings are . . . more likely to be spent on fungibles (food, clothes etc.), which are wasting assets at best, while the man's go, in particular, to buying the house, with its capital appreciation'. Gardner submits that the law's orthodox 'referability rules' redress the second kind of imbalance, but not the first. This, he submits, means that help is withheld where it is most needed. (See, further, Simon Gardner, 'Rethinking Family Property' (1993) 109 LQR 263.)

17.5 Quantification of the interest under the trust

17.5.1 Express declaration of trust

The quantification of interests under constructive trusts is first to be determined according to any express agreement made between the parties as to their respective shares. (Or it may be that the parties are not to have *shares* at all, but have expressly agreed to hold the land as joint tenants in equity (see *Goodman* v *Gallant* [1986] 2 WLR 236).) Only where there is no such express agreement as to shares will the court quantify the parties' entitlements according to whatever shares the parties can be assumed to have intended. You should recall from the start of the chapter that the standard Land Registry Form for the transfer of land (form TR1) asks joint transferees to express whether the beneficial (equitable) interest in the land will be held by them jointly under a beneficial joint tenancy or in shares under a tenancy in common. If the latter, the form asks them to express the shares in the equitable interest to be held. If the form is completed and signed it will constitute an express trust.

17.5.2 Resulting trust

It is in relation to the *quantification* of A's entitlement that the need to distinguish between resulting and constructive trusts is most important, but note that, after the decision in *Stack* v *Dowden*, the resulting trust is not relevant to quantifying interests where cohabitants hold land held in their *joint* names (see earlier).

In *Drake* v *Whipp* [1996] 1 FLR 826 the Court of Appeal stressed the importance of distinguishing between resulting and constructive trusts. In this case A and B purchased property which was conveyed into B's name alone. A had contributed 40 per cent of the original cost and a small proportion of the extensive conversion work subsequently undertaken on the property. The Court of Appeal held that she was entitled to a one-third share under a constructive trust. Under a resulting trust A would have been entitled only to one-fifth of the value of the converted house.

The correct date at which to quantify A's interest in the property of which B is legal owner is the date when A's interest is realised, in other words, the date when the joint residence is sold, or when B buys out A's interest.

As the judgment in *Drake* v *Whipp* illustrates, the quantification of the parties' respective beneficial entitlements under a resulting trust is determined by the extent of their respective financial contributions. It is a fairly mechanical calculus. Whatever each party puts in will 'jump back' to them under the resulting trust.

Springette v *Defoe* [1992] 2 FCR 561 was described by Dillon LJ, who sat in the case, as 'yet another . . . in which it falls to the court to decide the proportions of the beneficial interests of a man and a woman, who are not married to each other, in the proceeds of sale of a house which they have acquired in their joint names for the purpose of living together in it'. The reason the issue fell for determination by the court was because there had been no express declaration of the trusts upon which the property was to be held. It was also found as a matter of fact that the parties had not entered into any discussions relating to their respective shares in the property.

Having referred to *Rosset*, Dillon LJ stated that '[s]ince . . . it is clear in the present case that there never was any discussion between the parties about what their respective beneficial interests were to be, they cannot, in my judgment, have had in any relevant sense any common intention to the beneficial ownership . . . The presumption of a resulting trust is not displaced.'

Steyn LJ made the same point very succinctly: '[g]iven that no actual common intention to share the property in equal beneficial shares was established, one is driven back to the equitable principle that the shares are presumed to be in proportion to the contributions.' On that basis, the court calculated Miss Springette's share to be 75 per cent and Mr Defoe's share to be 25 per cent. In arriving at such neat proportions it is clear that the court was prepared to approximate the figures somewhat in order to produce an outcome that could be applied in practice without involving unnecessary accounting complexity.

17.5.3 **Constructive trust**

17.5.3.1 **Where a shared home is in joint names**

Stack v *Dowden* has established that where cohabitants are joint owners at law there is a strong presumption that they are joint owners in equity leading to equal shares of sale proceeds, and that it will be hard for a cohabitant in such a case to rebut that presumption in favour of unequal shares. However, the presumption of equality can be rebutted if that appears appropriate to the court, having taken into account the wide range of factors we considered at 17.4. Despite the wide range of factors, the exercise should not be allowed to disguise judicial creativity—Baroness Hale emphasised that the court is involved in a search for evidence of the parties' true intentions regarding the quantification of their respective shares. In that case it was deemed especially significant that Ms Dowden had made by far the greater financial contribution to the purchase of the home and did not pool her income with Stack's. They also had an arrangement by which it was understood precisely who should meet particular domestic expenses.

The *Stack* v *Dowden* approach to quantification agrees with that of Waite LJ that the court should 'undertake a survey of the whole course of dealing between the parties relevant to their ownership and occupation of the property and their sharing of its burdens and advantages' which 'will take into consideration all conduct which throws light on the question what shares were intended' (*Midland Bank plc* v *Cooke* [1995] 4 All ER 562). However, where Waite LJ proposed that '[o]nly if that search proves inconclusive does the court fall back on the maxim that *equality is equity*', the majority of their Lordships in *Stack* v *Dowden* start from a presumption of equality *where land is in joint names*, and the survey into the parties' dealings is used to see if an intention to rebut the presumption should be inferred.

 THINKING POINT

Does the approach of the majority in *Stack* v *Dowden* allow a claimant to have their cake and eat it? Suppose a cohabitant had made minor financial contributions to the purchase of land in joint names, but had contributed a great deal to domestic work and child care. How much would he or she get? Presumably half. If a cohabitant contributed more to the purchase price than the other cohabitant, how much would he or she get? Presumably, on the evidence of the actual decision in *Stack* v *Dowden*, more than half. It seems that the claimant wins both ways, and that the other cohabitant loses both ways.

17.5.3.2 **Where legal title to a shared home is in the sole name of one of the cohabitants**

Where legal title to land is in the sole name of one of the cohabitants, exact equality is presumably the last thing the parties intended, and Waite LJ's approach—of inferring equality as a last resort—is surely the correct one.

THINKING POINT

Imagine that you are a woman who has lived for 15 years with the legal owner of your quasi-matrimonial home. There was no express agreement of any sort in relation to your ownership of the house. You contributed half the initial deposit, but since then you have not been working and have not contributed a penny to the mortgage instalments. However, you have given birth to, and raised, two children and carried out the vast majority of all housework, cooking, shopping and gardening. What should be the extent of your equitable interest in the house?

From your direct financial contribution it can be inferred that at the date of purchase you were to have *some* beneficial interest in the house. All that remains is to quantify the extent of your interest—in relation to which, there is surely every reason to infer a common understanding that you were to have a half-share in the house.

CASE CLOSE-UP

Oxley v Hiscock [2004] EWCA Civ 546

Facts: an unmarried couple disputed the extent of their respective entitlements in their shared home, legal title to which was registered in the man's sole name. It was agreed that there had been no express agreement as to their respective shares and the man therefore contended that resulting trust principles should apply, which would give the woman about a one-fifth share based on her contribution to the initial acquisition of the home.

Held: at first instance Her Honour Judge Hallon held that in the absence of express agreement the presumption 'equality is equity' should apply, and awarded each party a half-share in the house. The Court of Appeal allowed the appeal. It was held (applying *Midland Bank v Cooke*) that a fair division of the proceeds of sale 'having regard to the whole course of dealing between them in relation to the property' was 60 per cent to H and 40 per cent to O. This approximated an assessment of the parties' total contribution to the current value of the home (being a £60,700 contribution by the man and a £36,300 contribution by the woman).

In the 'sole-owner' case *Graham-York v York* ([2015] EWCA Civ 72) the claimant received a reduced share despite her lengthy cohabitation with her former partner because mercenary considerations, rather than natural love and affection, had been at the forefront of the cohabitants' relationship.

17.6 Proprietary estoppel

A proprietary estoppel is a cause of action that arises in equity to prevent ('estop') the legal owner of certain property (A) from denying that another person (B) has, or might have, a proprietary interest in that property. The 'dealings' essential to establishing an estoppel are now taken to be: a representation made, or assurance given, by the owner of land (A) to another person B to the effect that B would acquire some interest in A's land, upon which assurance B has reasonably relied by act or omission in such a way that it would be detrimental to B (and unconscionable of A) if A were subsequently to resile from (go back on) his representation or assurance and assert his ownership of the land unencumbered by any rights claimed by B. Opinion is divided between those who consider that proprietary estoppel aims primarily to fulfil the claimant's expectation (e.g. S. Gardner, 'The Remedial Discretion in Proprietary Estoppel—Again' [2006] LQR 492) and those who consider that it aims primarily to compensate the claimant's detrimental reliance (e.g. B. McFarlane and P. Sales, 'Promises, Liability, and Detriment: Lessons from Proprietary Estoppel' [2015] LQR 610). The arguments on both sides were summarised in *Davies* v *Davies* [2016] EWCA Civ 463 where Lewison LJ opined, *obiter*, that the second approach might be preferable.

When a proprietary estoppel arises, it will be satisfied (or 'fed') by an equitable award that is fair and proportionate between the parties ('the essence of the doctrine of proprietary estoppel is to do what is necessary to avoid an unconscionable result' (*Jennings* v *Rice* [2003] 1 P&CR 8, Court of Appeal, at para. [56])). See, also, the decisions of the Court of Appeal in *Joyce* v *Epsom* [2012] EWCA Civ 1398, *Suggitt* v *Suggitt* [2012] EWCA Civ 1140 and *Davies* v *Davies* [2016] EWCA Civ 463). Often the appropriate remedy is a share of land under a constructive trust; sometimes an award of cash will suffice (see, for example, *Lloyd* v *Sutcliffe* [2008] EWHC 1329 (Ch)). If a representation is made on certain conditions, it is not enough to prove reliance on the representation. One must also show that reliance was detrimental, and that the detriment flowed from reasonable reliance on the representation (*Hunt* v *Soady* [2007] EWCA Civ 366, CA (Civil Division)). *Powell* v *Benney* [2007] EWCA Civ 1283 illustrates the point. The owner of a number of properties promised Mr and Mrs Powell that he would leave the properties to them in his will. They proceeded to improve the properties *on their own initiative*. When the representor died he left no will and his property passed to Benney on intestacy. The Court of Appeal called this a 'non-bargain' estoppel and upheld the first instance award of £20,000 as reasonable to meet the Powells' expectations.

Yeoman (next) is another case in which the claimant was merely awarded cash. The House of Lords could have decided that the case involved a proprietary estoppel which ought to be remedied by an award of cash, but their Lordships instead held that there was no estoppel. They took the opportunity to drastically rein in the scope of proprietary estoppel in commercial contexts, by holding that estoppel should not be allowed to disturb normal commercial dealings. *Yeoman* is a so-called bargain case, albeit one in which the bargain was still under negotiation as regards certain terms.

Q CASE CLOSE-UP

Yeoman's Row Management Ltd v *Cobbe* [2008] UKHL 55; [2008] 1 WLR 1752

Facts: A property developer entered into an oral agreement with the owner of a block of flats under which the developer undertook to obtain planning permission to demolish the block and replace it with new town houses. A formula was agreed on price and division of profits from the development. The developer spent 18 months acquiring planning permission to demolish the block to build new town houses. It was after planning permission had been obtained that the owner of the block purported to withdraw from the agreement. In the Court of Appeal, a proprietary estoppel was recognised in favour of the developer, which was remedied by awarding the developer a share in the increased value of the property attributable to the planning permission, but this was overturned by the House of Lords.

Held: There was no proprietary estoppel on these facts, so the developer was awarded a mere *quantum meruit* (sum deserved) sufficient to ensure that the land owner had not been unjustly enriched by the time and labour expended by the developer in pursuing the planning permission in accordance with the informal agreement. It was held that the developer had assumed the risk that the owner of the block would withdraw. The fact that withdrawal was unconscionable in the abstract did not suffice; it had to be shown that the owner had behaved in a manner traditionally considered to be unconscionable in this context. The evidence was the other way—namely, that the traditional practice was to allow parties to withdraw from an informal contract in such a case. The claimant's argument that both parties considered themselves to be bound 'in honour' to perform the contract was rejected.

In the same way that the radical decision in *Stack* v *Dowden* ought to be read so as to restrict it to its facts (i.e. domestic or 'romantic' joint legal ownership cases), so the *Yeoman* case ought to be construed restrictively to apply only to commercial cases (and perhaps only to joint venture cases). It is clear that proprietary estoppel will continue to thrive in non-commercial cases, as the decision in *Thorner* v *Major* (a.k.a *Thorner* v *Curtis*) [2009] UKHL 18; [2009] 1 WLR 776 makes clear. In this case the legal owner had left his farm to the claimant by will, but subsequently destroyed the will and died intestate. The claimant had worked for the deceased for nearly 30 years in the reasonable expectation (based on various hints, but no express representation) that he would inherit the farm. Proprietary estoppel was found in favour of the claimant and he was awarded the farm.

Judges frequently use the term 'proprietary estoppel' as if it were interchangeable with the term 'constructive trust'. Indeed, a clear example of the practice can be found in the seminal speech of Lord Bridge in *Lloyds Bank plc* v *Rosset*. Another clear example appeared a year later, in *Hammond* v *Mitchell* [1991] 1 WLR 1127 at 1137B, where Waite J used the terms 'proprietary estoppel' and 'constructive trust' interchangeably without any apparent unease. In this section we shall attempt to determine the meaning of the former term, and its proper relationship to the latter. We will discover that they are not synonymous.

At the start of this chapter, we observed that the formality requirements for the creation of trusts do not affect the creation or operation of resulting, implied or constructive trusts (s 53(2), Law of Property Act 1925). It is now worth noting that the requirement of writing in relation to *contracts* for the sale of land (Law of Property (Miscellaneous Provisions) Act 1989, s 2) is similar, in that it has no effect upon 'the creation or operation of resulting, implied or constructive trusts' (s 2(5)), which means to say that a failure of contractual formality does not preclude a finding of an informal trust. In fact, a merely oral agreement to sell land can be binding if the parties believed it to be so and if it is relied upon to a party's detriment, even if the sale was otherwise governed by a formal contract (*Matchmove Ltd* v *Dowding* [2016] EWCA Civ 1233; [2017] 1 WLR 749, Court of Appeal. Noted Boncey and Ng (2017) 2 *Conv* 146–57).

In *Yaxley* v *Gotts* [1999] Ch 162 the Court of Appeal confirmed that the social policy of simplifying conveyancing by means of formal contracts for the sale of land did not necessitate that unconscionable conduct be allowed to prevail. Their Lordships held that the 'constructive trust' exception to the requirement of contractual formality (s 2(5), Law of Property (Miscellaneous Provisions) Act 1989) could be taken to embrace any cases of proprietary estoppel which might equally well have been categorised as a case of constructive trust.

The most obvious role for proprietary estoppel is to remedy those cases, not covered by purchase money resulting and constructive trusts, where *after* the purchase A expends money or labour improving B's property in a way that cannot be shown to be referable to the mortgage instalments or otherwise referable to the purchase price.

17.6.1 The 'ingredients' of proprietary estoppel

As early as *Wilmot* v *Barber* (1880) 15 ChD 96, an attempt was made to lay down the defining ingredients, or '*probanda*', of proprietary estoppel. These *probanda* were reiterated in *Matharu* v *Matharu* (1994) 68 P & CR 93 at 102 by Roch LJ as being that:

- [A] has made a mistake as to his or her legal rights;
- [A] has expended some money or done some act on the faith of that mistaken belief;
- [B] must know of the existence of his legal rights which is inconsistent with the equity, if it exists;
- [B] must know of the other person's mistaken belief as to his or her rights;
- [B] must have encouraged [A] in his or her expenditure of money or in doing the other acts on which [A] relies, either directly or by abstaining from asserting his legal rights.

Oliver J in *Taylors Fashions Ltd* v *Liverpool Victoria Trustees Co Ltd* [1982] 1 QB 133 at 154 preferred a 'broad test of whether in the circumstances the conduct complained of is unconscionable without the necessity of forcing those incumbrances into a Procrustean bed constructed from some unalterable criteria'. This more relaxed approach would no doubt have commended itself to Lord Denning MR. In *Crabb* v *Arun District Council* [1976] Ch 179 Lord Denning MR said:

> The basis of this proprietary estoppel . . . is the interposition of equity. Equity comes in, true to form, to mitigate the rigours of the strict law. The early cases did not speak of it as 'estoppel' they spoke of it as 'raising an equity'. If I may expand what Lord Cairns LC said in *Hughes* v *Metropolitan Railway Co* (1877) 2 App Cas 439 at 448: 'it is the first principle upon which all courts of equity proceed', that it will prevent a person from insisting on his strict legal rights—whether arising under a contract, or on his title deeds, or by statute—when it would be inequitable for him to do so having regard to the dealings which have taken place between the parties.

The 'dealings' relevant to establishing an estoppel are now taken to be:

- a representation made, or assurance given, by the owner of land (A) to another person (B);
- to the effect that B would acquire some interest in A's land;
- upon which assurance B has quite reasonably relied by act or omission;
- in such a way that it would be detrimental to B (and therefore unconscionable of A) if A were subsequently to resile from his representation or assurance and assert his ownership of the land unencumbered by any rights claimed by B.

These elements of estoppel are not to be regarded as entirely distinct from one another. They are frequently compounded or amalgamated on particular sets of facts; the nature of the assurance will often be bound up in the reasonableness of the reliance and the nature of the reliance will often be inseparable from the detriment. This point was forcefully made by Robert Walker LJ in *Gillett* v *Holt* [2001] Ch 210 where his Lordship emphasised that 'detriment' is 'not a narrow or technical concept':

> The detriment need not consist of the expenditure of money or other quantifiable financial detriment, so long as it is something substantial. The requirement must be approached as part of a broad enquiry as to whether repudiation of an assurance is or is not unconscionable in all the circumstances. (at 232)

The facts of *Gillett* v *Holt* remind us somewhat of the basis on which the dastardly Mr Wickham tried to establish his claim in Jane Austen's novel *Pride and Prejudice*.

 OUTSIDE THE BOX

Jane Austen, *Pride and Prejudice*
We were born in the same parish, within the same park; the greatest part of our youth was passed together; inmates of the same house, sharing the same amusements, objects of the same parental care. *My* father began life in the profession which your uncle, Mr Phillips, appears to do so much credit to—but he gave up everything to be of use to the late Mr Darcy and devoted all his time to the care of the Pemberley property. He was most highly esteemed by Mr Darcy, a most intimate, confidential friend. Mr Darcy often acknowledged himself to be under the greatest obligations to my father's active superintendence, and when, immediately before my father's death, Mr Darcy gave him a voluntary promise of providing for me, I am convinced that he felt it to be as much a debt of gratitude to *him*, as of his affection to myself.

Or perhaps it is more accurate to say that *Gillett* v *Holt* reads like a Dickensian novel. (The facts of *Murphy* v *Burrows* [2004] EWHC 1900, (Ch), a case similar to *Gillett* v *Holt*, were actually described as 'Dickensian' by the judge.) The point is that there is often a striking human story behind the facts of legal cases in this area. Mr Gillett was 12 years old when Mr Holt (then a 38-year-old gentleman farmer) took him under his wing. Mr Gillett left school at the age of 16 at Mr Holt's suggestion and began a long career working on Mr Holt's farm. Mr Gillett's wife and children became in due course a surrogate family to Mr Holt (who had no immediate family of his own), a fact confirmed by Mr Holt's frequent assurances (often in public) that Mr Gillett would one day inherit the farm. However, the relationship between the men eventually cooled and ultimately broke down entirely. Mr Holt wrote Mr Gillett out of his will and Mr Gillett commenced action seeking to establish an interest in the farm under proprietary estoppel, on the basis of Mr Holt's assurances and Mr Gillett's detrimental reliance upon them. The judge at first instance held that Mr Holt's representation could not be considered irrevocable and that in any event Mr Gillett had suffered no detriment in reliance upon them. The Court of Appeal rejected any need to show that the assurance was irrevocable and held that, despite the obvious material benefits of Mr Holt's patronage, it would be detrimental to deny him an interest in the farm because he had forgone the opportunity to educate himself and make alternative provision for his retirement and old age. A most interesting feature is the detriment Mr Gillett was held to have suffered when Mr Holt paid the private school fees of Mr Gillett's eldest son. How is that detrimental, one might ask? The answer is that Mr Gillett had another son whom he then felt obliged to educate privately at his own expense!

Gillett v *Holt* was followed by the Court of Appeal in *Lloyd* v *Dugdale* [2001] EWCA Civ 1754, where their Lordships confirmed that if the person to whom an assurance is given forsook an opportunity he can be said to have suffered a detriment. So if X declines to take up an advantageous lease of Blueacre because he has been assured a lease of Redacre, the person (Y) giving the assurance may be estopped (assuming he is the owner of Redacre) from denying X's right to a lease of Redacre.

Gillett v *Holt* was also followed in *Century (UK) Ltd SA* v *Clibbery* [2004] EWHC 1870, Ch (transcript). If *Gillett* v *Holt* belongs in a novel by Charles Dickens, the facts of *Century (UK) Ltd SA* v *Clibbery* would be at home in a novel by Jilly Cooper: a Panamanian company owned and controlled by a racehorse trainer (Mr Allan) sought to recover possession of a substantial eight-bedroomed house in Newmarket from the mother of one of Mr Allan's mistresses. The defendant, Mrs Clibbery, claimed to have made several hours of video recordings (of horse races) for Mr Allan and carried out other secretarial and domestic work, as if she were his personal assistant. She claimed that this was in reliance on an expectation that she would be entitled to some interest in the house. The company succeeded in gaining repossession and damages for unpaid rent during the four years in which the defendant had resisted the claim to repossession. Blackburne J noted the argument that 'by living at The Gables Mrs Clibbery lost the opportunity of making other arrangements for her accommodation when she reached retirement age' but held that 'apart from a weekly pension of £175, Mrs Clibbery was unwilling to indicate what further resources she had access to' so that '[o]n the evidence it was quite impossible to assess to what extent (if at all) she had made a sacrifice of this kind'.

Inwards v *Baker* [1965] 1 All ER 446 is a classic illustration of the facts giving rise to the proprietary estoppel. Baker junior was keen to build himself a bungalow, but he could not afford the price of a vacant site. His father had some spare land. Baker senior said to his son, 'Why don't you build the bungalow on my land and make it a bit bigger?' Baker junior did exactly that, and made the bungalow his permanent home. Baker senior retained legal ownership of the fee simple to the land, and so the house also became Baker senior's property as a matter of law. All was well while both senior and junior were alive, but when senior died his will (made long before the bungalow was built) left the land in question not to Baker junior, but to Inwards. Inwards brought proceedings to recover possession of the bungalow.

The Court of Appeal held that Baker junior [A] had acquired, in equity, a right to occupy the land for life, and that this right was in principle binding against third parties who had notice of the equitable right. Lord Denning MR held that:

> if the owner of land [B] requests another [A], or indeed allows another, to expend money on the land under an expectation created or encouraged by [B] that he will be able to remain there, that raises an equity in [A] such as to entitle him to stay . . . and [quoting *Plimmer's Case* (1884) 9 App Cas 699, PC] . . . the equity arising from the expenditure on land need not fail 'merely on the ground that the interest to be secured has not been expressly indicated' . . . the court must look at the circumstances in each case to decide in what way the equity can be satisfied.

Danckwerts LJ, concurring with the conclusion of the Master of the Rolls, went on to state that:

> [i]t is not necessary, I think, to imply a promise. It seems to me that this is one of the cases of an equity created by estoppel, or equitable estoppel, as it is sometimes called, by which the person who has made the expenditure is induced by the expectation of obtaining protection, and equity protects him so that an injustice may not be perpetrated.

It is notable that neither Lord Denning MR nor Danckwerts LJ actually defined or named A's equitable interest. In the years following *Inwards v Baker* many judges and commentators assumed, quite understandably, that Baker junior's right was a particular equitable right *called* a proprietary estoppel. On first reading Danckwerts LJ appears to suggest as much. Upon closer examination, however, it seems that his Lordship was not describing Baker junior's equitable interest *as* an 'equitable estoppel', but merely stating that his equitable interest had been created *by* 'equitable estoppel'. The problem with *Inwards v Baker* is that there was never any need to specify the nature of the son's equity, because the son never asserted a right but merely defended Inwards' claim. He used his estoppel as a shield, not a sword, so the Court of Appeal was able to satisfy the estoppel by the award of a nebulous, innominate equity. If Inwards had been a purchaser rather than the beneficiary of a will the court might have felt constrained to be more specific about the nature of the son's equitable right.

THINKING POINT

Do you think that the equitable interest created by the equitable estoppel in *Inwards* v *Baker* could have been an interest under a resulting or constructive trust of the sorts considered earlier in this chapter?

An award of a *resulting* trust is not consistent with the facts of *Inwards v Baker*, for Baker junior did not get back an interest in the land equivalent only to that which he had put in by way of bricks, mortar and labour. On the contrary, he 'sowed' in bricks and mortar and 'reaped' a right to occupy his father's land for as long as he wished.

Perhaps, then, it was a *constructive* trust? That is a more plausible alternative. It will be recalled that Lord Bridge in *Rosset* held that to establish a constructive trust in land there must be either express agreement coupled with detrimental reliance thereon, or an agreement inferred from direct financial contributions to the purchase of the land. In *Inwards v Baker* the son would probably have qualified for an interest under a constructive trust on the former basis.

If a constructive trust is the remedy deemed to be appropriate to satisfy the proprietary estoppel, the claimant will end up with a trust which will be identical in its *operation* (if not its creation) to a constructive trust construed directly from the facts (i.e. constructive trusts of the *Rosset* type). It is hardly surprising, therefore, that the use of the terms 'proprietary estoppel' and 'constructive trust' have frequently been confused in the courts. That said, Professor Paul Matthews, sitting as a judge of the High Court, has pointed to the possibility of a technical distinction between the two. In *Culliford* v *Thorpe* [2018] EWHC 426 (Ch), he conjectured that one of the distinctions emerging between proprietary estoppel and common intention constructive trust may be that in the former the court has to weigh up the advantages and disadvantages of the promisee's position post-reliance, whereas in the latter '[i]t appears to be enough to show that the promisee has relied to his or her detriment on the agreement between the parties, such that it is unconscionable for the legal owner to renege on the agreement' (para. [76]).

Many years ago, Sir Christopher Slade, who sat as a judge of the Chancery Division between 1975 and 1982, urged the following simple three-fold distinction: '(1) [I]mplied and resulting trusts arising by virtue of contributions to the cost of acquisition of land; (2) constructive trusts arising by virtue of the doctrine of proprietary estoppel; [and] (3) other cases of constructive trusts' (*The Informal Creation of Interests in Land*, The Child & Co Oxford Lecture, 2 March

1984). Perhaps the law would have developed in an altogether more orderly way had Sir Christopher's three-fold division been enunciated in the superior courts.

17.6.2 **The impact of proprietary estoppel on third parties**

The remedial flexibility attaching to proprietary estoppel has the potential to deter third parties from purchasing the land from the legal owner. Where the constructive trust is institutional, the theory is that a purchaser can discover from making a simple inquiry whether or not the legal title is encumbered by any beneficial interest under a trust, and this interest can be overreached by payment of the purchase monies to two trustees (perhaps the legal owner and a friend of the legal owner who has been appointed as a second trustee). Where the legal owner is subject to a proprietary estoppel it will not be clear until a later court hearing whether or not the equitable claimant has a proprietary right or not. It might be that an award of compensatory or restitutionary damages will suffice to satisfy the equity; it may be that nothing short of a conveyance of the legal fee simple will suffice (see *Pascoe* v *Turner* [1979] 2 All ER 945). Whether or not the ultimate award is proprietary in nature is of fundamental concern to the purchaser because only proprietary interests will be binding upon him (see *National Provincial Bank* v *Ainsworth* [1965] AC 1175).

M.P. Thompson has argued that proprietary estoppels have the effect of introducing uncertainty into conveyancing ((1981) 125 Sol Jo 539). He submits (at 540):

> that the operation of proprietary estoppel should be limited to factual situations where money has been expended on the property, as a result of representations made: *Inwards* v *Baker* [1965] 2 QB 29; *Pascoe* v *Turner* [1979] 1 WLR 431. At least in this situation, when the fact of expenditure is disclosed to him, the purchaser can be certain that equities have arisen in favour of the person claiming the interest.

He refers approvingly to the judgment of Browne-Wilkinson J in *Re Sharpe* (*a bankrupt*) [1980] 1 All ER 198 at 204: 'Doing justice to the litigant who actually appears in court by the invention of new principles of law ought not to involve injustice to other persons who are not litigants . . . but whose rights are fundamentally affected by the new principles.'

Practically speaking, the prudent purchaser should probably work on the assumption that the estoppel will be remedied by the award of a constructive trust interest, and should therefore overreach that interest (i.e. remove it from the land) by paying purchase monies to all the trustees (being at least two in number or a trust corporation: s 2 of the Law of Property Act 1925).

 ## Summary

We have seen that there are three basic situations in which A may successfully claim a beneficial interest under an informal trust of land to which B is legally entitled:
- (Lord Browne-Wilkinson's category (A) resulting trust—from the *Westdeutsche* case) a resulting trust is presumed to arise where A has contributed in whole or in part to the purchase of land which is vested in the name of B (albeit that it may be vested in the

joint names of A and B). A resulting trust merely entitles A to an interest in the land equivalent to the proportion A's contribution bore to the whole purchase price. Because of this rigidity, a resulting trust solution will probably not be appropriate where A and B have agreed, expressly or by inference, that A will gain some larger interest in the land in return for A's contributions. It has been confirmed by the highest court in the land in *Stack* v *Dowden* (2007) and *Jones* v *Kernott* (2011) that the presumption of resulting trust based on initial financial contributions to purchase will *not* apply where land is held in the joint names of 'romantic' cohabitants who are unmarried (and not in a civil partnership).

- (Lord Bridge's first basis for establishing a constructive trust—from the *Rosset* case) a constructive trust arises where A and B by express words 'agree' that A is to have a beneficial interest in the land, and A has acted to her detriment in reliance upon that 'agreement'. In such circumstances B's conscience would be bound by A's claim, making B a constructive trustee for A. This constructive trust may be institutional if one takes the view that at the date of the court hearing the court is merely vindicating A's existing proprietary right. An alternative view is that the express 'agreement' (it is often just an express representation) raises an estoppel, for where A has relied upon it to A's detriment, it would be unconscionable for B to assert his 100 per cent legal entitlement against A, and B would be estopped from so doing. This proprietary estoppel must be 'fed' (satisfied) by an equitable award that is fair and proportionate between the parties. Such an award frequently takes the form of a constructive trust. If the estoppel analysis is the correct one, it is clear that in most of the reported cases the courts, when awarding the remedial constructive trust, do not explicitly refer to the estoppel stage (see, for example, *Aspden* v *Elvy* [2012] EWHC 1387 (Ch); [2012] 2 FLR 807). The better approach may be to limit proprietary estoppel to cases where A has effected improvements to the property after, or independently of, acquisition.

- (Lord Bridge's second basis for a constructive trust—from the *Rosset* case) where there is no express 'agreement', a common intention can be inferred from direct financial contributions to the purchase price (either by way of deposit, other purchase capital or mortgage instalments). It might also be inferred from later direct financial contributions (e.g. building an extension) as confirmed in *Stack* v *Dowden* and *Jones* v *Kernott*. It might even be possible to infer agreement from indirect financial contributions. The latter approach would be unorthodox, but the more flexible approach introduced by *Stack* v *Dowden* and confirmed by *Jones* v *Kernott* might open the way for such a development. As things stand it is only where the court cannot discern the parties' current intentions with regard to shares, that 'each is entitled to that share which the court considers fair having regard to the whole course of dealing between them in relation to the property'.

- The advantage of the constructive trust approach to financial contributions, over the resulting trust approach to financial contributions, is that an interest established by the constructive trust method will be quantified not merely at the level of the financial contribution, but at a level necessary to give effect to the underlying common intention of the parties. Hence a £10,000 contribution to the purchase of a £200,000 house might give rise to a half-share in the house if an agreement to that effect can be inferred from all the facts.

? Summative assessment exercise

Mr and Mrs Brown bought a house for their daughter Jenny to live in during her time as a student at university. The house cost £200,000 and for tax reasons was conveyed into Jenny's sole name. Mr and Mrs Brown paid £100,000 in cash and Jenny took out a mortgage to cover the balance of £100,000. It was understood that Mr and Mrs Brown would make payments into her account each month to cover the mortgage instalments as they fell due. Jenny's only financial outlay was £3,000 to cover stamp duty, the expenses of the purchase, removals and home insurance, but it was understood she would not have to pay a penny thereafter apart from the usual bills for gas, electricity and so forth. After one year of her university course Jenny invited Pete to live with her in the house. Pete was Jenny's long-term boyfriend and he had a steady job. From the moment he moved in, he started to pay the mortgage instalments instead of Mr and Mrs Brown. However, the house remained in Jenny's sole name. Jenny explained that her parents had paid a lot of money towards the house and wouldn't let her put the house in the joint names of her and Pete.

A year later Jenny and Pete split up. Advise the parties as to their likely interests in the house.

 Full specimen answers can be found at www.oxfordtextbooks.co.uk/orc/watt_directions5e/.

☐ The bigger picture

Despite the problems described in *Midland Bank plc* v *Cooke* (see 17.1.2), the Law Commission has rejected calls for cohabitants to be given the same rights as married couples and civil partners in the event of separation (Law Commission, 'Cohabitation: The Financial Consequences of Relationship Breakdown' (Law Com No 307) Cm 7182, July 2007). This is not surprising—just try and define 'cohabitant' and you will discover how hard it would be to draft laws to govern property distribution when cohabitants go their separate ways.

≡ Further reading

Dixon M.J. 'Proprietary estoppel: A return to principle?' (2009) 3 Conv 260
an article supporting the 2009 House of Lords decision in *Thorner* v *Major* (a.k.a. *Thorner* v *Curtis*)

Etherton, Sir Terence, 'Constructive Trusts and Proprietary Estoppel: The Search for Clarity and Principle' (2009) 73 Conv 104
overview of the law on constructive trusts and proprietary estoppel, focusing on the House of Lords' decisions in *Stack* v *Dowden* and *Cobbe* v *Yeoman's Row Management Ltd*

Ferguson, P. 'Constructive Trusts—A Note of Caution' (1993) 109 LQR 114
contends that a constructive trust must be different from a proprietary estoppel because the former arises independent of the courts' intervention

McFarlane, B. *The Law of Proprietary Estoppel* (2014) Oxford: Oxford University Press
a comprehensive practical and theoretical overview of the doctrine of proprietary estoppel

Sloan, B. 'Keeping Up with the Jones case: establishing constructive trusts in "Sole Legal Owner" scenarios' (2015) 35(2) *Legal Studies* 226–51
argues that judges have been too conservative in failing to take opportunities (however few) to move beyond the restrictive approach of *Lloyds Bank plc* v *Rosset* and allow novel outcomes in the light of *Jones* v *Kernott*

Hayton, D. 'Constructive Trusts of Homes—A Bold Approach' (1993) 109 LQR 485
regards the common intention constructive trust as in practice indistinguishable from equitable proprietary estoppel, responding to Ferguson (above)

 For links to selected cases, statutes, academic papers and official reports mentioned in this chapter please visit the online resources at www.oup.com/uk/watt_directions6e/.

18 Tracing

Introduction

We have already considered the extent of trustees' personal liability in an action for compensation or account (see Chapter 15). Now we ask, amongst other things, 'what should be done if the action proves worthless in practice because the trustees are impecunious or have been declared bankrupt, and are therefore unable to repay trust monies to the fund?' In such circumstances the beneficiaries may be able to trace the value of their trust property into bank accounts and into assets which have been bought with the trust property. It is important to realise that it is not the precise item of trust property itself which is sought in most cases, but the value of that property.

Tracing is often spoken of as being a remedy in itself—lawyers will refer to the 'tracing remedy'. In fact, this is not strictly accurate. Tracing is a process that leads to the ultimate remedy of recovering misapplied money or property.

It might help to imagine 'tracing' as a form of detective work. Take, for example, the following series of events: first, trustee Tim places trust monies in his private bank account and then, with monies from that account, he buys some shares which he transfers to Sam and Sally. Later, Sam sells her shares and gives Tim the cash proceeds of the sale, while Sally sells her shares and spends the proceeds on a party for her friends. Finally, Tim uses the money he has received from Sam and some of his own money to purchase a car. Where has the trust property gone?

The answer is far from obvious to the lay observer. It would be very helpful to have contemporaneous memoranda detailing the whereabouts of the trust property at every stage of every transaction, but without such documentary or other evidence it is necessary to rely on the presumptions raised by a number of rules of 'tracing'. It is these rules with which we shall be primarily concerned in this chapter.

The problem posed by this scenario is not made any simpler by the fact that the cash may have been earning interest, the value of the shares may have changed (indeed, dividends, or a bonus issue, may have been declared on them) and the car may have depreciated in value. Nevertheless, we should be able to conclude with some confidence that, as a piece of detective work, it will be easier to try to trace and recover the 'value' of the original trust assets than to attempt to trace and recover the original trust assets themselves. Generally, this is the aim of tracing. (The process of identifying the original assets as they pass from person to person and place to place is simply referred to as 'following'. In *Foskett* v *McKeown* [2001] 1 AC 102, House of Lords, Lord Millett stated (at 127) that '[f]ollowing is the process of following the same asset as it moves from hand to hand' whereas '[t]racing is the process of identifying a new asset as the substitute for the old'.) It is important to appreciate that in a tracing action, the claimant can trace the money 'not because it is the claimant's, but because it is derived from a fund which is treated as if it were subject to a charge in the claimant's favour' (*London Allied Holdings Ltd* v *Lee* [2007] EWHC 2061 (Ch) *per* Etherton J at para. [257] citing *El Ajou* v *Dollar Land Holdings* [1993] 3 All ER 717 *per* Millett J at 735j–736a).

18.1 The artificiality of the distinction between common law and equitable tracing rules

Tracing may take place at common law or in equity, and, for convenience in handling the older authorities, this chapter is divided along those lines. However, it is hoped that in the future it may be possible finally to put aside the artificial distinction between the legal and equitable rules for tracing.

Q | CASE CLOSE-UP

Foskett v McKeown [2001] 1 AC 102, House of Lords

Lord Steyn: 'in truth tracing is a process of identifying assets: it belongs to the realm of evidence. It tells us nothing about legal or equitable rights to the assets traced. In a crystal-line analysis Professor Birks ('The Necessity of a Unitary Law of Tracing' in *Making Commercial Law: Essays in Honour of Roy Goode* (1997), pp. 239–58) explained that there is a unified regime for tracing and that 'it allows tracing to be cleanly separated from the business of asserting rights in or in relation to assets successfully traced': at p. 257. Applying this reasoning, Professor Birks concludes, at p. 258,

> that the modern law is equipped with various means of coping with the evidential difficulties which a tracing exercise is bound to encounter. The process of identification thus ceases to be either legal or equitable and becomes, as is fitting, genuinely neutral as to the rights exigible in respect of the assets into which the value in question is traced. The tracing exercise once successfully completed, it can then be asked what rights, if any, the plaintiff can, on his particular facts, assert. It is at that point that it becomes relevant to recall that on some facts those rights will be personal, on others proprietary, on some legal, and on others equitable.

In *Trustee of the Property of FC Jones and sons (a firm)* v *Jones* [1996] 3 WLR 703, CA, Millett LJ had observed likewise that:

> [t]here is no merit in having distinct and differing rules at law and in equity, given that tracing is neither a right nor a remedy but merely the process by which the plaintiff establishes what has happened to his property. The fact that there are different tracing rules at law and in equity is unfortunate though probably inevitable, but unnecessary differences should not be created where they are not required by the different nature of legal and equitable doctrines and remedies. There is, in my view, even less merit in the present rule which precludes the invocation of the equitable tracing rules to support a common law claim; until that rule is swept away unnecessary obstacles to the development of a rational and coherent law of restitution will remain.

The facts of *Jones v Jones* were that the wife of one of the partners of a bankrupt firm of potato growers placed £11,700 from a joint bank account held in the name of her husband and another partner with brokers to invest in potato futures. When she ultimately realised her investment it was worth £50,760. She placed this sum in a deposit account with Raphaels plc. The judge at first instance held that she had received the money in a fiduciary capacity and was a constructive trustee. It was held on appeal that the defendant was not a constructive trustee. She had neither legal nor equitable title to the property, but was merely the *possessor* of it. The claimant trustee in bankruptcy had to bring his claim at common law and trace his property into the proceeds of the defendant's dealings; equity had no role to play. The chose in action constituted by the deposit of the trustee's money with the brokers belonged to the trustee, it was not a right to the original deposit, but to the current balance of the account with the brokers. The defendant would be unjustly enriched were she able to retain the monies and the huge profits she had made on them. (See G. McMeel, 'Misdirected Funds and Profits' [1997] Nott LJ 90.)

Lord Millett (as he now is) confirmed his objection to the distinction between legal and equitable tracing in the House of Lords in *Foskett* v *McKeown* [2001] 1 AC 102:

> Given its nature, there is nothing inherently legal or equitable about the tracing exercise. There is thus no sense in maintaining different rules for tracing at law and in equity. One set of tracing rules is enough . . . There is certainly no logical justification for allowing any distinction between them to produce capricious results in cases of mixed substitutions by insisting on the existence of a fiduciary relationship as a precondition for applying equity's tracing rules. The existence of such a relationship may be relevant to the nature of the claim which the plaintiff can maintain, whether personal or proprietary, but that is a different matter.

His Lordship was speaking *obiter* (he stated that this case was not 'the occasion to explore these matters further'), but despite his earlier belief that the distinction between legal and equitable tracing might be 'inevitable' (see *Jones* v *Jones* earlier) his Lordship would doubtless remove the distinction at the first opportunity. Note that in *Federal Republic of Brazil* v *Durant International Corp* [2013] JCA 071, Jersey's Court of Appeal confirmed that in Jersey tracing is an evidential process in which the challenge is the pragmatic one of demonstrating that current assets may be considered the substitutes of original assets. The process, in contrast to the tracing process in England, is not concerned to distinguish tracing in law from tracing in equity.

Foskett v *McKeown* is the leading modern case on tracing.

 CASE CLOSE-UP

***Foskett* v *McKeown* [2001] 1 AC 102, House of Lords**

Facts: M misappropriated money entrusted to him by a number of purchasers for the purchase of land in Portugal. M used some of this money to pay part of the premium on a life insurance policy. However, prior to this, M had by deed divested the beneficial interest in the policy in favour of his three children. M later committed suicide. The claimant, who was one of the prospective purchasers, claimed to be entitled to the proceeds of the policy. The trial judge decided that the purchasers were entitled to 53.46 per cent of the proceeds of the policy. The children appealed, arguing that the purchasers were only entitled to trace their money into the proceeds to the extent they could recover plus interest. The Court of Appeal held, by a majority, that since M did not have any beneficial interest in the insurance policy at the time the misappropriated money was used to pay the premiums, no resulting or constructive trust could be imposed upon the proceeds of the policy. The purchasers were only entitled to recover the money used to pay for the premiums plus interest. The Court of Appeal ([1997] 3 All ER 392) stated that the authorities were against the conclusion that the payment of the premiums meant that the payer became the owner of the policy. Hobhouse LJ suggested that 'it did not follow that if the value of an innocent party's asset has been increased by an amount greater than the expenditure that had been made using trust money that the innocent third party should besides making full restitution account as well for the additional increase in value'. This decision was reversed on appeal to the House of Lords ([2001] 1 AC 102).

Held: Lord Browne-Wilkinson: 'the question which arises in this case is whether, for tracing purposes, the payments of the fourth and fifth premiums on a policy which, up to that date, had been the sole property of the children for tracing purposes fall to be treated as analogous to the expenditure of cash on the physical property of another or as analogous to the mixture of monies in a bank account. If the former analogy is to be preferred, the maximum amount recoverable by the purchasers will be the amount of the fourth and fifth premiums plus interest: if the latter analogy is preferred the children and the other purchasers will share the policy monies *pro rata*.'

[In the Court of Appeal Hobhouse LJ had preferred the analogy of improvement of land, but Lord Browne-Wilkinson (agreeing with Lord Millett's analysis of this point) held that the analogy of monies mixed in an account was the correct one]:

'where a trustee in breach of trust mixes money in his own bank account with trust monies, the monies in the account belong to the trustee personally and to the beneficiaries under the trust rateably according to the amounts respectively provided. On a proper analysis, there are 'no monies in the account' in the sense of physical cash. Immediately before the improper mixture, the trustee had a chose in action being his right against the bank to demand a payment of the credit balance on his account. Immediately after the mixture, the trustee had the same chose in action (i.e. the right of action against the bank) but its value reflected in part the amount of the beneficiaries' monies wrongly paid in. There is no doubt that in such a case of monies mixed in a bank account the credit balance on the account belongs to the trustee and the beneficiaries rateably according to their respective contributions.'

Lord Millett described the case as a 'textbook example of tracing through mixed substitutions':

The claimants claim a continuing beneficial interest in the insurance money. Since this represents the product of Mr Murphy's own money as well as theirs, which Mr Murphy mingled indistinguishably in a single chose in action, they claim a beneficial interest in a proportionate part of the money only. The transmission of a claimant's property rights from one asset to its traceable proceeds is part of our law of property, not of the law of unjust enrichment. There is no 'unjust factor' to justify restitution (unless 'want of title' be one, which makes the point). The claimant succeeds if at all by virtue of his own title, not to reverse unjust enrichment. Property rights are determined by fixed rules and settled principles. They are not discretionary. They do not depend upon ideas of what is 'fair, just and reasonable'. Such concepts, which in reality mask decisions of legal policy, have no place in the law of property.

18.2 Tracing at common law

18.2.1 **General**

CASE CLOSE-UP

Agip (Africa) Ltd v Jackson [1990] 1 Ch 265, ChD

A senior officer of A Ltd innocently signed a payment order which was then forged and used by a fraudulent accountant in the employ of A Ltd. The accountant took the order to a Tunisian bank, who in turn requested a payment from Lloyds Bank plc, in accordance with the terms of the order. Lloyds Bank then made a payment over to the defendant's account, believing that it would be reimbursed by the recipient's New York bank. In doing so Lloyds took a delivery risk, as the New York bank had not yet opened for business. By the time the plaintiffs had discovered the fraud it was too late to stop the payment; nor could a refund be obtained from the defendants. The defendants claimed that they had acted innocently throughout and that the Tunisian bank, and not the plaintiffs, was entitled to bring the action.

Millett J: 'the common law has always been able to follow a physical asset from one recipient to another. Its ability to follow an asset in the same hands into a changed form was established in *Taylor* v *Plumer* 3 M & S 562. In following the plaintiff's money into an asset purchased exclusively with it, no distinction is drawn between a chose in action such as the debt of a bank to its customer and any other asset: *Re Diplock* [1948] Ch 465, 519. But it can only follow a physical asset, such as a cheque or its proceeds, from one person to another. It can follow money but not a chose in action. Money can be followed at common law into and out of a bank account and into the hands of a subsequent transferee, provided that it does not cease to be identifiable by being mixed with other money in the bank account derived from some other source. *Banque Belge pour l'Etranger* v *Hambrouck* [1921] 1 KB 321 . . .

Nothing passed between Tunisia and London but a stream of electrons . . . and accordingly the plaintiff's attempt to trace the money at common law must fail . . .

There is no difficulty in tracing the plaintiffs' property in equity, which can follow the money as it passed through the accounts of the correspondent banks in New York or, more realistically, follow the chose in action through its transmutation as a direct result of forged instructions from a debt owed by the Banque du Sud to the plaintiffs in Tunis into a debt owed by Lloyds Bank to Baker Oil in London.

The only restriction on the ability of equity to follow assets is the requirement that there must be some fiduciary relationship which permits the assistance of equity to be invoked. The requirement has been widely condemned and depends on authority rather than principle, but the law was settled by *Re Diplock* [1948] Ch 465.'

As long as the distinction between tracing at common law and tracing in equity persists, common law tracing cannot be used to identify assets to be the subject of an equitable claim, and equitable tracing cannot be used to identify assets to be the subject of a common law claim. The significance of this shortcoming is potentially very great because a common law claim is a personal claim against a *person* holding, or a *person* who has held, the property that is traced, whereas a proprietary claim in equity is a claim against the *property* currently held by the defendant. The latter is unaffected by the defendant's *personal* insolvency (see 18.3.1).

Common law tracing is possible where the defendant has received the claimant's property and that property still exists in an identifiable form, even if its precise form has changed. In *Banque Belge pour l'Etranger* v *Hambrouck* [1921] 1 KB 321 a cashier stole monies from his employer, paid them into a new bank account, and later made certain withdrawals. He paid some of the money to S, with whom he was living. S then paid these monies into her own deposit account. She spent the majority of the balance of this account. Only £315 remained in S's account at the date of the court hearing. It was held that the bank was entitled to trace its money. The £315 could be identified as the product of, or substitute for, the original money.

THINKING POINT

In which of the situations set out in Table 18.1 do you think that common law tracing could be used to trace the value of the £10,000 after the particular transaction has occurred? You should derive some guidance from the case of *Agip (Africa) Ltd* v *Jackson* [1990] 1 Ch 265 (earlier).

The solutions are as follows:

(a) tracing at common law would be permitted because there is a clear transactional link between the original £10,000 and the £10,000 worth of shares. The shares clearly represent the original cash—they are said to be its 'exchange product'. So it can be said that the trust property still exists, but has merely changed its form. This result should come as no surprise. After all, it is precisely the sort of transaction which occurs when a trustee makes a legitimate investment with trust monies. The cash was trust property to begin with and the shares are the same trust property at the end, except that the precise form of the trust property has changed;

(b) again, there is no difficulty here. This time the cash has changed hands, but it remains in an identifiable form. It does not matter that Debbie may have deposited £10,000 in £10 notes and that the bank might have transferred £10,000 in £50 notes. The property exists in an identifiable form throughout and can be traced through the various transactions. In theory, Debbie could point at the monies at any time and say 'they are mine'. Her trust property is a chose in action (a debt) which is good against the bank and then the building society;

Table 18.1 Common law tracing

The transaction	Does common law tracing succeed?
(a) Trustee Tim uses £10,000 of trust monies to purchase £10,000 worth of shares	☐
(b) Debbie pays £10,000 cash into Gold Bank plc which then transfers £10,000 in cash to Nunnery National Building Society at Debbie's request	☐
(c) Silver Bank plc transfers £10,000 by telegraphic transfer (think of it as a transfer over the telephone) to Banque Argent SA, France	☐
(d) X deposits £15,000 worth of krugerrands with Silver Bank plc with the instruction to pass them on to Banque Argent SA. In anticipation of the receipt of the krugerrands from Silver Bank plc, Banque Argent pays out £15,000 worth of krugerrands to Y	☐

(c) in this scenario common law tracing fails. This is because a telegraphic transfer involves the passing of electrons down a telephone line. The cash has ceased to exist in an identifiable form. The fact that there is £10,000 at one end of the telephone line and £10,000 at the other end will not suffice to permit tracing at common law. An onlooker might say 'there's the £10,000' when it is in the custody of Silver Bank plc, and 'there it is again' when it reaches Banque Argent SA. However, common law tracing will not be possible because it was not possible to identify the £10,000 in the intermediate stage. In this respect the common law appears to suffer from a Luddite inability to deal with the technological realities of the commercial world;

(d) in this situation Banque Argent are said to have taken a 'delivery risk'. They have made a payment out of monies before receipt of monies in. Clearly, the two sums of krugerrands must have been distinct. The transfer of krugerrands had yet to arrive when another £15,000 worth of krugerrands were paid out. It would therefore be impossible to identify the krugerrands paid out to Y as being the exchange product of the krugerrands originally held by X. Common law tracing would not be possible in this scenario.

This last example further illustrates the importance attached to identifying the thing itself, even if its form has changed, to trace at common law.

18.2.2 Defences to the common law restitutionary claim

We have so far considered tracing at common law from the point of view of the person attempting to trace their original property to an ultimate fund or asset. Generally, they do not wish to recover their original fund or asset, but wish to recover its value as represented in a new fund or asset which is identifiable as their original property in a new (substitute) form. Now we must put ourselves in the position of the defendant to a common law tracing action.

Suppose that the original owner of certain property claims to be able to identify property currently held by you as being their original property in a new form. What defences might you raise?

You should recall *Lipkin Gorman* v *Karpnale* [1992] 4 All ER 512 from Chapter 1; the facts of the case were that a partner in a firm of solicitors had used monies from his firm's client account to gamble at the 'Playboy Club' casino in London. The casino was the defendant to the action. Two defences to a restitutionary claim based upon common law tracing were identified (if either of these defences can be made out, the 'ultimate' property holder will not have to make restitution to the 'original' property holder, even though the latter had successfully carried out the tracing process).

 THINKING POINT

Can you guess why this defence was unsuccessful on this occasion?

First, the casino argued that it should not be required to make restitution to the claimant because it had provided consideration for the monies it had received, namely the provision of gambling services. It argued that because it had given consideration it had not been unjustly enriched by the receipt of the client account monies, and therefore should not have to make restitution. The court accepted that the provision of consideration could be a valid defence in certain circumstances, but it would not be so on the facts of the present case.

The defence did not succeed here because a contract for gambling services was (at the time of the case) not a legally enforceable contract (it now is: Gaming Act 2005, ss 334–5). Even though consideration had been given it could not be treated as *legal* consideration and so the casino was held to have been unjustly enriched.

Secondly, the casino argued that if it must be liable to make restitution it should only be liable to make restitution *net* of winnings that it had paid out to the gambling solicitor. It would be unjust, it argued, to require it to repay all the money that it had received without taking account of the money that it had paid out. This time the court accepted the defence. The casino would be excused having to make restitution, to the extent that the casino had altered its finances in *good faith* by paying winnings to the solicitor. This has been described as the 'change of position defence'. If this defence develops in the UK in the way that it has developed in other common law jurisdictions it is probable that the defence will succeed only where the activity constituting the 'change of position' (e.g. the paying out of winnings) would not have been undertaken had it not been for the receipt by the defendant of the monies which the claimant is seeking to recover.

 THINKING POINT

Can you imagine any other scenarios in which the 'change of position' defence might succeed?

One example might be where X receives £20,000 (in good faith) and builds (again, in good faith) a £20,000 swimming pool in his garden. X would not have built the swimming pool had he not received the monies; indeed, he could not have afforded to do so. Tracing might be possible at common law, in as much as the swimming pool can be said to represent the £20,000 fund in a new, but identifiable, form. But would it be just to require X to repay the £20,000 cash? Probably not! This sounds like a scenario in which the defence of change of position would succeed. X would say 'I have spent the money in good faith and I would not have done so were it not for the fact that I received the £20,000 in good faith. I have changed my position.' However, X has clearly been unjustly enriched by this process and it seems that the claimant would be entitled to a charge over the property to the extent to which its value has been increased by the swimming pool. So, if a £20,000 swimming pool adds, for example, £15,000 to the market value of the house and garden, the claimant would be entitled to a charge for £15,000 secured on the house and garden.

Having considered these possible defences to a restitutionary claim founded upon a tracing action at common law, it is worth noting that it will *not* be a defence for the defendant to show that they have disposed of the claimant's property. This is because the claim at common law is a personal claim and not a proprietary one. If the defendant has received, at some stage, my property in an identifiable form, I have a claim against him personally. It does not defeat my claim for the defendant to show at the date of the court hearing that they no longer hold that property. Only if the claim were proprietary would it be essential to show that the defendant still had the property in his hands. We will come to consider this distinction in more detail when we analyse tracing in equity.

18.2.3 **Problems for common law tracing**

The last section considered defences to the ultimate restitutionary claim brought when the common law tracing process has been successful, but the process itself can sometimes encounter difficulties and not infrequently fails. Some of those difficulties are considered in this section.

18.2.3.1 **Mixed funds**

It has been said that 'tracing runs into problems when it encounters mixing' (Professor Peter Birks, 'Mixing and Tracing' [1992] CLP 69). This is clear from the most primitive of examples.

Suppose I own a cow and it joins your herd of 1,000 cows. Will I be able to recover my cow if it is unmarked and indistinguishable from the majority of your herd? You now have 1,001 cows and you will have been unjustly enriched if you fail to return my cow. That I have a restitution-ary right seems beyond doubt, but tracing my particular cow would appear to be impossible. The tracing process has run into difficulties. A similar problem arises in modern commercial arrangements. Suppose I mistakenly pay £5 into your bank account, the balance of which was previously £1,000. You were aware of my error and have been unjustly enriched to the tune of £5. Again, it is clear that I should be able to establish a restitutionary claim, but how could I possibly trace my £5? It is, after all, indistinguishable from all the other £5s in the account.

In each of these situations, I am no more able to identify my property than I would be able to point to my share of the 'stream of electrons' passing on a telegraphic transfer. For this reason, common law tracing is not permissible through mixed funds. To trace through mixed funds we must attempt to trace in equity, to which we will shortly turn. It is often said that there is no tracing at common law *into* mixed funds. This is not true in a case where a fiduciary has mixed his own money with that of his principal. If it were true, a fiduciary could (by the simple expedi-ent of paying his principal's monies into his own current account) escape personal liability at common law for the tort of conversion (the tort of wrongfully 'converting' another's property to one's own use). In such a case it is more accurate to say that at common law it is not possible to trace *through* a mixed account. So common law tracing would fail if monies were withdrawn from a mixed account to buy an item of property.

18.2.3.2 **Trust beneficiaries tracing at common law**

> **THINKING POINT**
>
> Do you see any conceptual difficulty in permitting beneficiaries under trusts to trace their beneficial entitlements at common law?

There is a difficulty! Beneficiaries, as you will be aware, only have *equitable* interests and their rights are recognised only in equity. Accordingly, they will not be able to take advantage of the purely common law right to trace. Having said that, one way in which the beneficiaries might be able to take advantage of the common law right to trace is to compel the trustees to trace on behalf of the beneficiaries. The trustees hold the legal title to the trust property and are able to take advantage of legal, as opposed to equitable, rights of action. This will include the com-mon law tracing action. But on what basis could the beneficiaries be entitled to compel the trustees to trace on their behalf?

One argument is that the right to trace is a *chose in action*, in other words, it is a form of prop-erty consisting of a right to sue. Because trustees cannot hold any trust property for their own benefit, the benefit of the right to trace at common law must belong, in equity, to the benefi-ciaries. Accordingly, the beneficiaries are able to enjoy the benefit of that right by compelling the trustees to sue on their behalf. However, the exercise of an exclusively common law right by indirect action in equity would be highly unorthodox. There is authority to suggest, however, that beneficiaries can be subrogated to the trustees' right to sue if the trustees themselves are unwilling to exercise that right (*Parker-Tweedale* v *Dunbar Bank plc* [1990] 2 All ER 577); in such a case the trustees would be joined as parties to the common law action. However, such an action will only succeed where the trustees do in fact have a common law right to sue.

THINKING POINT

Can you think of a situation where the trustees would not have a right to sue for the recovery of property at common law?

A straightforward example is the situation where the trustees have themselves paid the trust monies away in breach of their trust. The beneficiaries want to recover the monies but may not do so via the trustees because the trustees are not permitted to 'derogate from their grant' to the third party against whom tracing is sought.

In conclusion, the tracing process at common law might not be available to beneficiaries, and even if it is available the process is liable to fail if it encounters a mixed fund. In addition, even if the tracing process is successful in itself, the claimant may fail to establish an ultimate restitutionary right if the defendant can show that he innocently gave consideration for it or changed his position by reason of receipt of the property. Should tracing at common law fail for any of these reasons it may be that the claimant will have more success with a tracing action in equity.

18.3 Equitable tracing

OUTSIDE THE BOX

'Dapplegrim' from *The Red Fairy Book* by Andrew Lang

The second time the Princess changed herself into a loaf, and laid herself on the table among four other loaves; and she was so like the other loaves that no one could see any difference between them.

But the youth again went down to the stable to Dapplegrim, and told him that the Princess had hidden herself again, and that he had not the least idea what had become of her.

'Oh, just take a very large bread-knife, sharpen it, and pretend that you are going to cut straight through the third of the four loaves which are lying on the kitchen table in the King's palace—count them from right to left—and you will soon find her,' said Dapplegrim.

So the youth went up to the kitchen, and began to sharpen the largest bread-knife that he could find; then he caught hold of the third loaf on the left-hand side, and put the knife to it as if he meant to cut it straight in two. 'I will have a bit of this bread for myself,' said he.

'No, dear friend, don't cut, it is I!' said the Princess again; so he had found her the second time.

Equitable tracing reaches the parts that tracing at common law does not reach! It will trace value into assets even where the form of the asset has changed—perhaps not from princess to bread, but, say, from cash to electrons to gold. There are three basic distinctions between the two forms of tracing.

First, the crucial advantage of equitable tracing is the fact that it is possible to trace in equity into mixed funds. This aspect is considered in depth in 18.3.3. Having said that, equitable tracing has its limits (see 18.3.2).

Secondly, another distinction is that beneficiaries under trusts are able to trace directly in equity, whereas they are not able to do so at common law.

Thirdly, the tracing action in equity is against identifiable property in the defendant's hands, whereas the tracing action in common law is against the defendant's general, personal funds. Whereas common law tracing may lead to a personal remedy, tracing in equity can lead to a proprietary remedy. It is to this last point that we now turn our attention.

18.3.1 Advantages of proprietary rights

Successful tracing in equity leads to a right in a thing (be it a bank account or a tangible asset, e.g. shares). A right in a thing is known as a proprietary right, or a right *in rem*. This can be contrasted with tracing at common law, which leads to a personal claim against a person holding, or a person who has held, the property that is being traced. However, a proprietary right should not be confused with 'real' rights, such as those established in land law. A 'real' right allows the recovery of specific, one might call it 'original', property, whereas a proprietary right permits recovery of value as represented by original or substitute property or a charge over original or substitute property in the hands of the defendant.

THINKING POINT

Proprietary remedies have certain advantages over personal remedies. Can you think of any?

There are several advantages:

- proprietary claims do not depend for their success upon the personal solvency of the defendant. It does not defeat the proprietary claim to discover that the defendant may owe more money to his various creditors than he can possibly hope to repay from his personal assets, nor does it defeat the proprietary claim if the defendant is declared personally bankrupt on that basis. His personal circumstances are, in theory, irrelevant to the success of the claimant's tracing action in equity. This is by far the most significant advantage of the proprietary claim over the personal claim. This is not to say that a personal claim is useless in the event of a defendant's insolvency, merely that the claimant with only a personal claim will have to join the queue of creditors with personal claims against the bankrupt's estate. If the claimant is able to establish a proprietary right to property in the defendant's hands, the claimant will be able to avoid the queue of creditors. If the claimant's proprietary claim is successful, the property which the claimant is claiming is treated as if it had never become part of the bankrupt's personal estate;

- a proprietary claim to property in the defendant's hands has the added advantage that the claimant can recover the property even if it has increased in value. This is so even if the defendant's shrewd investment was responsible for the increased value of the property. The claimant cannot be said to have been unjustly enriched by a windfall gained at the expense of the defendant's time or know-how, although it might be different if the windfall can be shown to have been acquired at the defendant's *financial* expense. As Lord Hoffmann observed in *Foskett* v *McKeown* (for the facts, see 18.1):

> Mr Murphy's children, claiming through him, and the trust beneficiaries whose money he used, are entitled to share in the proceeds of the insurance policy in proportion to the value which they respectively contributed to the policy. This is not based upon unjust enrichment except in the most trivial sense of that expression. It is, as my noble and learned friend says, a vindication of proprietary right.

- in a proprietary claim, interest accrues from the date that the defendant acquired the property. In contrast, the claimant in a personal action may usually claim the interest only from the date that the defendant's personal liability is established, i.e. the date of the court's judgment. Not infrequently the judgment will backdate the account for interest to the date of the writ, but no earlier;

- whereas personal actions may be time-barred under the Limitation Act 1980 either directly or by analogy (see 15.2.3) the Act will usually have no application to a proprietary claim (see 15.2.2.2);

- because the success of a proprietary claim depends upon the continued existence of the property in the defendant's hands it will often be possible to obtain an injunction preventing disposal of the property before the hearing. Such an injunction may be available under s 37(1) of the Senior Courts Act 1981.

For the advantages of proprietary claims see Figure 18.1.

Figure 18.1 Advantages of proprietary claims

The main strengths of proprietary claims are summarised by the 'Four Is':

Insolvency is no bar to a claim

Increase in value can be claimed

Interest accrues from the date that the defendant acquired the property

Injunction can prevent disposition of the property

18.3.2 Limits to equitable tracing

 THINKING POINT

As you have progressed in your study of land law and the law of trusts you will have acquired a cumulative understanding of equity and equitable concepts. With this understanding you might be able to think of some ways in which the claimant's ability to trace in equity may be limited. If you have any ideas jot them down and compare them with the following list.

18.3.2.1 Tracing against *bona fide* purchasers for value

It is well established that equitable tracing will not be permitted against a *bona fide* purchaser for value of the legal estate in property if that purchaser had no notice of the claimant's equitable claim to the property. This is a concept with which you should be very familiar from your study of land law.

Such a purchaser has, by definition, given consideration for the property in their hands, but what if the property is being held by an innocent volunteer—someone who has not given consideration but has received the property without notice of prior equitable claims? This brings us to the next section.

18.3.2.2 **Innocent volunteers**

When a claimant claims to be able to trace into property held by an innocent volunteer, equity has a dilemma. We have already seen that when property comes to an innocent *purchaser* without notice of the claimant's rights there is no dilemma because the presence of the consideration gives the purchaser an unanswerable claim at common law. Innocent volunteers have given no consideration for the property in their hands and can be said to have been unjustly enriched if it can be shown that the property in their possession properly belongs to another. The dilemma is choosing between two innocent parties.

> **THINKING POINT**
>
> Read the following analysis of *Re Diplock* [1948] 1 Ch 465. How was the dilemma resolved in that case?

In *Re Diplock* Lord Greene MR held that the volunteer should not be treated as strictly as a person standing in a fiduciary relationship to the person with the equitable claim. In fact, he went as far as to equate the equitable burden on the conscience of the volunteer with that of the equitable claimant. The result was that the volunteer did not have to treat the claimant's claim as paramount. The defendant volunteer (the charity in *Re Diplock*) was entitled to assert its own claims on the mixed fund to the extent that it was not unconscionable to do so. Put another way, equitable tracing will not be permitted against innocent volunteers who have mixed their own monies with those of equitable claimants if it would be inequitable so to permit.

The rationale given in *Re Diplock* for permitting tracing against innocent volunteers was that equitable claimants have 'rights of property' in mixed funds containing their monies and it would be unconscionable for the innocent volunteer to deny those proprietary rights. Hence the orthodox view is that the claimant must be able to prove that the funds they claim have at some time been held in the nature of property for them. In practical terms this has put on the claimant a requirement to show that the funds they claim have been held, at some stage, by some other person in a fiduciary capacity—to show, in other words, that some other person has held the funds knowing they belonged to (were the 'property' of) the claimant.

In *Foskett v McKeown* the House of Lords confirmed that the rules of tracing 'through a mixed fund' should be distinguished from 'those regulating the position when monies of one person have been innocently expended on the property of another':

> In the former case (mixing of funds) it is established law that the mixed fund belongs proportionately to those whose monies were mixed. In the latter case it is equally clear that money

expended on maintaining or improving the property of another normally gives rise, at the most, to a proprietary lien to recover the monies so expended. In certain cases the rules of tracing in such a case may give rise to no proprietary interest at all if to give such interest would be unfair: see *Re Diplock* [1948] Ch 465, 548.

It is clear from *Re Diplock* that the tracing rules operate less harshly against a wholly innocent volunteer. However, not every volunteer recipient is wholly innocent!

In *Boscawen v Bajwa* [1995] 4 All ER 769 the registered proprietor of a property charged it to a building society and exchanged contracts for the sale of the property to purchasers who had obtained a mortgage offer from a bank. The bank transferred cash to the purchasers' solicitors for the sole purpose of completing the purchase. The purchasers' solicitors transferred the money to the vendor's solicitors, who then paid it on to the building society in repayment of the vendor's mortgage arrears. The building society duly discharged the charge and forwarded the title deeds of the property to the vendor's solicitors. However, the sale fell through. Later, the claimant (who was a judgment creditor of the vendor) obtained a charging order absolute against the property. The question was whether the claimant's charge had priority to the equitable claim of the bank.

The Court of Appeal held that, as the bank's money could be traced into the payment to the building society and had been used towards the discharge of the latter's charge, the bank was entitled to a charge on the property by way of subrogation to the rights of the building society to the extent that the money had been used to redeem the charge and in priority to any interest of the claimant. Millett LJ rejected the claimant's claim, based upon *Re Diplock*, that the vendor and the bank had both contributed to the discharge of the building society's charge and should be entitled to the property in proportion to their contributions, allowing the claimant to assert its charge against the vendor's part. The present case, his Lordship declared, was very different from *Re Diplock*. In that case innocent volunteers had mixed trust monies with their own monies. In the present case the vendor and his solicitors were not innocent volunteers, although it was true that their actions fell short of dishonesty (because the vendor had relied upon the solicitors, and the solicitors had honestly believed that completion was imminent). The vendor must have known that any monies received by his solicitors would represent the balance of the proceeds of sale due *on completion*. He cannot possibly have believed that he could, at one and the same time, retain possession of the property and use and enjoyment of the proceeds of sale. Had he thought of the matter at all, he would have realised that the money was not his to mix with his own and dispose of as he saw fit. This was not wholly innocent behaviour and it followed that the more favourable tracing rules which are available to an innocent volunteer who subconsciously mixes trust money with his own could not be relied upon by the claimant in the present case. Incidentally, in *Boscawen*, Millett J indicated that he thought the defence to an action available after tracing property, whether at law or in equity, should be the 'change of position' formulation suggested by Lord Goff in *Lipkin Gorman* (see 18.2.2), rather than the 'inequitable' formulation applied in *Re Diplock*.

18.3.2.3 Need for a fiduciary

Equitable tracing will not be possible unless the property has at some stage been held in a fiduciary capacity (*Chase Manhattan Bank v Israel-British Bank (London) Ltd* [1981] 1 Ch 105).

If the property which is being traced is trust property it will readily satisfy this requirement because the legal title to trust property is by definition always held in a fiduciary capacity. In fact, Professor Birks suggests that a 'proprietary base', and not the presence or absence of a fiduciary, is the essence of the claim ('Mixing and Tracing' [1992] CLP 69). In modern commercial settings the presence or absence of fiduciary relationships seems to be an almost random factor, and the concept of what is and what is not a fiduciary relationship is surely too ill-defined to allow the right to trace in equity to turn upon it.

In fact the courts have shown a pragmatic willingness to 'discover' fiduciary relationships where the justice of the case demands that tracing succeed. The *Chase Manhattan* case illustrates this pragmatic approach. There, the claimant bank paid monies to the defendant bank by mistake. The monies had not previously been subject to any trust or fiduciary obligations, but Goulding J held that the conscience of the defendant bank became subject to 'a fiduciary duty' to respect the claimant's proprietary right *upon receipt* of the claimant's monies.

In *Nesté Oy v Lloyds Bank plc* [1983] 2 Lloyd's Rep 658 at 666 Bingham J confirmed that 'the receiving of money which consistently with conscience cannot be retained is, in equity, sufficient to raise a trust in favour of the party for whom or on whose account it was received'. (Here his Lordship was actually quoting Story's pre-Judicature Acts *Commentaries on Equity Jurisprudence*.) But Lord Mustill has urged greater restraint in the 'discovery' of fiduciary relationships. In *Re Goldcorp Exchange Ltd* [1994] 3 WLR 199 his Lordship observed that:

> [m]any commercial relationships involve . . . a reliance by one party on the other, and to introduce the whole new dimension into such relationships which would flow from giving them a fiduciary character would . . . have adverse consequences . . . It is possible without misuse of language to say that the customers put faith in the company, and that their trust has not been repaid. But the vocabulary is misleading; high expectations do not necessarily lead to equitable remedies.

18.3.2.4 Dissipation and destruction

Equitable tracing will not be permitted where the claimant's property has been dissipated or destroyed (*Borden (UK) Ltd v Scottish Timber* (1981)). In *Re Diplock* it was held that successful tracing presupposes 'the continued existence of the money either as a separate fund or as part of a mixed fund or as latent in property acquired by means of such a fund. If . . . such continued existence is not established, equity is as helpless as the common law itself.'

This limitation on the right to trace in equity is probably the easiest one to grasp. Because equitable tracing leads to a proprietary claim it depends for its success upon the continued existence of property in the defendant's hands. If the defendant has dissipated or destroyed the property the tracing action must fail. It would be necessary to have recourse to a personal action against the defendant (where possible) to recover the lost value of the property. Property need not be dissipated and destroyed by explosion or such like. One could, for instance, spend the fund on a holiday, or on a meal for friends. You should now remember the example scenario with which we began this chapter, and be some way nearer to a solution to the problems it raised.

It is also possible to dissipate monies by paying off unsecured debts. This is because the creditor will be a *bona fide* purchaser for value without notice. Using the fund to pay off secured debts produces a very different result: in such a case payment of the debt releases property ('the security for the debt') to which the tracing claim can continue to attach.

 THINKING POINT

Would it be fair to permit tracing in equity, even after dissipation, against the general funds of the defendant? Try to list some of the arguments for and against such an approach.

Against such an approach is the fact that the equitable claimant would be given priority over the general creditors of the defendant in the defendant's insolvency. In favour of the approach is the fact that it might be fair in certain situations to allow the claimant to fix a charge or lien over the defendant's property where it would be unjust to allow the defendant to set up the dissipation as a defence. The justice or injustice of permitting dissipation to be set up as a defence might tie in with the presence or absence of facts which show that the claimant has undergone a 'change of position' in dissipating the property in a way in which he would not have done had he never received the property in the first place.

Whether a general charge would be permitted after dissipation should, perhaps, depend upon whether or not the defendant is solvent. There would appear to be little injustice, with the availability of the defence of change of position, in permitting a charge against the general assets of a solvent defendant where this would cause no prejudice to the defendant's general creditors. Of course, the law instinctively recoils from making its conceptual coherence subject to the factual accident of solvency, but instances of result-led conceptualisation are not unknown elsewhere (see, for example, innominate terms in contract law).

In *Space Investments Ltd* v *Canadian Imperial Bank of Commerce Trust Co (Bahamas) Ltd* [1986] 1 WLR 1072 a bank had deposited trust monies with itself, having been authorised to do so. Lord Templeman stated, *obiter*, that equity might permit beneficiaries to trace their trust property into *all* the assets of the bank by placing a charge over the bank's assets. This approach, it is arguable, runs contrary to the principles of insolvency law in that it has the effect of promoting the equitable claimant to the position of debenture holder with priority over general creditors, but it might achieve fairness in the case of a solvent defendant. Figure 18.2 presents some obstacles to equitable tracing and claims.

Figure 18.2 Obstacles to equitable tracing and claims

The major obstacles to tracing and claiming in equity may be summarised in the mnemonic acronym 'FIDE':

Fiduciary must hold the property at some stage

Innocent volunteer recipients of misapplied trust property are not always bound by trust beneficiaries' claims

Dissipation or destruction of trust property is an absolute bar to a proprietary claim in equity

Equity's darling: the *bona fide* purchaser of a legal estate without notice of the trust has an unanswerable defence

18.3.2.5 **Summary**

18.3.3 Equitable tracing into funds and assets

The rules for equitable tracing vary according to whether the tracing is into mixed funds or unmixed funds and according to whether the funds remain in a bank account or have been used to purchase property.

18.3.3.1 Tracing into unmixed funds in a bank account

Generally, equity follows the law. If I give you £10,000 which you then place in an empty bank account, I can trace into the £10,000 which has been deposited into that account. I can trace in law and in equity, provided that the prerequisites and limits to those respective actions are observed. We have already noted that one of the great advantages of the equitable tracing action in this context is that trust beneficiaries can use it directly.

18.3.3.2 Tracing into assets purchased with unmixed funds

Here, the beneficiaries may recover the original assets or their exchange products. The court will order the person currently holding the property to make restitution to the trustees, who will then hold the property on the original trusts for the beneficiaries. The beneficiaries will, in effect, be entitled to 'adopt' the new asset as if it were an authorised investment.

 CASE CLOSE-UP

Foskett v _McKeown_ [2001] 1 AC 102, House of Lords

Lord Millett: 'the simplest case is where a trustee wrongfully misappropriates trust property and uses it exclusively to acquire other property for his own benefit. In such a case the beneficiary is entitled at his option either to assert his beneficial ownership of the proceeds or to bring a personal claim against the trustee for breach of trust and enforce an equitable lien or charge on the proceeds to secure restoration of the trust fund. He will normally exercise the option in the way most advantageous to himself. If the traceable proceeds have increased in value and are worth more than the original asset, he will assert his beneficial ownership and obtain the profit for himself. There is nothing unfair in this. The trustee cannot be permitted to keep any profit resulting from his misappropriation for himself, and his donees cannot obtain a better title than their donor. If the traceable proceeds are worth less than the original asset, it does not usually matter how the beneficiary exercises his option. He will take the whole of the proceeds on either basis. This is why it is not possible to identify the basis on which the claim succeeded in some of the cases.

Both remedies are proprietary and depend on successfully tracing the trust property into its proceeds. A beneficiary's claim against a trustee for breach of trust is a personal claim. It does not entitle him to priority over the trustee's general creditors unless he can trace the trust property into its product and establish a proprietary interest in the proceeds. If the beneficiary is unable to trace the trust property into its proceeds, he still has a personal claim against the trustee, but his claim will be unsecured. The beneficiary's proprietary claims to the trust property or its traceable proceeds can be maintained against the wrongdoer and anyone who derives title from him except a _bona fide_ purchaser for value without notice of the breach of trust. The same rules apply even where there have been numerous successive transactions, so long as the tracing exercise is successful and no _bona fide_ purchaser for value without notice has intervened.'

Further, because equitable tracing is a proprietary claim, the beneficiaries may also claim any increase in the value of the assets and any profits which have been made on the property whilst in the trustees' hands. On the other hand, if the trust property as represented in the current assets has decreased in value the beneficiaries will not wish to adopt the current assets as if they had been obtained by an authorised investment. Instead, the beneficiaries have the option of treating the new assets as security for the full value sought by taking a charge over the new assets (see *Re Hallett's* (1880) 13 ChD 696 at 18.3.3.3).

 THINKING POINT

How would you advise the beneficiaries of the trust to proceed if their trustee had misappropriated £20,000 from the trust and used the money to purchase: (a) shares which have risen in value to £40,000? (b) a new car?

In situation (a) the best advice would be to assert beneficial ownership of the shares as the direct exchange product of the misappropriated monies. This would give the beneficiaries a 'windfall' of £20,000. In situation (b) the best advice, in the light of the rapid depreciation of new cars, would be to fix the trustee with personal liability to repay the £20,000 and to place a charge over the car to secure the repayment of the £20,000.

18.3.3.3 Tracing the trustee's and the beneficiary's monies into bank accounts containing a mix of monies

If a trustee, or other fiduciary, mixes his own money with that of a beneficiary (whether a beneficiary under an orthodox trust or a beneficiary of the obligations owed by a fiduciary), it will not be possible to trace at common law *through* the mixed fund that results (see 18.2.3.1). It is, however, possible to trace in equity.

According to *Re Hallett's Estate* (1880) 13 ChD 696 CA the beneficiary in such a case will be entitled to a first charge over the mixed fund to the extent of their claim to the fund. In *Re Hallett's* the trustee had died leaving enough money in his mixed bank account to satisfy the beneficiaries, but the trustee's general creditors claimed that they should be entitled to the fund. It was held that the balance in the account must be treated as belonging to the trust because the trustee will be presumed to have withdrawn his own money first rather than to have withdrawn the trust money in breach of trust. (In the same way that the legal owner of land cannot assert at law that they have trespassed on their own land, a trustee cannot assert that they have done an act improperly which it is open on the facts to find that they have done properly.) This rule against 'improper assertion' appears to share the rationale of the maxim *equity imputes an intention to fulfil an obligation*.

By extension of *Re Hallett's*, a beneficiary will be entitled to trace into the 'lowest intermediate balance' in a mixed bank account. Trust monies will always be deemed to have been withdrawn from the account last (*James Roscoe (Bolton) Ltd* v *Winder* [1915] 1 Ch 62).

 THINKING POINT

What do you think would be the result if the balance in a mixed account was reduced to 'nil' and the trustee later paid £10,000 of their own monies into the account?

You might have thought that the courts would once again assume that the trustee had acted properly and decide that the payment into the account should be treated as a repayment of trust monies. In fact, payments into an account after a 'nil' balance are not to be treated as repayments of trust monies. This principle was confirmed in *Bishopsgate* v *Homan* [1994] 3 WLR 1270, one of the cases arising out of the Robert Maxwell scandal. In that case a pension account ended up in credit but the liquidators were not able to trace into those monies on behalf of the pensioners because there had previously been a 'nil' balance in the account (in fact the account had been overdrawn), indicating that all the trust monies must have been paid out at some point. Equitable tracing, as has been said before, depends upon the continued existence of the property in the defendant's hands. More recently, the Privy Council expressed willingness in *Federal Republic of Brazil* v *Durant International Corpn* [2015] UKPC 35; [2015] WLR (D) 358 to disapply the lowest intermediate balance rule where an overall scheme is established for some dishonest purpose such as hiding a bribe by money laundering (which occurred in this case). Their Lordships held that in such cases, equity's view should be holistic: the 'availability of equitable remedies ought to depend on the substance of the transaction in question and not upon the strict order in which associated events occur' (para. [38]).

One legal analyst suggests that the presumption that the trustee has withdrawn his or her own monies first is made on the basis that the trustee has been culpable in mixing the fund in the first place and therefore should be the one who suffers the loss (see Simon Gardner, *An Introduction to the Law of Trusts*, Oxford: Clarendon Press, 1990). However, in *Re Diplock* Lord Greene stated that the principle in *Re Hallett's* could be applied to mixed funds even where the mixing had been effected by an innocent volunteer. He disagreed with the view, adopted by the judge at first instance, that *Re Hallett's* could operate only where the mixing takes place in breach of trust, actual or constructive, or in breach of some other fiduciary relationship. Rather, Lord Greene MR stated that 'equity may operate on the conscience not merely of those who acquire a legal title in breach of some trust, express or constructive, or of some other fiduciary obligation, but of volunteers, provided that as a result of what has gone before some equitable proprietary interest has been created and attaches to the property in the hands of the volunteer'.

18.3.3.4 Tracing into assets purchased with mixed funds of trustees' and beneficiaries' monies

Here, because the assets have been purchased in part with the beneficiaries' monies and in part with the trustees' monies, the beneficiaries cannot claim the assets outright. Such cases are referred to as cases of 'mixed substitution'. This description applies where the substitute assets are purchased using a pre-mixed fund and where funds are mixed for the first time at the moment the 'substitute' assets are purchased.

In *Re Oatway* [1903] 2 Ch 356 the trustee bought shares with a mixed account, comprising his own monies and those of the trust. At the time of the purchase of the shares enough money remained in the account to meet the claims of the trust beneficiaries, but later the balance in the account was dissipated.

THINKING POINT

Do you think that the beneficiaries were entitled to a charge on the shares?

It was held that the beneficiaries were entitled to a charge over the shares. However, this result is rather puzzling at first sight. After all, did not *Re Hallett's* decide that the trustee was presumed to withdraw his own money first? In which case, should not the shares in *Re Oatway* have belonged to the trustee? The apparent conflict can be resolved when one recalls the thinking which seems to underpin the decision in *Re Hallett's*, namely that *equity imputes an intention to fulfil an obligation*. It would be entirely in keeping with the maxim to require that the trustee in *Re Oatway* should satisfy the claims of the beneficiaries before setting up a personal claim to the shares. As Ungoed-Thomas J stated in *Re Tilley's WT* [1967] Ch 1179: 'If a trustee mixes trust assets with his own, the onus is on the trustee to distinguish the separate assets and, to the extent that he fails to do so, they belong to the trust.'

A burning question in this area of the law is whether beneficiaries who have successfully traced their property into assets in the hands of the defendant should be able to claim increases in the value of those assets if the assets were bought with a mixed fund.

It had been argued, on the authority of an *obiter* statement of the Master of the Rolls in *Re Hallett's*, that the beneficiaries should be permitted to enforce only the original value of their charge (or 'lien'). For example, suppose that trustee Tam placed £5,000 of trust money in her own account and later purchased a car worth £20,000 with monies from that account. According to *Re Hallett's* the beneficiaries would be entitled to a charge on the security of the car representing their misappropriated funds. The value of the charge would therefore be £5,000. If the car should later prove to be a collectors' item worth £100,000 the *obiter* statement in *Re Hallett's* suggested that the beneficiaries should still be entitled to recover only £5,000.

If you feel an instinctive unease with this approach, you should pause to consider whether you would be happy for a debt secured by a charge (mortgage) on your home to increase in value simply because your home has increased in value! The fixed value charge argument suddenly appears to be more attractive, doesn't it? That, of course, is a quite different case, and the arguments against the fixed charge in the case of a trustee who has wrongfully mixed his own monies with those of the trust are quite overwhelming.

Indeed, an argument against the *Re Hallett's* approach appeared as early as the year that case was reported.

> **S. Williston, 'The Right to Follow Trust Property when Confused with Other Property' (1880) 2 *Harvard Law Journal* 28 at 29**
>
> If the trust fund is traceable as having furnished in part the money with which a certain investment was made, and the proportion it formed of the whole money so invested is known or ascertainable, the *cestui que trust* should be allowed to regard the acts of the trustee as done for his benefit, in the same way that he would if all the money so invested had been his; that is, he should be entitled in equity to an undivided share of the property which the trust money contributed . . . The reason in the one case as in the other is that the trustee cannot be allowed to make a profit from the use of the trust money, and if the property which he wrongfully purchased were held subject only to a lien for the amount invested, any appreciation in value would go to the trustee.

Re Tilley's WT [1967] 1 Ch 1179 was the first modern English authority to cast serious doubt upon the *Re Hallett's* fixed charge approach. It is authority for the recovery, in addition to the original value of the beneficiaries' property, of that proportionate part of the assets which is attributable to the beneficiaries' property. Ungoed-Thomas J stated that 'the beneficiaries are entitled to the property purchased *and any profits* which it produces to the extent to which it has been paid for out of trust monies . . . it appears to me, however, that the trust monies were not in this case so laid out' (emphasis added). On the facts of *Re Tilley's* the trust monies had not actually been 'paid out', strictly speaking, but had been used to reduce the trustee's overdraft at his bank; therefore the statement on this point was *obiter dicta*.

However, this *pro rata* solution has now been approved in the House of Lords in *Foskett v Mc-Keown*. Lord Millett stated that:

> [w]here a trustee wrongfully uses trust money to provide part of the cost of acquiring an asset, the beneficiary is entitled at his option either to claim a proportionate share of the asset or to enforce a lien upon it to secure his personal claim against the trustee for the amount of the misapplied money. It does not matter whether the trustee mixed the trust money with his own in a single fund before using it to acquire the asset, or made separate payments (whether simultaneously or sequentially) out of the differently owned funds to acquire a single asset . . . The primary rule in regard to a mixed fund, therefore, is that gains and losses are borne by the contributors rateably. The beneficiary's right to elect instead to enforce a lien to obtain repayment is an exception to the primary rule, exercisable where the fund is deficient and the claim is made against the wrongdoer and those claiming through him.

In so stating the rule, his Lordship disapproved the *obiter dictum* of Sir George Jessel MR in *Re Hallett's Estate* (1880) 13 ChD 696 at 709, where the Master of the Rolls appeared to suggest that in the case of a mixed substitution the beneficiary is *confined* to the lien (i.e. the charge).

THINKING POINT

Does this *pro rata* solution go far enough?

Arguably not. It might be asked why the trustee should be permitted to retain *any* of the profits made on the 'mixed asset' where they have been responsible for the mixing. This would appear to breach the 'inflexible rule' against allowing a fiduciary to profit from their trust (see 12.1). Certainly, if it can be shown that the trustee or fiduciary could not have obtained the profit 'but for' the use of the beneficiaries' monies in their hands—in other words, if the necessary causal or 'transactional' link can be made out—would the trustee not be profiting from their breach of trust by retaining any part of the profit made on the mixed asset?

On the other hand, if the beneficiaries are permitted to claim *all* profits made on the mixed fund or asset on the basis that the fiduciary must not profit from their breach, this could work great injustice against the fiduciary's general creditors in the event of the fiduciary's insolvency. As so often in this area of the law, the formulation of a unified theoretical approach is thwarted by the vastly differing outcomes in solvent and insolvent scenarios. See Figure 18.3.

18.3.3.5 Tracing into mixed bank accounts containing beneficiary's monies and monies of another trust or innocent volunteer

If a trustee places £10,000 of trust A into a current account which already holds £10,000 of trust B, and later withdraws £10,000 and spends it on a luxury cruise, who can claim the £10,000 left in the account?

Here is equity's traditional dilemma! How should a choice be exercised between two innocent parties? From your land law studies you may recall the maxim of equity that *where the equities are equal, the first in time prevails*. So, if a legal owner concludes a contract for land with X and then concludes another contract for the same land with Y, X's equitable estate contract will

Figure 18.3 Outline of procedure and remedy against dependant wrongfully in possession of trust assets

prevail (subject to the need to protect it by registration) because it was established first in time. This rule of 'first in time, first in right' is a rule of convenience. It is dispute resolution at its crudest. A different rule of convenience exists which is designed to produce a solution to the problem of the competing claims of A and B to the residue of the mixed fund in the scenario with which we began this section. It is called the rule in *Clayton's Case* and was developed to deal with similar problems which frequently occur in the banking world. The rule is designed to allocate the balance of an account when there have been a number of payments in and payments out of the account and will not be applied to scenarios other than those involving simple current accounts. The rule is that the first payment into the account is deemed to correspond to the first payment out of the account. Ironically, then, this rule of convenience achieves the opposite result to the maxim 'first in time, first in right'. The balance of a bank account will belong to the persons who made the most recent payments into it, so bringing about the result that the 'last in time is first in right'!

 THINKING POINT

If the rule in *Clayton's Case* were applied to the problem of A and B, which of them would be entitled to the £10,000 left in the account?

The answer is that A will be entitled to the balance because B's money was the first money to be paid into the account and is therefore assumed to be the first money paid out. Does this result seem fair? Can you think of a fairer solution?

The result does not seem at all fair. A rule which was designed to achieve a convenient solution to the complex accounting problems arising where there are numerous and frequent payments into and out of simple bank accounts produces a palpably inequitable result in the context of our representative breach of trust scenario.

A fairer result would have been for A and B to share the balance in the account *pari passu* their contributions. In other words, they should share the balance in proportion to their contributions, which in the case of A and B would mean allocating the balance half and half. This fairer approach was adopted in *Sinclair* v *Brougham* [1914] AC 398. In that case a building society had been wound up and the question arose of priority between outside creditors, shareholders and depositors. The assets remaining to be distributed could not satisfy all their claims and were divided *pari passu* between the claimants according to the amounts credited to them in the books of the society at the commencement of the winding up. (Note that *Sinclair* v *Brougham* was considered by the House of Lords in the *Westdeutsche* case (see 1.2.7). Their Lordships declined to follow *Sinclair* v *Brougham*, but in relation to a different point.)

Jessel MR would have approved of this approach. In *Re Hallett's* he described the rule in *Clayton's Case* as 'a very convenient rule, and I have nothing to say against it *unless* there is evidence either of agreement to the contrary or of circumstances from which a contrary intention must be presumed' (emphasis added).

There has also been modern support for a more equitable solution to the problem of cases like that of A and B. In *El Ajou* v *Dollar Land Holdings plc* [1993] 3 All ER 717 it was stated that the rule of convenience (the rule in *Clayton's Case*) must yield to the contrary intentions of the parties involved. Likewise, in *Vaughan* v *Barlow Clowes* [1992] 4 All ER 22 the Court of Appeal stated that the rule would not be applied if it was contrary to the intentions of the parties; nor if its application would be impractical (it is, after all, a rule 'of convenience'); nor, in fact, if the application of the rule would produce an unjust result (confirmed in *Commerzbank AG v IMB Morgan plc* [2005] 1 Lloyd's LR 298). In other words, even though the rule still exists (in *Charity Commission v Framjee* [2014] EWHC 2507 (Ch); [2014] WLR (D) 340, Henderson J stated (at para. [49]) that *Clayton's Case* is 'probably still the default rule') it has been emasculated and will apply in the future only to resolve otherwise irreducible accounting difficulties, and only then in current bank accounts. In one case the judge even suggested that the so-called 'rule' in *Clayton's Case* ought to be known as the 'exception' in *Clayton's Case*! (*Russell-Cooke Trust Co v Prentis* [2002] All ER (D) 22 (Nov), *per* Lindsay J.)

🔍 CASE CLOSE-UP

Foskett v McKeown [2001] 1 AC 102, House of Lords

Lord Millett: 'the tracing rules are not the result of any presumption or principle peculiar to equity. They correspond to the common law rules for following into physical mixtures (though the consequences may not be identical). Common to both is the principle that the interests of the wrongdoer who was responsible for the mixing and those who derive title under him otherwise than for value are subordinated to those of innocent contributors. As against the wrongdoer and his successors, the beneficiary is entitled to locate his contribution in any part of the mixture and to subordinate their claims to share in the mixture until his own contribution has been satisfied. This has the effect of giving the beneficiary a lien for his contribution if the mixture is deficient . . . Innocent contributors, however, must be treated equally *inter se*. Where the beneficiary's claim is in competition with the claims of other innocent contributors, there is no basis upon which any of the claims can be subordinated to any of the others. Where the fund is deficient, the beneficiary is not entitled to enforce a lien for his contributions; all must share rateably in the fund.'

It is worth clarifying that if the fund contains a mixture of the trustee's own money and monies from more than one trust, the courts will first apply the rules in 18.3.3.3 for distinguishing between the trustee's and beneficiaries' money. Then, the rules we have just discussed will be applied to ascertain the entitlements of the beneficiaries *inter se*.

Summary

- We have seen that there is a difference between tracing misapplied trust property and actually recovering it. Tracing is the process of following the value of the misapplied trust assets into substitute assets (e.g. the value of a coin can be traced into a book acquired with the coin) and since it is merely an evidential process (like detective work) it shouldn't make any difference that the property one is seeking to recover is equitable property under a trust rather than property owned absolutely.

- Tracing having been completed, the ultimate claim one brings to recover the misapplied trust property is an equitable proprietary claim. A proprietary claim has certain advantages, summarised by the 'Four Is':

  - insolvency is no bar to a claim;

- increase in value can be claimed;
- interest accrues from the date that the defendant acquired the property;
- injunction can prevent disposition of the property.

• However, the fact that the ultimate proprietary claim is an equitable claim has a reflex action on the tracing process leading to the claim, with the result that the courts still refer to 'tracing in equity', when it would be more logical to regard the evidential tracing process as neutral (or 'unitary'), i.e. having no distinction between equity and law. Because of the equitable nature of the claim, and because the equitable nature of the claim reflects an equitable character upon the tracing, there remain certain obstacles to tracing and claiming in equity. They are summarised by the mnemonic 'FIDE':

- *fiduciary* must hold the property at some stage;
- *innocent* volunteer recipients of misapplied trust property are not always bound by trust beneficiaries' claims;
- *dissipation* or *destruction* of trust property is an absolute bar to a proprietary claim in equity;
- *equity's darling*: the *bona fide* purchaser of a legal estate without notice of the trust has an unanswerable defence.

• Apart from the problematic 'equitable' label attached to the tracing process, the tracing itself is a relatively simple and logical one. It is a series of factual presumptions, and the golden rule is that the presumptions always operate in favour of the innocent and against the wrongdoer so far as possible. So if, for example, a trustee misapplies trust money by placing it in his own bank account, it will be presumed thereafter that he spends his own money first and leaves the trust money in his account, unless he uses money in his bank account to purchase a highly profitable asset, in which case he will be presumed to have acquired the asset for the trust.

? Summative assessment exercise

Trevor is a trustee of two trusts, Black's Settlement and White's Settlement, each comprising £50,000 in cash. The trust monies are kept in separate bank accounts. Trevor also has a private bank account in which he holds £100,000. Suppose that the following events take place, in the following order:

• Trevor withdraws all the monies from the Black's Settlement account and places them in his own private account;

• Trevor withdraws all the monies from the White's Settlement account and places them in his own private bank account;

• Trevor withdraws £100,000 from his own account in order to purchase a piece of fine art;

• Trevor withdraws £50,000 from his account and uses the monies to pay off the building society mortgage on his house;

• Trevor withdraws the balance of his private account and spends the monies on a luxury world cruise;

• Trevor finally pays £10,000 into his private account.

Trevor has just been declared bankrupt. His general creditors claim the work of fine art which is now worth £150,000, and the balance of monies in Trevor's private account. Advise the beneficiaries of the two trusts, who wish to recover the value of their misappropriated funds.

 Full specimen answers can be found at www.oxfordtextbooks.co.uk/orc/watt_directions5e/.

The bigger picture

Outside the trusts context, tracing contributes to detective work in money laundering contexts, where the knot of facts can be even harder to unravel. The requirement to show that the claimant's property is in the defendant's hands, and that it can be traced from the claimant to the defendant by an unbroken chain of connections, applies just as rigorously in the context of claims against criminal assets 'frozen' under the Proceeds of Crime Act 2002—see *The Serious Fraud Office* v *Lexi Holdings PLC (In Administration)* [2008] EWCA Crim 1443. Professionals dealing with financial matters are nowadays required to comply with a great many reporting and compliance procedures to prevent money laundering (perhaps especially with a view to combating laundering of terrorist funds). If you go on to work as a solicitor you will discover that modern practice is to require proof of every client's identity before you can act for them. We will consider an example involving banks in the next chapter.

Further reading

Birks, P. 'The Necessity of a Unitary Law of Tracing' in *Making Commercial Law: Essays in Honour of Roy Goode* (1997) Oxford: Clarendon Press 239
one of the earliest calls to remove artificial distinctions between tracing at common law and in equity

Millett, Sir P. 'Tracing the Proceeds of Fraud' (1991) 107 LQR 71
an excellent extrajudicial statement by the leading judge in the area

Smith, L. *Tracing* (1998) Oxford: Clarendon Press
a masterly treatment of the whole subject

Smith, L. 'Simplifying Claims to Traceable Proceeds' (2009) 125 LQR 338
argues that when the common law action for money had and received is deployed in relation to the proceeds of an unauthorised disposition, it can be understood as a common law claim to vindicate an equitable right to money held *in trust* for the claimant

 For links to selected cases, statutes, academic papers and official reports mentioned in this chapter please visit the online resources at www.oup.com/uk/watt_directions6e/.

19 The equitable liability of strangers to the trust

LEARNING OBJECTIVES

By the end of this chapter you should be able to:

- explain the rationale behind equitable liability for 'knowing receipt' of trust property;
- distinguish 'knowing receipt' from 'inconsistent dealing';
- assess the nature of a stranger's liability for dishonestly assisting in (or procuring) a breach of trust;
- advocate possible reforms of the law in this area.

Introduction

This book has contained a great many tales and fables. This chapter begins with a horror story. Imagine that you leave law school and one day qualify as a solicitor. You work in the corporate department, where you are called upon to advise a company director with regard to the restructuring of the company's property holdings and investments. You fail to realise that the scheme will wrongly place money in the director's personal control, in breach of the director's fiduciary duty to the company and in that sense in 'breach of trust'. You find yourself as a co-defendant in a civil action, where you are accused of dishonest assistance in a breach of trust. 'I am not the director or any kind of trustee', you respond. 'Maybe not', says the judge, 'but you can be liable as if you were a trustee . . . you should have read Gary Watt's textbooks at law school!' Okay, the last part is pure fantasy, but the threat to you is very real. In many of the reported cases discussed in this chapter it is a solicitor who is threatened with personal equitable liability, even though technically he or she is a stranger to the trust.

19.1 Liability of strangers distinguished from tracing

> The equitable doctrine of tracing and the imposition of a constructive trust by reason of the knowing receipt of trust property are governed by different rules and must be kept distinct. Tracing is primarily a means of determining the rights of property, whereas the imposition of a constructive trust creates personal obligations which go beyond mere property rights. (*Per* Sir Robert Megarry V-C in *Re Montagu's Settlement Trusts* [1987] Ch 264)

This quote usefully ties in the subject matter of this chapter with that of Chapter 18, which considered the nature and limits of equitable and common law tracing. Common law tracing is a personal action against the persons who have received the property that is being traced, whether or not they have since parted with that property. Equitable tracing, we noted, leads to a proprietary claim, a claim to property currently held by the defendant. This chapter looks at other forms of personal liability, whereby, on account of their behaviour, 'strangers' may be made liable in equity *as if they were* trustees. In such cases strangers are sometimes said to be liable as 'constructive trustees' (see, for example, the earlier quote from Sir Robert Megarry V-C), but that language is misleading, especially in cases where the stranger never takes formal possession of the trust assets, so in this chapter I will avoid that terminology where possible. Their Lordships in the UK Supreme Court have recently referred to strangers' personal liability in equity for 'knowing receipt' of misapplied trust property and 'dishonest assistance' in a breach of trust (the two types of personal liability in equity with which we are mainly concerned in this chapter) under the informal umbrella term 'ancillary liability' (*Williams v Central Bank of Nigeria* [2014] UKSC 10, Supreme Court, para. [9]).

19.2 'Strangers'

Suppose that trustee Tabitha and trustee Tim hold property on trust for Brenda and Bashir. The trustees appoint and pay a stockbroker to invest certain monies on behalf of the trust. If the stockbroker uses the monies for his own purposes he may be personally liable in equity. This means that even if the trust money is completely spent, the stockbroker will have to account to the trust from out of his own personal wealth.

This example illustrates that the imposition of personal liability in equity may coincide with other species of liability. For one thing, there is likely to have been a breach of contract by the agent in this situation for which the agent is liable to be sued by the trustees at common law. One major advantage of the imposition of liability in equity is that the beneficiaries are able to take direct action against the stockbroker in their own capacity.

Any commercial agent in a real dilemma as to the validity of a proposed course of action can apply to the court for a 'binding declaration' that the proposed course of action is proper, or apply for directions as to the best way to proceed. If the declaration is granted and the agent acts according to its terms the agent will effectively be immune to any subsequent action brought by a beneficiary (*Governor and Co of the Bank of Scotland v A Ltd* [2001] 1 WLR 751).

> ## 🔍 CASE CLOSE-UP
>
> ### *Barnes v Addy* (1873–4) LR 9 Ch App 244, Court of Appeal in Chancery
>
> Lord Selborne: 'those who create a trust clothe the trustee with a legal power and control over the trust property, imposing on him a corresponding responsibility. That responsibility may no doubt be extended in equity to others who are not properly trustees, if they are found either making themselves trustees *de son tort*, or actually participating in any fraudulent conduct of the trustee to the injury of the *cestui que trust*. But, on the other hand, strangers are not to be made constructive trustees merely because they act as the agents of trustees in transactions within their legal powers, transactions, perhaps of which a Court of Equity may disapprove, unless those agents receive and become chargeable with some part of the trust property, or unless they assist with knowledge in a dishonest and fraudulent design on the part of the trustees.'

19.3 Where tracing fails

In *Agip (Africa) Ltd v Jackson* [1989] 3 WLR 1367 common law tracing failed because money had been transmitted by telegraphic transfer: 'nothing passed between Tunisia and London but a stream of electrons', *per* Millett J. Further, equitable tracing was only partially successful in that case. Millett J stated that 'the tracing claim in equity gives rise to a proprietary remedy which depends on the continued existence of the trust property in the hands of the defendant'. The claimants could trace only into those monies which remained in the hands of the defendants. The judge continued: 'to recover the money which the defendants have paid away the claimants must subject them to a personal liability to account as constructive trustees and prove the requisite degree of knowledge to establish liability.'

The imposition of equitable liability (so-called liability as a 'constructive trustee') is frequently a last resort when tracing has failed. But it is also a remedy that can co-exist with the tracing process and is useful where tracing has been successful only in part.

This chapter examines three major bases for strangers' liability: liability as a '**trustee *de son tort***', liability for knowing receipt and liability for dishonest assistance in a breach of trust.

> **trustee *de son tort*** 'If one, not being a trustee and not having authority from a trustee, takes upon himself to intermeddle with the trust matters or to do acts characteristic of the office of trustee, he may thereby make himself what is called in law a trustee of his own wrong, i.e. a trustee de son tort': *per* Smith LJ in *Mara* v *Browne* (1896) 1 Ch 199 at 209.

19.4 Trusteeship *de son tort*

It is clear from this *dictum* that strangers who intermeddle in the business of a trust will be taken to have assumed a fiduciary duty to the beneficiaries of that trust. Indeed, they will be treated, for all purposes of liability, as if they had been expressly appointed to trusteeship of the trust. Of course, there would be no liability unless the stranger actually breaches the trust they have assumed.

19.5 Knowing receipt

A personal action is available in equity against a stranger to the trust who received trust property which they knew to be fixed with a breach of trust. In such a case, the stranger will be held personally liable. The remedy for knowing receipt is compensatory 'notwithstanding that it may also be described as restitutionary' (*Charter plc* v *City Index Ltd* [2007] 1 WLR 26, ChD). Where a recipient receives an asset knowing that a fiduciary has fraudulently transferred it at an undervalue and where the asset increases in value after the knowing receipt, the claimant's compensation includes any subsequent increase in the value of the claimant's 'undervalue part' of the asset (*Akita Holdings Ltd* v *Attorney General of the Turks and Caicos Islands* [2017] UKPC 7; [2017] 2 WLR 1153, Privy Council).

> **THINKING POINT**
>
> Can you think of any circumstances where the personal action would be useful?

The personal action is most useful where the claimant's property cannot be traced or can be traced but has depreciated in value. The disadvantage of this personal action to recover lost value is that, even if judgment is given for the claimant, he or she will have to 'join the queue' of creditors if the defendant is insolvent. A *personal* action is, in short, only as good as the defendant's *personal* solvency. If there are creditors with priority over the claimant, the claimant might be unable to recover their loss.

> **THINKING POINT**
>
> Suppose that a trustee uses trust monies, together with some of his own monies, to pur-
> chase shares as a gift to a favourite nephew. The nephew receives dividends on the shares
> over a period of two years before passing them on to his daughter as an 18th birthday
> present. In her hands the value of the shares plummets dramatically to the extent that they
> are nearly worthless. What actions may be open to the beneficiaries?

There is the personal action against the trustee for breach of trust (see Chapter 15). However,
if judgment against the trustee proves worthless (perhaps because the trustee cannot be traced
or has become insolvent) it should be possible to trace the value of the trust property through
to the shares held by the daughter. Tracing would have to take place in equity because the
shares were bought with a mixed fund. Of course, those shares are now practically worthless.
It is at this stage that the lost value of the shares might be recovered from the daughter or the
nephew by a personal action against them in equity on the basis of knowing receipt of misapplied trust property. In addition, if it is established that the nephew is liable in equity, he will be
liable to account to the beneficiaries for some or all of the profits which he made on the shares
while they were in his hands. The ultimate success of these personal actions depends in large
part upon the personal solvency of the various defendants. If the daughter and nephew are
insolvent, or impecunious, a judgment against them will be practically worthless.

Personal liability for knowing receipt depends upon proof of each one of the essential ingredients for liability. It is to those ingredients that we now turn.

19.5.1 'Knowing'

Certain preliminary notes should be made. First, in *Agip (Africa) Ltd* v *Jackson*, Millett J stated
that a recipient would not be liable for knowing receipt *until* they know about the breach of
trust. (Confirmed in *Criterion Properties plc* v *Stratford UK Properties LLC* [2003] 1 WLR 2108.)
So, if a stranger receives trust property but does not find out that it was fixed with a breach of
trust until a later date, the stranger will be liable as of that later date and not before. Secondly,
it is clear that a stranger will not be taken to have knowledge 'of a fact he once knew but has
genuinely forgotten' (*per* Megarry V-C in *Re Montagu's ST* [1987] Ch 264).

Knowledge that a trust is being claimed in litigation is generally insufficient to found liability. In
Carl Zeiss Stiftung v *Herbert Smith & Co* [1969] 2 Ch 276 an action was brought against one of
the United Kingdom's largest solicitors' firms alleging that fees which the firm had received
from a West German company comprised property which the West German company held in
trust for an East German company. Both of the German companies had been involved in litigation to decide which was entitled to the property. The Court of Appeal held that the solicitors'
firm had actual knowledge of the claim made by the East German company, but knowledge of
a claim that a trust existed was not enough to found personal liability in equity (in this case liability was sought on the basis of knowing assistance—dishonest assistance, as it is now—but
the same principle applies to knowing receipt).

Carl Zeiss was considered in *United Mizrahi Bank Ltd* v *Doherty* [1998] 2 All ER 230. There the
judge accepted that it could not be right for solicitors to be looking over their shoulders when
acting for a defendant in an action for breach of trust. However, the learned judge stopped
short of sanctioning in advance an act by the defendant solicitors which would allow them to

take their own fees out of the monies claimed by the claimant. The solicitors would have to take the risk (albeit not very great) that the defendants might lose and the solicitors be found liable for knowing receipt of trust monies applied in breach of trust.

One of the more complex aspects of fixing liability on a stranger for knowing receipt of trust property is ascertaining the degree of knowledge that is required to give rise to liability. Is it essential that the stranger *actually* knew that they were in receipt of property which has come to them directly or indirectly by reason of a breach of trust? Or is it sufficient that they *turned a blind eye to the obvious*, or even that they *should have been suspicious*?

Does a stranger, a bank for example, have to play detective in searching for evidence of fraud and money laundering in relation to monies it has received? Few would doubt that the bank should be liable if it had *actual* knowledge that the monies had come its way in breach of trust, but the difficult question is what degree of *constructive* knowledge should be sufficient to found personal liability in equity? This question will be addressed in the following sections.

19.5.1.1 The *Baden* categories

According to Peter Gibson J in *Baden* v *Société Générale* [1983] BCLC 325, knowledge is of five types:

- actual knowledge;
- wilfully shutting one's eyes to the obvious. This is sometimes referred to as 'Nelsonian blindness' (with allusion to an incident involving Vice-Admiral Lord Nelson at the Battle of Copenhagen, see later). It has been referred to as 'blind-eye knowledge' (*Credit Suisse (Monaco) SA* v *Attar* [2004] EWHC 374; *Manifest Shipping Co* v *Uni-Polaris Shipping Co* [2003] 1 AC 469, HL). In the *Manifest Shipping* case Lord Clyde held that such knowledge requires 'a conscious reason for blinding the eye. There must be at least a suspicion of a truth about which you do not want to know and which you refuse to investigate';
- wilfully and recklessly failing to make such enquiries as an honest and reasonable man would make;
- knowledge of circumstances which would indicate the facts to an honest or reasonable man;
- knowledge of circumstances which would have put an honest and reasonable man on enquiry.

Of these five categories of knowledge, types (1), (2) and (3) can be loosely grouped together as 'naughty knowledge', while types (4) and (5), being 'constructive' forms of knowledge, are more consistent with an innocent state of mind. Having said that, the reference to the 'honest' and 'reasonable' man in types (4) and (5) seems to import, or assume, an element of good faith.

 OUTSIDE THE BOX

Carola Oman, *Nelson* (Aylesbury: Hazell Watson & Viney Ltd) 1947

Nelson asked, 'in a quick manner', 'Do you know what's shown on board of the Commander-in-Chief? Number 39.' Stewart had to admit that he did not know what that number might signify. 'Why, to leave off action!' explained Nelson, adding, 'leave off action! Now damn me if I do.'

He gave a shrug, and addressing himself to Foley [his flag captain], said, 'You know, Foley, I have only one eye. I have a right to be blind sometimes.' He raised his spyglass to his [blind] right eye, and announced, 'I really do not see the signal'.

19.5.1.2 **Applying the *Baden* categories**

For the purpose of fixing liability for knowing receipt of trust property, it had originally been thought that knowledge in any of the *Baden* categories would suffice. However, subsequent decisions support a more restrictive approach. In *Re Montagu's ST* [1987] Ch 26 Megarry V-C held that only types (1), (2) and (3) would suffice. In summarising his findings the Vice-Chancellor doubted that *Baden* types (4) and (5) would suffice because, as he stated, 'I cannot see that the carelessness involved will normally amount to want of probity'. For Megarry V-C there needed to be some evidence of bad faith on the stranger's part before the stranger would be held liable. He further held that the concept of constructive notice (which you might recall from studying land law) should not be applied to personal actions where it is sought to fix equitable liability on strangers: 'The rules concerning a purchaser without notice seem to me to provide little guidance on this and to be liable to be misleading.'

It had been thought that liability based upon constructive knowledge of the *Baden* types (4) and (5) would be inappropriate to commercial transactions because the basis of commercial transactions should be trust and not suspicion (*Eagle Trust plc* v *SBC Securities Ltd* [1992] 4 All ER 488; *Cowan de Groot* v *Eagle Trust plc* [1992] 4 All ER 700), but, Scott LJ in *Polly Peck International plc* v *Nadir (No 2)* [1992] 4 All ER 769 pointed out that the *Baden* categories are not 'rigid categories with clear and precise boundaries. One category may merge imperceptibly into another.' For Scott LJ the real question is whether the stranger should have been suspicious. This flexible approach is now preferred. Thus in *Bank of Credit and Commerce International (Overseas) Ltd* v *Akindele* [2001] Ch 437, the Court of Appeal held that it need not be established that the defendant had acted dishonestly, but merely that his conscience was affected by what he knew. (This is reminiscent of the older formulation which asks whether the defendant's conscience became 'sufficiently affected for it to be right to bind him by the obligations of a constructive trustee'—*Re Montagu's Settlement Trusts* [1987] Ch 264 as applied in *Relfo Ltd (In Liquidation)* v *Varsani* [2012] EWHC 2168 (Ch).)

In *Papadimitriou* v *Crédit Agricole Corporation and Investment Bank* [2015] UKPC 13; [2015] WLR (D) 161, the Privy Council held that a defendant is deemed to have 'constructive notice' of knowledge that would have been revealed by a reasonably prudent reading of the apparent facts. In this case it was held that the recipient should have been suspicious of monies received via Liechtenstein and Panama because the expense of passing money through those jurisdictions could not be justified on commercial grounds and this should have alerted the defendant to the illegal money laundering (applying the analysis of Lord Neuberger of Abbotsbury MR in *Sinclair Investments (UK) Ltd* v *Versailles Trade Finance Ltd* [2012] Ch 453).

 THINKING POINT

Is it problematic to base the equitable liability of a stranger upon vague notions of 'conscience' and 'unconscionability'? (See Lord Nicholls in *Royal Brunei* v *Tan*, next.)

 CASE CLOSE-UP

Royal Brunei v Tan [1995] 3 WLR 64, Privy Council

Lord Nicholls: 'unconscionable is a word of immediate appeal to an equity lawyer. Equity is rooted historically in the concept of the Lord Chancellor, as the keeper of the royal con-

▶ CROSS REFERENCE

Recall the common law tracing action in *Lipkin Gorman* (Chapter 18), where we saw that liability for money 'had and received' does not depend upon knowledge.

> science, concerning himself with conduct which was contrary to good conscience. It must be recognised, however, that unconscionable is not a word in everyday use by non-lawyers. If it is to be used in this context, and if it is to be the touchstone for liability as an accessory, it is essential to be clear on what, in this context, unconscionable means.'

The reasoning in *BCCI (Overseas) Ltd* v *Akindele* was criticised in an *obiter* statement by Lord Nicholls of Birkenhead in *Criterion Properties plc* v *Stratford UK Properties LLC* [2004] 1 WLR 1846, HL. Lord Nicholls would prefer liability for receipt of trust property to be strict liability, in the sense that it should be based on the fact of receipt without proof that the recipient knew the receipt to be wrongful. Professor Birks also proposed (see (1989) LMCLQ 296) that wrongful recipients of trust property should be presumed strictly liable, subject to their being able to raise an adequate defence (for instance, proving that they had innocently purchased the asset received). This would have the result of aligning the approach of equity with that of the common law.

The clear advantage of strict liability for 'knowing receipt' is certainty in the law, which is, perhaps, especially important in the commercial sphere. However, strict liability would mean that banks and other commercial parties would be not only *attractive* targets to claimants (because they are usually solvent and wealthy), but also *easy* targets because they would be unable to raise the defence that they had acted honestly and did not 'know' that they had been involved in a breach of trust. In practice they would have to take out massive insurance against the risk of action being brought against them. In Australia the argument in favour of strict liability based on the reversal of unjust enrichment has been expressly disapproved (*Farah Constructions Pty Ltd* v *Say-Dee Pty Ltd* [2007] HCA 22). At the very least it must be fair to require a claimant to prove fault when the claimant is the sole adult beneficiary of a bare trust, for such a beneficiary can bring their trust to an end at any time. Why should a third-party recipient ('stranger') be *presumed* liable when the beneficiary of the bare trust was running the risk that their trustee might misapply the fund? (See G. Watt, 'Personal liability for receipt of trust property: Allocating the Risks' in E. Cooke (ed.), *Modern Studies in Property Law—Volume III* (2005) Oxford: Hart Publishing, p. 91).

It is not every suspicion that should be entertained. Certainly a bank should be slow to refuse a deposit into a customer's account. In *Tayeb* v *HSBC Bank plc* [2004] EWHC 1529 the court reminded banks that the proper way to respond to concerns about money laundering is to apply to court for a declaration of interim directions. That case concerned the transfer on 21 September 2000 of £944,114.27 to an account recently opened by a Libyan businessman at a Derby branch of the HSBC. The bank manager suspected money laundering, which in the circumstances was a perfectly reasonable suspicion, but his unreasonable response (as the court found it) was to send the money back to the transferring bank. In fact the transfer was perfectly legitimate and the claimant was awarded judgment in debt in the sum of £944,114.27 with interest from 21 September 2000. The judge held that the anti-money laundering procedures to which banks are subject 'do not necessarily lead to the bank having to disengage from the transfer and they certainly do not normally involve the retransfer to the payor, a course which would be most unlikely to protect the rightful beneficiary of the fund and which might well involve tipping off those criminally responsible' and that 'if banks are to be entitled to depart from their contracts with customers, on the basis of suspicion of unlawfulness and of general banking practice, that practice has to be clearly proved'. Of course, whether the court would have been quite so censorious had the bank followed the same course exactly one year later (post-9/11) may be doubted.

In *Bank of Credit and Commerce International (Overseas) Ltd* v *Akindele*, the liquidators of the bank had sought to recover US$6.79m from the defendant on the basis of personal liability for assistance in a breach of trust or wrongful receipt of trust property. In 1985, A had advanced US$10m to a company controlled by the bank under a false loan agreement. In 1988 A received US$16.79m under the agreement. The claimants argued that A's dishonesty could be inferred from his knowledge of the artificial character of the loan and from his receipt of the unusually high return of 15 per cent compound interest. The Court of Appeal held that the state of the defendant's knowledge in 1985 was not such as to make it unconscionable for him to enter into the transaction and, crucially, did not render it unconscionable for him to retain the benefits of the transaction in 1988, notwithstanding the rumours that were then circulating about the integrity of the bank's management. Compare this to *Goldspan Ltd* v *Patel* ([2012] EWHC 1447 (Ch)), in which a third party received £100,000 in the course of a series of transactions the honesty of which had been called into question. The recipient was permitted to retain the money because he had been owed £100,000 by the transferor.

THINKING POINT

Suppose that, in another case, a fake 'loan' were fabricated as part of a money-laundering scam? Do decisions such as this have the potential to play into the hands of fraudsters?

Thankfully other cases have confirmed that a defendant will not escape personal liability if it knowingly runs the risk of receiving misapplied trust assets (for example, *Armstrong DLW GmbH* v *Winnington Networks Ltd* [2012] EWHC 1; [2012] Ch 156 (Ch)).

19.5.2 'Receipt'

In *Agip (Africa) Ltd* v *Jackson* the judge at first instance, Millett J, stated that 'the recipient must have received the property for his own use and benefit'. The Court of Appeal in that case did not expressly deal with the issue. This raises the question whether a bank, which holds monies in an account into which monies had been placed by a trustee in breach of trust, will be liable for 'knowing receipt'.

THINKING POINT

Do you think that when a bank receives a deposit of monies it has received those monies for its 'own use and benefit'?

Millett J decided that the answer depends upon whether the bank placed the monies in an account in reduction of an overdraft or whether the bank merely acted as a conduit for the monies. In the former case there is, his Lordship suggested, beneficial receipt, while in the latter there is not. A cynic might argue that any time a bank receives monies for whatever purpose it benefits from the receipt, or will use the monies for its own benefit. Indeed, the receipt of monies to increase the credit balance of an account might actually be of greater benefit to a bank than the reduction of an overdraft. However, his Lordship argued that this apparently technical distinction was 'essential if receipt-based liability is to be properly confined to those cases where the receipt is relevant to the loss'.

19.5.3 **Inconsistent dealing**

A stranger might be liable for 'inconsistent dealing' with trust property. This category of liability is closely related to 'knowing receipt', as they have in common the receipt of trust property by a stranger, but there are also clear differences between them.

> **THINKING POINT**
>
> Suppose trustees appoint an agent and transfer trust property to that agent within the terms of their trust, and that agent receives the trust property lawfully and not for his own benefit. Could the agent be liable for 'knowing receipt' if he later sells the trust property and in a moment of impetuosity gambles the proceeds at a casino and loses it all?

No: there are two important factors missing. First, there had been no original breach of trust. Secondly, the agent has been appointed to carry out a task not for his own benefit, but for the benefit of the trust. As we have seen, 'knowing receipt' applies only to strangers who have received property for their own 'use and enjoyment'.

It is fairly clear that an action for 'knowing receipt' would not apply to this scenario, but it is possible that the stranger (the agent) could be liable in equity to account on the basis of 'inconsistent dealing' with the trust property.

For a stranger to be fixed with liability for inconsistent dealing they must have known that they had trust property in their hands, but need not have known the precise terms of the trust. (The chances are, of course, that very few genuine strangers to the trust would know its precise terms!)

It is important, however, that agents are not too readily fixed with liability. Lord Selborne in *Barnes* v *Addy* (1874) 9 Ch App 244 stressed the need to protect agents who have acted honestly and within the terms of their agency. If such agents are not protected, persons may in the future be dissuaded from undertaking the role of agent to trusts.

19.6 Dishonest assistance in (or procurement of) a breach of trust

This area of law was dramatically altered by the decision of the Judicial Committee of the Privy Council in *Royal Brunei Airlines* v *Tan* [1995] 3 WLR 64. It had previously been the law that where a dishonest and fraudulent venture had been undertaken by trustees, or other persons in a fiduciary position, a stranger might be liable for knowingly assisting in that design.

Following *Royal Brunei Airlines* v *Tan*, the original design of the trustees need not have been dishonest and fraudulent in order for the stranger to be liable as an accessory. On the contrary, the principal breach might have been quite innocently performed. The focus now is upon the accessory's (the stranger's) state of mind, whereas previously strangers would have been liable only if they had known of the trustees' dishonesty.

Liability under this heading has never been dependent upon the receipt of trust property by the stranger. This is a crucial difference between liability under this head and liability for 'knowing receipt' or 'inconsistent dealing'.

Millett J observed in *Agip (Africa) Ltd* v *Jackson*: 'The basis of the stranger's liability is not receipt of trust property but participation in a fraud.'

 THINKING POINT

Read the following summary of *Royal Brunei Airlines SDN BHD* v *Philip Tan Kok Ming* [1995] 2 AC 378, Privy Council. Was this a case in which the defendant's liability might properly have been described as liability 'as a constructive trustee'?

 CASE CLOSE-UP

Royal Brunei Airlines SDN BHD v *Philip Tan Kok Ming* **[1995] 2 AC 378, Privy Council**

An insolvent travel agency owed monies (ticket receipts) to the plaintiff airline, and held those monies on an express trust for the airline. The present action was brought against the principal director/shareholder of the travel agency. The plaintiffs sought to fix the defendant with liability on the basis of the defendant's knowing assistance in a dishonest and fraudulent design. The 'design' was the use of the airline's monies by the travel agency for its own business purposes in breach of the trust under which those monies were held. It was held that the defendant would be liable on the basis of his dishonest assistance in, or procurement of, the breach of trust. Lord Nicholls observed disapprovingly that courts had restrained themselves within the 'straitjacket' of Lord Selborne's *dictum* in *Barnes* v *Addy* (see earlier), with the result that liability for 'knowing assistance' had been confined to cases where the trustee had been dishonest. Lord Nicholls of Birkenhead considered the hypothetical case of an innocent trustee who is deceived into breaching his trust by a dishonest stranger and asked whether it could be right for the stranger to escape liability in such a case. His Lordship's conclusion was that the emphasis should be switched from the state of the trustee's mind to that of the stranger. Liability should not depend upon the *Baden* categories of knowledge (which his Lordship suggested should be forgotten), but upon whether the stranger had himself been dishonest. His Lordship made it clear that whereas dishonesty is a necessary and sufficient ingredient of accessory liability for breach of trust, 'knowingly' is better avoided as a defining ingredient. An objective test of dishonesty should be adopted, although his Lordship appeared prepared, in determining 'dishonesty', to consider the stranger's 'personal attributes . . . such as his experience and intelligence, and the reason why he acted as he did'.

It was stated at the outset of this chapter that it is inappropriate to describe a stranger's liability as liability 'as a constructive trustee' because the stranger does not control the trust property. That argument still holds good in the typical case of, for example, a solicitor advising a trust, but on the peculiar facts of *Tan* the defendant was actually the controlling director and the shareholder of the 'trustee' company. Accordingly, *Tan* itself is one of the few cases in which the stranger could genuinely be said to have been in control of the trustee, who in turn controlled the trust property. Accordingly, the defendant in *Tan* was sufficiently in control of the trust funds to call him a constructive trustee.

19.6.1 The four requirements for 'dishonest assistance'

The four basic requirements were set out in *Baden v Société Générale* [1983] BCLC 325, but they were modified by *Royal Brunei Airlines v Tan* (see J. Snape and G. Watt, 'A position of trust' (1995) 92(28) LSG 20), so they are now as follows.

19.6.1.1 Existence of a trust

It is not necessary to show that a formal trust exists; a fiduciary relationship is sufficient. So, for example, where a director of a company misappropriates company-owned property by passing it to a third party via the medium of the director's private bank account, the director's bank could be liable for dishonest assistance. There is no requirement for there to be trust property, and even if there were such a requirement, confidential information acquired by a fiduciary is capable of being trust property (*JD Wetherspoon Plc v Van de Berg & Co Ltd* [2009] EWHC 639 (Ch) (approved in *Novoship (UK) Ltd v Nikitin* [2014] EWCA Civ 908, Court of Appeal)).

19.6.1.2 Breach of the trust

Before *Tan* it had to be shown that a dishonest or fraudulent design existed, and that the trustee or fiduciary had been a party to it. It had to be something more than a mere breach of trust, which, as we have seen from previous chapters, can be committed innocently. Since *Tan*, an innocent breach of trust on the part of the principal fiduciary will suffice.

19.6.1.3 Assistance

It has to be shown that there was assistance in the breach of trust, and it must have been of more than minimal importance. This is a question of fact in each case. The 'assistance' requirement could be satisfied by proving that the stranger had been involved in an intermediate step in the process leading to the breach of trust.

Assistance seems to mean some kind of purposive conduct designed to advance and promote the unlawful object which breaches the trust: *Brinks Ltd v Abu-Saleh (No 3)* (1995) Times, 23 October. In this case, the claimant was the victim of a huge bullion heist which had been facilitated by the actions of one of its own employees who was in breach of his fiduciary relationship with the claimant. The claimant's case was that Mrs E, as part of the laundering of the proceeds, had accompanied her husband on trips to Zurich, at the instigation of P, one of those convicted of the robbery. The allegation was of accessory liability against Mrs E. Rimer J found as a matter of fact that Mrs E had simply accompanied her husband in the capacity of his wife and that this could not constitute 'assistance' for the purposes of accessory liability.

19.6.1.4 Dishonesty

Even before *Tan*, the view which generally prevailed in the courts was that a stranger must be shown to have had a dishonest intent in order to be fixed with liability for knowing assistance. As Millett J said in *Agip* at first instance, 'the true distinction is between honesty and dishonesty, and not between various levels of knowledge'. Where the defendant is, say, a solicitor, the test is whether an honest solicitor could have done what the defendant did given the knowledge of the facts that he had. It is not appropriate to apply the benchmark of an honest *and competent* solicitor, because it wrongly applies competency to determine honesty. The difference between negligence and dishonesty is not one of degree ('it is one thing to throw caution to the winds; that is likely to lead to negligent conduct. But even to do that to the nth degree does not involve crossing the dividing line and passing over to dishonesty': *Republic of Zambia* v *Meer Care & Desai (a firm)* [2008] EWCA Civ 1007 (CA)).

THINKING POINT

Tan has made the stranger's 'dishonesty' and not that of the principal/trustee/fiduciary the trigger of liability. Can you think of any justification for this change of emphasis?

Lord Nicholls considered the hypothetical case of a dishonest solicitor who had induced a trustee to misapply trust property in a manner which the trustee honestly believed to be permitted by the terms of his trust, but which the solicitor was fully aware constituted a breach of trust. 'It cannot be right', said his Lordship, 'that in such a case the accessory liability principle would be inapplicable because of the innocence of the trustee'. In the past, the error has been, he said, to make the principal's state of mind a prerequisite to the accessory's liability. The better view is to establish the accessory's liability on the basis of the accessory's own state of mind.

The developments in *Tan* did not represent a wholly novel departure from the existing law, but did bring clarity to the conflicting views expressed in lower courts. Since *Tan* it has been clear that dishonesty is a necessary ingredient of liability for 'knowing' assistance, which is why the label 'dishonest assistance' is used in this chapter. (The House of Lords in *Twinsectra Ltd* v *Yardley* [2002] 2 AC 164 approved Lord Nicholls' analysis in *Tan*: see 19.6.3, where the definition of dishonesty is considered at length.)

In fact, as long ago as 1969, the Court of Appeal had favoured an approach based on the defendant's dishonesty. *Carl Zeiss Stiftung* [1969] 2 Ch 276 was a unanimous decision of the Court of Appeal. On the question whether constructive notice or knowledge (the court preferred the neutral term 'cognisance') would suffice to establish liability for knowing assistance, Sachs LJ stated:

> It does not . . . seem to me that a stranger is necessarily liable even if it is established that he has such notice. As at present advised I am inclined to the view that a further element has to be proved, at any rate in a case such as the present one. That element is one of dishonesty or of consciously acting improperly, as opposed to an innocent failure to make what a court may later decide to have been proper inquiry.

This was confirmed, *obiter*, by the Court of Appeal in *Polly Peck International plc* v *Nadir (No 2)* [1992] 4 All ER 769 (a case primarily concerned with liability for knowing receipt), where Scott LJ opined that 'something amounting to dishonesty or want of probity must be shown'.

In *Polly Peck* Hoffmann LJ made an illuminating comparison between the actions for knowing assistance (which was subsequently relabelled 'dishonest assistance') and knowing receipt, and also clarified their common law counterparts. Hoffmann LJ stated that:

> [l]iability for knowing assistance is based upon wrongful conduct, namely knowing participation in a fraudulent breach of trust or fiduciary duty. Its common law analogy is conspiracy to defraud. Liability for knowing receipt is restitutionary, based upon the beneficial receipt of money or property known to belong in equity to somebody else. The equitable remedy depends upon the existence of a trust or fiduciary duty, but the breach of trust or duty need not have been fraudulent. The nearest common law analogy is money had and received.

Any commercial agent (such as a bank) that is in a real dilemma as to the propriety of a proposed course of action is well advised to apply to the court under r 40.20 of the Civil Procedure Rules, which provides simply that '[t]he court may make binding declarations whether or not any other remedy is claimed'. (See also, for interim declaratory relief, r 25.1(1)(b).) As Lord Woolf CJ observed in *Governor and Co of the Bank of Scotland v A Ltd* [2001] 1 WLR 751:

> it seems almost inconceivable that a bank which takes the initiative in seeking the court's guidance should subsequently be held to have acted dishonestly so as to incur accessory liability. The involvement of the court should . . . enable, in the great majority of cases, a practical solution to be determined which protects the interests of the public but allows the interests of a bank to be safeguarded.

19.6.2 The relationship between knowledge and dishonesty in cases of dishonest assistance

In *Tan* their Lordships substituted for the 'knowledge' requirement a requirement that the accessory be shown to have been 'dishonest'. Lord Nicholls stated that 'their Lordships' overall conclusion is that dishonesty is a necessary ingredient of liability. It is also a sufficient ingredient . . . "Knowingly" is better avoided as a defining ingredient of the principle, and in the context of this principle the *Baden* scale of knowledge is best forgotten.' However, Rimer J in *Brinks v Abu Saleh (No 3)* held that it is still necessary to show that the defendant had knowledge of the existence of a trust (or fiduciary) relationship, or at least of facts giving rise to such a trust. In *Heinl v Jyske Bank (Gibraltar) Ltd* [1999] Lloyd's Rep Bank 511 the Court of Appeal, purporting to follow *Tan*, held that 'dishonesty' means conscious impropriety and should be determined by reference to the third party's actual knowledge of the facts leading to the breach. Where Lord Nicholls had urged that the *Baden* scale of knowledge should be forgotten, Nourse LJ suggested that the *Baden* scale might still be useful in distinguishing different shades of knowledge. It is clear, however, that the defendant's knowledge is bound to inform the determination of the defendant's honesty or dishonesty. Lord Nicholls himself stated that 'in most situations there is little difficulty in identifying how an honest person would behave . . . an honest person does not participate in a transaction if he *knows* it involves a misapplication of trust assets' (emphasis added).

19.6.3 Defining dishonesty

Dishonesty is not as easy to define as one might think. For example, was Robin Hood dishonest?

 OUTSIDE THE BOX

J. Walker McSpadden, *Robin Hood*, 1904

'A yeoman am I, from Lockesley town. Men call me Robin Hood.'

'The saints forefend that you should treat me ill!' said the butcher in terror. 'Oft have I heard of you, and how you lighten the purses of the fat priests and knights. But I am naught but a poor butcher, selling this load of meat, perchance, for enough to pay my quarter's rent.'

'Rest you, my friend, rest you,' quoth Robin, 'not so much as a silver penny would I take from you, for I love an honest Saxon face and a fair name with my neighbours.'

The test of 'dishonesty' adopted by Lord Nicholls in *Tan* is, he says, 'an objective standard'; if a person knowingly appropriates another's property, he will not escape a finding of dishonesty 'simply because he sees nothing wrong in such behaviour'. Having said that, later on in Lord

Nicholls' judgment subjective considerations enter into this 'objective test'. He says that 'when called upon to decide whether a person was acting honestly, a court will look at all the circumstances known to the third party at the time. The court will also have regard to the personal attributes of the third party such as his experience and intelligence and the reason why he acted as he did.'

Lord Nicholls, when attempting to capture 'the flavour' of dishonesty in *Tan*, had approved Knox J in *Cowan de Groot Properties Ltd* v *Eagle Trust plc* [1992] 4 All ER 700, who had held that dishonesty is evidenced by 'commercially unacceptable conduct in the particular context involved'. Lindsay J in *HRT* suggested that this formulation could be misunderstood:

> It may, for example, be in one sense 'commercially unacceptable' for a bank to lend money without security or without investigating the title to the security it is offered by its borrower. It may thus be 'unacceptable' because too risky, but if the bank chooses to do so because, for example, it genuinely trusts the personal covenant of the borrower or is truly content to rely upon his assertion of his own beneficial title to the security he offers, that may involve conduct which is 'commercially unacceptable', if at all, only in relation to the bank's own position.

The complex question of the meaning of dishonesty in the context of accessory liability for 'dishonest assistance' finally came before the House of Lords in *Twinsectra Ltd* v *Yardley* [2002] 2 AC 164. Their Lordships held (Lord Millett dissenting) that the test to be applied is a combined subjective/objective test: a defendant will only be held to have been dishonest if it can be shown that *he knew* that ordinary honest people would have considered his actions to have been dishonest. Their Lordships were reluctant to apply a purely objective test when the outcome would be to stigmatise the defendant (often a professional person) as being 'dishonest'. (*Clydesdale Bank plc* v *John Workman* [2016] EWCA Civ 73, Court of Appeal, is similar in that respect.)

Lord Millett seemed equally concerned to avoid the casual imposition of that stigma, but his solution was to suggest that dishonest assistance should revert to its former description 'knowing assistance', with knowledge being the primary test of dishonesty. He combined this suggestion with his belief that the test for dishonesty should be a purely objective one—the defendant should be measured against an objective standard, albeit allowing that the objective standard against which the defendant is measured may be varied according to the defendant's subjective characteristics (i.e. a lower standard should be applied when judging the behaviour of a junior bank clerk than would be applied when judging a senior bank manager). All their Lordships purported to approve and apply the analysis adopted by Lord Nicholls in *Tan* so it may be somewhat surprising that they did not agree in their approach. It is this author's respectful submission that the test adopted by Lord Millett (an objective test appropriate to the subjective characteristics of the defendant) comes closest to that suggested by Lord Nicholls, but the majority were correct to conclude that Lord Nicholls intended to remove 'knowledge' as a defining ingredient. There is, however, much force in Lord Millett's argument (in spite of Lord Nicholls' apparent opinion to the contrary) that 'knowing assistance' would be a more appropriate description of this head of liability.

 CASE CLOSE-UP

***Twinsectra Ltd* v *Yardley* [2002] 2 AC 164, House of Lords**

Facts: Mr Yardley borrowed £1 million from Twinsectra Ltd. Leach, a solicitor, acted for Mr Yardley in connection with the loan, but did not deal directly with Twinsectra. Twinsectra dealt with another firm of solicitors, 'Sims', who represented themselves as acting on behalf of Mr Yardley. Sims paid the money to Leach and he paid it on to Yardley. Sims gave the following undertaking to Twinsectra:

- the loan monies will be retained by us until such time as they are applied in the acquisition of property on behalf of our client;
- the loan monies will be utilised solely for the acquisition of property on behalf of our client and for no other purposes;
- we will repay to you the £1 million together with interest calculated at the rate of £657.53, such payment to be made within four calendar months after receipt of the loan monies by us.

Contrary to the terms of the undertaking, Sims did not retain the money until it was applied in the acquisition of property by Yardley. On being given an assurance by Yardley that it would be so applied, they paid it to Leach. He in turn did not take steps to ensure that it was utilised solely for the acquisition of property on behalf of Yardley. He simply paid it out upon Yardley's instructions. The result was that £357,720.11 was used by Yardley for purposes other than the acquisition of property. The loan was not repaid. Twinsectra sued all the parties involved, including Leach. The claim against him was for the £357,720.11 which had not been used to buy property. The basis of the claim was that the payment by Sims to Leach in breach of the undertaking was a breach of trust and that Leach was liable for dishonestly assisting in that breach of trust.

Held: their Lordships allowed Mr Leach's appeal (Lord Millett dissenting).

Lord Hutton (with the majority) suggested that there are three possible standards which can be applied to determine whether a person has acted dishonestly: 'there is a purely subjective standard, whereby a person is only regarded as dishonest if he transgresses his own standard of honesty, even if that standard is contrary to that of reasonable and honest people. This has been termed the "Robin Hood test" and has been rejected by the courts. [See, for example, Sir Christopher Slade in *Walker* v *Stones* [2001] 2 WLR 623] . . . Secondly, there is a purely objective standard whereby a person acts dishonestly if his conduct is dishonest by the ordinary standards of reasonable and honest people, even if he does not realise this. Thirdly, there is a standard which combines an objective test and a subjective test, and which requires that before there can be a finding of dishonesty it must be established that the defendant's conduct was dishonest by the ordinary standards of reasonable and honest people and that he himself realised that by those standards his conduct was dishonest. I will term this "the combined test".'

Lord Hutton, approving 'the combined test', held that 'for liability as an accessory to arise the defendant must himself appreciate that what he was doing was dishonest by the standards of honest and reasonable men. A finding by a judge that a defendant has been dishonest is a grave finding, and it is particularly grave against a professional man, such as a solicitor. Notwithstanding that the issue arises in equity law and not in a criminal context, I think that it would be less than just for the law to permit a finding that a defendant had been "dishonest" in assisting in a breach of trust where he knew of the facts which created the trust and its breach but had not been aware that what he was doing would be regarded by honest men as being dishonest.'

Lord Millett expressed the contrary view thus: 'in my opinion Lord Nicholls was adopting an objective standard of dishonesty by which the defendant is expected to attain the standard which would be observed by an honest person placed in similar circumstances. Account must be taken of subjective considerations such as the defendant's experience and intelligence and his actual state of knowledge at the relevant time. But it is not necessary that he should actually have appreciated that he was acting dishonestly; it is sufficient that he was.'

And on the question of describing this head of liability, his Lordship asked: 'should we return to the traditional description of the claim as "knowing assistance", reminding ourselves that nothing less than actual knowledge is sufficient; or should we adopt Lord Nicholls' description of the claim as "dishonest assistance", reminding ourselves that the test is an objective one?'

He concluded: 'for my own part, I have no difficulty in equating the knowing mishandling of money with dishonest conduct. But the introduction of dishonesty is an unnecessary distraction, and conducive to error. Many judges would be reluctant to brand a professional man as dishonest where he was unaware that honest people would consider his conduct to be so. If the condition of liability is intentional wrongdoing and not conscious dishonesty as understood in the criminal courts, I think that we should return to the traditional description of this head of equitable liability as arising from "knowing assistance".'

Lord Hutton's test is a departure from that of Lord Nicholls in *Tan*. Lord Hutton's 'combined' test of dishonesty, with its clear subjective element (the defendant will not be liable if *he truly did not know* that objective onlookers would consider his actions dishonest), is not the same as Lord Nicholls' purely 'objective' analysis (the defendant is liable if objective onlookers would consider his actions dishonest). Despite this, the Privy Council has adopted a generous construction of Lord Hutton's speech to reach the conclusion that Lord Hutton was in fact in agreement with Lord Nicholls in *Tan* (see next).

CASE CLOSE-UP

Barlow Clowes International Ltd (in liquidation) v Eurotrust International Ltd [2005] UKPC 37; [2006] 1 All ER 333; [2005] 1 Lloyd's Rep 225, Privy Council

Facts: the case concerned a fraudulent off-shore investment scheme operated by Mr Clowes through Barlow Clowes International Ltd during the mid-1980s. He attracted about £140 million, mainly from small UK investors. Most of the money was spent for the personal benefit of Mr Clowes and his associates. Mr Clowes was eventually convicted and sent to prison. Some of the investors' funds were paid away during 1987 through bank accounts maintained by a company called International Trust Corporation (Isle of Man) Ltd ('ITC'). In proceedings in the High Court of the Isle of Man, Barlow Clowes (now in liquidation) claimed that the directors of ITC and, through them, ITC itself, dishonestly assisted Mr Clowes and one of his principal associates, Mr Cramer, to misappropriate the investors' funds.

Held: (following *Twinsectra Ltd v Yardley* [2002] 2 AC 164) that '[s]omeone can know, and can certainly suspect, that he is assisting in a misappropriation of money without knowing that the money is held on trust or what a trust means' and 'it was not necessary to know the "precise involvement" of Mr Cramer in the group's affairs in order to suspect that neither he nor anyone else had the right to use Barlow Clowes' money for speculative investments of their own.'

Lord Hoffmann: 'their Lordships accept that there is an element of ambiguity in [Lord Hutton's speech in *Twinsectra*] which may have encouraged a belief, expressed in some academic writing, that *Twinsectra* had departed from the law as previously understood and invited inquiry not merely into the defendant's mental state about the nature of the transaction in which he was participating but also into his views about generally acceptable standards of honesty. But they do not consider that this is what Lord Hutton meant. The reference to "what he knows would offend normally accepted standards of honest conduct" meant only that his knowledge of the transaction had to be such as to render his participation contrary to normally acceptable standards of honest conduct. It did not require that he should have had reflections about what those normally acceptable standards were.'

[NOTE: *Barlow Clowes* was followed in *Abou-Rahmah* v *Abacha* [2006] EWCA Civ 1492 (CA).]

In *Starglade Properties Ltd* v *Nash* [2010] EWCA Civ 1314, the Court of Appeal confirmed that the standard by which 'dishonesty' is tested does not vary just because some people might think that the standard is set too high: 'There is a single standard of honesty objectively determined by the court. That standard is applied to specific conduct of a specific individual possessing the knowledge and qualities he actually enjoyed' [para. 25].

 THINKING POINT

'It may be that unresolved conceptual difficulties relating to strangers' liability are no bad thing as equity seeks flexible tools to rationalise the complex transactional environment of the modern commercial world' (S. Gardner, 'Knowing Assistance and Knowing Receipt: Taking Stock' (1996) 112 LQR 56).

 # Summary

Figure 19.1 provides a diagrammatic summary of the main points of this chapter.

? Summative assessment exercise

Mr Sleeson, a solicitor, is a sole practitioner with access to his clients' accounts. He withdrew money from 'the client account' and placed it in his own private bank account which he holds with the Nelson Westminster Bank. Later, he withdrew monies from his private account and played at a casino in the city. He placed the winnings and the original withdrawals in his private account at the bank. This happened regularly and the bank manager suspected that something might be amiss, but turned a blind eye to Mr Sleeson's activities.

Eventually, Mr Sleeson 'went for the big gamble', lost all his money, and was declared bankrupt. The casino manager had accepted his bets because he 'knew that solicitors made a lot of money'.

Advise Mr Sleeson's clients who now seek to recover their lost funds.

 Full specimen answers can be found at www.oxfordtextbooks.co.uk/orc/watt_directions5e/.

Figure 19.1 Chapter summary

The bigger picture

Should the equitable liability of strangers to trusts be treated as a common law tort?

Professor Peter Birks said, some years before *Tan* (in the 1990–1 Butterworth Lectures), that 'there is no respectable modern reason why knowing assistance should not be regarded as a tort' ('knowing assistance' was, of course, the direct precursor to 'dishonest assistance'). Unfortunately, the Privy Council in *Tan* omitted to consider the potential of tortious liability as an alternative to liability as a constructive trustee in cases of assistance by strangers in breaches of trust. This omission is all the more surprising given that Lord Nicholls, delivering the opinion of the Judicial Committee of the Privy Council, made express reference to the related tort of procuring a breach of contract. As things stand at present, the tort of procurement of a breach of trust has not yet been acknowledged in the highest courts, although Hoffmann LJ in *Law Debenture Corpn v Ural Caspian Ltd* [1993] 2 All ER 355 added his support to the recognition of such a tort. The House of Lords in *Dubai Aluminium Co Ltd v Salaam* [2002] 3 WLR 1913 confirmed the orthodox view (see *Metall und Rohstoff AG v Donaldson Lufkin & Jenrette Inc* [1990] 1 QB 391) that procurement of, or assistance in, a breach of trust is not a tort, but the similarity between equitable liability for dishonest assistance and tortious liability at common law was made clear in that case by their Lordships' decision to hold that the partners of a solicitor liable for dishonest assistance may be held vicariously liable where the acts of dishonest assistance were rendered in the ordinary course of the firm's business. It has even been suggested that the equitable wrong of dishonest assistance should only be distinguished from tort for the purposes of domestic law and that 'its proper characterisation for the purposes of private international law is as a tort' (*OJSC Oil Company Yugraneft (in liquidation) v Abramovich* [2008] EWHC 2613 (Comm)).

 ## Further reading

Elliott, S.B. and Mitchell, C. 'Remedies for Dishonest Assistance' (2004) 67(1) MLR 16
considers types of compensation—substitutive and reparative

Gardner, S. 'Knowing Assistance and Knowing Receipt: Taking Stock' (1996) 112 LQR 56
an excellent article which doubts the faith we put in strict categories of liability

Gardner, S. [a note on the decision of the Court of Appeal in *City Index Ltd v Gawler* [2008] Ch 313] (2009) 125 LQR 20
argues that knowing receipt should be seen as a species of the normal trustee liability for failure to preserve trust property, which just happens to apply to those who are trustees because they receive illicitly transferred trust property

Lord Nicholls of Birkenhead, 'Knowing receipt: The need for a new landmark' in W.R. Cornish et al. (eds), *Restitution Past Present and Future: Essays in Honour of Gareth Jones* (1998) Oxford: Hart Publishing 231
a paper written extrajudicially by one of our leading judges. It argues for strict liability for knowing receipt.

 For links to selected cases, statutes, academic papers and official reports mentioned in this chapter please visit the online resources at www.oup.com/uk/watt_directions6e/.

20 Equity: doctrines and remedies

Introduction

Your legal studies are going very well, but you decide to audition for a TV talent show just to be on the safe side. You are successful and are chosen to sing in a newly created pop group. All goes well at first, but your launch gig is scheduled to take place on the day of your final examination in equity and trusts. You wouldn't miss that for the world and you refuse to perform unless a new date can be arranged. The manager of the group knows it would be pointless to sue you for common law damages, so he seeks the equitable remedy of specific performance in order to require you to take part in the launch gig. You are outraged, and decide to seek the equitable remedy of rescission to bring the contract with the manager to an end on the ground that the manager misrepresented before the contract that you could continue with your studies. You also seek an injunction prohibiting any performance of the group's 'launch' song without you, and (as you were the one who wrote it) you seek a search order to enter the manager's premises to seize the master disks of the studio recording so as to prevent the manager from distributing your song. By the end of this chapter you will have a good idea of your prospects of success.

Strange as it may seem, the preceding scenario represents the 'real world' of equitable remedies; pop groups and artists figure prominently in the modern cases. That said, there is no hiding the fact that the leading cases on equitable doctrines and remedies are often very old. We learned in Chapter 1 that equity is a body of law developed originally by the old Court of Chancery in constructive competition with the common law courts, but now applied (since the Judicature Acts 1873–5) by the unified Supreme Court of England and Wales. We also learned that equity, as a dimension of law, still performs the special function of restraining or restricting the exercise of legal rights and powers in particular cases, whenever it would be unconscionable for such rights and powers to be exercised to the full. In this chapter we will examine particular doctrines and remedies which have been developed over many centuries to help predict the way in which equity will operate in various types of case.

20.1 Equitable doctrines

❯ CROSS REFERENCE

See especially the maxims *equity imputes an intention to fulfil an obligation* and *equity sees as done that which ought to be done.*

It is not altogether clear what should and should not be included in the list of equitable doctrines. For example, should equitable estoppel (which we examined in Chapter 17) be included? It has been decided to include here only those well-defined doctrines which appear in the orthodox list. They were undoubtedly more significant historically than they are now, but we will examine them briefly because they still offer a valuable insight into the nature and operation of equity today.

20.1.1 Conversion

By the doctrine of conversion, 'money directed to be employed in the purchase of land, and land directed to be sold and turned into money, are to be considered as that species of property into which they are directed to be converted' (*Fletcher v Ashburner* (1779) 1 Bro CC 497, *per* Sir Thomas Sewell MR at 499). We considered an important example of this process in

Chapter 1, when we examined the specific performance of a contract for the sale of land. We saw that whereas at law the contract entitles the purchaser to a personal monetary remedy (damages), equity will order specific performance of the contract, and since specific performance ought to be done in the future, equity will consider it as done now. By this feat of imagination equity converts the purchaser's future right to personal damages into a present right in real property.

The doctrine of conversion as it applies to convert land into money is now of reduced relevance. Previously, where a trustee held land under a 'trust for sale', the trustee was deemed already to have sold the land, in accordance with the maxim *equity sees as done that which ought to be done*. Section 3 of the Trusts of Land and Appointment of Trustees Act 1996 has now abolished the doctrine of conversion in relation to trusts of land, with the result that land is no longer deemed to be money and money is no longer deemed to be land. However, a trust for sale of land created in a will taking effect before 1 January 1997 will still operate to convert the land into money or, where appropriate (as where personal property is subject to a trust for sale in order that the trustees may acquire land), to convert money into land.

Although the doctrine of conversion no longer operates to convert land into money by notionally regarding trusts for the sale of land as trusts of the proceeds of sale, it does still operate to convert money into land by notionally regarding contracts for the sale of land as having already sold the land to the purchaser. Therefore, even before the sale has been completed, this makes the purchaser the notional holder, not of purchase money, but of a present beneficial interest in the land (*Jerome v Kelly (Inspector of Taxes)* [2004] 1 WLR 1409 (HL)).

20.1.2 Reconversion

> **reconversion** 'That notional or imaginary process by which a prior notional conversion is annulled or discharged, and the notionally converted property restored . . . to its original actual quality' (*Snell's Equity*, 20th edn, Sweet & Maxwell, 1929).

The doctrine of **reconversion** is based on the following quaint maxim: 'equity, like nature, does nothing in vain' (*Benson v Benson* (1710) 1 P Wms 130). It applies to reverse conversion where conversion would be pointless, as where there is a sole adult beneficiary under a trust for sale of land and that beneficiary wishes to own the land absolutely as land and does not want his trustees to treat the land as if it had already been sold. The doctrine of conversion does not operate on trusts of land created since 1997, so the doctrine of reconversion is likely to be of historical interest only in the land context. It will still apply to other assets, such as shares. A case in that category is *Lloyds Bank plc v Duker* [1987] 1 WLR 1324 (see Figure 20.1), in which a wife was left a significant fraction (46/80ths) of her husband's residuary estate. She therefore claimed

Figure 20.1 *Lloyd's Bank plc v Duker*

to be entitled to 574 of her husband's 999 shares in a certain company (the company had a total of 1,000 issued shares). In fact, she never received the shares during her lifetime, and at her death left everything to Mr Duker.

The other beneficiaries objected that because he would be getting a majority shareholding in the company (which is worth more per share than any other holding), he would be acquiring more than the 46/80ths *value* of the estate to which he was entitled. They requested a sale of all the shares on the open market and an appropriate division of the proceeds. It was held that the executor had a duty to sell the shares. From this it followed that there had already been a notional sale and conversion into money in the hands of the executors (although the judge didn't expressly analyse it this way), and by ordering the sale to be carried out, Mr Duker's claim (although he didn't expressly put it this way) to have the notional sale proceeds reconverted into the company shares failed.

20.1.3 **Satisfaction**

The Rolling Stones could 'get no satisfaction', but then they probably never studied equity and trusts. Where A owes a sum of money to B, equity will require A to pay the debt while he is alive. However, if the debt has not been paid by the time of A's death and A's will contains no clause requiring his executors to repay his debts, a legacy (a bequest of a sum of money) left by A to B in his will is presumed to satisfy any outstanding debt for an equal or lesser sum owed by A to B prior to making his will. Equity sees as done that which ought to be done and imputes to A an intention to fulfil his obligation to B, provided the legacy is on terms which are as beneficial to B as repayment of the debt.

in loco parentis
'In the parent's place'. A guardian is said to stand in loco parentis to the child in his or her care (pronounced: 'inn low-co pair-entiss').

Another example of the operation of the doctrine is so-called ademption of a legacy by a portion. Where a child is bequeathed a specific legacy (such as '£1,000') in the will of a parent or person **in loco parentis** and that person, having written the will but before death, makes a lifetime donation in the same or greater sum and in substantially the same kind, the legacy can no longer be taken. It is said to have been satisfied by the lifetime donation through the process of 'ademption'. If the lifetime donation is for a lesser sum, the legacy can be taken to the extent of the difference only. Whether or not there is an ademption always turns, ultimately, on the presumed intention of the donor (*Hopwood* v *Hopwood* (1859) 22 Beav 488).

20.1.4 **Performance**

The doctrine of performance is a close relation to the doctrine of satisfaction and both doctrines share a common root in the maxim *equity imputes an intention to fulfil an obligation*. However, whereas one type of obligation, such as a debt, may be *satisfied* by something quite different, such as a legacy, *performance* always involves an action of the same kind as that which would be required to perform the particular obligation. Thus a promise by A that he will leave a legacy to B will be performed if A dies intestate (without making a valid will) and money passes to B on A's intestacy. Likewise, if A promises to acquire freehold land of a certain value and settle it on trust for the benefit of his wife-to-be, the purchase of freehold land of a lesser value may be held to be a partial performance of the promise (*Lechmere* v *Lady Lechmere* (1735) Cas t Talb 80). In that case there would have been no performance if A had acquired leasehold land because that is fundamentally different in type from the freehold land promised.

20.1.5 **Election**

The doctrine of election requires a party to choose between mutually exclusive courses of action. The common law version of the doctrine requires a claimant to choose between mutually inconsistent remedies before judgment is entered in his favour (on this form of election, see Chapter 15). In equity the doctrine provides that where a court judgment or a written instrument such as a will (*Codrington* v *Codrington* (1875) LR 7 HL 854) or trust deed confers a benefit on a certain person, that person must choose to take the benefit subject to *all* the requirements of the judgment or instrument, or else to reject the judgment or instrument and lose the benefits conferred by it (see, for example, *Frear* v *Frear* [2008] EWCA Civ 1320).

Despite its name, the equitable doctrine does not *confer* a right to choose; rather, it *restricts* the right to choose in the interest of fairness between the parties by ensuring that no party takes a benefit without taking an associated burden (*Nexus Communications Group Ltd* v *Lambert* [2005] EWHC 345, ChD). The equitable doctrine of election has its roots in the maxim *quod approbo non reprobo*: 'that which I approve, I cannot reject.' A modern example is provided by *First National Bank plc* v *Walker* (2001) 1 FLR 505, where the Court of Appeal held that a wife who was awarded the matrimonial home in divorce proceedings and had accepted the mortgage on the house as part of the award was not permitted, in subsequent repossession proceedings brought by the bank, to allege that the mortgage was invalid. She had elected to take the house and could not in conscience take it free of the mortgage.

20.1.6 **Summative exercise on equitable doctrines**

Table 20.1 contains the list of equitable doctrines in the left-hand column, and the right-hand column describes the various doctrines. Draw a line linking the doctrine to its proper description.

Table 20.1 **Equitable doctrines**

Conversion	Deems money to be land or other property, and deems property to be money (Choice C)
Reconversion	Reverses the process by which money is deemed to be land or other property, and property is deemed to be money (Choice D)
Satisfaction	Presumes that a legacy left by A to B in his will was intended to satisfy any outstanding debt for an equal or lesser sum owed by A to B prior to making his will (Choice E)
Ademption of a legacy by a portion	In certain cases deems a monetary gift in a will to have been satisfied by a lifetime donation made after the will was written where the donor is *in loco parentis* to the donee (Choice B)
Performance	Deems that an obligation to do a certain thing in a particular way is discharged in whole or in part by the act of doing the same thing in a different way (Choice F)
Election	This doctrine prevents a party from blowing hot and cold by taking the benefits of a transaction without taking the corresponding disadvantages (Choice A)

The solution (listed here in reverse order, so you don't cheat) is AFBEDC.

20.2 Equitable remedies

20.2.1 General

In *Co-Operative Insurance Society Ltd v Argyll Stores (Holdings) Ltd* [1998] AC 1 (HL), Lord Hoffmann affirmed that equitable remedies are 'flexible and adaptable to achieve the ends of equity'. But what are 'the ends of equity'? His Lordship approved the view expressed by the Lord Chancellor in *Wilson v Northampton and Banbury Junction Railway Co* (1874) LR 9 Ch App 279 at 284 that the purpose of equitable relief is to 'do more perfect and complete justice' than would be the result of leaving the parties to their remedies at common law.

The usual common law remedy for breach of contract or commission of a tort is an award of damages, but where in a particular case, or in a particular type of case, it would be unconscionable for the defendant to restrict the claimant to common law damages the court may award an equitable remedy against the defendant. For example, an injunction may be awarded to remedy the tort of trespass and the court may decree specific performance of a contract to acquire land, for in both these cases an award of damages is insufficient to achieve a just outcome: in the former case because an award of damages will be nominal unless real harm has been caused, and in any event an award of damages does not prevent future trespass; in the latter case because even if an award of damages were competent to meet the purchaser's legitimate expectations as to the investment value of the land, no amount of money will assist the purchaser to buy identical substitute land, since all land is unique.

20.2.1.1 Discretionary nature

Whereas common law remedies are available as of right, equitable remedies retain the discretionary nature of the early equitable jurisdiction, although the onset over the past two centuries or so of defined systems of precedent and law reporting have curtailed the original discretion somewhat, so that discretion is now exercised in accordance with fairly clear and sometimes rigid principles. We have already noted that the discretionary nature of equitable remedies can lead to the refusal of a remedy where the defendant comes to equity with unclean hands, but entirely innocent claimants may also be denied a remedy where to grant it would put the other party in breach of a contract with a third party (see *Warmington v Miller* [1973] QB 877). Other grounds for refusing an equitable remedy include the possibility that severe hardship will be caused to the defendant (reflected in the maxim *those who come to equity must do equity*). The question whether to award an equitable remedy calls for the court to exercise a very broad discretion. The court asks itself: '[i]s it just, in all the circumstances, that a plaintiff should be confined to his remedy in damages?' (*Evans Marshall & Co Ltd v Bertola SA* [1973] 1 WLR 349, *per* Sachs LJ).

20.2.1.2 Equitable remedies operate *in personam*

> *in personam* 'Against the person' or 'personal'. A remedy, such as an injunction, is said to operate *in personam* because it is enforced against a defendant personally. An *in personam* action is normally contrasted with an action *in rem*, which is a claim against property held by the defendant regardless of the defendant's identity.

An equitable remedy is awarded **in personam** against the particular defendant. It is not a law as such, but a direct order of the court against the individual. Failure to comply with the order is a contempt of court punishable by fine or imprisonment. However, the fact that remedies are sought *in personam* doesn't always mean that the defendant must be named. It can be sufficient to identify the defendant by description provided it is certain enough to enable potential defendants to be identified and distinguished from persons who are not potential defendants (*Bloomsbury Publishing Group Ltd* v *News Group Newspapers Ltd* [2003] 1 WLR 1633; *Hampshire Waste Services Ltd* v *Intending Trespassers upon Chineham Incinerator Site* [2004] Env LR 9). The fact that equitable remedies operate *in personam* means that they bind the persons against whom they are addressed and do not bind other persons (but see 20.2.3.7).

20.2.1.3 Final or interim remedy?

Equitable remedies are sometimes awarded as part of the final judgment in a matter, but some can also be awarded as interim remedies. Amongst the interim remedies listed as available under r 25.1 of the Civil Procedure Rules 1999 are injunctions, freezing orders and search orders, all of which are considered in detail in this chapter. In the process of examining individual remedies we will discover that there are a great many safeguards in place to ensure that the claimant does not gain an unfair advantage and that the defendant does not suffer an unfair detriment from the award of interim remedies.

20.2.2 Specific performance

At common law the person who makes a contractual promise has the option to perform or not perform. He might choose to breach his promise and to pay damages. In this sense equity is something of a spoilsport, for equity requires a promise to be performed whenever damages would not be an adequate remedy. However, because an order or 'decree' of specific performance is (like all equitable remedies) discretionary, it will be refused if the claimant has not kept his side of the bargain. This is in accordance with the maxim *those who come to equity must come with clean hands*.

We have already noted that specific performance is only available where damages are inadequate. The reason for this is that the decree of specific performance is ordered to remedy unconscionability, and there is nothing unconscionable in offering damages where they are adequate. This leaves us with the task of determining when common law damages are and are not 'adequate'. In the following sections we will see that the adequacy of damages turns to a large extent upon the nature of the subject matter of the contract that has been breached. The availability of specific performance can also turn on pragmatic considerations such as extreme difficulty in quantifying damages and political considerations such as the protection of free speech (even if it is the free speech of a far-right group: see *Verrall* v *Great Yarmouth Borough Council* [1981] QB 202, where the court ordered specific performance of a licence to occupy premises in which it was intended to hold a National Front conference).

Specific performance is a court order to perform a specific positive obligation, typically a contractual obligation. Whereas some equitable remedies, such as certain injunctions, may be ordered as interim measures before the final hearing of a matter, specific performance is a final order made only at the conclusion of the full trial.

20.2.2.1 Land

We considered specific performance of land at 1.2.5. We noted there that all land is unique (even identical homes on modern housing estates are located in utterly unique portions of three-dimensional space, benefiting from subtly distinct views, lighting, shade and so forth) and this means that there is a very strong presumption in favour of specific performance of contracts for the sale of land.

20.2.2.2 **Personal property**

Damages will usually be adequate where the contract was to purchase personal property, such as chairs (even antique 'Hepplewhite' chairs, provided they could be considered 'ordinary articles of commerce': see *Cohen* v *Roche* [1927] 1 KB 169). Damages are adequate in such cases because, as the Vice-Chancellor put it in *Falcke* v *Gray* (1859) 4 Drew 651, 'you only have to go into the market' to 'buy another equally good article', but damages will not be adequate where the property is unique or equivalent property cannot be readily acquired on the open market; such was the case in *Falcke* v *Gray* itself, where the subject of the contract was a pair of antique china vases of 'unusual beauty and rarity' (although specific performance was in that case refused on other grounds). Nor will damages be adequate where the property is of 'peculiar and practically unique value to the plaintiff.' (*Behnke* v *Bede Shipping Co* [1927] 1 KB 649. In this case an experienced ship valuer gave evidence that he was aware of 'only one other comparable ship'.)

20.2.2.3 **Sale of goods**

According to the Sale of Goods Act 1979, s 52(1), '[i]n any action for breach of contract to deliver specific or ascertained goods the court may, if it thinks fit, on the plaintiff's application, by its judgment or decree direct that the contract shall be performed specifically, without giving the defendant the option of retaining the goods on payment of damages.'

20.2.2.4 **Shares**

See *Oughtred* v *IRC* and *Neville* v *Wilson* at 3.2.1.

20.2.2.5 **Contracts of employment, contracts for services and contracts for a particular service**

The Trade Union and Labour Relations (Consolidation) Act 1992, s 236 prohibits any court order for specific performance of a contract of employment and any injunction which would compel an employee to do any work or attend at any place for the doing of any work. There are a number of reasons for this rule, and the reasons explain why the courts will generally refuse to order specific performance of *any* contract to provide on-going personal services, whether or not it is an actual contract of employment.

One reason is public policy: 'Courts are bound to be jealous, lest they should turn contracts of service into contracts of slavery' (*De Francesco* v *Barnum* (1889) 45 ChD 430). The risk of enforcing something akin to slavery is increased where the contract requires the service provider to work closely with someone over a prolonged period of time with whom they do not wish to work.

Another reason is the problem of supervision. If the contract is to perform a defined task, the court will not order specific performance if the contract cannot practically be enforced: as the maxim says, 'equity will not act in vain'. So, for example, trying to force a pop star to produce an album will be pointless if he or she might deliberately produce a bad one: see next.

 CASE CLOSE-UP

CH Giles & Co Ltd v Morris [1972] 1 WLR 307, ChD

Megarry J: 'if a singer contracts to sing, there could no doubt be proceedings for committal if, ordered to sing, the singer remained obstinately dumb. But if instead the singer sang flat, or sharp, or too fast, or too slowly, or too loudly, or too quietly, or resorted to a dozen of the manifestations of temperament traditionally associated with some singers, the threat of committal would reveal itself as a most unsatisfactory weapon: for who could say whether the imperfections of performance were natural or self-induced? To make an order with such possibilities of evasion would be vain; and so the order will not be made. However, not all contracts of personal service or for the continuous performance of services are as dependent as this on matters of opinion and judgment, nor do all such contracts involve the same degree of the daily impact of person upon person. In general, no doubt, the inconvenience and mischief of decreeing specific performance of most of such contracts will greatly outweigh the advantages, and specific performance will be refused. But I do not think that it should be assumed that as soon as any element of personal service or continuous services can be discerned in a contract the court will, without more, refuse specific performance.'

If the contract is not to perform a defined task but to perform on-going duties over a prolonged period of time, the problem of supervision is an even more serious one. The court will not order specific performance of such a contract if that would require constant supervision by the court. Constant supervision is not merely impracticable (*Ryan* v *Mutual Tontine Westminster Chambers Association Ltd* [1893] 1 Ch 116), it also raises the spectre of the court system being clogged by repeated applications to renew or vary the order.

Q CASE CLOSE-UP

Co-Operative Insurance Society Ltd v Argyll Stores (Holdings) Ltd [1998] AC 1, House of Lords

Facts: the claimants were landlords of a shopping centre and the defendant's supermarket was the main tenant. In the defendant's lease the defendant had covenanted to keep its premises open for retail trade during the usual hours of business in the locality, but when the supermarket became unprofitable the defendant closed the supermarket, having given the claimants only one month's notice to find a new tenant. At first instance the judge granted an order for damages to be assessed but refused an order for specific performance. The Court of Appeal, by a majority, allowed an appeal by the claimants and ordered specific performance. The settled judicial practice *not* to grant specific performance of an agreement to carry on a business was affirmed, although it was recognised that the grant or refusal of specific performance remains a matter for the discretion of the judge and the settled practice might be departed from in exceptional circumstances.

Held: the decision of the Court of Appeal was reversed. Lord Hoffmann distinguished 'orders which require a defendant to carry on an activity, such as running a business over a more or less extended period of time' from 'orders which require him to achieve a result'. The courts will be more willing to make the latter sort of order because the order is limited in time.

The courts have ordered specific performance of building contracts (e.g. *Wolverhampton Corpn* v *Emmons* [1901] 1 KB 515) and repairing covenants (e.g. *Jeune* v *Queens Cross Properties Ltd*

[1974] Ch 97). The courts have even ordered defendants to perform an obligation to appoint a porter to supervise an office block, on the basis that the task of finding the porter was well defined and had to be performed within two months (*Posner* v *Scott-Lewis* [1987] Ch 25). Prolonged employment can be contrasted with a case such as *Araci* v *Fallon* [2011] EWCA Civ 668, in which champion jockey Kieren Fallon was required by an order of specific performance to ride a particular horse in a specific one-off race (the Derby).

20.2.2.6 **Damages in lieu of specific performance**

Equity will decree specific performance in lieu of ('in the place of') a common law remedy of damages to achieve more perfect justice, but since the Chancery Amendment Act 1858 (21 & 22 Vict c 27) (known as 'Lord Cairns' Act') equity has been able to award common law-type damages in lieu of specific performance (see now the Senior Courts Act 1981, s 50). At first sight this seems nonsensical. If specific performance is awarded where damages are inadequate, when can it ever be appropriate for a court to award damages instead of specific performance? The answer is that sometimes it is simply not *practicable* to award specific performance, even though the decree of specific performance would be just and desirable.

Even though damages may be awarded in lieu of specific performance, it makes no sense to talk of a common law analogy to specific performance, and it is therefore inappropriate to apply the common law limitation period for contract to bar an action for specific performance (*P&O Nedlloyd BV* v *Arab Metals Co* [2006] EWCA Civ 1717). For more on limitation periods, see 15.2.1.

Lord Cairns' Act also applies to authorise the award of damages in lieu of an injunction: see next.

20.2.3 **Injunctions**

The effect of an injunction will be to stop the defendant from doing something (a 'prohibitory' injunction) or to require the defendant to do something (a 'mandatory' injunction) or, exceptionally, to prevent the defendant from committing a wrong which has not yet been committed, but is threatened. The latter is the so-called *quia timet* injunction (meaning 'because he fears'). An example of a prohibitory injunction is one which prevents a trespasser from entering onto the claimant's land. An example of mandatory injunction is one which requires a person to pull down a wall that was wrongly built on another person's land. The various types of injunctions are considered in detail later.

THINKING POINT

Can you see the close similarity between a decree of specific performance and a mandatory injunction? What, if any, is the difference between them?

As with the equitable remedy of specific performance, injunctions are only available at the court's discretion and where damages would not be adequate. It is also required that the party seeking the injunction has a legal (or equitable) right which the injunction would protect. In *Day* v *Brownrigg* [1878] D 11 (CA) the claimant whose house had carried the name 'Ashford Lodge' for 60 years was refused the injunction he sought to prevent his next-door neighbour from giving his house the very same name. Sir George Jessel MR held that no right of the claimant was infringed by the defendant renaming his house in this way.

Injunctions operate *in personam*. This means, as we have already noted, that to breach an injunction is not to break a legal rule but, rather, to act in contempt of court—an offence that is punishable by fine or even imprisonment. In *Shalson v Russo* [2003] EWHC 1637 (Ch) a fraudster was imprisoned for two years for breaching an equitable injunction freezing his assets (for 'freezing orders', see 20.2.3.7).

Injunctions may be made at the final hearing of a matter, in which case they will often be made on detailed terms designed to ensure that the parties will not resort to litigation in the future, or injunctions may be made in a preliminary hearing before the hearing of the merits of the case, in which case it is said to be 'interim' (formerly 'interlocutory', meaning 'between hearings'). Interim injunctions are frequently made to deal with some emergency and for this reason some may be sought by an 'application without notice' to the other party (previously called an *ex parte* application).

20.2.3.1 Interim (formerly 'interlocutory') injunction—overview

> The standard form of court order for an interim injunction contains the following fearsome warning to the defendant:
>
> (1) This Order [prohibits you from doing] [obliges you to do] the acts set out in this Order. [You should read it all carefully. You are advised to consult a Solicitor as soon as possible]. You have a right to ask the Court to vary or discharge this Order.
>
> (2) If you disobey this Order you may be found guilty of Contempt of Court and [any of your directors] may be sent to prison or fined [and you may be fined] or your assets may be seized.

The defendant to an injunction has it tough, but the applicant doesn't have it all his own way. The applicant must give the court an undertaking to pay any damages which the respondent (and any third party) might suffer as a result of the injunction (e.g. loss of profits if a business activity is brought to a halt) to the extent that the court considers the applicant ought to pay.

The requirement to give an undertaking to pay damages is so onerous for applicants of modest means that they frequently prefer to delay their application until they are quite sure they can prove their claim in the final hearing. In *Mortimer v Bailey* [2005] Build LR 85 the applicants delayed their application for an interim injunction to halt and remove building works until the building works were very nearly complete. The judge refused the interim order because it was so close to the date of the final hearing, but at the final hearing awarded a mandatory injunction to have the building (it was an extension to their home) pulled down. Previously it had been thought that delay in seeking an interim injunction would amount to acquiescence so as to prevent the applicant from seeking an injunction, but the Court of Appeal recognised that the applicants' modest means justified their refusal to risk an injunction until they were sure of their case. The court ordered the defendant to pull down the extension on the basis that they had run the risk that the court would order a mandatory injunction to that effect (see G. Watt, 'Building at Risk of Injunction' (2005) 69 Conv 14).

In *Regan v Paul Properties DPF No 1 Ltd* [2006] EWHC 2052 the fact that the defendant continued development in the face of the applicant's strong protests was given as a reason for refusing to enforce the applicant's undertaking to pay the defendant's damages. Usually, though, the court will enforce an undertaking to pay damages if at the final hearing it appears that the ion should not have been awarded in the first place (*SmithKline Beecham plc* v *Apotex Europe Ltd* [2006] EWCA Civ 658).

20.2.3.2 Interim injunction–prohibitory

An interim prohibitory injunction operates before the final hearing of the matter to stop the defendant from doing something that is infringing the applicant's legal or equitable rights. In the leading case of *American Cyanamid Co* v *Ethicon Ltd* [1975] 2 WLR 316 (HL) Lord Diplock laid down a number of helpful guidelines to the circumstances in which it is appropriate to award such an injunction. The respect in which his Lordship's guidelines are held has tended to imbue them with the status of statutory rules, but it should not be forgotten that the award of an injunction is ultimately discretionary, albeit guided by principle.

The claimant in the case was an American company that owned a patent covering certain medical products. The defendants, also an American company, were about to launch on the British market a product which the plaintiffs claimed infringed their patent. The plaintiffs applied for an interim (then an 'interlocutory') injunction which was granted by the judge at first instance with the usual undertaking in damages by the plaintiffs. The Court of Appeal reversed his decision on the ground that no *prima facie* case of infringement had been made out. The House of Lords allowed the appeal.

THINKING POINT

An extract from Lord Diplock's speech is set out in the next box. Highlight or underline as many distinct guidelines as you can, and compare your answer to the summary which follows the extract.

CASE CLOSE-UP

American Cyanamid Co v Ethicon Ltd [1975] 2 WLR 316, House of Lords

Lord Diplock: 'the court no doubt must be satisfied that the claim is not frivolous or vexatious, in other words, that there is a serious question to be tried . . . unless the material available to the court at the hearing of the application for an interlocutory injunction fails to disclose that the plaintiff has any real prospect of succeeding in his claim for a permanent injunction at the trial, the court should go on to consider whether the balance of convenience lies in favour of granting or refusing the interlocutory relief that is sought . . . As to that, the governing principle is that the court should first consider whether, if the plaintiff were to succeed at the trial in establishing his right to a permanent injunction, he would be adequately compensated by an award of damages for the loss he would have sustained as a result of the defendant's continuing to do what was sought to be enjoined between the time of the application and the time of the trial. If damages in the measure recoverable at common law would be adequate remedy and the defendant would be in a financial position to pay them, no interlocutory injunction should normally be granted, however strong the plaintiff's claim appeared to be at that stage. If, on the other hand, damages would not provide an adequate remedy for the plaintiff in the event of his succeeding at the trial, the court should then consider whether, on the contrary hypothesis that the defendant were to succeed at the trial in establishing his right to do that which was sought to be enjoined, he would be adequately compensated under the plaintiff's undertaking as to damages for the loss he would have sustained by being prevented from doing so between the time of the application and the time of the trial. If damages in the measure recoverable under such an undertaking would be an adequate remedy and the plaintiff would be in a financial position to pay them, there would be no reason upon this ground to refuse an interlocutory injunction.

. . . Where other factors appear to be evenly balanced it is a counsel of prudence to take such measures as are calculated to preserve the status quo. If the defendant is enjoined temporarily from doing something that he has not done before, the only effect of the in-terlocutory injunction in the event of his succeeding at the trial is to postpone the date at which he is able to embark upon a course of action which he has not previously found it necessary to undertake; whereas to interrupt him in the conduct of an established enter-prise would cause much greater inconvenience to him since he would have to start again to establish it in the event of his succeeding at the trial . . . The extent to which the disad-vantages to each party would be incapable of being compensated in damages in the event of his succeeding at the trial is always a significant factor in assessing where the balance of convenience lies, and if the extent of the uncompensatable disadvantage to each party would not differ widely, it may not be improper to take into account in tipping the balance the relative strength of each party's case as revealed by the affidavit evidence adduced on the hearing of the application. This, however, should be done only where it is apparent upon the facts disclosed by evidence as to which there is no credible dispute that the strength of one party's case is disproportionate to that of the other party. The court is not justified in embarking upon anything resembling a trial.'

These guidelines present judges with a simple algorithm, as set out in Figure 20.2.

Of course, this simple algorithm masks a number of more complex questions of discretion, the crucial one being to determine the 'balance of convenience' between the parties. One has to ask, if the injunction is refused and the applicant wins at trial, whether damages at trial will be an adequate compensation for pre-trial losses. Conversely, one has to ask, if the injunction is granted and the defendant wins at trial, whether the applicant's undertaking to pay damages will adequately compensate the defendant for pre-trial losses. The answer to these questions largely turns upon the extent of the losses and the ability of a party to pay if they lose at trial. If the court is undecided on the balance of convenience, it will generally preserve the status quo (*Cottage Foods Ltd* v *Milk Marketing Board* [1984] 1 AC 130).

The preceding short extract from the *American Cyanamid* case does not identify all the factors which might bear on the balance of convenience between the parties. Other factors include the following:

- the presence of hardship or extreme personal circumstances (see, for example, *Patel* v *Ali* [1984] Ch 283, where the defendant underwent the amputation of a leg at a time when she was pregnant and her husband was in prison);

- loss of employment (*Fellowes* v *Fisher* [1976] QB 122 (CA): the injunction was refused on the balance of convenience because there was no clear evidence that the claimants would suffer any damage if the injunction was refused, but if it was granted the defendant would lose his job);

Figure 20.2 Whether to grant a prohibitory interim injunction?

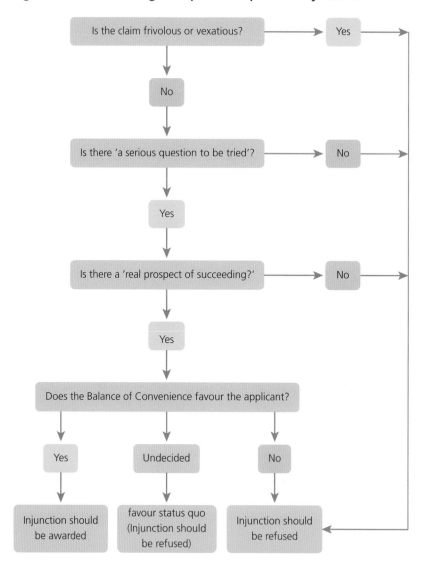

- closing of business (in *Potter Ballotini* v *Weston Baker* [1977] RPC 202 an injunction was refused because it would have unfairly required closure of the defendant's business);

- a prohibitory injunction cannot be used to force an employee into a position of having no choice other than specifically to perform a contract of services (see specific performance at 1.2.5);

- where the injunction restricts freedom of expression it is usually required to demonstrate more than a 'real prospect' of success, but exceptions will be admitted where necessary (see *Cream Holdings Ltd* v *Banerjee* [2004] UKHL 44; [2005] 1 AC 253 (HL) and *Douglas* v *Hello! Ltd (No 3)* [2005] EWCA Civ 595; [2006] QB 125 (CA));

- the fact that 'equity will not act in vain' means that an injunction will not be granted if it can do no practical good. Thus in *BBC* v *HarperCollins Publishers Limited* et al. [2010] EWHC 2424, the BBC failed to secure an injunction to prevent publication of a book revealing the secret identity of 'The Stig', a character in the TV programme *Top Gear*. The judge observed that 'the identity of Mr Collins as The Stig is [already] in the public domain'.

20.2.3.3 Interim injunction—mandatory

In *Locabail International Finance Ltd* v *Agroexport 'The Sea Hawk'* [1986] 1 WLR 657 the Court of Appeal approved the following *dictum* of the esteemed Chancery judge, Megarry J:

> the court is far more reluctant to grant a mandatory injunction than it would be to grant a comparable prohibitory injunction. In a normal case the court must, *inter alia*, feel a high degree of assurance that at the trial it will appear that the injunction was rightly granted and this is a higher standard than is required for a prohibitory injunction (*Shepherd Homes Ltd* v *Sandham* [1971] Ch 340, ChD).

The court won't grant an interim mandatory injunction if it would have an effect equivalent to specific performance, unless specific performance would itself be an appropriate order. In *Page One Records Ltd* v *Britton (Trading as 'The Troggs')* [1968] 1 WLR 157, ChD, the manager of 1960s pop group The Troggs asked the court to award him an interim injunction to restrain the group from engaging any other manager. He had produced The Troggs' song 'Give It To Me', but when it came to an injunction, the court declined to give it to him. The applicant's request for an injunction to prevent the employment of another manager was interpreted as being, in effect, a mandatory injunction compelling the group to continue to employ the applicant, which would in turn be tantamount to ordering the applicant specifically to perform his contract for personal services. The applicant was therefore refused his injunction . . . for his own protection! With hindsight, the parties could have saved themselves a great deal of trouble and expense—The Troggs reunited with Page at a later date. If The Troggs are a little out of date, the reader may be interested to know that the Stone Roses' failure fully to capitalise in the 1990s on the immense popularity they had achieved at the end of the 1980s can be put down in large part to the fact that they were trapped in a legal battle with their management and, from 1990, were prevented from releasing any music until the 'Second Coming' album appeared in 1994. (I must thank my editor, a Roses fan I think, for bringing this to my attention.)

20.2.3.4 Damages in lieu of injunction

Just as Lord Cairns' Act authorises the award of damages in lieu of specific performance, so it authorises the award of damages in lieu of an injunction (*Jaggard* v *Sawyer* [1995] 1 WLR 269 (CA)). Damages are awarded when an injunction would be desirable but impracticable. Classic instances include cases where a vital industry is causing an on-going nuisance to landowners and where houses have been built in breach of a restrictive covenant. In *Wrotham Park Estate Co* v *Parkside Homes Ltd* [1974] 1 WLR 798 Brightman J awarded damages in lieu of a mandatory injunction to pull down several houses because '[t]he erection of the houses, whether one likes it or not, is a fait accompli and the houses are now the homes of people'.

However, the courts are ever mindful to ensure that the builders of houses and the creators of nuisance are dissuaded from thinking that they are immune to injunctions which would tear down their houses and close down their factories. In *Shelfer* v *City of London Electric Lighting* [1895] 1 Ch 287 Lindley LJ opined that the jurisdiction to award damages instead of an injunction should be exercised only in exceptional cases. In that case an electric lighting company had erected powerful engines and other works on land near to a house, causing structural damage to the house. The Court of Appeal ordered the nuisance to cease. To have awarded damages instead would have sent out the message that the law allows tortfeasors to purchase the right to commit torts. For the same reason, the courts are quite willing to order the demolition of buildings erected with reckless disregard for breach of restrictive covenants (*Mortimer* v *Bailey* [2004] EWCA Civ 1514: see 20.2.3.1).

20.2.3.5 *Quia timet* injunction

Prevention is better than cure when it comes to administering justice, as Coke's Institutes state: 'preventing justice excelleth punishing justice'. From this it follows that '[a]lthough the claimant must establish his right, he may be entitled to an injunction even though an infringement has not taken place but is merely feared or threatened' (*Snell's Equity*, 28th edn, London: Sweet & Maxwell, 1982, p. 630). The threshold requirement for the award of a **quia timet** injunction is 'convincing evidence of real danger of actual violation' (*Angela Drury* v *Secretary of State for the Environment, Food and Rural Affairs* [2004] EWCA Civ 200 (CA)). The claimant must establish a strong case: 'no one can obtain a *quia timet* order by merely saying "Timeo" ("I am afraid")' (*A-G for the Dominion of Canada* v *Ritchie Contracting and Supply Co Ltd* [1919] AC 999 at 1005, *per* Lord Dunedin).

> **quia timet**
> 'Because he fears.' A *quia timet* injunction is ordered where a civil wrong is threatened but has not yet been committed.

🔍 CASE CLOSE-UP

Redland Bricks Ltd v Morris [1970] AC 652, House of Lords

Facts: a judge awarded a mandatory injunction requiring the defendant clay digging company to fill in a pit so as to restore support to the claimant's neighbouring land. The defendant appealed.

Held: allowing the appeal, that albeit there was a strong probability of grave damage to the claimant's land in the future and damages were not a sufficient remedy, the appellants had not behaved unreasonably, and since the mandatory injunction imposed upon them an unqualified obligation to restore support without any indication of what work was to be done, the injunction would be discharged.

Lord Upjohn: 'my Lords, *quia timet* actions are broadly applicable to two types of cases. First, where the defendant has as yet done no hurt to the plaintiff but is threatening and intending (so the plaintiff alleges) to do works which will render irreparable harm to him or his property if carried to completion. Your Lordships are not concerned with that and those cases are normally, though not exclusively, concerned with negative injunctions. Secondly, the type of case where the plaintiff has been fully recompensed both at law and in equity for the damage he has suffered but where he alleges that the earlier actions of the defendant may lead to future cases of action . . . of which that which is before your Lordships' House is typical, where the defendant has withdrawn support from his neighbour's land or where he has so acted in depositing his soil from his mining operations as to constitute a menace to the plaintiff's land. It is in this field that undoubted jurisdiction of equity to grant a mandatory injunction, that is an injunction ordering the defendant to carry out positive works, finds its main expression, though of course it is equally applicable to many other cases.'

The right that the claimant 'must establish' is normally a private right, but bodies with a statutory function may be awarded a *quia timet* injunction to protect the public from threatened criminal or other harm. In *Law Society of England and Wales* v *Shah* [2015] EWHC 2711 (Ch); [2015] 1 WLR 2094, Chancery Division, the Law Society successfully invoked the court's supervisory jurisdiction under the Solicitors Act 1974 s 41(4)(c) to obtain an injunction prohibiting a former solicitor from holding himself out as a solicitor, or undertaking reserved legal activities, where there was evidence that he was likely to do so unless restrained.

20.2.3.6 Search order (formerly '*Anton Piller* order')

This order allows a claimant to search the defendant's premises and seize things, especially documents, which the claimant will need to prove a legal claim against the defendant. In theory the search is not forcible, but the defendant is ordered to give his permission to be searched and is provided with the incentive of prison for contempt of court if he refuses. Established by the Court of Appeal in *Anton Piller KG* v *Manufacturing Processes Ltd* [1976] Ch 55 on the basis of long-standing case law, this order now has a statutory basis. The Civil Procedure Act 1997 provides that in the case of any existing or proposed proceedings the court may make an order for the purpose of securing (a) the preservation of evidence which is or may be relevant, or (b) the preservation of property which is or may be the subject matter of the proceedings or as to which any question arises or may arise in the proceedings (s 7). Such an order may direct any person to permit any person described in the order to enter premises in England and Wales, and while on the premises to take any of the following steps, so far as the terms of the order allow:

- to carry out a search for or inspection of anything described in the order; and
- to make or obtain a copy, photograph, sample or other record of anything so described; and
- to retain for safe keeping anything described in the order.

The Civil Procedure Rules 1999 summarise it as being an 'order requiring a party to admit another party to premises for the purpose of preserving evidence etc' (r 25.1). The order may also direct the person subject to the order to provide any information or article described in the order; however, an order made under the 1997 Act does not affect any right of a person to refuse to do anything on the ground that to do so might tend to expose him or his spouse to proceedings for an offence.

So we know what a search order *does*, but *when* will it be granted? A search order is a draconian measure and will be granted sparingly. The decision whether or not to award a search order lies, as it does for all injunctions, in the discretion of the court, but the court will be guided by the wisdom of earlier cases.

In the original case, AP Ltd, a German company, claimed that MP Ltd, its English agent, had been passing on confidential information to certain of AP's rival German companies. AP Ltd applied for an interim injunction to permit, inter alia, entry of MP's premises to inspect documentation and to remove documentation to the custody of AP's solicitors. AP undertook to issue a writ forthwith to support the action for breach of confidence and AP was granted its injunction. MP appealed. The appeal was allowed. Lord Denning MR held that in very exceptional circumstances, where the plaintiff has a very strong prima facie case to show that the defendant has caused or will cause very serious damage to the plaintiff, and where there is clear evidence that the defendant possesses vital evidence which might be disposed of so as to defeat justice, the court could by order permit the plaintiff's representatives to enter the defendant's premises to inspect and remove such material. The order could in such very exceptional circumstances be made without notice to the other party (at that time called an *ex parte* application). It was stated that where such an injunction is granted the plaintiff must act carefully and with full respect for the defendant's rights. One aspect of this is that the applicant's solicitors should photocopy confiscated documentation and return the originals to their owner. From this and subsequent cases, it is possible to identify the following factors as general prerequisites to an order:

- an extremely strong *prima facie* claim against the defendant;
- a real risk of serious damage to the defendant if the search order is refused;
- clear evidence that the defendant has the target assets in his possession;
- a clear risk that the defendant will destroy, conceal or dispose of the target assets.

The last factor is perhaps the most difficult. It has been held that a search order is inappropriate where the defendant will probably comply with an ordinary order to deliver up the assets; indeed, it has been said that the defendant must be akin to a 'fly by night pirate' for a search order to be justified (*Lock International plc v Beswick* [1989] 1 WLR 1268).

The search order has proved to be most useful in dealing with cases of alleged audio and video piracy. In *Columbia Picture Industries Inc v Robinson* [1987] Ch 38 the company sought an *Anton Piller* injunction against an alleged 'video pirate' (a person who, according to the judge, 'manufactures and trades in video cassettes which infringe the copyright in cinematographic films'). On one issue the dispute ultimately came down to the films *For Your Eyes Only* and *Star Wars*. If there is some dispute as to the proper ownership of certain items, such as alleged pirate tapes, they should not be retained by the plaintiff or his solicitor; they should be passed, subject to an undertaking that they be produced in court, to the defendant's solicitor.

The beneficiary of a search order is not allowed to use force (not even when seeking to recover pirated *Star Wars* films). Where a search order has been executed in an excessive and oppressive manner the court may order aggravated damages against the applicant and possibly, since solicitors executing such orders do so as officers of the court, exemplary damages.

 THINKING POINT

As a result of the Human Rights Act 1998, we can add to the applicant's worries the risk that a disproportionate search may be a potential breach of Art 8 of the European Convention on Human Rights (*Rank Film Distributors Ltd v Video Information Centre* [1982] AC 380; *Chappell v United Kingdom* 10461/83 [1989] ECHR 4 (30 March 1989)).

20.2.3.7 Freezing order (formerly 'Mareva injunction')

This is a prohibitory interim injunction by which the defendant is prevented from dealing with his assets in any way which might defeat the claimant's prospects of enforcing a legal judgment against the defendant. Originally developed in judicial decisions, including the decision of the Court of Appeal in *Mareva Compania Naviera SA v International Bulkcarriers SA* [1975] 2 Lloyd's Rep 509, the order now has statutory force. The Civil Procedure Rules 1999 describe it as an order 'restraining a party from removing from the jurisdiction assets located there' or 'restraining a party from dealing with any assets whether located within the jurisdiction or not' (r 25.1(f)). It is not the purpose of the order to give a claimant security for his claim or give him any proprietary interest in the 'frozen' assets (*Gangway Ltd v Caledonian Park Investments (Jersey) Ltd* [2001] 2 Lloyd's Rep 715 at para. [14], *per* Colman J). As Lord Bingham of Cornhill put it: 'The ownership of the assets does not change. All that changes is the right to deal with them' (*Customs and Excise Commissioners v Barclays Bank plc* [2006] 1 CLC 1096, [2006] UKHL 28 (HL) at para. [10]).

THINKING POINT

What can count as an 'asset' subject to a freezing injunction? Are beneficial interests under trusts subject to freezing? What about if the trust is a discretionary trust?

In *JSC BTA Bank* v *Solodchenko* [2010] EWCA Civ 1436; [2011] 1 WLR 888, it was held (at para. [49]) that a trustee's trust assets should only be frozen if it seems that the apparent trustee is actually the beneficiary of the assets. In *JSC Mezhdunarodniy Promyshlenniy Bank* v *Pugachev* [2015] EWCA Civ 139, the Court of Appeal confirmed (at para. [26]) that the potential beneficiary of a discretionary trust could not be regarded as the owner, either legally or beneficially, of any of the trust assets.

In *Mareva Compania Naviera SA* v *International Bulkcarriers SA*, the case that founded the freezing injunction and formerly gave it its name, MCN owned a ship, the *Mareva*, which it let to IB on a charter bound for the Far East. IB subsequently sub-chartered the vessel to the president of India on a voyage charter to India. The Indian High Commission paid £174,000 into IB's London bank. Out of these monies IB paid two instalments of the fees they owed to MCN, but failed to pay a third instalment which had fallen due. The judge at first instance granted an injunction against IB in favour of MCN, with a view to preventing dissipation of the balance of monies in the London bank. Lord Denning MR upheld the injunction on the basis that 'it is only just and right that this court should grant an injunction'. His Lordship stated that if IB should have any grievance about the injunction when they came to hear of it, they would be permitted to apply to court to attempt to have it discharged.

We saw earlier that one can discern in the cases certain prerequisites to the grant of a search order. The same is true of a freezing order:

- a freezing order will not be awarded on an interim basis unless the claimant issues, or undertakes to issue, definable substantive proceedings (*Fourie* v *Le Roux* [2007] UKHL 1 (HL). In this case it was held that the applicant should have failed at first instance because when he applied for the injunction he hadn't even 'worked out what proceedings he was going to bring to which the freezing order would be relevant');
- the applicant must establish a good arguable case;
- the applicant must establish that the defendant has assets in the jurisdiction (where assets are abroad, the applicant may seek a worldwide freezing order: see later);
- the applicant must demonstrate that the target assets are likely to be destroyed, removed or dissipated.

Although a freezing order is directed at the defendant and operates *in personam*, it *can* affect third parties:

A standard form of injunction is annexed to the Practice Direction on Interim Injunctions 25PD.10. The prescribed standard form contains the following penal notice:

IF YOU [ ] DISOBEY THIS ORDER YOU MAY BE HELD TO BE IN CONTEMPT OF COURT AND MAY BE IMPRISONED, FINED OR HAVE YOUR ASSETS SEIZED

ANY OTHER PERSON WHO KNOWS OF THIS ORDER AND DOES ANYTHING WHICH HELPS OR PERMITS THE RESPONDENT TO BREACH THE TERMS OF THIS ORDER MAY ALSO BE HELD TO BE IN CONTEMPT OF COURT AND MAY BE IMPRISONED, FINED OR HAVE THEIR ASSETS SEIZED

In *Customs and Excise Commissioners* v *Barclays Bank plc* [2006] 1 CLC 1096; [2006] UKHL 28 the House of Lords was called upon to determine whether a bank, notified by a third party of a freezing order granted to the third party against one of the bank's customers, affecting an account held by the customer with the bank, owes a duty to the third party to take reasonable care to comply with the terms of the injunction. Lord Bingham of Cornhill held that it would be 'unjust and unreasonable that the Bank should, on being notified of an order which it had no opportunity to resist, become exposed to a liability which was in this case for a few million pounds only, but might in another case be for very much more' (at para. [23]).

In *Independent Trustee Services Ltd* v *GP Noble Trustees Ltd* [2009] EWHC 161 (Ch), the applicant company applied to vary a freezing order made on a without notice application by the respondent company. The applicant wanted to release funds to help it to defend an action brought by the respondent company. It was held that a balance had to be found between permitting the applicant to spend funds which might belong to the respondent and refusing to allow the respondent to spend the funds. On the evidence, the respondent had an arguable proprietary claim to the monies and it was arguable that F was a vehicle for fraud. The variation was refused. Crucially, the person subject to the injunction must be a party to proceedings, thus a wife should not be subject to an injunction in proceedings brought against her husband: *BCS Corporate Acceptances Ltd* v *Terry* [2016] EWHC 533 (QB); [2016] 2 P & CR DG9.

In *JSC BTA Bank* v *Ablyazov (No 10)* [2013] EWCA Civ 928; [2014] 1 WLR 1414, Beatson LJ usefully identified three guiding principles to govern the grant of an injunction: (a) the enforcement principle, which is concerned to stop the injuncted defendant 'dissipating or disposing of property which could be the subject of enforcement if the claimant goes on to win the case'; (b) the principle of flexibility, which is that 'the jurisdiction to make a freezing order should be exercised in a flexible and adaptable manner so as to be able to deal with new situations and new ways used by sophisticated and wily operators to make themselves immune to the courts' orders'; (c) the principle of strict construction, which is that the terms of the order 'should be clear and unequivocal, and should be strictly construed'.

20.2.3.8 Worldwide freezing order

Although a freezing order is usually used to prevent assets from being taken outside the English jurisdiction, it is effective *in personam* against any person made a defendant to proceedings in an English court, and is not defeated by the mere fact that the assets subject to the injunction are based outside the jurisdiction of the English court. In *Derby & Co Ltd* v *Weldon (Nos 3 & 4)* [1990] Ch 65 (CA) the claimant sought a *Mareva* injunction against a number of defendants, including a Panamanian company and a Luxembourg company, neither of which appeared to have any assets within the UK. It was held that the purpose of the *Mareva* injunction was to prevent frustration of a court order and, although normally confined to assets within the jurisdiction, it could be used in relation to foreign assets, subject to the ordinary principles of international law. Because the injunction operated *in personam* it did not offend against the principle that courts should not make orders to take effect in foreign jurisdictions. Their Lordships did suggest, however, that the existence of sufficient assets within the jurisdiction would be an excellent reason for refusing a worldwide injunction.

STATUTE

Lord Chief Justice's Practice Direction (Mareva Injunctions and Anton Piller Orders) [1994] RPC 617, [1994] 1 WLR 1233, High Court

Lord Taylor of Gosforth CJ, Sir Stephen Brown P and Sir Donald Nicholls V-C:

'the terms of this order do not affect or concern anyone outside the jurisdiction of this court until it is declared enforceable or is enforced by a court in the relevant country and then they are to affect him only to the extent that they have been declared enforceable or have been enforced UNLESS such person is: (a) a person to whom this order is addressed or an officer or an agent appointed by power of attorney of such a person; or (b) a person who is subject to the jurisdiction of this Court and (i) has been given written notice of this order at his residence or place of business within the jurisdiction of this Court and (ii) is able to prevent acts or omissions outside the jurisdiction of this Court which constitute or assist in a breach of the terms of this order.'

The worldwide freezing order is especially useful in an age when fraud crosses national borders. When the BCCI group of banks collapsed as the result of international fraud on a grand scale, a worldwide freezing order (then known as a 'worldwide *Mareva* injunction') was granted to the liquidators against a director and an employee of BCCI with a view to making them personally liable for the losses which (it was alleged) had resulted from their fraud (*Re BCCI (Overseas) Ltd (No 9)* [1994] 2 BCLC 636).

CASE CLOSE-UP

The 'Dadourian Guidelines' on the grant of a Worldwide Freezing Order ('WFO') (Dadourian Group International Inc v Simms [2006] 1 WLR 2499, Court of Appeal) (paraphrased)

(1) the grant of permission should be 'just and convenient' and 'not oppressive to the parties to the English proceedings or to third parties who may be joined to the foreign proceedings';

(2) consideration should be given to 'granting relief on terms' (for example, extending to third parties the requirement of giving an undertaking for costs) and to 'the proportionality of the steps proposed to be taken abroad' and to 'the form of any order';

(3) 'The interests of the applicant should be balanced against the interests of the other parties . . . and any new party likely to be joined to the foreign proceedings';

(4) 'Permission should not normally be given in terms that would enable the applicant to obtain relief in the foreign proceedings which is superior to the relief given by the WFO';

(5) the decision whether or not to grant permission should be based on all the relevant information reasonably obtainable in the available time such as the judge would require to reach an informed decision (including evidence as to the applicable law and practice in the foreign court, the nature of the proposed proceedings to be commenced, the assets believed to be located in the jurisdiction of the foreign court and the names of the parties by whom such assets are held);

> (6) the standard of proof requires proof of a 'real prospect' that such assets are located within the jurisdiction of the foreign court in question;
>
> (7) the risk of dissipation of the assets;
>
> (8) 'normally the application should be made on notice to the respondent, but in cases of urgency, where it is just to do so, the permission may be given without notice to the party against whom relief will be sought in the foreign proceedings but that party should have the earliest practicable opportunity of having the matter reconsidered by the court at a hearing of which he is given notice.'

Interim freezing injunctions (domestic and worldwide) may be made to support foreign courts, provided that the foreign state is a Regulation State within the meaning of s 25(1) of the Civil Jurisdiction and Judgments Act 1982 or is a signatory to the Brussels Convention or the Lugano Convention. In *Fourie v Le Roux* [2007] UKHL 1 (HL) it was held that an interim injunction may be made in support of foreign litigation only if the injunction is genuinely acting as relief relevant to the final remedy sought. There must also be a genuine nexus between UK territory and the interim relief sought. These restrictions govern the circumstances in which it is appropriate to grant interim relief in support of foreign litigation, but in no way restrict the extent of the relief awarded if it is appropriate to exercise it (see, also, *Albon (t/a NA Carriage Co) v Naza Motor Trading Sdn Bhd* [2007] EWCA Civ 1124). In *Banco Nacional de Comercio Exterior SNC v Empresa de Telecomunicationes de Cuba SA* [2007] EWCA Civ 723 (CA) two orders were made at first instance: one to freeze the defendant's assets in England and another (a WFO) to freeze assets elsewhere. The orders were made to support a judgment made by a court in Turin. The Court of Appeal set aside the WFO on the basis that there was no connection between the UK-based assets and assets which might be covered by the WFO. (Cancelling the WFO also had the merit of avoiding conflicts with similar orders made in other jurisdictions (see Art 47 of Council Regulation (EC) 44/2001). It may be a rare case in which a WFO is ordered against a defendant who is not UK-resident.)

20.2.4 **Rescission**

Rescission is an equitable remedy by which a specific contract or other transaction is rendered unenforceable in law. It is, in a sense, a decree of specific non-performance. It directly and comprehensively prevents unconscionable assertion of legal rights and has therefore been described as 'one of the most common and natural occasions for the exercise of equitable jurisdiction' (R. Wooddeson, *A Systematical View of the Laws of England*, Dublin, 1794). As a pre-condition to rescission it must be possible to effect *restitutio in integrum* (*New Sombrero Phosphate Co v Erlanger* (1877) 5 ChD 73).

> **restitutio in integrum**
> To put the parties back into the position they were in prior to entering the rescinded agreement.

The requirement to effect **restitutio in integrum** is not absolute in relation to transactions entered into by persons in breach of a fiduciary relationship. In such a case, where rescission is called for on grounds of public policy, it will be ordered where the court can 'do what is practically just, though it cannot restore the parties precisely to the state they were in before the contract' (*O'Sullivan v Management Agency and Music Ltd* [1985] 3 All ER 351 (CA): see 12.1.2).

Professor Lionel Smith argues that the right to rescind can be regarded as an equity attaching to an asset in whosoever's hands it might come, until it comes to a good faith purchaser for value without notice (*The Law of Tracing*, Oxford: Oxford University Press, 1997, 365–7). For example, in *Shalson v Russo* [2003] EWHC 1637 (Ch) it was held that, upon rescission of a contract for misrepresentation, the beneficial title which passed to the representor under the contract revested in the representee so that the representee could trace through the exchange products of the original property, including in the hands of third parties. The same approach is taken where the rescission is based, not in misrepresentation, but on a mistake (*Bainbridge v Bainbridge* [2016] EWHC 898 (Ch). Noted Salmons (2016) 22(10) *Trusts & Trustees* 1098–1103). Rescission may be ordered on a number of grounds, including mistake and undue influence.

20.2.4.1 **Mistake**

The circumstances in which a transaction may be rescinded for mistake depend upon whether the transaction is contractual or non-contractual. In the case of a contract, a fundamental mistake as to the facts or their legal consequences may be a ground for rescission (*Bell v Lever Bros Ltd* [1932] AC 161 (HL)). In the case of a non-contractual (unilateral) transaction, apart from cases of mistake induced by fraud, undue influence or misrepresentation, the transaction will stand unless there was such a serious mistake as to the nature and effect of the transaction as would render it unjust for the transaction to stand, although a mere mistake as to the 'consequences or the advantages to be gained by entering into' the transaction will not be a ground for rescission (*Gibbon v Mitchell* [1990] 1 WLR 1304). This rather difficult distinction between 'effect' and 'consequence' has been criticised (see J. Hilliard, '*Gibbon v Mitchell* Reconsidered: Mistakes as to Effects and Mistakes as to Consequences', Parts 1 and 2 (2004) 6 PCB 357, (2005) 1 PCB 31).

20.2.4.2 **Undue influence**

Undue influence is a ground for rescinding many types of transaction, including contracts, mortgages and even the resignation of a trustee (*Daniel v Drew* [2005] EWCA Civ 507 (CA)). There are two broad forms of unacceptable conduct amounting to undue influence. The first comprises overt acts of improper pressure and coercion; the second is a relationship in which one party has taken unfair advantage of a position of strength (*Royal Bank of Scotland plc v Etridge (No 2)* [2002] 2 AC 773). In certain types of relationship, such as those in which it is 'the duty of one party to advise the other or to manage his property for him', undue influence is presumed, provided the complainant can prove as a matter of fact that the trust-like relationship existed and that the transaction was exceptional and therefore calls for an explanation. Benefits conferred by the vulnerable party will not be examined if they are unexceptional, otherwise no parent could confidently accept so much as a birthday present from their child (*Royal Bank of Scotland v Etridge* [2002] 2 AC 773, *per* Lord Nicholls of Birkenhead at 798, approving *Allcard v Skinner* (1887) 36 ChD 145). In *Minder Music Ltd v Sharples* [2015] EWHC 1454, the Intellectual Property Enterprise Court held that it did not suffice for the claimant to show that a bargain was hard, unreasonable or foolish or that there was unequal bargaining power between the parties. The bargain had to be unconscionable in the sense that one of the parties had imposed the objectionable terms in a morally reprehensible manner.

 THINKING POINT

We should always bear in mind that the jurisdiction to set aside contracts for undue influence is used sparingly. A court of equity, it must be remembered, is not a court of morality. Professor Wooddeson recognised more than two centuries ago that '[t]o rescind every contract incompatible with the nicest principles of honour and morality, tends to terminate all commercial intercourse' (*A Systematical View of the Laws of England*, Dublin, 1794).

It should be noted that the receipt of legal advice is usually sufficient to rebut the presumption of undue influence (but not always: see, for example, *Wright v Hodgkinson* [2005] WTLR 435). The saddest cases are not commercial ones, but cases of serious family strife. In *Re Edwards (deceased)* [2007] EWHC 1119 a mother's will was set aside after it emerged that one son had discharged her from a nursing home against medical advice and unduly influenced his mother to write his siblings out of her will. *Thompson v Foy* [2009] EWHC 1076 (Ch) is another case of a mistreated mother, but this time the claim of undue influence failed. She had allowed her daughter to become registered owner of a house the mother had bought in Spain. The daughter borrowed money against the house and the mother claimed to rescind the daughter's title on the ground of undue influence, to the prejudice of the mortgagee. This was not allowed, because the daughter's wrongdoing against the mother came after the charge in favour of the mortgagee.

20.2.5 **Rectification**

The equitable remedy of rectification is an aspect of the general equitable jurisdiction to relieve from the consequences of mistake (*Gibbon v Mitchell* [1990] 1 WLR 1304, *per* Millett J at 1307; *Gallaher Ltd v Gallaher Pensions Ltd* [2005] EWHC 42 (Ch)) or fraud (*Collins v Elstone* [1893] P 1). It has proved most useful in the case of mistakes in contracts and wills, and in cases where a party's advisers should have appreciated that they did not understand the terms of the arrangement (in *Bhatt v Bhatt* [2009] EWHC 734 (Ch) the mistake to be rectified arose from the party's poor grasp of the English language). For rectification there has to be: (a) clear evidence of the trustees' subjective intention; (b) a flaw in the document so that it did not give effect to that intention; (c) a specific intention to achieve something different from what had been done; (d) an issue capable of being contested even though all relevant parties consented to the proposed rectification (*Racal Group Services Ltd v Ashmore* [1995] STC 1151).

 CASE CLOSE-UP

***RBC Trustees (CI) Ltd v Stubbs* [2017] EWHC 180 (Ch); [2017] 2 P & CR DG5**

Facts: trustees applied, with the support of the settlor and beneficiaries, for rectification of a trust deed under which the original trusts had been revoked and resettled to remove the life interests of certain beneficiaries' ex-spouses. The solicitors had been instructed to remove the life interests of the former spouses, but had unnecessarily resettled the assets on new trusts, with serious adverse tax consequences for the remaining beneficiaries.

Held: rectification granted. A mistake as to tax was not a sufficient reason for rectification, but here the intention had been primarily to remove the former spouses and only secondarily to do so in a tax efficient way. Also, the mistake produced a contestable issue—namely, whether the beneficiaries were now entitled under the original or the substituted trusts.

20.2.5.1 **Contracts**

The court has jurisdiction to rectify an agreement if there was a common continuing understanding between the parties with regard to a particular provision of the agreement, but the court requires 'convincing proof' that the concluded instrument did not represent the parties' common intention (*Joscelyne* v *Nissen* [1970] 2 QB 86). Contracts may also be rectified in favour of one party, where it is 'inequitable that [the other party] should be allowed to object to the rectification', as might occur if the former party entered the contract under a unilateral mistake of which the latter party was aware (*Thomas Bates & Son Ltd* v *Windham's (Lingerie) Ltd* [1981] 1 WLR 505 at 515–16, *per* Buckley LJ). For rectification to be ordered in such a case, the defendant's conduct in suppressing his knowledge of the mistake must be 'such as to affect the conscience' (*George Wimpey UK Ltd* v *VI Construction Ltd* [2005] EWCA Civ 77). The defendant's conscience is unlikely to be affected unless the mistake was one which was to his benefit.

20.2.5.2 Wills

If a court is satisfied that a will is so expressed that it fails to carry out the testator's intentions, in consequence of a clerical error or of a failure to understand his instructions, it may order that the will shall be rectified so as to carry out his intentions (Administration of Justice Act 1982, s 20; see, for example, *Marley* v *Rawlings* [2014] UKSC 2, where one spouse accidentally signed the other spouse's will).

Crucially, the court has the power to rectify a settlement to give effect to the intentions of the parties to an agreement. It is not necessary for the parties to have agreed precisely the form of words they wished to be inserted into the settlement (*Stephenson* v *Stephenson* [2004] All ER (D) 35 (Mar)). Where a solicitor makes a mistake in drafting a will, the test to be applied is whether or not the solicitor had applied his mind to the significance and effect of the words used. An error through mere inadvertence should be rectified (*Re Segelman (deceased)* [1996] 2 WLR 173).

Sometimes quite remarkable mistakes are corrected, as in *Lawie* v *Lawie* [2012] EWHC 2940 (Ch), where a discretionary trust established for the benefit of the settlors' grandchildren accidentally omitted to include the settlors' children within the class of potential beneficiaries. Rectification was ordered in part because the trusts, as initially created, gave the trustees no practical choice of potential beneficiaries.

20.2.6 Account

> **account** A process by which the court assesses the sum due from one person to another, and the remedy of payment of the sum due that is ordered at the end of the assessment process.

An action for an **account** was at one time available at common law, but Chancery procedure for taking accounts was 'so superior that by the eighteenth century the common law action for an account had come to be superseded by equitable proceedings for an account' (*Tito* v *Waddell (No 2)* [1977] Ch 106). For us, account is especially relevant as an order made in favour of a beneficiary against a defaulting trustee. It requires the production of the trust's financial accounts and requires the trustee to give an account of his dealings with the trust property and make up any shortfall to the fund. A trustee will also be required to account for unauthorised profits made by reason of his trusteeship. The fiduciary duty to account for unauthorised profits is particularly important and is considered in depth in Chapter 12. Account is also very useful for requiring a defendant to disgorge profits made from unauthorised use of confidential information (*A-G* v *Guardian Newspapers Ltd (No 2)* [1990] 1 AC 109).

20.2.7 **Subrogation**

Like other equitable remedies, subrogation 'arises from the conduct of the parties on well settled principles and in defined circumstances which make it unconscionable for the defendant to deny [the claimant's claim]' (*Boscawen v Bajwa* [1996] 1 WLR 328 (CA)).

 CASE CLOSE-UP

Burston Finance Ltd v Speirway Ltd [1974] 1 WLR 1648

Walton J: '[subrogation] finds one of its chief uses in the situation where one person advances money on the understanding that he is to have a certain security for the money he has advanced, and, for one reason or another, he does not receive the promised security. In such a case he is nevertheless to be subrogated to the rights of any other person who at the relevant time had any security over the same property and whose debts have been discharged, in whole or in part, by the money so provided by him, but of course only to the extent to which his money has, in fact, discharged their claim' (at 1652B–C).

In *Boscawen v Bajwa* [1996] 1 WLR 328 (CA) a building society made an advance for the purchase of a property to be secured by a first legal charge. The purchase fell through after the vendor's solicitors, to whom the purchasers' solicitors had transferred the money, had used it to discharge a mortgage on the property. The claimants, the vendor's judgment creditors, having obtained a charging order against the property, claimed against the vendor and the building society an order for possession and sale of the property. The building society succeeded in its counterclaim to be entitled, by way of subrogation, to the rights of the mortgagee and, therefore, to a charge on the proceeds of sale of the property in priority to the claimants.

 CASE CLOSE-UP

Filby v Mortgage Express (No 2) Ltd [2004] EWCA Civ 759, Court of Appeal

Facts: the appellant Mrs Filby had divorced from her husband. When they were married he had forged her name on a mortgage deed and the mortgage monies were used, in part, to pay off an earlier mortgage. Mrs Filby claimed that she was not bound by the terms of the later mortgage (the one she had not signed), but the later mortgagee, having redeemed the earlier mortgage, claimed to be subrogated to the earlier mortgagee's unsecured personal rights against Mrs Filby.

Held: Mrs Filby's appeal was dismissed and the later mortgagee was awarded subrogation to the earlier mortgagee's claim plus 13 years of unpaid interest on the claim.

May LJ: 'the remedy of equitable subrogation is a restitutionary remedy available to reverse what would otherwise be unjust enrichment of a defendant at the expense of the claimant. The defendant is enriched if his financial position is materially improved, usually as here where the defendant is relieved of a financial burden—see Peter Birks, *An Introduction to the Law of Restitution*, p. 93. The enrichment will be at the expense of the claimant if in reality it was the claimant's money which effected the improvement. Subject to special defences, questions of policy or exceptional circumstances affecting the balance of justice, the enrichment will be unjust if the claimant did not get the security he bargained for when he advanced the money which in reality effected the improvement, and if the defendant's financial improvement is properly seen as a windfall. The remedy does not extend to giving the claimant more than he bargained for. The remedy is not limited to cases where either or both the claimant and defendant intended that the money advanced should be used to effect the improvement. It is sufficient that it was in fact in reality so used. The remedy is flexible and adaptable to produce a just result. Within this framework, the remedy is discretionary in the sense that at each stage it is a matter of judgment whether on the facts the necessary elements are fulfilled . . .

Applying these principles, for reasons which I have expressed in the course of this judgment, I consider that the judge reached the correct decision in the present case for the correct reasons. The claimants are entitled to a right against Mrs Filby equivalent to the unsecured personal rights of Midland Bank against her arising under the joint loan account. No security in law arises from the fact that, as things happened, the claimants sold the property and realised the proceeds of sale.

. . . The harsh realities in the present case include that, if you borrow money from a bank, the bank will charge interest; and that the Midland Bank account was a joint account for which Mrs Filby was severally liable to the bank. To the extent that the payment of £60,801 reduced the Midland Bank loan, Mrs Filby was relieved from a liability for interest and to that extent also she was enriched.' [para. 67]

 ## Summary

Rather than simply list everything we have covered in this chapter, let us repeat the exercise we carried out earlier in relation to equitable doctrines, but this time in relation to the much larger topic of equitable remedies. Table 20.2 contains the list of equitable remedies in the left-hand column, and the right-hand column describes the various remedies. Your task is to draw a line linking the doctrine to its proper description. Don't forget, though, that in the final analysis, equitable remedies are discretionary and even if we think we can tick the boxes, the courts still have the potential to surprise us.

Table 20.2 Equitable remedies

Specific performance	An order made before the final hearing which stops the defendant from doing something in the meantime (Choice A)
Interim prohibitory injunction	Allows a claimant to enter the defendant's premises to seize things (Choice B)
Mandatory injunction	Prevents the defendant from dealing with his assets in any way which might defeat the claimant's prospects of enforcing a legal judgment against him (Choice C)

(continued)

The solution to the problem is as follows (in reverse order): JEIHDCBFKAG.

Table 20.2 Equitable remedies (*Continued*)

Quia timet injunction	An order preventing persons from dealing with assets based outside the jurisdiction of the English court (Choice D)
Search order (formerly '*Anton Piller* order')	A process by which the court assesses the sum due from one person to another and requires it to be paid (Choice E)
Freezing order (formerly '*Mareva* injunction')	An order preventing the defendant from committing a threatened wrong (Choice F)
Worldwide freezing order	Requires a promise to be discharged whenever the common law remedy of damages would be inadequate (Choice G)
Rescission	Renders a contract or other transaction unenforceable and aims to put the parties back into their original positions (Choice H)
Rectification	Relieves against the consequences of mistake, especially in the case of contracts and wills (Choice I)
Account	Where the applicant is entitled to some benefit due to the defendant, this order will notionally place the claimant in the shoes of the defendant with a view to receiving that benefit (Choice J)
Subrogation	An order made at the final hearing which requires the defendant to do something (Choice K)

? Summative assessment exercise

We commenced this chapter with a scenario in which you were chosen to be a member of a newly created pop group. It was suggested then that by the end of this chapter you would have a good idea of your prospects of success in the various claims raised by the scenario. Do you? Look at the scenario again and try and answer it in the light of all that you have learned throughout this chapter. The Online Resource Centre accompanying this book contains a guide solution to the problems raised by the scenario.

Of course, it is also important to test yourself with essay questions. Here is one based on aspects of this chapter:

As a general rule, someone who, with the knowledge that he has clearly enforceable rights and the ability to enforce them, stands by whilst a permanent and substantial structure is unlawfully erected, ought not to be granted an injunction to have it pulled down. (*Gafford v Graham* (1999) 77 P & CR 73 (CA), *per* Nourse LJ at 73–4)

Are there any exceptions to the 'general rule'?

 Full specimen answers can be found at www.oxfordtextbooks.co.uk/orc/watt_directions5e/.

The bigger picture

In this chapter we have been largely concerned with equitable doctrines. We might be suspicious that doctrines should have nothing to do with the exercise of so free-spirited and flexible a force as equity. Oliver Goldsmith expresses similar suspicion about doctrines in his novel *The Vicar of Wakefield* (1766), where Dr Primrose (the so-called 'Vicar of Wakefield'), commenting on a fellow clergyman, says:

> I thought he seemed rather devout than learned, and began to think he despised all human doctrines as dross. Yet this no way lessened him in my esteem; for I had for some time begun privately to harbour such an opinion myself.

But it is precisely because equity has potential for arbitrary and unpredictable application that doctrines are so necessary. Equitable doctrines are precepts by which judicial discretion has traditionally been guided and restrained, and they should not lightly be thrown off. Just as they guide discretion, so they themselves are guided by the spirit of the equitable maxims that we examined in Chapter 1.

Further reading

Davies, P.S. 'Rectification versus Interpretation: The Nature and Scope of the Equitable Jurisdiction' (2016) 75(1) CLJ 62–85
argues that mistakes in written contracts should be corrected under the equitable doctrine of rectification rather than the common law of interpretation

Hodge QC, D. *Rectification: The Modern Law and Practice Governing Claims for Rectification for Mistake*, 2nd edn (2015) London: Sweet & Maxwell
Comprehensive practical treatment of claims for rectification for mistake

Mason, Sir A. 'The Place of Equity and Equitable Remedies in the Common Law World' (1994) 110 LQR 238
a sweeping, visionary and controversial statement on the present and future place of equity and equitable remedies by a distinguished Commonwealth judge

O'Sullivan, D., Elliot, S. and Zakrzewski, R. *The Law of Rescission* 2nd edn (2014) Oxford: Oxford University Press
comprehensive treatment of the law relating to the remedy of rescission in England and Wales

Ridge, P. 'Equitable Undue Influence and Wills' (2004) 120 LQR 617
argues that the distinction between the equitable doctrine of undue influence and the probate doctrine of undue influence is unjustified

Swadling, W. 'Rescission, Property, and the Common Law' (2005) 121 LQR 123
argues that if there was no mistake as to the subject matter of the transfer or as to the identity of the transferee 'a defrauded vendor should be allowed to rescind his contract of sale' but 'it should not carry with it any revesting of title'

 For links to selected cases, statutes, academic papers and official reports mentioned in this chapter please visit the online resources at www.oup.com/uk/watt_directions6e/.

Glossary

ab initio From the beginning (pronounced 'ab in-ish-ee-oh').

account A process by which the court assesses the sum due from one person to another, and the remedy of payment of the sum due that is ordered at the end of the assessment process.

accumulation of income Instead of being spent or otherwise applied, trust income is sometimes retained by the trustees and accumulated. Accumulation of income is not the mere retention of income for administrative purposes. It is the process of adding income to capital. As Harman LJ put it in *Re the Earl of Berkeley* [1968] Ch 744 at 772: 'Accumulation to my mind involves the addition of income to capital, thus increasing the estate in favour of those entitled to capital and against the interests of those entitled to income.'

acquiescence The decision by an injured party not to take action in response to the wrong done. Acquiescence may be a ground for barring a claim.

ad valorem **stamp duty** A tax charged as a percentage of the value transferred by a document.

advancement A statutory power granted to trustees (which may be altered, enlarged or removed by the trust instrument) under which the trustee can apply trust capital for the benefit of beneficiaries even though the beneficiaries are not yet strictly entitled to it.

beneficial joint tenants Where legal title to land is in the joint names of two or more persons who are also joint owners in equity, the co-owners are said to be beneficial joint tenants. Husband and wife will often be beneficial joint tenants.

bequest A gift of personalty made by will. Personalty means personal property, so the term includes all forms of property apart from land. The one exception is leases, which for historical reasons are treated as personalty.

bona fide Good faith (pronounced 'bone-a fyde' or 'bonna fye-dee').

bona vacantia Vacant goods, i.e. ownerless property. In England and Wales ownerless property will usually pass to the Crown or the Duchy of Lancaster (pronounced 'bone-a vak-ansh-ee-a' or 'bonna vak-ant-ee-a').

capacity 'Legal competency or qualification' (*Oxford English Dictionary*).

certum est quod certum reddi potest That is certain which can be made certain (pronounced 'sir-tumm esst quad sir-tumm red-dee poh-test').

cestui que trust The one who trusts, i.e. the beneficiary of a trust (pronounced 'settee key trust').

civil partnership A registered relationship between two people 'of the same sex' (Civil Partnership Act 2004).

'class' Persons who come within a certain category or description defined by a general or collective formula, and who, if they take at all, are to take one divisible subject in certain proportionate shares' (*per* Lord Selborne LC, *Pearkes* v *Mosely* (1880) 5 App Cas 714 at 723).

compound interest Interest calculated annually by adding to the capital the simple interest which has arisen during the previous year. Compound interest for the following year is calculated on the compound sum of capital and simple interest. The following year accumulated compound interest is added to capital, and the process repeated. It is, essentially, interest on interest.

constructive trust A trust imposed by the court on the legal owner of an asset to prevent that person asserting beneficial ownership of the asset in bad conscience to the prejudice of the true beneficial owner.

covenant This is a promise contained within a deed is called a 'covenant'. A covenantee (i.e. a person to whom a promise is made by deed) is not a mere volunteer because the deed itself (or, traditionally, the seal on the deed) is deemed to satisfy the common law requirement of consideration. Any party to the deed can enforce the covenant against the person who made the promise (the covenantor). A person is a party to a deed when they are named in the deed and signed it.

CREST An electronic share settlement and securities depository system introduced to the UK Stock Exchange in 1996. Since 2002 it has been administered by a company called Euroclear.

cy près Old law French for the 'the nearest thing', literally 'that which is near' (pronounced 'sea-pray').

debt 'A monetary obligation owed by one person to another which is an item of value because it can be transferred to a third party by way of sale or security for a loan' (Michael Bridge, *Personal Property*, 2nd edn, Oxford: Blackstone Press, 1996, p. 4).

delegatus non potest delegare This is the classic maxim which summarises the trustees' duty of personal service. It means 'the delegate has no power to delegate'.

devise A gift or trust of realty made by will. Realty means real property, so the term would include land apart from leases.

discretionary trust This arises where there is an obligation upon the donee of certain property to distribute it amongst a certain class of beneficiaries, but with discretion as to the manner of distribution. The obligation to distribute makes it a trust, the discretion as to the manner of distribution makes it a discretionary trust. The trustee under such a trust 'is under a duty to select from among a class of beneficiaries those who are to receive, and the proportions in which they are to receive, income or capital of the trust property' (*per* Warner J in *Mettoy v Evans* [1990] 1 WLR 1587).

donatio mortis causa A gift made *inter vivos* in expectation of the donor's imminent death, but which is not fully effective until the donor's death.

dualism In its most extreme form, the belief that, despite the Judicature Acts, equity remains utterly distinct from the common law.

'effective date' of a disposition This varies according to whether the disposition was made *inter vivos* or by will. An *inter vivos* deed of gift or trust is effective at the date of its execution. A testamentary gift or trust is effective, not at the date of execution of the will, but at the date of the testator's/testatrix's death.

equitable maxim This is a traditional judicial principle developed in the old Court of Chancery which serves as a guide to the exercise of discretion in the application of equitable doctrines and the award of equitable remedies.

fee simple The largest and best form of land ownership in English law.

fiduciary (As an adjective) descriptive of a duty of exclusive loyalty owed in law by one person to another and descriptive also of certain offices (the paradigm being trusteeship) under which a fiduciary duty is always one of the duties owed. (As a noun) descriptive of persons owing a fiduciary duty: although a trustee is the paradigm fiduciary, the term 'fiduciary' is often used as shorthand to indicate 'a fiduciary other than a trustee'.

fully secret trust This is where X formally leaves property to Y by his will in circumstances where Y is informally made aware by X during X's lifetime (and Y expressly or impliedly accepts) that Y is to hold the property as trustee for the benefit of Z.

fusion In its most extreme form, the belief that, after the Judicature Acts, equity and the law are indistinguishable.

gift subject to conditions precedent The intended donee of such a gift will not be entitled to the gift unless he or she *first* satisfies a particular condition, e.g. he or she might have to qualify as a barrister before the gift vests.

gift subject to conditions subsequent Such a gift vests unconditionally in the donee, but will be *forfeited* if the donee subsequently breaches a condition to which the gift was subject, e.g. the gift of land to a person might come to an end in the event of their moving to live abroad.

half-secret trust This is where X *formally* leaves property by his will to Y *expressly* 'on trust' for another, but where Y is only *informally* made aware of the identity of that other. It will be clear on the face of the will that Y is *not* the beneficial owner of the property.

in loco parentis 'In the parent's place'. A guardian is said to stand *in loco parentis* to the child in his or her care (pronounced: 'inn low-co pair-entiss').

in personam A remedy, such as an injunction, is said to operate *in personam* because it is enforced against a defendant personally. An *in personam* action is normally contrasted with an action *in rem*, which is a claim against property held by the defendant regardless of the defendant's identity.

in rem A right is an *in rem* right (also known as a 'proprietary right') where it is enforced against assets in the defendant's hands in which or over which the claimant has a proprietary interest, thus it is not defeated by the defendant's personal insolvency.

intermediate income Income arising from a gift, including a trust, during the period between the effective date of the trust (e.g. the date of the testator's death, in the case of a trust made by will) and the date that the beneficiary's interest vests in possession.

inter vivos Also known as a 'lifetime' trust. A trust is said to be *inter vivos* if it is effective within the lifetime of the settlor. The person setting up an *inter vivos* trust is called a 'settlor'.

intestacy The legal scheme for distributing the estates of people who die without leaving a valid will.

investment The process by which assets are applied with the intention of producing income and/or capital growth over the medium to long term.

'issue of the marriage' and 'marriage consideration' Issue will include children and even grandchildren, but not children of a previous marriage (unless their interests are 'interwoven' with those of the children of the marriage (*AG v Jacob Smith* [1895] 2 QB 341)), nor, it seems, 'illegitimate' children (despite the Family Law Reform Act 1987). The notion that children of a marriage have provided consideration is, according to Buckley J in *Re Cook's ST* [1965] Ch 902, a deliberate 'fiction'. In fact, the treatment of marriage as consideration is itself a fiction, not least because it functions as if it were common law consideration, even though strictly speaking it was a creation of the Court of Chancery.

laches Delay or 'laxness' in bringing a claim. A claim against a defendant will be barred by reason of the claimant's *laches* if there was such a delay in bringing the claim as is likely to prejudice the defendant's fair trial or otherwise offend the public interest in finality of litigation.

'lives in being' Persons alive at the 'effective date' of the grant, or persons in their mother's womb at that time who are later born (see *Re Wilmer's Trusts* [1903] 2 Ch 411). However, for the purpose of the rule against remoteness of vesting 'lives in being' include only 'relevant' or 'measuring' lives in being. These descriptions usually correspond to those persons who are expressly or impliedly referred to in the instrument by which the disposition is effected. Thus the lives in being at the date of execution of an *inter vivos* gift to 'such of my grandchildren as qualify as lawyers' include not only the grandchildren, but also the settlor and any of his children who are then alive. The grandchildren were expressly referred to, the reference to the settlor and his children is implicit.

maintenance A statutory power granted to trustees (which may be altered, enlarged or removed by the trust instrument) under which the trustee can apply trust income for the benefit of infant beneficiaries of the trust.

mandate A binding instruction given to an agent.

marriage settlement 'A legal arrangement by which property is given or secured when a couple get married' (*The Oxford Dictionary of English*, 2nd edn, Oxford: Oxford University Press).

overreaching This process enables a purchaser of land to take free of the beneficiaries' interests provided he pays all the trustees and the trustees are at least two in number or a trust corporation.

'perpetuity period' For the purpose of this rule this is the period ending 21 years after the death of all 'lives in being'.

proselytise 'To convert or attempt to convert (someone) from one religion, belief, or opinion to another' (*The Oxford Dictionary of English*, 2nd edn, Oxford: Oxford University Press, 2003).

protective trust A trust established by the settlor to protect the beneficiary (who cannot be the settlor) from the beneficiary's creditors. Sometimes called a 'spendthrift' trust, because it was traditionally employed to protect spendthrift children of the settlor. Protective trusts are used to protect beneficiaries from financial calamity and their own folly. It has been said that 'a protective trust shows the furthest extent to which English law will permit property to be denied to creditors': Maudsley & Burn's *Trusts and Trustees* (5th edn, Oxford: Oxford University Press, 1996).

quantum meruit The literal translation of this Latin phrase is 'as much as he has deserved'. According to the *Oxford Dictionary of English*, 'a reasonable sum of money to be paid for services rendered or work done when the amount due is not stipulated in a legally enforceable contract' (2nd edn, Oxford: Oxford University Press, 2003).

quia timet 'Because he fears'. A *quia timet* injunction is ordered where a civil wrong is threatened but has not yet been committed.

reconversion 'That notional or imaginary process by which a prior notional conversion is annulled or discharged, and the notionally converted property restored . . . to its original actual quality' (*Snell's Equity*, 20th edn, London: Sweet & Maxwell, 1929).

restitutio in integrum To put the parties back into the position they were in prior to entering the rescinded agreement.

restitution There is no simple definition of restitution, and if there is, it is disputed on account of its simplicity. For present purposes we will adopt Professor Andrew Burrows' simple (and disputed) proposition that 'Restitution is the law concerned with reversing a defendant's unjust enrichment at the plaintiff's expense' (*The Law of Restitution*, 1993, London: Butterworths, p. 1).

'right of survivorship' This is where an asset, such as land or the balance of a bank account, is owned 'jointly' (i.e. not in shares) so that each owner can be said to own the whole of the asset; on the death of one joint tenant the surviving joint tenant (or joint tenants) remains owner of the whole by 'right of survivorship'. It is important to realise that survivorship is not a process of inheritance. The joint tenant who survives does not inherit anything. He or she was already owner of the whole.

secret trust This is a trust binding on property passed under a will, but which does not comply with the formalities required by the Wills Act. It is effective because it binds the conscience of the person to whom the property passes under the will, that person having accepted the trust when the testator was still alive.

sham trust There being no *bona fide* reason for the creation of any trust, the description 'trust' is applied to an arrangement in order to conceal the true ownership of the property.

simple interest Interest calculated, usually on an annual basis, on the capital monies due from the trustee to the trust.

some useful terms 'Monotheism' is belief in one God; 'polytheism' is belief in more than one god; 'atheism' is belief in no god at all and 'agnosticism' is a belief that neither affirms nor denies the existence of a God or gods.

specific performance An equitable remedy taking the form of an order of the court requiring performance of a contract; it is awarded where the court will not permit the defendant to breach his contract and pay common law damages by way of remedy.

sui juris Adult and of sound mind (pronounced 'soo-ee your-is').

testamentary Any trust which comes into effect upon the death of the person setting up the trust is said to be 'testamentary'. The person setting up such a trust is called a 'testator' (if male) and a 'testatrix' (if female).

'the three certainties' certainty of intention = a certain intention to create a trust (i.e. words and conduct which create an imperative obligation); certainty of subject = certainty with regard to the assets (property) subject to the trust and the shares in which it is to be held by the beneficiaries; certainty of object = certainty with regard to beneficiaries or purposes of the trust.

trustee *de son tort* 'If one, not being a trustee and not having authority from a trustee, takes upon himself to intermeddle with the trust matters or to do acts characteristic of the office of trustee, he may thereby make himself what is called in law a trustee of his own wrong, i.e. a trustee *de son tort*': *per* Smith LJ in *Mara* v *Browne* (1896) 1 Ch 199 at 209.

types of interest These are 'vested in interest', 'vested in possession' and 'contingent'. The difference between the two types of vested interest can be illustrated quite simply by taking the classic trust 'to A for life and B in remainder'. In such a trust, both A and B are entitled to an interest, their interests have both 'vested in interest'. However, only A can claim to be entitled to the *present use and enjoyment of the trust property*, B has to wait until A dies. So it is said that only A's interest has 'vested in possession'. Where an interest might never be acquired, as in the case of a gift that is dependent upon the happening of an uncertain event, e.g. 'to A when he qualifies as a barrister', A's interest is said to be 'contingent' and as such it has not 'vested' in either sense of the word.

unconscionable This is a hard word to define, but in the opinion of this author it describes the conduct of asserting a legal right or power in a way which in the particular context is oppressive or otherwise unjust to the party against whom the right or power is asserted.

unincorporated association 'My Lords, an unincorporated association is, as I have said, not a legal entity. It is a number of legal persons having mutual rights and duties in accordance with rules which constitute the contract under which they have agreed to be associated. The property of the association is owned by or on trust for the individual members and subject to the rules. The liability of the individual members for the debts incurred for the purposes of the association is governed by the ordinary law of contract and agency. The rights of the members, as against each other, to avail themselves of the common property and facilities are governed by their contract' (*Eastbourne Town Radio Cars Association* v *Customs and Excise Commissioners* [2001] UKHL 19, para. [32]; [2001] 1 WLR 794, 803, HL, *per* Lord Hoffmann).

volunteer Where a promise is made voluntarily in favour of a person, the person claiming the benefit of the promise is said to be a volunteer. A volunteer does not give contractual consideration for the performance of the promise.

Index

A

M